26 . n .

OXFORD HISTORICAL MONOGRAPHS

Government Without Administration

State and Civil Service in Weimar and Nazi Germany

JANE CAPLAN

CLARENDON PRESS · OXFORD
1988

Oxford University Press, Walton Street, Oxford OX2 6DP
Oxford New York Toronto
Delhi Bombay Calcutta Madras Karachi
Petaling Jaya Singapore Hong Kong Tokyo
Nairobi Dar es Salaam Cape Town
Melbourne Auckland
and associated companies in
Berlin Ibadan

Oxford is a trade mark of Oxford University Press

Published in the United States
by Oxford University Press, New York

British Library Cataloguing in Publication Data
Caplan, Jane
Government without administration : state
and civil service in Weimer and Nazi
Germany.—(Oxford historical monographs).
1. Germany. Public administration.
Bureaucracy, 1918-1945
I. Title
350'.001'0943
ISBN 0-19-822993-3

Library of Congress Cataloging-in-Publication Data
Caplan, Jane.
Government without administration.
(Oxford historical monographs)
Bibliography.   Includes index.
1. Civil service—Germany—History—20th century.
2. Germany—Politics and government—1918-1933.
3. Germany—Politics and government—1933-1945.
4. National socialism. I. Title. II. Series.
JN3961.5.C37 1989   354.43006   88-12481
ISBN 0-19-822993-3

Set by Downdell Ltd., Abingdon, Oxon
Printed in Great Britain
at the University Printing House, Oxford
by David Stanford
Printer to the University

TO
MY TEACHERS

The bureaucracy is the imaginary state alongside the real state; it is the spiritualism of the state. Hence everything acquires a double meaning: a real meaning and a bureaucratic one; in like fashion, there is both real knowledge and bureaucratic knowledge.

Karl Marx, *Critique of Hegel's Doctrine of the State* (1843).

PREFACE

The historian of National Socialism today faces an immense body of scholarly literature that has accumulated in the thirty-odd years since the archives left by the regime became open to public use. Much of the most recent research has focused on the internal structure and workings of the Nazi regime, investigating such questions as the of role the NSDAP in the new state, the organization of the institutions of central and local government, and the power of Hitler. The Nazi regime had a shattering, if temporary, effect not only on the way that Germany was governed, but also on the idea of government as such. If no coherent remodelling process took place, this was not for want of programmes for reform. On the contrary, the regime was rife with rival visions of how to realize the Nazis' promise of a political New Order—and later, how to extract the Nazi party from the paralysis which institutionalized power seemed to have brought. For if the regime as a whole appears as a monstrous concentration of dynamic, unstoppable power, to many of its representatives and contemporaries its political institutions hardly realized their original aspirations for a refounded national state. The zeal of National Socialism was displaced, catastrophically, to the exercise of domination in the form of terror, genocide, and war; meanwhile, the state apparatus as such was managed in a way that amply bore out Hitler's insistence that the state was not an end in itself but a means to other ends. Historical research has thus had the effect of exposing the extent to which the Nazi regime was not in practice the totalitarian monolith that it once successfully projected as its public image. It is now commonplace to regard this interpretation as superseded by a new image of the Third Reich as a fragmented and disorganized parody of the German state. According to this view, Nazi Germany was not an efficient machine, but a system of semi-institutionalized conflict whose exponents wanted, in a sense, the power of government without the ballast of administration. The regime progressively and parasitically consumed the administrative structures on which it rested, proving incapable of generating the conditions for its own stabilization and reproduction, in terms either of institutions or of policy-making procedures.

I take up the question of the Nazi state in the final chapter of the book. What I want to emphasize here is the extent to which this changing image of Nazi Germany as a political structure may be seen as an artefact of the research process itself, rather than as a progressively revealed truth about its essential nature. It is true that one of the principal reasons for the shifts in our understanding of the Nazi regime is the relatively recent availability of the massive archival resources on which close analysis depends. Still, it is hard to believe that there is a unified and coherent history of National Socialism which cumulative research is voicing more and more adequately. Surely, the undiminishing fascination of National Socialism as a topic of scholarly research—indeed, as a theme in popular culture—cannot be explained only by the proposition that there is still more to be learned, in an additive sense, about the years 1933-45. That brief episode in human history has already attracted a collective research effort whose disproportion to its time-span, compared with other epochs, can only be guessed at. The 'gap theory' beloved of modern scholarship cannot account for the dense palimpsest that is now the record of research into National Socialism; there is something else at work here. This is, I think, the fact that the receding history of National Socialism continues to act as a mirror into which we look for new evidence not about itself, but about ourselves. By this I mean that it is still legitimate to look to this piece of not very past history for clues to the political and moral issues of the present, whether these are conceived as continuities or as parallels with the past. Whether or not this is evident and acknowledged in our work, what draws many to the study of Nazi Germany is the hope that we will learn more from it than simply new evidence about yet another of its protean aspects and actions. There is a sense in which this evidence is always produced to be marshalled into some agenda extraneous to itself; or rather, the significance of the Third Reich as an object of historical study is that nothing significant *is* extraneous to it. At any rate, I cannot think that anyone would admit to being drawn to the study of National Socialism by a pleasure in the contemplation of the past; nor by a merely scholarly or antiquarian interest in precise reconstruction or specialist micro-details. The bigger agenda is always looming.

Of course, National Socialism is not unique in functioning as an historical sounding-board for present concerns. Many historical events or processes that our culture regards as epochal do this. But National Socialism's particular fulfilment of this function may still be unique for the time being, in that the regime continues to operate as the standard by which political breakdown and depravity are measured. Perhaps the time will come when this is no longer the case. I do not intend this in a trivializing sense. But we are already faced with a challenge to rework the historical 'meaning' of National Socialism, notably its place in German history. It may still be too difficult, *pace* Marx, for present generations to accomplish this particular task. Certainly, the effort of reinterpretation is both a painful and a highly political affair, as the currently raging *Historikerstreit* demonstrates.

The subject of this study, therefore, reflects my own interest in the continuing dilemmas raised by the relationship between rationalization and liberty, by the effects of the division of labour in complex societies, and by the political meaning of claims to representational universality. In this book, I approach these issues through a detailed study of policy-making by bureaucratic process. My subject is the structure of the administration and the role of the bureaucracy in Nazi Germany; I focus primarily on the policies developed by the Reich interior ministry for the interior administration and its personnel. As such, the book offers a detailed study of one programme of political reform under National Socialism, and sets out to explain both the sources of this programme and the reasons for its defeat. In addition, I have chosen to set my discussion of the Nazi period in the context of the history of the bureaucracy in Germany since the nineteenth century. This is partly because the content and conditions of civil-service policy-making under National Socialism are less intelligible without this background, but also because this perspective permits an attempt to locate the National Socialist state in the longer process of German state formation.

The book centres on two sets of issues, therefore; the first deriving from the role of the civil service in German political history, and the second from current debates about the history of National Socialism. It has been relatively uncontroversial to assume that, from the mid-nineteenth century, the German civil service was an ideologically coherent group, imprinted with the interests and attitudes that its élite shared with other members of Germany's ruling orders. The German civil servant (*Beamte*) carried in his briefcase a docket endorsing his membership in a privileged caste, which effaced his other social characteristics. This classic image rests on the assumption that, in constituting the identity, self-image, and social coherence of civil servants, as individuals and as a group, collective or *ständisch* values continued to play a stronger role than any other influences from their background or working relations. In practice, too, this special identity was anchored in the legal status of the *Beamte*, who worked on a non-contractual basis and enjoyed the unusual material advantages of lifelong tenure, secure salaries, and pensions and other allowances. The career civil service or *Berufsbeamtentum* was thus incommensurable with either workers in the labour market or independent professionals, but was bound together and marked out by its special status and privileges. According to this model, the civil service was bound to be largely opposed to the 1918 revolution, and entered the Weimar Republic as an alien and hostile group that was also determined to protect its privileges at any cost. In common with other members of the old élites, the civil service then compromised, if uneasily, with National Socialism in the crisis after 1930. Its inherent tendency to preserve order and continuity, as well as a more active sympathy with Nazi anti-republicanism, led the bureaucracy to lend its crucial stabilizing and legitimating support to the regime in the early months of 1933. Subsequently, however, civil servants who identified their own and Germany's interests with the classic bureaucratic traditions of legality, rationality, and hierarchical order were marginalized and discounted by the political leadership.

My aim in this book is not to displace this account entirely, but to correct and deepen it in some critical respects. To begin with, it is important to note the extent to which the late nineteenth-century civil service (or, more properly, civil services) in Germany did not in practice resemble the model by which they have tended to be understood. It is perfectly true that the bureaucratic system did generate a strong corporate identity, based on the surviving traditions of the *Stand*, on the distinction between state and civil society, and on the highly elaborate rules and procedures of the civil service. However, this had already begun to erode as Germany urbanized and industrialized, and as the state's tasks expanded and shifted. By the beginning of the twentieth century, Germany's civil service was no longer a small and relatively homogeneous corps of officials, but a large and diverse collectivity of public employees. Some of its members had developed a strong sense of their own interests in the matter of salaries, and had joined together to form staff associations to represent them; another smaller segment added to this a concern for the subaltern status to which intensive governmental control of civil servants' official and private behaviour reduced them. Senior bureaucrats and ministers, the élite of the public service, watched these developments anxiously, and in Prussia began to weigh administrative reforms with which to reduce the cost of the civil service by restricting its members' material privileges. In other words, well before 1918 the status of the civil service was a contradictory one, and the stage was being set for battles in which state and civil service were not synonyms but antagonists.

In subsequent chapters I discuss the civil-service policies of the Weimar Republic in the light of this evidence, focusing first on the terms of the Weimar Constitution and the early civil-service policies of the republic, and then on the legal and financial status of civil servants in the later 1920s. Here I emphasize the diversity of influences operating in civil-service affairs, including the political parties, the civil-service staff associations, and academic and judicial opinion. The picture that emerges suggests that the familiar problem of how to democratize the civil service in order to assimilate it into the republic was not the only pressure on the institution during this period. Of considerable importance was the fact that governmental policies to reduce the cost of the administration after 1918 challenged the traditional privileges of civil servants at the same time as these were anchored in the Weimar Constitution itself. In addition, conservative academics and some élite civil servants shared an anxiety that the established values of the civil service were being undermined and displaced by the secular process of bureaucratization. The mass of lower-ranking civil servants was caught in the paradoxical position of having to defend, by quasi-trade-unionist means, the material rights which, in theory, had been guaranteed by the constitution. In this sense, civil servants were poised between ideologies and strategies of *ständisch* self-defence and of democratic participation, or of resistance to and embracement of the new political and constitutional system. Government policy itself veered between similar poles, and fuelled civil servants' fears on a number of critical occasions. In the early 1920s, tenure rights were temporarily abridged in the interests of retrenchment, while in the early 1930s the same imperative led Brüning to cut salaries drastically. Neither the traditionalism of the shrinking conservative and middle parties nor the class politics of the left appeared acceptable as a means for the effective defence of civil servants' collective interests, and thus the way was open for a different politics to capture their support.

I therefore go on to examine the appeal of the NSDAP to civil servants as voters and members before 1933, as well as governmental attempts to control the party's growing influence within the bureaucracy. Although the NSDAP made increasingly strenuous efforts to capture the civil-service vote in the early 1930s, the party was hampered by its reputation for disdaining the civil service both as a bureaucratic institution and as a caste of pen-pushing *Spiessbürger*. It appears that civil servants did not join the NSDAP in large numbers before 1933, but that the party was able to attract their vote after 1930. But the membership figures may not tell the full story, given the disciplinary and informal pressures against civil servants joining the radical parties. The circumstantial evidence of informal party organization and of governmental anxiety suggests that the NSDAP was in fact able to mobilize civil servants during the depression by presenting itself as the potential champion of both their material and their status interests.

The core of the book is a study of selected aspects of civil-service and administrative policy-making in the Nazi regime after 1933, from the point of view of central government and of the Reich interior ministry in particular. The principal theme here is the attempt by the interior ministry, under Wilhelm Frick, to achieve a comprehensive programme of administrative reform, pivoted on a reconstructed and powerful bureaucratic ēlite. These ambitious plans for what amounted to a new bureaucratic regiment were not only unrealistic in terms of the administrative effort and concentrated authority they demanded, but they also fell foul of other National Socialist factions who were not interested in vesting the interior ministry with such substantial power. In addition, the Nazi polity was unable to generate an alternative concept of the public functionary to replace the rejected images of the faceless bureaucrat and the authoritarian Prussian official. Interior-ministry policy remained poised between activism and ineffectuality, and in his attempts to pursue his grand vision Frick was driven to construct an ever more alarming picture of a civil service in crisis. This discourse of crisis was built on claims that the civil service was suffering from a collapse of recruitment, severe financial distress, status anxiety, and deteriorating morale. It intensified during the war, which aggravated the problems of staffing and morale and also shifted the distribution of power within the regime, with the ultimate effect of ousting Frick and replacing him with the head of the SS and police, Heinrich Himmler.

The book concludes by situating the themes disclosed by these empirical investigations in the context of a discussion of the Nazi state, which I relate in turn to the problem of German state formation and political representation since the nineteenth century. In the long run, the Third Reich remained part of, rather than a resolution to, the political crisis of representation that had launched it. If it lived politically on borrowed capital—the stored-up resilience of a developed and sophisticated state apparatus—it also inherited the tensions and contradictions of that system, and proved incapable of creating a functioning alternative.

J. C.

ACKNOWLEDGEMENTS

If writing sometimes seems a species of solitary confinement, learning is above all a social process; my debts here are numerous, but also a pleasure to pay. I was originally launched on the research from which this book derives by Martin Broszat, and by my dissertation supervisors at Oxford, James Joll and Peter Pulzer. I owe a similar debt of gratitude for early and sustained encouragement to Tim Mason and Hans Mommsen; also to Pat Thompson, editor of the Oxford Historical Monographs, for his annual requests for progress reports. Among the many other friends and colleagues who at different times have given me the benefit of their advice, and spurred and chided me into finishing this book, I would like to thank in particular David Abraham, David Blackbourn, Tom Childers, David Crew, Geoff Eley, Richard Evans, Michael Geyer, John Gillis, Michael Harloe, Hans-Adolf Jacobsen, Gareth Stedman Jones, Ellen Kennedy, Ian Kershaw, Andreas Kunz, Charles Medalen, Bob Moeller, Jeremy Noakes, Gillian Sutherland, and, last but far from least, the members of the German Women's History Study Group (Bonnie Anderson, Renate Bridenthal, Atina Grossmann, Amy Hackett, Deborah Hertz, Itsie Hull, Marion Kaplan, Molly Nolan, and Joan Reuterschan). To Mary Poovey I give my special thanks for sustaining me through the final work on the manuscript. This bare listing of names is hardly adequate to express my gratitude for so much assistance and support, but I hope that you will all recognize how much I have learned from you. Such merits as this book may have are testimony to the importance of shared collegial work, with these friends and in numerous seminars and colloquia over the years; but, in the now traditional disclaimer, the mistakes are all my own.

This book could also not have been written without the help of the many archives and libraries in which I worked, and of the institutions which employed and funded me. I made ample use of both the human and documentary resources of the Bundesarchiv in Koblenz, following its vertical peregrinations from the ninth to the ground floor of the Wöllershof and up again to Karthause; I thank its many archivists and its *Lesesaal* staff, whose friendliness and flexibility helped me to revise my conventional notions of the German *Beamte*. I received similarly generous assistance from the staffs of the Bundesarchiv-Militärarchiv, Freiburg; the Institut für Zeitgeschichte, Munich; the Bundestag Library; the library of the Deutscher Gemeindetag, Cologne; the Berlin Document Centre; the Prussian Geheimes Staatsarchiv; the Wiener Library; the British Library; the Bodleian Library; Cambridge University Library; the library of the University of Pennsylvania; and the library of Bryn Mawr College.

I would also like to acknowledge with thanks the financial support of the German Academic Exchange Service, the Anglo-German Group of Historians, the Volkswagen Fund, and the British Academy. I received additional support from the Principal and Fellows of Newnham College and the Provost and Fellows of King's College, Cambridge; and from Bryn Mawr College, in the form of the Rosalyn R. Schwartz Lectureship and a junior leave year.

I thank Croom Helm Ltd. for permission to reprint in Chapter 4 material originally published in my essay 'Speaking the Right Language', in T. Childers (ed.), *The Formation of the Nazi Constituency 1919-1933*.

Before I equipped myself with a computer, Chris McFarland, Lorraine Kirschner, Deanne Bell, and Edith Ianucci typed many drafts for me with care, patience, and cheerfulness. Kathleen Smith helped me to compile the bibliography. More recently, I have had the pleasure of working with Ivon Asquith and Robert Faber at the Oxford University Press, and I am also grateful to Nicola Pike for her meticulous and constructive copy-editing. Since there seems to be nowhere else to put this important but essentially mundane item of information, I will end on an appropriately bureaucratic note by stating that, except where indicated, all translations in the text from the German are my own.

CONTENTS

Abbreviations   xvi

1: 'The Illusion of the State': The German Bureaucracy
   in the Nineteenth Century   1

2: Politics and Depoliticization, 1918-1923   14

3: The Failure of Reform, 1923-1933   58

4: National Socialism and the Civil Service before 1933   102

5: Administration in the Nazi State: Reforms and
   Retreats, 1933-1937   131

6: Maintaining the *Gleichschaltung*: The Organization of
   Civil Servants in Nazi Germany   189

7: The Politics of Remuneration, 1937-1939: A Case Study   229

8: The Crisis of Policy, 1939-1945   260

9: State Formation and Political Representation in
   Nazi Germany   321

Bibliography   339

Glossary   372

Index   375

ABBREVIATIONS

ADB	Allgemeiner Deutscher Beamtenbund
ADGB	Allgemeiner Deutscher Gewerkschaftsbund
AOG	*Arbeitsordnungsgesetz*
AöR	*Archiv des öffentlichen Rechts*
APSR	*American Political Science Review*
BA	Bundesarchiv, Koblenz
BBG	*Berufsbeamtengesetz (Gesetz zur Wiederherstellung des Berufsbeamtentums,* 7 April 1933)
BDC	Berlin Document Centre
BNSDJ	Bund Nationalsozialistischer Deutscher Juristen
BRÄndG	*Beamtenrechtsänderungsgesetz* (30 June 1933)
BVP	Bayrische Volkspartei
DAF	Deutsche Arbeitsfront
DBB	Deutscher Beamtenbund
DBG	*Deutsches Beamtengesetz* (26 January 1937)
DDP	Deutsche Demokratische Partei
DGT	Deutscher Gemeindetag
DNVP	Deutschnationale Volkspartei
DR	*Deutsches Recht*
DRA	*Deutscher Reichsanzeiger*
DV	*Deutsche Verwaltung*
DVBl	*Deutsche Verwaltungsblätter*
DVFP	Deutschvölkische Freiheitspartei
DVO	*Durchführungsverordnung*
DVP	Deutsche Volkspartei
GBV	Generalbevollmächtigter für die Reichsverwaltung
GBW	Generalbevöllmächtigter für die Wirtschaft
GS	*Gesetzsammlung*
GStA	Geheimes Staatsarchiv
HA	NSDAP-Hauptarchiv
HfK	Hauptamt für Kommunalpolitik
HJ	Hitlerjugend
IfZ	Institut für Zeitgeschichte

JAO	*Justizausbildungsordnung* (22 July 1934)
JCH	*Journal of Contemporary History*
JMBl	*Justizministerialblatt*
JMH	*Journal of Modern History*
JöR	*Jahrbuch des öffentlichen Rechts*
KPD	Kommunistische Partei Deutschlands
LR	*Landrat*
MBliV	*Ministerialblatt für die innere Verwaltung*
NSBZ	*Nationalsozialistische Beamten-Zeitung*
NSDAP	Nationalsozialistische Deutsche Arbeiterpartei
NSV	Nationalsozialistische-Volkswohlfahrt
OKW	Oberkommando der Wehrmacht
OVG	Oberverwaltungsgericht
PAV	*Personalabbauverordnung* (27 October 1923)
PK	Parteikanzlei
RBG	*Reichsbeamtengesetz* (1873; reissued 1907)
RDB	Reichsbund der Deutschen Beamten
RDStrO	*Reichsdienststrafordnung* (26 January 1937)
RGBl	*Reichsgesetzblatt*
RGS	*Reichsgrundsätze* (24 May 1921, 14 October 1936)
RhB	Reichsbund der höheren Beamten
RM	Reichsmark
RMBliV	*Reichsministerialblatt für die innere Verwaltung*
RPL	Reichspropagandaleitung
RVG	Reichsverwaltungsgericht
RVBl	*Reichsverwaltungsblatt*
SA	Sturm-Abteilung
SD	Sicherheitsdienst
S Sch	Sammlung Schumacher
SPD	Sozialdemokratische Partei Deutschlands
SS	Schutzstaffel or Sammlung Sänger
StdF	*Stellvertreter des Führers*
VB	*Völkischer Beobachter*
VjhZ	*Vierteljahreshefte für Zeitgeschichte*
VO	*Verordnung*
WHW	Winterhilfswerk
ZADR	*Zeitschrift der Akademie für Deutsches Recht*
ZgStW	*Zeitschrift für gesamte Staatswissenschaft*

1

'The Illusion of the State': The German Bureaucracy in the Nineteenth Century

No student of modern German political history can afford to ignore the role of the civil service. 'It is plain', wrote Hermann Finer fifty years ago, 'that energies as mighty as those which England devoted to the creation of parliamentary institutions were in Prussia turned to the establishment of administrative institutions.'[1] In one sense, this simply asserts a historical fact, but the terms of Finer's comparison suggest something more: that for Prussia, and subsequently for Germany, the bureaucratic state has had the character of a defining national institution. Just as English history was once fashionably represented as a story of parliamentary progress, so a comparably whiggish view of German history could see it as the development of the administrative, legal, and ideological institutions which constituted the Prusso-German *Rechtsstaat* of the late nineteenth century. For if Germany is 'the classical land of the civil service', as Otto Hintze claimed,[2] it has also been the classical land of scholarship about this institution. From Hegel and Marx to Hintze, Weber, Michels, and beyond, the historical and theoretical study of administration and bureaucracy has owed much of its pertinence and authority to German scholars, who drew largely on the experience of their own society. Indeed, Karl Mannheim once asserted that 'the majority of books on politics in the history of German political science are *de facto* treatises on administration'.[3] The development of the civil service and state administration in nineteenth-century Germany was thus accompanied by a sophisticated scholarship which simultaneously inscribed it in a particular reading of Germany's political history.

This scholarship has given rise to a historiography which tends to share a number of common assumptions and points of orientation, and from which a classic account of the bureaucracy's history can be

---

[1] H. Finer, *The Theory and Practice of Modern Government* (London, 1932), ii. 1184.
[2] O. Hintze, *Der Beamtenstand* (Leipzig, 1911), 39.
[3] K. Mannheim, *Ideology and Utopia* (New York, 1936), 105.

constructed.[4] Its paradigm was the history of the Prussian bureaucracy from its origins in the early eighteenth-century Prussian monarchy's drive towards dynastic absolutism, and the attempt to impose a single authority in place of the dispersed hierarchies of a semi-feudal system of rule. Although eighteenth-century Prussian officialdom continued to share many characteristics with the political and social system in which it grew, and was far from displacing the aristocratic power structure, it already constituted a distinctive type of politico-administrative system under Frederick William I. It was defined by independence from personal loyalties other than to the king, and by conformity to specified norms of structure and procedure, including collegial and hierarchical organization. The day-to-day organization of government business was routinized, the allocation of work minutely detailed, working hours regulated, and lateness and absenteeism penalized. The state service also had a certain social significance as a new élite that opened further avenues of advancement and offered fresh measurements of rank and status. In the course of the eighteenth century, Prussian state servants acquired notable privileges, including exemption from taxation, a special jurisdiction, and protection from slander and libel (*Beamtenbeleidigung*). Balancing this was the notion of duty (*Pflicht*) which the official owed to the state, and which formed the crux of the civil-service ethic. The important principles of impersonal service and security of tenure, however, were not established. Before the nineteenth century, officials were still the king's servants, not the 'state's', and the threat of instant dismissal was an ever-present disciplinary force. In this sense, eighteenth-century officialdom did not yet constitute a professional civil service.

None the less, the first half of the century saw the beginning in Prussia of the system of specialized qualification and closely supervised training that became the hallmark of the professional German civil service. Legal qualification was required for jurists, a largely bourgeois profession which was not subject to the *Ämterprivileg* (the reservation of official posts to the nobility); and cameralistics influenced the practical orientation of administrative training. Well before the end of the century, entrance and final examinations were formally prescribed

---

[4] This account is drawn chiefly from the writings of O. Hintze and G. Schmoller; see also F. Hartung, *Studien zur Geschichte der preussischen Verwaltung*, i. *Vom 16. Jahrhundert bis zum Zusammenbruch des alten Staates im Jahre 1806* (Berlin, 1942); H. Rosenberg, *Bureaucracy, Aristocracy, and Autocracy: The Prussian Experience 1660-1815* (Boston, 1966); and H. Hattenhauer, *Geschichte des Beamtentums* (Cologne, Berlin, Bonn, and Munich, 1980).

for candidates for most of the upper ranks, and clerks too were trained and examined. A period of unpaid in-service training or apprenticeship was also standard by the mid-century, originating in the older practice by which the surplus of jurists had worked for nothing while waiting for a post to become vacant. These processes influenced the class composition of state service, of course. Lower-class youths' access to university was increasingly narrowed from the early eighteenth century, and a long unpaid apprenticeship was, and remained, virtually impossible for them. The examination system was also far from universally effective, and patronage continued to limit the penetration of merit as the organizing principle of the service.

The reforms of the late eighteenth and early nineteenth century constituted a virtual refoundation of German officialdom, as the political and social effects of the Enlightenment and the French Revolution redirected the theory and practice of the state and its tasks.[5] The personal quality of princely rule was overlaid by the concept of the constitutional state; *ständisch* hierarchy and patrimonial privilege, mercantilism and monopoly, were contested by liberal theories of the individual and of economic and civic rights. But, given the political and international status of the German states, it was inevitable, if paradoxical, that the decomposition of the 'night-watchman state' should be above all a bureaucratic process, in which the power of the state advanced rather than retreated. The reform of the body politic began with the reform of its limbs, the bureaucrats. Starting with the Prussian *Allgemeines Landrecht* (1794) and the Bavarian *Hauptlandespragmatik* (1805), officialdom was withdrawn from its personal subjection to the monarch and reconstructed, for the first time, as a state or civil service. The king symbolized the state, and civil servants continued to take a personal oath of loyalty to him; but henceforth it was the law that constituted the substance of their obligation and regulated their own official status.[6]

[5] B. Wunder, *Geschichte der Bürokratie in Deutschland* (Frankfurt, 1986), 22 ff; H.-J. Henning, *Die deutsche Beamtenschaft im 19. Jahrhundert* (Stuttgart, 1984), 15-16; also in general R. Koselleck, *Preussen zwischen Reform und Revolution: Allgemeines Landrecht, Verwaltung und soziale Bewegung von 1791 bis 1848* (Stuttgart, 1967).

[6] For the nineteenth century, in addition to sources already cited, see A. Lotz, *Geschichte des deutschen Beamtentums* (Berlin, 1914); J. Gillis, *The Prussian Bureaucracy in Crisis, 1840-1860: Origins of an Administrative Ethos* (Stanford, 1971); R. Morsey, *Die oberste Reichsverwaltung unter Bismarck 1867-1890* (Münster, 1957); J. C. G. Röhl, 'Higher Civil Servants in Germany, 1890-1900', *JCH*, 2/3 (1967), 101-21; L. W. Muncy, *The Junker in the Prussian Administration under William II, 1888-1914* (New York, 1970); H. Fenske, 'Preussische Beamtenpolitik vor 1918', *Der Staat*, 12 (1973), 339-56.

One of the most important manifestations of this was the development, within the new field of public law (*öffentliches Recht*), of a specific legal construct of civil-service status (*Beamtenverhältnis*). In place of the private contract that had previously regulated the relationship between prince and official, the nineteenth-century codifications of civil-service law began to refer to this as a *Treueverhältnis*, a bond of loyalty. The *Beamte* was thus no longer the equal partner in a contract, but the unequal beneficiary of a one-sided act of state. The *Dienst- und Treueverhältnis* rested originally on the Enlightenment belief that sovereignty was a trust exercised for the common good, and that its servants were not private individuals following merely private interests. By entering the state service, and offering it the full right to dispose of his labour power, the *Beamte* renounced his character as a private individual, and with it his right to pursue his economic interests in the market. The state therefore undertook to compensate him for his withdrawal from economic activity by guaranteeing him and his family a 'standesgemässer Unterhalt': a socially appropriate standard of maintenance, which included sick pay, a pension, and, on his death, dependants' allowances (*Hinterbliebenenversorgung*). In 1880, von Gerber gave a classic formulation of the 'alimentation' principle, in which civil-service remuneration was explained as being not a salary or

a rate of pay assessed according to his service . . . The essence of the German public service lies in the fact that it is a lifelong profession, on which one embarks only after a prolonged preparation and after renouncing every other commercial livelihood, but in which one expects on the part of the state the provision of a level of maintenance consistent with one's social status.[7]

The creation of a non-contractual civil-service status was in some respects a deliberate anachronism in an increasingly capitalist society for which freedom of contract was a cardinal virtue, and it emphasized the unique status of the civil servant as the executive arm of the sovereign. It had an ambiguous effect on the position of civil servants in the nineteenth-century constitutional monarchies, poised as they now were in a new tension between their rights as citizens and their duties as public officials. This was particularly evident in the case of Prussia, and after 1870 in the Reich.[8] On the one hand, civil servants stood

---

[7] C. F. von Gerber, *Grundzüge des deutschen Staatsrechts* (Leipzig, 1880), 120.

[8] See principally H.-J. Rejewski, *Die Pflicht zur politischen Treue im preussischen Beamtenrecht 1850–1918* (Berlin, 1973); E. Brandt. (ed.), *Die politische Treuepflicht: Rechtsquellen zur Geschichte des deutschen Berufsbeamtentums* (Karlsruhe and Heidelberg, 1976).

materially and ethically at the disposal of the sovereign, who claimed the right to regulate their entire range of behaviour. As the Prussian deed of appointment put it: 'It is expected that [the appointee] will be loyal and obedient to His Majesty the King and His Royal Household, will conscientiously fulfil the duties of his office, and will always conduct himself in a manner befitting a royal official.'[9] This was no empty formula. In the course of the nineteenth century, its effect was to subject civil servants' private as well as public lives to intense scrutiny and control. Everything, from clothing and social contacts to the conduct of wife, children, and servants, had to be orderly and *standesgemäss*; a civil servant's political behaviour—in the context of public participation in general as well as at election times—was closely scrutinized for any evidence of indiscipline.[10] As a court decision of 1863 stated:

Not everything which does not fall under the penal law in general and which is not as such forbidden to everyone in the state can be regarded as appropriate and seemly for a civil servant. In his off-duty conduct as well he must remain aware of the obligation he owes the state in consequence of his official status as a civil servant.[11]

Failure to live up to this standard could result in disciplinary proceedings; but good behaviour would be rewarded by official recognition and public esteem.

Although this gave the state a tremendous formal and informal power over its officials, there was another side to the situation. The devotion and commitment with which the *Beamte* served the state were matched by the state's guarantee to him of lifelong tenure. In contrast to judges, whose tenure was primarily a guarantee of judicial independence, the *Beamte*'s right had a material as well as an ethical character. It was intended not only to prevent corruption, but also to relieve him of the anxiety that if he lost his job he would also lose his livelihood. As the field of public law developed, the circumstances under which civil servants—*Beamte* proper—could be dismissed or demoted were specified; disciplinary codes elaborated the norms of behaviour and the penalties for non-observance. The development of tenure was a complex process, and was never absolutely universal throughout

---

[9] Cited in H.-J. Henning, *Das westdeutsche Bürgertum in der Epoche der Hochindustrialisierung 1860-1914: Soziales Verhalten und soziale Strukturen*, i. *Das Bildungsbürgertum in den preussischen Westprovinzen* (Wiesbaden, 1972), 117.

[10] Ibid., *passim*.

[11] Cited in Rejewski, *Pflicht zur politischen Treue*, p. 75.

Germany. A number of leading offices—state secretaries, *Oberpräsidenten*, and the like—were also deliberately excluded from the tenure system; these *politische* or *disponible Beamte* could be retired at any time. But the 'political' *Beamte* were peculiar, in that they were regarded as spokesmen for the government and were expected to give it their active support. In principle, for the rest of the civil service, the *Beamtenverhältnis* connoted lifelong employment as the counterpart to the total commitment it demanded; 'royal service and a secure existence'[12] were the certainties on which the *Beamte*'s life turned.

No less important in shaping the character of the nineteenth-century civil service was the shift towards legal studies as the primary qualification for entry into the higher ranks of the administration.[13] This movement was especially marked in Prussia, where a university training and formal examinations in law were prescribed as a condition of entry in 1817. The quality of academic law also altered; it was increasingly tailored to the needs of future judges and lawyers, and concentrated on private law to the virtual exclusion of public law. Students had to master such quantities of legal data that there was also little time for the other recommended fields of study for prospective administrators, such as administrative technique, fiscal affairs, rural economy, and the like. Cribs and crammers became the main source of information; hurried and cursory study produced overfilled but superficial minds. Although the South German states held on to the cameralistic tradition somewhat longer, it was the Prussian *Juristenmonopol* that became the model, producing a corps of administrators well fitted to apply the positivistic standard of law that had by now replaced an earlier and more generous constitutionalism.[14] With few interruptions, the later nineteenth century also saw a chronic surplus of qualified jurists, so that fully examined candidates had to wait many years for an established appoint-

---

[12] Henning, *Westdeutsches Bürgertum*, p. 121.

[13] W. Bleek, *Von der Kameralausbildung zum Juristenprivileg: Studium, Prüfung und Ausbildung der höheren Beamten des allgemeinen Verwaltungsdienstes in Deutschland im 18. und 19. Jahrhundert* (Berlin, 1972); C. von Delbrück, *Die Ausbildung für den höheren Verwaltungsdienst in Preussen* (Jena, 1917); E. Geib, 'Die Ausbildung des Nachwuchses für den höheren Verwaltungsdienst', *AöR*, 80 (1955/6), 307-45; C. J. Friedrich, 'The Continental Tradition of Training Administrators in Law and Jurisprudence', *JMH*, 1 (1939), 129-48; W. F. Bruck, *Das Ausbildungsproblem des Beamten in Verwaltung und Wirtschaft* (Leipzig, 1926).

[14] For the importance of positivism in nineteenth-century German constitutional theory, see P. von Oertzen, *Die soziale Funktion des staatsrechtlichen Positivismus: Eine wissenssoziologische Studie über die Entstehung des formalistischen Positivismus in der deutschen Staatsrechtswissenschaft* (Frankfurt, 1974).

ment, on top of the two or three years they had already served as trainees. This further restricted the social sources of recruitment to the senior ranks, notably in Prussia, where trainees were subject to a property qualification before establishment. In Prussia, professionalization thus failed to weaken social exclusivity: between 1835 and 1918, 90 per cent or more of senior civil servants in one region were from the upper classes (including a large contingent from civil-service families), compared to percentages in the 50s for Bavaria.[15]

The insistence on a university training for the senior civil service, and the exclusion of those without independent means, also closed off an important avenue of social mobility within the Prussian civil service, between the 'subaltern' and the higher ranks. Unpaid aspirants to the senior grade were no longer permitted to work in the subaltern service while awaiting establishment; conversely, 'subaltern' officials who were highly educated but lacked the full academic qualifications, were no longer able to rise into the ranks of the *Räte*.[16] This marked an increasingly rigid social stratification within the civil service as its size and diversity expanded. Hierarchies of precedence, titles, honours, and uniforms distinguished the ranks of *Räte* in the highest grade (*höherer Dienst*), and demarcated them from the subaltern officials, who initially lacked full *Beamte* status. In Prussia and some other states, the lower levels of the subaltern service were filled almost exclusively from the military, where short-service NCOs were guaranteed civil-service appointment on discharge; the higher subaltern ranks continued to be filled by well-educated civilians, including men who had failed the examination for the senior grade. These two groups of, respectively, *Versorgungsanwärter* and *Zivilsupernumerare* were the precursors of the lower grade (*unterer* or *einfacher Dienst*) and the superior grade (*gehobener Dienst*) of the civil service. In the course of the century, many officials from both levels of the subaltern service were able to acquire full *Beamte* status, the process varying in speed and scope from state to state.[17] Although categories of non-*Beamte* state employment continued to exist in large numbers—the *Angestellte* (clerks), and the *Arbeiter* (manual employees)—the drift towards *Beamte* status swept up numerous classes of previously untenured officials.

---

[15] Wunder, *Geschichte der Bürokratie*, p. 80; also W. Schärl, *Die Zusammensetzung der bayrischen Beamtenschaft 1806-1918* (Kallmünz, 1955), 79-83; Röhl, 'Higher Civil Servants in Germany', pp. 115 ff.

[16] This was not the case in Württemberg, where all senior officials rose from the ranks; Hattenhauer, *Geschichte des Beamtentums*, pp. 263-4.

[17] Wunder, *Geschichte der Bürokratie*, pp. 58-60, 81-7.

The growth in the number of *Beamte* was also determined by the expansion of the sphere of state activity and administrative employment in the second half of the nineteenth century. Between 1875 and 1907, employment in the civil administration almost trebled;[18] while the German labour force grew by 50 per cent between 1882 and 1907, the personnel of the civil administration expanded by 127 per cent, increasing from about 7 to over 10 per cent of the gainfully employed.[19] As well as staffing the traditional agencies of the administration— whether as ministerial officials, *Landräte* and the like, or as clerks and copyists—public employees were by the end of the century working in huge numbers in newer areas such as transport, communications, and the growing field of municipal enterprise: the number of *Beamte* employed in the postal administration, for example, increased from 34,000 in 1869 to 260,000 in 1913. Women's representation in public employment, previously restricted to elementary education, became somewhat more diverse and numerous after the mid-century, when they were allowed—under discriminatory conditions—into the telegraph and counter services of the postal and railway systems, and worked in increasing numbers in the social and welfare sector.[20]

By the end of the nineteenth century, these developments had set the scene for growing tensions over the definition, composition, and coherence of the civil service. Although the nobility and upper classes continued to dominate the senior grade of the service, especially in Prussia and, after 1870, in the Reich, the complexion of the institution as a whole was deeply affected by its growth and diversification. The extension of *Beamte* status to wide groups of employees had mixed implications, from the point of view both of the state and of the employees themselves. From the latter's point of view, the acquisition of *Beamte* status brought, as we have seen, considerable social and economic advantages, but at the same time subjection to rigid

---

[18] Ibid. 72.

[19] J. P. Cullity, 'The Growth of Governmental Employment in Germany, 1882-1950', *ZgStW*, 123 (1967), 205.

[20] L. Hauff, *Die Entwickelung der Frauenberufe in den letzten drei Jahrzehnten* (Berlin, 1911), 38-41, 63-74, 76-9; C. Hahn, 'Der öffentliche Dienst und die Frauen: Beamtinnen in der Weimarer Republik', in Frauengruppe Faschismusforschung, *Mutterkreuz und Arbeitsbuch: Zur Geschichte der Frauen in der Weimarer Republik und im Nationalsozialismus* (Frankfurt, 1981), 50-2. Women were not admitted to the higher grade until after the war; for the status of the wives of senior civil servants, see S. Meyer, 'Die mühsame Arbeit des demonstrativen Müssiggangs: Über die häuslichen Pflichten der Beamtenfrauen im Kaiserreich', in K. Hausen (ed.), *Frauen suchen ihre Geschichte* (Munich, 1983), 172-94.

disciplinary and behavioural standards. The balance of interest for the state was exactly the reverse. Disciplinary control hedged the advance of social democracy and trade-unionism in mass employment areas like the railways, and the social and material rewards of *Beamte* status might help to bind their beneficiaries more closely to the political status quo. On the other hand, the material privileges—tenure, salary, and pension— which civil servants were now active in claiming and extending, were enormously expensive and increasingly burdensome to states with limited fiscal resources; the same was true for the now vastly expanding municipalities. Reducing the size and cost of the *Beamtentum* by imposing strict legal criteria for the establishment of *Beamte* posts was a key and contested element in the Prussian government's incomplete plans for administrative reform in the years before 1914.[21] It was to remain an equally critical and contentious issue after 1918 as well.

The expectation that *Beamte* could be held at a healthy distance from the changing society around them was thus not entirely fulfilled. By the 1890s, civil servants were grouping into professional associations, stratified by rank, branch, and locality, in order to protect and advance their material status. Some of these associations functioned mainly as social groups or consumer co-operatives, but others cautiously expressed the aspirations of their members in the permitted forms of petitions and electoral addresses. Not surprisingly, it was the mass employment areas like the railways and the postal service that generated some of the earliest and largest of these associations. Although they were all subject to a strenuous state supervision that was intended to crush any incipient signs of social democracy or other political indiscipline, this was not entirely successful in some areas, notably the postal service. Even before the First World War brought a new twist of radicalization to the civil service, some of its rank-and-file members had made contacts with the trade-union movement and with the more liberal political parties. Though the concrete effects of affiliation should not be exaggerated, it is striking that by 1911 almost 60 per cent of German *Beamte* were members of an association of some kind.[22]

[21] P. R. Duggan, 'Currents of Administrative Reform in Germany 1907-1918' Ph.D. thesis (Harvard, 1968).

[22] Hintze, *Beamtenstand*, p. 5. For the early development of civil-service associations and other political activities, see A. Falkenberg, *Die deutsche Beamtenbewegung nach der Revolution* (Berlin, 1920), ch. 2; F. Winter, *Der Deutsche Beamtenbund: Seine Entstehung und Entwicklung* (Berlin, 1931), 7-20; Rejewski, *Pflicht zur politischen Treue*, pp. 99-105, 132-49; G. Kalmer, 'Beamtenschaft und Revolution: Eine sozialgeschichtliche Studie über die Voraussetzungen und Wirklichkeit des Problems', in K. Bosl (ed.), *Bayern im Umbruch* (Munich, 1969), 201-20.

These facts stand in some contrast to the image of the civil service that was still being purveyed by its encomiasts of the time. To its distinguished historians like Otto Hintze or Gustav Schmoller, as well as to dozens of lesser academic and professional apologists, the civil service of imperial Germany was, for all its faults, the apex of an historic process of development that had been taking place since the eighteenth century.[23] Its distinctive quality was its combination of disinterest and independence, which guaranteed its capacity to work genuinely for the public good, and enabled Germany to escape the pitfalls of a parliamentary system of government. Hegel's ideal of the 'universal class' presided over this nineteenth-century ideology:

> What the service of the state really requires is that men shall forgo the selfish and capricious satisfaction of their subjective ends; by this very sacrifice, they acquire the right to find their satisfaction in, but only in, the dutiful discharge of their public functions. In this fact . . . there lies the link between universal and particular interests which constitutes both the concept of the state and its inner stability.[24]

This was reflected in the observation of the rector of Strasbourg University in 1891, that 'No kind of rule is endured so easily or accepted so gratefully as that of high-minded and highly educated civil servants. The German State is a State of the supremacy of officialdom—let us hope that it will remain so.'[25] It was also expressed more rhetorically in Hintze's catalogue of the 'lofty virtues which the civil service has never lacked: legal expertise, a sense of duty, selfless industry, a corporate consciousness, an unyielding sense of justice, simple loyalty', and in his claim that 'it is very hard to construct either a juridical or an economic concept of [civil-service] status. There is in it something unique, something irrational, which can only be grasped in terms of history.'[26]

Possibly there had been an historical reality to which this intellectual account corresponded in the period between the Reform Era and the 1840s, in which, as John Gillis has put it, 'the bureaucracy occupied a position comparable to that enjoyed by Plato's guardian class'.[27] But

---

[23] See D. Lindenlaub, *Richtungskämpfe im Verein für Sozialpolitik: Wissenschaft und Sozialpolitik im Kaiserreich vornehmlich vom Beginn des 'Neuen Kurses' bis zum Ausbruch des Ersten Weltkrieges (1890-1914)* (Wiesbaden, 1967), i. 238-60.

[24] G. W. F. Hegel, *Philosophy of Right*, trans. T. M. Knox (Oxford, 1967), §294; see also §§202 and 205.

[25] Quoted in L. von Mises, *Bureaucracy* (New Haven, 1944), v.

[26] Hintze, *Beamtenstand*, p. 17.

[27] Gillis, *Prussian Bureaucracy*, p. 16.

this had been but a brief episode in the history of the German civil service, corresponding to the balance of political and social forces between the decline of absolutism and corporatism and the development of class society and the constitutional monarchy. Even at the time, Marx had argued in his critique of Hegel that 'the bureaucracy is a network of *practical* illusions, or the "illusion of the state"'.[28]

The 'illusion of the state' suggested that the bureaucracy could be extracted from civil society, or act as the bridge between civil society and the state, and that its members formed a unique *Stand* or estate. Obviously, this was not entirely an illusion. Bureaucracies do generate corporate identities and interests, and these constitute a powerful ethical system which helps to dissolve the ties of family, class, religion, and region. The legal status of the German civil service was peculiar, as we have seen; it provided the basis for an elaborate code of norms and sanctions, a daily repertoire of standards and behaviour that affirmed its distinctiveness to insiders and outsiders alike. Moreover, the idea of the *Ständestaat* still held real authority throughout the nineteenth century as an ideology and structure of social order, within which it was possible to generalize a strong ethos of loyalty to the state as the guarantor of public safety. But the closure of the civil service was impossible to maintain in practice, however important it was to the defence of the status quo. Even before the end of the nineteenth century, it was evident to some observers that bureaucratic image and reality were out of kilter in Germany. Weber—whose name is virtually synonymous with the study of bureaucracy—was himself an acute and pessimistic critic of the German civil service and its apologists by the turn of the century; so were some of its own members.[29] By then, the specifically Prusso-German discourse about the civil service had begun to merge with a more general debate about the role of bureaucracy and administrative control in a society in which the scope of governmental and private managerial activities was vastly expanding, and suggesting new directions for the organization of public life.[30] In 1911, Otto Hintze even surmised that Germany faced a choice 'between the

[28] K. Marx, 'Critique of Hegel's Doctrine of the State', in K. Marx, *Early Writings* (Harmondsworth, 1975), 107. See also V. M. Perez-Diaz, *State, Bureaucracy and Civil Society: A Critical Discussion of the Political Theory of Karl Marx* (London, 1978), ch. 2.

[29] D. Beetham, *Max Weber and the Theory of Modern Politics* (London, 1974), ch. 3; W. J. Mommsen, *Max Weber and German Politics 1890-1920* (Chicago and London, 1984), 163-72; L. E. Schücking, *Die Reaktion in der inneren Verwaltung Preussens* (Berlin, 1908).

[30] J. Kocka, 'Otto Hintze, Max Weber und das Problem der Bürokratie', *Historische Zeitschrift*, 233 (1981), 65-105.

strengthening of social democracy or the extension of civil-service status'.[31] By this he meant that if the growing popular demand for the kind of economic security offered by the *Beamtenverhältnis* were not met by the state, the social democrat promise of planned social welfare would become irresistible. On top of this thesis that civil servants might come to share some of their distinctive privileges with the population at large, the growth of a new sector of white-collar workers suggested a repositioning of the civil service itself, as many of its functions—if not its status—were reproduced in the activities of the *Privatbeamte* and the *Angestellte*. This 'new *Mittelstand*' was a novel actor on the social and political stage, and though its identity and import were not fully addressed by politicians and social theorists until after the war, its impact was already being felt before then.[32] Before 1914, in other words, the *ständisch* assumptions behind civil-service status were already being ruffled by changes inside and beyond the institution.

Recent scholarship has paid more attention to the evidence of cracks in the armour of the late Wilhelmine state, and has become more sceptical of the claims advanced by defenders of its political and social institutions, including the bureaucracy. The apolitical cover of late nineteenth-century Germany has been lifted, to expose the forms of political expression that were active below its surface.[33] We have become more familiar with the extent to which the upper echelons of the civil service were suffused with corruption, patronage, and inefficiency, and with the fact that portions of the rank and file were not quite as servile and self-satisfied as their contemporary image suggested.[34] By the turn of the century, not all civil servants regarded themselves as synonymous with the state, in so far as this was identified as the government of the day. 'State' and 'government' were separable concepts for the mass of civil servants who were not themselves ministers. This was true for the ēlite bureaucrats like the 'canal rebels'

[31] Hintze, *Beamtenstand*, p. 72.

[32] On white-collar work, see in particular J. Kocka, *Die Angestellten in der deutschen Geschichte 1850-1980* (Göttingen, 1981); see also Chapter 3, pp. 70-3, below.

[33] See in general D. Blackbourn and G. Eley, *The Peculiarities of German History* (Oxford, 1984); also R. Koshar, *Social Life, Local Politics, and Nazism: Marburg 1880-1935* (Chapel Hill, 1986).

[34] e.g. P.-C. Witt, 'Der preussische Landrat als Steuerbeamte 1891-1918: Bemerkungen zur politischen und sozialen Funktion des deutschen Beamtentums', in I. Geiss and B.-J. Wendt (eds.), *Deutschland in der Weltpolitik des 19. und 20. Jahrhunderts* (Düsseldorf, 1973), 205-19; also the evidence reviewed in Fenske, 'Preussische Beamtenpolitik', and J. Caplan, '"The Imaginary Universality of Particular Interests": The "Tradition" of the Civil Service in German History', *Social History*, 4/2 (1979), 299-317.

of 1899, whose self-interest brought them into open conflict with Miquel and Bülow; and for the lesser civil servants who saw the government as an employer, if of a special kind, with whom they had to negotiate their own demands. The civil service itself was not the homogeneous ethical corps it represented to its champions, but an increasingly diverse, expensive, and unwieldy bureaucratic apparatus, numbering well over a million persons by the outbreak of the war. In other words, the German civil service was a dynamic and contested system, however rigid and immobile it might have looked on the surface and at the top. As it did to so many of Germany's institutions, the First World War brought challenges that were met only partially or with difficulty. Though the administration did not collapse, the strains on its efficiency and on the loyalty of its personnel were such that by 1918 the call for the reform of the civil service was as irresistible as it was for the German polity as a whole.[35]

---

[35] Apart from the general histories already cited, for the war see J. Kocka, *Klassengesellschaft im Krieg: Deutsche Sozialgeschichte 1914-1918* (Göttingen, 1973), 82-5; Duggan, 'Currents of Administrative Reform', chs. 4-6; and for examples of contemporary reform proposals, A. Grabowsky (ed.), *Die Reform des deutschen Beamtentums* (Gotha, 1917), and B. Drews, *Grundzüge einer Verwaltungsreform* (Berlin, 1917). For the history of the civil service in the war and post-war, see Andreas Kunz, *Civil Servants and the Politics of Inflation in Germany, 1914-1924* (Berlin and New York, 1986), which I received too late to consult for this work.

2

Politics and Depoliticization
1918-1923

I

'Not until the revolution', wrote Arnold Köttgen in 1928, 'did the *Berufsbeamtentum* really become a genuine problem.'[1] Despite its qualifications, his statement implies that the civil service had been unproblematic before 1918—a claim which, as the previous chapter has suggested, was only partly true. The implication that it was the revolution alone that generated difficulties for a previously untroublesome institution needs sceptical assessment, given the accelerating tendency during the Weimar period to deploy the contrast between pre-war stability and Weimar turmoil in the general campaign against the republic. The civil service was an easy pawn to play in this game. Nevertheless, the revolutionary process and its outcome did mark a decisive break in several obvious respects. First, it was self-evident that it was a major political rupture: it established a new form of state and constitution, and this could hardly fail to represent a new departure for the servants of the state. But what was also new was the broad recognition in political discourse that the relationship between the political and administrative aspects of the state was unfixed and contentious. If this recognition had been confined before the war to relatively narrow and specialist circles of debate, after 1918 it became a prominent theme of public argument, inside and outside the government.[2] Secondly, the revolution expressed and developed a complex of social tensions from which civil servants were no more immune than other social groups. It was, after all, a process of class struggle among other things, and called into question the structure of social relations as well as the relationship between state and civil society.[3] For the participants in the embryonic

[1] A. Köttgen, *Das deutsche Berufsbeamtentum und die parlamentarische Demokratie* (Berlin and Leipzig, 1928), 1.

[2] For amplification of this, see K. D. Bracher, *Die Auflösung der Weimarer Republik: Eine Studie zum Problem des Machtverfalls in der Demokratie* (Düsseldorf, 1978), 163 ff.

[3] Recent historical research has stressed the revolution as a social conflict in particular. For a review of the issue, see W. J. Mommsen, 'The German Revolution 1918-1920: Political Revolution and Social Protest Movement', in R. Bessel and

government in November 1918, as for the established republican state after 1919, the problem of the bureaucracy presented itself in threefold form: the interconnected problems of the civil service as a *Stand*; as the personnel of the modern administrative state; and as a linchpin of political stability. Whether it would be possible to combine a solution to these problems in a single coherent policy became a profound dilemma for the young republic.

The existing literature on the problem of the bureaucracy in the revolution and the republic has tended to explore and emphasize the institutional hostility of the civil service to parliamentary democracy, its unwillingness to accept the terms of party politics, and its contribution to the decomposition of the parliamentary system after 1930.[4] As a general description of the bureaucracy and some of its leading members this can hardly be disputed, and yet it also tends to see the bureaucracy as an institution defined primarily by its structural unity and continuity, giving this relatively more explanatory weight than the processes of change and internal division that were also part of civil servants' experience in the post-war years. As Peter-Christian Witt has argued in his study of the Reich finance administration in the 1920s, however, it

E. J. Feuchtwanger (eds.), *Social Change and Political Development in Weimar Germany* (London, 1981), 21-54; for a review of recent literature, see also R. Rürup (ed.), *Arbeiter- und Soldatenräte im rheinisch-westfälischen Industriegebiet: Studien zur Geschichte der Revolution 1918/19* (Wuppertal, 1975), 'Einleitung'. In *Der Hüter der Verfassung* 2nd edn. (Berlin, 1962), 149-65, Carl Schmitt discusses the problem of what he saw as the ambiguity of the civil servant's status given the dissolution of any distance between state and society in contemporary Germany.

[4] There has been no monographic study of Reich civil-service policy comparable to the Prussian research of W. Runge, *Politik und Beamtentum im Parteienstaat: Die Demokratisierung der politischen Beamten in Preussen zwischen 1918 und 1933* (Stuttgart, 1965). Surveys include Bracher, *Auflösung*, ch. 7; H. Fenske, 'Monarchisches Beamtentum und demokratischer Staat: Zum Problem der Bürokratie in der Weimarer Republik', in *Demokratie und Verwaltung: 25 Jahre Hochschule für Verwaltung Speyer* (Berlin, 1972), 117-36; R. Morsey, 'Beamtenschaft und Verwaltung zwischen Republik und "Neuem Staat"', in K. D. Erdmann and H. Schulze (eds.), *Weimar: Selbstpreisgabe einer Demokratie* (Düsseldorf, 1980), 151-68; E. Frank, 'The Role of the Bureaucracy in Transition', *Journal of Politics*, 27 (1966), 724-53; H. Mommsen, 'Staat und Bürokratie in der Ära Bruning', in G. Jasper (ed.), *Tradition und Reform in der deutschen Politik: Gedenkschrift für Waldemar Besson* (Frankfurt, 1976), 81-137. Prussia continues to attract the most attention; apart from Runge, see also H.-K. Behrend, 'Zur Personalpolitik des preussischen Ministeriums des Innern: Die Besetzung der Landratsstellen in den östlichen Provinzen 1919-1933', *Jahrbuch für die Geschichte Mittel- und Ostdeutschlands*, 6 (1957), 173-214; H. Möller, 'Die preussischen Oberpräsidenten der Weimarer Republik als Verwaltungselite', *VjhZ*, 30 (1982), 1-26; L. Muncy, 'The Junkers and the Prussian Administration from 1918 to 1937', *Review of Politics*, 9 (1947), 482-501; E. Pikart, 'Preussische Beamtenpolitik 1918-33', *VjhZ*, 6 (1958), 119-37. Further and contemporary references are cited below.

is only empirical research that can reveal the actual contours of continuity and tradition: it is not reasonable simply to infer them from the silence of structural persistence.[5] Although very little research of this kind exists, either for the years 1918-19 or later, what there is suggests that the image of the 'closed civil service *Stand*'[6] has been cultivated to such an extent that it obscures other realities of the bureaucracy: the degree of differentiation within the civil service, and the fluctuations of political experience and position in the 1920s and early 1930s.

The conventional image of civil-service hostility to, indeed, structural incompatibility with, the parliamentary republic is one that has been drawn largely from the study of the relationship between the origins and the fall of the republic. As one representative summary puts it:

Already mostly bound by origins and education to the monarchical-authoritarian tradition, the greater part of the bureaucracy in the Reich and in the Länder had been unable to reconcile with the party state of the Weimar Republic their traditional conception of the 'servant of the state' as the guardian and representative of a disciplined society. Party politics . . . earned the barely concealed contempt of the old civil servants, who saw in the state a higher point of power and order . . . the true higher purpose of the state after the end of the monarchy was identified with the eternal and supra-individual Nation . . .[7]

In one sense, of course, this is true; yet how is it to be reconciled with the fact that in Weimar the Reichstag consistently contained more civil-servant deputies than in the empire?[8] Or that the DNVP, the most traditional of the conservative parties, had its own large complement of deputies mainly from the senior grade, the most ēlite representatives of the old civil-service order?[9] Or that the DDP, which consciously saw

---

[5] P.-C. Witt, 'Reichsfinanzminister und Reichsfinanzverwaltung: Zum Problem des Verhältnisses von politischer Führung und bürokratischer Herrschaft in den Anfangsjahren der Weimarer Republik', *VjhZ*, 23 (1975), 1-2, 21 ff.

[6] Bracher, *Auflösung*, p. 169.

[7] M. Broszat, *The Hitler State: The Foundation and Development of the Internal Structure of the Third Reich* (London, 1981), 11.

[8] Figures given in F. Poetzsch-Heffter, 'Vom Staatsleben unter der Weimarer Republik', *JöR*, 17 (1929), 71; A. Falkenberg, *Die deutsche Beamtenbewegung nach der Revolution* (Berlin, 1920), 95; H. Schmahl, *Disziplinarrecht und politische Betätigung der Beamten in der Weimarer Republik* (Berlin, 1977), 215. Schmahl breaks the figures down according to party, and also gives civil-service membership in the Prussian Landtag. Discrepancies between the figures in these sources are due to different methods of categorizing *Beamte* (including or excluding teachers, judges, etc.).

[9] Stated in G. Hoffmann, *Sozialdemokratie und Berufsbeamtentum: Zur Frage nach Wandel und Kontinuität im Verhältnis der Sozialdemokratie zum Berufsbeamtentum in der Weimarer Zeit* (Hamburg, 1972), 61.

itself as the representative of civil-service interests, repeatedly identified the parties of the left as magnets for civil-service voters?[10] How was it, finally, that this pervasive sense of bureaucratic resistance to the terms of pluralist politics could coexist with a level of civil-service associational membership that remained consistently higher than trade-union membership throughout the republic?[11]

At the very least, evidence of this kind suggests a defensive mobilization by civil servants, and a willingness to make use of the techniques offered by a political system which they may have affected to despise. But beyond this, its very variety also indicates that it may not always make sense to speak of the civil service as a homogeneous group, even in a republic in which it was in many respects an outsider. In the 1920s, only some 2 per cent of Reich civil servants were in the higher grade of the service, to which the ascription of an élite corps homogeneity is most applicable. Almost half of all civil servants in Germany were employed in the *Betriebsverwaltungen*, such as the postal and railway systems, where working conditions were quasi-industrial; and some tens of thousands of civil servants in the 1920s were women, excluded virtually by definition from any easy identification with a traditional élite.[12] In terms of mass organization, 1918 saw a temporary convergence

[10] This was claimed by speakers at DDP party and executive committee meetings, e.g. 28 Sept. 1919 (Hartmann: 'Many voters have run off to the extreme left. This is happening especially among *Angestellte* and *Beamte*'); 19 July 1922 (Erkelenz: 'Workers, *Angestellte* and *Beamte* . . . will go to the left, and then we shall have exactly what we now want to avoid, a socialist majority'): see K. Wegner and L. Albertin (eds.), *Linksliberalismus in der Weimarer Republik: Die Führungsgremien der Deutschen Demokratischen Partei und der Deutschen Staatspartei 1918–1933* (Düsseldorf, 1980), 92, 269–70. See also H. Schüstereit, *Linksliberalismus und Sozialdemokratie in der Weimarer Republik* (Düsseldorf, 1975), ch. 8; W. Schneider, *Die Deutsche Demokratische Partei in der Weimarer Republik 1924–1930* (Munich, 1978), 184–6. The DDP consistently had the highest proportion of civil-servant members in its Reichstag delegation of any political party, though of course its parliamentary representation shrank drastically after 1919; see Schmahl, *Disziplinarrecht*, p. 215.

[11] Associational membership is examined in A. Kunz, 'Stand versus Klasse: Beamtenschaft und Gewerkschaften im Konflikt um den Personalabbau 1923/24', *Geschichte und Gesellschaft*, 8 (1982), 55–86. For an example of the complex situations that could arise from this new level of associational mobilization, see E. Pikart, 'Berufsbeamtentum und Parteienstaat: Eine Fallstudie', *Zeitschrift für Politik*, NF 7 (1960), 225–40. For an early statement in favour of political activism by senior civil servants, see the report of the second delegate conference of the RhB, 22–3 March 1919 (copy in BA R 43I/2630).

[12] For further discussion of the composition of the civil service in the 1920s, see Ch. 3, pp. 60–1, below; also Kunz, 'Stand versus Klasse', p. 61; for women civil servants, see C. Hahn, 'Der öffentliche Dienst und die Frauen: Beamtinnen in der Weimarer Republik', in Frauengruppe Faschismusforschung, *Mutterkreuz und Arbeitsbuch: Zur Geschichte der Frauen in der Weimarer Republik und im Nationalsozialismus* (Frankfurt, 1981), 49–78.

of the vast majority of civil servants—over a million—into affiliation with the Deutscher Beamtenbund (DBB), which was pro-republican and officially neutral in party terms, although it was led by the DDP deputy Ernst Remmers. In subsequent years this unity fell apart, first with the secession in 1921 of the Reichsbund der höheren Beamten (RhB), with some 60,000 members; this was followed by the loss in 1922 of some 350,000 more members who formed the trade-union-affiliated Allgemeiner Deutscher Beamtenbund (ADB).[13] In other words, civil servants formed part of that temporary, but remarkable convergence of anti-authoritarian sentiment that swept Germany in 1918-19, although, like most participants, they were less clear about their positive aims and tactics than they were about what they were rejecting.

The extent to which the leaderships of such large and heterogeneous associations could accurately 'represent' the interests and aspirations of their widely dispersed memberships is debatable, of course. This is especially true of the DBB before the splits of 1921-2, when its membership amounted to a million or more. What does seem clear, however, is that the politicization and activism of the DBB and its membership in 1918 was not simply a sudden, panicked response to the threats presented by revolution and the possibility of civil war. Hugo Preuss was to refer later to civil servants' 'panic-stricken fear' that their rights would be abrogated by the new state,[14] but this was something that was vented especially during the drafting of the constitution, in the spring

---

[13] Apart from the DBB and ADB, the other umbrella associations (*Spitzenverbände*) to which local and departmental groups were affiliated were: the Reichsbund der höheren Beamten (RhB), whose membership grew from about 23,000 in 1918 to a steady 100,000 from the mid-1920s; the Christian-nationalist Gesamtverband Deutscher Beamtengewerkschaften (GDB), which took its 150,000 members into the DBB in 1926; and the nationalist (Hirsch-Düncker) Ring Deutscher Beamtenverbände (RDB), which had about 65,000 members at its maximum in 1924. The *Spitzenverbände* were officially recognized for negotiating purposes by the government; see Reich interior ministry to Reich chancellery, 22 Apr. 1924 (BA R 43I/2650). The DBB was instrumental in the establishment of an interior-ministry department for civil-service affairs in 1920; see documentation in BA R 43I/990, ff. 3-50. See also Kunz, 'Stand versus Klasse', pp. 58-61; Falkenberg, *Deutsche Beamtenbewegung*; E. Lederer and J. Marschak, 'Der neue Mittelstand', *Grundrisse der Sozialökonomik*, 9 (Tübingen, 1926), 129; E. Schron, 'Deutscher Beamtenbund (DBB) 1918-1933', and D. Fricke, 'Reichsbund der höheren Beamten (RhB) 1918-1934', in D. Fricke (ed.), *Handbuch der bürgerlichen Parteien und anderer bürgerlicher Interessenorganisationen* (Leipzig, 1968), i. 422-8, ii. 493-500. See also *Deutscher Beamtenbund: Ursprung, Weg, Ziele* (Bad Godesberg, 1968); A. Bartels, 'Die deutsche Beamtenbewegung', in A. Erkelenz, *Zehn Jahre Deutscher Republik*, (Berlin, 1929), 344-51.

[14] Quoted in Schmahl, *Disziplinarrecht*, p. 35; Preuss was writing in 1923.

of 1919. By that time, the contours of the post-revolutionary state were emerging clearly, and the struggle for the protection of special interests had become distinct from any more comprehensive revolutionary vision. Before that, however, the involvement of civil servants in the revolution, wary though it was, can be seen as the culmination of an older process of voluntary organization on behalf of their political and employment interests. In November 1918, this typically involved issuing a profession of loyalty to the emerging regimes in Reich and *Länder*, together with claims for job and pension security, and for political rights. Civil servants also demanded to be included in the workers' councils, and established their own *Beamtenräte* to represent their interests.[15]

These claims were met more than half-way by the Reich and *Land* regimes that were struggling to establish their legitimacy in November 1918. Thus, Ebert's initial appeal to civil servants on 9 November was highly conciliatory, even conservative in tone, summoning them to stay at their posts in the name of *Volk* and *Vaterland* rather than in the spirit of the new republic.[16] In a sense this was inevitable, given the political strategy of the SPD leadership. The alternative to calling the existing administration to co-operate in familiar and sedative language, was indeed to risk large-scale, high-level bureaucratic resistance, and thus to be thrown into the embrace of the radical politico-administrative structure represented in embryo by the workers' and soldiers' councils. This was anathema, of course, to Ebert's strategy of achieving the political transition to republican democracy with the maximum of order and continuity, and the minimum of open rupture with the past. The

---

[15] Evidence for the behaviour of civil servants during the revolution is not abundant. For a model study, see G. Kalmer, 'Beamtenschaft und Revolution: Eine sozialgeschichtliche Studie über die Voraussetzungen und Wirklichkeit des Problems', in K. Bosl (ed.), *Bayern im Umbruch* (Munich, 1969), 201-61. See also S. Miller, *Die Bürde der Macht: Die deutsche Sozialdemokratie 1918-1920* (Düsseldorf, 1978), 163-75; Hoffmann, *Sozialdemokratie und Berufsbeamtentum*, pp. 30-51; E. Kolb, *Die Arbeiterräte in der deutschen Innenpolitik 1918-1919* (Düsseldorf, 1962), ch. 10; W. Elben, *Das Problem der Kontinuität in der deutschen Revolution 1918-1919* (Düsseldorf, 1965); A. J. Nicholls, 'Die höhere Beamtenschaft in der Weimarer Zeit: Betrachtungen zu Problemen ihrer Haltung und ihrer Fortbildung', in L. Albertin and W. Link (eds.), *Politische Parteien auf dem Weg zur parlamentarischen Demokratie in Deutschland: Entwicklungslinien bis zur Gegenwart* (Düsseldorf, 1981), 195-207. For an example of senior civil servants' attitudes, see the 'Aufruf an alle höheren Verwaltungsbeamten des Reiches und der Bundesstaaten', circulated by the Berufsverein höherer Verwaltungsbeamten, 31 Dec. 1918 (GStA Rep. 184/221).

[16] Text in E. R. Huber, *Dokumente zur deutschen Verfassungsgeschichte*, ii (Stuttgart, 1964), 512; discussed in Miller, *Bürde der Macht*, p. 163; Hoffmann, *Sozialdemokratie und Berufsbeamtentum*, p. 31.

transitional structure of the Berlin government reflected and enacted this choice. Civil servants at the highest levels—ministerial advisers and the like—were left relatively untouched, and they performed exactly the task of securing order and legitimacy which had been allotted to them. The concentration of administrative authority on these, more or less intact, inherited central offices severely, and deliberately, limited the scope of action available further down the hierarchy and away from the centre. Ministerial civil servants in Berlin routinely resisted local political pressure for personnel changes in the field, or simply stalled by not answering complaints. This strategy was maintained for months, despite mounting demands both from the councils and from the SPD rank and file for an immediate and effective personnel purge, without which they believed democracy could not be safeguarded.[17]

The failure to embark on a systematic revision of administrative structure and personnel was thus not an error of judgement, nor was it a course of action forced by the lack of any alternative. It was a deliberate policy choice which established the priorities of the SPD leadership, not without the initial, though increasingly grudging, connivance of the USPD leaders. It has been suggested that it was not the old civil service that sabotaged the revolution by its active resistance, but the political leadership that voluntarily and intentionally placed the bureaucracy in a position in which it would necessarily have the effect of braking the momentum of revolutionary change.[18] The SPD leadership's priority was to stabilize a defeated and disordered nation, and Ebert especially was convinced that this was impossible without the collaboration of the existing administration. Thus, the solution of an immediate problem was approached by means which incurred a potential danger for the republic in the future.

This does not mean that any alternative would have succeeded better, or would have been more acceptable to civil servants. The social and political cleavages in Germany were far too deep, and the hostility of the radical left towards the imperial administration was far too strong, for any convergence of revolutionary and democratic impulses to have been likely of prolonged success. Moreover, as the following years were to confirm, it was extraordinarily difficult in practice to combine

---

[17] See Kolb, *Arbeiterräte*, pp. 362 ff; Behrend, 'Personalpolitik', pp. 195 ff; for intra-governmental relations in the early months of the republic, see principally Elben, *Problem der Kontinuität*, and E. Matthias, *Zwischen Räten und Geheimräten: Die deutsche Revolutionsregierung 1918/19* (Düsseldorf, 1970).

[18] Miller, *Bürde der Macht*, p. 174.

enmity to bureaucratic authoritarianism as a structure with support for the rights of individual state employees as workers. Indeed, this was to be one of the presiding dilemmas of Weimar civil-service policy, as we shall see. Yet this was also one of the impulses behind the early civil-service policy of the republic, including the drafting of the constitution. The revolution itself showed that the construction of a legitimate relationship between the state and its servants was perilously similar to allowing the republic to be recaptured by an un-reconstructed administrative apparatus. Yet it also demonstrated the extent of civil-service claims for their dissociation from the traditional entailments of *Stand*. Efforts to disaggregate employment rights from *ständisch* status persisted at least until the early 1920s, when they were drowned by new pressures and divisions in the civil service. In the early years, however, civil servants were represented by associations committed to a concept of their members' aims and interests that straddled some of the distance between service and employment, between private privilege and public right, between the archaic and the modernizing. How these ambiguities would be disentangled, articulated, and resolved would depend partly upon the flow of political argument. It was the constitution that carved out one of the principal channels for this, and it is to this that we must now turn.

II

The drafting of the constitution after January 1919 became the first occasion for taking up the question of administrative structure and reform that had been in the offing since November 1918.[19] The two

[19] There has been no monographic study of the Weimar Constitution since W. Apelt, *Geschichte der Weimarer Verfassung* (Munich and Berlin, 1964; orig. edn., 1946). Apelt was an assistant of Preuss's in the Reich interior ministry in 1918-19 and later an academic jurist; his comprehensive work reflects both perspectives, but is inevitably not based on public archival sources, and also lacks both full references and a bibliography. G. Schulz, *Zwischen Demokratie und Diktatur: Verfassungspolitik und Reichsreform in der Weimarer Republik, i. Die Periode der Konsolidierung und der Revision des Bismarckschen Reichsaufbaus 1919-1930* (Berlin, 1963), 1-212, is the most comprehensive recent study of the development of the constitution, in the light of regional tensions in particular. See also T. Eschenburg, *Die improvisierte Demokratie: Gesammelte Aufsätze zur Weimarer Republik* (Munich, 1963). Both F. Hartung, *Deutsche Verfassungsgeschichte vom 15. Jahrhundert bis zur Gegenwart* (Stuttgart, 1969; orig. edn., 1950), and H. W. Koch, *A Constitutional History of Germany in the Nineteenth and Twentieth Centuries* (London, 1984), are surveys, Koch's being as much a political as a constitutional history. For recent interpretations of the context and fate of the constitution, see e.g. H. Potthoff, 'Verfassungsväter ohne Verfassungsvolk? Zum Problem von Integration und

aspects that concern us most here are the form in which the constitution guaranteed the terms of public service, and its handling of the Reich's administrative structure. Both of these delineated lines of policy that were to be of great importance both for the republic and for the Nazi state.

It has long been argued that the guarantee of civil servants' vested rights contained in Article 129 of the Weimar Constitution, a guarantee which included the right of tenure, saddled the new republic with a crippling burden from the past, and demonstrated the power of a privileged group to mortgage Germany's political future to its own interests. The crucial parts of Article 129 declared that: 'Civil servants are appointed on life tenure, unless otherwise provided by statute. Pensions and dependants' allowances are to be statutorily regulated. The vested rights of civil servants are inviolable. . . . Only under the conditions and procedures as statutorily provided may civil servants be temporarily suspended from office, provisionally or finally retired, or transferred to a post with an inferior salary.'[20] The critical sentence here was: 'The vested rights of civil servants are inviolable', for this by implication abridged any other authority that might otherwise be derived from the constitution or other statutory sources to tamper with tenure and material benefits. As such, the article has been seen as one of the cardinal errors of the republic, and certainly it was to store up unexpected trouble for the future.[21] As long as civil servants took

Desintegration nach der Novemberrevolution', in G. A. Ritter (ed.), *Gesellschaft, Parlament und Regierung: Zur Geschichte des Parlamentarismus in Deutschland* (Düsseldorf, 1974), 339-54; E. Friesenhahn, 'Zur Legitimation und zum Scheitern der Weimarer Verfassung', in Erdmann and Schulze (eds.), *Weimar*, pp. 81-108. The constitution itself is reprinted in Huber, *Dokumente*, iii. 129-56, and in English translation in R. Brunet, *The New German Constitution* (New York, 1922), appendix. Contemporary studies of the constitution were abundant, of course; I have consulted principally G. Anschütz, *Die Verfassung des Deutschen Reiches* (Bad Homburg, 1960; orig. edn., 1921); G. Anschütz and R. Thoma (eds.), *Handbuch des deutschen Staatsrechts*, 2 vols. (Tübingen, 1932); F. F. Blachly and M. Oatman, *The Government and Administration of Germany* (Baltimore, 1928); H. de Grais and H. Peters, *Handbuch der Verfassung und Verwaltung in Preussen und dem Deutschen Reich* (Berlin, 1926); W. Jellinek, 'Revolution und Reichsverfassung', *JöR*, 9 (1920), 1-128; O. Meissner, *Das neue Staatsrecht des Reiches und seiner Länder* (Berlin, 1921); Axel Frhr. von Freytagh-Loringhoven, *Die Weimarer Verfassung in Lehre und Wirklichkeit* (Munich, 1924).

[20] For a review of contemporary opinion on the vested rights, see H. Bruns, *Das Prinzip verfassungsrechtlicher Sicherung der Beamtenrechte* (Cologne, 1955), 20 ff.

[21] For this judgement, see e.g. A. Brecht, 'Personnel Management', in E. H. Litchfield (ed.), *Governing Post-War Germany* (Ithaca, 1953), 264; Bracher, *Auflösung*, pp. 162-72. For a more circumspect contemporary view, see Freytagh-Loringhoven, *Weimarer Verfassung*, pp. 321-8. Note, however, the tradition of anchoring civil-service law in the constitution; see B. Wunder, *Geschichte der Bürokratie in Deutschland* (Frankfurt, 1986), 29, 112.

oath of loyalty, the provisions of Article 129 made it impossible to dismiss them (unless they belonged to the small group of untenured 'political' *Beamte*), and thus it stood squarely in the way of administrative reform after 1919. At the same time, the oath was no real guarantee of loyalty, as we shall see, and so an invaluable policy instrument—the right to dismiss political recalcitrants—was apparently given away for nothing. Moreover, the fact that service status was enshrined in the constitution, rather than being relegated to ordinary statute law, made certain that it would always tend to be elevated to an affair of state, instead of remaining a more mundane aspect of administrative policy. Once again, this was to become enormously problematic in later years, as the extent of the guarantee was tested in the courts and in political debate.

The dangers of Article 129 were by no means hidden from the drafters of the constitution, and in fact the original draft contained no references at all to the status, rights, or duties of civil servants. Preuss's January draft aimed to confine the constitution to a restatement of the relations between the Reich and the constituent states; it specified only the two fundamental liberal rights of equality before the law and freedom of conscience and religion.[22] However, in the course of the constitutional committee's deliberations in the spring of 1919, this parsimonious Bismarckian protocol was transformed into the distended document it eventually became—what Delbrück called a 'hypertrophy'. The constitution became, in effect, a magnet for every interest that could represent itself as more than sectional, and the political parties were not slow to realize the dividends they could draw from sponsoring appropriate concerns. The claims of civil servants were advanced as part of these processes, and of course they had the unusual advantage of being easily represented as integral to the public good. This quality was not unique to the civil service—the articles on the *Mittelstand* and the family, for instance, incorporated a similar invocation of the public interest—but it drew on a unique authority, and allowed the parties to the right of the SPD, notably the DNVP, to champion the civil servants' cause without appearing entirely partisan. In March, the DBB met with the constitutional committee to press its insistence on security of tenure for civil servants as a matter of national interest. Even the SPD committee members were persuaded by this, and retreated from

[22] Apelt, *Weimarer Verfassung*, pp. 59 ff.

their party's formal commitment to the Erfurt programme's demand for
an elective bureaucracy. This left only the USPD attached to a radical
reform of the bureaucracy, and allowed the SPD to join in the general
rush to sponsor the interests of civil servants. But it did not do this with
great energy and enthusiasm, and whether it managed to attract many
civil servants into its ranks is doubtful. However, in the constitutional
committee the SPD representatives did prompt discussion of subjective
material rights in such matters as disciplinary law, equal opportunity,
and the administrative equivalent of the works councils (the *Beamtenvertretungen*), thereby exposing the reluctance of the DNVP to back its
concern for the civil service with real support for officials' personal
rights.[23]

No less important a reason for the inclusion of Article 129 was the
fact that it was in a real sense the pay-off for the regime's appeals for
bureaucratic co-operation since November 1918. It was the practical
realization of these verbal commitments to respect the rights of civil
servants, and any retreat from this risked a massive defection of loyalty.
Deeply opposed though he was to overloading the constitution with
specific commitments, Preuss recognized the force of this argument. 'I
am enormously sympathetic to every suggestion for limiting the basic
rights', he said in the committee debates in May:

But I beg you nevertheless to include at least some of this article [Article 39b,
an early version of the codification of rights which became Article 129]. It is
certainly doubtful whether it is the right tactic to hand out a gift to every
interest [*Stand*]—flowers to that one, fruit to this. But that is what has now
happened. From the very beginning the civil service has been very nervous;
they were worried especially that their entire status might be abolished as a
result of the upheavals, even though this was in fact scarcely a practical
possibility. If you omit the second paragraph, there will be *great alarm among
civil servants*. Precisely the stipulation of tenured appointment for civil servants
. . . the inviolability of vested rights—it is this clause that I regard as desirable in
the interests of calming civil servants, and this above all because now that it has
been requested its deletion would surely cause alarm.[24]

---

23 The SPD's position is discussed in detail in Hoffmann, *Sozialdemokratie und
Berufsbeamtentum*, pp. 68-72, and for Ebert's views, pp. 75-80; see also Schmahl,
Disziplinarrecht, pp. 37 ff., and Falkenberg, *Deutsche Beamtenbewegung*, pp. 51 ff. See
also documentation, including a statement of the principles of the SPD policy, by Ebert,
9 July 1919 (BA R 43I/2551).
24 *Verhandlungen der verfassungsgebenden Deutschen Nationalversammlung*, 336,
Anlagen zu den stenographischen Berichten, (Session 33, 30 May 1919), 382.

By means of arguments such as this, through the pressure exerted by the DBB, and the responses of the party representatives in the constitutional committee and the National Assembly, Article 129 became part of Section 2 of the Weimar Constitution, one of a group of four articles (128-31) dealing with civil servants.[25] Koch-Weser criticized the entire second section of the constitution for confusing existing law with guidelines for future legislation,[26] and Article 128 contained three separate commitments. The first declared that all citizens had free access to public office 'in accordance with statute and with regard to their qualifications and abilities'—a clear statement of rights. The next paragraph declared the repeal of all measures discriminating against women in the civil service. This again was a clear statement of rights, but one which, as we shall see, was violated by the state for most of its existence. The final paragraph stated that the principles of civil-service status would be regulated by Reich law: this was a commitment to a future act of legislation, and one that was never fulfilled. Article 129, as we have already suggested, was thoroughly unclear on whether it guaranteed an individual right or the existence of an institution. Did it, in other words, guarantee each and every civil servant's right to tenure, to a *standesgemäss* income, to pensions and dependants' allowances? Or was it rather a commitment to the preservation of civil-service status as a system, with no assurance about the situation of any individual member? Finally, the provisions of Article 130 were deeply ambiguous. It began with a rhetorical flourish in the spirit of Naumann: 'Civil servants are the servants of the community, not of any party', and continued with: 'All civil servants are guaranteed freedom of political opinion and association'. This newly granted right clearly met the democratic standards demanded by the DBB, liberals, and the SPD, freeing civil servants from restrictions on their political activity. Yet it did this through the creation of an absolute right, which was not even circumscribed by a specific provision analogous to that of Article 118, which qualified the general exercise of civil rights by subjecting them to 'the limits of the general law'. The tension between the two parts of

---

[25] The other articles declared equal access to civil-service appointment, and pledged a Reich civil-service law (128); stated that civil servants were 'servants of all, not of a party'; guaranteed freedom of political opinion and association; foresaw civil-service councils (*Beamtenvertretungen*, on the model of the works councils) (130); and regulated legal liability for official acts (131). Article 176 provided for the administration of an oath of loyalty, and Article 39 guaranteed the right of civil servants to run for election to Reichstag and Landtag.

[26] Cited in Apelt, *Weimarer Verfassung*, p. 116.

Article 130 was blatant and troubling, given the depth of political divisions in post-war Germany, and it was to become the subject of heated debate in later years. While the first sentence clearly suggested that political neutrality would be expected of civil servants, the second, with equal clarity, promised them wide freedom of political behaviour. This ambiguity was the more threatening in that Weimar's political parties did not share a consensus in support of the new constitution. It was thus possible to argue that a civil servant affiliated to the KPD or DNVP in 1920, for example, or to the NSDAP in 1932, was abusing his or her rights.

The provisions of the constitution established the terms in which governmental freedom of action in civil-service policy would have to be negotiated, and in which the civil-service associations manoeuvred between the concepts of collective rights in employment, the demands of public interest, and the appeal to the privileges of *Stand*. If the constitutional committee acted under political constraint in 1919, this was to extend a deep shadow into the future of governmental policy; while the ambiguity of interest and language left a space in which civil servants would ultimately be willing to respond to new forms of *ständisch* collectivism, having failed, with Germany, to make a clean break with the past in 1918-19.

Section 2 of the Weimar Constitution was, as a whole, one of the most blatantly improvised aspects of what Preuss at an early stage had labelled 'Die Improvisierung des Parlamentarismus'.[27] Nevertheless, even the first section, which dealt with the relationship of Reich and *Länder* and which was the heart of Preuss's original project, revealed great deficiencies as far as administrative policy was concerned. These were the consequence of the strong competition of interests in play, especially the resistance to the drift towards a more unitary state. It has been argued that the revolution did not weaken particularism, but strengthened it.[28] Preuss's aim of combining a unitary constitutional

---

[27] In an article in *Norddeutsche Allgemeine Zeitung*, 26 Oct. 1918, reprinted in H. Preuss, *Staat, Recht und Freiheit: Aus 40 Jahren deutscher Politik und Geschichte* (Hildesheim, 1964), 361-4.

[28] This point is made strongly by Apelt, *Weimarer Verfassung*, pp. 62 ff. For further discussion of the federal problem, see primarily Schulz, *Demokratie und Diktatur*; E. Eimers, *Das Verhältnis von Preussen und Reich in den ersten Jahren der Weimarer Republik (1918-1923)* (Berlin, 1969); also H. Jacob, *German Administration since Bismarck: Central Authority versus Local Autonomy* (New Haven and London, 1963); H.-P. Ehni, *Bollwerk Preussen? Preussenregierung, Reich-Länder Problem und Sozial-demokratie 1928-1932* (Bonn and Bad Godesberg, 1975); R. Schlesinger, *Federalism in*

structure with parliamentary democracy thus contained a basic contradiction. The objective may have been to use the end of the old ruling dynasties to effect a fundamental territorial and political rationalization of the German state, and to push the centralization of sovereign authority as far as was required to achieve this. But it was frustrated by the refusal of the *Länder* to accept the necessary degree of political concentration, even if this were accompanied by broad administrative decentralization. This refusal meant that a determined curtailment of regional particularism would be incompatible with the principles of parliamentary democracy—it would, to use Apelt's word, be a 'Gewaltherrschaft', a rule of force.[29] Although this was only latent in Weimar while the matter remained unresolved, it was to emerge fully after 1933, when the problem of regionalism was subjected to brutal solution. At any rate, the version of Section 1 of the constitution which emerged from the deliberations of the constitutional committee and the National Assembly was far from meeting Preuss's original objectives; this was the result in particular of pressure from Bavaria, both in its socialist and conservative incarnations. It is hardly an exaggeration to conclude that what survived of the principle of strong federal unity was secured more by the status and powers of the president than by the actual Reich-*Land* dispositions. In other words, German unity was premised on the capacity of the presidency to become the centre of a plebiscitary dictatorship, and this was to become one of the major sources for the enhancement of executive power.

The tension between the power of the Reich to maintain central control, and the unwillingness of the *Länder* to let this become effective, bedevilled all aspects of administrative policy in Weimar. As Arnold Brecht wrote in 1931, after years of intimate and frustrating familiarity with the issues, and in the middle of the last phase of public discussion of constitutional reform, the Weimar Republic had stopped half-way along the road to becoming a unitary state (*Einheitsstaat*).[30] It was saddled by its constitution with a politically and administratively obstreperous structure, and was burdened by the disparity of the *Länder*

Central and Eastern Europe (New York, 1945), part 2; F. Menges, *Reichsreform und Finanzpolitik: Die Aushöhlung der Eigenstaatlichkeit Bayerns auf finanzpolitischem Wege in der Zeit der Weimarer Republik* (Berlin, 1971).

[29] Apelt, *Weimarer Verfassung*, p. 63.

[30] A. Brecht, *Reichsreform: Warum und Wie?* (Berlin, 1931), 9. See his *Federalism and Regionalism in Germany: The Division of Prussia* (New York, 1945), and his two volumes of autobiography, *Aus nächster Nähe: Lebenserinnerungen eines beteiligten Beobachters 1886-1927* (Stuttgart, 1966), and *Mit der Kraft des Geistes: Lebenserinnerungen zweite*

in size and population, by the idiosyncracies of internal borders, and by the overlapping and confusion of a dual administrative system. In the years of relative stabilization after 1924, plans for the further resolution of this unsettled structure were slowly developed, and the need for a more formal level of unity was now better recognized by the bourgeois parties (apart from the unregenerate BVP). The debates involved three different projects of reform: 'Verfassungsreform', or constitutional reform in the strict sense; 'Reichsreform', or changes in the territorial and sovereign relations between Reich and *Länder*, or between *Land* and *Land*; and 'Verwaltungsreform,' which was administrative reform not involving constitutional relations. There were some achievements in the realms of *Reichsreform* and *Verwaltungsreform*—the rationalization of internal borders, the amalgamation of some smaller units, the redrawing of administrative boundaries—and larger-scale plans matured towards the summoning of a conference of *Länder* in 1929 and 1930. But the chances for reform by parliamentary means were already narrowing by then, as the democratic character of the state was critically compromised under Brüning, and the movement towards executive and authoritarian solutions began. As early as 1924, the Reich economic minister, Hamm, had written: 'I start from the assumption that the struggle over the constitution is less a struggle among constitutional lawyers which will be settled in clauses and articles, but rather a struggle for the political soul of the German people.'[31] In the end, it was to be both.

In sum, then, the Weimar Constitution expressed problematic compromises in spheres of great importance for the civil service. First, in the civil-service articles in Section 2, the constitution faltered between guaranteeing the civil service as a traditional state institution, and guaranteeing individual civil and employment rights. Up to about 1924, state policy was to be caught in the political contradictions of meeting democratic pressure for a purge of anti-republican elements from the civil service, while at the same time trying to maintain the constitutional commitments. The problem of political control arose

Hälfte 1927-1967 (Stuttgart, 1967); abbreviated English version published as *The Political Education of Arnold Brecht: An Autobiography 1884-1970* (Princeton, 1970). Arnold Brecht (1884-1977) was a career civil servant in the Reich justice ministry (1910-18), the chancellery (1918-21), the Reich interior ministry (1921-7), and the Prussian administration (1927-33), in all of which posts he had a primary responsibility for *Reichsreform*.

31 Quoted in Schulz, *Demokratie und Diktatur*, p. 608.

again after 1929, with the threat presented by the NSDAP, by which time the issue of civil servants' rights was to be handled rather differently. Secondly, the constitution straddled unitary and federal state systems. This, together with the irritations it engendered, obstructed the adoption of increasingly necessary administrative reforms. It also made it harder than political divisions already did for any progress to be made towards uniformity of practice in administrative and civil-service policy—for example, in training, promotion, and salary practices—and it sapped the will to provide the new civil-service law promised by the constitution. The result was the accumulation of an enormous legacy of administrative problems and frustrations, bequeathed in the end to the Nazi state.

III

Despite the compromises of 1919, a commitment to create a civil service that was more appropriate to the democratic republic did survive among the moderate bourgeois parties and the SPD, and in fact became unavoidable as the locus of the threat to Weimar shifted from left to right. In principle, it demanded at least four linked strategies. First, the imposition of some sort of test of political reliability to determine eligibility for office, and a procedure for dealing with those who refused or failed it. Secondly, a reform of recruitment, so that the pool of possible candidates could be widened in terms of political sympathies, social origin, and confession (gender was not an issue in this sense— rather the reverse). Thirdly, a reform of training, in order to ensure that it functioned as a process of instruction in skills, not as an initiation into a caste. Finally, a reform of the structure of administration, in conformity with principles of accountability to elected government, and in order to eliminate the subaltern mentality associated especially with the Prussian field administration.

In practice, these strategies would look different depending upon the rank of civil servants, and the kind of work they did. Thus, Reich and Prussian practice had long sanctioned one important distinction according to rank, in their creation of the category of 'political' (*disponible*) civil servants. This permitted the discretionary suspension of such high-ranking officials as state secretaries, departmental heads, and leading officials in the field administration. It was relatively simple for the republic to retain and extend these provisions, but the new state also faced a general dilemma that had not existed previously. This was the problem of how to meet the simultaneous demands both for a democratically staffed and structured bureaucracy, and for political freedom for individual civil servants. It was an unwelcome but inescapable fact that some civil servants would use the rights granted them under the constitution to undermine the republic of which they were in theory the representatives and servants. The governments of Reich and *Länder* had to decide at what point civil servants' political activity would demand intervention. Where, in particular, ought the limits of political reliability to be drawn? Should the boundary of the impermissible lie with official acts and decisions, or with off-duty behaviour as well? Should it extend to beliefs and opinions too, whether or not acted upon? Unless the political principles behind such regulation were made absolutely clear, the policies and methods would seem all too reminiscent of the controls exercised over the civil service in the empire.

Although the problem was not of the republic's own making, the fact that it remained a controversial issue was due almost as much to the deviations of government policy as to the persistence of hostility to the republic among civil servants. Only the Prussian government really took up the challenge of devising a machinery of democratization which did not merely replicate the subaltern supervision of imperial Germany. Even there, the SPD-promoted policy of politicizing senior posts as far as possible (i.e. ensuring that they were held by persons of reliable political views) led to controversy and to some curious ironies. In a celebrated case in 1920, in which the Prussian SPD finance minister, Lüdemann, dismissed two of his senior officials for allegedly working against him, Lüdemann appeared in the furore that followed as the defender of the state's traditional control over its civil servants' political beliefs. His detractors in the DVP and DNVP, meanwhile, offered themselves as proponents of the more up-to-date and restrained concept of civil-service neutrality.[32] It is also true that the issue had far more relevance for Prussia than it had for *Länder* such as Baden or Württemberg with their more liberal traditions. As Ludwig Haas pointed out in a DDP committee meeting in November 1921, when discussing the claims of political reliability and technical competence: 'We all want all posts to be filled with competent people, but we must also demand that

---

[32] See Pikart, 'Berufsbeamtentum und Parteienstaat', and documentation in GStA Rep. 90/23256. For a discussion of the issue of politicization versus neutralization, see T. Eschenburg, *Der Beamte in Partei und Parlament* (Frankfurt, 1952); for the contemporary debate see Köttgen, *Deutsches Berufsbeamtentum, passim*.

they are committed to the republic. In Baden only the ministerial posts were political appointments; otherwise the old civil-service apparatus continued, for there the civil service took the right attitude. In Prussia this was not the case.'[33] Prussia was the most polarized *Land* in sociopolitical terms, and its coalition governments had little choice but to deal with the problems created by the relentless conservatism of East Prussia, and by the radicalism of the Ruhr and Berlin. Elsewhere, no sustained democratization campaigns were undertaken; intermittent bouts of activity, prompted largely by the political emergencies of the early 1920s, were followed by neglect or reversal. The high point of any national consensus for direct intervention came in 1922 with the *Republikschutzgesetze*, which did aim to clarify the precise limits of compatibility between civil servants' civil liberties and their official obligations. Yet this was a short-lived moment. In the eyes of the rightwards-moving Reich government, the law was to be not the plateau for future practice, but a peak from which a swift descent was made. Within eighteen months, it was also followed by the *Personalabbauverordnung* (PAV), a major cost-cutting effort to reduce the personnel of the administration by some 25 per cent, which may also have been used covertly to purge the civil service, but this time of the left.[34] Outside Prussia, therefore, it is not a matter of looking at a policy that failed, but of trying to find policies at all.

It was inevitable, however, that one of the first acts of the republic should be to institute a new oath of loyalty for civil servants, and equally inevitable that this should be greeted by the right with contempt and hostility. Civil servants had been released from their oaths of loyalty to the old regimes in the weeks after 9 November, as the heads of state abdicated, and had existed in a kind of limbo until August 1919, when the new wording was issued: 'I swear loyalty to the constitution of the Reich'.[35] This may seem an unexceptionable formula, but

---

[33] DDP committee meeting, 11 Nov. 1921, in Wegner and Albertin (eds.), *Linksliberalismus*, pp. 222-3.

[34] This is asserted by Schmahl, *Disziplinarrecht*, p. 74, but disputed by Morsey, 'Beamtenschaft und Verwaltung', p. 158 n. 17, on the grounds that Schmahl's evidence is insufficient. Kunz, 'Stand versus Klasse', does not discuss the issue directly, but implies (p. 77) that sources for its investigation might exist among Reich finance-ministry records.

[35] In German, 'Ich schwöre Treue der Reichsverfassung'; for a detailed discussion of the oath, see H.-W. Laubinger, 'Die Treuepflicht des Beamten im Wandel der Zeiten', in K. König et al. (eds.), *Öffentlicher Dienst: Festschrift für Carl Hermann Ule* (Cologne, 1977), 99-104; and Schmahl, *Disziplinarrecht*, ch. 3. See also Jellinek, 'Revolution und Reichsverfassung', p. 84; H. Daniels, 'Pflichten und Rechten der Beamten', in Anschütz

it elicited great dismay from conservatives, who baulked at the explicit reference to the constitution. Their preference was, not surprisingly, for something less defined and (in their eyes) politically rebarbative, such as the state, or Reich, or perhaps people. The conservative academic Köttgen's account of the oath graphically illustrates the reasons for this kind of objection, and its possible implications. Having previously argued that 'only the nation can at present act as the mediator between the civil service and the state', he insisted that this relationship had to be contained in some tangible object:

This is especially true in the case of the oath, which is the primary outward sign of this link between state and civil servant. The form of the oath laid down by presidential order in accordance with Article 176 of the constitution takes no account whatsoever of this requirement. An oath to the constitution, which after all is no more than a lifeless law, fails to satisfy reasonable demands on this score. [Here Köttgen makes a footnote reference to a critique by the DNVP.] The civil-service oath under the constitutional monarchy was sworn to the monarch personally, and an inner bond of loyalty [*Treueverhältnis*] to him was established; even though constitutional loyalty was also sworn on top of this, it had only a secondary significance. An inner bond to a legal norm is positively unthinkable. [Here another footnote quotes a suitably dismissive comparison between the constitution and the town-planning law, in support of this argument.] . . . What is missing for the civil service here is any outward, meaningful documentation of the personal bond between civil servant and the state. The civil servant does not serve a lifeless constitution, but the living nation, in respect of which alone he can display the kind of devotion which is rightly expected of him: he cannot do this with an abstract, legalistic norm.[36]

Taken literally, this turbid disquisition was equivalent to a total repudiation of the rule of law: if a 'legal norm' was so inefficacious in this context, why should it compel obedience in any other? But Köttgen was correct in finding something problematic in the meaning of the oath, even though the real problem lay in its legal implications rather than in its lack of a living object. The big question was whether the oath could legally restrain civil servants from activities aimed at changing the constitution, or whether this would be an illicit abridgement of their civil rights. In other words, did civil servants owe a *special* degree of duty to the constitution; and if so, how did this tie in with their

and Thoma (eds.), *Handbuch*, ii. 43, and E. Brandt, *Die politische Treuepflicht: Rechtsquellen zur Geschichte des deutschen Berufsbeamtentums* (Karlsruhe and Heidelberg, 1976), especially the introduction by H. Mommsen, 'Beamtentum und demokratischer Verfassungsstaat', 17-36.

[36] Köttgen, *Deutsches Berufsbeamtentum*, pp. 117-18.

constitutional emancipation as citizens like any others? Once the issue was broached, it had to be pursued into the further question of whether such a duty extended to any act by a civil servant, or only to those committed in an official capacity, and whether it also covered beliefs and convictions. The DNVP's civil-service committee declared that *deutschnational* civil servants would not regard the oath as restricting their right to work towards the achievement of 'andere staatliche Zustände' by constitutional means. The SPD, conversely, demanded that any civil servant who expressed reservations about the implications of the oath should be treated as having refused it, and hence as liable to penalization.[37] After some vacillation, the Reich government decided in December 1919 that the oath represented a commitment of loyalty to the constitution in the performance of official duties. It was not to be construed as limiting 'inner convictions', nor as placing restrictions on a civil servant's right to engage in legal activities directed at changing the form of the state.[38] In this way, the provisions of Article 130 were at first allowed to exist undiminished.

This absolutism was not equal, however, to the political strains of the early 1920s, as the Kapp *putsch* and the wave of political assassinations in 1921 and 1922 were to demonstrate. But it is worth noting that the republic's oath differed from its predecessors in two ways. First, it enlisted an implicit recognition that the constitution was a public document open to revision, rather than something definitionally incapable of change (except by legitimate succession), such as the person of a monarch, or the metaphysical eternity of the nation. As such, it introduced the notion of compliance with legal procedures for effecting revision. Secondly, the 1919 interpretation repudiated control over 'inner convictions' and thus marked a break with the traditional concept of *Treue*, which had extended to the entire person of the civil servant and demanded a total personal commitment to the service of the state. In the past, this had obviated the need for a precise and comprehensive enumeration of a civil servant's legal obligations (likewise, of the state's obligations to civil servants), and had blurred the distinction between official and private life. But with the advent of the republic, it was unavoidable that the political implications of a civil servant's obligations would become highly contentious. The early attempt to

---

[37] Schmahl, *Disziplinarrecht*, pp. 43 ff.

[38] In Prussia this was explained to civil servants before they took the oath, and a statement to that effect was printed on the back of the certificate they received; see ibid. Schmahl also points out (p. 75) that *Länder* with SPD or KPD coalition governments were unwilling to rely on the *Treuepflicht* as the basis for civil-service policy.

relax obligations in favour of maximizing civil rights severed the previous continuum that had been supposed to connect the public and the private, and shattered the unitary concept of the *Treue- und Gehorsamsverhältnis*. The old ethic had masked the fact that the law itself had been incomplete and imprecise, and had allowed the issue to be evaded to some extent—though, as we have seen, civil servants had already begun to contest it before the war. An academic like Köttgen might be conceded a theoretical point in drawing attention to the loss of certainty, but this could not be said of the party-political right. Spokesmen for the DNVP and DVP conveniently ignored the tension between their cultivated traditionalism on the one hand, and their eagerness on the other to ensure that conservative civil servants should not be constrained by that very traditionalism in their newly acquired right to subvert the constitution. In fact, as we shall see shortly, the strains of the 1920s forced a return to older concepts of *Treue*, in an effort to attach civil servants to the republic without adopting an overtly politicizing policy. This also anticipated the reinforcement of a unitary and toughened political and personal supervision after 1933.

The Kapp *putsch* can be seen as the first real test of civil servants' loyalties after the establishment of the republican state.[39] By joining the general strike for the republic, they passed the test, yet it was not clear whether this was because the alliance with the republic still existed, or because order and the status quo were under threat. The aftermath of the *putsch* provoked calls for closer political control of senior officials, which suggests that its lessons were less heartening for those who, like Chancellor Wirth, were now willing to acknowledge that the enemy was to the right. There was indeed a difference in the responses of senior and lower officials to the *putsch*. Broadly speaking, senior ministerial officials in Berlin, who were the first to face directly the challenge of Kapp's action, were willing to rely on the non-committal formula of duty to the established order as the basis for their refusal of co-operation. This formula almost certainly masked an educated guess about the likelihood of Kapp's success. For them, neutrality rather than the active defence of the republic was the motif, and they were strongly opposed to the strike action that was quickly undertaken by the public sector in general. Middle and lower civil servants on the other hand, responded

---

[39] For the Kapp episode, see principally J. Erger, *Der Kapp-Lüttwitz-Putsch: Ein Beitrag zur deutschen Innenpolitik 1919/20* (Düsseldorf, 1970), and G. Jasper, *Der Schutz der Republik: Studien zur staatlichen Sicherung der Demokratie in der Weimarer Republik* (Tübingen, 1963), from which the following account is drawn. See also Pikart, 'Berufsbeamtentum und Parteienstaat'.

actively to the call for strike action that was issued by the SPD members of the Bauer cabinet and ratified by the DBB.

The attitude taken by senior civil servants, both in the Berlin ministries of Reich and Prussia and in the field, was somewhat less niggardly than that of the Reichswehr generals, however. The latters' response to Noske's proposal for armed resistance was epitomized in Seeckt's ambivalent statement, at the crucial meeting on the night of March 12, that 'We can't conduct a manœuvre with live ammunition between Berlin and Potsdam'.[40] Although Seeckt was not in direct command, of course, and the actual commander, Reinhardt, supported Noske, his comment was taken by Noske as tantamount to a declaration that the Reichswehr would not be dependable. Rather than test the correctness of his interpretation, the government took the prudent decision not to issue orders for armed resistance to Kapp. But, it did immediately instruct senior civil servants to stay at their posts while refusing to co-operate with the *putschists*. In fact, this is what most of them did unbidden; Brüning describes how a number of senior officials in the welfare ministry made their way to work by three-hour journeys on foot.[41] The lack of co-operation came as a shock to Kapp when he tried to take over the ministries on March 13 (a Saturday, incidentally), and his fellow *putschists* reacted with bewilderment. Meeting with refusals by civil servants either to stand down or to go home, the *putschists* responded indecisively, detaining them briefly and then releasing them; force was neither threatened nor used. The only substantial section of officials to desert to Kapp were from the police and security forces (Sipo), who provided telephonists to staff the otherwise abandoned communications centres, for instance (Arnold Brecht had presciently ordered the usual switchboard operators to stay off work for a week). The government had withdrawn to Dresden, leaving a group of senior men like Brecht, Albert, von Haniel, and Wever to organize the bureaucratic obstruction, and to try to maintain some kind of administrative presence and continuity, while at the same time contriving to ignore Kapp's claims to be their new political master. They formally refused to take any orders from Kapp or his ministerial nominees, therefore, but at the same time they worked to prevent an administrative

[40] Quoted in Erger, *Kapp-Lüttwitz-Putsch*, p. 143; Erger disputes the authenticity of the more famous claim, 'Reichswehr does not fire on Reichswehr', cited for example in E. Eyck, *A History of the Weimar Republic*, i. *From the Collapse of the Empire to Hindenburg's Election* (New York, 1967), 150.

[41] H. Brüning, *Memoiren 1918–1934*, i (Munich, 1972), 68.

vacuum. Most famously, Schröder instructed the Reichshauptkasse to issue no money to anyone not equipped with the necessary authorization; the Reichsbank was also to refuse any unauthorized demands. In what must have been uneasy hours of joint occupation of the ministries, Kapp's colleagues confronted the stonily unco-operative civil servants with the inconsistency between their desertion of their monarch in November 1918 and their invocation of 'higher duty' in this new emergency. Evidently, the officials countered this dig at their professional integrity by pointing out that in 1918 the chancellor had instructed them to work with Ebert, and that they had shortly afterwards been formally released from their oath to king and Kaiser. Now, however, in March 1920, they were under equally precise instructions from the legal order (in the persons of Ebert and Bauer) *not* to co-operate with the *putschists*.

There was a good deal of truth in that claim, and a certain irony in the fact that at this juncture the republic was the beneficiary rather than the victim of civil-service traditions. Only a few higher officials opted openly for Kapp, mainly in East Prussia. More behaved circumspectly, and others responded in the same way as the conservative *Regierungspräsident* in Kassel, Springorum, who summoned his staff, instructed them to remain loyal to Bauer's government, and issued telegrams in the same vein to his field staff. The oath of loyalty was the formal basis for these decisions, underpinned by the maladroitness of the *putsch*. There was neither motive nor encouragement for senior civil servants to demonstrate anything more than a temperate sense of duty during these March days. The strike call was issued by the SPD members of the government, not in the name of the government itself, which officially called on civil servants to stay at their posts. This circumspection derived from a fear of opening the door to counteraction by the left, a fear which senior civil servants were likely to have shared. In that sense, March 1920 echoed some of the calculations of November 1918.

The revolutionary division between senior and lower-ranking civil servants was also repeated in 1920. This was partly a reflection of the different ways in which they were affected by the *putsch*. Senior civil servants in leading posts had no choice but to decide upon their response to Kapp more or less immediately, whereas lesser officials were faced neither by such an urgent individual choice nor by the same pressure of time—the fact that the *putsch* began on a Saturday absolved many of them from an immediate test of loyalty. The DBB, however, convened as many executive members as it could on Sunday 14 March, and decided by thirteen votes to three to support the government by striking in those parts of the country where it was no longer in full control. Voting by affiliated organization revealed that those in favour of strike action represented about half a million members, those against, about 54,000.[42] An action committee of seven executive members was elected and given powers to decide further responses as necessary. The DBB leadership later split on the question of calling off the strike on the night of 17/18 March, after Kapp's retreat. Meeting in Stuttgart on the evening of March 17, five members of the action committee took Kapp's decision as sufficient evidence that the emergency was over, and signed an instruction that DBB members should return to work. But the DBB leaders in Berlin rejected this call, on the grounds both that it was unauthorized and that the situation was by no means clearly resolved, in Berlin or elsewhere. They thought that the strike should not be abandoned until order had been fully restored. This difference of opinion was not due simply to a discrepancy in the information available in Stuttgart and Berlin; it was a political disagreement. The Berlin statement ended with the words: 'We will not stab the workers in the back', and its authors went into active partnership with the Allgemeiner Deutscher Gewerkschaftsbund (ADGB) and the Allgemeiner freier Angestelltenbund (Afa-Bund) to draw up the programme of demands which the strike movement was now insisting on. Again, it is difficult to assess the range of civil servants' opinions about this transparent advance to a class offensive. The strikers' demands included a call for the effective participation of workers' organizations in the reconstruction of Reich and *Land* governments—a sign that potentially fundamental *political* change was anticipated; also that soldiers who had mounted the *putsch* and officials who had collaborated in it should be detained and tried; that Noske should resign; that 'reactionaries' should be purged from public offices and the administration should be democratized (an old demand of the radical rank and file in 1918-19); and a range of social and economic demands which also echoed the aspirations of the revolution. The strike in support of this programme was not called off until 20 March, when a compromise—in effect a defeat for the strikers— was reached; but that is a different story.

The Kapp *putsch* alone did not produce an immediate sharp break in

---

[42] See the account in *Deutscher Beamtenbund*, pp. 36-42; H. Potthoff, *Gewerkschaften und Politik zwischen Revolution und Inflation* (Düsseldorf, 1979), 264-8; also H. H. Biegert, 'Gewerkschaftspolitik in der Phase des Kapp-Lüttwitz-Putsches', in H. Mommsen *et al.* (eds.), *Industrielles System und politische Entwicklung in der Weimarer Republik* (Düsseldorf, 1974), 190-205.

civil-service policy, but it did have the effect of deepening political divisions within the organization of civil servants, and contributed largely to the eventual splintering of the DBB in 1921 and 1922. The absence of large-scale or individually significant defections among civil servants absolved the government from immediate radical action, even though many voices were raised (not only on the left) for a purge of the civil service, judiciary, and police. But inaction was encouraged by the loss of strength on the democratic left in the June elections, and by the exclusion of the SPD from Fehrenbach's ministry. Thus, it was not until 1922 that effective measures were adopted 'for the security of the republic' (*zum Schutze der Republik*), as a result of the building of the Weimar coalition under Wirth, the accumulation of pressure on the republic as its domestic and international situation deteriorated, and a succession of right-wing attacks on leading politicians—the Erzberger murder in August 1921, and an acid attack on Scheidemann and the murder of Rathenau in June 1922. Some *Länder*—Thuringia and Prussia—had already been considering or had adopted protective measures, and Rathenau's murder provided the final shocking impetus to action at Reich level. Wirth's famous accusation—'Der Feind steht rechts'—was made in the Reichstag debate on 30 June 1922, and the bundle of instructions and statutes adopted in June and July was aimed deliberately and selectively at that quarter.

Thus, when the Reich at last took specific steps to enforce a certain standard of political behaviour on civil servants, and to expand the category of 'political' civil servants, it was as part of a wider programme of defence for the republic. It amounted to an explicit, though reluctant, recognition that 'traditional' standards of neutrality were no longer appropriate, though the outraged DNVP tried to insist that they were and that the proposed legislation was nothing but party-political chicanery. The July 1922 Law Concerning the Duties of Civil Servants for the Security of the Republic[43] amended the 1907 Reich civil-service law in three principal ways. First, it specified that civil servants were 'duty bound in their official activities to support the republican state power as provided in the constitution [*verfassungsmässige republikanische Staatsgewalt*]'. Secondly, it restricted the manner in which civil servants could take part even in lawful anti-republican or pro-

---

[43] *Gesetz über die Pflichten der Beamten zum Schutze der Republik*, 21 July 1922 (*RGBl*, 1922, i. 590). Note that the law deliberately referred to 'republic' rather than the more abstract 'constitution'. For an account of the law's development see Schmahl, *Disziplinarrecht*, ch. 4.

monarchical political activities. And thirdly, it brought the two most senior ranks of civil servants wholesale into the category of 'political' officials. However, a provision which would have allowed the establishment of a new disciplinary senate, appointed by the president and bypassing the perhaps not wholly dependable existing machinery, was dropped in the course of debate. Instead, the statute drew attention to the need for its application in particular to civil servants whose duties directly involved the security of the republic.

The nettle of political control had been grasped at last. The *Schutzgesetze* as a whole were adopted only after a battle with some of the *Länder*, notably Bavaria and Württemberg, which were extremely sensitive about the Reich's encroachments on their political independence. Bavaria also had strong political reservations about the law relating to civil servants, and failed to issue regulations of its own, as it was empowered to do by the law.[44] The DNVP, of course, launched a major battle against the law, and despite its political intentions, this did expose the uncomfortable fact that the government had retreated from its own previous stance on the relationship between civil servants' rights and duties. Unrestricted political freedom was not, it appeared, compatible with the security of the republic. The only alternative— apart from an intensive and urgent political purge, for which there was no support at national level—was to reinstate some form of control over civil servants' political behaviour on and off duty. The new law was the only statutory statement of how this control would operate, and even here its wording did little more than echo existing formulas. For practical purposes, the principal source of control for all but the handful of 'political' *Beamte* remained the unreformed civil-service disciplinary code, which was rooted in precisely those conceptions of duty from which the republic had tried to some extent to distance itself: the *Treuepflicht* and the *Pflicht zu achtungswürdigem Verhalten*.[45] These were supposed to refer respectively to the content of an act and to its form (and acts alone were at stake here: thought remained free), but in practice this distinction was not a very clear one. For example, the fact

44 Neither Baden nor Württemberg issued comparable legislation; both *Länder* had inherited a more liberal civil service than elsewhere, and Württemberg had never known the category of the 'political' civil servant; see Schmahl, *Disziplinarrecht*, pp. 70-1; Fenske, 'Monarchisches Beamtentum', p. 125; also D. R. Tracey, 'Reform in the Early Weimar Years: The Thuringian Example', *JMH*, 44 (1976), 207-8.
45 A new disciplinary code (*Reichsdienststrafordnung*) was in fact under discussion between 1925 and 1927; see Schmahl, *Disziplinarrecht*, pp. 77-9, and Hoffmann, *Sozialdemokratie und Berufsbeamtentum*, pp. 208-21.

that the constitution itself provided a legal process for constitutional change (Article 76) was held to legitimize civil servants' participation in activities aimed at achieving such change; but whereas ordinary citizens were only bound to constitutional methods, civil servants were also under an obligation to protect the reputation of the state. Thus, the *Schutzgesetze* and the penal code made certain criticisms of the republic an offence in themselves (e.g. bringing a minister into disrepute). What civil servants faced were not necessarily entirely different charges from those risked by other citizens, but additional and heavier penalties. For example, a civil servant who wrote a defamatory newspaper article was fined 100 RM by an ordinary court, but then lost his job when his case came up before the disciplinary tribunal.[46] On the other hand, these decisions were not always based on obviously political criteria, but might reflect a pedantically exact reading of the law. Thus, ceremonies celebrating Constitution Day had to be held in all state offices on pain of disciplinary charges, but civil servants could only be 'urged' to participate; they could not be penalized for staying away. Inevitably, by the early 1930s civil servants were being brought to book for defaming National Socialist ministers, under the general rubric of 'undermining confidence in members of a *Land* government'—an unhappy legal consequence at administrative level of the political problems of the republic by this date.

The 1922 legislation was essentially defensive, and cannot be seen as an effective means to repair the gaps left by the events of 1918–19. It by no means solved the problem of reconciling civil servants' rights and duties, and, in so far as a solution was attempted, it was done at the cost of reviving pre-war concepts of duty. It is hard to gauge the law's success in controlling political activity. Its application in Prussia has been researched, but there the law was employed as part of a wider attack on the problem of political disaffection in the civil service, and it can hardly be taken as exemplary for the *Schutzgesetze* alone. Elsewhere, comprehensive research is still lacking, though it is probably safe to say that there was no vigorous campaign to enforce the law. The most

---

[46] Schmahl, *Disziplinarrecht*, p. 93, where a range of similar cases is cited to illustrate the ways in which civil servants could fail in their duty to preserve public respect for the state. For example, proceedings were opened against civil servants who described the republic in insulting terms ('built on the sand of desertion and treason'), or who lampooned the national colours ('black-red-mustard'). Schmahl points out, however, that penalties were only selectively imposed; it should also be noted that the bulk of his evidence comes from Prussia, where it can be assumed that the law was more stringently applied.

significant aspect of the law from our point of view is that it relied on disciplinary procedures rather than overt political intervention as the mechanism of control. This was probably inevitable, and at least partly accounted for the survival of the inherited standards of imperial disciplinary law in the republic, thus carrying an element of continuity in policy. By contrast, the process for enforcing civil servants' political obligations to the state under the republic provided no real precedent for the radical and comprehensive political interventionism which was perpetrated by the Nazi regime after 1933. The Nazi propaganda contention that the civil service was subjected to an unparalleled degree of political interference under the republic was thus less than truthful, even before the opprobious comparison with post-1933 practices exposed the hypocrisy of their claim.

Nevertheless, although Prussia cannot be taken as representative of the whole of Germany, its government did undertake a sustained and multifarious campaign to democratize its bureaucracy. It can be discussed, therefore, as an example of what a national policy might have comprised. In this, as in other realms of policy, Prussian energy and success can be contrasted with Reich weakness and failure, not least because in civil-service politics the Prussian government embarked on its most radical and creative period just at the moment when the break-up of the Weimar coalition signalled retreat and reaction at the national level. The credit for this lay with Carl Severing and Albert Grzesinski, the two social democrats who dominated the interior ministry between 1920 and 1932.[47] Because of the length of Severing's tenure of office, the conduct of civil-service policies in this period became known as the 'Severing system', though Grzesinski was the more radical of the two. But apart from differences in their personal political temperament, both were caught up in the web of political dependencies which the coalition system entailed. Thus, ironically, Severing's freedom of action was limited by his own state secretary, Meister, a DVP member whom Severing himself had chosen as a conciliatory gesture to his coalition partners. Relations between them were poor, but although Meister apparently asked to retire, Severing could not risk complying in case it inflamed political tensions within the coalition. A longer-lasting

[47] Their periods in office were as follows: Severing: Mar. 1920-Apr. 1921, Nov. 1921-Oct. 1926, Oct. 1930-July 1932; Grzesinski: Oct. 1926-Feb. 1930. Severing was also Reich interior minister in the Müller cabinet, June 1928-Mar. 1930. For Severing, see his memoirs, *Mein Lebensweg*, 2 vols. (Cologne, 1950); for Grzesinksi, see his *La Tragie-Comédie de la République allemande* (Paris, 1934), and A. Glees, 'Albert C. Grzesinksi and the Politics of Prussia, 1926-1930', *English Historical Review*, 89 (1974), 814-34.

problem was that the Prussian finance ministry, whose approval was required for senior civil-service appointments, was in fiscally unsympathetic hands (mainly those of the DDP's Höpker-Aschoff) after November 1921.

A summary of the policies adopted in this period will indicate the kinds of strategy available in the republic, and will provide a context for later discussions of Nazi policy.[48] The data discussed here refer to a small and select number of officials in the interior field administration: those 490 men (*sic*) who, as *Oberpräsidenten, Regierungspräsidenten, Landräte,* and *Polizeipräsidenten,* were the linchpins of administration and security in the field. In 1918, these were the men who had the power, the experience, and the political inclination to engage in 'bureaucratic sabotage' against the republic, both directly and by influencing their subordinates. They were also, like senior ministerial officials, 'political' *Beamte* subject to dismissal at any time without disciplinary process. In the course of the revolution, the *Räte* had been given powers of supervision over the first three categories in December 1918; they were evidently able to secure some shakily legal dismissals by mid-1919 (when their authority was finally suppressed), but they had never exercised a right of reappointment. This remained, therefore, in the hands of the Berlin government, which equipped itself with two new instruments in February 1919, modifying inherited civil-service law which otherwise remained in force. The first of these altered the terms and qualifications for the appointment of *Landräte* by liberalizing the voting procedure in the Kreistag (which had the right of nomination) and abolishing the technical qualifications for appointment; it thereby opened this key post to a wider pool of formally untrained candidates. The other measure confirmed existing government powers to retire 'political' civil servants compulsorily, and offered the new option of voluntary retirement to anyone with ten years' service who felt morally unable to work for the republic. However, neither measure was used in such a way as to produce a sweeping purge, except among the *Oberpräsidenten,* of whom nine out of twelve were replaced by the time of the Kapp *putsch.* All these new nominees were members of one of the coalition parties, and, significantly, none had won a transfer from branches of the interior administration: all of them came from municipal and local government, the legal profession, or the labour movement.

---

[48] The following account draws on Runge, *Politik und Beamtentum*; Pikart, 'Preussische Beamtenpolitik'; and Behrend, 'Personalpolitik'. See also O. Braun, *Von Weimar zu Hitler* (New York, 1940); Severing, *Mein Lebensweg.*

The *Oberpräsident* was, of course, a peculiar official, who stood outside the field hierarchy and acted more as a regional representative of the government; their replacement could hardly have been unexpected. But elsewhere in the key 'political' posts, the degree of change was far less drastic. It was true that half the *Regierungspräsidenten* (17 out of 34) had been replaced by March 1920, and 10 out of 25 *Polizeipräsidenten* (in the latter case, most of the new appointees were non-career men from the SPD bureaucracy). But only 42 of some 405 *Landräte* were new appointments by the same date, and of these (as also of the new *Regierungspräsidenten*), the large majority were transfers from within the administration, and thus were themselves pre-1918 appointments.

The slow progress of real democratization (as opposed to shifts within the system) caused great offence in the SPD. The bourgeois parties, though more concerned to ensure an 'orderly' process of change, were also anxious about the survival of so many senior officials (at the cost, incidentally, of jobs for their own nominees). But the reasons for this were neither exclusively lack of will nor absence of opportunity, but a mixture of both. Thus the first Prussian interior minister, Hirsch, had resigned in frustration at the lack of movement, but his successor, Heine, chose to meet conservative resistance by a policy of deliberate caution and reserve. Heine was certainly trying to develop a long-term perspective on democratization, but this involved both sacrifice and risk; and it was inevitable that he should be dismissed after the Kapp *putsch* and the calls for a more active policy.

In fact, the Kapp *putsch* did mark a clear break with the immediate past in Prussia, by contrast with the Reich. Severing entered the ministry with an obligation to honour the agreement with the trade unions that unreliable officials would now be replaced by 'men with a firm backbone against reactionary temptation', as he put it in his memoirs.[49] This policy was then developed along each of the two lines suggested by the 1919 changes in appointment practice. The power of dismissal was more vigorously used, and, as a necessary corollary, more appointments were made of people without formal training, the so-called 'outsiders' (*Aussenseiter*). These methods were used in sequence. Dismissal was an immediate, almost an emergency policy, which would remain exceptional (short of a total change in the nature of civil-service law), but the reform of rules on qualification and training could be developed more strategically. Dismissals (strictly speaking, compulsory suspension) came in two waves: one immediately after the Kapp *putsch*,

[49] Severing, *Mein Lebensweg*, i. 281.

the other in 1922 in the wake of the *Republikschutzgesetze*. By the end of 1920, a further ninety-six 'political' civil servants in the field administration had lost their jobs, including eighty-eight *Landräte*, the huge majority of them in the eastern provinces; mostly they were replaced by *Aussenseiter* from the SPD or DDP. The situation was more difficult in 1922, because the political implication of the *Republikschutzgesetze* was that civil servants would have to give evidence of active engagement with the republic, and not just refrain from opposing it. Even though this inference was not actively drawn in Reich policies, in Prussia it led to pressure from the left for the government to recognize it, even at the cost of dismissing men who were members of the coalition parties. The result was that a smaller number of 'political' posts were purged once again, though demands for a fuller attack on the *Landräte* were resisted. The new appointees were largely career civil servants (not *Aussenseiter*), and were drawn from among members of the bourgeois coalition parties. This was the last action that could be described as a purge, though Grzesinski returned to a somewhat more aggressive policy during the referendum campaigns of 1926 and 1930, when a handful of officials were retired for misconduct.

Compulsory suspension was only part of the machinery of political intervention, since it was restricted to 'political' officials. Coercive control of this kind could also be exercised through the disciplinary system, as we have seen; and beyond this, there was more indirect control that could be achieved through a selective appointment policy. Appointment policy offered wider scope for influencing the membership of the higher civil service, since more posts fell vacant through 'natural' means, such as transfer and retirement, than as a result of coercive action.[50] The issue for a democratizing appointments policy was twofold. First, how could selective criteria be employed in order to alter the political and confessional balance of the administration? Secondly, how could the entry qualifications and career structure of the higher grade of the service be modified, given that the long periods of university education and in-service probationary training imposed an

[50] There has been no study of recruitment and appointment policy below the senior level of the civil service, which is why so many generalizing assertions about the composition and attitudes of civil servants remain unproven, or at best, educated guesses. There has been no research on the extent to which political criteria may have operated at subordinate levels, nor into the equally interesting question of the effect of changing industrial training and management practices on the civil service (for example, psychometric assessment of job aptitude was adopted by the Reich postal service in the 1920s).

obvious social bias? To a considerable extent, these two questions were interdependent: only changes in the training system could provide a wider catchment of potential candidates for the higher grade, and thus allow the practice of a selective appointment policy. As we have already seen, rules governing eligibility for appointment as a *Landrat* had been relaxed in 1919; and in July 1920, a formal amendment to the 1906 administrative civil-service training law was adopted. This relaxed a number of general regulations about admission to the higher grade, and facilitated the appointment of so-called *Aussenseiter* by empowering the authorities 'Exceptionally, to declare as eligible for the higher administrative grade such other persons as shall be deemed suitable for appointment as a higher civil servant by virtue of their specialist [*fachlich*] training so long as they shall also have had three years' previous experience in a branch of the public administration.'[51] This was a cautious instrument (it had been prompted by the DDP). Far from throwing open the higher grade to 'outsiders', what it really did was to facilitate internal promotion within the civil service — an innovation certainly, but hardly equivalent to that mass invasion of unqualified aliens that critics deplored. Indeed, although the employment of *Aussenseiter* was one of the most contentious aspects of Prussian civil-service policy during this period, this was more because it was a convenient and visible target for critics than because it was either radically new or used to reckless effect. For a start, it was not unprecedented: similar powers had existed before 1918, and there was no sudden or massive expansion in their use after 1920. Among East Prussian *Landräte*, the percentage of *Aussenseiter* was 11 per cent in 1905, 6 in 1916, and 18 in 1925; according to a detailed breakdown of 296 posts, only 28 (9.5 per cent) were newly filled by *Aussenseiter* as permanent appointments under the republic.[52] Similarly, Runge shows that although the number of juristically trained administrative civil servants decreased after 1919, the average in 1929 was still 72 per cent overall; he concludes that the power to appoint *Aussenseiter* was used sparingly, and that the training post of *Regierungsassessor* remained the standard route of entry.[53] Moreover, those civil servants who remained in office in 1919 tended to be promoted, so on the whole the upper ranks were filled by regular in-service promotion, not by people brought in over the heads of the career civil servants. As far as the other indices of democratization are

51 *Gesetz, betr. Änderung des Gesetzes über die Befähigung zum höheren Verwaltungsdienst vom 10. August 1906* (*GS*, 1920, 388).
52 Behrend, 'Personalpolitik', pp. 202-3.
53 Runge, *Politik und Beamtentum*, pp. 191 ff.

concerned, the proportion of men of noble birth fell considerably, as Table 1 shows.[54]

TABLE 1. Social Origin of Prussian Civil Servants ('Political' Posts), 1916-1930

Post	Total		Nobles		Bourgeois	
	1916	1930	1916	1930	1916	1930
Oberpräsident	12	12	11	1	1	11
Regierungspräsident	36	32	20	4	16	28
Landrat	485	405	264	81	221	324
Polizeipräsident	28	41	20	3	8	38
TOTAL	561	490	315	89	246	401

The influence of the Centre party, as well as a generally more equit-able appointments policy, was demonstrated in the increase in the number of Catholics in the higher civil service.[55] Confessional and political questions were taken seriously by policy-makers, but apparently not discrimination on grounds of sex.[56] The Weimar Constitution included a declaration of equality between men and women (Article 109), and expressly abolished discrimination against women in the civil service (Article 128). Yet these statements of principle tell us nothing about practice, and the provisions of the constitution were repeatedly violated by Reich and *Länder*, formally and informally. The grossest formal abrogation was the *Personalabbauverordnung* of 1923, which forcibly retired certain categories of women in the public service. Even

---

[54] Grzesinski, *La Tragie-Comédie*, p. 151; changes in totals 1916-30 reflect border changes and also the incorporation into the Prussian state administration of the post of *Polizeipräsident*.

[55] Runge, *Politik und Beamtentum*, p. 188.

[56] For a preliminary study of women in the civil service, see Hahn, 'Öffentlicher Dienst'; see also J. Stephenson, *Women in Nazi Society* (London, 1975), ch. 1; R. Bridenthal and C. Koonz, 'Beyond *Kinder, Küche, Kirche*: Weimar Women in Politics and Work', in R. Bridenthal et al. (eds.), *When Biology Became Destiny: Women in Weimar and Nazi Germany* (New York, 1984), 33-65; H. L. Boak, 'Women in Weimar Germany: The "Frauenfrage" and the Female Vote', in Bessel and Feuchtwanger (eds.), *Social Change and Political Development*, pp. 163-5. The Marie-Elisabeth Lüders Nachlass (BA) is a rich source of information from the hands of one of the most prominent protagonists of women's rights in the Weimar Republic.

before that, however, women were subject to various forms of discrimination. For example, married women might be covertly pressured to resign; the fringe benefits available to women, whether married or not, were often lower than those for men; and salary levels were depressed by means of lower gradings.[57] This might still leave women in the public service working under better terms than those in private employment (especially as far as pay was concerned), but it did not fulfil the spirit of the constitution. A handful of notable individuals achieved senior appointments as 'political' civil servants, the best known of these being Gertrud Bäumer (the ex-president of the Bund Deutscher Frauenvereine) in the Reich interior ministry, and Klara Mende in the ministry of economics. But in 1924, there were no more than fifty women in senior public-service posts, and in 1923 (on the eve of the *Personalabbau*), nine out of eighteen Reich authorities employed not a single *Beamtin* (though all employed women, sometimes in senior positions, as *Angestellte*). Of the total of 61,462 women civil servants at the same date, no fewer than 60,883 were employed in the postal system, and it can be safely assumed that by far the majority of these were telephonists and counter-hands.[58] In the absence of detailed research, it may be tendentious to assert that this division of labour reflected a policy of deliberate discrimination, aimed at keeping women confined within particular sectors of public employment. The existence of a sex-segmented labour force in the public sphere certainly reflected the wider experience of German women in the economy. At any rate, it would be stretching credibility to imagine that appointment authorities in the 1920s were engaged in a sincere but unsuccessful search for women qualified for appointment to the upper echelons of the bureaucracy.

There remains the question of the political affiliations of senior civil servants, and the degree of success in ensuring the appointment of persons committed to the republic. This has been the subject of exhaustive investigation for Prussia, and virtual neglect for other *Länder*.[59]

57 Hahn, 'Öffentlicher Dienst', p. 64.

58 'Übersichten über den Personalstand nach dem Stande vom 1. Okt. 1926', Reich finance ministry, 7 Jan. 1927, *Drucksachen des Reichstags*, III. Wahlperiode 1924-7, 2895.

59 Runge, *Beamtentum und Politik*, offers an exhaustive study of Prussian appointments; Pikart, 'Preussische Beamtenpolitik', pp. 130-7, reconstructs the standard appointment procedure as far as the evidence allows; for Prussia, see also H.-P. Ehni, 'Zum Parteienverhältnis in Preussen 1918-1932', *Archiv für Sozialgeschichte*, 11 (1971), 246-55, and Möller, 'Die preussischen Oberprasidenten'. Fenske, 'Monarchisches Beamtentum', is the only national survey.

In Prussia, Severing and Grzesinski pursued a vigorous policy of selective appointment, based on a fairly formalized system in which each coalition party nominated candidates in proportion to its strength. By 1929, some 70 per cent of the leading 'political' posts in the Prussian field administration were held by members of the SPD, DDP, Centre party, and DVP. This was certainly a considerable achievement by comparison with the situation ten years before, but it still left numerous key officials whose political tendencies were of uncertain relation to the republic. Moreover, in the context of a known system of political patronage, party membership might indicate little about the ideological and professional principles of a civil servant—the more so in the case of Centre and DVP members, whose sense of patriotic duty might well override any more specific commitment to the republic as such. The appointments themselves reflected tensions within the governing coalitions as much as any determined strategy towards creating a republican leadership corps, and should not be seen simply as unambiguous tributes to the effectiveness of this policy. Thus, in the autumn of 1929, Grzesinski felt it necessary to resist his own party's pressure for the appointment of social democrats to three vacant posts, distributing them instead to nominees of the Centre party and DVP; this was done partly to strengthen the coalition, partly also in the hope of braking the DVP's movement to the right.[60] This was the kind of act that allowed the propaganda attacks from the right to make an elision between *Aussenseiter* and *Parteibuchbeamte*—an elision which also concealed a further equation with 'unqualified'. The effect was to produce a composite image of a civil service corrupted by the appointment of untrained outsiders selected wholly on political grounds. But the elision was misleading in a number of respects. Political considerations governed appointments of all qualified personnel, not just *Aussenseiter*. Moreover, in Prussia it does not appear that political amenability excluded professional competence: despite DNVP and later Nazi claims that Prussia's appointments policy had saddled the administration with proven incompetents, there were in fact only a handful of cases in which civil servants had to be recalled on those grounds. Nevertheless, the controversy did underscore three facts about Prussian policy: that it was a patronage system; that, in the absence of any effective new concept of constitutional loyalty, this had to be mediated through loyalty to a particular party; and that the issue of

[60] Runge, *Beamtentum und Politik*, p. 76.

politicization versus neutrality in the civil service remained visible, contentious, and unresolved. Political controls outside Prussia were varied, and less complete.[61] The scale of the problem was somewhat different in the smaller *Länder*. In Prussia, the non-ministerial civil-service senior grade numbered some 1,600 posts altogether, 540 of which were 'political'. Elsewhere, this grade numbered no more than a few hundred in any one *Land*—300 in Saxony, 100 in Baden, for example. Saxony's senior civil service had been notoriously conservative before 1918, and included a high proportion of nobles; the South German *Länder* were much less dominated by an agrarian nobility, though even a relatively liberal region like Baden had had few Catholics and no social democrats among its senior officials before 1918. The concept of the 'political' civil servant was not universal in Germany; it was not known in Württemberg civil-service law, for example. Similarly, the degree to which an effective *Juristen-monopol* existed by 1918 varied from *Land* to *Land*. It was this lack of uniformity in training (which inhibited the transfer of civil servants from *Land* to *Land* and between *Länder* and Reich), as much as any desire to expand the bases of recruitment, that acted as the stimulus towards a comprehensive training scheme in the 1920s.

Liberal opinion had long been canvassing the idea of a training reform to undermine the *Juristenmonopol* in its heartland of Prussia. The breaching of the *Juristenmonopol* where it existed was also a crucial element in any democratization policy, because of the exclusionary effects of its lengthy and costly educational and training procedures. Moreover, debates on training reform also raised the question of what was practically appropriate for the training of leading administrators in a modern bureaucracy: law and more law, or administrative technique, economics, and the like? As one contributor put it: 'In the end the criterion for the administration should not be admissibility [*Zulässig-keit*] but utility [*Zweckmässigkeit*]. Whatever seems useful should also be admissible.'[62] For some protagonists in the debates, this meant that logically there should be separate specialized training systems for recruits into the administrative and the judicial arms of the civil service

---

61 See Fenske, 'Monarchisches Beamtentum', from which this account is drawn.

62 W. Norden, 'Zur Ausbildungsfrage der höheren Verwaltungsbeamten', *ZgStW*, 86 (1929), 109. See also A. von Batocki *et al.*, *Staatsreferendar und Staatsassessor: Reformvorschläge für das Ausbildungs- und Berechtigungswesen der Juristen und Volkswirte* (Jena, 1927); W. F. Bruck, *Das Ausbildungsproblem des Beamten in Verwaltung und Wirtschaft: Geschichtliches und Reformvorschläge* (Leipzig, 1926); Freiherr von Scheurl, 'Probleme der Juristenbildung', *AöR*, NF5 (1923), 137-81.

respectively, as had been the practice in Prussia. This would allow future administrators to be trained in more than just the law, without overloading prospective jurists with irrelevant information. The other side of the argument, however, was that this would undermine the unity of the leadership corps, result in a semi-trained class of legally ignorant administrators, and make the achievement of a nationally uniform training system that much more difficult.[63]

In the event, little was achieved in the way of structural reform, though the effect of republican appointment policy was to reduce somewhat the percentage of top civil servants qualified in law.[64] As we have seen, training regulations in Prussia were amended in 1920 to allow the appointment of formally unqualified persons, and at the same time the administrative component in the regular process of in-service training for career recruits was slightly strengthened. In 1927, the separation of administrative and judicial training was suspended, a move that may have been intended as temporary though it survived until after the Nazi seizure of power. The Reich government was by this time trying to develop more uniform national guidelines on training, and in 1930 an inter-*Land* declaration was issued which represented agreement in theory on a joint training system. It would involve a seven-year sequence of university education and in-service training, to include only six months in an administrative office, though it did at least widen the university syllabus to include more economics and public law.[65] This was a timid step, and had no binding force. Both the political implications of alternative training systems, and the difficulty of securing agreement among the *Länder* for any Reich-sponsored rationalization, obstructed the achievement of national reform in this sphere, as was also to be the case in the wider field of civil-service law reform.

In one matter, however, the exigencies of national policy demanded action at Reich level, despite the network of competing interests involved. The crisis of hyper-inflation which hit Germany in 1923 presented the national government with an inescapable need to slash the costs of administration. Five years after the first battle over civil-service tenure rights, another was to begin.

---

[63] The matter was under discussion at Reich ministerial level in the later 1920s: see the series of ministerial exchanges and committee protocols in BA R 43I/2621 and 2622. See also Nicholls, 'Höhere Beamtenschaft', pp. 199-207, and E. Geib, 'Die Ausbildung des Nachwuchses für den höheren Verwaltungsdienst', *AöR*, 80 (1955/6), 307-45.

[64] Runge, *Politik und Beamtentum*, pp. 190-200.

[65] *Bekanntmachung*, 26 Sept. 1930 (*RMinBl*, 1930, 547).

IV

As in other European countries, war, demobilization, and inflation led in Germany to a pronounced expansion in the personnel of the public administration. In less than a decade, 1914-23, the total complement of civil servants in the Reich and *Land* administrations increased by about 40 per cent, with comparable or greater growth in other classes of public employment.[66] Retrenchment in this, as in other areas of economic policy, was delayed by the Reich government's strategy of tolerating a measure of inflation in order to sustain the post-war boom, until the onset of uncontrollable hyper-inflation with the Ruhr occupation in January 1923.[67] In October 1923, two weeks after the passage of the Enabling Act, the Reich government decreed a programme of national cut-backs in administrative personnel by issuing the *Personalabbauverordnung* (PAV), or Decree to Reduce Reich Personnel Expenditure.[68] In one sense, this was a belated aspect of the demobilization process, and belonged to the general elimination of exceptional state powers that accompanied the end of the war and the post-revolutionary reaction. It was also part of what was intended to be a comprehensive programme of administrative simplification and financial restraint, adopted partly under pressure from the Reparations Commission and partly in the context of the broad movement of rationalization that swept Germany in the 1920s. And finally, for the civil service it was the beginning of a

---

[66] See Kunz, 'Stand versus Klasse', pp. 61-3; O. Schwarz, *Die Entwicklung der Ausgaben und Einnahmen Deutschlands, Englands, Frankreichs und Italiens vor und nach dem Weltkriege (Anhang: Die Beamtenvermehrung seit Kriegsbeginn)* (Magdeburg, 1921); *Der Personalstand der öffentlichen Verwaltung im Deutschen Reich am 31. Marz 1928 und am 31. Marz 1927 (Einzelschriften zur Statistik des Deutschen Reiches*, 18; Berlin, 1931), 13-14, 17; J. P. Cullity, 'The Growth of Governmental Employment in Germany, 1882-1950', *ZgStW*, 123 (1967), 201-17, surveys long-term trends. For a fuller discussion of civil-service size and composition in the 1920s, see Ch. 3, pp. 60-1, below.

[67] For the results of recent research into German inflation, see G. D. Feldman *et al.* (eds.), *Die deutsche Inflation: Eine Zwischenbilanz / The German Inflation Reconsidered: A Preliminary Balance* (Berlin, 1982), and in particular, A. Kunz, 'Verteilungskampf oder Interessenkonsensus? Einkommensentwicklung und Sozialverhalten von Arbeitnehmergruppen in der Inflationszeit 1914 bis 1924', pp. 347-84. Further publications of the inflation research project of the Berlin Historische Kommission are forthcoming.

[68] *Verordnung zur Herabminderung der Personalausgaben des Reichs*, 27 Oct. 1923 (*RGBl*, 1923, i. 999); amended 28 Jan. 1924 (*RGBl*, 1924, i. 39). Kunz, 'Stand versus Klasse', is an exhaustive and judicious evaluation of the decree and its effects. Art. 18 required the *Länder* to adopt the main provisions of the decree, and empowered them to issue their regulations in decree form too. See also Schulz, *Demokratie und Diktatur*, pp. 527-38; K. B. Netzband and H. P. Widmaier, *Währungs- und Finanzpolitik der Ära Luther 1923-1925* (Tübingen, 1964), 120-9; G. Lassar, 'Reichseigene Verwaltung unter der Weimarer Verfassung', *JöR*, 14 (1926), 60-8.

reform programme that aimed ultimately to modernize the terms of public employment in Germany.

The immediate origins of the PAV lay in discussions conducted in the Reich finance ministry in the course of 1923 about a law to enforce a statutory retirement age for the civil service. The RBG imposed no compulsory age for retirement: 'incapacity' (*Dienstunfähigkeit*) had to be proven in each case, a cumbersome procedure that was increasingly inappropriate in such a large-scale enterprise as government employment. Moreover, the only provision in the RBG which gave any leeway in the firing of civil servants for administrative reasons was so narrowly framed that it was only possible when the post itself was being eliminated from the establishment (§24). The Reich finance ministry, whose own establishment was one of the agencies most swollen by the effects of the inflation, proposed issuing a straightforward expansion of existing powers: 'Tenured Reich civil servants may be provisionally retired under payment of an allowance [*Wartegeld*] if the civil-service establishment of their administrative branch is to be systematically reduced by authority of a decision by the Reich government.'[69] The proposed order of priority for such retirements reflected those adopted in the earlier process of demobilization in the non-state sector. It discriminated against the 'economically secure' (usually a euphemism for a woman married to an employed man), the unmarried, and those married but childless: but the top priority for suspension was anyone deemed no longer capable of performing his or her duties.

The inter-ministerial discussions of this plan over the summer of 1923 were supposed to be highly confidential, but they took place against a background buzz of press publicity about the problem of the 'overgrown' bureaucracy. Rumours of government plans, if not actual leaks, were rife.[70] The finance ministry was evidently fortified by the sense that 'public opinion' was backing its efforts, and urged that a 'somewhat more merciless' attitude be taken in framing the necessary powers.[71] Those that were finally taken in the PAV, after discussions with the *Länder*, were in a sense not 'more merciless' than the original suggestion, but they were far more sweeping. They amounted, in fact, to a serious attack on tenure and related rights.

[69] Reich finance minister to Reich ministers, 25 June 1923 (BA R 43I/2612).

[70] Kunz, 'Stand versus Klasse', pp. 68-9, 74-5.

[71] Chancellery memo (Graevell), Sept. 1923 (full date not given); also Reich finance minister (Hilferding) to state secretary in the Reich chancellery (von Rheinbaben), 10 Sept. 1923, alleging demands from the public and from Reichstag members for an 'accelerated and rigorous' policy; both BA R 43I/2612.

The PAV began by amending the RBG, in order to relax the terms under which civil servants could be transferred, and to set sixty-five as the compulsory retirement age in all but a few specified posts. Article 2 permitted voluntary early retirement from age fifty-eight, where this was in the interests of reducing the personnel of the administrative branch in question. There then followed the original focus of the law, the creation of powers provisionally to retire tenured civil servants. Among other provisions, new appointments were frozen, pensions were to be subject to means-testing, and, in an originally unplanned but crucial extension of the scope of the measure, Article 15 contained the laconic instruction that '*Angestellte* are to be dismissed'. In addition, there was a blatant abrogation of the constitution in the provision that a married woman civil servant or teacher could be dismissed at the discretion of her employing authority, provided that in its view, 'her economic situation appeared secure' (Article 14). In subsequent execut-ive instructions, it was added that this security was to be assumed in cases where a woman was married to another civil servant—an ironic as well as a discriminatory assumption, given the way in which the PAV attacked his tenure too. Women's pension rights were also abridged. The article thus demonstrated the extreme fragility of the legal gains ostensibly made by women since 1918. The state itself was setting a significant precedent for the vociferous campaigns against women's right to work which were to reach their climax in the 1930s.

The stated objective of the PAV was to reduce the complement of *Reichsbeamte* by between 5 and 25 per cent, though the timetable provided in the decree only covered the first 15 per cent (Article 8). These were to be off the books by the beginning of April 1924, a target which was not only met in time, but exceeded, as Table 2 from the finance ministry's official report in May 1924 shows.[72]

Altogether, the percentage of jobs lost in the public sector was 24.9, but, as the table shows, this masks the fact that the effect on each of the three categories of public employment, *Beamte*, *Angestellte*, and *Arbeiter*, was very different. The percentage of *Beamte* who lost their jobs only slightly exceeded the interim figure of 15 per cent foreseen in the decree, though rights to increase this to the full extent allowed by law were specifically reserved. But the PAV had set no precise limits on

---

[72] Compiled from tables in *Denkschrift des Reichsfinanzministeriums über den Personalabbau*, Berlin, 15 May 1924, 2, 3 (copy in BA R 431/2613). This data covers the Reich only; there appears to be no comparable compilation for the *Länder* and local government.

TABLE 2. Personnel Reductions in the Reich Administration, 1923-1924

Branch	Beamte		Angestellte		Arbeiter	
	Total on 1.10.23	No. dismissed by 31.3.24	Total on 1.10.23	No. dismissed by 31.3.24	Total on 1.10.23	No. dismissed by 31.3.24
Central Reich authorities	105,976	7,207	51,394	24,350	50,046	13,411
Reichsbahn	425,852	85,749	861	568	576,083	186,658
Post, Telegraph, Reich printers	294,127	41,551	8,492	5,279	79,383	32,065
TOTAL	825,955	134,507 (16.3%)	60,747	30,197 (49.7%)	705,512	232,134 (32.9%)

reductions among *Angestellte* and *Arbeiter*, and in the end these were much more heavily hit than *Beamte* were. *Arbeiter*, the least protected contractually, suffered the largest numerical depletion, though the percentage job-loss for them was still a good deal lower than it was for *Angestellte*: the latters' numbers were reduced by almost half. Obviously, this was somewhat less than the wholesale elimination announced in summary terms by the PAV. Yet, given that the personnel reduction process as a whole achieved the 25 per cent proposed for *Beamte* alone, it is self-evident that in the end the *Beamte* were spared by the sacrifice of *Angestellte*, many of whom would have been doing basically the same kind of work. At any rate, the government aimed all its defensive justifications of the exercise at the ears of *Beamte*, telling them that the reductions of 1923 were actually in their own interests, for they would otherwise have become the victims of subsequent and more serious measures which would erode the institution of the career civil service as such. What this threat meant was left unsaid; but it was no doubt intended partly as a rather backhanded way of expressing a continued governmental commitment to the civil service as an institution.

The civil-service associations had put maximum and partially successful pressure on the government to convert the *Beamtenabbau* into this wider *Personalabbau*.[73] But, despite what they managed to salvage for their members, the PAV still drew their criticism as a dangerous assault on the rights of civil servants and on the stability of the institution. Indeed, the mixture of warnings and fears of alienation among civil servants that was voiced in different quarters at this time echoed the tones of 1918–19. The spokesmen for the associations, meeting with Stresemann in November, expressed disappointment that the personnel cut-backs had not been preceded by a systematic and comprehensive review of administrative structure, for it made the PAV appear to be a negative attack lacking any sense of positive strategic planning.[74]

[73] Kunz, 'Stand versus Klasse', pp. 68–80, discusses in detail the process by which this took place, and the part played by the civil-service associations in limiting the damage to be inflicted on their memberships; see also documentation in BA R 43I/2612 and 2613. Note that the PAV did not grant any new powers to dismiss *Angestellte* and *Arbeiter*, since these were already untenured jobs, but Art. 15 did create a statutory obligation to dismiss *Angestellte*.

[74] Minutes of meeting between representatives of the civil-service associations and Stresemann, 14 Nov. 1923 (BA R 43I/2612); the file contains other examples of the associations' protests against the decree, and see also the minutes of one such meeting between Marx and the associations, 19 Feb. 1924, reprinted in *Akten der Reichskanzlei: Die Kabinette Marx I und II*, ed. G. Abramowski (Boppard, 1973), i. 381–3.

Whether such a review would have served the associations' interests any better was doubtful, as future plans for streamlining the civil service were to indicate, but presumably the rhetoric was intended to impress.

However, the PAV itself was basically an emergency measure, and was defended as such by the government. Although most of its provisions were not statutorily repealed until August 1925,[75] the personnel cut-backs were ended by cabinet decision in June 1924, by which time their immediate purpose had been completed.[76] After August 1925, the government retained powers to supervise new appointments of Reich civil servants, to freeze some vacancies, and to facilitate compulsory transfers. In addition, the constitutionally dubious powers to dismiss married women civil servants were retained, though with some amendments.[77] Finally, although the wholesale discharge of *Angestellte* ceased, new appointments were forbidden.

The retention of these powers indicates that the PAV was also something of a provisional substitute for a more systematic reform of administrative structure and civil-service law—an objective that was to be pursued, though with little success, in the mid-1920s. Figures computed in 1931, showing that the number of *Angestellte* had more than doubled between 1913 and 1928 while *Beamte* had grown by only one-third, suggest that the PAV could not reverse a secular trend towards the recomposition of public employment, as we shall see below.[78] Like other measures in the stabilization period 1923-35, the *Personalabbau* marked the end of the post-war, post-revolution period, and the beginning of an era of reconsolidation: a period of structural trade-offs which made a political market-place of what had shortly before been a revolutionary encounter. In itself and in its effects, it was an ambiguous measure. It both undermined and protected civil servants' rights, repeated and corrected the constitutional commitment of 1918-19, and offered civil servants a continuation of their special

[75] By the somewhat confusingly entitled *Gesetz über Einstellung des Personalabbaus und Änderung der Personalabbauverordnung*, 4 Aug. 1925 (*RGBl*, 1924, ii. 181).

[76] Minutes of cabinet meeting, 16 June 1924 (BA R 43I/2613).

[77] While PAV Art. 14 rendered women civil servants liable to compulsory and summary dismissal at any time (on condition of their adequate economic security), the 1925 amendment stipulated three months' notice, and introduced eligibility for severance allowances in lieu of pension; women civil servants were also entitled to request their own release, on similar conditions. In general, the effect of the amendment was to ameliorate somewhat the harshness of the original decree, while retaining its discriminatory spirit.

[78] *Der Personalstand der öffentlichen Verwaltung*, p. 17; see Ch. 3, p. 61, below.

status without guaranteeing this. When the Reich government moved to the right from the end of 1923 onwards, it proved possible to reformulate the basis of state and civil-service collaboration, as the DBB moved into a corporatist relationship with the state as employer. In this context, Stresemann's assurance to the civil-service associations in November 1923 was more than just resounding rhetoric: 'Now that two of the three institutions which held the nation [*Reich*] together, the monarchy and the army, have vanished, the *Berufsbeamtentum* is the last clamp that is holding the nation together.'[79] But what this meant to the government and to the civil service was, as it turned out, two rather different things.

---

[79] See n. 76 above.

3

The Failure of Reform
1923–1933

I

The period of 'relative stability' between inflation and depression was as short-lived and as equivocal for civil servants as it was for the Weimar Republic in general. Between the two periods of political and economic emergency that sandwiched the 1920s lay a thin layer of relief, which for civil servants centred largely on the 1927 salary law. The 1920s were far from secure for those who had survived the depredations of the *Personalabbau*. Even though it was completed within six months, and the main legal powers were abrogated eight months after that, the threat of further administrative rationalization was never entirely lifted. This was partly due to the continuing debates of the 1920s about the unfinished work of the constitution, which left so much scope for administrative reform. Little of this came to any conclusion, however. It was all the more galling to civil servants, then, that post-inflation governments argued for strict conservatism in administrative expenditure, while costly structural defects such as overlapping competences or unnecessarily duplicated offices eluded political solution. These bugetary constraints were particularly tight at Reich rather than *Land* level. In December 1923, the Reich cabinet established a three-man administrative review commission, headed by the *Sparkommissar*, Saemisch, the president of the Reich audit office. The commission, comparable to Britain's Geddes Committee, grew out of earlier efforts at fiscal retrenchment, and it had wide-ranging powers to review the entire budgetary operations and administrative structure of the Reich.[1] It stayed at work for the rest of the republic's life, a fiscally mandated but professionally alarming machinery for controlling the structure and personnel of the Reich's administration. As a result of its operations, civil servants faced promotion blocks and generally reduced career

[1] G. Schulz, *Zwischen Demokratie und Diktatur: Verfassungspolitik und Reichsreform in der Weimarer Republik*, i (Berlin, 1963), ch. 13; Dr M. Saemisch, *Der Reichssparkommissar und seine Aufgaben* (Berlin, 1930); H. James, *The German Slump: Politics and Economics 1924-1936* (Oxford, 1986), ch. 3.

opportunities; they were constantly reminded of the loopholes in the security of their vested rights; and they saw increasing anomalies and inequities in the status of civil servants employed by different authorities, as *Land* and local governments sought their own ways of meeting or ducking their financial problems. Moreover, they could see these issues thrown into the limelight of political and constitutional debate, as politicians and academics continued to thrash out questions about the republic's legitimacy, and the structure and status of its functionaries. The heavy sense of history and obligation with which much of this debate was invested could, however, become a burden rather than an honour to its bearers, if the old language was used to undermine in practice the traditions that it lauded in theory. For civil-service politics in the 1920s was characterized by two uneasily concurrent themes which finally severed the residual special relationship between civil servants and the state.

On the one hand, on the basis of the constitution and through the Deutscher Beamtenbund, civil servants recovered something of their special relationship to the state, albeit on the new basis of mass organization rather than the traditional bonds of obligation. Through the DBB, civil servants sought as a pressure group to preserve and exploit their inherited institutional status, rejecting the more radical alternative offered by the Allgemeiner Deutscher Beamtenbund with its overtly trade-unionist stance. The popularity of the DBB over the ADB was manifest in their membership statistics. In 1918, the DBB had about a million affiliated members; this fell to some 774,000 by 1922, as members seceded to form other organizations, but rose again to over a million in 1930, partly as a result of reaffiliations. By contrast, the ADB reached a maximum of 354,000 in 1924, falling steeply to 166,000 four years later, a low from which it barely recovered.[2] The DBB secured tangible benefits for its members from the close relationship it was able to cultivate with the centrist governments of the mid-1920s, the major achievement being the 1927 salary law. But this success—the fruit of a convergence of momentarily favourable circumstances—was unexpectedly short-lived. Its early denouement in the heavy salary cuts imposed by Brüning less than three years later was not simply the consequence of worsening economic conditions, but was at least partly due to the other tendency in civil-service affairs that had developed in the previous decade. This was the perception in academic and government circles of

[2] A. Kunz, 'Stand versus Klasse: Beamtenschaft und Gewerkschaften im Konflikt um den Personalabbau 1923/24', *Geschichte und Gesellschaft*, 8 (1982), 58.

a widening gap between the implications of the traditional *Berufsbeam-tentum*, and its practicability in the context of a bureaucratized mass society. The bureaucratic state of the twentienth century was becoming something very different from the *Beamtenstaat* of the nineteenth. This had already begun to emerge as a problem before the war, but it became more urgent as post-war Germany demonstrated its fiscal inability to maintain its inherited obligations to a mass civil service. The per capita costs of public administration doubled between 1913-14 and 1925-6.[3] At the end of the 1920s, there were about 1.6 million *Beamte* proper in all areas of the public service in Germany, and about 1.2 million other public employees. Of the *Beamte*, a little less than half (48.7 per cent) were occupied in the administration itself, while most of the rest (44 per cent) worked for public utilities.[4] These, principally the railways and the postal service, were regarded in a rather different light from the rest of the administration, being seen as commercial enterprises rather than as state activities *per se*. Indeed, in the narrowest official definition, the 'general administration' (*allgemeine Verwaltung*) employed no more than 7 per cent of the 1928 civil-service complement. In terms of overall state activity, certain traditional sectors, such as the military, had been declining in relative importance since before the end of the nineteenth century (and in the case of the military, the drop in absolute as well as relative numbers was precipitate after 1918). The public utilities were assuming a larger proportion of state employment in the same period, while sectors such as public health, which had barely existed before the turn of the century, were showing major growth by the mid-1920s. In addition, the social legislation of the 1920s, which introduced agencies such as the employment offices and the industrial arbitration system, was creating new professional careers in the public administration, demanding previously unknown skills.[5] Moreover, it was these newer

---

[3] *Statistisches Jahrbuch für das Deutsche Reich*, 1928, 530.

[4] See principally *Der Personalstand der öffentlichen Verwaltung im Deutschen Reich am 31. März 1928 und am 31. März 1927* (*Einzelschriften zur Statistik des Deutschen Reichs*, 18; Berlin, 1931), and 'Der Personalstand der öffentlichen Verwaltung im Deutschen Reich am 31. März 1927', a special supplement to *Wirtschaft und Statistik*, 1930, 6; figures also discussed in E. Lederer and J. Marschak, 'Der neue Mittelstand', *Grundriss der Sozialökonomik*, 9 (Tübingen, 1926), 128-31.

[5] J. P. Cullity, 'The Growth of Governmental Employment in Germany, 1882-1950', *ZgStW*, 123 (1967), 202-4 (note that in table 1, col. 3, the figure for 'Armed Forces' should be preceded by a minus sign, as also the figures in col. 4 for 'Transportation' and 'Other'). See also L. Preller, *Sozialpolitik in der Weimarer Republik* (Düsseldorf, 1978; orig. edn., 1949); H. Jacob, *German Administration since Bismarck: Central Authority versus Local Autonomy* (New Haven and London, 1963), 73 ff.

sectors that were responsible for the fall in the proportion of public-service jobs held by *Beamte*, which even the PAV had not been able to reverse. Whereas in 1913 *Beamte* had held 88.8 per cent of public-sector jobs and *Angestellte* 11.2 per cent, by 1927 the proportion of *Beamte* had fallen to 66.7 per cent, while *Angestellte* held 13.5 per cent of posts and *Arbeiter* 19.8 per cent.[6] This was a major shift in the structure of public employment which organized civil servants resisted, even as the government and some theorists sought to exploit the tendency in order to limit the reach of *Beamte* status.

What this meant was that Germany's bureaucratic apparatus was becoming both larger and more diverse than ever. This not only entailed mounting costs to the state in salaries and especially in pensions, but it also generated fears about an uncontrollable bureaucratization of German life—with social and political consequences which to some observers loomed as large as the financial ones. The origins and effects of this process, which was common to all the developed countries, were debated nowhere more vigorously than in Germany. There the inheritance of the *Beamtenstaat* combined with the effects of the rationalization movement of the 1920s to present a particularly pronounced, and in some ways contradictory example of this generic bureaucratic phenomenon. Some saw bureaucratization as an effect of a crisis of cultural creativity which was afflicting Europe as a whole;[7] others, as an aspect of the increasing rationalization of modern industrial capitalism, with its creation of a new class of white-collar workers—clerks, managers, administrators, and the like.[8] But from any angle of vision, the advance of bureaucratic organization in industry, commerce, and the state was raising taxing questions about the specificity of *Staatsbeamte* status. To some extent, this was a continuation of the process of enquiry initiated by Weber and Hintze into the nature, origins, and development of bureaucracy in general and the German civil service in particular. One problem of demarcation had already

---

[6] T. Ramm, 'Labor Relations in the Public Sector of the Federal Republic of Germany: The Civil Servant's Role', in C. M. Rehmus (ed.), *Public Employment Labor Relations: An Overview of Eleven Nations* (Ann Arbor, 1975), 103.

[7] e.g. E. Michel, 'Das Beamtenproblem, II: Die Krise', *Deutsche Republik*, 3, (1929), 1501-7.

[8] e.g. Lederer and Marschak, 'Der neue Mittelstand'; see also J. Kocka, *Die Angestellten in der deutschen Geschichte 1850-1980* (Göttingen, 1981), chs. 4 and 5. The role of women in this is discussed in C. Hahn, 'Der öffentliche Dienst und die Frauen: Beamtinnen in der Weimarer Republik', in Frauengruppe Faschismusforschung, *Mutterkreuz und Arbeitsbuch: Zur Geschichte der Frauen in der Weimarer Republik* (Frankfurt, 1981), 49-78.

been faced in this literature—that between *Privatbeamte* and *öffentliche Beamte*—and the tendency was to solve it by emphasizing not only the specificity of the civil servant's tasks as the state's representative, but also the uniqueness of his 'Seelenverfassung', as Hintze put it in 1911.[9] Conservative anti-positivists persisted in this thinking after 1918, indeed, stressed it even more heavily in order to preserve their inordinate claims on behalf of the civil service's significance. Thus, Arnold Köttgen concluded one of his many discussions of the question: 'In the final analysis, therefore, the specificity of the civil servant rests on a psychological basis alone. The distinction between the civil servant and the employee [*Arbeitnehmer*] is not primarily a question of legal status, but is rather to be explained solely in terms of the specific mental attitude of the civil service.'[10] The disdain for legalistic definition was a hallmark of anti-positivism; the assertion that the essential nature of the civil servant was insusceptible of legal definition opened up the space for an alternative idealist conceptualization. Hans Gerber, an extreme representative of this school of thought, reduced the Hegelian tradition to the point of banal parody with his discussion of the organic relationship between state, civil service, and people, and argued that since law is like religion in having a spiritual as well as a rational content, 'the civil service is most aptly to be compared to a religious order or to the Catholic clerical hierarchy'.[11] Even when attempting a practical definition of civil-service status and tasks, Gerber remained irredeemably idealist (and virtually impossible to render into intelligible English):

It has recently been more and more vigorously emphasized that the civil-service problem is in essence a problem of conviction [*ein Gesinnungsproblem*]. Anyone of whom it can and must be demanded that he accept that his professional relationship to the state [is structured by] this unique conviction, which must be grasped intellectually as a public responsibility, can be allowed to participate in

---

[9] O. Hintze, *Der Beamtenstand* (Leipzig, 1911), 17.

[10] A. Köttgen, *Beamtenrecht* (Breslau, 1929), 15. See also his 'Die Entwicklung des deutschen Beamtenrechts und die Bedeutung des Beamtentums im Staat der Gegenwart', in G. Anschütz and R. Thoma (eds.), *Handbuch des deutschen Staatsrechts*, ii (Tübingen, 1932), 1-19, and his more exhaustive discussion in *Das deutsche Berufsbeamtentum und die parlamentarische Demokratie* (Berlin and Leipzig, 1928); also his 'Aufgaben und verfassungsrechtliche Stellung des Berufsbeamtentums im modernen Staat', in F. Berber (ed.), *Zum Neuaufbau der Verfassung* (*Jahrbuch für politische Forschung*, 1; Berlin, 1933), 101-28.

[11] H. Gerber, 'Vom Begriff und Wesen des Beamtentums', *AöR*, NF18 (1930), 64; the content of the essay makes it clear that Gerber intends his clerical language not just metaphorically but essentially. Köttgen, *Deutsches Berufsbeamtentum*, pp. 274-5, concludes with a similarly sacerdotal, though here more metaphorical, analogy.

the institutional organism [*Organschaft*] as a civil servant. Where the question of such conviction is not decisive, there the private employee [*Privatangestellte*] has his place.[12]

This position was closely related to the concept that the only meaningful oath was an all-embracing act of self-dedication, rather than a formal commitment to abide by a given constitutional and legal situation. Behind Gerber's tortuous syntax lurks the suggestion that civil-servant status, as a question of 'conviction', is a quality already possessed by certain people: a vocation, an inherency which fits them for this peculiar public responsibility, and which the state in a sense is called upon to mobilize. Against this, Köttgen's definition of the *raison d'être* of the civil service in Weimar Germany may seem a model of sober common sense: 'The task of the bureaucracy is the protection of the stability of the state, and it is called upon to act as a counterbalance to the fluctuating political forces represented in the party.'[13] Yet it would be wrong to see in this simply a conventional and pragmatic understanding of the role of a permanent bureaucracy in a parliamentary democracy, just as it would be a mistake to read Gerber's rhetoric as merely extreme idealist verbiage. Both writers were advancing opinions which had a wide resonance among conservative politicians and academics, and which also had highly practical implications for the status of the German civil service in law. Philosophy and jurisprudence legitimated more widely held political opinions. Conservative politicians wanted to dispute the Weimar Republic's claim to 'really' represent the political life of the nation. Academics like Gerber and Köttgen were reasserting the primacy of the civil service as the representative of the nation as a whole, against the pretensions of democratic representation theory. Their views belonged in the current of political debate that was swept forward by the wave of anti-positivist publication in political theory in the late 1920s.[14] Hostility to parliamentary democracy was functional to the construction of a conservative theory of sovereign representation: to the fragmentation of the people in parliament was

[12] H. Gerber, 'Bericht', in H. Gerber and A. Merkl, *Entwicklung und Reform des Beamtenrechts* (Veröffentlichung der Vereinigung der deutschen Staatsrechtslehrer, 7; Berlin and Leipzig, 1932), 36.

[13] Köttgen, *Deutsches Berufsbeamtentum*, p. 123, and also pp. 242 ff; and H. Nawiasky, *Die Stellung des Berufsbeamtentums im parlamentarischen Staat* (Munich, 1926).

[14] K. Sontheimer, *Antidemokratisches Denken in der Weimarer Republik* (Munich, 1978), esp. ch. 14; J. Meinck, *Weimarer Staatslehre und Nationalsozialismus: Eine Studie zum Problem der Kontinuität im staatsrechtlichen Denken in Deutschland 1928 bis 1936* (Frankfurt and New York, 1978), pts. 1 and 2.

counterposed the unification of the people in the institution of the *Berufsbeamtentum*.

This did not mean, however, that the civil service as it actually existed in the 1920s was seen as an adequate institutional vehicle for this idea. Anxious though Köttgen was to redeem the significance of the civil service in the new political conditions of parliamentary democracy, he also examined the ways in which this might demand a modification of some of the traditions of the civil service—a modification whose purpose, of course, would be to preserve its essence intact. Thus, this thinking led him to propose a very restrictive definition of true *Beamte* status, limiting it to those officials whose work was part of the public functions of the state as a sovereign authority. For Köttgen, the essence of the civil service was compromised when *Beamte* status was extended to officials who performed tasks that could just as well be undertaken by private or commercial enterprises—the administration of the railways or of the welfare system, for example. This minimalist conception of the state and its functions was perhaps the effect rather than the cause of his commitment to a restricted élite of civil servants, whose true *raison d'être* was as a 'community of conviction'.[15] Thus, he argued:

It is advisable to make a more parsimonious use of the civil service in the future, compared with the situation up to now. Two reasons may be adduced in particular here. The demands made by the parliamentary state on its civil service are infinitely greater than those of the past. If these enhanced demands were to be imposed upon an excessively large group of people, this would inevitably result in failure. Quite apart from this, however, it has already been exhaustively demonstrated that in a parliamentary state civil servants must be accorded the most varied range of privileges which in themselves forbid too

---

[15] Köttgen's term is 'Gesinnungsgemeinschaft', which he contrasts with 'Berufs-gruppe' or 'occupational group'; *Deutsches Berufsbeamtentum*, p. 90, and also p. 272: 'The social structure of the civil service in the parliamentary state must also be interwoven in some form or another with the structure of the nation as a whole. Here it is a matter of decisive import that the essential focus of solidarity for the civil service can never lie in economic or professional attributes, which deserve at most secondary consideration. At a number of points in our previous discussion, the outstanding significance for the civil servant of the concept of the state has become evident. If, then, we are looking for a social form of solidarity [*sozialen Verbindungsform*] for the civil service, it is this point that must here be in the foreground. The integration of the civil service can take place only in the form of a community of conviction. A shared professional ethos is the sole conceivable core of a modern civil service, just as it was this indeed that elevated the old *Beamtenstand* far above the meaning of a simple agency of particular interests.' On the related issue of the professions and their status, see K. H. Jarausch, 'The Crisis of the German Professions 1918-33', *JCH*, 20/3 (1985), 379-98.

extensive a use of civil servants. The necessity of lifetime tenure alone makes it impossible in many cases to appoint civil servants to a range of offices.[16]

In other words, the conservative defence of the *Berufsbeamtentum* required an abridgement of precisely those rights which had been confirmed by the constitution in the name of continuity and legitimacy. For, if the distinction between public and private office was an issue as old as the bureaucracy itself, and had been a staple of nineteenth-century political and social theory, the question which had become more pressing after the First World War was the distinction *within* the public service between different classes of employee. Köttgen's clear aim in the late 1920s was to facilitate the re-emergence of a real élite of civil servants from the protean mass bureaucracy: an élite which would be capable of 'counterbalancing' the organs of parliamentary government, or in other words, of challenging the latter's monopoly of sovereign authority. But interest in the problem of the relationship of élite to mass in the civil service was not confined to conservative political theorists alone. In different ways, the state, the political parties, the civil-service associations, and, not least, academic sociologists and labour lawyers were all closely concerned with the question.

Weimar governments in the 1920s were deeply concerned at the economic and political costs of maintaining a mass *Beamtentum*. As an emergency cost-cutting measure, the PAV achieved the negative aim of stemming the tide of *Angestellte* in the public service. However, partly as a result of the civil-service associations' pressure, it had not permanently abridged the costly constitutional rights enjoyed by *Beamte* proper. But if civil servants' rights were thus unassailable once acquired, the alternative was to restrict the number of state employees who had access to them. In the mid-1920s, therefore, Weimar governments attempted to fix a statutory definition of *Beamte* status (*Beamtenverhältnis*) for the first time, a definition which might radically narrow eligibility for the status and its benefits. Although fiscal motives were prominent here, there was also a conservative tendency that contained more than a faint echo of some of the academics' positions. Thus, Sparkommissar Saemisch himself saw other, larger dangers in

[16] Köttgen, *Deutsches Berufsbeamtentum*, pp. 260-1; and see pp. 57-75, 85 ff., 145 ff., 260-4. See also A. Köttgen, 'Zur Frage des Erwerbs der Beamteneigenschaft', *AöR*, NF 18 (1930), 232: 'There must be two objectives here [in the jurisdictional practice of the Reichsgericht]. In the first place, a sharp demarcation and specification of the *Berufsbeamtentum* as an institution, the character of which has today lost far too much of its precision.'

the uncontrolled growth of *Beamte* numbers. After estimating the number of *Beamte* in 1930 at some 1.5 million, he went on to argue:

This number appears disproportionate by comparison with the total population. It is clearly desirable on financial grounds to achieve a considerable reduction in this number. I need only refer to the massive expansion of pension costs in recent years. But in my view this is less important than the fact that there is widespread and bitter opposition in Germany to the expansion of civil-service status, and that this breeds attacks on the career civil service [*Berufsbeamtentum*] as such. The dangers of this development can hardly be overestimated in my opinion.[17]

In other words, bureaucratization carried with it a taint which might infect the *Berufsbeamtentum*, conceived of as an institution distinct from the bureaucracy in general. The priority for Saemisch, as for some other members of the 1920s cabinets and their advisers, was to safeguard that institution, and thereby underline the specificity of its status and role.

Reich governments made two attempts at legislating a definition of *Beamte*: the first in 1924-7 as part of a programme of administrative reform; and the second in 1930-2 when the economic crisis endowed the question with renewed urgency.[18] The issue was not what rights a civil servant enjoyed after appointment as such, but what was the legal foundation and mark of the acquisition of civil-servant status. Neither Reich nor *Länder* law, taken over from pre-war Germany, contained any substantive statutory definition of civil-servant status.[19] The effect was that the task of demarcating it from other forms of employment was

---

[17] Saemisch, *Reichssparkommissar*, p. 45. For examples of public criticism of the civil service, see the 25-pp. collection of press-cutting material submitted to the interior ministry by the DBB, 30 Dec. 1926 (copy in BA R 43I/2554). In a sense, Saemisch's objective was precisely the reverse of what the PAV had ultimately achieved, in that he wanted to reduce the number of *Beamte*, and consign work to contractual employees as far as possible—though within the context of a massive streamlining of the administration.

[18] See documentation in BA R 43I/2553-6; also G. Hoffmann, *Sozialdemokratie und Berufsbeamtentum: Zur Frage nach Wandel und Kontinuität im Verhältnis der Sozialdemokratie zum Berufsbeamtentum in der Weimarer Zeit* (Hamburg, 1972), 138-51.

[19] See Köttgen, *Beamtenrecht*, pp. 30-5; id., *Deutsches Berufsbeamtentum*, pp. 139-48; W. Jellinek, 'Die Rechtsformen des Staatsdienstes: Begriff und rechtliche Natur des Beamtenverhältnisses', in Anschütz and Thoma (eds.), *Handbuch*, ii. 20-33 (includes a listing of valid Reich and *Land* laws); for Prussia, see also A. Brand, *Das Beamtenrecht: Die Rechtsverhältnisse der preussischen Staats- und Kommunalbeamten* (Berlin, 1928), 15-22, and H. Helfritz, 'Die Entwicklung des öffentlichen Rechts in Preussen', *JöR*, 14 (1926), 246-69; for other *Länder*, see E. Rosenthal, 'Der staatliche Aufbau des Landes Thüringen', *JöR*, 12 (1923/4), 88; W. Apelt, 'Die Entwicklung des

left to academic debate in theory, and to judicial decision in practice. Although the lack of definition was often remarked upon as somewhat paradoxical,[20] the existence of such a statutory lacuna was hardly unusual in itself: uncodified conventions frequently play a large role in legal and constitutional practice, so too the use of the courts to fill such gaps. But there were particular reasons for the attempts to achieve a statutory definition in the Weimar period. As suggested above, both fiscal and ideological concerns were prominent, the more so because after 1918 the courts were delivering very generous judgements on the question to numerous appellants pressing their claims to civil-servant status and rights. By the late 1920s, the *Land* administrative courts and the Reichsgericht had established the convention that 'Hoheitsakte', or acts executed by power of the state, could be performed only by persons with *Beamte* status; anyone who could prove that their work fell under this elastic definition could thus raise a claim to such status.

The whole question was an extremely thorny one, both legally and politically. A central problem was whether a statutory definition should be formal or substantive. Should civil-servant status be acquired as the effect of a formal procedure, namely, the issue of a due certificate of appointment? Or should it, on the other hand, be derived from a substantive enumeration of the attributes of office, much as the courts' practice affirmed? Critics of the latter procedure argued that a substantive definition would not put an end to the legal uncertainty, but would open the way to endless litigation as state employees pressed their individual claims in the courts. But the formal definition was seen by its opponents as potentially unsettling to civil servants already in office, for many of them had never received due certification of appointment and would thus risk being retrospectively deprived of their status and rights. In both bouts of governmental discussion, the interior ministry (under Jarres and later Wirth) tended to espouse a substantive definition; this was seen as an expression of its staff's protective attitude

öffentlichen Rechts im Freistaat Sachsen 1923-1930', *JöR*, 19 (1931), 41; C. Sartorius, 'Die Entwicklung des öffentlichen Rechts in Württemberg in den Jahren 1925-1931', *JöR*, 20 (1932), 184-5 (Württemberg's new 1929 civil-service law was the most comprehensive in Germany); H. Gmelin, 'Die Entwicklung des öffentlichen Rechts in Hessen von 1923 bis Ende 1928', *JöR*, 17 (1929), 179-80; and H. Liermann, 'Die Entwicklung des öffentlichen Rechts in Baden bis Ende 1928', *JöR*, 17 (1929), 148-9.

[20] See e.g. Köttgen, *Beamtenrecht*, p. 30: 'Thus the concept of the civil servant [*Beamtenbegriff*] has up to the present not been able to extract itself from literary debate, and again and again disagreements turn up all over the place and often surprisingly about the nature of civil-servant status.'

to the interests of civil servants, which was also disclosed in the ministry's tendency to play up the risks of their alienation. The finance ministry, on the other hand, pushed for a highly restrictive and watertight formal definition, especially after 1930 when the successful claims to *Beamte* status—and thus to retrospective salaries and prospective pensions—which had been made by *Angestellte* were imposing an intolerable additional burden on the Reich's critically strained finances.[21]

It was in fact the economic crisis of the depression that led to the resumption of discussions in 1930, after these had lapsed three years earlier when the interior ministry had changed hands and its reform programme was decelerated.[22] By then the problem was a matter of extreme urgency for the finance ministry, which adopted a highly unusual procedure in a desperate attempt to force a solution. Instead of communicating its desires directly to the interior ministry, which was formally responsible for the policy area and in theory still had a draft law under consideration, the finance ministry produced its own definition in consultation with the justice ministry, and then circulated this to the entire cabinet. This was a deliberate circumvention of the usual formalities, and was obviously intended to rap recalcitrant ministerial knuckles as well as to push the issue to a conclusion. Up to a point, it was a successful gambit. The cabinet overwhelmingly preferred the finance ministry's draft, and despite residual opposition from the interior ministry, a proposed law 'on the foundation [*Begründung*] of civil-servant status' was ready for presentation in the Reichstag by the end of September 1931.[23] The draft recommended a formal definition of civil-servant status in future, by means of certification of appointment, and offered a measure of protection for existing civil servants who did not have this. It also specifically disallowed existing contractual employees (*Angestellte*) from acquiring civil-servant status, whatever the substantive nature of their work.

This bill represented a defeat for the interior ministry, which made

21 See the official memorandum to the finance ministry's draft law 'on the foundation of civil-servant status', as submitted to the Reich chancellery, 23 Sept. 1931 (BA R 431/2556). In an exemplary decision of the Reichsgericht on 11 Oct. 1929, a Prussian local-government official won his appeal for civil-servant status on the grounds that his post as head of the coal and housing office involved 'obrigkeitliche Aufgaben', and this overrode the fact that he had no formal certificate of appointment as a *Beamte*; see *Entscheidungen des Reichsgerichts in Zivilsachen*, 125 (Berlin and Leipzig, 1929), 420-2.

22 See Hoffmann, *Sozialdemokratie und Berufsbeamtentum*, pp. 150-1.

23 See n. 21 above. The draft was entered as *Drucksachen des Reichstags*, VII. Wahlperiode, 1932, 278.

no effort to expedite its passage through the Reichstag. By February 1932 it had made its way through the Reichsrat, but no room had been made for it on the Reichstag agenda. However, the widespread awareness that legislation was imminent was leading to a rush to the courts, as individual employees tried to get their civil-servant status certified before the curtain fell. Civil servants themselves viewed the bill with suspicion and apprehension: indicatively, the DBB and ADB had opposed it in draft, though the RhB had been less critical, for reasons which will be discussed below. In May, the finance ministry made another bid to speed its passage. It had sometime previously instructed its field officials that 'sovereign functions' (*hoheitliche Funktionen*) were no longer to be assigned to *Angestellte*, for fear that it would lead to 'the so-called "automatic acquisition" of civil-servant status"' through the courts. But this order was easier to issue than to implement, as the ministry itself went on to explain:

This instruction . . . is, however, leading to intolerable problems in practice. The collection of Reich taxes, likewise the collection of *Land*, local government, and church taxes in so far as these are administered by the [Reich] finance offices, and furthermore the [tax] supervision system . . . can in many cases no longer be effectively carried out . . . It is impossible to substitute *Beamte* for these *Angestellte*, because the existing establishment of *Beamte* may not be increased . . . This state of affairs is bound to have its effect on the tax yield; how critical this is in the current budgetary situation needs no further emphasis.[24]

Despite this note of urgency, no immediate action was taken and the bill remained in limbo until after the Nazi take-over of power. A revised version was then incorporated into the compendium Law for the Amendment of Regulations in Civil-Service, Salary and Pensions Law, of June 1933—a great dustbin of a statute into which all the odds and ends that had eluded regulation in the 1920s were swept, along with

24 Reich finance minister (Dietrich) to Reich interior minister (Groener), 28 May 1932 (copy in R 43I/2556, f. 153). The finance ministry saw itself in a no-win situation. It had inherited a shortage of experts, and the tax changes after 1930 imposed additional burdens on an already stretched administration. It was not empowered to increase its establishment of *Beamte*, and would normally have tried to fall back on the employment of *Angestellte* as temporary staff. But if *Angestellte* enjoyed the prospect of acquiring civil-service status through the courts, this would amount to a back-door and unplanned increase in ministerial staff. The ministry was thus avoiding appointments, to the detriment of tax collection. No doubt the ministry played up the threat this represented to the already disastrous fiscal situation of the Reich government in order to enhance its case for statutory reform.

new, specifically Nazi rules.[25] The significance of this will be discussed in Chapter 5. What needs further consideration here is the wider context of issues in civil-service law raised by the problem of definition. Although conservative academics may have dominated discourse about the civil service by the beginning of the 1930s, they held no monopoly in the broader debate in the Weimar Republic on the role of the state and of the bureaucracy in contemporary society. Full discussion of this would go beyond the scope of this study, but the political and intellectual history of modern Germany assured a central place for debate on these questions, not least among liberals and the left. Fuelled by the twin traditions symbolized by Weber and Kautsky, and spurred on by the establishment of the new German state in 1918, this debate ramified in the 1920s into a complex discourse about the social function of law and the state, about organized capitalism, corporatism, rationalization and bureaucratic organization, and ultimately about the social sources of political legitimacy and domination. One important aspect of this may be summarized as an enquiry, especially on the left, into the social conditions for effective and progressive democracy; sub-themes of this were provided by investigations into the composition and political identity of the petty bourgeoisie, and into the social links between the state and the working class.[26] Though at first sight these may seem to be utterly unconnected questions, in fact there was a close association between them, and one that was of great practical significance for the

[25] *Gesetz zur Änderung von Vorschriften auf dem Gebiete des allgemeinen Beamten-, des Besoldungs- und des Versorgungsrechts*, 30 June 1933 (*RGBl*, 1933, i. 433), §§1-6; see Ch. 5, pp. 149-52, below.

[26] The literature on these themes is large and developing. For social democratic ideas, see initially D. Abraham, 'Labor's Way: On the Successes and Limits of Socialist Politics in Interwar and Post-World War II Germany', *International Labor and Working Class History*, 28 (1985), 1-24, and references therein; also R. Saage (ed.), *Solidargemeinschaft und Klassenkampf: Politische Konzeptionen der Sozialdemokratie zwischen den Weltkriegen* (Frankfurt, 1986). Representative contemporary writers in this tradition include O. Kirchheimer: e.g. his essays 'Weimar—und was dann? Analyse einer Verfassung', and 'Zur Frage der Souveranität, both in his collection *Politik und Verfassung* (Frankfurt, 1964), 9-95, and 'Verfassungsreform und Sozialdemokratie', in his *Funktionen des Staats und der Verfassung: Zehn Analysen* (Frankfurt, 1972), 79-99; H. Heller: e.g. 'Politische Demokratie und soziale Homogenität', in his *Gesammelte Schriften* (Leiden and Tübingen, 1971), ii. 421-33 (on Heller, see also C. Müller and I. Staff (eds.), *Der soziale Rechtsstaat: Gedächtnisschrift für Hermann Heller 1891-1933* (Baden-Baden, 1984)); F. Neumann: 'The Social Significance of the Basic Laws in the Weimar Constitution', *Economy and Society*, 10 (1981), 329-47; O. Kahn-Freund: *Labour Law and Politics in the Weimar Republic* (Oxford, 1981). On *Angestellte* in Weimar, see H. Speier, *Die Angestellten vor dem Nationalsozialismus: Ein Beitrag zum Verständnis der deutschen Sozialstruktur 1918-1933* (Göttingen, 1977).

politics of the civil service. For both derived from the same preoccupation with the politics and sociology of class, and both ultimately debouched into the same question of whether and how the transition from Weimar's hybrid socio-liberal democracy to full-scale socialism might take place.

For social democratic theorists like Theodor Geiger, or Emil Lederer and Jakob Marshak, establishing the class location of the petty bourgeoisie or *Mittelstand*—especially the 'new' petty bourgeoisie of white-collar workers, of which civil servants were seen as a component—was an essential prerequisite to developing an appropriate theory and strategy for socialist politics in Weimar. Classic Marxist social theory in Germany had viewed the petty bourgeoisie as a group destined to disappear, of course, as the continuing process of friction between capitalists and proletariat pulverized its autonomy and dispersed the fragments to the proletariat.[27] Debate on this question had been reanimated by the appearance of the new petty bourgeoisie by the turn of the century—clearly a social and occupational group produced by capitalism, and not a mere relict of a superseded mode of production. The question of its social identity and political destiny was thus an important one. Was it still possible to salvage the two-class theory, and see the new petty bourgeoisie as a group awaiting enrolment in the working class? Might it, alternatively, demand recognition as an independent class, requiring the reworking of class theory? Or might the petty bourgeoisie, as conservative social theory argued, be a permanent buffer zone in society, a staging post for class mobility and an elastic guarantee of social harmony? There was a certain additional resonance to these questions in the case of the civil service, given the tradition of assigning it a place outside society, a place in fact designed for, and required by, the function of social reconciliation with which it had been endowed in nineteenth-century political theory. Geiger's answer to this was equivocal: 'Class society has no *Mittelstand* as a third front; it has only a bloc of those who are outside the solidarity of class [*einen Block der klassenmässig nicht Solidarisierten*]; i.e. a zone which is not yet permeated by the principle of class stratification.'[28] The question was, then, whether and how an identification of the new *Mittelstand* with the working class could be achieved.

It was in keeping with the left's view of the Weimar Republic as a

[27] See e.g. A. Leppert-Fögen, *Die deklassierte Klasse: Studien zur Geschichte und Ideologie des Kleinbürgertums* (Frankfurt, 1974), pt. 1.
[28] T. Geiger, 'Panik im Mittelstand', *Die Arbeit*, 10 (1930), 639.

stage on the road to socialism, and with the theoretical tradition that ratified this judgement, that a central role in the process of binding the new petty bourgeoisie to the working class was assigned to social rather than political policy. The term *Sozialpolitik*—social politics, rather than social policy—stood for more in Weimar than the discrete enactments of the state in the realm of labour and welfare law. It connoted, rather, a comprehensive and strategic concept of social solidarity, embracing not simply legislation but the whole process of social articulation and the organization of labour. It has been justly pointed out that in the 1920s 'Sozialpolitik and social reform emerged as alternatives to the defeated attempts at socialization and socialism'.[29] One might extend this by suggesting that, for the social democratic left, this concept of *Sozialpolitik* was a functional alternative to the supersession of the state-society dichotomy which was otherwise supposed to be delivered by socialist revolution; while, outside the left, *Sozialpolitik* offered liberals a modern vision of attainable social harmony.[30] The German left had its own long tradition of conducting class conflict by other means, of course, and Weimar in the 1920s was the site of a distinctive version of this—a hybrid composite of displaced class struggle, corporatism, and rationalization.

It was social politics in this sense that was the corner-stone of the pioneering study of the new *Mittelstand* by Lederer and Marschak, published in 1926, which built up to a discussion of the origins and objectives of organized-interest activity by white-collar workers and civil servants.[31] In this perspective, it was the status of the new *Mittelstand* as employees—as, therefore, a species of worker—that guaranteed their potential for enrolment in the ranks of the proletariat, where their true interests lay. Hence it was their organization on behalf of economic demands that was the crucial register of their relationship to the wider labour movement. This rested of course on a highly debatable, though firmly established tradition of deriving ideological potential in more or less unmediated form from economic location; but apart from that, the appropriateness of this model as a source of practice was already precarious, especially in the case of civil servants. For if the employment status of *Angestellte*—a distinctive one in some legal respects—itself presented certain obstacles to their identification with

[29] D. Abraham, *The Collapse of the Weimar Republic: Political Economy and Crisis* (New York, 1986), 221.
[30] See e.g. Preller, *Sozialpolitik*, pp. xvii–xviii.
[31] Lederer and Marschak, 'Der neue Mittelstand', pp. 131–9.

the cause of labour, how much more problematic this was for civil servants, whose occupational status was wholly foreign to the quintessence of proletarianism, the sale of labour power through free contract. How could civil servants become aligned with labour, when their status in law was designed precisely to distinguish them from contracted labour? Building connections between civil-service and labour politics was thus far from straightforward. There were attempts to do this, on both sides of the potential alliance, but they were fraught with contradictions.

In a sense, these contradictions were exemplified in the very way in which civil servants had entered the republic in 1918-19—on the one hand, as newly emancipated citizens, partners, and participants in the process of Germany's democratic self-renewal; on the other, as a peculiar institution of anything but equal citizens, viewed with suspicion by the left. But for a short period, the first of these images was cultivated by democratic politicians and by the leaders of the DBB, as they explored the way in which the caste rigidity of the civil service might be broken down, without losing the vested rights whose protection appeared tightly bound up with status. This, indeed, was the nub of the problem: did civil servants require a distinctive legal status, either to secure their material interests or because the nature of their public office demanded it? Or was it in their interests, both as employees and as citizens of the new republic, to concede that the day of the *öffentlich-rechtliches Treue- und Gehorsamsverhältnis* was past, that the very term connoted a superseded patrimonial authoritarianism? The DBB initially contained proponents of both positions, and in the first few years of the republic the more radical position had a slight edge, as if the fail-safe of the constitution provided a certain security from which change could at least be contemplated. But by 1923, as we have seen, the DBB had split, with the majority preferring to retreat to the safety of the constitution rather than risk a radical rupture. The DBB repudiated any interest in a radical reform of civil-service law, though it did still try to carve out a middle course between this and the mere survival of tradition. The radical aim of abolishing or narrowly restricting civil-servant status was confined to the ADB. Only this group, composed largely of *Betriebs-beamte*, was openly and aggressively in favour of assimilating civil-service law to labour law. The ADB argued that the state was an employer like any other, that only the handful of 'political' civil servants needed a special status, and that the persistence of legal status distinctions between different classes of workers was incompatible with the principles of the new Germany.[32]

Against this, no political party was prepared to commit itself formally to such a radical position, and some were of course deeply opposed to it. The Centre and the DDP were committed to the retention of special civil-service law, though also to the existence of powers that would ensure that the republic could rely on the loyalty of its officials. The right-wing parties, the DVP and DNVP, had fewer qualms about 'loyalty': for them, neutrality in the traditional sense was sufficient and correct, and the preservation of civil-servant status was a foregone conclusion. Not surprisingly, it was the parties of the left that had the greatest difficulty in defining their position, since they had to face the contradiction between the theory and the practice of class struggle. In 1924, the SPD's laboriously developed civil-service programme described its policy on this score in impenetrably delphic language: 'Retention of the public-law status of civil servants in the framework of German labour law in general.'[33] The KPD's 1927 programme represented an attempt to define civil servants solely in class terms, eschewing any references to the law. It insisted that the KPD made

a sharp distinction between civil servants of the lower and middle salary groups on the one hand, and the upper civil servants [Oberbeamten] on the other. It is absolutely opposed to the increasingly apparent tendency to award special financial and legal advantages to upper civil servants at the expense of lower, thereby giving them the same kind of privileged status as directors, board members and shareholders in private enterprises.[34]

The party programme went on to oppose any 'general abolition of civil servants' rights', and to support a uniform civil-service law for the whole of Germany, one which would not include a 'differentiation between the so-called ranking and industrial civil servants [Hoheits- und Betriebsbeamten]'.

At first sight this may seem paradoxical—a reversal of precisely the radical position represented by the ADB, which had argued for such a

[32] For examples of this ADB position, see H. L. Brill, Der Kampf um die Erhaltung des Berufsbeamtentums (Berlin, 1926), and H. Potthoff, Grundfragen des künftigen Beamtenrechts (Berlin, 1923).

[33] Programme reprinted in A. Freymuth et al., Sozialdemokratie und Berufsbeamtentum (Berlin, 1927), 28-30. See Hoffmann, Sozialdemokratie und Berufsbeamtentum, pp. 118-37, for a discussion of the programme, and pt. 2, passim, for SPD views on the relationship between civil servants and workers.

[34] Reprinted in Deutscher Beamtenbund: Ursprung, Weg, Ziele (Bad Godesberg, 1968), 181-3; the civil-service programmes of the DNVP, DVP, Centre, DDP, SPD, and NSDAP are also reprinted here, pp. 177-83.

distinction in the name of progressive politics. How was it that the KPD could argue for recognizing class differences between the different echelons of the civil service, and yet reject a legal distinction which seemed likely to support and further the class alliances desired by the party? The answer lies in the way that the implications of civil-service law reform had been transformed between the early and mid-1920s. Immediately after the revolution, the demand for assimilating civil-service and labour law had been a radical demand, advanced in the name of emancipating both civil servants and other citizens from the legacy of the *Obrigkeitsstaat*. Civil servants would cease to be a separate caste, but would retain their material rights, rebaptized as 'social gains' (*soziale Errungenschaften*), and functioning now as a model for progress by other groups of workers too. The state would cease to be an embodiment of authoritarianism, and would become instead a model employer. The residual special status of a small group of *Hoheitsbeamte*, envisaged as something like an extension of the category of 'political' civil servants, would carry with it not the privilege of tenure, but rather the liability to suspension. In other words, for most state employees tenure would be reconceptualized as job security, and this and other rights would form a model of employment practice. By the mid-1920s, however, the conditions for this scenario no longer existed. The left was marginalized in the Reich government, and technocratic rather than democratic government had taken the place of authoritarian rule.[35] The limitation of civil-servant status was now, as we have seen, more a weapon in the hands of those politicians and academics who wanted either to reduce the spiralling costs of the traditional system, or to construct a new civil-service élite. To concede a new system of distinctions between the élite and the mass of civil servants, therefore, no longer appeared to be a means of isolating the former and safeguarding the latter, but was likely to confirm the privileges of one group and degrade the status of the other. Thus, the changing political context of civil-service affairs saw shifts in the positions and alliances adopted by the protagonists. The 1927 salary law was the most tangible reward for the conventionalism espoused by the DBB as it abandoned

---

[35] See P. Haungs, *Reichspräsident und parlamentarische Kabinettsregierung: Eine Studie zum Regierungssystem der Weimarer Republik in den Jahren 1924 bis 1929* (Cologne and Opladen, 1968); M. Stürmer, 'Parliamentary Government in Weimar Germany, 1924-1928', in A. J. Nicholls and E. Matthias (eds.), *German Democracy and the Triumph of Hitler* (London, 1971), 59-77; H. Mommsen, 'Staat und Bürokratie in der Ära Brüning', in G. Jasper (ed.), *Tradition und Reform in der deutschen Politik: Gedenkschrift für Waldemar Besson* (Frankfurt, 1976), 81-5.

its residual radicalism, while the history that led up to it provides a microcosm of the tension between radicalism and traditionalism in civil-service affairs.

II

Whatever the shortcomings of a political theory that derived class consciousness from economic status, it was true that salary scales and salary structure were powerful determinants of shared and conflicting interests in the civil service. The politics of both the Reich government and the civil-service associations in the 1920s were marked by great tensions over the principles of the salary system, tensions that expressed deep divisions over the nature of a fiscally responsible and equitable system of remuneration. The salary system was clearly a matter of the first importance for a state whose finances were as turbulent as Germany's in the 1920s, and the vicissitudes of government policy mostly followed the path of its fiscal history, if sometimes in unexpected ways. At the crudest level, therefore, there was the question of the amount of the funds available for civil-service pay, and the economic and political priorities governing their disbursement. But the technical intricacies of the salary system also lent themselves to very elastic applications and manipulations, with results that could affect groups of civil servants as profoundly as decisions about overall funding. Thus, the salary cuts imposed by Brüning from 1930 were by no means the first time that Weimar's civil servants had felt the economic effects of political opinions about their status; while even the 1927 salary law, often represented as simply an over-generous hand-out to an imperious interest group,[36] expressed a clear commitment to a particular concept of the civil service, and a rejection of previously chosen priorities.

Perhaps the cardinal aspect of the internal structure of the salary system was the question of differentials between grades and within their incremental scales. The relationship between the highest and lowest salary levels was a clear index of the hierarchical and social principles embodied in the system. This was also expressed in the overall shape of the system: the more complex it was, and the more numerous were its scales and levels, the more hierarchical and unequal were its effects. Simplification denoted egalitarianism, and this was a visible principle of policy in the early years of Weimar, as the republican governments

[36] e.g. E. Eyck, *A History of the Weimar Republic*, ii (New York, 1967), 135-7.

made some attempt to embody their social principles in civil-service salary law. The broad tendency of these early years, therefore, was a move towards a more egalitarian system, though this was not solely the effect of new democratic priorities, but continued a trend that had already been discernible before and during the war. The 1909 Reich salary law had inaugurated the tendency for differentials to be narrowed, both by amending the internal structure and by giving proportionately larger salary increases to the middle and lower grades of the service. The trend continued during the exceptional strains of wartime and post-war inflation. Between 1914 and 1917, average real salaries in the civil service had fallen by between 46 and 58 per cent. This was followed by further sharp falls in real income in 1920, and then by a hiccuping sequence of ups and downs during the hyper-inflation of 1922-3. Stabilization—though not at full pre-war levels—followed in 1924.[37] Throughout these processes, differentials were narrowed further, with lower civil servants consistently retaining a higher proportion of their purchasing power than the other grades from 1917 onwards. At the absolute low point of March 1920, higher civil servants' real income stood at no more than 20.4 per cent of its 1913 figure, and middle civil servants' at 29.2 per cent, while for lower civil servants the figure was as high as 51 per cent. This narrowing of differentials both in and after the war was the effect of deliberate discrimination in favour of lower-paid civil servants, and included, for example, the introduction of flat-rate child and housing allowances.[38] Wartime policy had not aimed to satisfy principles of social justice as such, however, but more to maintain the morale of an increasingly embittered section of the civil service whose disaffection might threaten the stability of the regime.[39] Nevertheless, whatever its motivation, the

[37] *Wirtschaft und Statistik*, 1925, 43; see also A. Günther, 'Die Folgen des Krieges für Einkommen und Lebenshaltung der mittleren Volksschichten Deutschlands', in R. Meerwarth *et al.*, *Die Einwirkung des Krieges auf Bevölkerungsbewegung, Einkommen und Lebenshaltung in Deutschland* (Stuttgart, Berlin, Leipzig, and New Haven, 1932), 250-1; and for a full discussion, A. Kunz, 'Verteilungskampf oder Interessenkonsensus? Einkommensentwicklung und Sozialverhalten von Arbeitnehmergruppen in der Inflationszeit 1914 bis 1924', in G. D. Feldman *et al.* (eds.), *Die deutsche Inflation: Eine Zwischenbilanz / The German Inflation Reconsidered: A Preliminary Balance* (Berlin, 1982), 347-84.
[38] H. Völter, 'Die deutsche Beamtenbesoldung', in W. Gerloff (ed.), *Die Beamtenbesoldung im modernen Staat* (Munich and Leipzig, 1932), 40-1; P. Quante, 'Die Kinderzulagen in der deutschen Beamtenbesoldung', *Zeitschrift des preussischen statistischen Landesamts*, 62 (1922), 232-6.
[39] J. Kocka, *Klassengesellschaft im Krieg: Deutsche Sozialgeschichte 1914-1918* (Göttingen, 1973), 73-4; K.-L. Ay, *Die Entstehung einer Revolution: Die Volksstimmung in Bayern während des Ersten Weltkrieges* (Berlin, 1968), 94-6.

pre-war and wartime tendency emerges clearly in retrospect, and it formed the context in which the early republican governments adopted a more socially conscious salary policy.

At the end of 1919, the Bauer government decided to embark on a thorough review of salary law, in order to restore some order to a system disorganized by piecemeal responses to inflation, and to incorporate new personnel recently added to the Reich civil service (the staffs of the Reichsbahn and the customs service, for example). The salary law of April 1920 was the only major item of civil-service law to be adopted by the National Assembly at the behest of the SPD-led coalition (by then headed by Müller).[40] It was influenced by the civil-service associations in their most radical phase, and reflected both formally and substantively some of the democratic aspirations of 1918-19. Formally, the 1920 law greatly reduced and simplified the number of salary groups (*Besoldungsgruppen*), i.e. the major divisions of the salary system. From a total of 180 under the 1909 law, the number was trimmed to no more than twenty. The reduction reflected not only the DBB's concern for a less highly segmented system, but also a major change of emphasis in the principles of salary law. As the official memorandum to the law explained, civil-service salaries were no longer premised on the traditional system of alimentation, the grading of provision according to rank, but on the principle of payment according to qualifications and job content or merit.[41] The social priorities of the law were also evident in the internal structure of the system, which reduced to a new low the technical calculation of the differential (*Spannung*) between the lowest and highest salaries. Where the 1909 law had set the salary of senior posts at between 6.7 and 8.6 times that of the lower, the comparable figure in 1920 was 4.0. Expressed as a proportion of 1913 rates, this meant that salary levels in 1920 varied sharply according to grade, with senior officials receiving no more than about 35 per cent of their pre-war income, compared with some 48 per cent for the middle grade and 78 per cent for the lower.[42] Similarly, there was a considerable degree of overlap (*Verzähnung*) between the highest salary payable in one group

[40] *Besoldungsgesetz*, 30 April 1920 (*RGBl*, 1920, i. 805).
[41] Völter, 'Die deutsche Beamtenbesoldung', pp. 24, 74. This, too, built on a trend evident during the war, but was the most explicit implementation of it to date.
[42] Kunz, 'Verteilungskampf oder Interessenkonsensus?', pp. 354-60 and table 1; also Völter, 'Die deutsche Beamtenbesoldung', pp. 27-8. The method for calculating representative salaries and differentials for the three grades was enormously complex and open to much debate among the interested parties: see e.g. the assertions and arguments made in the Reich finance-ministry memorandum, 'Die Entwicklung der Besoldung der Reichsbeamten von 1897 bis Dez. 1924', 22 Jan. 1925, (*Drucksachen des Reichstags*, III. Wahlperiode, 407), 5-7, and the DBB's rebuttal, 'Stellungnahme des Deutschen

and the lowest in the next. Social objectives were equally explicit in the decision to give proportionately larger seniority increments at the lower end of a salary scale than at the higher. This was intended to take account of the heavier demands on the income of younger people who might be expected to be married and have growing families. The child allowances introduced during the war were continued, and were paid at a flat rate of 40 to 60 RM per month depending on the age of the child. As a final example of the law's principles, the old housing allowance (*Wohnungszuschlag*) based on rental costs only was expanded into a local weighting system (*Ortszuschlag*), which rested on a wider comparison of all living expenses—something the civil-service associations had been pressing for.

The salary system enacted in 1920 was poised in fact between three alternative criteria which were rapidly becoming the focus of heated debate and setting the framework for subsequent arguments about salary policy. The traditional alimentation system, with its emphasis on the *standesgemässer Unterhalt*, or provision according to rank, was rivalled by two newer concepts. There was the idea of merit (*Leistung*), whereby salary should be determined by qualification and job content, on the basis of comparable pay for comparable work. And there was the principle of social justice (*soziale Gerechtigkeit*), with its implication that the state should not only act as a model employer in terms of salary rates and other benefits, but should also ensure that the overall salary system did not allow the infiltration of ēlitism in the guise of structure. Each concept clearly reflected a different politics, indeed a different ideology of the state, at least in theory. Alimentation expressed the traditional concept of the civil servant attached to the state not by a contract, but by a mutual obligation: duty and loyalty on his side, welfare (*Fürsorge*) on the state's side. Academic theory and judicial practice tended to uphold this traditionalism, resisting any suggestion that civil-service salaries should be seen as payment for work or time, and arguing that alimentation was the kernel of the non-contractualism which defined *Beamte* status.[43] The merit principle, by contrast, was clearly a far more recent concept, appropriate to a competitive technocratic society in

Beamtenbundes zur Denkschrift des Reichsministers der Finanzen über die Besoldung der Beamten', 19 Mar. 1925, 3-5 (copies in BA R 431/2567).

[43] Völter, 'Die deutsche Beamtenbesoldung', p. 75, citing the Reichsgericht; also O. Sölch, 'Insbesondere Besoldungen und Hinterbliebenenversorgung', in Anschütz and Thoma (eds.), *Handbuch*, ii. 68-9: 'It is to be desired that legislation will not abandon the premiss of alimentation [*Unterhaltstheorie*] and will resist every temptation to assimilate civil-service salary law and provisions for pensions and dependants' allowances to the wage and insurance law of *Angestellte* and workers'; Nawiasky, *Stellung des Berufsbeamtentums*, p. 14.

which the structure of salaries could function as a means of job control and organization as well as to offer rewards for skill and performance. Social justice, finally, suggested that a more complex set of principles and interests than economic calculation alone should determine the practice of the state and the status of its functionaries.

The civil-service associations were divided over the issue. The RhB, representing senior civil servants, took a somewhat equivocal position. On the one hand it argued that civil servants' pay must be sufficient to guarantee a 'suitable' standard of living, including outlay on education and cultural pursuits, but at the same time, it recognized the operation of a merit principle to some extent, and conceded that the salary system must contain elements of both *Leistung* and *Unterhalt*. A traditionalist vocabulary thus conveyed a more pragmatic practical stance; both were aimed at the RhB's main objective in the 1920s, which was to recover pre-war salary levels by means of a fresh expansion of differentials. The DBB, meanwhile, saw the merit principle as the appropriate standard for the calculation of salaries in a modern society. As we shall see below, it took the position that social change was tending to level the objective needs of all members of society, thus eliminating the justification for differentials assessed according to social status. It therefore argued that comparable work should be recompensed by comparable pay, irrespective of sex and social rank, and that the salary system should be structured in a simple and uniform manner which left no room for élitist privileges. Although it would complete the picture neatly to show that the 'social justice' principle was espoused by the progressive wing of the civil-service movement, this was not in fact the case. In practice, a salary system based on social principles was too close to the paternalism of alimentation, and it was not entirely welcome to the ADB or to the DBB in its more radical moments. The separation of need from social status was conceptually and practically difficult as long as civil-servant status continued to be *sui generis*. Thus the ADB argued that wives' and children's allowances should not be separate payments, but should be incorporated into basic pay rates, creating what was in effect a family wage.[44]

[44] RhB, DBB, and ADB programmes in Völter, 'Die deutsche Beamtenbesoldung', pp. 99-102. For the RhB, see also A. Bohlen, *Besoldungsreform und höhere Beamte* (Berlin [1925]), and W. Maschke, *Der höheren Beamten niedrige Besoldung* (Berlin, 1927), both RhB publications (copies in BA R 431/2580). For the DBB, see its 'Stellungnahme', 19 Mar. 1925, 5. For the traditionalist views of the GDB, see H. Gast, *Die Beamtenbesoldung im Reich und in den Ländern* (Berlin, 1922). Hoffmann, *Sozial-demokratie und Berufsbeamtentum*, pp. 181-92, discusses SPD views on salary policy. For

In other words, in the actual situation of the 1920s, when the reform of civil-service status along progressive lines was unlikely to be achieved, it was the merit principle that came to dominate policy discussions. The successful entry of this concept into the political discourse of the civil service was further evidence of the extent to which the language and values of rationalization had invaded the German public sphere in the 1920s. The merit principle was an obviously rationalizing concept; its adoption into the 1920 salary system recognized the objective changes in the structure, size, and functions of the administration which have already been discussed. Yet the fact that judicial and conservative academic opinion remained relatively impervious to the new terminology is also a reminder of how little synchrony there may be in the movements of different institutions in an historical period. The political issues at stake in the definition of the civil service, the ambiguities of its actual status and authority in the republic, together with the undoubted power of tradition and the attractiveness of the concepts and vocabularies it made available—all this ensured that there would be no radical break with the past. Rather, civil-service policy and interest representation in the 1920s reveal a mixed, shifting, and sometimes anomalous flow of discourses and practice, and a competition of interests struggling to appropriate an effective programme and language of representation.

This can be further illustrated by looking at the debates between the principal associations and the Reich government in the mid-1920s. The period between the stabilization crisis and the issue of the new salary law in December 1927 was marked by persistent agitation for increases in civil-service salaries. These had been fixed at an extremely low level against the gold mark in December 1923, a fact which had aroused enormous dissatisfaction among civil servants. (It should also be remembered that this was the period of the *Personalabbau* and the beginning of the moves towards administrative rationalization, which were equally disquieting to civil servants.) By the end of 1924, as the financial situation improved, five upward revisions of the 1923 rates had brought real salaries nearer to the 1913 rates than at any time since the war, again with lower civil servants doing proportionately better than the higher ranks. The battle for a full rescheduling of salary rates

a discussion of civil servants' expenditure patterns, see S. Coyner, 'Class Consciousness and Consumption: The New Middle Class during the Weimar Republic', *Journal of Social History*, 10 (1977), 310-31, and the source on which this is based, *Die Lebenshaltung von 2000 Arbeiter-, Angestellten- und Beamtenhaushaltungen* (*Einzelschriften zur Statistik des Deutschen Reichs*, 22; Berlin, 1932).

was joined early in 1925, with the publication of a finance-ministry review of salary developments, and a major policy response by the DBB.[45] At issue was not only the question of a pay increase, but the structure and the future of the 1920 salary system. The DBB was committed to maintaining the principles of 1920, while also securing higher rates of pay. Its principal complaint, therefore, was that the finance ministry was using the inflation and stabilization crises as, in effect, a smoke-screen for the restoration of the pre-war structure of pay differentials.

The ministry's report took 1913 as the yardstick for its review of salary movements, thus implicitly representing this year as the norm, despite the fact that quite different standards had since been adopted in the 1920 legislation. Of course, the ministry noted that differentials had been narrowing, and it did imply approval of this, up to a point. But it also argued that the process had already gone too far, and it was careful to present this in language appropriate to the concept of merit:

Since 1913, indeed since 1897, the income of civil servants in the middle and upper salary groups has been considerably less increased than that of the lower salary groups. As a result, there has been a narrowing of differentials in civil servants' income, in terms both of basic rates and even more notably of total pay [i.e. including allowances]. This means that superior education and more demanding and responsible work is being less rewarded, by comparison with inferior education and work of lesser importance, than was previously the case.[46]

In response to this, the DBB depicted Germany as a society in which real class differences were being progressively narrowed by economic development, and in which real needs and expectations were converging across the social spectrum:

The transition from the authoritarian state to the people's state is a result and a reinforcement of this development. The people's state is committed to a concept of community. It confers on all the same rights and duties. It summons the entire people to consider and decide important questions. It demands an inner sense of commitment and deep attachment to the whole. It acknowledges no partitions within the people, it aims to mitigate and reduce distances and differences.[47]

The DBB memorandum can be seen as a transitional text measuring the extent of its distance from both left and right—though more explicitly

---

[45] See n. 42 above.
[46] Reich finance ministry, 'Entwicklung der Besoldung', p. 19.
[47] DBB, 'Stellungnahme', p. 2.

from the right as embodied in the current financial regime of Luther. It offered a vision of social integrity in opposition to the cloven images of both the 'authoritarian' and the 'class' state, and advanced it in the name not of the republic but of history and the people. The republic was depicted as little more than the automatic political expression of a long-term and profound process of social transformation, the effect of Germany's industrialization. The chief consequence of this, for the DBB's purposes, was a secular process of social convergence in the German population: 'The various strata of the people are . . . converging in their claims, their needs and their style of life.'[48] Crucially, this had to be recognized as the effect of long-term technical progress, and not mistakenly attributed to contingent events such as the war and the inflation. The government's salary policy, obsessed with the minutiae of comparability with pre-war norms, thus missed the point and flew in the face of history. The issue was not an outmoded system of differentials, but the fixing of a minimum income, 'out of which can be satisfied those needs which are recognized as essential in terms of general development and the economic situation'.[49] But, according to the DBB, the effect of the cumulative revisions of 1924 had been to reintroduce something like the pre-war differential system, arbitrary as it was by contemporary standards. It accused the finance ministry of the misleading implication that salary improvements for the lower-paid civil servants were necessarily achieved at the expense of the higher-paid. The DBB position was that the first priority was to ensure a basic minimum income; only then should 'higher quality work [*hoherwertige Leistungen*] be recompensed to its full value'. It took a critical view of those who were obsessed with their relative income status, 'even if this can be excused as an opinion belonging to the time of the authoritarian state, with its divisions into estates and classes'. But, as it went on to argue, attacking the ministry's position: 'that such principles should be officially recognized and confirmed, that the values of class struggle should be thus encouraged in the civil service, must be deplored by anyone with a modicum of political acumen'.[50] Finally, the DBB summarized its critique by asserting that 'the division of civil servants into three sharply distinct strata contradicts the principle of national community [*Volksgemeinschaftsgedanken*] and leads to the formation of classes in the civil service'.[51]

[48] Ibid.   [49] Ibid. 3.
[50] Ibid. 7.   [51] Ibid. 10.

Clearly, the DBB had abandoned the ground of shared interests among the waged and the salaried which it had briefly espoused in the period of the revolution. In doing so, it probably made an accurate calculation of the arguments that were likely to appeal to the retrenchment regime of the mid-1920s: the call to class identity was obviously not among these. Yet it is not quite clear what alternative ground the DBB now stood on—or rather, what is interesting about its position is its extreme eclecticism. On the one hand, there is the clear commitment to the principle of the minimum wage, an archetypal social-justice principle with trade-unionist overtones. This was the keystone of the DBB position, since it supported the argument against the 1913 differential structure, and was clearly in the interests of the lowest-paid civil servants. Yet at the same time, the DBB advanced the market principle of merit as a further ideological weapon against the old differential structure, based as this had been on the alimentation principle; though here it is compromised in practice by the priority given to the minimum-wage principle. Finally, there is the broad social vision proposed as the alternative to the divisions of class and estate, in the rather imprecise but capacious notion of the national community. In the circumstances, the ambiguity is as telling for its profuse associations as for its exclusions. What it seems to do most clearly is to establish a visible place for the civil service in the neutral space of the nation. The term 'Volksgemeinschaft'—common enough at the time as an image of national solidarity—avoids the awkward precision of a political terminology which risked recalling both the imperial state that the DBB entirely repudiated, and the republican state with its unclear legitimacy. Read in the context of the document as a whole, the term also conveniently amalgamates the traditional and the modern. There is no opprobrium in linking the civil service with the historical totality of the people; and yet, as the historical preamble sets out, this increasingly coherent national community is the necessary outcome of the modern tendency towards greater economic and social homogeneity. Here is equality purged of its overtones of radical levelling, and reinstated as the product of a technical development. The DBB's stance seems to pick up the frequency of rationalization, without having to whistle the tune out loud. The result is a portrait of national and professional harmony that draws unmistakably on the most traditional iconography of the German civil service, yet does so in colours tinged with modernity.

In some ways, the document is a masterly compound of these differ-ent forms; in others, however, its pluralism seems more emblematic of the helplessness of civil-service association politics in the 1920s than of any versatility. While the republic was contested, so also was the status of the civil service. The ADB chose to take one way out by embracing a clear trade-union position, but this condemned it to marginalization among civil servants, while the social democratic and trade-union movements were not welcoming to this white-collar constituency. The DBB chose to defend a relatively radical position with conservative arguments, aiming no doubt to broaden its appeal. Yet it could not disguise the priority it gave to the lower- and medium-paid civil servants, nor its rejection of ēlitism within the civil service. Its aspiration to lead a reconstructed professional community was dashed. The RhB maintained its attack on the post-war salary system on exactly the ground repudiated by the DBB: it objected to the convergence the DBB praised, and argued the social benefits of restoring to Germany's civil-service ēlite the cultural superiority they had once enjoyed.[52]

In the mid-1920s, these were all voices in the wilderness. Despite mounting pressure from the associations and from Reichstag motions, and despite growing evidence of resentment among civil servants at their exclusion from the economic recovery of the post-inflation years, no government would take the economic risk of embarking on a salary increase. Yet at the same time, it was clear that some revision of the 1920 law would come in time: and it was also clear—this was the DBB's main complaint—that meanwhile the trend was reversing towards a more traditionalist salary structure. The impetus towards new legislation was provided by two developments: the expiration in April 1926 of the national ceiling on civil-service salaries (imposed in 1920 in order to maintain uniform salary scales throughout Germany); and the formation of Marx's fourth cabinet in January 1927. The end of the national ceiling unleashed the threat of a new round of leap-frogging salary increases and supplements from *Land* and local governments protective of their autonomy, in a revival of regional particularism deplored by the Reich government.[53] The new cabinet had shifted rightwards to

---

[52] Bohlen, *Besoldungsreform*. See also the comments on the finance-ministry memorandum by two senior chancellery civil servants, Graevell and Offerman, who were especially critical of the levelling effects of current salary law (note to Chancellor Luther, 14 May 1925, in BA R 431/2567); this document illustrates the quasi-official opportunities open to senior *Beamte* to defend their own interests.

[53] §1 of the *Gesetz zur Sicherung einer einheitlichen Regelung der Beamtenbesoldung (Besoldungssperrgesetz)*, 21 Dec. 1920 (*RGBl*, 1920, i. 2117), made the 1920 salary law

include the DNVP; it also saw the appointment as finance minister of the Baden Centre party politician, Heinrich Köhler, an ex-civil servant and well-known friend to his profession.[54] At the end of March, Köhler was authorized to announce to the Interfractional Committee that, 'despite the difficult financial situation', the Reich government would submit proposals for a revision of the salary system by the end of the year.[55] By June, this had become a public commitment to a pay increase by the autumn.[56]

Sincere as Köhler's motivations may have been, his conduct of his campaign was inept. He faced a sharp division of opinion within his own party; his initial plans for giving priority to increases for the lower-paid aroused opposition within the higher civil service and had to be revised; and his attempt to curtail cabinet discussion of his plans was unwise, especially as the final increases were a good deal higher than the percentages first mooted. Moreover, as a rule, civil-service pay increases imply tax increases and are popular with no one but civil servants; public sympathy could hardly be expected, however justified the improvements might seem to those receiving them.[57]

binding on civil servants employed by *Länder*, local government, and public corporations by stating that their pay could not be higher than that of corresponding *Reichsbeamte*. The law was evidence of the greater influence in civil-service law exerted by the Reich government in the Weimar Republic compared with previously; see L. Waldecker, 'Entwicklungstendenzen im deutschen Beamtenrecht', *AöR*, NF 7 (1924), 131-3. In practice, however, uniformity was more easily claimed than achieved: direct correspondences between greatly varying systems were hard to establish, and there were many ways to evade the spirit of the *Besoldungssperrgesetz*. Prussia, for example, had a shorter working week than the Reich, better leave allowances, and so on; material on this and similar cases in BA R 431/2567 and 2587, and minutes of cabinet meetings and ministerial discussions reprinted in *Akten der Reichskanzlei: Das Kabinett Müller II*, ed. M. Vogt, i. (Boppard, 1970), 194-9, 292-3.

[54] For Köhler, see his memoirs, *Heinrich Köhler: Lebenserinnerungen des Politikers und Staatsmannes 1878-1949*, ed. J. Becker (Stuttgart, 1964). He ascribed the indifference of civil servants to the collapse of the monarchy in 1918 to their alienation from a state that had paid them so poorly for years, and felt that the republic was running a similar risk (p. 252).

[55] Minutes of cabinet meeting, 27 Mar. 1927 (BA R 431/2568). The background to the 1927 salary revision is discussed in Haungs, *Reichspräsident und parlamentarische Kabinettsregierung*, pp. 217-29; Schulz, *Demokratie und Diktatur*, pp. 549-62; Völter, 'Die deutsche Beamtenbesoldung', pp. 16-17.

[56] Reich finance-ministry press release, 17 June 1927 (BA R 431/2568).

[57] The salary law was the immediate provocation to the rural protest movement that swept Oldenburg in the winter of 1927-8 and signified the beginning of the NSDAP's exploitation of *Mittelstand* discontent; see J. Noakes, *The Nazi Party in Lower Saxony 1921-1933* (Oxford, 1971), 108-12; K. Schaap, *Die Endphase der Weimarer Republik im Freistaat Oldenburg 1928-1933* (Düsseldorf, 1978), 34; J. Noakes and G. Pridham (eds.), *Nazism 1919-1945*, i. *The Rise to Power 1919-1934* (Exeter, 1983), 59-61.

Finally, Köhler's sense of timing was acute, but dangerous: 1927 was the last transitional year under the Dawes Plan arrangements, and thus the last year in which government expenditure might be increased before the beginning of repayments in full in 1928. Although Köhler argued strongly that the new rates could be paid for out of the continuing upward movement of the economy and the resultant expansion of the tax base, he does not appear to have convinced all of his colleagues. Fears were voiced that the salary increases would lead to pressure for wage increases and hence to a price rise; there was insistence that the promulgation of the law must be accompanied by an official statement that it would not mean tax increases.[58]

The draft was prepared in strict confidentiality, without the active participation of the civil-service associations—which of course gave a certain advantage to the senior civil servants involved in the drafting. But early in September, Köhler leaked the main financial provisions in a speech to the DBB in Magdeburg; at the time he was criticized for this breach, but he defended it as being necessary in order to dispel disquieting rumours about the government plans then circulating among civil servants.[59] The problem for Köhler was that the trade-union wing of the Centre party, led by Stegerwald and Imbusch, was deeply hostile to the proposed increase in pay scales, not least because of the level to which the proposed increases had been raised since the first discussions. Brüning, too, was among the chief critics of the law, and though Köhler professed in his memoirs to have silenced Brüning's opposition, it appears that the latter was not in fact reconciled.[60] The atmosphere of disquiet was further fuelled by the leaking to the press of a memorandum drawn up by the American agent-general for reparations, Parker Gilbert, in which he criticized the rising trend of government expenditure and the salary revision in particular.[61] He alleged that the extra cost to Germany as a whole would be between 1,200 and 1,500 million marks a year (Köhler's Magdeburg speech had been deliberately vague on this point, revealing only a proportion of the expected cost). The government was castigated for its remarkable neglect of the possible effect of the salary increase on

---

[58] Minutes of ministerial meeting, 13 Oct. 1927 (BA R 431/2570).
[59] Köhler, *Lebenserinnerungen*, p. 255. He spoke of increases of the order of 18 to 25 per cent, as opposed to the 10 per cent originally planned.
[60] H. Brüning, *Memoiren 1918-1934*, i. (Munich, 1972), 133-7, in a section entitled 'Fateful Developments'.
[61] Parker Gilbert memorandum, 20 Oct. 1927, submitted to the Reich finance ministry (copy in BA R 431/1424).

the Germany economy, and finally for its failure to combine salary revision with a realistic programme of administrative rationalization—the sole justification for such a measure, in Parker Gilbert's eyes. In private, in fact, the cabinet had already broached both these issues a week earlier, while some days later Köhler dismissed Parker Gilbert's arguments in another cabinet meeting.[62]

The impression conveyed by these proceedings is of a government anxious to make the best of a bad job and to be shot of a measure that was opening unwelcome rifts in the coalition. On the other hand, a last-ditch attempt was made, apparently with Marx's connivance, to incorporate an element of administrative reform into the law as it was about to go before the Reichstag in December. The Centre party fraction at that point submitted a number of amendments to the bill.[63] One called for 'economical budgeting' and administrative reform, specifying among other things that the *Länder* must embark on a full-scale rationalization campaign, and proposing the means-testing of pensions. Another dealt with changes in the financing of the postal administration, while the last was a scheme for a new bout of rationalization at Reich level. This included a proposal, adopted as law after what Brüning described as 'the most difficult battle of my parliamentary career',[64] for every third civil-service post to lapse from the establishment as it fell vacant. After some battles with the Centre party fraction, the bill was finally passed into law by the Reichstag on 14 December, its provisions backdated to 1 October.[65] The seriousness of the split in the Centre party is indicated by the fact that thirteen of its deputies abstained in the final vote, eight absented themselves from the division and one, Imbusch, voted against it. Otherwise, only the KPD opposed the measure; the coalition partners supported it, of course, as the SPD and the NSDAP did also.

The tensions in the Centre party were to reappear less than three years later, when Brüning introduced a series of emergency cut-back measures which reduced civil-service salary scales to almost exactly the pre-1927 rates. At that time, as we shall see, the party began to pay dearly for its leader's 'betrayal' of civil servants' interests, but it seems that the loss of support it suffered then had been prepared for to some

---

[62] Minutes of ministerial meeting, 13 Oct. 1927 (BA R 43I/2570); minutes of cabinet meeting, 24 Oct. 1927 (BA R 43I/1424).

[63] Copy in BA R 43I/2570, together with memorandum by chancellery state secretary, Pünder, 8 Dec. 1927; the complex entanglement of the salary law in Reich-*Länder* relations is discussed by Schulz, *Demokratie und Diktatur*, pp. 558-63.

[64] Brüning, *Memoiren*, i. 136.

[65] *Besoldungsgesetz*, 16 Dec. 1927 (*RGBl*, 1927, i. 349).

extent by the vacillations of 1927. The DBB had already expressed disquiet at the party's lack of solidarity on the salary issue in 1927;[66] and although it had made its submissions to the cabinet when the reform had first been announced, neither it nor the other umbrella associations were formally consulted during the drafting of the measure. In the end, moreover, whatever Köhler's own first intentions, the 1927 system represented a notable reversal of the principles of 1920 and thus a slap in the face for the DBB, not to mention the ADB. In the absence of open consultation, it seems clear that the permanent bureaucracy of the finance ministry managed to use its own means to ensure that the trend away from 1920 was not interrupted. Thus, the index of differentials increased from 1 : 4 to 1 : 6; the number of salary groups was increased from twenty to fifty-eight; and the principle of a large overlap between groups was undermined. Local weighting was calculated in such a way that there was now a steeper graduation between the highest and lowest amounts paid. Special supplements *(Stellenzulage)* of up to 1,000 RM per year for posts of particular responsibility were reintroduced. These were highly unpopular among those who were not eligible for them (and were opposed in principle by the DBB and ADB), because they were a back-door method of granting selective pay increases; indeed, they were to be widely used by and for higher civil servants during the 1930s pay freeze. As well as this, of course, the salary scales themselves were considerably increased, by up to 25 per cent in some cases. This was the main selling point of the law to civil servants, and yet the circumstances—the lack of official consultation, the grudging attitude of the leading coalition party, the rumpus at the last minute—conspired to make it seem less than a triumph for its own beneficiaries. If the civil-service lobby had appeared undesirably powerful to the nation at large, to its own membership it seemed only just adequate as a defender of its interests. Altogether it was a measure more radical in its disruptive than in its positive effects. Although the salary increases were certainly welcome to civil servants, the manner of their achievement was not likely to strengthen confidence in the government's willingness to treat its officials as negotiating partners.

---

[66] See chancellery memo of phone call from DBB chairman, Flügel, 5 Dec. 1927, requesting a meeting to discuss 'certain tendencies' in the Centre party (the request was refused) (BA R 431/2570).

III

If the 1927 salary law advanced a particular model of the civil service alongside its primary purpose of raising pay scales, so the pay cuts imposed by Brüning in the fiscal crisis of the early 1930s involved more than just a balancing of the state budget. Brüning's austerity programme was part of a political strategy conceived on the grand scale and premised on the achievement of a fundamental financial reform. This would be the keystone in a comprehensive project of German recovery, construed as a set of linked initiatives on the economic, constitutional, and international fronts. Moreover, for Brüning, as for many conservatives, *Vernunftrepublikaner*, and disappointed liberals, the depression was something more than a global economic crisis. In Germany, it was also seen as an expression of the structural defects of the Weimar Republic, and a crisis in the old sense of the word—an occasion, however unwelcome in its symptoms, for finally curing those defects by means of fundamental changes in constitutional and administrative practice. In a sense, the failed administrative rationalization of the 1920s was politicized as the constitutional reformism of the early 1930s. Behind the emergency of fiscal crisis there lurked, none too invisibly, the grander vision of a refoundation of post-war Germany.

Whatever the precise development of Brüning's reform plans—the retreat from the Reichstag, the reliance on the presidency, the plans for a restoration of the monarchy, the moves towards a unitary state—the bureaucracy obviously occupied a critical place. It was both the object and the instrument—and potentially the obstacle—for the achievement of Brüning's strategy. With economic collapse, a *Primat der Reparationspolitik*, and the threatening insolvency of the state the dominant economic issues after 1930, an effective fiscal reform would also have to tackle the thorny and intractable issue of administrative rationalization, and the fiscal relationship between Reich and *Länder*. In both of these matters, the burdensome costs of administration were key issues. Brüning's intention was to attack both the total size and cost of the administration, and the rates of civil-service pay, yet his animus in the latter question seems to have been the more intense, inspired partly by the defeat he had suffered in 1927. In his view, an effective financial *Sanierung* demanded first of all a determined roll-back of the 1927 salary rates. This would then be followed by a stiff programme of administrative and personnel rationalization throughout Germany, a policy which was integral to his vision of a politically and administratively streamlined state.[67]

It is in the context of this overall strategy that his determination to 'force back the power of the organizations, above all of the DBB'[68] must be understood. He saw the DBB as one of the great obstacles to the fulfilment of his vision of a restabilized Germany, and he contrasted its intransigence with the relative pliability of the trade unions. In Brüning's eyes, the 1927 law had literally been a tribute to the power of organized interest groups, a pay-off made at the expense of Germany's future security and stability. Yet it is abundantly clear that his animosity towards the DBB expressed no preference for democratic and parliamentary practice as such. It was not because the DBB circumvented the electoral system by its pressure-group tactics that Brüning abhorred its influence. Rather, his views derived from the illusions he shared with current conservative opinion about the traditional virtues of the civil service: a vision of a profession imbued with its service ethic, which could only be compromised and vitiated by the crude egoism of the interest group. This helps to explain the apparent paradox that it was the increasingly bureaucratic regime developed under Brüning's chancellorship that was also responsible for policies that were so profoundly antagonistic to civil servants. The fact that Brüning failed to recognize the extent to which their political loyalties were shaken by his policies was due less to his ignorance or arrogance than to his outdated understanding of the role of the civil service. The point that he missed was that the nature and terms of the civil service's relationship with the state had been shaken and displaced since the war, even if this was partly disguised by the fact that it had not acquired a clear new status. The rhetoric of the interest group as expressed by the DBB was not firmly established, it was true, either among civil servants and their spokesmen or among politicians. It had not fully supplanted the language of service—or perhaps it is more accurate to suggest that the relationship between service ethic and private interest had not been clearly recast. Yet confidence in the state as the reliable guarantor of civil servants' interests was also far from secure by 1930, and thus the necessary practical concomitant to the service ethic was missing. The

---

[67] K. D. Bracher, *Die Auflösung der Weimarer Republik: Eine Studie zum Problem des Machtverfalls in der Demokratie* (Düsseldorf, 1978), pt. 2, chs. 2 and 3; id., 'Brünings unpolitische Politik und die Auflösung der Weimarer Republik', *VjhZ*, 19 (1971), 113-23; Mommsen, 'Staat und Bürokratie', pp. 85 ff., 102 ff.; Brüning, *Memoiren*, i, ch. 2; James, *German Slump*, pp. 67-71.

[68] Brüning, *Memoiren*, i. 183.

appeal to selflessness, on its own, had no magic left; and yet it is clear from the responses of the civil-service organizations, and from the electoral shifts of civil servants' loyalties, that they did continue to *expect* more protection from the state as of right, and were deeply alienated by disappointment. Within a short time this made them prey to a new rhetoric from the Nazi right, which promised to protect them by a joint commitment to *both* a renaissance of the civil service *and* a refoundation of the relationship between state and community which would not simply return to the defective terms of the monarchical *Obrigkeitsstaat*. In these circumstances, it was especially inopportune that both Brüning's governmental style and his constitutional ideas leant so heavily on precisely that tattered historical model, with so little attempt at refurbishment. This may also have helped to drive a wedge between the élite civil servants for whom the images of the past held a promise of resurgence, and those below them who had long signalled their dissatisfactions with it.[69]

At one level, of course, the civil-service associations were quite unanimous in denouncing the effects of Brüning's policies where they hurt most—their pockets. Between December 1930 and December 1932, a series of presidential emergency decrees reduced salaries and pensions by cumulative cuts of between 19 and 23 per cent.[70] On top of that, public officials had been assessed for a *Reichshilfe*, or national levy, of 2.5 per cent for six months from July 1930;[71] while the intricate system for calculating pensionable service was revised in such a way as to limit the state's heavy commitments.[72] Although it was perhaps churlish that, as Brüning himself pointed out, the first emergency decree in

[69] See the perceptive comments in W. Besson, *Württemberg und die deutsche Staatskrise* (Stuttgart, 1959), 241-50; also Mommsen, 'Staat und Bürokratie', pp. 88-92. There is more than a reminiscence of Sparkommissar Saemisch in Brüning's position here.

[70] *Verordnung des Reichspräsidenten zur Sicherung von Wirtschaft und Finanzen*, 1 Dec. 1930 (*RGBl*, 1930, i. 517), imposing a fixed 6 per cent cut in salaries, pensions, and dependants' allowances; *Zweite Verordnung des Reichspräsidenten zur Sicherung von Wirtschaft und Finanzen*, 5 June 1931 (*RGBl*, 1931, i. 279), imposing graduated cuts of between 4 and 8 per cent, and reducing child allowances up to the fourth child; *Vierte Verordnung des Reichspräsidenten zur Sicherung von Wirtschaft und Finanzen und zum Schutz des inneren Friedens*, 8 Dec. 1931 (*RGBl*, 1931, i. 699), imposing a fixed 9 per cent cut, with a slightly lower cut in pensions. These provisions were valid until 31 Jan. 1936.

[71] By the *Verordnung des Reichspräsidenten zur Behebung finanzieller, wirtschaftlicher und sozialer Notstände*, 26 July 1930 (*RGBl*, 1930, i. 311).

[72] By the *Dritte Verordnung des Reichspräsidenten zur Sicherung von Wirtschaft und Finanzen und zur Bekämpfung politischer Ausschreitungen*, 6 Oct. 1931 (*RGBl*, 1931, i. 537).

December 1930 reduced salaries 'precisely to the amount that had been agreed between the finance ministry and myself in 1927'[73]—i.e. before the last-minute revisions had taken the package through the roof—it was certainly no coincidence that by 1932 the total series of reductions had almost exactly matched the entire increase accorded in 1927 (indeed, at one point the cabinet had debated simply repealing that law wholesale).[74] This linkage was deliberately established by Brüning, and was deeply resented by the civil-service associations, whose spokesmen bitterly repudiated the inference that it was their salary increase that had thrown the state into its fiscal crisis.[75] For Brüning, however, the associations stood in the role of saboteurs. The salary cuts were part of a larger package of government expenditure cuts which was itself tied to his heroic vision of German resurgence; a refusal to co-operate with any one component carried with it the opprobrium of frustrating the entire design. At a certain level, it may have been true that Brüning simply did not give a high priority to civil servants' reactions, and he certainly did not intend to be held to ransom by them. He was strongly backed in this by the Centre's trade-union wing, represented in his cabinet by that inveterate critic of civil servants, Adam Stegerwald. In another sense, however, one gets the impression that Brüning also wanted to make an example of the bureaucracy, as if to punish it for betraying its heritage of self-sacrifice. A token of this was his expectation that municipal civil servants could be progressively replaced by unsalaried honorary officials, 'as is consistent with the spirit and values of a healthy local administration'.[76] An interesting idea, perhaps, in certain circumstances, but in the midst of a depression something that could only be seen as a threat to jobs. Brüning's appeals to the civil service to collaborate with him in making his policies work managed also to mingle enticement with menace, and perhaps a hint of *Schadenfreude*. Presenting his first emergency decree

---

[73] Brüning, *Memoiren*, i. 232.

[74] Mommsen, 'Staat und Bürokratie', p. 110.

[75] See e.g. the minutes of the meeting between Brüning and DBB leaders, 30 May 1930, at which the proposed *Notopfer* was discussed (BA R 431/2571). (The files R 431/2363-70 and 2571-3 are filled with numerous letters of protest against the decrees from the civil-service associations, the majority coming from the RhB, DBB, and ADB.) In Sept. 1930, the industrialist Paul Silverberg had pointed out the need to distinguish between the 1927 salary rates for individual civil servants, which he thought not excessive, and the aggregate cost of salaries to the Reich; the latter *was* inordinate, and was the result of the still unsolved problems of administrative excess; see Mommsen, 'Staat und Bürokratie', pp. 103-4.

[76] Brüning, *Memoiren*, i. 393; see also p. 411.

to the Reichsrat in November 1930, he reminded his audience of the privations afflicting all classes in Germany, and professed to believe that civil servants would understand their pay cut as 'a sacrifice [that] fuses them closely with the whole nation [*am stärksten in das Volksganze einfügt*]'.[77] In a meeting with the DBB leadership six months earlier, he had already argued that: 'Since the civil service is so closely linked with the state, it must have a special interest in seeing order introduced into the state's finances'[78]—a forked tongue indeed.

To the associations, Brüning's punitive stance and his willingness to expose civil servants to the unproven insinuation of co-responsibility for the depression was symptomatic of the breakdown of confidence between state and civil service. Indeed, the widening gap between the two could not be bridged by the conventional rhetoric of partnership, however diligently reiterated. It was signalled by the different concerns voiced by each side, by their unwillingness to recognize the other's arguments, and not least by the interruption of communications, for Brüning repeatedly refused the associations' urgent requests for consultations after the summer of 1930, and reduced encounters to a minimum. The associations responded with outrage, their complaints about unfairness quickly developing into warnings about the growing radicalization of their members. Brüning may well have felt that the associations had cried wolf too often, and that his predecessors had shown excessive weakness in yielding to such blackmail.[79] At any rate, he gave little sign of taking these claims seriously, even when they were echoed by members of his own cabinet.[80] Although the associations had so little

[77] 4 Nov. 1930 (copy in BA R 43I/2367).

[78] Meeting of 30 May 1930; see n. 75 above. See also his very similar urgings in a meeting with representatives of all the civil-service umbrella associations, 27 June 1930 (minutes, dated 1 July 1930, in BA R 43I/2365); and his remarks in the Reichstag, 16 Oct. 1930, in which he also undertook to protect the civil service against the 'irresponsible smear campaign' to which it was being subjected (*Stenographische Berichte*, 444, V. Wahlperiode, 18).

[79] In Dec. 1929, the Müller cabinet had considered and rejected a civil-service pay cut as one response to the mounting deficit. As Hilferding put it: 'Considerable reductions in civil-service salaries might perhaps become necessary, but this would be politically impossible, even with Art[icle] 48, which would be directly unconstitutional. This kind of catastrophe policy is not feasible. Would incite a storm which no government would survive, not even a dictatorial one'; minutes reprinted in *Akten der Reichskanzlei: Das Kabinett Müller II*, ii, doc. 367, 1212-14; see also minutes of cabinet meeting, 5 Feb. 1930 (doc. 434). Subsequent cabinets split over the issue of a *Notopfer*, though the majority accepted it as a preferable alternative to a salary cut; see docs. 455, 457, 458 (ministerial discussions of fiscal plans).

[80] e.g. in the cabinet meetings of 19 Dec. 1930 (BA R 43I/2682) and 13 Apr. 1932 (BA R 43I/2684). See also the exchange between Dietrich and Brüning in Jan. 1931, in

success in challenging Brüning face to face, let alone in being consulted in policy-making, they maintained a barrage of critical letters and memoranda to the chancellor. While these could do little else but concede the severity of the economic situation, they also argued repeatedly that the policy of pay reductions was mechanical, discriminatory, and ineffective;[81] that the burdens were unfairly distributed between the ranks;[82] that the 1927 pay scales had not been excessive given the growing prosperity of the late 1920s;[83] and that the whole policy was quite possibly illegal.[84]

The latter question was serious. It demonstrated once again the practical problems that arose from the constitutional guarantee of civil servants' vested rights—rights that were actually better protected in the constitution than those civil rights that were subject to suspension under Article 48. The civil-service associations used Article 129 to argue that the government was not legally empowered to tamper with civil servants' salaries and pensions in a manner that might prove adverse to them. Thus the DBB warned Brüning that: 'The civil service has till now always been loyal to the constitution and the state; it regards the present constitution as particularly sacrosanct because the constitution guarantees civil servants' rights. For this reason everything must be done to prevent anything that represents an attack on the vested rights of civil servants.'[85] The RhB similarly reminded Brüning of the extent to which the state was dependent on the loyalty of its

which the former called for a meeting between civil-service representatives and the president to allay the process of radicalization and improve morale (BA R 43I/2650, ff. 254-6). See also Ch. 4, pp. 126-7, below.

[81] From numerous possible examples, see DBB to government, 11 June 1930 (BA R 43I/2364), and RhB to chancellery, 8 Oct. 1930 (BA R 43I/2366). The DBB also published a 50-pp. critique of the government's policies, 'Die deutsche Beamtenschaft zur Notverordnung vom 5. Juni 1931: Kritik und Forderungen des DBB' (copy in BA R 43I/2378).

[82] This point was repeatedly pressed by the RhB especially; see its submissions to the chancellery, 10 Mar. 1931 (BA R 43I/2571), and 19 Aug. 1931 (BA R 43I/2572); also A. Bohlen, *Die höheren Beamten nach drei Gehaltskürzungen* (Berlin, 1931). The ADB and DBB tended to argue that the government's economic policy in general spared the rich and laid excessive burdens on the poor; see notes from the ADB, 26 Sept. 1930 (BA R 43I/2366) and DBB, 27 Oct. 1930 (BA R 43I/2367).

[83] See e.g. notes from the RhB, 6 June 1930 (BA R 43I/2364); and 10 Oct. 1930 (BA R 43I/2366).

[84] See e.g. RhB to Brüning, 19 Aug. 1931 (BA R 43I/2572); chancellery memo (von Hagenow) of conversation with Flügel of the DBB, 27 Nov. 1930 (BA R 43I/2571); ADB to Brüning, 18 Sept. 1931 (BA R 43I/2373).

[85] Minutes of meeting between Brüning and DBB leaders, 30 May 1930 (BA R 43I/2571).

officials, and went on to argue that: 'Income [*Gehalt*] is a form of provision according to rank [*standesgemässer Unterhalt*], granted in accordance with merit [*Leistung*]. A cut in income is warranted only, if at all, when the cost of living has fallen (not when it is in the process of falling).'[86]

Behind these arguments lay a complex legal situation, with the courts and academic opinion divided on the truth of the matter.[87] The basic question was whether, on the one hand, Article 129 established the right to a specific pay scale (what was called a 'ziffernmässige Garantie') which could be enforced as an individual claim and which virtually ruled out any reduction of pay scales other than by constitutional amendment; or whether the constitution offered only an institutional guarantee of civil-service status as such, a guarantee that could not be reduced to individual claims. On the whole, judicial opinion tended towards the second interpretation, especially because the 1927 salary law, and most *Länder* laws, specifically reserved the right to amend salary and pension rates by simple statute. Yet the issue was legally trickier in the case of those *Länder* which, like Bremen or Lübeck, had failed to include this specific reservation in their legislation; and trickier still in relation to pensions, which were deemed to be withheld pay and would thus in a sense be subject to illegal retrospective cuts. The problems were concrete enough for the Reich government to insert a clause in most of its emergency orders asserting that vested rights were not affected—yet this statutory commitment seemed more formal than real as far as its immediate effects were concerned. It certainly did not stifle the opinion among many civil servants that they were already suffering an illicit abridgement of their rights. Still, there was a certain irony in the fact that, as Carl Schmitt pointed out disapprovingly, the *ziffernmässige Garantie* actually implied that a contractual relationship existed between civil servant and state. This relationship was entirely foreign to the concept of public-law status and vested rights themselves—yet it was under precisely this banner that the DBB and RhB attacked the pay cuts.[88]

---

[86] RhB to Brüning, 19 Aug. 1931 (BA R 43I/2572).

[87] See Dr H. Bruns, *Das Prinzip verfassungsrechtlicher Sicherung der Beamtenrechte* (Cologne, 1955), 69-78, for a review of contemporary opinion; also Mommsen, 'Staat und Bürokratie', pp. 116-19. The matter was discussed by Reich and Prussian ministers on 11 Sept. 1931 (minute in BA R 43I/2556; and see associated material in R 43I/2373).

[88] C. Schmitt, 'Wohlerworbene Beamtenrechte und Gehaltskürzungen' (1931), in his *Verfassungsrechtliche Aufsätze* (Berlin, 1958), 174-80; see also Völter, 'Die deutsche Beamtenbesoldung', pp. 81-4; Köttgen, *Beamtenrecht*, p. 55.

Though this may have been a little short on logic, the RhB's argument that pay should be reduced only as the cost of living fell was very pertinent, for the reductions were not in fact related to the changes in the cost of living, and civil servants' real incomes did indeed fall faster, at least until early 1932. Meanwhile, as the DBB and ADB pointed out, the lower ranks were frequently worse hit than the upper by the impact of the reductions—a social injustice which was to fuel much resentment against those who seemed to have been spared, and which was to be vigorously exploited by the NSDAP.[89]

The social inequity of the pay cuts was paralleled in related measures which had divisive or discriminatory effects. For one thing, it was impossible for uniform personnel practices to be enforced throughout the country, since the Reich government could only indirectly influence the budgetary policies of the *Länder* and local governments. However, heavy pressure was exerted by the Reich, which used its fiscal authority to exact expenditure cuts from the *Länder*; meanwhile, the *Länder* at times resisted such pressures and at other times exploited them to cover their own desperately needed cuts, fearing to take the opprobrium on themselves. All semblance of uniformity was lost as state and local authorities resorted piecemeal to pay cuts, promotion bars, and similar measures to reduce their personnel costs, producing a patchwork of policies that only a forcible centralization could bring under control—as was ultimately to be attempted after 1933.[90]

More deliberately discriminatory was the adoption in May 1932 of new statutory powers to dismiss married women from the civil service. This law reactivated and extended the powers exercised by the Reich government between 1925 and 1929 under the residual authority of the PAV.[91] It created permissive and prescriptive powers: women

[89] Mommsen, 'Staat und Bürokratie', pp. 114-15; Völter, 'Die deutsche Beamtenbesoldung', pp. 87-9.

[90] James, *German Slump*, pp. 73-109. The emergency decrees required the *Länder* to enact comparable pay reductions. In addition, however, the Dietramszeller decree (*Notverordnung zur Sicherung der Haushalte von Ländern und Gemeinden*, 24 Aug. 1931; *RGBl*, 1931, i. 453) empowered the *Länder* to impose further reductions by decree, in order to alleviate their deteriorating fiscal situation. This not only exposed salary regulation to a new level of confusion, but was of dubious legality; see Bruns, *Das Prinzip*, pp. 75-6; Bohlen, *Die höheren Beamten*, pp. 14-15.

[91] *Gesetz über die Rechtsstellung der weiblichen Beamten*, 30 May 1932 (*RGBl*, 1932, i. 245). The amended PAV had lapsed in 1929, when its extension would have required a two-thirds majority in the Reichstag. See Hahn, 'Öffentlicher Dienst', pp. 74-6; also H. Boak, 'Women in Weimar Germany: The "Frauenfrage" and the Female Vote', in R. Bessel and E. J. Feuchtwanger (eds.), *Social Change and Political Development in Weimar Germany* (London, 1981), 164-5, and B. Greven-Aschoff, *Die bürgerliche Frauenbewegung in Deutschland 1896-1933* (Göttingen, 1981), 172-9.

employed by the Reich authorities could leave the civil service at their own request, but they could also be compulsorily dismissed under certain conditions, as long as they were deemed economically secure, i.e. were supported by another income earner. In either case, the women would forfeit their pension rights in exchange for a one-off severance payment. The measure was opposed by the major civil-service associations (though some of the women's associations reluctantly accepted it), but it was supported in the Reichstag by all the political parties, with the exception of the Staatspartei (which abstained) and the Communists (who voted against it). It was adopted in the context of the enormously visible cosmetic campaign against so-called *Doppelverdiener*, or double earners, which was widely backed across the political and social spectrum in depression Germany.[92] The term 'double earner' in fact applied only to 'working wives', and was built on a long tradition of hostility towards women's professional employment. The official justifications of the policy of excluding married women from the civil service rested on two equally specious arguments. It was asserted as a general principle that married women were in practice unable to combine their duties as employees and as housewives. Evidence for this was found in the statistics on absenteeism among civil servants, which allegedly showed that the rate among married women was twice as high as for men or for single women.[93] These statistics were hotly disputed, but it was clear that for some opponents of married women's work the very *fact* of their marriage was sufficient evidence against them, irrespective of any measurable effects. Thus, in 1931 the state secretary in the postal ministry replied to a complaint by Marie-Elisabeth Lüders (a prominent member of the Staatspartei Reichstag fraction and one of the most vigorous opponents of discrimination):

I am unable to share the objection you make that nothing would be more deleterious to the stability of marriage and the family than the dismissal of married women civil servants. On the contrary, it is more in keeping with moral prescriptions and with the preservation of family life that a married woman should be able to devote her activities primarily to the family. It has been

---

[92] See the memorandum, 'Zum Problem der Doppelverdiener' (Mar. 1931), in BA Nachlass Lüders, vorl. 153; also J. Stephenson, *Women in Nazi Society* (London, 1975), 81-4; Hahn, 'Öffentlicher Dienst', pp. 74-6; Boak, 'Women in Weimar Germany', pp. 164-5.

[93] *Drucksachen des Reichstags*, III. Wahlperiode, 1924-5, Unterausschuss 5b, 27: 'Regierungserklärung zu Artikel 14 der Personal-Abbau-Verordnung', 7 Apr. 1925, para. 1 (copy in BA Nachlass Lüders, vorl. 153).

proven that the double duties of civil servant and housewife are not compatible, and the majority of married women themselves readily recognize this.[94]

The attitude of the postal ministry was important, because it was in this administration that by far the majority of women in the Reich civil service were still to be found: they were now liable to summary dismissal at the discretion of their employer.[95]

In the same communication, the state secretary reiterated the older accusations about absenteeism, added the charge that married women were abusing their employment to secure pension rights by underhand means, and referred to threats to circumscribe women's rights in the civil service even further if reasonable measures against married women were not adopted. He also advanced the second strategic argument in the armoury of discrimination, namely, that women took jobs away from men, and that this was insupportable in a time of deep economic crisis. Yet the argument that 'double earners' should give way to male bread-winners was, if anything, even less convincing than the morality argument. Indeed, the whole campaign against double earners was based on the entirely false premiss that women held jobs that might otherwise be available to men. In general terms, the labour market was far too sex-segmented for such an assumption to be justifiable. Any detailed investigation of the real prospects for such substitution would reveal that in practice very few jobs were to be gained by dismissing women, and fewer still by restricting dismissals to economically secure married women. With married women representing only about 5 to 6 per cent of female civil servants and *Angestellte* (as compared to some 20 per cent of all working women), the numbers liable to dismissal would be tiny—no more than a few thousand at most, in all areas including teaching.[96] To suggest that such a handful of jobs would have any appreciable impact

[94] Sautter to Lüders, 3 Jan. 1931 (BA Nachlass Lüders, vorl. 135).

[95] Figures for 1926 show 45,886 *Beamtinnen* in the postal administration, compared with 448 in the other Reich authorities (*Reichshoheitsverwaltungen*); see Reich finance ministry's 'Übersichten über den Personalstand nach dem Stande vom 1. Oktober 1926', *Drucksachen des Reichstags*, III. Wahlperiode, 1924-7, 2895 (copy in BA Nachlass Lüders, vorl. 153). Other concentrations of women were in teaching and in the social services. Hahn, 'Öffentlicher Dienst', p. 77, gives postal-administration figures for subsequent years (these were published annually in the *Statistisches Jahrbuch*): in 1932, at the passage of the law, there were 36,217 *Beamtinnen* here. There is no reason to suppose that relative numbers in the Reich authorities had altered by then.

[96] Figures for *Beamtinnen* alone were not calculated. It was in any case hard to estimate how many of these married women would be liable to dismissal, since not all would be 'economically secure'. For attempts to do this, see the memorandum, 'Zum Problem der Doppelverdiener' (see n. 92 above), and Lüders' annotations thereon.

on the labour market at a time when over 4.5 million people were registered unemployed was ludicrous—yet not patently so, it seems, for the law was adopted and the campaigns continued. Clearly, the issues at stake in this affair were not wholly economic—except perhaps for the women whose lives and livelihoods were most immediately threatened. Women's right to work in certain jobs was endemically contested and restricted throughout the Weimar period; the policies to be adopted after 1933 merely gave permanent sanction to an already established practice.

IV

'In the past few weeks I have held numerous meetings and addressed civil servants in particular. My experience is that because of the inadequacy of their trade-union leadership, civil servants are taking an almost unreservedly negative attitude towards the government's measures.'[97] Thus warned one of the Centre party's own civil-service spokesmen and organizers, Hubert Gast, in an appeal to Stegerwald in October 1931. As a remedy, he urged among other things that more strenuous efforts should be made to convince civil servants of the dire emergency in which the nation found itself, so that they might begin to understand the sacrifices being demanded of them. But this was what Brüning refused to do, largely because of his determination to break the civil service's power to hold the government and his policies to ransom, as he saw it. However, the stakes in this were larger than the momentary economic status of civil servants at a time of fiscal crisis. For Brüning, as we have seen, the ultimate objective was the refoundation of the German state on a basis that would permanently emancipate it from thralldom to the power of organized interest groups. In an illusionary bid to roll back the administrative history of modern Germany as an interventionist state, Brüning pursued a vision of élitist leadership and civic culture from which the bureaucracy as such was excluded (a vision which, incidentally, was to surface again in the wartime political plans of the conservative resistance).[98]

For civil servants threatened by this vision, the invocations of sacrifice seemed increasingly threadbare. Such power as they enjoyed to

---

[97] Gast to Stegerwald, 27 Oct. 1931 (BA R 43I/2572).

[98] See H. Mommsen, 'Social Views and Constitutional Plans of the Resistance', in H. Graml *et al.*, *The German Resistance to Hitler* (London, 1970), 55-147.

secure their interests derived not from the prestige of a hallowed national institution, but from the prosaic practical influence of their representative associations. The conservative aspect of the revolution in 1918 had enabled the civil service as an interest group to get a foot in the door of the republic in the name of history, and in the first few years of Weimar a possible, if uneasy, path of collaboration on the basis of a shared social liberalism had opened out. The opportunism of the largest civil-service association, the DBB, was signalled in its willingness to move to the right along with the Reich governments in the mid-1920s, when the corporatist partnership between the government and the recognized associations delivered precisely that participation in the making of civil-service policy which the authoritarian paternalism of pre-war Germany had excluded. This was no less important a gift of the revolution than the more trumpeted survival of the *Berufsbeamtentum* as a homogeneous corps: indeed, the homogeneity of the civil service was no longer something that could be taken for granted in the 1920s. By the early 1930s, the hollowness of an official rhetoric which lauded the traditions while the institutional practice was being eroded was all too tangible. Brüning's optimistic (or cynical) expectations were met by the extreme narrowness of the DBB's conception of the constitution as simply an instrument for the protection of sectional rights. Moreover, with the loss of any special relationship with the state, the fear that the civil service would lose *all* its rights was widespread. Thus, in September 1931, even the radical ADB, in a major critique of government policy on both pay and civil-servant status, conjured up an image of the civil service delivered up to the tyranny of administrative discretion unfettered by legal process: 'Now it seems that decisions about whether civil-servant status exists at all are to be withdrawn from the courts' judgement in terms of objective characteristics, and given over to the one-sided discretion of the administration. With this, civil-servant status simply ceases to exist as a legal entity [*Rechtsverhältnis*].'[99] There is no sense of any mutuality or reciprocity between the state and its servants in this, only distance, a looming gap. It indicates the depth of the crisis of confidence that permeated the civil service by the early 1930s, a crisis which the NSDAP exploited as readily as it did the other fissures which by then were tearing German society asunder.

[99] ADB to Brüning, 18 Sept. 1931 (BA R 431/2373).

4

National Socialism and
the Civil Service before 1933

I

Before 1933, the publicly professed attitude of the NSDAP towards the civil service was characterized by a profound ambivalence which was to leave its mark on the policies of the party in power. Standing outside the political system until its participation in a number of *Länder* coalitions in the early 1930s, the Nazi party was hardly loath to identify the civil service with the despised republican state. Indeed, civil servants were the state's agents, not only in the execution of national policy, but also in the repression and harassment of the Nazi movement. They were the police who spied on and broke up Nazi gatherings, the local officials who banned meetings and demonstrations, the public prosecutors who arraigned Nazis in the courts, the judges and gaolers of the movement's martyrs. It was equally inevitable that the NSDAP would use the condition of the civil service as another stick with which to beat the republic, depicting it as the instrument of a craven political leadership, an institution corrupted by political favouritism and pork-barrel patronage. Behind these negative representations, however, hovered an alternative image of the civil service as the object, rather than the agent, of republican mismanagement. *This* civil service was the victim, not the perpetrator: its members were forced to uphold an unpopular state, to see their once honourable profession degraded by the admission of aliens and outsiders, to contend with inadequate salaries, diminished pensions, and insecure tenure rights.

Equivocation, opportunism, and a lack of control over party spokesmen all played a part in constructing this contradictory standpoint, and the party's commitment to the institution and sympathy for its members was always in question. But the negative image of the civil service was also profoundly rooted in National Socialist ideology, notably in Hitler's *Weltanschauung*. At issue was not simply the civil service as it actually existed in the 1920s, but the bureaucracy as the embodiment of a polity whose power to ward off racial disaster Hitler always thought was uncertain. *Mein Kampf* betrays a pervasive despair at the capacity of the state—of politics as such—to perform its protective function *vis-à-vis* the *Volk*. This fear could be precisely located by Hitler. Purporting to explain how the Jews had recently contrived to evade the natural watchfulness of the German people and pass themselves off as Germans, he assailed the state's inability to realize that, whatever the guise, 'he is always the same Jew':

That so obvious a fact is not recognised by the average head-clerk in a German government department, or by an officer in the police administration, is also a self-evident and natural fact; since it would be difficult to find another class of people who are so lacking in instincts and intelligence as the civil servants employed by our modern German State authorities.[1]

This was the same Hitler of the later *Table Talk*, which is peppered with deeply contemptuous asides about the vices of bureaucrats and lawyers.[2] Although this extreme note of savage odium for the state and its officials was more latent than prominent before 1933, it powered the visible antagonism between the Nazi party as *Kampfbund* and the bureaucracy as a rule-bound system, epitomized in the contrast between the street-fighting SA man and the pen-pushing clerk, between the will and the paragraph. But the lesson also depended on the more metaphysical contrast drawn between the instinctively alert and self-protective *Volk*, and the state that could be duped and deceived into betraying the interests of the racial community—the state that is ultimately undependable as the guarantor of racial survival. Unlike the more common comparison, made by the Nazis as by other political parties, between the 'good' civil service of the past and the 'bad' civil service of the present, this imagery was timeless and beyond history. It subsisted in a fantasy world of nameless powers and uncontrollable threats, and expressed that profound disbelief in the defensive capacity of the ordered polity which was so fundamental to Hitler's ideology, and which became so prominent in the policies of the later 1930s and the war.[3]

The dilemma of the relationship between *Volks-* or *Parteigenosse* and administrator was to become ineluctable after 1933, as the regime faced

<hr/>

[1] A. Hitler, *Mein Kampf* (London, 1939), 262.

[2] See e.g. *Hitler's Table Talk 1941-44*, introd. H. Trevor-Roper (London, 1973), 103-6, 373-7.

[3] See T. Mason, 'Intention and Explanation: A Current Controversy about the Interpretation of National Socialism', and H. Mommsen, 'Hitlers Stellung im nationalsozialistischen Herrschaftssystem', in G. Hirschfeld and L. Kettenacker (eds.), *The 'Führer State': Myth and Reality. Studies on the Structure and Politics of the Third Reich* (Stuttgart, 1981), 23-72.

the practical challenge of generating a governing system that would transcend the defects of bureaucracy. In the drive for power before then, however, the main problem for the Nazis was to straighten out some of the contradictions in their public position. Adept though the party was at having it all ways, its spokesmen were obliged to devote considerable efforts to assuaging the alarm provoked among civil servants by its public pronouncements, and to fending off repeated allegations that the party was *beamtenfeindlich*—hostile to civil servants— a charge that came from both democratic and conservative opponents. In the party's own historical archives, the first references to civil-service matters—police reports and press clippings from Bavaria from early 1923—cover attempts by Hitler to explain and defend the NSDAP's position. One special meeting held for the purpose, at which Hitler spoke on 'The National Socialist Movement and Civil Servants and White-Collar Workers', attracted an audience of some four to five thousand people, described in a police report as belonging to 'the better classes', mainly middle and lower civil servants with a sprinkling of senior officials. The themes were predictable: the civil service was being infiltrated by 'Jewish elements' and by other undesirables who were despoiling its prestige; the state was at the mercy of political parties which were incapable of protecting it from its external enemies (this was shortly after the French occupation of the Ruhr). Defending himself against the earlier charges, Hitler made a typical attempt to distinguish between what the Nazis attacked and what they defended in the civil service. Thus the party did not, as had been alleged, oppose civil-service pensions, but was simply in favour of a pension system for all citizens; similarly, it was not the civil service as such that drew Nazi fire, but only those officials who owed their jobs to political patronage.[4]

Clearly there was a tension between the critique and defence of the civil service, and attempts at resolution always risked betrayal by the incautious remarks of some of the party's more intemperate spokesmen, both from within the civil service and outside it. The NSDAP's repeated claims that it was the victim of deliberate and malicious campaigns of misrepresentation by its opponents could only go so far towards assuaging civil servants' doubts that this was a party they could trust. But as far as a coherent pro-civil-service position was developed in the party, two approaches or languages can be detected: one which

[4] Meeting reported in *VB* 7 [?] Apr. 1923; Bavarian police report 405 (undated), and report by Polizeidirektion Munich to Bavarian Staatsministerium, 11 Apr. 1923 (HA reel 70, folder 1514, together with similar material).

stressed a corporatist imagery, and the other material interests. The former was more likely to be found in discursive than in occasional political statements—in books and pamphlets rather than leaflets and public speeches—while the defence of civil servants' material interests became the dominant note in Nazi propaganda in its opportunistic exploitation of the economic crisis after 1930. The corporatist approach was obviously the more traditionalist, and drew on the established imagery of the German civil service as a homogeneous *Stand*, bound together by a code of service and sharing a common prestige. The language that this view of the civil service evoked from the right was, as we have seen, generally hyperbolic, and the Nazi version was no exception—indeed, the line between them was indistinct:

The civil servant is the custodian of the welfare of the state and the people; he is the Guardian in the Platonic sense. The people's honour is sacred to him. He serves it with a passionate heart, and offers it every sacrifice. Any derogation of this precious possession strikes him more heavily than if it were his own property. 'I serve' is his motto . . . Genuine and truthful in his whole outlook, abjuring weakness, hostile to the counterfeit, German, not fashionable—in short, Existence not Appearance.[5]

Before 1933, this ethical approach sustained repeated Nazi calls for the 'restoration' (*Wiederherstellung*) of the civil service, a demand which conjured up the image of a corrupted and damaged institution which the party promised to refound in a pristine purity. The contrast between the abasement of the civil service in the republic and the eminence it had once enjoyed was a common enough theme of Nazi discourse; to quote *Mein Kampf* again, in a more positive moment:

The most outstanding trait in the civil service and the whole body of the civil administration [in the empire] was its independence of the vicissitudes of government, the political mentality of which could exercise no influence on the attitude of the German State officials. Since the Revolution this situation has completely changed. Efficiency and capability have been replaced by the test of party-adherence; and independence of character and initiative are no longer appreciated as positive qualities in a public official. They rather tell against him.[6]

The frequency of this vocabulary of restoration suggests that it was seen as an effective means of recruiting the interest and support of civil servants; and yet it was not without its defects as a propaganda vehicle.

---

[5] [H.] Müller, *Beamtentum und Nationalsozialismus* (Munich, 1931), 36-7.
[6] Hitler, *Mein Kampf*, pp. 236-7.

For one thing, exposing and deploring the contrast between the pre-1918 civil service and its Weimar counterpart was a commonplace of all right-wing political propaganda in the 1920s, as we have seen. There was nothing distinctively National Socialist about it—Hitler's words could as easily have tripped from the pen of a DNVP or DVP politician. If the NSDAP wanted to achieve a conspicuous political profile, this simple contrast between the past and the present was inadequate. Moreover, the implication that National Socialism was primarily about restoring the past rather than creating the future in a new mould was out of keeping with the party's own revolutionary pretensions. Even though a degree of caution in balancing promises of restoration and rupture might be prudent in addressing civil servants, the former could not be allowed to dominate. A second problem with this approach was that, as already suggested, a disparaging contrast of Weimar civil servants with their predecessors slighted the officials along with the republic, suggesting that they were as worthless as the state they served. Not only was this a very negative image with which to appeal to civil servants, but, as opponents of the Nazis were not slow to point out, it suggested a strenuous future purge of the civil service if it ever fell into Nazi hands.

The language of the NSDAP's own civil-service programme may also have had discouraging overtones, though presumably not for nationalist-minded civil servants, who felt that they would be exempt from any such purification. The nine-point programme committed the NSDAP to the maintenance of the professional civil service with its constitutionally guaranteed rights, and went on to demand the dismissal of all political appointees, Jews, and other 'aliens', and the preferential reappointment of veterans and short-term service personnel (*Versorgungsanwärter*).[7] The party's social concerns were expressed in calls for an upward revision of pay scales, especially for the lower ranks, and for state assistance in the provision of housing—the latter an important consideration for civil servants, who were required to live where they were posted. It also attacked the mortgaging of the Reichsbahn to the Dawes loan, and opposed any further 'Dawesization' or privatization of public utilities.

The civil-service programme was issued in 1924, a year in which two

---

[7] Programme reprinted in NSDAP Reichsorganisationsleitung, *Quo Vadis Deutsches Berufsbeamtentum?* (Frankfurt, 1932), 23-4; also in an anti-Nazi pamphlet published by the ADB, *Der Nationalsozialismus eine Gefahr für das Berufsbeamtentum* (Berlin, 1932), 5, where its date is wrongly given as 1929; and in *VB*, 8 July 1926.

Reichstag elections gave German voters the chance to pass judgement on the disastrous sequence of events in 1923-4. Despite the limited recovery of the democratic parties in the December vote, the 1924 elections together testified to the instability of republican and parliamentary sentiment in Germany, and continued the trend towards the strengthening of the right that had begun in 1920. The Nazi/*völkisch* movement devoted considerable attention to civil-service issues, no doubt because of the fortunate coincidence of the election year with the unsettling consequences of the PAV. In addition, the effects of inflation on public-sector salaries and the still insecure status of the *Berufsbeamtentum* were exploited in Nazi/*völkisch* election leaflets with appeals to both the corporatist and material interests of civil servants, especially where the two coincided. Their propaganda condemned the PAV and called for its repeal, and identified the salary and appointment policies of the Reich government as further threats to the survival of the professional civil service. Although the DVP and DNVP had more success in mobilizing civil-service discontent in these elections, it does appear that the Nazi/*völkisch* movement chalked up a better electoral performance among civil servants than among white-collar employees, and thus that there were some political advantages to be scored in this sector.[8] It is not clear from the propaganda alone, of course, where civil-service support for the Nazi movement lay, and what motivated these voters. Possibly the appeals to the interests of lower-ranking civil servants were successful in garnering some support from those to whom the DNVP was too much a party of the traditional élites (though it should be remembered that the DNVP itself had a broad base of support).[9] It is possible that, given the state of the Nazi movement itself in the post-*putsch* year of 1924, it was *völkisch* sentiment that dominated both appeals and responses, and that voters were attracted both by the extreme anti-Semitism and by the somewhat traditionalist cast of the propaganda. It was only the subsequent dramatic change in the fortunes of the NSDAP during and after 1930 that permits us, after all, to interpret 1924 as the first stage in a pattern of crisis-related voting, and it is important to remember that the Nazi party of 1924 was a very different movement from that which fought the campaigns of the early 1930s.

[8] See T. Childers, *The Nazi Voter: The Social Foundations of Fascism in Germany, 1919-1933* (Chapel Hill, 1983), 97-8 and 101-2 especially.
[9] Evidence discussed most recently by R. Hamilton, *Who Voted for Hitler?* (Princeton, 1982), e.g. 87-8.

At any rate, the Nazi/*völkisch* Reichstag fraction of fourteen members that was left at the end of 1924 included a man whose political personality in some ways linked the two wings of the movement, and who was later to be one of the most prominent figures in the Nazi regime's civil-service policy. Wilhelm Frick, known to contemporaries as 'the Royal Bavarian Nazi',[10] was a career civil servant whose links to the November *putsch*, as a member of the Bavarian political police, had been enough to earn him a suspended prison sentence in 1924. He was one of the few Nazi/*völkisch* deputies to survive the December 1924 election, and after the definitive break between the NSDAP and the DVFP in March 1927, Frick became leader of the now seven-strong NSDAP Reichstag fraction. Until the fraction was augmented in 1930, Frick acted as the party's most frequent spokesman on civil-service affairs, a subject that was presumably close to his heart. The subjects of his speeches and of party motions and interpellations were consistent with the repetitive themes of party propaganda outside the Reichstag. For example, Frick and his party put themselves forward as the particular champions of those civil servants who had lost their jobs under the PAV. These *Wartestandsbeamte* lived in a limbo of wretched insecurity, with small payments in lieu of pensions, and the distant prospect, usually empty in practice, of reappointment. Nazi demands usually linked the dismissal of Jewish and political appointees to the reinstatement of these *Beamte*, or proposed amending the PAV so that it would amount to purging the civil service of these 'alien' groups.[11] Frick also hinted that the PAV itself had been a covert purge: 'Through the infamous *Personalabbau* it was principally politically suspect civil servants who were dismissed, to be replaced by party big shots and other favourites who needed a job.'[12] The other repeated theme of 1920s propaganda, inside and outside the Reichstag, was the salary and pensions system. The high pensions of Reich ministers, legally treated as civil servants, and of senior civil servants (both being political appointees) were contrasted with the wretched state of *abgebaute Beamte* and with the minimal emoluments of lesser officials. A series of Nazi amendments to the 1927 salary bill proposed abolishing both ministerial pensions and the supplements payable to senior ministry officials,

[10] See W. S. Allen (ed.), *The Infancy of Nazism: The Memoirs of Ex-Gauleiter Albert Krebs* (New York, 1976), 259.

[11] See W. Frick, *Die Nationalsozialisten im Reichstag 1924-1931* (Munich, 1932), 149 (motions 25/II and 1137/III), 150-1 (motion 464/II).

[12] Ibid. 156.

improving seniority calculations for *Versorgungsanwärter* and disabled veterans, and increasing child allowances.[13] Frick's speech on this occasion played on the inequity of the proposed increases—with some justification, as we have seen—and implied that they were bribes to ensure the loyalty of senior officials. Far from the higher grades deserving the best increases, Frick declared that: 'We are of the opposite opinion: it is precisely the higher and highest civil servants, who are changing this republic from on high, who ought to inflict privation on themselves first of all, and feel at first hand how bad things are for the German people.'[14]

The repeated use of words formed from *hohe* ('high') in this quotation underlines the extent to which the Nazi party identified itself with the interests of lower-level officials, separating itself and them from the senior echelons. This belonged to the technique of disaggregation that characterized Nazi political propaganda: the identification of specific social and occupational groups in the population who could then be addressed with a message tailored to their ears alone. This was by no means an exclusively Nazi technique—all the Weimar parties targeted segments of the electorate with specific political propaganda— but it was developed with greater sophistication and cynicism by the NSDAP than by any other party.[15] The method was well adapted to the bid to represent the NSDAP as the party for the entire people, and was used especially in the thrust for an electoral majority after 1928. Competing promises could be offered to different audiences, and their contradictions then effaced in the rhetoric of the grand set pieces of party propaganda, the speeches by Hitler, Goebbels, and the like. The civil service presented the party with a double field of disaggregation. Institutionally, an effort was increasingly made to sever the civil service not only from its identification with the existing republican state, but also from a previous history which enveloped it in the anodyne language of tradition, and called up the politics of restoration rather than rupture. Secondly, Nazi propagandists sharpened the distinction between so-called 'aliens' and the truly German civil servant, as well as that between the ēlite civil servant complicit in the decline of Germany, and the ordinary official who ranked among the victims of this—hence, a 1931 pamphlet, 'Die Bonzen im Speck, das Volk im Dreck!', which

13 Ibid. 151-3.
14 *VB*, 17 Dec. 1927, 3, and p. 2 for report on child allowances; also *VB*, 15 July 1927, 3.
15 See Childers, *The Nazi Voter, passim*.

included an attack on the high salaries of senior civil servants.

Between them, these approaches helped to anchor a new concept of the civil service marked with a Nazi stamp: no longer a *Stand* representing the sovereignty of the state, but a genuinely German body representing the *Volksgemeinschaft*. Thus, the evolving Nazi ideal of the civil service did not simply repeat the generic concept of the institution inherited from the *staatserhaltende* discourse of the empire and still practised by the conservative right. Although the traditional corporatist imagery never entirely vanished from Nazi propaganda, its effect of unifying civil servants in a synthetic abstract ideal was crossed by an alternative approach, which sought to expose the differing interests and affiliations of civil servants, and to suggest how the institution might be reconvened as a truly national creation. Prominent in this was a form of political address which attacked the élitism associated with the right and the class consciousness cultivated by the parties of the left, both of which were presented as inimical to the shared interests of the real nation.

This became clear after 1930, when the NSDAP's wavering support of civil servants' material interests solidified into an aggressive and sustained attack on those groups and politicians most closely associated with the Brüning salary reduction policy. Coverage of civil-service issues was stepped up in the party press and other publications, while Nazi deputies savaged the government and the other political parties in the Reichstag for their handling of civil-service pay cuts. Along with the dramatic expansion in the NSDAP's Reichstag fraction in September 1930 came twelve civil servants, trumpeted by the party as genuine *Berufsbeamte*, unlike the party clients who represented the SPD.[16] In 1931, the party issued an emergency programme for the civil service, calling on the government to repeal 'all special legislative measures directed against civil servants', and demanding in particular the abrogation of the *Republikschutzgesetze*, the recent Prussian ban on civil-servant membership of the NSDAP, and the emergency decrees.[17]

The five major election campaigns of 1932 gave the party a final unparalleled opportunity to exploit and deepen the discontent of civil servants. Materials surviving from four of these campaigns (the two

[16] Speech by J. Sprenger (one of the newly elected), 9 Dec. 1930, *Stenographische Berichte*, 444 V. Wahlperiode, 453.

[17] Programme submitted to Brüning by Sprenger on the day of its adoption by the NSDAP, 20 Sept. 1931 (copy in BA R 431/2380). Also reprinted in *Der Nationalsozialismus eine Gefahr*, p. 7.

rounds of the presidential election, the Prussian Landtag election, and the July Reichstag election) show that the NSDAP's central Reichspropagandaleitung (RPL) drafted some 131 propaganda leaflets aimed at different voter groups and circulated to the *Gaue* for distribution throughout the country.[18] Civil servants received the highest number of these leaflets—twenty-two in all, or about one in six of the total issued. Probably this attention was partly due to the exceptional occupational clarity of the civil-service group, and to its sheer size. Yet it must also be the case that the Nazi propaganda leadership—Goebbels chief among them—saw civil servants as a worthwhile target for a party in search of voters. Their grievances against the Brüning and Papen governments, their desertion by their professed friends, and their commitment to some version of the national interest in times of crisis offered the Nazis ample opportunities for electoral seduction. RPL instructions accompanying each batch of leaflets identified the tactics to be adopted in the campaigns, and carefully selected the grounds on which to fight. For the Prussian Landtag election, the presiding slogans were 'Prussia must become Prussian again/We are the last of the Prussians/Smash Severing and his party';[19] for the second round of the presidential election a fortnight earlier, the *Gaue* were directed to pay particular attention to the 'German *Spiessbürger*', women, civil servants, and pensioners in an attempt to wean them from their commitment to Hindenburg.[20] The Reichstag election, finally, was fought primarily on the issue of the emergency decrees, with the emphasis on NSDAP opposition to them.

Remarkable in the run of leaflets addressed to civil servants were the relentless attacks on the SPD and the ADB, as well as the Centre and the DBB, and the almost exclusive focus on civil servants' material interests rather than on their corporate identity. Thus, a leaflet in the

[18] The materials are collected in HA reel 15, folders 286-89; my thanks are due to Thomas Childers for drawing my attention to this collection.

[19] RPL instructions, 2 Apr. 1932 (HA reel 15, folder 286).

[20] RPL instructions, 23 Mar. 1932 (HA reel 15, folder 288). Shortly before this, a Nazi civil-service organizer in Munich interpreted the presidential vote to an audience of fellow Nazi *Beamte*: 'The Brüning government has nothing left for civil servants. It is doubtful whether under this government the civil servant will continue to get his pay or pension. Much of the blame for the present emergency must be borne by the civil servants themselves, because of their *spiessbürgerlich* attitudes.' One of his listeners suggested that 'civil servants . . . only voted for Hindenburg out of nervous anxiety [*Angstmeierei*], so that everything would be nice and fine again'; Munich Polizeinachrichtendienst 770, report of meeting of NSBO Fachgruppe Beamte, 17 Mar. 1932 (HA reel 89, folder 1867, 18).

Prussian Landtag series headed 'Achtung Beamte!', warned civil
servants that the ADB was part of the Iron Front's conspiracy to
prevent a Nazi parliamentary majority and had internationalist connections incompatible with the interests of the German civil service.[21]
Similarly, a leaflet entitled 'Der Nationalsozialismus eine Gefahr für
das Berufsbeamtentum?', was a defence of the NSDAP's record and
programme against allegations assembled in the ADB publication of the
same title.[22] Others in the Prussian series made it clear that the party's
aim here was to compete with the left for the votes of lower-ranking
civil servants;[23] even a leaflet headed 'The Dissolution of the *Berufsbeamtentum*' linked this threat to the 'hunger wages of civil servants',
and asserted darkly that 'A starving civil service will gradually become
the moral prey of unleashed booty hunters'.[24] Similar themes were
taken up in the Reichstag election leaflets, while for the second round of
the presidential election, responding to the RPL's instructions to attend
to the *Spiessbürger*, there was a more deliberate emphasis on the
NSDAP's commitment to the principle of the *Berufsbeamtentum*. Many
leaflets also vigorously denounced the allegations made by other parties
that the Nazis were hostile to the *Berufsbeamtentum* and would have no
respect for civil servants' rights once in power.

This was, as we have already noted, a tricky issue for the party. By the
early 1930s, the brutal and opportunist nature of the party was no doubt
clear to many, and evidence was also accumulating that it would not
allow professional rights or traditions to stand in the way of its political
agenda. The two issues on which the Nazis were probably most
vulnerable were their attitudes to civil servants' *wohlerworbene Rechte*,
which for many party members were corporate privileges incompatible
with the egalitarian principles of the *Volksgemeinschaft*, and to their
right of freedom of speech and opinion, a precept of which the Nazis
themselves were somewhat less than observant. Jakob Sprenger, by then
the NSDAP's spokesman for civil-service affairs, voiced his party's
equivocation when he declared in the Reichstag in December 1930 that:
'A well-ordered state which has evolved a professional civil service from
the principle that the civil servant will perform his functions out of a
sense of duty, on the strength of his bond of solidarity with the people,
does not need to lay any emphasis on vested rights. It would be a matter

---

[21] HA reel 15, folder 286.   [22] Ibid.
[23] e.g. 'Beamte Augen auf!', ibid.   [24] Ibid.

of course that if the civil servant did his duty, the state would take corresponding care of him.'[25]

Opponents could seize on evidence such as this, publicizing a similar statement by Arthur Greiser in the Danzig assembly in 1930: 'Today every citizen has his vested rights. If "vested rights" is supposed to mean special privileges for civil servants, we reject that view.'[26] A favourite tactic of the party in fending off such hostile accusations was to turn the table on the record of the accuser. The party press regularly covered speeches and statements by opponents in order to expose their 'real' views about the civil service; thus, in a 1932 article, Grzesinski, now police president in Berlin, was denied any right to speak on behalf of civil servants since he was a *Parteibuchbeamte* who owed his job to party patronage.[27] A long programmatic pamphlet issued by the NSDAP, also in 1932, mixed protestations of the party's belief in the *Berufsbeamtentum* ('The NSDAP ... declares that it stands firmly for the professional civil service, and that it would create such a professional civil service if it did not already exist') with pointed criticisms of opinions and policies from other parties calculated to undermine the principle of the professional civil service.[28] A leaflet for the 1932 Prussian Landtag elections, headed 'The National Socialists want to deprive civil servants of their rights', proclaimed belligerently:

LIES! Each more stupid and contemptible than the next!
Who took away the civil servant's *freedom of expression*!
Who has *cut his salary* with ever *new emergency orders*!
Who has taken away from him every *security for the future* by an *irresponsible financial policy*!
THE SOCIAL DEMOCRATS AND THE CENTRE!
They're the ones making policy in Prussia!
These parties have no right to act as accusers!
They are the accused![29]

It went on to defend the party on an equally tricky score—the question of a purge of the civil service, which was repeatedly promised in party propaganda. This had remained a fixed element in the Nazi position since the 1924 programme (and had also been implied in point 6 of the

---

[25] See n. 16 above.

[26] Quoted in *Der Nationalsozialismus eine Gefahr*, p. 7. A similar collection of material can be found in H. Klotz, *Nationalsozialismus und Beamtentum* (Berlin, 1931).

[27] 'Wenn ein Parteibuchbeamter spricht!', *NSBZ*, 20 July 1932, 201.

[28] *Quo Vadis Deutsches Berufsbeamtentum?*, pp. 3, 5 ff, 13 ff.

[29] HA reel 15, folder 286.

1920 party programme); it was justified by the argument that the only way to restore the *Berufsbeamtentum* was a strict policy of dismissing party appointees and other 'unsuitables' (Jews were less commonly referred to as such in the early 1930s propaganda material). Thus, Goebbels devoted a pamphlet written for the 1932 Prussian Landtag elections to the old Prussian virtues of the civil service ('dutifulness, discipline, and authority . . . that was what was great, yes greatest about Prussia'), contrasting them with their current abjection.[30] Elsewhere the party argued for 'a thorough-going cleansing of the civil service' and asserted that: 'The NSDAP will not rest until this civil service [the old Prussian ideal] is once more restored in its old purity and independence'. At the same time it claimed that: 'The right to freedom of political opinion is guaranteed in a National Socialist state. No civil servant will be dismissed because he does not belong to the NSDAP'—yet also argued that no 'internationalists' could remain in the service of the state.[31]

Whether this kind of thing was seen more as a threat or a promise by civil servants is hard to know. Certainly it was seized on by the party's opponents as evidence of the NSDAP's intentions, and it appears that the experience of Nazi rule in some *Länder* before 1933 caused great disquiet. This was notably so in Oldenburg, where the Nazis unexpectedly took power after the May 1932 Landtag elections.[32] Between May and the July Reichstag election, Gauleiter Röver, now prime minister, moved circumspectly. He renounced his own first month's salary as a propaganda gesture (on Hitler's instructions), and used the Reich's emergency decrees to order a reduction in ministerial and senior civil-service salaries. But the crudity and demagoguery of Röver's political style were soon apparent, and civil servants became the particular butt of the party's public pronouncements. In September, wider civil-service salary cuts were promulgated, and intervention in personnel policies was stepped up. A freeze on most promotions and appointments was imposed, a number of officials were forcibly retired, and party members were substituted. One of these cases involved replacing a *Regierungspräsident* with an *Angestellte*—so much for the NSDAP's commitment to the *Berufsbeamtentum*—while another

---

[30] J. Goebbels, *Preussen muss wieder preussisch werden!* (Munich, 1932) (copy in BA Zsg. 3/1137).

[31] *Quo Vadis Deutsches Berufsbeamtentum?*, pp. 9, 18.

[32] K. Schaap, *Die Endphase der Weimarer Republik im Freistaat Oldenburg 1928-1933* (Düsseldorf, 1978), 191-265; J. Noakes, *The Nazi Party in Lower Saxony 1921-1933* (Oxford, 1971), 222-32.

involved a serious and rancorous conflict between the Nazi *Regierungs-präsident* of Lübeck and the DNVP mayor of Eutin, which developed into a major scandal. All the main civil-servant associations issued strenuous protests, and it seems more than likely that the NSDAP's civil-service policies contributed to the party's loss of votes in the November Reichstag elections: the 8.3 per cent loss in Oldenburg state was twice the Reich average, while in the heavily administrative city of Oldenburg the decline, at 15.8 per cent, was even steeper. In Braun-schweig, too, where the Nazis were in coalition from October 1930, and in Thuringia, where there was Nazi participation in 1931 and 1932, the Nazis exerted what pressure they could on appointments policy, especially in the police forces.[33] In a private letter in February 1930 Hitler explained his intentions in nominating Frick as the Nazi candidate for the Thuringian interior ministry. Describing him as a trained and fanatical man, he declared that: 'As interior minister Dr Frick will undertake a slow cleansing of the administrative and civil-service body from the red residues of the revolution. Dr Frick will here introduce with ruthless determination a nationalization which will show the other bourgeois governments what we understand by this word.'[34] Frick was later described, by a fellow-Nazi, as having carried out a financially inevitable personnel reduction and administrative rational-ization on fairer terms than the 1923 *Personalabbau*, in that senior civil servants were made to bear the brunt of the measures.[35]

As this last example suggests, participation in government brought the Nazis mixed rewards in terms of the party's reputation among civil servants. Office-holding exposed the Nazis' inexperience—indeed, their unfitness for rule—as well as the gaps between their rhetoric and their practice. Civil servants could hardly have failed to notice the crude political jobbery operated by Röver, or the fact that tax cuts benefiting the Oldenburg peasantry were supported by their own salary reductions. Active involvement in government also implicated the NSDAP in Germany's political and economic crisis, instead of leaving it free to barrack the efforts of others from the safety of the sidelines. If

---

[33] For Oldenburg, see Noakes, *The Nazi Party*, p. 230; for Braunschweig, E.-A. Roloff, *Bürgertum und Nationalsozialismus: Braunschweigs Weg im Dritten Reich* (Hanover, 1961); for Thuringia, F. Dickmann, 'Die Regierungsbildung in Thüringen als Modell der Machtergreifung: Ein Brief Hitlers aus dem Jahre 1930', *VjhZ*, 14 (1966), 454-64.

[34] Letter of 2 Feb. 1930 (addressee unknown), in Dickmann, 'Regierungsbildung in Thüringen', p. 462.

[35] H. Fabricius, *Dr Frick: Der revolutionäre Staatsmann* (Berlin [1933]), 37 ff.

the limited evidence from Oldenburg is any guide, civil servants may have found the Nazis less attractive in power than in opposition—a view of which the party was well aware by November 1932, of course, since it appeared to be shared by others among the German electorate. Nevertheless, although the ambiguities in Nazi attitudes to the civil service were thus never fully masked, not even by the more astute propaganda of the early 1930s, evidence about other means of mobilizing civil servants' support for the party suggests that it did exert a considerable pull among certain groups. Mass propaganda was not the only tactic employed by the NSDAP in these years: it also recruited and organized party members, apparently with growing success.

II

Although individual civil servants began joining the NSDAP in small numbers from the very beginning, no effort was made to court them as a group until the early 1930s. The party's early radicalism had discouraged the formation of any special interest groups, especially for such quintessential members of the petty bourgeoisie. The earliest such groups, the Hitler Youth and the National Socialist German Student Association, both formally founded in 1926, were clearly aimed at generational rather than occupational groups, and thus did not affect the principle; while the SA and SS were a different matter altogether. It was not until the later 1920s, when the party leadership turned from the unsuccessful strategy of organizing an urban working-class following towards the recruitment of a broader and more middle-class constituency, that the potential of existing and new affiliated groups began to be taken more seriously.[36] Even then, it was lawyers, not civil servants as such, who were the first to be organized into an occupational affiliate, the Bund Nationalsozialistischer Deutscher Juristen (BNSDJ), established in 1928. Although there might have been a certain amount of overlap between the two categories in theory, in practice the BNSDJ was not a mass-membership association, numbering only 700 by January 1932.[37]

The leadership's unwillingness to sanction the establishment of some kind of civil servants' group, even as a base for party recruitment,

---

[36] For the party's new strategy, see D. Orlow, *The History of the Nazi Party: 1919-1933* (Pittsburgh, 1969), 118 ff., 149 ff.; and M. Kater, *The Nazi Party: A Social Profile of Members and Leaders, 1919-1945* (Cambridge, Mass., 1983), 56-71.

[37] Report from BNSDJ directorate to H. Frank, 18 Jan. 1932 (BA NS 22/847).

sprang from a number of deep-seated reservations. We have already examined the party's ambivalence towards civil servants, and seen that it did not dissipate until government economic policies rendered them attractive as a reservoir of potential voters. To this was added the suspicion felt by Hitler and Gregor Strasser in the 1920s towards powerful sub-organizations within the NSDAP, in particular anything that smacked of a Nazi trade union; thus, even the NSBO was not founded until 1929 and was not intended to function as a trade union as such.[38] However, it is clear that by 1930 civil servants sympathetic to the party were meeting and organizing themselves informally, their relationship to the party itself being somewhat unclear. In November 1930, for example, a Hamburg police report identified a 'Vereinigung nationalsozialistischer Beamten', allegedly founded at the instigation of the NSDAP Reichsleitung in 1929, which had become active since the Reichstag elections: 'For the most part postal civil servants belong to it; its membership numbers are not at present known . . . Civil servants are being recommended not to enrol in the party itself if there is any danger that they would lose their jobs. They are to be entered in the list of the nameless.'[39] Scattered evidence of this kind is confirmed by a later survey of the party's organizational work among civil servants, which in most *Gaue* dated from 1930-2.[40] By this time, the party head-quarters had received a number of unsolicited proposals arguing for the foundation of a Nazi civil-service section or association. One of these pointed out that the Nazis enjoyed little support among traditionalist civil servants, and that the party had poor prospects if the existing pattern of political appointments persisted (something of an exaggeration); the author urged the establishment of a Nazi front organization, nominally independent of the NSDAP itself, and open to nationalist civil servants.[41] Another stressed the advantages to the party of harnessing the energies and experience of civil servants: for example, they could collect information on their colleagues for use by a future Nazi government, or use their jobs to influence current

---

[38] See T. W. Mason, *Sozialpolitik im Dritten Reich: Arbeiterklasse und Volksgemeinschaft* (Opladen, 1977), 69; also Orlow, *History of the Nazi Party*, pp. 176, 196-7.

[39] Lagebericht Hamburg, 29 Nov. 1930 (copy in HA reel 70, folder 1514, 42).

[40] The NSDAP's organizational work was reviewed on a *Gau*-by-*Gau* basis in the *Almanach der Deutschen Beamten*, published in 1934 by the Reichsbund der Deutschen Beamten, 54-74.

[41] 'Memorandum über die Schaffung eines Beamtenbundes', by Treff (a Berlin municipal councillor and party member since 1926), 3 Nov. 1931 (BA NS 26/1411).

policy-making.[42] It was in response to such pressures that Strasser issued a directive in January 1930 forbidding the establishment of independently financed sections for civil servants or any other occupational groups.[43] While informal discussion groups were permitted, Strasser argued that the subdivision of the party membership into a series of sections with specialized economic interests would cause the NSDAP to disintegrate into a mere association of *Standesgruppen*.

Strasser's directive was partly an attempt to maintain central control over all party activities (the control of finances was crucial in this), and the stages by which civil-service organization proceeded subsequently illustrate the importance attached to this. Pressure for more authority in this sphere was evidently being exerted by Jakob Sprenger, the middle-ranking postal official and *Gauleiter* elected to the Reichstag in 1930 who had been given fractional responsibility by Frick for civil-service questions. Early in 1931, Sprenger was given departmental authority in the NSDAP headquarters as the party's expert adviser on the civil service (his title was *Beamtenfachberater* or *-sachbearbeiter*), and was empowered to appoint a *Gausachbearbeiter für Beamtenfragen* in each *Gau*.[44]

However, this was not to be seen as the first step in the establishment of a civil-service membership section. A headquarters circular of April 1931 to *Gau* organizers reiterated the earlier veto, and instructed them to confine their public activities to ideological propaganda, avoiding any direct involvement with civil servants' interests and grievances.[45] Organizers were also warned to work with great circumspection, in view of the hostile attitude of the state authorities to the NSDAP. It is clear that this need for caution was another reason for the slowness with which organization proceeded. By 1931, as we shall see, a number of *Länder* had issued restrictions on civil servants' activity for the NSDAP, and although there were difficulties in enforcing these regulations effectively, they were obviously seen as threatening by some civil servants. The party thus had to give some thought to circumventing the problem of harassment.

[42] 'Vorschlag zur Bildung von Beamten-Gruppen' (1930), signed by Karsch and Gutmann (BA NS 26/1411).

[43] NSDAP Organisations-Abteilung I, Anordnung des Organisationsleiters, 16 Jan. 1930 (BA S Sch. 218).

[44] This process is reconstructed from documentation in BA NS 22/361 and S Sch. 218, which does not include a specific directive to this effect.

[45] NSDAP Organisations-Abteilung I, Abteilung Beamtenfachberater, 1931, RdSchr. I, 29 Apr. 1931 (BA S Sch. 218).

Nevertheless, during 1931 party activity among civil servants became more energetic, spurred on both by Sprenger's ambition and by pressure from below. It was still very irregular, however. In the absence of a Nazi civil-service association of some kind, individual civil servants were now becoming attached to the NSBO, but this was highly unsatisfactory given the historic differentiation between *Beamte* and workers, and must have led to some friction. In the summer, Strasser and Sprenger ordered civil servants to leave the NSBO; they could form their own informal groups, but the ban on a Nazi association remained in force.[46] Sprenger was now also involved in the familiar process of defending and extending his powers within the party, presaging the greater battles for control that took place after 1933. At the end of 1932, he drafted an instruction to Nazi ministers and fraction leaders in the *Länder*, insisting that they clear their civil-service policies with him in advance; similarly, he demanded that his department be given sole authority to evaluate the political standing of ministerial civil servants, thus centralizing another dispersed process.[47] He was also trying to negotiate an understanding with the DBB, pressing it to hold to its non-party stance while the NSDAP in effect infiltrated it. Evidently this attempt was abandoned towards the end of 1932, following what Sprenger saw as repeated attacks on his party by the DBB.[48]

Meanwhile, Sprenger was also travelling widely through Germany, speaking at the increasing number of meetings now being held for civil servants by the NSDAP, and setting up the skeleton of an organizational structure. He was assisted in this by his industrious deputy for propaganda, Hermann Neef, a customs official who was later to be put in charge of the Nazi organization of civil servants in the Third Reich, after Sprenger had moved on to higher things. In December, Sprenger published the first issue of the *Nationalsozialistische Beamten-Zeitung* (*NSBZ*), a fortnightly paper that was to appear regularly until 1943 and that was claiming 80,000 subscribers by 1933. Sprenger continued to press for a more formal party organization for civil servants, and in April he and Strasser came to an agreement to authorize the establishment of Nazi 'Beamtenarbeitsgemeinschaften' at local (*Ort*) level, to which Nazi 'sympathizers' (*Anhänger*) could be attached. Finally, in

---

46 Reichsorganisationsleiter I, Anordnung 5/31, 29 Aug. 1931 (HA reel 70, folder 1514, 50).

47 Sprenger to Hauptstabsleiter Glaser, 22 Nov. 1932; Sprenger to Strasser, 18 July 1932 (BA NS 22/361).

48 Documentation in ibid. See also H. Mommsen, *Beamtentum im Dritten Reich* (Stuttgart, 1966), 28, and Orlow, *History of the Nazi Party*, p. 59.

May, a formal civil-service department was set up within the party, headed by Sprenger and based in his home town of Frankfurt-am-Main.[49] The Beamtenabteilung was to be assigned 'all persons having civil-service status in public law who are members of the party. They are to be organized in local groups.' Once again, the establishment of a Nazi civil-servant association as such was expressly forbidden, though in practice the party was now becoming more deeply involved in civil servants' interests.

With formal or informal sanctions against NSDAP membership by civil servants common until mid-1932, the party also had to make arrangements for 'sympathizers' to associate themselves without being full members: these were people who 'supported [the party] materially and ideologically and paid regular subscriptions to the Beamtenabteilung';[50] they were later claimed to have numbered 120,000 by 1933.[51] A Berlin police report of April 1932, summarizing confidential NSDAP instructions on propaganda work among civil servants, gives some indication of party tactics.[52] Objectives were now said to include 'safeguarding the professional interests [*Standesbelange*] of associated civil servants', and active participation in professional activities:

The Nazi groups are to attempt to exert influence in the local civil-service professional associations, with the aim of suppressing contrary political opinions in these associations as far as possible ... Further, in elections for civil-service representatives [to the equivalent of works councils] representations should be made to suitable organizations for the inclusion of Nazis in the lists presented by these organizations ...

The Nazis threatened to nominate their own lists if these requests were refused—an example of the kind of pressure exerted on the DBB. Propaganda and recruitment were to be arranged through agents (*Vertrauensleute*) in each office; they were to maintain contact with other members in their office, and to hold meetings for wider

49 Documentation in BA NS 22/361.

50 Neef (Hauptamt für Beamte) to *Stabsleiter*, Reichsorganisationsleitung, 25 June 1935 (BA NS 22/346).

51 This figure is given in E. Mursinsky and J. Brill, *Die Organisation der national-sozialistischen Beamten* (Berlin, 1940), 4: in the light of the much lower *NSBZ* subscription figure (80,000) it seems exaggerated.

52 Mitteilung Nr. 8 des Polizeipräsidiums (I) Berlin vom 15. April 1932, 'Versuche zur Zersetzung der Beamtenschaft' (HA reel 89, folder 1867). The folder contains other miscellaneous information on the subject, including e.g. copies of party membership forms drawn up for civil servants, and police reports of public and closed party meetings in Munich.

audiences. Anyone who showed any interest was to be urged to join up 'if this is compatible with his professional interests'; others were to be enrolled as sympathizers; great efforts were to be devoted to the sale of the *NSBZ*. The agents were to make monthly reports to the *Gau* representatives, and regular contact was to be maintained with other party organizations.

Theoretically, then, the NSDAP leadership had stuck to their rejection of an independent civil-service association sponsored by the party—an important decision, given the high degree of organization among Germany's civil servants. The leadership's dislike of sectional organizations, and the special risks of organizing *Beamte* were largely responsible for this, as we have seen. But by 1932 the tentative steps to contain pressures for a more active effort had been overtaken, not least by the rewards the party now hoped to reap from cultivating the votes of civil servants. By then, the NSDAP had in Sprenger a man who enjoyed some standing in the party at large as a *Gauleiter* and Reichstag member, and in Hermann Neef an assiduous junior organizer who did an enormous amount of leg-work in the expectation of a prominent party career; they also had a national office and a network of local organizers; and a national newspaper—altogether a considerable apparatus established in a relatively short time. However, for all the effort expended on the organization of civil servants in the Nazi party and the range of surviving evidence of these activities, it remains difficult to quantify accurately the actual success of the party. The NSDAP's own *Partei-Statistik*, issued in 1935, shows that only a handful of civil servants joined the party before 1933, and that their representation in the total membership was in fairly close proportion to their representation among the employed population as a whole. In September 1930, 7,992 civil servants (excluding teachers) were party members; this was 6.2 per cent of the current total of 129,500, while civil servants formed some 6 per cent of employed persons. On the eve of the Nazi take-over in January 1933, the comparable figures were 44,080 out of some 720,000, which represented a slight fall in the civil-servant proportion of membership, to 5.2 per cent.[53] These figures, though not in themselves wholly reliable, can be compared with the recent findings of Michael Kater, who confirms the unexceptional membership figures and suggests that the proportion of civil servants among new members of the NSDAP fell between 1930 and 1932, rising only from mid-1932,

[53] Figures compiled from the *NSDAP Partei-Statistik* (Berlin, 1935), ii, 53, 70; also Orlow, *History of the Nazi Party*, p. 239, and Kater, *The Nazi Party*, table 1, p. 241.

especially among higher civil servants.[54] However, the value of these crude figures remains limited as an index of the popularity of the NSDAP among civil servants. In the absence of information on the propensity of civil servants to join other political parties, it is impossible to tell whether those joining the NSDAP followed or broke a wider pattern. The SPD published a survey of its membership in 1930, showing civil servants as 3.1 per cent of its 100,000 members, which would make it attractive to about half the numbers drawn by the NSDAP.[55] We have no such quantified information for the other major parties, but only a set of conventions which assert the appeal of the DNVP and DVP to higher civil servants, the DDP and Staatspartei to the more liberal, and the Centre to Catholics from the middle ranks. Another factor that weakens the value of membership figures was, as we have seen, the existence of arrangements for civil servants who wanted to express their solidarity with the NSDAP while avoiding the possible penalties of outright membership. If we take at face value the 120,000 alleged *Anhänger* before 1933, this would treble at a stroke the numbers of civil servants acknowledging some relationship with the party, and would immediately transform the NSDAP into a party of considerable appeal to civil servants. Yet one must be cautious in reading this evidence, partly because of its unreliability in stemming from undocumented party sources, and partly because we do not know how many potential members from other occupational strata were deterred from joining by fear of disadvantage, or, indeed, how similar considerations might have affected other political parties. Finally, the fact that tens of thousands of *Beamte* flocked into the NSDAP *after* 1933 is not in itself conclusive evidence of a pent-up desire to join, given the obvious advantages by then of belonging to the party in command of the state. Nevertheless, 20.7 per cent of civil servants were party members by 1935, the largest proportion of any of the major occupational categories —a fact which was to be of some concern to the party leadership.

The quantifiable evidence is, in other words, almost as ambiguous as the party's own record of concern for civil servants. Still, although it would be foolish to rely on the evidence of the 'sympathizer' numbers claimed by the NSDAP and of the post-1933 membership rush, it

---

[54] Kater, *The Nazi Party*, pp. 59-61, 68-70. See also his 'Sozialer Wandel in der NSDAP im Züge der nationalsozialistischen Machtergreifung', in W. Schieder (ed.), *Faschismus als soziale Bewegung: Deutschland und Italien im Vergleich* (Göttingen, 1983), 30, 34.

[55] R. N. Hunt, *German Social Democracy 1918-1933* (Chicago, 1970), 103.

would also be unreasonable to discount it altogether. It seems safe to say that the pre-1933 membership figures alone do not tell the whole story, and that there was more support for the NSDAP than they indicate. This impression is reinforced by the other evidence, notably from government sources, that suggests the existence of growing anxiety at the extent of the party's reach into the civil service after 1929.

III

Government concern about the relationship of civil servants and the NSDAP died down after the events of 1923, and until 1929 there was little official attention to the NSDAP in the political monitoring of the civil service.[56] However, ordinary civil-service law gave the state some powers to control civil servants' political activities, as we have seen. Reich and *Länder* had their disciplinary codes, and the Reich also had the stronger authority assigned by the 1922 amendment to the Reich civil-service law, adopted as part of the group of laws for the protection of the republic. (The main part of these expired in 1929, and they were not renewed in their original form, but the amended civil-service law remained in force.) Nevertheless, the degree of acceptable control continued to give rise to dispute, while both the powers available and the standards applied varied among the employing authorities. In the mid-1920s, it was the KPD that had excited more official concern as a threat to the republic, but by the end of the decade attention was shifting to the right wing once again. The agitation around the Young Plan referendum, and then the precipitate and alarming growth of support for the NSDAP, provoked both the Reich and Prussian governments to start monitoring the behaviour of civil servants more closely. In October 1929, the Prussian minister-president, Braun, warned civil

---

[56] See H. Schmahl, *Disziplinarrecht und politische Betätigung der Beamten in der Weimarer Republik* (Berlin, 1977), chs. 6, 9. Government policies are discussed in detail in the following sources (mainly dealing with the Reich and Prussia), to which my account is indebted: H.-P. Ehni, *Bollwerk Preussen? Preussenregierung, Reich-Länder Problem und Sozialdemokratie 1928-1932* (Bonn and Bad Godesberg, 1975), chs. 3-4; R. Morsey, 'Staatsfeinde im öffentlichen Dienst: Die Beamtenpolitik gegenüber NSDAP-Mitgliedern', in K. König *et al.* (eds.), *Öffentlicher Dienst: Festschrift für Carl Hermann Ule* (Cologne, 1977), 111-35; R. Morsey, 'Beamtenschaft und Verwaltung zwischen Republik und "Neuem Staat"', in K. D. Erdmann and H. Schulze (eds.), *Weimar: Selbstpreisgabe einer Demokratie* (Düsseldorf, 1980), 151-68; H. Mommsen, 'Die Stellung der Beamtenschaft in Reich, Ländern und Gemeinden in der Ära Bruning', *VjhZ*, 21 (1973), 163-4.

servants that support for the referendum would constitute a violation of the *Treuepflicht*, while the Reich government declared that it would collect information on civil servants actively engaged in it. That few cases came to light—a mere forty-three out of the total of 339,000 *Reichsbeamte*—might perhaps be seen as evidence of the efficacy of the Reich government's announcement.[57] But this was only the beginning of the process of political radicalization that now swept through Germany. The Prussian local-government elections on 17 November 1929 brought the first signs of an NSDAP breakthrough, and the Prussian government prepared to stiffen its position. A few days later, the cabinet resolved that in future 'members of parties or organizations that publicly declare their desire for the violent overthrow of the existing governmental system shall neither be appointed as civil servants, nor promoted or confirmed in office'. It was doubtful, however, that there would be any legal authority to dismiss civil servants.[58]

At the same time, the Prussian government made the first of several efforts to persuade the Reich to follow suit. Although these remained unsuccessful, the Prussians persisted in their own tough stance. After some delay, the so-called *Radikalenerlass* was issued in June 1930, naming the NSDAP and KPD as 'organizations whose objective is the violent overthrow of the existing state', and declaring that: 'A civil servant who takes part in such an organization, who works for it or otherwise supports it, thereby violates the special duty of loyalty that derives from his civil-servant status, and renders himself guilty of a disciplinary offence.'[59] In the next six months, this lead was followed by Baden, Hessen, and Hamburg, though with somewhat less stringent regulations.[60] Among the other larger *Länder*, Bavaria issued no instructions, while the Württemberg government restricted itself to a warning against anti-constitutional activities, without specifying any organizations by name. *Länder* in which the Nazis enjoyed cabinet representation also refused any regulations, and in Thuringia, Frick used his authority as interior minister to issue a ban on membership in, or activities for, the KPD. Prussia remained the most interventionist

[57] Morsey, 'Staatsfeinde', pp. 113-14.

[58] Prussian cabinet session, 21 Nov. 1929 (copy of minutes in BA R 43I/2555).

[59] Resolution of the Prussian cabinet, 25 June 1930 (*MBliV*, 1930, 599), reprinted in Schmahl, *Disziplinarrecht*, p. 211.

[60] See Schmahl, *Disziplinarrecht*, pp. 160 ff; H. Rehberger, *Die Gleichschaltung des Landes Baden 1932/33* (Heidelberg, 1966), 82-9; J. H. Grill, *The Nazi Movement in Baden, 1920-1945* (Chapel Hill, 1983), 203-5.

state, which was consistent with its willingness to adopt the more activist civil-service policy that has been discussed above.[61] It also enjoyed the most effective backing from its courts. In March 1931, the Prussian disciplinary court for non-judicial civil servants handed down a landmark decision in an appeal case by declaring that: 'Activity by a civil servant on behalf of the NSDAP constitutes a disciplinary offence, since it [the NSDAP] intends the overthrow of the existing state system [*bestehende Staatsordnung*] by violent means.'[62] The case in question concerned a Regierungsinspektor Hasse in Stade, a *Kreisleiter* and an NSDAP member since 1929. He had previously been warned about his activities, and had been compulsorily transferred in 1930, before the June *Radikalenerlass*. He was taken before a disciplinary court when he refused to stop working for the party, and had been dismissed from his job. Similarly, in April 1931, the Prussian Staatsgerichtshof rejected an NSDAP appeal against the legality of the June decree.[63] However, although any civil servant associated with the NSDAP risked proceedings in principle, in practice only the most active campaigners and party office-holders were likely to face arraignment. Indeed, in April 1933, when the Nazi commissarial justice minister, Hans Kerrl, conducted a survey of the Prussian judicial authorities charged with administering the decree in their bailiwicks, two of the twelve respondents claimed not to have applied it, four expressed varying degrees of misgiving about it, one argued that opposition to the decree would have been ineffective, four were not in office at the time, and only one (in Frankfurt-am-Main) stated that the NSDAP had indeed been a revolutionary party before 1933.[64]

In any event, the validity of the Prussian decree was short-lived. Following the loss of the coalition majority in the April 1932 elections, the Landtag voted to rescind it. After Papen's *Preussenstreich* in July, Bracht lifted all restrictions on activities for the NSDAP, and one-sided regulations affecting the KPD alone were confirmed or reinstated. Only the wearing of civil-service uniforms at public rallies was banned.[65]

[61] See Ch. 2, pp. 41-9, above. One of the architects of that policy, Severing, now Reich interior minister in Müller's cabinet, tried unsuccessfully to promote joint action by the Reich government (see documentation in BA R 431/2555).

[62] *Deutsche Juristenzeitung*, 1931, 713, citing decision of 9 Mar. 1931. The Prussian cabinet had discussed the case the previous October; see minutes of its session, 2 Oct. 1930 (GStA P 134/3112a); also Ehni, *Bollwerk Preussen?*, pp. 191-2.

[63] Morsey, 'Staatsfeinde', p. 116.

[64] Prussian justice ministry to *Kreisgerichtspräsidenten* and *Oberlandesgerichtspräsidenten*, 4 Apr. 1933 (GStA P 135/3157).

[65] Prussian interior-ministry circular, 5 Aug. 1932 (*MBliV*, 1932, 787); reprinted in Schmahl, *Disziplinarrecht*, pp. 212-13.

Later in the year, Bracht amnestied those civil servants disciplined during the Young Plan referendum campaign; and in October 1932, the Prussian Oberverwaltungsgericht declared that the now abrogated decree had been unconstitutional. In Baden, Hessen, and Hamburg, too, the regulations were weakened or abandoned in the latter half of 1932, reflecting the changed political atmosphere in Germany.

The attempts to control Nazi activity by civil servants were hampered not only by the lack of concert, but also by the absence of a clear direction by the Reich government and of legal unanimity on the question of the NSDAP's constitutionality. The academic literature tended to be more yielding to the party's protestations, whereas the courts inclined to view it as containing at least an anti-constitutional tendency which might well become dominant. Of course, the NSDAP leadership was now anxious to maintain a legalist façade in its drive for power. Hitler's declaration at the Ulm officers' trial came only months after the Prussian *Radikalenerlass*, but this still did not stifle debate about the constitutionality of the ends as well as the means of the party. However, where civil-service disciplinary courts lacked the additional authority of an instrument like the Prussian decree, the *Treuepflicht* was likely to be more narrowly constructed, and civil servants were not brought to book unless their alleged offence took place in aggravated circumstances, such as when they were on duty.[66]

Above all, it was of the utmost significance in the worsening political climate of the early 1930s that Brüning's cabinet failed to act decisively, despite repeated pressure both from the Prussian government and from its own members. The question was first raised in a full cabinet in December 1930, but Brüning refused further discussion for the next fifteen months, leaving it to individual ministers to deal with the problem in their area of jurisdiction as each saw fit.[67] Apart from Groener, who, as interior minister in Brüning's reshuffled cabinet after October 1931, had responsibility for public order, the ministers who expressed most concern about the scope of Nazi activity were the finance minister, Dietrich, and Schätzel, the postal minister. Both men headed departments with large field agencies which between them employed hundreds of thousands of personnel, and they were increasingly alarmed by the evidence of NSDAP activity and recruitment. In the initial cabinet review of the issue in December 1930, Schätzel asserted that: 'in his administration the National Socialists had actually

---

[66] Schmahl, *Disziplinarrecht*, pp. 169-71.
[67] Cabinet minutes, 19 Dec. 1930 (BA R 431/2682).

won their greatest number of supporters among higher civil servants', while Schleicher drew attention to the problems caused by Nazi members among the border police (*Grenzschutz*) in areas where the NSDAP was strong and security a sensitive issue. In August 1931, Dietrich took notice of the Hasse case in Prussia, and through Wirth tried to set up a joint meeting with Brüning, unsuccessfully.[68] By the beginning of 1932, it seemed that Schätzel was no longer certain of his earlier opinion, expressed in December 1930, that NSDAP membership alone should not be grounds for initiating disciplinary proceedings against a civil servant, but his request for a cabinet discussion of the issue was evaded by Brüning. It was not until mid-April, during the cabinet discussion of Groener's proposed ban on the SA and SS, that the question was broached again at this level.[69] Once again, Dietrich and Schätzel were the most vocal. Schätzel claimed that: 'The National Socialists are practising such a degree of terror in the civil service that constitutionally appointed officials are being completely intimidated'; and Dietrich, that ministers were 'basically defenceless' because they lacked clear authority or guidelines, while the disciplinary authorities were 'amicably disposed' to Nazi civil servants.

Other evidence tends to confirm the implication that by 1932 the Nazis had been successful in making inroads into the uniformed civil service, including the *Betriebsverwaltungen*. Information collected by the Berlin police and forwarded to Pünder by the Prussian government in 1931 indicated that the majority of the forty-five or so civil servants registered as members of the Berlin SA were from the postal service.[70] Some of the problems encountered by Sprenger in demarcating between his civil-service department and the NSBO clearly arose from the propensity of personnel in the *Betriebsverwaltungen* to adhere to Nazism. An analysis of the 1934 complement of officials in the Nazi civil-service organization shows that, of the fifty-one who were pre-1933 party members, the largest contingent (eighteen) had been *Beamte* in the postal and telegraph service; eight came from the customs and

---

[68] Reich finance minister to Reich interior minister, 18 Aug. 1931 (BA R 431/2557).
[69] In Jan. 1932, Dietrich and Schätzel had again asked for a meeting; this was eventually arranged by Pünder, but cancelled on Brüning's orders on 4 Mar., owing to the presidential elections; see Groener to Pünder, 26 Jan. 1932, and subsequent documentation in BA R 431/2557. The postal ministry was particularly concerned at this time about Sprenger, whom they considered a fit subject for a disciplinary case; see copy of the ministry's letter to Wirth, 13 Feb. 1932, in ibid. Minutes of cabinet meeting on 13 Apr. 1932 in BA 431/2684.
[70] Copy of Berlin *Polizeipräsident* report, 2 Mar. 1931 (BA R 431/2682).

finance administration, and five from the Reichsbahn; the majority of these had been active in Sprenger's network before 1933.[71] It is also notable that all except five of these officials had been employed in the intermediate or superior grade of the civil service (four were not *Beamte*, and the other was the senior civil servant and prominent Nazi propagandist, Hans Fabricius). Sprenger, the middle-ranking postal official, and his deputy, Neef, the junior customs officer, thus perfectly epitomized the organization they led.

Brüning's policy of leaving matters to the discretion of individual ministers was a failure, therefore, judged both by their reactions and by the evidence of Nazi mobilization. Yet, even in April 1932 it was clear that he would not countenance effective measures. Justice minister Joel told his cabinet colleagues that only some kind of exceptional law naming the NSDAP would be legally adequate—a course of action he had doubts about, and one rejected by Brüning for fear of jeopardizing the current delicate political bargaining between the Centre and the NSDAP. It was indeed emblematic of the compromised and, in Dietrich's word, 'defenceless' position into which ministers had by now been backed, that the only concrete proposal Joel could offer was the issue of a declaration to senior civil servants, assuring them of the government's 'protection' in their attempts to stifle undue Nazi agitation.

The failure by the Reich government to act strongly in this matter was not, of course, its sole or most egregious political error between 1930 and 1932, nor would such action have meant much on its own. Indeed, it is hardly likely that it could have taken place in isolation, for it would have involved the reversal or inexistence of central planks in Brüning's policy: the exclusion rather than incorporation of the NSDAP, and a less pugnacious disregard for civil servants' interests and anxieties. For the latter remained the paramount cause of disaffection. As civil-servant members of his own party bitterly observed to Brüning in 1931: 'In our opinion it cannot be the job of the Centre to contribute through salary reduction measures to the advance establishment in the civil service of a firm support for the Third Reich desired by a certain party.'[72] On its own, a ban on Nazi recruitment of

---

[71] Figures compiled from information in *Almanach der Deutschen Beamten*, pp. 96-108. In 1929, the Reichstag deputy, Ludwig Hass, had warned the government that the para-military Reichsbahn police were 'entirely on the radical right'; see document 366 in *Akten der Reichskanzlei: Das Kabinett Müller II*, ed. M. Vogt (Boppard, 1970), ii. 1208.

[72] Communication to Brüning from the civil-service advisory group of the Centre party of Lower Saxony, 11 May 1931 (BA R43I/2369).

civil servants would, for many of them, have removed a symptom but not the cause, and the non-Nazi associations were in any case divided over the constitutionality of such a policy, given the provisions of Article 129 of the constitution.[73] Yet the evidence confirms how little regard Brüning had for the problem itself, and how weak was the situation in which he left not only his own ministers, but also the more interventionist *Länder* governments.

Thus, by 1932 the NSDAP had succeeded in tapping the varied discontents of at least a portion of the civil-service constituency, who could enjoy the neat coincidence of self- and public interest in their support of the party as members, sympathizers, or voters. More opportunistically than astutely, the Nazis alternated between a negative critique of the civil service, stressing its moral degradation and its subordination to a politically corrupt regime, and a positive imagery of reconstruction. The latter offered the possibility of a civil service dedicated to the Nazi ideal of the state as an institution designed to safeguard the creative labour of its citizens and to protect them from domestic and foreign exploitation. The forms of argument deployed in Nazi propaganda were consistent with the party's populism, with its stand against *Bonzen*, élites, and cliques of privileged insiders. In political discourse, they were the equivalent of the party's economic anti-capitalism, and contributed to that reformulation of the relationships between class and nation which had led the NSDAP to pivot its electoral strategy on the *Mittelstand*. This may have been a cynical electoral manœuvre, but it also recognized that this group represented a viable political space between the languages of class and of élite. However, the opening this offered was not simply the result of strategic choices by the NSDAP, but reflected the changes in German social structure and political discourse which had dispersed the reality of *Stand* without establishing an effective political response. It was in this sense that the *Mittelstand* was available for a peculiarly ideological appeal in the inter-war years—not so much as a genuinely pre-industrial 'survival', but as a social group previously excluded from the polarities of German political argument. The civil service, as we have seen, had

---

[73] The DBB entered a protest against the Prussian government's June 1930 decree on 29 July 1930, citing an administrative court decision of 1921 that simple membership of a political party did not constitute a disciplinary offence (GStA P 135/3157). The ADB, by contrast, pressed for stronger measures: see its communications to Brüning of 16 Jan. 1932 (BA R 43I/1650) and 18 Mar. 1932 (BA R 43I/2683). For a response on behalf of the BNSDJ, see R. Neubert, 'Beamtentum und Nationalsozialismus', *Deutsches Recht*, 1931, 77-86.

not been exempted from this interplay of social change and political stagnation. Shaky though the NSDAP's appeal may have been, it was sufficient in the crisis years of the early 1930s to attract civil servants into its widening political orbit.

5

Administration in the Nazi State: Reforms and Retreats 1933-1937

I

The efforts devoted by the NSDAP to capturing the civil-service vote were not matched by a comparable energy in cultivating contacts with influential figures in the administration or developing policies for a future Nazi government. Compared with the attention paid to economic issues and to industrialists' circles, for example, the administration was virtually ignored before 1933.[1] The NSDAP took little part in the widely debated issues of constitutional and administrative reform before 1933, and simply committed itself to 'the creation of a strong central state power for the Reich', as the 1920 programme put it. It is true that Hitler wanted Frick's spell as Thuringian interior minister in 1931 to serve as an experiment for a future national government, but such evidence as we have does not suggest that the party leadership undertook any systematic review of this experience or sponsored other serious planning for the future. Moreover, apart from the neglect of top administrators by the party's leadership, its own organizational structure and political style before 1933 offered little security for a systematic and coherent administrative policy after a Nazi take-over. Despite the party's propagandistic commitment to fundamental changes in the nature and purposes of rule, there was a massive gap between its pretensions and its preparations; as Dietrich Orlow has put it: 'The NSDAP was a means to power, not a test laboratory for a new society in miniature.'[2] The

---

[1] It is instructive that one of Göring's most sensitive civil-service appointments in Feb. 1933 was Ludwig Grauert, a lawyer who, as sometime head of a steel employers' association, was one of the NSDAP's contacts in industrialist circles (Grauert took over the police department in the Prussian interior ministry; some weeks later he was appointed state secretary); see K. D. Bracher, W. Sauer, and G. Schulz, *Die nationalsozialistische Machtergreifung* (Cologne and Opladen, 1962), 491.

[2] D. Orlow, *The History of the Nazi Party: 1919-1933* (Pittsburgh, 1969), 296. See also H. Mommsen, 'National Socialism: Continuity and Change', in W. Laqueur (ed.), *Fascism: A Reader's Guide* (Harmondsworth, 1976), 154-7; J. Nyomarkay, *Charisma and Factionalism in the Nazi Party* (Minneapolis, 1967); M. Broszat, 'Soziale Motivation und Führer-Bindung des Nationalsozialismus', *VjhZ*, 18/4 (1970), 398 ff.

pre-1933 party was an unstable combination of institutionalization and charisma, organization and indiscipline, polarized between the decentralized nature of party activity in the *Gaue*, and Hitler's unbounded leadership. Organizational developments in the years of rapid growth after 1930 were particularly suggestive of future Nazi standards and styles. Between 1930 and 1932 the NSDAP's bureaucratic and leadership apparatuses proliferated wildly as the party struggled to digest the influx of supporters and the shift in its political strategy. But the painstaking administrative reforms introduced by Gregor Strasser between June and September 1932 were a mere interlude, for in December, in the wake of Strasser's disgrace, Hitler demolished the structure he had established and returned the party to its fragmented hyperactivism—a move which augured ill for the fate of a future Nazi state.[3]

It is more than probable, therefore, that thinking about administrative reforms and civil-service policies under a future Nazi or coalition government was confined to that small group of senior civil servants attracted to the party in the early 1930s, many of whom had lost their jobs as the price of their allegiance to National Socialism. Evidence on these early connections and initiatives is fragmentary, and it is unclear whether any members of the party leadership itself—Frick would be the obvious candidate—were actively involved. But both of Frick's future state secretaries, Hans Pfundtner and Wilhelm Stuckart, were pre-1933 party members; their rather different experiences with the party before the seizure of power were doubtless due to their respective ages and social backgrounds. Stuckart, a judicial civil servant and son of a railway worker, had joined the NSDAP as a student in 1922. Although, following the NSDAP's dissolution in 1923, he had not rejoined until 1930, he worked actively with the party as an unpaid legal adviser, and resigned from his civil-service post in 1932, under threat of disciplinary action.[4] Twenty years his senior, Hans Pfundtner had already forfeited his civil-service post in 1919 by refusing to take the oath of loyalty. He applied to join the NSDAP in March 1932, the day after he left the DNVP; thereafter he solicited Göring, Goebbels, and Funk at various times to take advantage of his experience in the civil service and the fact that he was on the managing committee of the élite and far right National Club.[5] In June 1932, Pfundtner submitted

[3] Orlow, *History of the Nazi Party*, pp. 175-82, 187-209, 257-96; P. D. Stachura, *Gregor Strasser and the Rise of Nazism* (London, 1983), 67-73.

[4] BDC Stuckart.

[5] Documentation in BA R 18/5330 and 5331.

to Funk a set of proposals for a nationalist administrative reform programme, notable both for the casualness with which he was prepared to treat 'the so-called "vested rights of civil servants"', and for his call for a strenuous programme of administrative centralization.[6]

The rebuffs Pfundtner received to his repeated and obsequious solicitations of party patronage were probably not untypical of the experience of other senior officials who shared his age and background. These men were of no interest to a party leadership which put a premium on active engagement and which had no wish to be publicly associated with such egregious archetypes of the old Germany. Thus Hans Heinrich Lammers, a *Ministerialrat* in the interior ministry and a colleague of Pfundtner's in the National Club, cut no more ice than Pfundtner as a self-appointed contact man to the senior bureaucracy.[7] Not dissimilar was the experience of the two heads of the NSDAP's own Innenpolitische Abteilung (department for home affairs), a rudimentary planning office established in the Munich Reichsleitung in 1931, and staffed by six mainly voluntary officials. Though the existence of the department testifies to a certain party interest in political planning, neither Helmut Nicolai nor Ernst von Heydebrand und der Lasa (nephew of the conservative politician) seem to have been highly regarded in party circles. Both were nationalist civil servants of the old school, born respectively in 1895 and 1884, whose political activities had temporarily cost them their jobs in the early 1930s, and who worked on a semi-voluntary basis for the Reichsleitung. Helmut Brückner, the *Gauleiter* of Silesia, doubted Nicolai's suitability for party membership, describing him in 1931 as too much the intellectual and corps student; later, Gauleiter Loeper, with whom Nicolai was sent to work in 1933 as a *Regierungspräsident*, damned him as 'nothing more than an arrogant bureaucrat who lacks the slightest understanding of the inner meaning of National Socialism'.[8] Nicolai and von Heydebrand produced a series of detailed proposals for administrative reform, intended to fulfil the party's programmatic commitment to a strong central state. At the time, these schemes appeared marginal to the drive for political power, and Nicolai

---

[6] Memo, 'Vorschläge für Verwaltungsmassnahmen einer nationalen Regierung im Reich und Preussen', in R 18/5314; reprinted in H. Mommsen, *Beamtentum im Dritten Reich* (Stuttgart, 1966), 128-35, and see also p. 29; also Bracher, Sauer, and Schulz, *Machtergreifung*, pp. 409-10.

[7] Ibid. 409.

[8] List of personnel of department, 3 Aug. 1932, and personal information on Nicolai and the department, in BDC Nicolai; see also Bracher, Sauer, and Schulz, *Machtergreifung*, pp. 411-12.

was trying to get out of the department at the end of 1932. In 1933, these men and their schemes were to fill the vacuum left by the party leadership's failure to prepare more actively for the take-over and reconstruction of the German state—but with an aura that they were external to the real purposes of National Socialism as such.

In this context, Wilhelm Frick, who was appointed Reich interior minister on 30 January 1933, was an outsider in the Nazi movement, and it was something of an anomaly that he managed to find and maintain the place he occupied among the party cadres. Born into a middle-class family in 1877, Frick had undergone the usual training for the senior administrative civil service, and had spent most of his career in the Bavarian police administration until his complicity in the Munich *putsch* forced his resignation. He then made a second career as a Reichstag deputy and was the only Nazi member of the January 1933 cabinet to have had prior government experience. Albert Krebs, the Hamburg *Gauleiter* who was expelled from the party in 1932, described him as a 'free conservative' in the nineteenth-century sense, whose 'ideological purity' was less dependable than 'his obedience and fulfilment of duty'; he was generally known in more revolutionary party circles under the sobriquet 'the Royal Bavarian Nazi'.[9] More a civil servant than a politician, Frick had nevertheless contrived to impress Hitler with his devotion to National Socialism,[10] and was a committed if not compelling propagandist for the party before 1933. No doubt it was more than this mutual bond with Hitler that led first to Frick's appointment as the NSDAP's Reichstag fraction leader, and then, in January 1933, as Reich interior minister. Rather, in both capacities, Frick's standing as an old-school civil servant was of tactical service to the party, a token of its respectability—but one which did not apparently need to be duplicated.

Frick's position as Reich interior minister was to be crucial in determining the shape of the administrative and civil-service policies of the Nazi regime when the interior ministry itself underwent a radical transformation. In the Weimar Republic and earlier, the bulk of administrative work was the responsibility of the *Länder* administrations, of course, not of direct Reich agencies.[11] The Reich interior ministry's

[9] W. S. Allen (ed.), *The Infancy of Nazism: The Memoirs of ex-Gauleiter Krebs 1923-1933.* (New York, 1976), 259-62.

[10] F. Dickmann, 'Die Regierungsbildung in Thüringen als Modell der Machtergreifung: Ein Brief Hitlers aus dem Jahre 1930', *VjhZ*, 14 (1966), 461.

[11] See H. Jacob, *German Administration since Bismarck: Central Authority versus Local Autonomy* (New Haven and London, 1963), chs. 3 and 4; F. Medicus, *Das Reichsministerium des Innern* (Berlin, 1940), ch. 2.

supervisory authority extended across the fields of constitutional, administrative, and civil-service affairs, together with some aspects of health, welfare, and education, but it had no field administration of its own. In other words, in the interior as in other policy areas, the federal structure of the Weimar Constitution mandated the separation of legislative and administrative activities, and a system of executive delegation. As we have seen, this hybrid of federalism and centralism was found to be profoundly unsatisfactory in many ways, not least because it was fragmented, uncoordinated, and wasteful of personnel and resources. The republic had inherited a system under severe strain, and not all the reform schemes of the 1920s had been anti-democratic in spirit. However, Weimar's reformist aspirations had been defeated by particularism and political instability. The worsening political situation after 1930 gave a tremendous stimulus to conservative centralizing impulses, both political and administrative, the clearest example being the coup against Prussia in July 1932. By 1933, the linkage of defederalization and deparliamentarization had already been clearly established.

The National Socialist government thus drew on existing currents and models of structural reform for the process of political and constitutional *Gleichschaltung* it sponsored after 1933. The combination of political necessity, programmatic commitment, and vast inexperience within the NSDAP leadership itself meant that wide responsibilities now devolved on the main Reich and Prussian ministries, with their staffs of trained bureaucrats. In other words, although the NSDAP leadership had not cultivated the senior bureaucracy or studied the issues, it was now heavily dependent on them and on the few men in its own ranks who straddled both worlds. This was to be true not only of the first stages of the seizure of power, for among the main priorities of the senior bureaucracy after 1933 was the retention of a professionally trained and vocationally committed civil service. The development of strategies for constitutional and administrative reform (*Reichsreform* and *Verwaltungsreform*) was thus accompanied after 1933 by policies designed to reproduce the *Berufsbeamtentum* and to bolster the authority of its élite; and one important reason for the abandonment of these larger reforms by the political leadership was the reliance on the ministerial bureaucracy they enforced.

The most ambitious of these strategies were developed in the interior ministry, and by some other experienced administrators, such as the Prussian finance minister, Popitz, or the Reich finance minister,

Krosigk.[12] While aiming to secure his ministry's leadership, Frick acted as the channel by which experts and ideas that had failed to make headway under the republic came to influence the wayward process of state formation under National Socialism. The reform programme sponsored in the interior ministry after 1933 had four principal elements. First, the parliamentary system was to be abolished at national, *Land*, and local level, so that democratically elected assemblies and accountable executives were excluded from the political process. Secondly, a unitary state was to replace the federal system of the Weimar and Bismarckian constitutions, a process which would involve abolishing the sovereignty and independent authority of the *Länder*, subordinating them to the Reich government, and incorporating their administrative apparatuses with that of the Reich. Thirdly, the majority of the field administrative apparatuses were to be concentrated by incorporation in the machinery of the Reich interior administration, giving it not only its own field system for the first time, but an extensive and powerful network of agencies. The purpose of this was to combat the tendency towards the fragmentation of administration at the intermediate level, or *Mittelinstanz* (i.e. the *Länder*, and below them, the *Regierungen* or districts), by constructing a single coherent and coordinated administrative machinery under the supervision of one Reich ministry. This would deliver a huge accretion of power to the interior ministry. In place of a series of separate field apparatuses attached hierarchically to the specialist ministries, the interior ministry aimed to establish a single administrative structure under its own control. Finally, administration was to be decentralized and executive powers were to be delegated to subordinate agencies, so that the Reich authorities would set the broad lines of policy and supervise their implementation, but would not be directly involved in their execution.

This set of interlocked objectives was not in itself incompatible with the more propagandist conception of national political unity espoused by the Nazi party leadership, but there were two crucial points of divergence in its further implications. In the first place, given the provenance of this programme, it assumed a central role for the state bureaucracy as initiators, supervisors, and executors of administrative government; conversely, the potentially problematic role of the Nazi

[12] The outstanding source for these policies remains Bracher, Sauer, and Schulz, *Machtergreifung*. See also M. Broszat, *The Hitler State* (London, 1981); E. Peterson, *The Limits of Hitler's Power* (Princeton, 1969); P. Diehl-Thiele, *Partei und Staat im Dritten Reich: Untersuchungen zum Verhältnis von NSDAP und allgemeiner und innerer Staatsverwaltung* (Munich, 1966); and Mommsen, *Beamtentum*.

party in government and administration was not fully explored. Secondly, it was conceived initially as a systematic programme of reform; one of Nicolai's early drafts outlined it as a series of stages which would culminate in the promulgation of a new constitution.[13] But the course of the Nazi seizure of power quickly made it clear that neither of these assumptions was reliable. Far from being a smooth transition to a centralized administrative state, the Nazi take-over proved to be an unstable and multifaceted political struggle which reached no fixed or final resolution.

In spite of this, however, the main elements of the reform project were never abandoned by Frick. Rather, he continued to act as if he were working towards his ultimate objective, a centralized and concentrated administration in which his ministry would play the pivotal role; as part of this, he insisted on his overriding authority in civil-service matters as *Beamtenminister*. Thus, the civil-service policies of the 1930s were shaped as much by Frick's unrenounced ambitions as by the political interventionism of a party power structure that remained relatively autonomous from the state. Frick himself was increasingly caught in his fractured status as the Nazi minister who had most in common with the bureaucratic élite. He was clearly seen by such nominal party colleagues as Hess, Bormann, Goebbels, and Hitler himself as the source of a bureaucratic deformation of the Nazi regime; yet, though he found himself defending the fragile status of the professional civil service, he was also unable to gain the respect or practical support of colleagues from outside his own ministry.

II

The conflict between long-term planning and improvisational opportunism was only one of the fault lines that ran through the Nazi regime from its earliest weeks. Equally early to surface were conflicts between centre and periphery, between the institutions of leadership and of execution, and, more generally, among the plurality of government institutions, as it became clear that collegial and hierarchical structures of decision-making were breaking down and collapsing into their atomic parts. The complexity of these multiple structural frictions is obscured if they are reduced to the single dualism of party and state, for

13 Undated general plan for constitutional reform [1933] (copy in R 18/5439).

important though this division obviously was, it was also overdetermined by the others. True, the party-state contrast was inevitably experienced as overriding in the early months of the regime, for National Socialism was bound to be seen as external and posterior to the state, as a force that, by the take-over of power, assaulted and overwhelmed existing institutions. Yet the precise demarcations between party and state quickly became unclear, the more so in that the political impulse to develop a coherent strategy of take-over or reconstruction was not sustained by the regime as a whole. Party and state did exist as real dual or parallel institutions, and the issue of their interrelation was critical for the self-representation of the regime. But the concept also offered a pliable metaphor for conflicts whose origins lay elsewhere within the proliferating institutional structures and ideological contradictions of the 'Third Reich', and which were not comprehended by the limited contrast of the dualist model.

In the spring of 1933, however, the seizure of power pre-eminently involved the monopolization by the National Socialist party of the political and administrative institutions of the state, as well as the destruction of political and social opposition. In a process parallel to the subjugation of the democratically elected assemblies, Nazi activists moved to gain control over the apparatuses of national, regional, and local administration by expelling known opponents and other unsympathetic civil servants from office, and by securing the appointment of politically reliable alternatives. Mixed in with this, and mocking the party's own virulent critique of alleged Weimar standards, was a spoils system for 'deserving' party members, usually in inferior civil-service posts. These pressures frequently met resistance from civil servants dismayed at the violation of normal procedures, whatever their own political proclivities. And increasingly, as the Nazi regime tightened its grip after the March elections, the issue of central control—a problem for the party as well as for the state—became uppermost. *Gleichschaltung* and *Reichsreform* were thus the context of the new regime's civil-service policy.

In his Sportpalast speech of 10 February, Hitler called for 'the re-establishment of integrity among our people, integrity in every sphere of life, integrity in our administration, integrity in public life'.[14] For the civil service, this announced the beginning of the purge long promised in the Nazi party's propaganda. Where the new rulers had the power—in Prussia and in some of the Reich ministries, for example—immediate

14 *Das Archiv*, 1933, i. 99.

use had been made of the statutory right to suspend 'political' civil servants (a category which included such crucial posts as state secretary, *Oberpräsident, Polizeipräsident, Regierungspräsident*, and *Landrat*), and to replace them with more acceptable appointees, who legally did not need to be professionally qualified civil servants. Thus, Lammers succeeded Planck as head of the Reich chancellery on 30 January; Pfundtner replaced Zweigert as interior-ministry state secretary at the beginning of February; and a number of other ministries also received new state secretaries.[15] Similarly, by mid-February, Göring, the new Prussian minister-president, had replaced twelve Prussian *Polizeipräsidenten* and six other leading provincial officials; before the end of March, a total of seventy-one Prussian political personnel had been replaced—and this was on top of the purge already carried out by Bracht after the Papen coup.[16] By now, the political situation had shifted further towards the Nazis' advantage in Germany as a whole, following the national, *Land*, and local elections (outside Prussia, local elections were not held, but seats were redistributed in proportion to the Reichstag vote). The lawlessness which had already characterized many actions by party members and SA men against unpopular local and municipal officials intensified. Throughout Germany, mayors and other city officials were forced out of office by various forms of pressure, threat, and terror, and sometimes by literal physical expulsion or arrest; often, taking up Hitler's demand for 'integrity', allegations of corruption were added in justification. Discipline in the civil service threatened to break down as denunciations, allegations, and petitions multiplied.[17] By May, some seventy *Oberbürgermeister* and over 500 leading municipal officials had been ousted, with the larger cities being especially hard hit.[18] The elections on 5 March also ushered in the political subjugation of those *Länder* not already under Nazi control, a process again accompanied by forced personnel changes as newly appointed 'special commissioners' took over from the local police authorities.[19] In Bavaria, where Held refused to resign, von Epp

[15] Ibid. 11, 126.

[16] Ibid. 112; W. Runge, *Politik und Beamtentum im Parteienstaat* (Stuttgart, 1965), 327-49; see also Bracher, Sauer, and Schulz, *Machtergreifung*, pp. 490-1.

[17] The Prussian government, for example, made repeated attempts to control these: see its instructions of 28 Feb., 16 Mar., 28 Apr., 22 June, 3 and 20 July (*MBliV*, 1933, 257, 282, 510, 731, 803, 860).

[18] H. Matzerath, *Nationalsozialismus und kommunale Selbstverwaltung* (Stuttgart, Berlin, Cologne, and Mainz, 1970), 80-1; Bracher, Sauer, and Schulz, *Machtergreifung*, p. 446.

[19] Broszat, *The Hitler State*, pp. 96-104; Bracher, Sauer, and Schulz, *Machtergreifung*, pp. 460 ff.

became the first commissioner to take over a *Land* government, the forerunner of the *Reichsstatthalter* who were to be appointed throughout Germany at the beginning of April. In a meeting with leading officials on 12 March, von Epp and his commissioners tried to calm the nerves of the civil service, with his new interior minister, Wagner, expressing the hope that although 'in 1918 it was hard for you as state officials to adjust to the new circumstances, at the very least I anticipate that it has been somewhat easier for you to come to terms with the present situation'. Regierungspräsident Röhmer may then have spoken for his colleagues when he commented that: 'The interior administration's attitude to the new revolution is quite different from . . . that of 1918, which was greeted only with gnashing of teeth.'[20]

The pseudo-legitimacy of the Nazi take-over of power was obviously an important factor in generating support for the new government among senior civil servants, and their work then contributed to its further legitimation. Following Hitler's repeated insistence, from mid-March, that the national revolution must now be pursued in an orderly fashion under central direction, the Reich interior ministry began to develop policies intended to accomplish just that.[21] Central to these were measures intended to tighten both Nazi and Reich control over the state apparatuses of the Reich and *Länder*. Although the Enabling Act of 23 March and the first Law for the Co-ordination of the *Länder* with the Reich of 31 March both appeared to recognize *Länder* sovereignty, they were followed within a week by the first steps towards the abolition of *Länder* independence. On 7 April, the second co-ordination law mandated the appointment of ten Reich commissioners (*Reichsstatthalter*) for the *Länder*.[22] Appointed by the president on the chancellor's nomination, the *Reichsstatthalter* fulfilled a double function. They advanced the movement towards executive control by substituting for

---

[20] O. Domröse, *Der NS-Staat in Bayern von der Machtergreifung bis zum Röhm-Putsch* (Munich, 1974), 90-2; also circular of Bavarian interior minister, 17 Mar. 1933 (BA SS 374). See also P. Sauer, *Württemberg in der Zeit des Nationalsozialismus* (Ulm, 1975), 67.

[21] For Hitler's appeal on 10 Mar., see Bracher, Sauer, and Schulz, *Machtergreifung*, p. 468; for his speech on 24 Apr., *Das Archiv*, 1933, p. 274. For repeated references by Göring to the fact that the 'national revolution' was over, see e.g. *MBliV*, 1933, 533 and 649 (decrees of 6 and 29 May); and see Reich interior-ministry instructions, 10 July 1933, reiterating this (copy in BA R 43II/1263).

[22] *2. Gesetz zur Gleichschaltung der Länder mit dem Reich*, 7 Apr. 1933 (*RGBl*, 1933, i. 173). Some of the smaller *Länder* were amalgamated for this purpose; in Prussia, the chancellor took on the office, but its rights were exercised by Göring, who added them to his existing powers as minister-president and interior minister; Broszat, *The Hitler State*, pp. 106-12.

the *Land* governments, and, with their mandate to 'ensure compliance with the principles of policy established by the Reich chancellor', they initiated the constitutional subordination of the *Länder* to the Reich. On top of this, since all but one of them were NSDAP *Gauleiter*, they also represented a significant step towards the integration of the party in the structure of government.

The same day saw the promulgation of the regime's first item of civil-service legislation, the Law for the Restoration of a Professional Civil Service (BBG).[23] For Frick and others, the reform of civil-service law, on both an emergency and a longer-term basis, was a major priority. Preparations for a measure enabling the government to dismiss civil servants irrespective of tenure, which had been in hand by the last week of March, had been brought to a swift conclusion by the Reich interior ministry.[24] The most notorious of the powers created by the BBG empowered the government to dismiss politically and racially undesirable officials from the public service, but the law was more than a mechanism for a political purge. In the first place, its speedy adoption signalled the determination of the Reich interior ministry, supported by the cabinet, to recover and extend central authority over personnel decisions in the civil service, threatened as they were by the unregulated intervention of local party activists.[25] Secondly, the drafts of the law, as well as commentaries on the final version, make it clear that one of its aims was to permit another round of administrative retrenchment on the model of the 1923 PAV.[26] In his Reichstag speech on 23 March, Hitler had called for 'the devoted loyalty and work of the professional civil service', and promised that 'there will be no interventions except where the state of the public finances compels it, and then only with the strict proviso of absolute fairness'.[27] The available options for financial

[23] *Gesetz zur Wiederherstellung des Berufsbeamtentums*, 7 Apr. 1933 (*RGBl*, 1933, i. 175).

[24] The preparation of such a measure was agreed at the cabinet meeting on 24 Mar. 1933, the day after the adoption of the Enabling Act (minutes in BA R 43I/1460). Details in Mommsen, *Beamtentum*, pp. 39-61; see also Broszat, *The Hitler State*, pp. 244-5; Peterson, *Limits of Hitler's Power*, pp. 88-90; Bracher, Sauer, and Schulz, *Machtergreifung*, pp. 496-509.

[25] The NSDAP Reichsleitung had issued instructions on 14 Mar. that personnel proposals must be submitted to the Reich authorities through the local *Gauleitung* (reprinted as Prussian interior-ministry circular, 16 Mar., *MBliV*, 1933, 282).

[26] This was generally admitted at the time, e.g. by Hanns Seel, the interior-ministry official in charge of work on the BBG, in 'Das Beamtenrecht des Dritten Reiches', in H. Frank (ed.), *Deutsches Verwaltungsrecht* (Munich, 1937), 156-7; and by Pfundtner, in his radio speech on the law, reported in the *Frankfurter Zeitung*, 13 Apr. 1933.

[27] *DRA*, 71, 24 Mar. 1933.

savings were either a further turn of Brüning's salary screw, for which there was no enthusiasm in the cabinet,[28] or some move to reduce costs by cutting staff. Two of the BBG's clauses, therefore, created powers that overrode existing tenure protection, permitting summary transfer to other posts (§5) and compulsory retirement in the interests of administrative simplification (§6).[29] As we shall see, these clauses were also the first steps in a broader programme of civil-service law reform.

The other major powers created by the law were blatantly political and racist, facilitating a full-scale purge of the public service. Successive clauses enforced the dismissal without pension of 'unqualified' officials, i.e. anyone who did not have 'the prescribed or usual training, or other qualifications [*sonstige Eignung*]' (§2), and the dismissal with reduced pension of those 'whose previous political behaviour affords no guarantee that they will give permanent and unconditional support to the national state' (§4). Subsequent amendments added the following powers: §6(1) permitted honourable retirement in the interests of administrative convenience, without specifying that vacated posts could not be refilled;[30] §2(a) belatedly regularized the legally dubious dismissal of Communists under §2;[31] and §4(2) retrospectively applied the provisions of §4 to civil servants who had already retired before the promulgation of the BBG.[32]

These were powers of unprecedented scope. In a single powerful instrument, they combined, perverted, and enormously extended the scattered and far less effective equipment with which republican

---

[28] Papen had already rejected this; see cabinet minutes, 18 Nov. 1932 (BA R 43I/1458-9). In July, it was again agreed that further salary cuts were not advisable (cabinet minutes, 14 July 1933, BA R 43I/1464).

[29] Under §5(2), civil servants could request retirement instead of transfer; posts vacated under §6 could not be refilled. §5 borrowed directly from the PAV, while §6 extended the somewhat unspecific provisions of §24 RBG.

[30] *Gesetz zur Änderung des BBG*, 23 June 1933 (*RGBl*, 1933, i. 389). This provision took account of cases where §§2-4 were inapplicable, and §§5 and 6 inadequate.

[31] *Gesetz zur Ergänzung des BBG*, 20 July 1933 (*RGBl*, 1933, i. 518). This was necessitated by the lack of any legal authority for the interpretation that Communists were to be automatically regarded as 'unqualified' under the terms of the original §2 (which had been applied in preference to §4 because its terms were more severe); see the first DVO, 11 Apr. 1933 (*RGBl*, 1933, i. 195), and Mommsen, *Beamtentum*, pp. 47-8. On 8 Mar., the Reich interior ministry had already asked for the names of all civil servants arrested for communist activity in order to initiate disciplinary actions: 'Civil servants active on behalf of Communism can in my opinion no longer be allowed to remain in the Reich service' (GStA Rep. 90/2326).

[32] *3. Gesetz zur Änderung des BBG*, 22 Sept. 1933 (*RGBl*, 1933, i. 655). §§5, 9(3), 10(1), 11, and 12 were also retrospective; see R. Echterhölter, *Das öffentliche Recht im nationalsozialistischen Staat* (Stuttgart, 1970), 44-5.

governments in the Reich and the *Länder* had at various times tried to reduce administrative expenditure, democratize appointments, and defend the civil service from subversion. Clauses 2-4 enacted the NSDAP's long-stated commitment to purge the civil service of 'non-Aryans', political enemies, and persons without formal qualification, a term which in the Nazi vocabulary was synonymous with republican party appointees. On the other hand, §§5 and 6 imitated legislation which the party had equally strenuously criticized before 1933, but created powers which senior bureaucrats had long sought. The law's claim to 'restore the professional civil service' was thus somewhat double-edged, and something of an effort was devoted to justifying it in public. Pfundtner was deputed to explain the act in a radio broadcast, in which he argued that a 'ruthless purge' was necessary to rid the civil service of persons who had brought it into disrepute.[33] Sanctimoniously recasting his privately cynical disregard for civil servants' rights, he told his audience that the law was to create a civil service 'that in spirit is not primarily concerned about material advantage but, as once before, sees unremitting self-sacrifice in the performance of its duties as its highest purpose, and proves itself worthy of the national trust that is given into its hands'.

Mainly because the law was recognized as encroaching severely on civil servants' rights, its validity was limited to six months, after which existing civil-service law was to come back into force.[34] However, this brief duration proved inadequate, for two reasons. It soon became clear that the amount of work the purge involved had been underestimated, and, moreover, that the additional powers the law created could not be dispensed with immediately. Hitler had expected six months to be too little, in view of the fact that the same process in Italy had lasted two years, and his warning was accurate.[35] The law applied to the Reich, *Länder*, local authorities, and public corporations, and affected the entire corps of public officials, including *Angestellte* and *Arbeiter* as well as *Beamte*, together with retired and suspended officials, and, to some extent, the dependants of deceased officials—equivalent to millions

[33] See n. 26 above. See also *NSBZ*, 20 May 1933; Göring's speech to the Prussian Landtag (*DRA*, 19 May 1933); Goebbels in *Der Angriff*, 18 July 1933.

[34] See Frick's comments to a meeting of ministers, 27 Apr. 1933 (minute in BA R 43II/423a; (reprinted in Mommsen, *Beamtentum*, pp. 159-60).

[35] Hitler's view reported by Göring in ministerial conference of 25/6 Apr. 1933 (minute in GStA Rep. 318/882); see also Prussian cabinet meeting, 5 May 1933 (minute in GStA P 134/6334); and also Mommsen, *Beamtentum*, pp. 44, 52-3. The purge of the Austrian civil service after the *Anschluss* also took longer than foreseen; see Seyss-Inquart to Reich chancellery, 17 Dec. 1938, and subsequent documentation in BA R 43II/423.

of cases, all of which had to be individually scrutinized.[36] The investigation and attestation of racial origins and political background involved extensive research at great cost in time and money; the licensing of exemptions from the basic stipulations was also very time-consuming.[37] 'Non-Aryan' *Frontkämpfer*, for instance, were exempt from the racial provisions, as also were 'non-Aryans' whose fathers or sons had been killed at the front; similarly, §2 was not supposed to be rigidly enforced against persons deemed to have had a genuine change of heart. In such cases, a bureaucratic process had to decide what constituted service at the front, or how sincerity was to be adjudicated. Additionally, there were complex provisions to mitigate the law's financial effects in cases of hardship, plus a general stipulation—demanded by Hitler—that the law should not be too harshly applied, partly in order to protect Germany's reputation abroad, but mainly in order to avoid excessive unrest among those affected.[38] Quite apart from the casework that engulfed local offices, a heavy burden fell on the Reich ministries, to which final decisions were reserved. This was an important provision of the law, in that it offered a safeguard against local or unofficial pressures which would be damaging to central authority as well as to the morale of civil servants. Amending laws in 1934, therefore, allowed for unfinished cases to be withdrawn or revised in favour of a civil servant as long as the decision had become pending by 30 September 1934.[39]

Given the amount of work involved, it was something of an achievement that the process of initiating cases under §§2-4 was achieved more or less on time. Although no authoritative comprehensive analysis of the law's effects exists, the Reich interior ministry conducted an inquiry in November 1933, and some of these records have survived, along with other fragmentary figures.[40] The great variations they reveal in the effects of the law were due largely to the employment practices of the different administrations. The Reich finance ministry reported that

[36] The discussion here is confined to *Beamte* alone.

[37] The work involved in the local implementation of the BBG is discussed in K. Teppe, *Provinz, Partei, Staat: Zur provinziellen Selbstverwaltung im Dritten Reich untersucht am Beispiel Westfalens* (Münster, 1977), 36-52.

[38] Reported by Göring; on the other hand, Hitler insisted on a strict application of the racial clause; see n. 35 above.

[39] Law of 22 Mar. 1934 (*RGBl*, 1934, i. 203); the amending law of 26 Sept. 1934 (*RGBl*, 1934, i. 845) extended the validity of §§5 and 6 *sine die*, until the issue of the new civil-service code. Note that the BBG expressly excluded legal appeals against retirement, dismissal, or transfer (§7).

[40] The effects are discussed in Mommsen, *Beamtentum*, pp. 53-61.

1,312 civil servants in its jurisdiction had been retired or dismissed, and 108 transferred, with 501 cases still pending; completed cases represented about 2 per cent of the staff investigated.[41] The Prussian judicial administration was more heavily affected, with 1,432 officials dismissed or retired—three-quarters of them on racial grounds—272 transfers, and 100 undecided cases; here, completed cases came to 3.6 per cent of the total staff.[42] In June 1934, the *Völkischer Beobachter* reported that 212 of the 1,513 higher civil servants of the labour administration had been dismissed or retired: at 14 per cent, this reflects the fact that the labour administration was a republican creation, staffed more heavily with 'outsiders' than the older branches. In the Prussian police administration, where Daluege claimed to have applied the strictest criteria, dismissals and retirements in the eleven categories surveyed averaged 7.7 per cent.[43] According to a 1937 statistical breakdown for the interior administration, of the 1,663 senior civil servants in the Prussian interior administration, 211 (12.5 per cent) were 'dealt with' (*behandelt*) under §§2-4, and 258 (15.5 per cent) under §§5 and 6. The numbers affected in the non-Prussian *Länder* were a good deal lower: of the total of 2,339 senior civil servants, 106 (4.5 per cent) were affected by §§2-4, and 143 (5 per cent) by §§5 and 6. For the remaining grades of the civil service, 1.13 per cent were affected by §§2-4, and 2.33 per cent by §§5 and 6 in Prussia; the comparable figures for the other *Länder* were 1.79 and 3.72 per cent.[44] The discrepancies between Prussia and other *Länder* were probably due not only to the effects of Prussia's republican appointments policy, but also to the closer influence exercised by the Reich in Prussia.

Altogether, the purge itself directly affected about 1 to 2 per cent of the professional civil service, though its indirect effects were certainly more widespread.[45] Standards doubtless varied widely, as the figures already discussed suggest, though Jewish officials, known Communists,

[41] Lists sent by the finance ministry to the interior ministry, 2 Dec. 1933 (BA R 2/22559).
[42] Prussian justice-ministry report to Prussian interior ministry, 30 Nov. 1933 (BA P 135/6334). For the background and effects of the racial clause, see U. D. Adam, *Judenpolitik im Dritten Reich* (Düsseldorf, 1979), 51-71, and K. A. Schleunes, *The Twisted Road to Auschwitz: Nazi Policy towards German Jews 1933-1939* (Urbana, Chicago, and London, 1979), 105-9.
[43] Daluege to Hitler, 3 Feb. 1934 (R 43I/2290).
[44] E. Schütze, 'Beamtenpolitik im Dritten Reich', in H. Pfundtner (ed.), *Dr. Wilhelm Frick und sein Ministerium* (Berlin, 1937), 51.
[45] An unauthenticated statement by Herman Neef in 1937 put the totals dismissed under §§2 and 4 at 5,433, and under §3 at 1,984, or 0.7 per cent of the total civil service; *NSBZ*, 31 Oct. 1937, 555-6.

social democrats, and Centre party members or sympathizers, were the most common victims. A close study of the Munich city administration shows that the authorities recommended far more penalties than were eventually confirmed, and set extremely stringent criteria for judgement and mitigation. Denunciations were rife; attempts were made to settle old political scores on the flimsiest of evidence; and there was extensive cross-use of clauses in order to ensure dismissals or to exact the most severe penalty available.[46] Although two-thirds of the city's proposals were turned down, practices such as these must have confirmed the Reich government's worst fears about the effect of the purge on civil servants' morale, and encouraged its efforts at mitigation. Moreover, there were complaints that both the political and administrative clauses were being used against civil servants associated with the NSDAP's coalition partners, and even to get rid of some party members (presumably on administrative grounds).[47]

However, although §§2–4 went out of force in September 1933, and brought the acute phase of the purge itself to an end, the clauses that were more generally administrative in intent (§§5 and 6, as amended) were repeatedly extended, ultimately until January 1937.[48] The unexpectedly long life of these clauses resulted not from misjudgements about the time it would take to implement them, but from the derailing of expectations about the speed of civil-service law reform. In some ways, it was disingenuous for ministry spokesmen to proclaim that the BBG was only a temporary measure pending the 'restitution' of existing law, for it is clear that the Reich interior and finance ministries were planning an extended programme of law reform, to which the BBG was only a preliminary. Though the overtly political clauses of the BBG were intended to administer a short sharp shock, the administrative clauses were the first move towards transforming the shape of civil-service law by achieving the comprehensive reform that had eluded

[46] H. M. Hanko, 'Kommunalpolitik in der "Hauptstadt der Bewegung" 1933-1935: Zwischen "revolutionärer" Umgestaltung und Verwaltungskontinuität', in M. Broszat *et al.* (eds.), *Bayern in der NS-Zeit*, iii. *Herrschaft und Gesellschaft im Konflikt* (Munich and Vienna, 1981), 370-402 (Hanko's evidence shows that 3.5 per cent of *Arbeiter* eventually lost their jobs, compared with 1 per cent of *Beamte*); Mommsen, *Beamtentum*, p. 55, briefly discusses the application of the BBG in Hamburg; and see also H. Dimpker, *Die 'Wiederherstellung des Berufsbeamtentums': Nationalsozialistische Personalpolitik in Lübeck* (Kiel, 1981).

[47] See interior-ministry circulars in response, 1 Aug. 1933, 2 Feb. 1934 (both BA R 43II/447; the first is reprinted in Mommsen, *Beamtentum*, pp. 166-7), and 11 May 1936 (BA R 43II/426; reprinted in ibid. 68); see also n. 53 below.

[48] 6th amending law, 26 Sept. 1934 (*RGBl*, 1933, i. 845), Art. 1 (2).

Weimar governments. As such, they drew on ideas and drafts which had previously been circulating ineffectively in the ministries, and which now found a home in the early legislative enactments of the new regime.

During the drafting of the law, the Prussian finance minister, Popitz, had proposed that the government simply equip itself with 'a general power of dismissal', a suggestion which reflected his fiscal and administrative interest in the weakening of tenure rights.[49] Although this course had not been followed, on the grounds that it would cause more unrest than the enumeration of specific grounds for dismissal, the amendment to §6 adopted in June 1933 in effect created such a power. The clause now had a somewhat hybrid quality, for what had prompted the amendment was the need for powers to get rid of certain categories of politically unwelcome local officials (notably *Bürgermeister*) in cases where none of the BBG's other clauses sufficed.[50] In any case, it was the administrative clauses of the law that were resorted to for political purposes when the overtly political clauses could not be used for any reason. This cross-use of clauses—and it worked in reverse, too, to mitigate as well as to sharpen the law's operation—makes it difficult to distinguish entirely between the BBG's political and administrative applications.[51] Almost all of the available evidence shows that cases under §§5 and 6 were by far the most numerous category, often totalling more than the combined number of cases under the remaining clauses. Whether this use of administrative powers disguised a political content almost certainly varied among the different branches of the administration. For example, the §6 cases in Munich were allegedly entirely political,[52] while, conversely, it is certain that the financial and postal administrations made use of the BBG to streamline their large staffs. Thus, the postal administration had disposed of about 5,400 *Beamte* under §6 by 1934;[53] and a similar breakdown of 503 cases in the

[49] Mommsen, *Beamtentum*, p. 42.

[50] *Regierungspräsident* in Münster to Grauert, 3 May 1933, and Grauert to Reich chancellery, 5 May (GStA Rep. 77/10); also minute of Prussian cabinet meeting, 5 May 1933 (GStA Rep. 90—Sitzungsprotokolle); *Begründung* to draft of the June law, 20 May 1934 (copy in BA R 43II/423); and Matzerath, *Nationalsozialismus*, pp. 74-5.

[51] See examples among 189 cases compiled in the Prussian interior ministry (GStA Rep. 77/3221-31); also cases in the tax administration (see n. 54 below).

[52] Hanko, 'Kommunalpolitik', pp. 394-5, argues this, but gives few details.

[53] Ministerial discussion, 23 Feb. 1934 (BA R 2/22014). The ambiguous nature of §6 is underscored by the fact that Bormann reached (belated) agreement with the interior ministry in Jan. 1937 that it was not to be applied to civil servants who had joined the party before 1933; StdF circular 4/37, 9 Jan. 1937 (BA NS 6/vorl. 225).

lower ranks of the tax administration shows that 326 decisions were taken under §6 and 42 under §5, against only 36 under the political clauses.[54] Of the §6 cases, 145 represented the final push given to *Wartestandsbeamte* who had remained on the books since the PAV;[55] and most of the other 181 officials who were retired were allegedly too old, too ill, or too incompetent to be of further service. Clearly, the larger departments found the BBG useful as a means of improving the quality of their otherwise immobile staffs.

The hybrid character of the BBG, as both a cynical political purge and an act of administrative renewal, enacted a pattern of mixed intentions that was to become characteristic of civil-service policy in Nazi Germany. At this stage, however, it is clear that there was a considerable identity of interests among those responsible for the legislation; indeed, the majority of its guiding hands in the cabinet were men with a civil-service background or of nationalist persuasion.[56] Pfundtner and Seel, the interior-ministry officials who piloted the law through the drafting process, saw it as an integral measure of political and administrative reform, which demanded an attack on tenure in defiance of existing law and the vested rights of civil servants.[57] For all of these men, the alleged politicization of the civil service under Weimar required a political solution, and they saw no contradiction in the law's claim to 'restore the civil service' by purging its ranks. On the other side, Hitler, and Göring too, were evidently concerned for pragmatic reasons to minimize the disruptive effects of the law, whether by limiting its duration or by interpreting its application generously in certain cases. Thus, the initial purge of the civil service by the National Socialist regime bore the marks of its origins in a coalition of Nazi, nationalist, and bureaucratic interests. Because the German civil service was so large and ramified, a single universally applicable measure— unprecedented in German civil-service law—was the most appropriate

[54] Documentation from the Oberfinanzdirektion in Hamburg, in BA R 2/22539-47; also Mommsen, *Beamtentum*, pp. 59-60.

[55] Predictably, given the NSDAP's championing of the victims of the PAV before 1933, this and other evidence of the Nazi government's lack of concern for them afterwards caused much resentment; see Neef to interior ministry, 21 June 1933 (GStA P 134/3235; also documentation in BA R 43II/462a).

[56] Namely, Frick, Krosigk, Gürtner, Göring, and Popitz, together with Papen and Hugenberg; see H. Seel, *Erneuerung des Berufsbeamtentums* (Berlin, 1933), 4.

[57] Seel (born 1876, NSDAP member since Aug. 1932) was described by Pfundtner as 'the father of the BBG' in a note to Krohn (labour ministry), 14 June 1933 (BA R 18/5529); see Seel, *Erneuerung*, and his commentary, *Gesetz zur Wiederherstellung des Berufsbeamtentums* (Berlin, 1933).

means to exert authority over it, and this procedure was also consistent with the powerful current towards administrative centralization. If the alternative to an uncontrolled rank-and-file party campaign against civil servants was a legalized and centrally directed purge, this initially strengthened the hand of the ministerial bureaucracy itself, and encouraged the belief that the Nazi regime would see the resurgence of a strongly centralized executive state.

III

In the eyes of the ministries responsible for civil-service policy, the BBG was seen as an emergency measure, pending a comprehensive recodification of civil-service law. In the meantime, the regime also adopted an interim reform measure which succeeded in clearing up an accumulation of loose ends in civil-service law, as well as in adapting parts of the Reich's civil-service code to the political conditions of Nazi rule. Discussions on these reforms proceeded directly from the debates that preceded the Nazi seizure of power. Financial desiderata continued to be one of the prime considerations, and the hand of Popitz, the Prussian finance minister and expert in the fiscal aspects of administrative reform, is clearly visible in the schemes adopted after January 1933. By April at the latest, the Reich finance ministry, in collaboration with the Reich interior ministry and the Prussian finance ministry, was urgently engaged in drafting a complex piece of legislation which affected numerous financial and legal aspects of civil-service law.[58] The thirteen sections of this compendious *Beamtenrechts-änderungsgesetz* (BRÄndG) encompassed an enormously diverse field and were in no sense a coherent codification of civil-service law. Its stated purposes were to create powers for further administrative rationalization and retrenchment, to restrict 'double earning', and 'to eliminate certain complications and irregularities that have arisen . . . as a consequence of the fact that an excessively broad interpretation of the constitutional provisions protecting civil servants' "vested rights" has limited the implementation of essential measures'.[59]

As this official memorandum indicated, the new legislative process created by the Enabling Act made it possible to adopt some significant

[58] Cabinet minutes, 25 Apr. 1933 (BA R 43II/422).

[59] Official memorandum to the *Gesetz zur Änderung von Vorschriften auf dem Gebiete des allgemeinen Beamten-, des Besoldungs- und des Versorgungsrechts*, 30 June 1933 (*RGBl*, 1933, i. 433), *DRA*, 162, 14 July 1933, 1.

measures which had proved impossible under Weimar for both political and constitutional reasons. Among the most important of these was the draft law 'on the foundation of civil-servant status', which had been under discussion since 1930 and had twice made it as far as the Reichsrat.[60] It was now incorporated in the BRÄndG in a new version, so that for the first time a substantive definition of civil-service work and a formal specification of status were introduced into German law. Proceeding from the argument that the absence of such a definition had been responsible for the excessive and costly expansion of the *Beamtentum* proper since the war, the BRÄndG established two criteria for the creation of civil-service posts. They had to be 'permanently necessary [*dauernd erforderlich*]', and must involve either 'entrustment with official sovereign business [*die Wahrnehmung obrigkeitlicher Aufgaben*]' or matters of state security; further, 'official sovereign business' excluded work which was no different in kind from that performed in the private sector, or which consisted merely of mechanical, clerical, or simple office duties.[61] This narrow substantive definition of civil-service work was followed by an amendment to the *Reichsbeamtengesetz* (RBG) stipulating that civil-servant status was established by the formal process of issuing a certificate of appointment as a *Beamte*; again this was an innovation in German law.[62] In further amendments, the RBG was made to conform to the discriminatory standards of the new regime. Racial restrictions were tightened to exclude the appointment in future of anyone of 'non-Aryan' parentage or married to a 'non-Aryan'; similarly, new appointees were to have 'the prescribed or usual training or other special qualification' and must 'guarantee [their] unconditional support for the national state'; moreover, women were excluded from established appointment until the age of thirty-five, in order to limit competition with men.[63] Between them, these new

[60] See Ch. 3, pp. 68-70, above.

[61] BRAndG, Ch. I, §1; further instructions issued by the interior ministry, 26 Feb. 1935 (*MBliV*, 1935, 289). See also *DRA*, 162, 1; C.-O. Ebeling, *Grundlagen und wesentliche Merkmale des Beamtenverhältnisses im nationalsozialistischen Staat* (Hamburg, 1936), chs. 7-9; O. G. Fischbach, 'Voraussetzungen für die Schaffung von Beamtenstellen', *Beamtenjahrbuch*, 11 (1935), 659-67; G. Wacke, 'Zwischen Arbeitsrecht und Beamtenrecht', *ZADR*, 16 (1937), 496-9; H. Seel, *Die Neuordnung des Beamtenrechts* (Berlin, 1933), 41 ff.

[62] Ch. II, §3(1), amending RBG, §1; see also further instructions issued by Prussian finance ministry, 14 Apr. 1934 (*MBliV*, 1934, 623).

[63] §3(2). Note that the racial conditions specified in the instructions to the law issued on 8 Aug. (*RGBl*, 1933, i. 575) were stricter than those later adopted under the Nuremberg laws (see instructions to *Reichsbürgergesetz*, 14 Nov. 1935; *RGBl*, 1935, i. 1333).

regulations substantially narrowed the definition of posts to which the rights of civil servants attached, the acquisition of civil-servant status by any individual official, and individual eligibility for appointment.[64]

The law introduced a series of other novel and far-reaching regulations. Like the BBG, its major provisions were directly valid for the *Länder*, local authorities, and public corporations, and represented another massive step towards the creation of uniform civil-service law throughout Germany. An important section of the law reiterated the stipulations in the Brüning emergency legislation that *Länder* and local authorities should reduce their salaries to the comparable Reich levels, and attempted to dispose of the constitutional inhibitions against this.[65] Fiscal considerations were also behind new regulations easing the transfer of civil servants between different authorities (Chapter V), which was normally a complex and costly process. Sharpening anti-feminist policies introduced before 1933, the law reinforced existing powers to compel women to leave the civil service and extended their applicability to all public authorities. Thus, married women lost their right to appeal against dismissal through the courts, the length of notice was reduced from a maximum of a quarter to a month, and severance payments were reduced; moreover, as well as discriminating against women by raising the age for established appointment, the law expressly abrogated §128(2) of the constitution and stipulated that they could now legally be paid less than men (Chapter III).[66] In a similar attack on 'double earning' (Chapter IV), the regulations on civil servants' right to take supplementary employment were tightened up, partly on the grounds that civil servants owed their entire labour power

---

[64] Anyone appointed expressly as a civil servant prior to the law was to be regarded as such, with or without certification; but the acquisition of civil-servant status by anyone who had not received such express appointment was forbidden, irrespective of prior commitments or legal judgements, or of arguments about the nature of his work (§5). By 1934, at least 10,000 civil-service posts had been degraded to *Angestellte* posts; see Blomberg to Reich interior ministry, 29 Feb. 1936 (GStA P 134/3138).

[65] Ch. VIII, and Ch. XIII, §§77 and 80; note, however, that these provisions were strictly speaking illegal, because the Enabling Act did not entitle the Reich government to delegate its powers to individual ministers or to the *Land* authorities; see Echterhölter, *Öffentliches Recht*, pp. 16-17. For an example of the legal and constitutional problems which led to this attempted solution, see the submission from the Anhalt state government to the Reich chancellery, 23 Mar. 1933 (BA R 43II/429).

[66] See J. Stephenson, *Women in Nazi Society* (London, 1975), 157 ff.; D. Winkler, *Frauenarbeit im 'Dritten Reich'* (Hamburg, 1977), 49 ff.; T. W. Mason, *Sozialpolitik im Dritten Reich: Arbeiterklasse und Volksgemeinschaft* (Opladen, 1977), 134-5; also Ch. 3, pp. 97-100, above. The interior ministry tried to calm anxieties about the dismissal policy in an Oct. circular (reprinted 21 Nov. 1933, *MBliV*, 1933, 1365).

to the state, partly as a gesture towards the unemployment crisis. A further section of the law (Chapter VII) stipulated that a civil servant sentenced to a year or more in prison would automatically lose his job or forfeit his pension, instead of undergoing separate disciplinary proceedings.

Unlike the BBG, the BRÄndG was a highly technical measure which disposed in summary fashion of some of the major outstanding problems in civil-service law. Although it was largely bureaucratic in origin and spirit, only the political circumstances of the now entrenched Nazi regime permitted its passage; it thus illustrates the powerful intercalation of interests at work in the first year after the seizure of power. Together the BBG and BRÄndG provided the basic legislative framework for civil-service policy for the first four years of the Nazi regime, pending the long-delayed issue of the new civil-service code (work on this began in 1934, but it was not finished until January 1937). In the meantime, however, the practical conditions of civil-service and administrative policy had been profoundly affected by further development of political relationships in the regime. Three areas of policy were directly significant here: progress in *Reichsreform*; the structural status of the Nazi party in relation to government policy-making and execution; and the question of the Nazification of the civil service.

IV

The Reich interior ministry continued to enjoy the initiative in *Reichsreform* until 1935. Although this did not quite constitute the orderly progress towards the establishment of a unitary state foreseen by Nicolai in 1933, the thrust of policy was clearly in that direction. The critical steps in this process were the Law for the Reconstruction of the Reich (*Neuaufbaugesetz*), adopted in January 1934; the second *Reichsstatthalter* law of January 1935; the centralization of the judicial administration; and the amalgamation of most of the Prussian ministries with those of the Reich.[67] The *Neuaufbaugesetz*, unanimously passed by the new Reichstag elected in November, rewrote the territorial provisions of the Weimar Constitution by abolishing the *Länder* assemblies, transferring their sovereignty to the Reich, and subordinating their governments to

[67] The discussion that follows draws largely on Bracher, Sauer, and Schulz, *Machtergreifung*, pp. 593-612; Diehl-Thiele, *Partei und Staat*, pp. 37-73; and Broszat, *The Hitler State*, pp. 104-20; individual page references will be reduced to a minimum.

the Reich.[68] No less important, the *Reichsstatthalter* were placed under the supervision (*Dienstaufsicht*) of the Reich interior ministry, thus abridging their role as Hitler's delegates (Article 3) and giving them a status somewhat comparable to that of the Prussian *Oberpräsidenten*; and the Reich government was empowered to create new constitutional law (Article 4).

In subsequent months and years, this brief statute was the source of much legislation designed to give meaningful content to its lapidary declarations. In the course of 1934, the majority of the Prussian ministries were amalgamated with those of the Reich; for the first time this gave the Reich interior ministry direct control over a large field apparatus, and also reinforced the influence of Prussian administrative and bureaucratic models in the Reich government. The judicial system was centralized under the control of the Reich justice ministry by legislation issued in 1934 and 1935; meanwhile, supporting measures eased the procedures for transferring personnel within these new joint ministries and their apparatuses. However, the *Neuaufbaugesetz* also sowed some of the seeds of the administrative confusion that was to vitiate the interior ministry's attempts to establish itself as the focal point of a centralized administrative system. To an extent, the ministry was the author of its own problems, which illustrate the contradictory tendencies towards concentration and polyocracy in the Third Reich. On the one hand, its willingness to allow the other Reich ministries to implement the law in their jurisdictions, as long as it was allowed overall supervision, conformed to the tendency of National Socialist government to decompose into its individual ministerial or equivalent parts. But on the other hand, Frick and his officials were naïve if they supposed that their claim to be *primus inter pares*, as the ministry for constitutional, administrative, and civil-service affairs, would simply be accepted.[69] In fact, Frick's colleagues refused to concede this claim, while accepting the invitation to run their own shows. As a result, the process of defederalization resulted in the creation not of a concentrated

---

[68] *Gesetz über den Neuaufbau des Reichs*, 30 Jan. 1934 (*RGBl*, 1934, i. 75). The abolition of the Reichsrat followed on 14 Feb. (*Gesetz über die Aufhebung des Reichsrats*; *RGBl*, 1934, i. 89). See H. Nicolai, *Der Neuaufbau des Reiches nach dem Reichsreformgesetz vom 30. Januar 1934* (Berlin, 1934), which includes extracts from Hitler's speech on the law to the Reichstag, and Frick's radio speech; C. Schmitt, 'Das neue Verfassungsgesetz', *VB*, 1 Feb. 1934; W. Frick, *Wir bauen das Dritte Reich* (Berlin, 1934).

[69] This is the argument in Bracher, Sauer, and Schulz, *Machtergreifung*, p. 600. See also Frick's circulars to Reich and *Land* authorities, 21 Mar. 1934 (copy in BA R 43II/1309), and 23 Apr. 1934 (copy in BA R 43II/418).

administrative structure under the supervision of the interior ministry, but rather of a series of separate administrative hierarchies attached to each of the specialist ministries or supreme Reich authorities, in fields such as transport, posts, or the economy. This fragmentation of the administrative machine into a 'pluralism of centralized administrative systems'[70] was a constant reminder of the failure of the interior ministry's ambitions, and a spur to continued efforts to realize them. Yet not only was the interior ministry unable to build up the unified structure originally envisaged, but it was increasingly blamed for the administrative confusion that followed. Between 1933 and 1936, ten new supreme Reich authorities were established, many with their own field apparatuses. These included four ministries carved out of the interior ministry's old jurisdictions, and more than outweighed the examples of concentration achieved in 1934. The residual *Länder* continued to vary enormously in size and population; *Land* and *Gau* borders bore no relation to one another; the district organizations of the Reich ministries were equally uncoordinated. In 1938, Frick pointed out that the distribution of district offices at the *Mittelstufe* presented the following variegated picture: 18 '*Länder*' (his quotation marks), 28 finance offices, 29 Reichsbahn directorates, 46 Reichspost directorates, 38 propaganda offices, and 15 army and 14 aviation districts; in the field of the labour ministry alone, there was equally little co-ordination, with 14 labour offices, 12 welfare offices, and 16 trustee offices.[71]

This problem of horizontal co-ordination was paralleled by the problem of hierarchical reorganization, which turned especially on the status of the *Reichsstatthalter*, and the shape of the *Mittelinstanz*, or intermediate level of the administration. As soon as the abolition of *Länder* independence began, basic questions arose as to what kind of administrative structure was to be established in their place. Though the *Neuaufbaugesetz* made the basic constitutional changes, it hardly began to address the new administrative ones. The issues here were rather complex, and focused in particular on the role of the *Reichsstatthalter*, and of the Prussian *Oberpräsidenten*, on whom the former were increasingly modelled. The point about the *Oberpräsident* was that he had never been part of the administrative field hierarchy, but answered to the interior ministry for the broad conduct of government in his district. Most importantly, this meant that the *Oberpräsident* had no power to issue instructions to the *Regierungspräsidenten*; the latter

---

[70] Bracher, Sauer, and Schulz, *Machtergreifung*, p. 604.
[71] Frick to Lammers, 5 Dec. 1938 (BA R 43II/703).

remained directly subordinate to the interior ministry, and were the middle link in the administrative chain that ran, broadly speaking, from central ministry to local *Landrat*. The question that arose again and again was whether this dual system, now complicated by the addition of the autonomous relationship between Führer and *Gauleiter*, should be perpetuated and generalized throughout Germany, or whether, and how, the *Reichsstatthalter/Oberpräsidenten-Gauleiter* might be given more substantial powers in the field. Related to this was the question of their answerability—whether to Hitler, which would tend to reinforce the role of the party in government and encourage a new form of regional particularism; or to the Reich interior ministry, which would connote centralization and the pre-eminence of the administrative apparatus. These were intricate political questions, not least because they raised a host of issues to do with the nominal and actual relationships of the party and some of its leading figures to the institutions of the state.

Plans circulating in the interior ministry in 1934-5 suggest that if the ministry felt it could exercise effective control over the *Reichsstatthalter*, it was ready to use them as the pivot of a new territorial and administrative division of the nation. But things were not so simple in practice. Even as the interior ministry worked to assert its authority over the complex politico-administrative structure of the *Länder*, the *Reichsstatthalter* contested their apparent subordination to it under the *Neuaufbaugesetz*. Friction also arose over the extent of their rights in relation to the residual *Land* governments and administrations, now that these had been nominally incorporated in a unitary Reich system. Drawing on their extramural legitimacy as *Gauleiter* and defenders of National Socialism against the ministerial bureaucracy, the *Reichsstatthalter* made personal appeals to Hitler, behind the back of the interior ministry.[72] In June, an attempt by Frick to get Hitler to ban this kind of informal approach, and to confirm his ministerial authority, met with a typically ambiguous response: Hitler accepted 'in principle' Frick's argument that the ministerial line of communication was the primary one, but also asserted that 'exceptions' had to be made in 'cases of particular political significance'. It can hardly have helped Frick's position that a few months later, at the party's Nuremberg rally in September, Hitler delivered his dictum that: 'It is not the state that commands us, but we who command the state'—a declaration that was

---

[72] Documentation on these disputes, notably Gauleiter-Reichsstatthalter Loeper's attempts at clarification, in BA R 43II/1376.

immediately translated by party members as giving the NSDAP the right to control the state in all its activities.[73] In an fresh attempt to resolve the situation in the ministry's favour, the interior ministry began in September to plan a second *Reichsstatthalter* law, which was issued in January 1935.[74] Although this met ministry objectives to the extent of designating the *Reichsstatthalter* as 'permanent delegates of the Reich government' (§1), it did not abolish the dualism of *Reichsstatthalter-Land* government by amalgamating the office of *Reichsstatthalter* with that of *Ministerpräsident*. Instead, a permissive clause merely allowed Hitler to make such joint appointments; but it was used in only two *Länder*, Hessen and Saxony. Moreover, it compromised the authority of §1 by simultaneously declaring that the *Reichsstatthalter*'s task was 'to ensure that the lines of policy determined by the Führer and Reich chancellor are observed'; in addition, the office was appointed by Hitler and held at his pleasure, and to Hitler too was reserved the power to determine the territorial extent of the *Reichsstatthalter* jurisdictions. Like the Prussian *Oberpräsidenten*, the *Reichsstatthalter* were now equipped with the right to require information (*Unterricht*) from subordinate *Land* and Reich agencies in their area, but they could only issue direct orders in exceptional cases (§2(1)). As the delegates of the Führer and chancellor, they also had the power to nominate the members

[73] The ostensive context of Hitler's declaration at Nuremberg was his explanation of how 200,000 people had been induced to assemble there: foreigners, he said, did not understand that loyalty and desire were enough motivation, and assumed the state must have commanded attendance. But, as he said: 'Nicht der Staat befiehlt uns, sondern wir befehlen dem Staat' (soundtrack, L. Riefenstahl, 'Der Triumph des Willens'). For examples of attempts to clear up the widespread decoding of these words by party members, see e.g. statements by Frick (*Germania*, 27 Nov. 1934) and Göring, in the Prussian cabinet, 16 Oct. 1934 (GStA Rep. 90/2339).

[74] *Reichsstatthaltergesetz*, 30 Jan. 1935 (*RGBl*, 1935, i. 65); see Diehl-Thiele, *Partei und Staat*, pp. 70-3. The status of the Prussian *Oberpräsidenten* had already been regularized in this way in Nov. 1934 (2. *VO über den Neuaufbau des Reichs*, 27 Nov. 1934; *RGBl*, 1934, i. 1190); §10 of the *Reichsstatthaltergesetz* also included special provisions for Prussia, with the effect that Hitler acted as *Reichsstatthalter* for Prussia, delegating his powers to the *Ministerpräsident*. On the relationship now established between *Reichsstatthalter/Oberpräsident* and *Regierungspräsident*, see Diehl-Thiele, *Partei und Staat*, chs. 2 and 3, and P. Hüttenberger, *Die Gauleiter: Studie zum Wandel des Machtgefüges in der NSDAP* (Stuttgart, 1969), 89-91; for contemporary accounts, see W. Stuckart and W. Scheerbarth, *Verwaltungsrecht* (Leipzig, 1941), 56-61, 67-70, and A. Köttgen, *Deutsche Verwaltung* (Berlin, 1944), 67-9. For examples of the dissatisfaction of the *Reichsstatthalter* with their status, see in particular memoranda written by Sauckel in 1936 and 1937, the second of which led to the reforms in the *Reichsstatthalter*'s role introduced in Austria after the *Anschluss*; see memos of 27 Jan. 1936 (BA R 43II/494), and 22 Nov. 1937 (BA R 18/5442), also further documentation on the latter in BA R 43II/1310b; and see also Ch. 8, pp. 264-6, below.

of the *Land* governments (§5), and to appoint *Land* civil servants. But the crucial question of whether the Reich interior ministry would be able to make good its supervisory authority could not be decided by a statute, especially one which still left so much unclear.

At this relatively high point, however, the interior ministry lost the initiative in *Reichsreform*, and within months Hitler had effectively imposed a moratorium on further work, bringing the whole process to an abrupt standstill. The immediate cause was the development of intense and disruptive competition about the strategy of reform between the Reich interior ministry and the party. In June 1934, Hess had appointed the Bavarian interior minister, Adolf Wagner, to his staff as head of a new 'Referat Reichsreform'. Wagner secured the services of a number of heavyweight experts, including the geopolitical theorist, Karl Haushofer, approached the Reich interior ministry in search of advice and collaboration, and began to promote active public discussion of his own proposals.[75] This severely compromised the independent work of the ministry, which, through Nicolai and his colleague, Medicus, was quietly pursuing its own plans, under the shelter of a ban on public discussion of *Reichsreform* issued to the party on Hitler's instructions in 1933.[76] But as a result of the renewed publicity, and of the increasingly acrimonious relations between the Reich interior ministry and the Wagner unit, the January 1935 *Reichsstatthalter* law was evidently the last measure Frick was able to accomplish before the issue became too hot. In March, Hess issued a reminder to the party of Hitler's veto.[77] The effect appears to have been more devastating for the interior ministry than for the party, however. Nicolai, whose plans had become less and less solicitous of party interests, was forced out of the ministry, disgraced by a scandal which had cost him his party mem-

[75] Documentation on these matters is in BA R 18/373 and 375, beginning with Nicolai to Frick, 8 June 1934; and Medicus memo for Frick, 12 June 1934, re 'Reorganization of Reich (Organization and Jurisdiction of the *Reichsgaue*)' (both BA R 18/375). The complex political and administrative pattern of relationships is illustrated by the fact that, as Bavarian interior minister, Wagner was now subordinate to the Reich interior ministry; but as a *Gauleiter* and a member of Hess's staff, he was a free agent. His plans envisaged a massive degree of decentralization; the weight of independent government would fall on the periphery of the *Reichsgaue*, not on the Reich ministries, which were to be radically reduced in number and size.

[76] StdF announcement, 29 Sept. 1933 (BA NS 6/vorl. 215).

[77] NSDAP Anordnung 46/35, 14 Mar. 1935 (BA R 43II/373). See also instructions to the German press, 27 Mar. 1935 (BA SS; this collection contains many similar instructions, indicating the sensitivity of the matter; e.g. 25 Jan. 1937, 18 Feb. 1937, 20 Jan. 1938, 20 Jan. 1939, etc.).

bership.[78] In April, the *Regierungspräsident* in Hildesheim reported that far from having a calming effect, Hess's order had given the impression 'that the constitutional ministry [Verfassungsministerium, i.e. interior ministry] is unable to prevail against certain opposition which derives from purely personal interests'. By May, Medicus was complaining that: 'At all corners questions of administrative reform are being wrecked or obstructed by the fact that up to now we lack any basis for *Reichsreform*, whether organizational or regional.' Finally, in November, Hitler was reported to have instructed Frick that '*all* territorial reform measures are to be abandoned'; and in December, the ministry accepted that 'all questions relating to *Reichsreform* will be allowed to lapse for the foreseeable future'.[79]

By the time this decision became known, the complexity of the structural situation and the intensity of the rivalries (both within the party and between it and the state) were such that only a determined intervention could have clarified the path for further action. But Hitler, the only possible source of such an authoritative and active decision, chose instead to leave things as they were, irrespective of the arbitrary point the reorganization process had reached. From his point of view, this had the merit of keeping state power unevenly distributed between the competing sources of his regime's stability—bureaucratic and personal, state, quasi-state, and party institutions—without finally fixing its disposition.[80] But although this characteristically passive decision absolved Hitler from taking a firm stand on matters in which he was intrinsically uninterested, it did not create a fixed and static situation. Rather, the absence of any clear structure of decision-making or firm guidelines for policy meant that the future would see shifting and unregulated modifications in the balance of power, rather than planned and co-ordinated ones.

---

[78] BDC Nicolai. For his views on the incorporation (and nullification) of the party in the state, see his memo to Frick, 13 June 1934 (BA R 18/375).

[79] *Regierungspräsident* in Hildesheim, *Lagebericht*, 4 Apr. 1935; Medicus memo, 14 May 1935; interior-ministry memos, 13 Nov. and 27 Dec. 1935 (all BA R 18/373). Hitler had already instructed that the issue of *Reichsreform* was not to be discussed at the Nuremberg congress; see Bormann to Metzner (interior ministry), 2 Sept. 1935 (BA R 18/5029).

[80] Hitler's motives are examined by Broszat, *The Hitler State*, pp. 118-19; see also H. Mommsen, 'Hitlers Stellung im nationalsozialistischen Herrschaftssystem', in G. Hirschfeld and L. Kettenacker (eds.), *The 'Führer State': Myth and Reality. Studies on the Structure and Politics of the Third Reich* (Stuttgart, 1981), 43-72.

V

Under these circumstances, the interior ministry was obliged to drop its expansive plans for administrative reform for the next several years, and to concentrate on lesser measures of civil-service law reform.[81] But although some of the most difficult constitutional issues and disputes with party authorities had thus been put into abeyance, the ministry still had to cope with the party's determination to secure its hand in civil-service policies, in terms both of projected reforms and of the day-to-day process of bureaucratic work. The positions from which the party did this were various, from the officially sanctioned role of the Führer's deputy in legislation and appointments, to the illicit interventions of local party officials. During the seizure of power, rank-and-file party members and subordinates in the party's hierarchy throughout Germany had taken it upon themselves to interpret and secure the party's interests in the administration. In the earliest days, influencing appointments and dismissals was naturally their principal, though not exclusive, interest. Most of their actions were of dubious or non-existent legality, and were strongly resisted, not only by the state but, for reasons of political expediency, by Hitler and Göring as well. Apart from the innumerable interventions in personnel questions before and after the passage of the BBG, individuals or offices in the party were engaged in a broad range of unauthorized activities, such as forcing civil servants to join the NSDAP;[82] nominating representatives in state offices;[83] distributing questionnaires on political affiliation;[84] demanding that civil servants outside the party sign an undertaking to obey party directives;[85] and interfering in the administration of §§2-4 of the BBG.[86] Actions like these were epidemic in the first few months

---

[81] Pfundtner reported to a Dec. 1936 conference of Lammers, Körner, Sommer, and Wienstein that Hitler had instructed Frick that 'apart from a few cases of territorial consolidation [*Flurbereinigung*], *Reichsreform* should proceed primarily in the area of the standardization of law'; minutes, 9 Dec. 1936 (BA R 43II/494). In the following years, work proceeded in 3 selected areas—the civil-service and disciplinary codes, the incorporation of *Land* civil servants in the Reich, and the reform of training for senior *Beamte*—until in 1938, Germany's territorial annexations mandated a new round of major administrative reform; see Ch. 8, below.

[82] See statement forbidding this by Krosigk, *Reichsbesoldungsblatt*, 6 Apr. 1933.

[83] Correspondence between Fachschaft IV A of the NS Beamten-Arbeitsgemeinschaft and the Reich chancellery, Feb. 1933 (BA R 43F/4015).

[84] Correspondence between Landesfinanzamt Kassel and finance ministry, July to Sept. 1933, concerning *Kreis* and *Gau* initiatives (BA R 2/22583).

[85] Complaint from Stahlhelm chief in Pomerania, 27 May 1933; GStA Rep. 77/1.

[86] See Göring's instructions to Prussian ministers forbidding this, 4 Oct. 1933 (*JMBl*, 1933, 495). See also Matzerath, *Nationalsozialismus*, pp. 61-81.

of 1933, and were the cause of endless friction and disputes as local Nazis demanded unprecedented rights to question or sabotage bureaucratic procedures. For their different reasons, both Hitler and the ministries were anxious to regulate the forms of party involvement in civil-service and administrative politics. The process was caught up in the twin tendencies towards both the diffusion and concentration of power: the appointment of the *Reichsstatthalter* in April 1933 was balanced by the designation of Hess, the Führer's deputy (*Stellvertreter des Führers*, or StdF), as an observer at cabinet meetings in June, and as a full cabinet member in December.[87]

Neither Hess's appointment nor the establishment of the *Reichsstatthalter* was able to staunch the flow of unauthorized interventions, especially by the *Gauleiter*. Whether or not they were also *Reichsstatthalter*, the *Gauleiter* endlessly insisted on their right to monitor or interfere in administrative business (and on protecting their claims against other party offices).[88] The problematic relation of 'party and state' was never to be fully resolved, but subsisted as a series of conflicts and debates at every level, covered by a veneer of slogans. Nevertheless, in subsequent years Hess was able to develop extensive watch-dog powers over the civil government, plus a range of subsidiary rights of consultation.[89] In July 1934, against Frick's objections, he was given extensive rights of prior consultation in the preparation of all departmental legislation, a power which at the very least offered wide opportunities for obstructive behaviour.[90] From 1938, he was also to be consulted during the drafting of Führer decrees.[91] The reluctance of ministries to comply with this regulation is demonstrated by the fact that Hess was soon driven to complain repeatedly that his staff was

[87] *Gesetz zur Sicherung der Einheit von Partei und Staat*, 1 Dec. 1933, §2 (*RGBl*, 1933, i. 1016); Diehl-Thiele, *Partei und Staat*, p. 225.

[88] Hüttenberger, *Gauleiter*, ch. 3; Diehl-Thiele, *Partei und Staat*, chs. 1-3, *passim*. See also J. Klenner, *Verhältnis von Partei und Staat 1933-1945: Dargestellt am Beispiel Bayerns* (Munich, 1974), esp. ch. 7. A statement by Krosigk in 1963 describes how the *Gauleiter* saw themselves as entitled to issue direct orders to administrative agencies in their regions; Krosigk to Baum, 3 Mar. 1963 (IfZ ZS 145).

[89] Checklist, 14 May 1941, in BA R 43II/1213a; also StdF announcement B24/40, 11 May 1940 (copy in BA R 18/5318); and see A. Norbeck, *Die Formen der Zusammenarbeit von Partei und Staat auf dem Gebiet der Verwaltung*, Ph. D. thesis (Munich, 1938).

[90] Unpublished Führer decree, 27 July 1934; Frick's objections were stated in a letter to the Reich chancellery, 8 June 1934 (both BA R 43II/1197). In 1935, Hess's right of consultation was extended to cover all statutory instruments published in the *Reichsgesetzblatt*; Diehl-Thiele, *Partei und Staat*, pp. 231-2; Mommsen, *Beamtentum*, pp. 77-8; W. Sommer, 'Die NSDAP als Verwaltungsträger', in H. Frank (ed.), *Deutsches Verwaltungsrecht* (Munich, 1937), 170.

[91] Reich chancellery circular, 7 June 1938 (BA R 2/31905).

receiving drafts too late for effective comment.[92] Hess's other major power in civil-service affairs was his acquisition, in September 1935, of a rather vague right of 'consultation' (*Beteiligung*) in appointments and promotions in the most senior and sensitive civil-service posts.[93] In practice, what Hess got was a right to veto proposals from the relevant nominating authority, rather than his own right of nomination, and this procedure was confirmed two years later when new regulations were issued under the 1937 civil-service law. As we shall see, his exercise of these powers, and his efforts to build them into a right of permanent intervention in appointments and promotions, were to cause tremendous problems for the interior ministry as it attempted to operate an orderly personnel policy.

To utilize his powers, Hess had built up a staff of specialists at his headquarters in the Brown House. The men most directly involved in administering the party's role in civil-service and administrative policy were the members of department III, established in 1934 with a brief to supervise 'constitutional questions'.[94] This turned out to be a curiously hybrid formation: a party office staffed entirely by professional civil servants. In order for the department's staff to be capable of carrying out their tasks, it was virtually inevitable that they should be experienced above all in the ways of the administrative bureaucracy. Thus, the first head of the department, Walter Sommer, was a career civil servant, initially on secondment from the Thuringian interior ministry, though he had also been a member of the NSDAP since 1928. His colleagues were likewise all trained civil servants, on secondment from a variety of *Länder* and Reich ministries—the normal procedure

[92] Reich chancellery circular, 27 Oct. 1934 (BA R 43II/1197); similarly, interior-ministry circular, 2 Mar. 1935 (BA R 43II/1198); Hess to Lammers, 21 Dec. 1935 (BA R 43I/1490); and Bormann to Reinhardt (finance ministry), 23 Dec. 1935 (BA R 2/31905).
[93] His move was prompted by Hitler's take-over of appointment rights after his assumption of the Reich presidency (see Führer decrees of 1 Feb. 1935; *RGBl*, 1935, i. 73 and 74). Hess's right was accorded by the *Erlass über die Beteiligung des Stellvertreters des Führers bei der Ernennung von Beamten*, 24 Sept. 1935 (*RGBl*, 1935, i. 1203; documentation in BA R 43II/421 and GStA Rep. 90/2339). Hess had announced this impending decree somewhat prematurely: see StdF circular 76/35, 26 Apr. 1935 (BA NS 6/vorl. 218), announcing procedures for the submission of information by subordinate party offices. He soon had to deal with bureaucratic problems of late and contradictory reports: see instructions 52/36, 30 Mar. 1936 (BA NS 6/vorl. 22) and 1/37, 7 Jan. 1937 (NS 6/vorl. 225).
[94] D. Orlow, *The History of the Nazi Party: 1933-1945.* (Pittsburgh, 1973), 130, 139-43; Broszat, *The Hitler State*, pp. 248-9; Diehl-Thiele, *Partei und Staat*, pp. 216-24. Klopfer, later head of the department, said it had been created in order to 'translate' ministerial correspondence for Hess (IfZ ZS 352).

for providing any minister without portfolio with a staff.[95] Hess disliked an arrangement which left his officials open to pressure from their parent authorities, and which may have imparted an undesirably provisional air to his office. As business expanded in 1935, he began to push first for the transfer of a nucleus of his staff to the Reich budget, and then, progressively, for its expansion.[96] From 1936, therefore, the StdF staff appeared as a separate title (Kap. I. Tit. I) in the interior-ministry budget plan (Einzelplan V), which bureaucratically speaking was a highly irregular arrangement.[97] In any case, it resulted in a somewhat paradoxical state of affairs. Hess's staff was financially the responsibility of the NSDAP, which was itself massively subsidized by the state, but bureaucratically it stood under the nominal auspices of a government minister.[98] Within four years, the senior staff employed on this basis had grown from two to twenty, and resembled a small, top-heavy ministry; by 1944, the total had reached thirty-three posts.[99] To build up his staff's numbers and status, Hess had repeatedly insisted on rapid promotions in defiance of the standard procedures; neither Frick nor Krosigk was able to resist this momentum, though Krosigk's ministry usually lodged a vain pro forma protest after the interior ministry had given way.[100]

[95] List of the department's 11 chief officials, 5 Mar. 1936 (BA R 2/11903). I am grateful to Professor Michiyoshi Oshima, of Keio University, for drawing my attention to this material.

[96] See the extensive exchanges between Hess and Reinhardt of the Reich finance ministry, plus internal-ministry memos, from Feb. 1935 (ibid.).

[97] In 1939, this arrangement covered about half the number of *Beamte* employed on Hess's staff; the rest remained on secondment. In 1943, the staff (now part of Bormann's party chancellery) was transferred to the budget of the Reich chancellery, under the same conditions; see Lammers to finance ministry, 9 Apr. 1943 (ibid.).

[98] Party finances after 1933 were a complicated affair; income derived partly from investments and membership fees, and partly from ever-expanding state subsidies, with the bulk paid over to the party treasury as a lump sum out of the Reich budget (Einzelplan XVII, Kap. 14: 'Beitrag an den Reichsschatzmeister der NSDAP'); these funds were destined for a variety of party uses. The subsidy grew from about 66 m. RM in 1933 to over 400 m. by 1942; see memo for Krosigk, 20 May 1943 (BA R 2/31906); and a post-war deposition concerning the subsidy policy by Schmidt-Schwarzenberg, section head in the finance ministry, 12 June 1948 (IfZ ZS 511); also Orlow, *History of the Nazi Party: 1933-1945, passim.* Information on the means by which other subsidies were paid, and on the problems of auditing their use, can be found in a number of BA files, not all of which were clearly catalogued at the point at which I used them: R 2/31905, R 2/31013, and R 2/11913 a and b; R 18/5288; NS 1/421.

[99] 1944 budget listing in BA R 43II/1079c. According to Diehl-Thiele's evidence, the total staff of the entire office may have reached 400 by 1944, 200 of them lawyers (*Partei und Staat*, p. 218 n. 47).

[100] Of 28 promotions approved between 1937 and 1943, 18 violated one or other of the rules designed to prevent excessively frequent, or earely promotion (figures compiled

Thus, Hess established a staff of bureaucrats capable of monitoring state policies, and he was able to reward these mainly younger men by guaranteeing them rapid advancement. The reverse side of this reliance on trained *Beamte* was that they had been schooled as civil servants and could be expected to act as such. Although there was a certain advantage in the fact that they spoke the same language as their counterparts in the ministries, it also meant that bureaucratic solidarity might win out over party interests. Moreover, there was some suggestion that the parent authorities regarded 'their' civil servants as their representatives in the party headquarters, much as Reinhardt or von Helms were supposed to be the party's trustees in the finance and interior ministries respectively.[101] At the very least, the fact that state and party were sharing the use of a single body of administrators allowed for a degree of interlocking that was characteristic of more than one political institution in Nazi Germany, and that flowed, broadly speaking, from the persistent lack of clarity about the party's status in the governing apparatuses of the Third Reich. In the context of this unresolved relationship between two centres of power and legitimacy, it was perhaps unsurprising that each should take on some of the features of the other.

The unreliable character of the staff of department III resulted in constant interference in its affairs by another of Hess's departmental chiefs, Helmuth Friedrichs. The head of department II (party affairs), Friedrichs was a party man through and through, and deeply contemptuous of all bureaucrats.[102] In this he resembled his sponsor, Martin Bormann, who took over the StdF office after Hess's flight to England in May 1941 (when it was also renamed the party chancellery). Unlike Hess, who was dilatory and inefficient and willing to rely on his subordinate staff, Bormann was extremely assiduous in running his office, and was in every way more personally ambitious than his predecessor. Bormann found it very difficult to work either with Sommer, whose resignation in 1941 seems to have been engineered by

from proposal forms in BA R 2/11903; some additional documentation on these proposals in R 43II/1213). For the finance ministry's ultimate sense of helplessness in respect of these demands, see internal memo (by Kallenbach), 9 Nov. 1944 (BA R 2/4502). Hess's policy resembled that of other recently established or fast-expanding authorities also engaged in constant battles for exceptional treatment for their officials; see pp. 171-4, below.

[101] Broszat, *The Hitler State*, p. 260 n. 22.

[102] See his bitter comments on bureaucrats in his report on the 1935 Nuremberg rally (BA NS 26/vorl. 395); also statements under interrogation by Gerhard Klopfer, head of department III, 1941-5 (IfZ ZS 352).

him, or with his successor, Gerhard Klopfer. Despite his leading position in the party chancellery, Klopfer ended up supporting Himmler after the latter's appointment as interior minister, on the grounds that he was 'the only bulwark' against the threat that 'the whole civil service in Germany was disintegrating [*kaput geht*]'.[103] Klopfer's alienation from an office that he had joined as a young *Regierungsrat* in 1935, and in which he had made a rapid career, is evidence of the strains we have been discussing, but also of the direction that the party's civil-service policy was to take under Bormann, especially in relation to appointments.

How to ensure the political reliability of the administrative apparatus was a headache that had vexed party leaders, nationally and in the *Gaue*, since the first weeks of the regime.[104] It was one thing to purge the civil service of men and women deemed undesirable; it was another matter to decide upon the criteria for future personnel policies and who would test and apply them. The four possible solutions were, first, to insist on a test of political commitment to National Socialism at the time of appointment or promotion; secondly, to combine appropriate party and state offices in the same person; thirdly, to establish some kind of parallel system of political commissars to oversee the administration; and fourthly, to ensure that existing and future civil servants were schooled in the principles of National Socialism. All of these alternatives were adopted at different times, and their influence can be seen at work in some of the legislation already discussed. However, each of them also raised a number of problems, and carried disadvantages from the point of view of the party, the ministries, or both.

The fourth of these alternatives, suggesting policies of training reform and political indoctrination, was inevitably a long-term strategy, useless for the immediate challenges of 1933.[105] Realistically, it was the first three strategies that offered themselves as immediate responses to the problems facing the regime in 1933, but in practice, the options narrowed down fairly quickly to the first two. Commissars were widely used in the first few months after 30 January, but proved to be only an

---

[103] See Klopfer's statement under interrogation, 14 Nov. 1945 (IfZ ZS 464). Sommer had left the StdF staff in May 1941 to head the newly established Reich administrative court; within a year, he had been expelled from the party and from his new post, possibly also at Bormann's behest; see correspondence between Bormann, Hess, and Frick, Jan. to May 1941 (BA R 18/5533); Führer decree, 3 Apr. 1941 (*RGBl*, 1941, i. 201); and BDC Sommer.

[104] On this question generally, see Mommsen, *Beamtentum*, ch. 4.

[105] See pp. 183-8, and Ch. 6 below.

interim provision.[106] No systematic hierarchy of party agencies parallel with the structure of the state was established, nor was the state apparatus remodelled to fit the organizational structure of the NSDAP. Rather, a loose, partial, and ambivalent dualism of party and state evolved, in which some parallelisms could be detected, and some party and state offices were held in *Personalunion*. The prime example of this was of course Führer and Reichskanzler Hitler himself, but there were other instances in the combination of *Gauleiter* with *Reichsstatthalter*, or of *Kreisleiter* with *Landrat* or *Bürgermeister*. However, in the absence of any commitment to a systematic dual structure of power, the party was thrown back on to efforts to gain and expand its political influence over the personnel policies of the state administration. 'Party' here could mean individuals and offices as varied as the *Gauleiter* and the Hauptamt für Kommunalpolitik, as well as the StdF *Stab* whose main object was to ensure its central control of the whole process.[107] The ministries, for their part, resisted the exertion of such influence in so far as it conflicted with their house authority, with bureaucratic procedures, and, in some cases, with the principles of a professional and vocational civil service. Although all professed their commitment to the establishment of a politically reliable civil service, the means by which this was to be achieved were the object of persistent dispute.

As the Nazi regime came to power in 1933, its earliest efforts had been devoted to identifying suitably qualified Nazi sympathizers to take the place of officials forced into retirement or dismissed. Typical was a list submitted to the Prussian interior ministry in April 1933; it contained fifty-one nominations to senior posts, annotated with comments such as 'party member', 'probably stands between DNVP and NSDAP; wife party member; highly recommended', or 'not a party member, but long sympathetic'.[108] Inevitably, however, it had quickly become clear in 1933 that the party had far too few suitably qualified candidates to fill the numerous posts deemed to require politically sympathetic occupants. The stage was thus set for what was to become an unending battle with the ministries over the rival significance of professional and political qualification, as well as over the question of

---

[106] Bracher, Sauer, and Schulz, *Machtergreifung*, pp. 460 ff., 509 ff.

[107] See e.g. the prolonged efforts between 1938 and 1941 by the NSDAP's Hauptamt für Kommunalpolitik to secure an official role in local-government appointments (documentation in BA NS 25/685, 689, and 763).

[108] List dated 6 Apr. 1933, and probably submitted by Gauleiter Kube, head of the NSDAP's Landtag fraction (BA R 18/7951; see also extensive documentation in GStA Rep. 77/2).

which posts ought to require a test of political eligibility, and how and by whom this was to be established. The Reich and Prussian institution of the 'political' civil servant offered some precedent for the most sensitive posts; after extension in the Weimar Republic, it included senior ministerial posts such as state secretary and section head, and Prussian field posts such as *Regierungspräsident*, *Polizeipräsident*, and *Landrat*, and these were the ones on which an active personnel policy was concentrated after 1933. However, party complaints at the slow pace of change prompted Frick to issue instructions in July 1933 that only civil servants 'reliable in a National Socialist sense' should be entrusted with personnel affairs; while a year later, he ordered that clerks in personnel departments should also be 'in principle members of the NSDAP'.[109] To demonstrate what personnel officers could achieve, Hans von Helms, an *alter Kämpfer* installed as personnel officer in the Prussian interior ministry's police department in January 1933, reviewed his successes up to mid-1934 in raising the proportion of party members in the senior ranks of the police administration. For example, the number of pre-1933 party members among the 135 senior officials had almost doubled between 1933 and mid-1934, while in the Berlin police presidency the percentage had gone from 10 to 33 per cent. But at the same time von Helms was bitterly critical of the political complexion of most senior officials in his ministry; and he also pointed out that only some 69 of the ministry's 270 *Beamte* were party members, of whom only 18 had joined before 1933.[110]

Von Helms set his arguments in the context of a discussion of the structural problem of party–state relations, and his final memorandum points up two issues in particular. In the first place, certifications of political reliability had to be reliable themselves. From the party's point of view, the best means of ensuring this for an existing civil servant was to allow party officials access to his personnel records before a promotion or transfer. From the Reich interior ministry's point of view, this was a breach of confidentiality; in any case, the ministry took the view that the BBG and BRAndG between them had disposed of the problem of unreliability among the existing establishment. But the

[109] Interior-ministry instructions of 17 July 1933 (copy in BA R 2/22583) and 10 July 1934 (copy in BA R 43II/421). In Aug. 1935, Frick circulated a demand from Bormann for information on progress achieved; the returns do not appear to have survived (GStA Rep. 318/805). For some evidence on earlier implementation in the labour administration in 1934, and on party efforts (by a local *Amt für Beamte*) to influence this, see ibid.
[110] BDC von Helms; Mommsen, *Beamtentum*, pp. 65-6, 171-3.

pressure for an authoritative ruling from subordinate administrative offices, which bore the brunt of local party pressure, caused Frick to issue formal instructions in December 1934. These provided that files could only be handed over to the StdF (and that party requests would therefore have to go through him), but that verbal information could discretionarily be given to *Gauleiter* and *Reichsleiter*.[111] However, this initiated a process of progressive extensions of the right of access, in which the ministry gradually gave ground.[112] It was somewhat unclear exactly which appointments and promotions required political certification. Local party offices seemed to think that they could object to any unwelcome decisions, but after Hess had been given the right to participate in senior appointments and promotions in 1935, the interior ministry took the view that it was these alone that required certification.[113]

This view touched on the second problem implied in von Helms's 1934 discussion of personnel policies. Party membership was an obvious standard for political reliability, but what was its real value? In 1933, it was a plausible test of political commitment to National Socialism, as von Helms's memo suggested; but as civil servants sensibly flocked to join a party that put such a premium on political affiliation, so they devalued the meaning of membership as well as altering the character of the party itself. Hitler had already declared in December 1933 that it was 'not necessary' for all leading civil servants to be party members,[114] but the number of National Socialist civil servants in a ministry or departmental office continued to figure in party circles as the common-

[111] Interior-ministry circular, 29 Dec. 1934 (*MBliV*, 1935, 27); reprinted in Mommsen, *Beamtentum*, p. 182.

[112] Documentation in BA R 43II/426. See ministry instructions 5 Mar. and 2 Apr. 1935 (*MBliV*, 1935, 316 and 547), 2 Nov. 1936 (*RMBliV*, 1936, 1491), and 8 Sept. 1937 (*RMBliV*, 1937, 1504); also StdF instruction 2/37, 8 Jan. 1937 (BA NS 6/vorl. 225). For the procedure by which state offices obtained political certifications from the party, see StdF instruction 119/35, 14 June 1936, and interior-ministry instructions, 8 Oct. 1936 (*RMBliV*, 1936, 1329), 28 Jan. 1937 (*RMBliV*, 1937, 169) and 18 Dec. 1937 (BA R 2/22583); also labour-ministry circular, 24 Feb. 1938 (GStA Rep. 318/820). The StdF found it hard to keep up with the work involved; see vom Helms to finance ministry, 26 Apr. 1938 (BA R 2/22583).

[113] Interior ministry to Prussian minister-president, 27 Jan. 1936 (GStA Rep. 318/820). See also e.g. Gau Baden Amt für Beamte to HfB, 30 June 1935 (BA R 2/22583). On the practice of political certification in general, see D. Rebentisch, 'Die "politische Beurteilung" als Herrschaftsinstrument der NSDAP', in D. Peukert and J. Reulecke (eds.), *Die Reihen fast geschlossen: Beiträge zur Geschichte des Alltags unterm Nationalsozialismus* (Wuppertal, 1981) 107-25.

[114] Hitler was responding to a query by Hess, during cabinet discussion of the Law for the Unity of Party and State, 1 Dec. 1933 (BA R 43II/1196).

est gauge of progress towards Nazification.[115] By 1935, however, civil servants were vastly overrepresented in the NSDAP: 20 per cent of them were members, and 80 per cent of these had not joined until after the seizure of power.[116] Their membership was more likely to be evidence of prudence than of persuasion; they were liable to be not *alte Kämpfer* but *Konjunkturritter*. It was also far from clear that it was to the party's benefit for large numbers of civil servants to become members. True, the party made generous use of their skills in running its own vast bureaucratic machine; but this only underscored a general dilemma that faced the NSDAP after 1933—its reduction to a massive bureaucratic institution without a clear political mission.

The problem of the party's overall role in Nazi society and the state, including the composition of its membership, had become a matter of deep concern to many of its leaders and spokesmen within a few years of the seizure of power.[117] Whether party stalwarts were entangled in administrative work, or civil servants were assumed to need party membership as a job qualification, the character of the party as a *Führerorden*, or vanguard of believers, was severely compromised. The practice of joint office-holding (*Personalunion*) stirred considerable doubts, despite its superficial attractions as a political mechanism. In 1934, Hitler had expressed the view that it was in principle undesirable, and in 1937, Hess had ordered all such instances to be dissolved.[118] In December 1939, Helmuth Friedrichs, head of Hess's department II, drafted a long and vehement memo summing up the party's suspicions

---

[115] Among numerous examples of individual appointment cases, see exchanges between the Prussian interior ministry and Gauleiter Jordan, Weinrich, and Simon in 1934 (GStA Rep. 77/3 and 5), and exchanges between Bormann and Frick in 1936 and 1937 (GStA Rep. 90/2339 and 2340). For examples of ministerial censuses of party membership in their departments, see 'Übersicht über die Zugehörigkeit Angehöriger des Reichswirtschaftsministeriums und des Preussischen Ministeriums für Wirtschaft und Arbeit zur Partei, SA und SS. Stand vom 1. Januar 1935' (BA R 43II/1141); and interior-ministry circular on candidates for *Landratsämter*, 31 Aug. 1936 (BA R 18/7951).

[116] *NSDAP Partei-Statistik*, i. *Parteimitglieder* (Munich, 1935), 70.

[117] See the discussions by Orlow, *History of the Nazi Party 1933-1945*; J. Noakes, 'The Nazi Party and the Third Reich', in J. Noakes (ed.), *Government, Party and People in Nazi Germany* (Exeter, 1980), 11-33; M. Broszat *et al.* (eds.), *Bayern in der NS-Zeit*, i. *Soziale Lage und politisches Verhalten der Bevölkerung im Spiegel vertraulicher Berichte* (Munich and Vienna, 1977), 387-569; J. H. Grill, *The Nazi Movement in Baden, 1920-1945* (Chapel Hill, 1983), esp. ch. 11; A. L. Unger, *The Totalitarian Party: Party and People in Nazi Germany and Soviet Russia* (Cambridge, 1974); and see also Ch. 6 below.

[118] Hitler's view recorded in a note from Lammers to Wagner, 30 Sept. 1934 (BA R 43II/497); Hess's instruction 29/37, 19 Feb. 1937.

about the whole concept.[119] The excessively close interrelation of party and state had, he suggested, diluted the party's vigour by entangling it in administration and identifying it with an unloved bureaucracy. Worse: 'even the oldest National Socialist fighters, once they hold state office, not only allow their bureaucracies to bring them into positions of conflict with the party as such, but can even be used as a cloak for measures that contradict the essence of Nazism, without their noticing it'. Friedrichs read this as confirmation of the civil service's ambition to obtain the leading political role, and to exclude the party entirely. The issue was indeed one of enormous importance for the interior ministry, with its hopes for the role of the *Reichsstatthalter* in the *Mittelinstanz* and its sentimental commitment to the historic figure of the *Landrat* as the archetype of the versatile administrator. Nevertheless, although the drift was against formal *Personalunion*, the practice was never wholly discontinued, and Bormann was still making vain attempts to ban it as late as February 1945.[120]

The question of civil servants' party membership and their political qualification in general was as interesting to the ministries as it was to Hess and his staff. The fundamental question was whether political affiliation could be allowed to take precedence over professional qualification in personnel decisions. Already, the rank and file of the civil service had been made the subject of political attentions after 1933 which wrought havoc with normal standards of bureaucratic practice. The Nazi party's attitude was that politically undesirable civil servants should be subject to negative sanctions, while 'deserving National Socialists' should enjoy positive discrimination in the civil service. This produced a myriad of special provisions and allowances for party members. In June 1933, civil servants who had received disciplinary penalties in the course of the 'national uprising' were amnestied or allowed to have their cases reopened.[121] In the depths of the depression, however, probably the most important advantage enjoyed by party

---

[119] Copy in BA S Sch. 218. The issue of joint office-holding was also prominent in an exhaustive 267-pp. analysis of the party's problems and future written in 1942, probably by Gauleiter Karl Röver (pp. 6-14) (BA NS 20/109).

[120] See instructions issued by Bormann, 16 Feb. 1945 (copy in BA R 18/2003). One reason for the party's reluctance to dissolve joint office-holding by *Kreisleiter* was the financial cost of their salaries to the NSDAP. For full details, see Mommsen, *Beamtentum*, pp. 112 ff., 223-41; Diehl-Thiele, *Partei und Staat*, pp. 173-200; and Matzerath, *Nationalsozialismus*, pp. 237 ff.

[121] *Gesetz über die Aufhebung der im Kampf für die nationale Erhebung erlittenen Dienststrafen und sonstigen Massnahmen*, 23 June 1933 (*RGBl*, 1933, i. 390).

members was preferential access to jobs in the public sector.[122] The institution of the *Versorgungsanwärter*—the uniformed policeman, or short-service soldier for whom virtually all lower public-service posts were reserved—lent itself readily to extension to party members or sympathizers. A start was made in July 1933, when 50 per cent of appointments to *Angestellte* posts were reserved for 'deserving fighters for the national uprising', i.e. members of the NSDAP, the SA, and the SS.[123] From 1934, the budget began to reserve the uncommitted 10 per cent of lower civil-service posts for them and for severely disabled veterans.[124] Benefits were progressively extended; within a few years, for example, they included the taking into account of full-time work for the party, SA, and SS in seniority calculations, as well as simplified examinations, early establishment, and preferential promotion.[125] Conversely, politically and racially undesirable civil servants were barred from promotions.[126] 'Final' regulations on preferential appointments were issued in 1937; these discriminated in favour of pre-1930 party members in all lower civil-service appointments, and provided for conversion of a number of *Arbeiter* and *Angestellte* posts into civil-service posts (*Beamtenstellen*).[127] This was a highly unorthodox procedure, of course, which flew in the face of precedent. Moreover, the opportunities for favouritism and corruption offered by this entire system of party patronage can well be imagined. And although the professed object was to find civil-service jobs for unemployed National Socialists, it appears that eligibility was exploited not only to find but to switch jobs: in 1935, almost 90 per cent of the party members appointed

[122] For discrimination in favour of unemployed party members in general, see Mason, *Sozialpolitik*, pp. 135-7.

[123] Interior-ministry circular, 12 July 1933 (reprinted 28 Aug. 1933; *MBliV*, 1933, 1005; documentation in BA R 43II/1207). Pre-1933 party members were also getting preferential treatment from the labour department's employment exchanges; e.g. StdF *Stab* instruction to *Gauleiter*, 2 Oct. 1933 (BA NS 6 vorl. 215), and Prussian government circular, 11 Apr. 1934 (*MBliV*, 1934, 661).

[124] Documentation for 1934 and 1935 budgets in BA R 43II/758.

[125] Finance-ministry circulars, 26 May 1936 (seniority) (copy in GStA P 134/3212); 21 Dec. 1934 (examinations) (*MBliV*, 1935, 691); 22 Dec. 1934 (establishment) (*MBliV*, 1934, 769) and 26 Oct. 1933 (promotions) (copy in BA R 2/22559); also Mommsen, *Beamtentum*, pp. 70-4, 166 ff.

[126] Interior-ministry circular, 21 June 1934 (copy in BA R 43II/452; documentation in BA R 43II/421a).

[127] Interior-ministry circulars, 1 Apr. 1937 (*MBliV*, 1937, 515) and 19 Nov. 1937 (reprinted in Mommsen, *Beamtentum*, pp. 177-9). See also documentation on implementation in Prussia 1938-40 in BA R 18/5802.

to civil-service posts were not unemployed, but were simply bettering themselves.[128]

The issues involved were even more serious, of course, for the senior grade of the civil service. From a bureaucratic point of view, strict standards and procedures for training, appointment, and promotion were critical for upholding not only the rules which defined the nature of administrative hierarchy, but also the authority of ministers in their own houses. The essence of bureaucracy was its adherence to rules, and nowhere was this more strongly defended than in relation to its own constitution. Part of the German bureaucratic tradition was the development of strict rules on qualification and seniority for appointment and promotion, notably for senior civil servants; permitting the appointment of professionally unqualified 'outsiders' had been one of the most contentious issues in administrative policy during the Weimar years. Appointments and promotions in the senior grade of the civil service had been covered since 1921 by a series of 'Reich principles' (*Reichsgrundsätze*, or RGS) which set out the minimum qualifications at each stage of the career. For the initial appointment as a *Regierungsrat*, a candidate either had to have completed the prescribed training as an *Assessor*, or (to allow for the appointment of outsiders) had to be at least thirty-two years of age and have had three years' experience in the Reich, state, or local administration. Promotion to *Oberregierungsrat* required three years' seniority; promotion to *Ministerialrat* a further three years' experience, and a minimum age of thirty-five.[129]

These procedures were bound to be called into question in 1933. Not only did party officials striving for Nazification have little sympathy for such essentially bureaucratic mechanisms, but the heads of newly founded or rapidly expanding ministries also found them extremely irksome. The RGS did empower the interior and finance ministries to license certain exceptions, and Frick and Krosigk declared themselves willing to be reasonably generous; but at the same time, they reissued the RGS as a signal of their commitment to the principle of qualification by training and seniority.[130] In practice, the regulations were rendered virtually inoperative as the procurement of exceptions was consistently abused. As we have seen, the StdF *Stab* repeatedly

---

[128] See Blomberg to Hess, 29 Feb. 1936 (BA R 2/21906). Blomberg was concerned about ensuring that enough posts would be made available to the growing numbers of *Versorgungsanwärter* following the reintroduction of conscription.

[129] The regulations had been issued in the form of an interior-ministry circular to Reich ministries, 24 May 1921 (copy in BA R 18/5994).

[130] Interior- and finance-ministry circular, 26 July 1933 (copy in BA R 2/22535).

demanded promotions for its civil servants in defiance of the rules. Hess, or Bormann acting on his behalf, used their rights in relation to personnel policy to make increasingly ambitious demands on the interior ministry; they also exceeded their powers by making counter-nominations when approached for their views on a ministry candidate. In the spring of 1936, for example, Hess declared that only party members should be appointed as *Regierungspräsidenten*; a year later, Bormann insisted that the same should be true for the post of *Oberpräsident*'s deputy; and there was similar friction over the political qualification of *Landräte*.[131] From the ministry's point of view, this not only defied the principle of qualification, but was also tantamount to excluding professional civil servants from the apex of the civil-service career.

Among the new state departments, the worst offenders were the new propaganda and aviation ministries, which were equipping themselves with entire staffs from top to bottom. In 1934, the finance ministry attempted vainly to hold back a surge of promotions demanded by Goebbels, insisting that he 'not promote civil servants seconded to your ministry at such an early age that they soar way above their contemporaries in their parent departments'.[132] In this and later years, the finance and interior ministries were constrained to sanction, reluctantly, twenty-two of Goebbels's twenty-eight requests for out-of-line promotions. These included a 27-year-old with no seniority, whom Goebbels wanted to elevate to a post which had stringent age and seniority conditions, and an unqualified *alter Kämpfer*, whose three promotions in four years all violated the RGS.[133] By 1942, two-fifths of the ministry's senior civil servants lacked professional training, while the number of *Angestellte* in the propaganda ministry was also large and disproportionately unqualified.[134]

---

[131] Hess to Frick, 24 Mar. 1936, and see also Popitz to Frick, 2 Sept. 1936 (GStA Rep. 90/2339); Bormann to Frick, 19 Mar. 1937, and Frick to Bormann, 7 Apr. 1937 (GStA Rep. 90/2340). The *Oberpräsidenten*, who were also *Gauleiter*, of course, were equally energetic in seeking the nomination of party members in preference to qualified civil servants; see memo by Körner (Prussian minister-president's office), 29 Nov. 1937 (ibid.).

[132] Krosigk to Goebbels, 24 Apr. 1934 (BA R 55/45). These exceptionally rapid careers were extremely costly in budgetary terms, and were the more disturbing to peers in that fiscal constraints mandated a very restricted promotion policy as a rule.

[133] Documentation on the case of Krause, nominated for the post of *Oberregierungsrat* (BA R 18/5994); and on Müller, first nominated for promotion in Mar. 1938 (BA R 43II/455c).

[134] Figures given in propaganda-ministry memo, 'Vorschlag über die Heranbildung des Nachwuchses für den höheren Dienst im Ministerium und den Reichspropagandaämtern', 12 Aug. 1942 (BA R 55/vorl. 27).

In an attempt to restore disciplined standards of practice, the interior and finance ministries, in consultation with the StdF *Stab*, prepared a revised version of the RGS which was issued in 1936 under Hitler's signature, with Frick, Reinhardt, and Hess as co-signatories.[135] The regulations were a clear declaration of commitment in principle to a professionally qualified civil service, largely reiterating the 1921 stipulations on qualification and seniority for appointments and promotions. But they also took account of political pressures in a number of respects, though without capitulating entirely to party interests. Thus, 'reliably National Socialist candidates' [*national-sozialistisch bewährte Anwärter*]' could serve a significantly reduced probation, but only if they had also proved their professional abilities by exceptional performance in the prescribed examinations (§4). In response to party demands, full-time work for the NSDAP and its associated organizations (SA, SS, DAF, etc.) was taken into account for probation (§4); similarly, periods of both full-time and 'zealous [*eifrig*]' voluntary work for the party counted towards the field experience that was required before promotion to *Ministerialrat* (§12). In the important and disputed question of political qualification for promotion, the new RGS specified that, in addition to proven professional ability and a sound career record, promotions would be restricted to civil servants who 'with regard to [their] previous political record unconditionally warrant, and since 30 January 1933 [have] proven, that [they] unreservedly support and effectively represent the National Socialist state'.[136] This fell short of making promotion conditional on party membership, and it did not exclude any political groups as such (e.g. ex-social democrats). However, the regulations did allow for the exceptional appointment or promotion of pre-1933 party members who had given 'significant service' to the movement (§17). They also responded to party pressures for a more egalitarian career structure by permitting promotion between grades, though this was made relatively difficult by the age and seniority conditions prescribed (§15).[137]

135 *Reichsgrundsätze über Einstellung, Anstellung und Beförderung der Reichs- und Landesbeamten*, 14 Oct. 1936 (*RGBl*, 1936, i. 893); see Mommsen, *Beamtentum*, pp. 79 ff. They did not apply to local government. See also Dr Wittland, 'Die Reichsgrundsätze über Einstellung, Anstellung und Beförderung der Reichs- und Landesbeamten', *Beamtenjahrbuch*, 11 (1936), 599–614.

136 §8; note the transmutation of the 'national' state of the BBG and BRÄndG. The clause also set racial conditions for both the civil servant and his spouse.

137 The RGS were amended in June 1938, to reduce the terms of probationary service (*RMBliV*, 1938, 969); see Ch. 6, p. 214, below.

The issue of the RGS did not bring to an end disputes about the relative weight of political and professional qualification. Although the regulations defended the principle of professional qualification, they simultaneously allowed exceptions to be made to many of their provisions. These powers were delegated to the interior and finance ministries, but Hitler also reserved to himself the capacity to license exceptions to *any* of its other clauses as he saw fit (§17). This loophole—a typically all-embracing let-out which virtually contradicted the ostensible purpose of the law—may well have been included at Hess's behest. At any rate, it was to be exploited by his office as a means of demanding an expanded role in personnel decisions. By 1939, Hess was insisting on decision-making rights and a level of political qualification which went far beyond the statutory definitions that had been achieved meanwhile.

VI

Chief among these was the comprehensive codification of civil-service law issued in January 1937. Often described by its framers as 'the crowning work' of the regime's civil-service policy, the *Deutsches Beamtengesetz* (DBG) was indeed a crucial component of the interior ministry's reform strategy. It was symptomatic of the obstacles to the ministry's programme, however, that the DBG—originally intended to come into force when the BBG expired in September 1934—should have taken so much longer to bring to completion. Serious work on it had begun in the Reich interior ministry in 1934, under Pfundtner's supervision.[138] In format, the law was modelled closely on the 1873 RBG, and the tone of the earliest drafts also came directly from that law. Legalistic in terminology, devoid of any strong political emphases, these were functional measures that revealed an unbroken continuity with the assumptions of an earlier era in both format and content.[139] At this stage, the interior ministry may have believed that its version could be adopted more or less as it stood, for in August Pfundtner was still assuming that the law could be made ready for cabinet decision by September.[140] By November, however, this expectation had been

[138] In June 1934, Pfundtner told dept. IV of the Reich interior ministry that the new civil-service law and disciplinary code were to be settled 'before the end of the summer'; note of 11 June 1934 (BA R 18/5438).

[139] Copies of drafts dated June and Aug. 1934 in BA R 18/5547.

[140] Note to dept. IV, 10 Aug. 1934 (BA R 18/5438; reprinted in Mommsen, *Beamtentum*, p. 203).

disappointed. Referring to Prussia's long experience in civil-service law, Popitz observed that the current draft lacked 'music', and offered some sharp criticisms; of more importance was the fact that Hess was not satisfied with it.[141] Pfundtner's irritation with both these standpoints is revealed in his comment that if 'something *entirely new* is to be created in the field of civil-service law . . . this can hardly be realized without undermining principles of the professional civil service that have been tried and tested for centuries and that even survived the period of Marxist rule'.[142] From now on, the drafting of the law became a battleground between the conflicting interests in renovation and innovation.

Work on the law began again virtually from scratch, with drafts now picking up the 'music' demanded by Popitz and expected by Hess. Where earlier versions had opened by defining civil servants 'within the meaning of the act', by March 1935 the preamble was striking a new note: 'A professional civil service rooted in the German nation, imbued with the National Socialist ideology, and bound in loyalty to the Leader of the German Reich and nation, Adolf Hitler, constitutes a keystone of the National Socialist state. Accordingly the government has remodelled the duties and rights of German civil servants in the following law.'[143] Detailed discussions began in earnest when this draft was circulated to the Reich ministries and to Hess, who raised a number of serious objections. He insisted that the preamble and opening paragraphs of the law were of the utmost importance, and must constitute a 'powerful' statement of the law's principles.[144] Where the first section of the March draft had spoken of the civil servant as 'the executant of the state's National Socialist will', Hess substituted the more precise formulation, 'the executant of the will of the state borne by the National Socialist German Workers' Party'. At his demand, the reference to civil servants' 'rights and duties' in the preamble was dropped, and the law was purged of any implication that they possessed subjective rights *vis-à-vis* the state.[145] Related to this, too, was his reluctance, shared by

[141] Pfundtner note to Frick, 8 Nov. 1934 (BA R 18/5524; reprinted in Mommsen, *Beamtentum*, pp. 203-4).

[142] Note of 8 Nov. Pfuntdner had already refused to yield supervision of the DBG to the Reich chancellery; note to Frick, 18 Oct. 1934 (BA R 18/5292).

[143] Draft dated 31 Mar. 1935; GStA Rep. 90/2329. It was followed by drafts on 31 May, 14 June, and 12 Dec. 1935, 11 Jan. 1936 (all ibid.), 18 Dec. 1936, 9 and 15 Jan. 1937 (GStA Rep. 90/2330).

[144] Hess to interior ministry, 26 Apr. 1935 (GStA Rep. 90/2329).

[145] Thus the proposed section on 'Rights of the Civil Servant' was retitled 'Safeguards [*Sicherung*] for the Legal Status of the Civil Servant'. On the question of subjective public rights, see also Ch. 6, pp. 199-203, below.

Hitler, to see any provisions on civil servants' pensions and dependants' allowances incorporated in the law, far less anything that increased their entitlements.[146]

Predictably, Hess's main objections were to the draft's weaknesses in taking account of the status and claims of the NSDAP in relation to the civil service. For example, he wanted transfers of civil servants who occupied a wide range of party, SA, or SS offices to be conditional on his agreement, rather than his consultation, as the interior ministry had proposed for a much narrower group (§35).[147] Similarly, he argued that part-time or honorary office in the party should be included in the calculation of pensionable service. But by far the most contentious issue was whether civil servants had the right or duty to go outside official channels in matters that affected the NSDAP. Specifically, Hess wanted a right for the party to be informed of any matter injurious to the NSDAP which was discovered by a civil servant in the course of his official duties (§42(2)). It was not so much the importance of the information itself that was at stake, as the fact that Hess's proposal would give the StdF a base from which to interfere in civil-service affairs. Frick found it hard to satisfy either Hess or his own fellow ministers, who were outraged at this proposed breach of the principles of official secrecy and internal discipline. His own suggestions—creating a special complaints commission, or allowing an official to go over the head of his immediate superior and inform a higher authority—met with vehement opposition from ministers, and were equally unacceptable to Hess.[148]

This deep disagreement was the principal reason for the repeated delays in the issue of the DBG. An attempt to secure a ruling by Hitler failed, as did the search for compromises on this and other tricky questions, including civil servants' answerability in party courts (§7) and, of course, the role of the StdF in appointments.[149] By January 1936, Frick had a new draft ready which he described as 'kabinettsreif' and 'extremely urgent'.[150] He felt keenly the risk that further delay

---

[146] For Hitler's views, see note from Killy to Lammers, 1 Feb. 1936 (BA R 43II/419a; reprinted in Mommsen, *Beamtentum*, pp. 206-7).

[147] References are to clauses as numbered in the final law.

[148] See notes from the education, post, transport, economics, propaganda, and foreign ministries, and correspondence in BA R 43II/420; reprinted in Mommsen, *Beamtentum*, pp. 208-11; see also pp. 99-100.

[149] A ministerial conference on 4 June 1935 recognized that deadlock had been reached, and agreed to turn this and other issues over to Hitler (minutes in GStA Rep. 90/2329). On 25 June, Lammers reported to Frick that Hitler wanted to discuss them further with Hess, and that he saw no urgency for passing the law (BA R 43II/420a).

[150] Interior-ministry circular, 16 Jan. 1936 (BA R 43II/419a).

might drive individual ministers to issue *ad hoc* solutions to particularly pressing problems, thereby compromising his own authority as civil-service minister. Once again, he hoped that outstanding disputes would be decided by Hitler, but the list remained long and daunting. Not only did §§7, 35, and 42(2), remain unresolved, but also such crucial issues as the granting of exemptions from the racial restrictions on appointment (§25); the question whether candidates for appointment, many of whom would be only in their teens, must prove that they had mastered National Socialist ideology (§26); and the new categorization of 'political' posts (§44). Moreover, Hitler and Hess remained stubborn in their refusal to sanction any draft that contained financial provisions, and once again Hitler was arguing that there was no great urgency for passing the law.[151] The Reich chancellery's expert, Killy, counselled accommodation to the situation as it stood; he suggested that the current lack of clarity about 'certain ideas and situations' constituted an unfavourable climate for the adoption of such a fundamental law, and expressed the hope that matters might be resolved 'in the English manner' by 'letting things sort themselves out and then legalizing these organic developments in due course through an appropriately exhaustive statute'.[152]

Despite Frick's misgivings, it appears that at least the first stage of this process occurred, since active work on the DBG apparently ceased for the next six or seven months. In his anxiety to get things moving again, Frick then began to yield to Hess's demands. Between September 1936 and January 1937, a series of compromises on §42(2), still the main sticking-point, was negotiated between Frick, Hess, and Bormann.[153] The wording Frick eventually agreed to was hardly ideal: it permitted civil servants who were party members to communicate information that was damaging to the NSDAP to the StdF as well as to their ministry or supreme authority; non-party members were given the option of bypassing the usual channels and informing their ministry. The majority of ministers, including Göring, rallied once again to express their strongest opposition to this proposal; Hess remained obdurate, and the passage of the law was once more in jeopardy. The deadlock was broken, paradoxically, by Hitler himself, who finally

151 Killy to Lammers, 1 Feb. 1936, and Lammers's handwritten marginal note recording Hitler's view (BA R 43II/419a; reprinted in Mommsen, *Beamtentum*, pp. 206-7).
152 Ibid., 207.
153 Full details in ibid. 100-2, and documents reprinted pp. 212-22.

agreed to make the ruling that he had refused eighteen months earlier. Though the background of this is unclear, it appears that towards the end of 1936 Hitler indicated his readiness to see some of the less fundamental and delicate issues of *Reichsreform* taken up again. In particular, he was reported to have authorized active work on a number of linked legislative initiatives under preparation in the interior ministry, including the DBG.[154] His decision on the offending §42(2) was that all civil servants, if they chose not to use the usual channels, should have the option of reporting directly to their supreme authority or else to the Führer himself, as head of state.[155] Hitler's formula thus nullified the hopes of Hess and Bormann that the DBG would endow the StdF *Stab* with a permanent watch-dog role in administrative business. But a last-ditch attempt by Bormann to block the passage of the law failed, and in the cabinet meeting of 26 January 1937 the last few problems were ironed out and the law was formally approved.[156]

In an essay on 'Die NSDAP und das Deutsche Beamtengesetz' published in February 1937, Hess's subordinate, Walter Sommer, suggested that the negotiation of the law had exemplied the role of the StdF in legislation: a somewhat ironic comment.[157] Hess and Bormann's main contribution to the DBG had been to delay it while they tried to promote their interests, and then to attempt sabotage. But the final version represented a compromise between ministerial insistence on maintaining the integrity of civil-service policy, and the party's demands for due regard to be paid to its political interests. The vexatious struggle over §42(2) ended in a formal defeat for Hess, which was confirmed in the subsequent decision that Lammers, not Hess, would act as the channel for information submitted to Hitler.[158] As far as the other bones of contention were concerned, the balance sheet was mixed. Full-time work for the NSDAP or its formations, including before 1933, was accepted for the calculation of pensionable service (§§85 and 179(8)). On the other hand, Hess had to accept tight

[154] Reported at state secretaries' conference, 9 Dec. 1936; see n. 81 above. It was at this meeting that Hess's representative, Sommer, had presented his new proposal for §42(2).

[155] Memo by Lammers, 13 Jan. 1937; BA R 43II/420a; reprinted in Mommsen, *Beamtentum*, p. 220.

[156] See Lammers's memos on this sequence of events, 26 Jan. 1937 (BA R 43II/420a and R 18/5550; reprinted in Mommsen, *Beamtentum*, pp. 220-1).

[157] In *DVBl*, Feb. 1937, 81-3.

[158] Führer decree, 20 July 1937 (*RGBl*, 1937, i. 875); and Reich chancellery circular, 16 Sept. 1937 (BA R 43II/580).

limitations on the categories of those civil servants who, as party office-holders, could not be transferred without consultation with him (§35). Equally, the freedom of a civil servant who was a party office-holder to give political reports on other civil servants was partially restricted by considerations of official secrecy.[159] It was also important that the category of 'political' civil servants, subject to dismissal at Hitler's will, was expanded (§44).

A number of other issues were left to subsequent decision. Among these, the answerability to party courts of civil servants who were party members (§7(4)) was never finally settled.[160] On another important question—the grounds and procedures for the compulsory retirement of civil servants whose political reliability came to be doubted (§71)—subsequent decisions set the limits far wider than the DBG itself had intended. These powers were the counterpart to the political criteria for appointment established elsewhere in the DBG (§26(3)), but both the clause and its executive instructions were framed in such a way as to limit the party's capacity to exploit it. First, the wording restricted the application of §71 to officials who were judged to be 'no longer' reliable supporters of the Nazi state, thus preventing its retrospective use. Secondly, the power to initiate investigations and proceedings remained within the civil-service hierarchy, who used it sparingly; although the StdF had the right to insist on proceedings against any civil servant who had left or been expelled from the NSDAP, he had no further rights in relation to them, except to be informed of the outcome.[161] Moreover, §171 of the DBG, in conjunction with §6(2), expressly excluded the use of judicial decisions as evidence of unreliability, thus formally protecting the independence of the judiciary. In 1938, Hitler expressed a desire to make §71 applicable to judicial decisions, and in general to weaken the principle of judicial tenure. This was deflected, but not entirely successfully, by Lammers and Gürtner, the justice minister; Lammers issued a circular to the Reich authorities which reiterated the provisions of §171, but instructed them

[159] *VO zur Durchführung des Deutschen Beamtengesetzes*, 29 June 1937, re §26 (*RGBl*, 1937, i. 669). See also StdF instructions on this, 71/36, 13 May 1936 (BA NS 6/vorl. 223); 96, 5 Aug. 1937 (NS 6/vorl. 226); and 11/38, 21 Feb. 1938 (NS 6/vorl. 228).

[160] Mommsen, *Beamtentum*, pp. 103–4; also correspondence between the StdF *Stab*, the HfK, and the Saxon Amt für Kommunalpolitik, 1938–42 (BA NS 25/839); and Bormann to interior ministry, 26 Jan. 1938, together with ensuing correspondence (BA R 2/31906).

[161] VO, 29 June 1937 (see n. 159 above), re §71. Documentation on 14 cases of alleged unreliability, many of which arose from religious scruples, can be found in BA R 43II/447 and 448; see also Broszat, *The Hitler State*, pp. 230–3.

to apply stricter criteria than hitherto in the evaluation of a civil servant's official behaviour.[162] These pressures for a tougher political stand intensified during the war, and culminated in the Reichstag decision of April 1942, which gave Hitler the right to dismiss any official at will. Not long thereafter, Bormann also secured the right to initiate cases under §71.[163]

If some of the political implications of the DBG were unprecedented and strongly contested, there were other provisions that, though less spectacular, constituted significant innovations in civil-service law.[164] For example, the law removed certain matters from the competence of the civil courts, transferring them to the less independent Reich administrative court system: this was stipulated for civil servants' financial claims against the state (§142) and for third-party claims against an official (§147). In addition, civil servants lost their legal right to salary increments, which could now be withheld for sub-standard performance (§21). The code formalized the episodic discrimination against women contained in Weimar measures and in the BRÄndG, by stating that women were not eligible for tenured appointment until the age of thirty-five, compared to twenty-seven for men (§28). Moreover, married women were to be dismissed if they were deemed economically secure, or at their own request. They received a tax-free severance payment in lieu of all other claims, provided that they were not married to a man with two or more Jewish grandparents (§§63-5).[165] As a whole, the DBG incorporated the previously separate laws

---

[162] Lammers' circular, 12 July 1938, and preceding correspondence (BA R 22/20753); also StdF circular 136/38, 1 Sept. 1938 (BA NS 6/vorl. 231). Documents on 13 cases brought against judges are in BA R 22/20788. See also H. Weinkauff, 'Die deutsche Justiz und der Nationalsozialismus: Ein Überblick', in *Die deutsche Justiz und der Nationalsozialismus*, i (Stuttgart, 1968), 120-2; Mommsen, *Beamtentum*, pp. 104-6; and Broszat, *The Hitler State*, pp. 254-5.

[163] *Beschluss des Grossdeutschen Reichstags*, 26 Apr. 1942 (*RGBl*, 1942, i. 247); Ch. 6, p. 228, below; it does not appear that Hitler used this power extensively; see also A. Wagner, 'Die Umgestaltung der Gerichtsverfassung und des Verfahrens- und Richterrechts im nationalsozialistischen Staat', in *Die deutsche Justiz*, p. 219. Bormann's new powers were announced in the 6th DVO to the DBG, 29 July 1942 (*RGBl*, 1942, i. 483).

[164] Discussed in R. Schneider *et al.*, *Kommentar zum Deutschen Beamtengesetz* (Berlin, 1937); also O. G. Fischbach, *Deutsches Beamtengesetz*, 2nd edn. (Berlin, 1940), and A. Brand, *Das Deutsche Beamtengesetz*, 4th edn. (Berlin, 1942). See also Ch. 6 below.

[165] This regulation was not enforced against women in the lower echelons of the postal and telegraph services; see VO, 29 June 1937 (n. 159 above), re §63. In view of the labour shortage during the war, it was amended to annul the automatic dismissal of married women, to allow their temporary reappointment, and to grant requests for dismissal for pregnant women and women with school-age children only; see 2nd and

on dependants and on accident assistance, but disciplinary law was now treated in a distinct and enlarged disciplinary code.[166] Although the DBG was not the springboard for a more confident and decisive period of civil-service and administrative policy, it was by no means an irrelevance. Together with the disciplinary law, it constituted a massive codification comparable in form, if not in scope, to the codification work of late imperial Germany. In the technical sense of providing a single, uniform legal instrument in a field which had hitherto been the province of numerous separate enactments as well as considerable lacunae, it was thus no mean achievement. Moreover, as Broszat has suggested, the DBG 'was a rare example of what a united cabinet could achieve under Hitler', in terms of defending a coherent civil-service policy against the encroachments of Hess and Bormann.[167] However, the effectiveness of the measure was severely compromised by the fact that it stood virtually on its own, lacking the companion measures of administrative reform to which it was ostensibly the centre-piece. Nor was it the hoped-for conclusive measure that would seal the interior ministry's authority, and the integrity and competence of the civil service as the agency of administration in the Nazi state. Rather, as a piece of legislative machinery, the DBG was not competent to represent or resolve the complex power struggles and divisions of interest that continued to focus on civil-service affairs.

Clear evidence of this fact was provided by the question of the role of the StdF in appointments and promotions, which, as we have seen, had been the subject of unremitting dispute since 1933. The RGS had not clarified his power to sanction promotions, while the DBG also left the matter for later resolution by Führer decree (§31). This was duly issued in July 1937, and closely followed the 1935 pattern; although the decree itself only reiterated Hess's right to be 'heard', subsequent executive instructions interpreted this as giving him a right of veto.[168] Hess, as we have seen, had made active use of his rights since 1935, and he now exploited the additional loophole offered by the exceptions

3rd *VO über Massnahmen auf dem Gebiet des Beamtenrechts*, 3 May 1940 (*RGBl*, 1940, i. 732) and 7 Oct. 1942 (*RGBl*, 1942, i. 577); also the 9th VO to DBG, 22 June 1943, re §63 (*RGBl*, 1943, i. 367).

[166] *Reichsdienststrafordung* (RDStrO), 26 Jan. 1937 (*RGBl*, 1937, i. 71); DVO, 29 June 1937 (*RGBl*, 1937, i. 690).

[167] Broszat, *The Hitler State*, p. 253; also Mommsen, *Beamtentum*, pp. 91-2.

[168] *Erlass des Führers und Reichskanzlers über die Ernennung der Beamten und die Beendigung des Beamtenverhältnisses*, 10 July 1937; and DVO, 12 July 1937 (*RGBl* 1937, i. 769 and 771).

clause of the RGS by interpreting it as giving the party the final say in any disputed nomination. Hess also claimed that he now had Hitler's express backing for his view that all senior civil servants (*Ministerialrat* upwards) must be party members. Ministers raised a host of objections to this—that it would be impractical, especially in the technical branches; it would penalize anyone who had refrained from joining the party in order not to appear opportunist; it discriminated against those caught out by the NSDAP's 1937 freeze on new memberships; it would deter recruits to the profession. Frick suggested that one way round the problem would be to confer automatic party membership on politically impeccable older civil servants. This was hardly likely to be acceptable to the party, however, and in June 1939, Lammers secured a compromise ruling from Hitler that party membership was only 'desirable' at this stage.[169]

The continuing wrangles showed that Hess and Bormann would not cease to test the limits of the qualified powers conferred on them by statute. After all, the StdF *Stab* had only existed for a few years, and ideas on its role and future were still developing. Given their objectives to 'Nazify' the civil-service élite and gain more authority in personnel policy, there were certain weaknesses in the strategy employed up to this point. For one thing, reviewing nominations in the StdF *Stab* absorbed an enormous amount of time, often in unproductive routine decisions. For another, the question of what party membership meant as such was still problematic. By the end of the 1930s, therefore, it appears that the StdF *Stab* was shifting away from emphasis on simple membership as the political test for civil servants as a group. Instead, it wanted a more exacting standard applied to the élite of civil servants, with party membership no longer expected of the rank and file (including many in the lower posts of the senior grade). This was argued by Walter Sommer, as Hess's spokesman, at an important conference on personnel policies attended by representatives of the StdF *Stab* and of certain ministries in August 1938.[170] The NSDAP, he suggested, was no longer particularly interested in a civil servant's political qualification at the time of appointment, but wanted stricter criteria than hitherto to be applied when an official was being considered for promotion to a key post. At that stage, it would no longer be enough that a civil servant was 'politically reliable' (as current legislation

---

[169] Full details in Mommsen, *Beamtentum*, pp. 80-6, 182-97.
[170] Minutes of conference on 31 Aug. 1938 (copy in GStA Rep. 90/2340).

stipulated); he must not only be a party member, but he must have proven 'political genius and . . . sensitivity'.

It was significant that Sommer's remarks also dwelt on a question in which he happened to have a strong personal interest: the training of the next generation of the civil-service élite.[171] The personnel strategy he was proposing looked to the future, and he was very concerned about the coming challenge of securing good recruits now that other careers beckoned more enticingly. The ultimate aim, he suggested, was 'to train a civil-service corps that was no longer distinguishable in any way from the party's leadership corps'; what this training would look like was something that his office was increasingly concerned with. Not long before these remarks, in fact, Sommer had been in the middle of a major clash between his office and the interior ministry over the principles of training reform. Once again, the issues had turned on the problematic relationship of professional and political standards.

VII

The interior ministry had initially taken up the reorganization of training for the higher civil service towards the end of 1934. It was seen by Frick as complementary to the DBG, and it proceeded with the same aims of standardization and the defence of bureaucratic procedures. Training policies at this time were far from uniform. Despite the statement of common principle issued by the *Länder* in 1930, there had been no consistency in the pre-1933 training programmes for either the administrative or the judicial branch of the higher civil service (*höherer Dienst*).[172] In most of Germany outside Prussia, candidates in these two principal branches shared a joint training. They took the same university law curriculum, culminating in the first state examination in law (*erste juristische Staatsprüfung*); their subsequent apprenticeship or in-service training as *Referendare* (trainees) also followed a single pattern, consisting primarily of sequences of work in the courts and other government and judicial agencies, and ending with a second state examination (the *grosse Staatsprüfung*). This qualified them

---

[171] See also Chs. 6, p. 214, and 8, pp. 280-94, below.
[172] For the history of training policy, see E. Geib, 'Die Ausbildung des Nachwuchses für den höheren Verwaltungsdienst', *AöR*, 80 (1955/56), 307-45; A. von Batocki *et al.* (eds.), *Staatsreferendar und Staatsassessor: Reformvorschläge für das Ausbildungs- und Berechtigungswesen der Juristen und Volkswirte* (Jena, 1927); Ch. 2, pp. 49-50, above.

as *Assessoren* (assistants), eligible for probationary civil-service appointment when a position became open. Prussia, by contrast, whose higher grade recruited many more candidates than the much smaller administrations of the other *Länder*, had traditionally divided its judicial and administrative training after the first state examination, conducting a separate in-service scheme for *Referendare* in the interior administration. However, this system had been suspended in 1927; as the Nazis came to power, therefore, a joint training was *de facto* the norm throughout Germany—until, in June 1933, Prussia re-established its separate administrative training.[173]

Much of the subsequent debate about training policy now turned on this question of joint versus separate training, which was more than simply a technical issue. The progress of defederalization meant that by 1934-5 the Reich justice and interior ministries both controlled national administrative apparatuses for whose reproduction they were also responsible. The achievement of a national joint training system was integral to Frick's strategy for making the interior administration the nucleus of a reconstructed and standardized national administration, and was vital if the interior administration was to have access to a pool of candidates from which to draw men of high quality. By comparison with the annual intake of some 900 into the judicial system, the interior's 150-200 recruits did not represent a critical mass, and in terms of image would look more like an exception if separately trained than the norm which the ministry aspired to represent. On top of this, Frick wanted a uniform training for the non-technical specialized branches of the administration (finance, local government, welfare, transport, etc.), in order to defeat any tendency towards the development of independent training schemes in these areas. Also important here was the idea of expanding the practical training of young men, so that they would 'know something about life and not stick only to the letter of the law', as Pfundtner put it.[174]

Not all of Frick's colleagues were convinced that his was the best strategy. Men schooled in the Prussian tradition, like the Prussians

[173] Prussian interior-ministry instruction, 'Annahme von Regierungs-referendaren', 20 June 1933 (*MBliV*, 1933, 738). This adopted the same racial criteria for acceptance as instituted by the BBG, but set no political conditions; an earlier judicial instruction had imposed demands for 'Volksverbundenheit, soziales Einfühlungsvermögen, Verständnis für die gesamte völkische Entwicklung', etc. (24 Apr. 1933; *JMBl*, 1933, 130); see also Prussian justice ministry to provincial judicial offices, 28 July 1933 (GStA P 135/2661).

[174] For the interior ministry's views, see Pfundtner memo for Frick, 8 Nov. 1934 (BA R 18/5438).

Popitz and Schulenburg, were strongly committed to its separate training, which for them was the core of a system built on practical knowledge and all-round experience.[175] What was more important was the fact that the Reich justice ministry was unwilling either to concede sufficient time during the *Referendarzeit* for training experience in the administration, or to agree to a shared training system unless it was absolutely uniform. The German judicial administration underwent a more complete process of centralization in 1934-5 than the interior administration, and the Reich justice ministry was able to move faster to establish uniformity in its own sphere. By 1935, it had issued new national regulations for the training both of *Referendare* and of judges and public prosecutors (*Richter* and *Staatsanwälte*), and was evidently reluctant to agree to the adjustments proposed by the interior ministry.[176] But a decision of some kind was overdue, because the JAO had invalidated some of the *Länder* training regulations for the administrative civil service. At the beginning of 1936, therefore, Frick conceded defeat for the time being, and announced his plans for a separate administrative training.[177]

Frick's main aim was to create 'a uniform type of administrative assistant' (the *Verwaltungsassessor*, as opposed to the judicially trained *Gerichtsassessor*) who would be qualified to move freely among all the non-technical branches, including local government, and help the development of a coherent and co-ordinated national administrative system. The training scheme borrowed from the Prussian model, but gave greater weight to practical experience in branches outside the interior administration itself. A university legal training was to remain the basis for admission as a *Referendar*, but Frick hoped that prospective entrants would begin to seek practical experience outside the

175 For Popitz, see H. Herzfeld, 'Johannes Popitz: Ein Beitrag zur Geschichte des deutschen Beamtentums', in *Forschungen zu Staat und Verfassung: Festgabe für Fritz Hartung* (Berlin, 1958), 343-65; for Schulenburg, see H. Mommsen, 'Fritz-Dietlof Graf von der Schulenburg und die preussische Tradition', *VjhZ*, 32/2 (1984), 213-39, and *Beamtentum*, pp. 34-8, 137-42, 146-9. Göring, too, was committed to the separate administrative training; see his speech in the Prussian Landtag, 18 May 1933.

176 The judicial regulations were the *Justizausbildungsordnung* (JAO), 22 July 1934 (*RGBl*, 1934, i. 727), and the *Verordnung über die Laufbahn für das Amt des Richters und Staatsanwalts*, 29 Mar. 1935 (*RGBl*, 1935, i. 487). For Frick's reading of Gürtner's views and his ministry's position (apparently not entirely the same), see memo by Frick, 18 May [1935] (BA R 18/5567). Gürtner was also said to oppose a joint system of qualification for fear that candidates rejected for the administration on political grounds would seek employment in the judicial service; see exchange between Lammers and Pfundtner, 15 and 19 Jan. 1937 (BA R 43II/450a).

177 Frick to StdF, Prussian minister-president, Prussian finance minister, and Reich finance and labour minister, 3 Feb. 1936 (R 43II/450a).

law in their vacations. A three-year training period followed, to include eight months in the court system, ten months in a *Landratsamt*, and shorter periods in local-government, police, finance, and welfare offices, as well as other administrative agencies. These proposals met with the initial approval of the ministries approached by Frick, apart from the finance ministry, which felt that its needs were best met by recruitment from the ranks of the *Gerichtsassessoren*.[178] As plans developed and were more widely circulated, however, it became clear that the specialist ministries were concerned that the new regulations might limit their freedom of choice to recruit *Gerichtsassessoren*, a point which in fact was not fully clarified in the regulations which were finally issued.[179]

More problematic was the response of Hess's office to the draft legislation, which Frick circulated at the end of December 1936, aiming to issue it at the same time as the DBG.[180] If one part of Frick's strategy was to standardize training and keep it under his ministry's control, another equally important objective was to maintain the principle that only fully qualified professionals who saw the civil service as a lifelong career should staff the senior ranks of the administration. His draft contained few concessions to party interests as such, apart from provisions that exempted a handful of offices (including *Reichsstatthalter*, *Oberpräsident*, and *Polizeipräsident*) from the regulations, and allowed the principle of qualification by training to be suspended in exceptional cases (§12). But Hess now proposed a totally different formula for regulating admission to the senior civil service, one which rode roughshod over the principles nurtured by the interior ministry. Instead of a careful specification of training procedures for a professional career, Hess's spokesman, Sommer, presented a highly abbreviated draft law 'on qualification for the higher civil service', which essentially declared as qualified not only 'anyone who has completed the training prescribed in a training regulation . . . to be

---

[178] Minutes of conference attended by representatives of the above, 25 Feb. 1936 (ibid.).

[179] See queries raised by e.g. finance and education ministries, Jan. 1937 (ibid.); also internal discussion in the labour ministry, 22 Feb. 1936, and ensuing documents (GStA Rep. 318/835). The measure as passed did allow for candidates trained according to the JAO to be appointed as *Regierungsassessoren* under certain circumstances, but left unclear the source of recruitment to the specialist administrations; see W. Sommer, 'Die Ausbildung des Nachwuchses der höheren Verwaltungsbeamten', *DVBl*, Aug. 1937, 360-3.

[180] Frick to Reich ministries, 29 Dec. 1936 (BA R 43II/450a).

issued by the Reich interior ministry', but also 'anyone who without this training has been declared qualified'.[181] Eligible for this declaration were civil servants with a minimum of five years' established service, and career officials of the NSDAP and its associated formations. This formula was completely unacceptable to the interior ministry, of course: as Pfundtner pointed out, it equated highly qualified *Verwaltungsjuristen* with utterly unqualified political outsiders, and discounted the whole idea of a vocationally committed and hierarchically organized profession.[182] Accordingly, Frick tried to ignore Hess's intervention, and circulated a final revised draft for ministerial approval in April, as if the StdF *Stab* had raised no objections.[183] Hess was incensed, and demanded that Frick withdraw the law until the whole issue of his counter-draft had been discussed. Frick beat a tactical retreat under this attack, and withdrew the law from the cabinet agenda. However, using his powers under §164 of the DBG, he issued it as an administrative decree in June.[184] Further protests by Hess followed, and implementation of the already published measure was temporarily suspended, on Hitler's insistence. Finally, in September, Hitler withdrew his objections to the measure, but only after assurances from Frick that there would be '*no monopoly* of administrative lawyers in administrative posts'.

The interior ministry had thus preserved one of its major priorities, the protection of a professionally trained and vocationally committed senior civil service, but at the price of abandoning the combined training system, and only after fighting off Hess's attempts to subvert its objectives. It is hardly surprising that Frick and his colleagues did not regard the decree as the final word, but were to revive the whole issue of training reform a few years later.[185] In the meantime, as the following chapters will show, the problem of defending ministry priorities had expanded into what its protagonists saw as a struggle for the

181 Copy, dated 6 Jan. 1937, in BA R 18/5550.

182 Pfundtner to Frick, 9 Jan. 1937 (ibid.).

183 Draft and official memo circulated 12 Apr. 1937 (this and following documentation in BA R 43II/450a). Goebbels was also opposed to the measure, as was Hitler himself.

184 *VO über die Ausbildung für den höheren Dienst in der allgemeinen und inneren Verwaltung*, 29 June 1937 (*RGBl*, 1937, i. 666). §164 of the DBG empowered the government, and in certain circumstances individual ministers, to issue training regulations by administrative decree (*Verordnung*); Frick had not wanted to adopt this procedure initially, because the DBG did not come into force until July, and because a statute (*Gesetz*) was required so that the new regulations could legally supersede *Länder* law. The greater prestige of a statute was also important.

185 See Ch. 8, pp. 280-94, below.

survival of an historic national institution. The conflict over the regulation of training epitomized the struggle for control of the reproduction of the civil service as a particular kind of institution. This was repeated in the new uncertainties and confusions about the professional identity and authority of the civil service that accompanied its assimilation into National Socialist political ideology.

6

Maintaining the *Gleichschaltung*: The Organization of Civil Servants in Nazi Germany

The DBG was a major addition to the formidable body of public law which, since the mid-nineteenth century, had established a pattern of close supervision of civil servants' private lives as well as their official rights and duties. Even in the Weimar Republic, disciplinary law still regulated their behaviour and personality as a matter of course; the political restraints imposed by such special legislation as the *Republik-schutzgesetze* were only part of this broad pattern of supervision. The corpus of civil-service law as a whole covered such matters as the regulation of training, appointment, and retirement, salaries and pensions, and the sphere of disciplinary law. Most of this underwent more or less change under National Socialism, though in many ways a basic continuity overrode the political rupture. Some changes—the DBG and RDStrO themselves, for example—represented the achievement of long-delayed projects of statutory consolidation, as well as the partial incorporation of specifically National Socialist principles. Other revisions, both statutory and quasi-formal, pursued more exorbitant visions of professional status and behaviour. In some cases, these drew on older models of the role of the professional civil servant, but in other respects they belonged to the core Nazi project of social and political transformation. The contradictory nature of the components in this Nazi 'revolution' has long been recognized, as also the failure to accomplish very much in practice. 'Beneath the cover of Nazi ideology,' wrote David Schoenbaum twenty years ago, 'the historic social groups continued their conflicts like men wrestling under a blanket.'[1] This placed impossible demands on the ordinary citizens who were required to assimilate or adapt to the indistinct tenets of Nazi ideology and its supposed incarnation in the new *Volksgemeinschaft*. But if National Socialism produced not a phalanx of re-educated believers, but rather a

---

[1] D. Schoenbaum, *Hitler's Social Revolution: Class and Status in Nazi Germany 1933-1939* (New York, 1966), 286. See also D. Peukert, *Inside Nazi Germany: Conformity, Opposition and Racism in Everyday Life* (New Haven and London, 1987), esp. 243-9.

'fracturing or atomisation of opinion', as a recent judgement suggests,[2] this was not for want of effort. No revision of the meaning or effects of Nazi ideological practice has yet dislodged the fundamental image of a society permeated by political propaganda and organization, and by the compulsive monitoring of public morale. However ambiguous the results of this hyperactivity, the tentacles of Nazi propaganda reached into every household and work-place—to be ignored or rejected, perhaps, yet remaining as an insistent background noise to daily life. By 1934, more than one German adult male in five was a member of the NSDAP, while many of the rest, and millions of women and young people too, belonged, whether willingly or under duress, to one of the party's formations or associations. It is probably less apt to call this political structure a machine than an amoeba, or a miasma, that shrouded and disoriented many of those who had not voluntarily succumbed to it. Boring and pointless though much of the party's activism was, however, it represented an unprecedented level of mobilization, even in such a complex and public society as twentieth-century Germany.

The transformation of ideological practice after 1933 created a paradoxical situation for civil servants. On the one hand, they were familiar with the tradition of an interventionist state that had long claimed the right to regulate the public and private behaviour of its officials. Nazi interventionism could thus be seen to some extent as simply a new version of an old story. But the new, and surely unwelcome twist was that National Socialism demanded the *active* engagement of civil servants rather than their passive conformity to prescribed rules; and it stated its new claims in enigmatic, contradictory, and even hostile terms compared with the relatively unequivocal and complaisant pronouncements of the imperial state. As a consequence, civil servants were pulled this way and that by the contrary and sometimes capricious demands placed on them, and they also found themselves and their shortcomings more publicly and officially pilloried than before.

I

Ordinary civil servants and their concerns were addressed by three principal sources of official pronouncements: the NSDAP's Hauptamt

---

[2] I. Kershaw, *Popular Opinion and Political Dissent in the Third Reich* (Oxford, 1983), 384-5.

für Beamte (HfB) and its mass-membership association, the Reichsbund der deutschen Beamten (RDB); governmental and party policies and directives concerning standards of behaviour, and rights and duties; and the public press, especially the party press. The minority of civil servants who consulted the professional journals also had access to a more academic debate about the nature of the Nazi state and the role of the civil service within it. Between them, these institutions generated a clamour of instructions and advice on what constituted correct behaviour for the public servants of the Third Reich.

The HfB and RDB emerged towards the end of 1933 as a result of the *Gleichschaltung* of existing civil-service associations, though it took several more years to work out an acceptable legal formula for the dissolution of these.[3] The exact lines of demarcation between the RDB and other party organizations with a foot in the public sector were also slow to be settled, and fear of absorption by the gigantic and powerful DAF (which organized *Angestellte* and *Arbeiter*) persisted.[4] As with all the *gleichgeschaltete* organizations, the RDB bore little resemblance to its republican predecessors: it was emphatically not an interest group representing civil servants *vis-à-vis* the state, nor was it supposed to be seen as a *ständisch* body—the two most obvious models.[5] Its tasks were to educate its members as 'exemplary National Socialists', to make them mindful of their special position in the nation as agents of the Führer's will, to support the government's civil-service policies, to sponsor welfare and self-help projects, and to further the professional education of civil servants.[6] This hardly promised more than an ancillary role for the organization, and in fact its future irrelevance was sealed in July 1933 when Jakob Sprenger, the party's original civil-service organizer,

---

[3] In common with many other professional organizations, the civil-service associations offered their support to the new regime in 1933; see e.g. letters from the DBB, RhB, Preussisches Beamtenbund, and others in Feb. and Mar. (GStA Rep. 90/613 and BA R 43I/2651); for an exception, see ADB to Hindenburg, 25 Feb. 1933 (ibid.). The old civil-service associations were dissolved by law on 27 May 1937 (*RGBl*, 1937, i. 597); and see documentation on this from *c*. 1934 in BA R 22/4462.

[4] See Reich interior-ministry circular, 27 Dec. 1934 (R 43I/421). Further information on the HfB and RDB in E. Mursinsky and J. Brill, *Die Organisation der national-sozialistischen Beamten* (Berlin, 1940), and the *Almanach der Deutschen Beamten* (Berlin, 1935). See also H. Neef, *Das Beamtenorganisationswesen im nationalsozialistischen Staat* (Berlin, 1935), and his *Fünf Jahre nationalsozialistischer Beamteneinheitsorganisation* (Berlin, 1938).

[5] See Reich interior-ministry circular, 26 Mar. 1934 (BA R 43I/2651); H. Neef, *Die politisch-weltanschauliche Reorganisation der deutschen Beamten im Sinn und Geist des Nationalsozialismus* (Berlin 1935), 7.

[6] Constitution, published in *Organisationsbuch der NSDAP* (Munich, 1937), 246-51.

moved on to higher office as *Reichsstatthalter* in Hessen, leaving the civil service to his ineffectual deputy, Hermann Neef.

Born in 1904, Neef had made his career in the middle grade of the customs service. He joined the NSDAP and SA in 1923, and was a *Stadtverordneter* and NSDAP organizer in Berlin between 1929 and 1931. There followed a period of obscurity when he resigned from the Berlin city council after a family scandal, but his patron, Sprenger, managed to protect him and preserve his standing in the party, such as it was. When the Nazis came to power, Neef's status rose: he became a member of the Reichstag and head of the HfB and RDB, and after some prodding, the finance ministry was induced to promote him to a rank more commensurate with his party role.[7] However, despite the valiant efforts of his propaganda machine to foster an image of him as a seasoned member of the highest councils of state, neither Neef nor his apparatus were ever more than rank outsiders in the real business of civil-service policy (even if, appropriately, the HfB/RDB employed more staff than any comparable Nazi organization). The ambitions of Neef and his local organizers to secure a permanent role in policy-making and appointments procedures were quickly squashed by the more powerful arms of Hess and Frick.[8] The organizations themselves eventually fell victim to the manpower drive in February 1943, when they were both disbanded and Neef himself was dispatched to less glamorous duties in an anti-aircraft gun crew.

The significance of the HfB/RDB, therefore, lies in its downward contacts with the mass membership rather than in its nugatory status in the process of policy-making. Supposedly, it was not compulsory but only 'desirable' for civil servants to join the RDB, but by 1938, 98 per cent had decided that voluntary compliance was in their best interests, thus allowing the RDB to trumpet its claim to be the 'Einheitsorganisation' of the entire German civil service.[9] The organization they joined was busy with the kind of frenetic but ultimately aimless energy that animated the Nazi party after 1933, as it tried vainly to find a new role in a state that was now its own. Between 1934 and 1938, the HfB/RDB central staff grew from 250 to 680. About ten thousand

[7] BDC Neef; documentation on his promotion in BA R 18/2132.

[8] Neef was not consulted, for example, about the DBG; see HfB to Reich chancellery, 16 Jan. 1937, and chancellery memo (Killy), 23 Jan. (BA R 43II/420a). In the same year, the *Gaue* ÄfB lost their competences in the political evaluation of civil servants; see StdF instruction 84/37, 15 July 1937.

[9] Neef, *Fünf Jahre*, p. 3; see also his speech to the first 'Deutscher Beamtentag' in 1937, in *NSBZ*, 31 Oct. 1937, 555-6.

meetings were held annually, with an aggregate attendance of two million. The nine propaganda camps established between 1936 and 1938 had been attended by 18,000 men, with another 3,000 enrolled in speakers' courses. The RDB also ran convalescent homes and medical services, financed low-cost mortgage and housing schemes, awarded financial aid for needy civil servants and their families, encouraged sports and athletic activities, played an important part in the provision of further training and refresher courses for civil servants, and collaborated with the twin pillars of populist politics, the *Kraft durch Freude* and *Schönheit der Arbeit*.[10] The *NSBZ*, which claimed to have a million subscribers, replaced the 400 or so civil-service publications of the 1920s, just as the RDB itself had superseded Weimar's 900-odd associations. The fact that this single organization now occupied the place once shared among the multifarious associations of the republic was represented by Neef as a fundamental achievement, a microcosm of what the Third Reich had accomplished for Germany itself: 'A united Reich needs a united civil service, a National Socialist people a National Socialist corps of public officials, and this in turn professional unity and integrity.'[11]

Neef himself symbolized this declaration of unity. His voice dominated the public stage through innumerable speeches and pamphlets, hammering home platitudinous and uncontroversial slogans about the new Germany, and generally trying to boost the morale of his depressed audience. The main themes were predictable and repetitive, consisting of attacks on the record of the republic, explanations and defences of Nazi civil-service policies, and the construction of a revised imagery with which to represent the civil servant to himself and to the populace. All this was also intended to prop up the myth of symmetry and design in the new German state, especially in relation to the role and status of the party. The presiding image was the substitution of an organic community of co-operation for the corruption and bureaucratism of the Weimar Republic, a substitution which enabled the civil servant to become truly the servant of the people instead of an abstract state. After 1933, 'The state was no longer a mystical and transcendent personality, as it was in some epochs of German history, but became an administrative organism in the hands of the people.'[12] Thus, 'nomination to civil-servant status is a mark of faith on the part of the Führer . . . and

10 Neef, *Fünf Jahre*, pp. 16–22; also *Almanach, passim.*

11 Neef, *Fünf Jahre*, p. 8.

12 H. Neef, *Die politische Forderung an den Beamten in Recht und Gesetzgebung* (Berlin, 1937), 3.

thus . . . of the people themselves'.[13] The civil servant should see himself as the 'mediator between the will of Adolf Hitler as Führer of the Reich, and the German people as nation',[14] or as 'a true soldier of the Führer on the field of administration',[15] whose task was not simply to 'discharge his duties without professional error or reproach, but [to] dedicate his life to the national community, free from self-seeking, a model of dutiful service and unshakeable loyalty'.[16]

The organic theme was developed in more sustained fashion in some of the HfB's educational materials, which drew on the imagery of feudalism to describe the status of the civil servant and, especially, his relationship to the Führer.[17] Placing both the civil service and National Socialism in a synthetic and largely imaginary historical lineage, these claimed that the feudal duties of *Treue* and *Gehorsam* owed by civil servants were core Germanic values which had been buried by centuries of racial impurity and national weakness, apart from a brief resurgence in eighteenth-century Prussia. Since then, the state had been degraded to the level of an economic enterprise, empty of moral worth, with the values contained in the *Treue- und Gehorsamsverhältnis* replaced by a merely external and formalistic concept of duty: 'It was no longer an honour to serve such a state. The moral content of the civil service had drained away.'[18] The establishment of the Third Reich had now healed this fractured history and restored a real continuity with the Germanic and Prussian order. The civil servant was invited to see himself as the Führer's vassal; his oath was not simply a commitment to the correct performance of his official duties, but established a liege relationship that lasted until death.[19]

The propaganda may appear crude, yet it drew upon ideas that had been commonplace in nineteenth-century academic thought, and that the right still clung to after 1918.[20] Conservatives who, after 1918, had watched with alarm the signs that civil-service status might be assimi-

---

[13] Ibid. 4.

[14] J. Vogel (ed.), *Deutsches Berufsbeamtentum: Kernsätze aus Reden, Schriften und Aufsätzen des Reichsbeamtenführers Herman Neef* (Berlin, 1942), 103.

[15] H. Neef, *Das Soldatentum des deutschen Beamten* (Berlin, 1936), 16; see also E. Ritgen and H. Wiese, *Wehrmacht und Beamtentum* (Berlin, 1937).

[16] Neef, *Fünf Jahre*, p. 6.

[17] See in particular H. Schneider (ed.), *Richtlinien Propaganda und Schulung*, issued by the HfB in 1936/7, 1937/8, and 1938/9; also Hauptschulungsamt der NSDAP, *Beamtenschulung* (1944).

[18] *Richtlinien*, 1937/8: 'Beamtenverbände und Systemzeit'.

[19] See ibid., and *Beamtenschulung*, '1944-45 Jahresplan', p. 44.

[20] See W. Wiese, *Der Staatsdienst in der Bundesrepublik Deutschland* (Neuwied and Berlin, 1972), ch. 3.

lated to labour law welcomed the renewed emphasis on the personal relationship between the *Beamte* and his *Dienstherr*.[21] The Nazi state in fact revised the civil-service oath in two stages. After a first revision in December 1933, it was finally rewritten after Hindenburg's death: 'I will be loyal and obedient to the leader of the German state [*Reich*] and nation, Adolf Hitler, observe the laws and conscientiously fulfil my official duties.'[22] As one commentator observed, implying the primacy of the leader above the law: 'The significance of the oath of loyalty to the leader is not confined to its promise to "observe the laws", but demands a lasting commitment, through an inner devotion to the person of the leader, to the political order that is represented in him.'[23] Or, in Neef's more emotive words:

This relationship . . . is not simply a constitutional or ordinary legal one, but is like that of the Germanic vassal, who for life and death in all circumstances and at all times knows and feels that he is bound to his leader. Through this personal bond with the leader the civil servant receives a proof of trust, in the same way that members of the National Socialist movement and its formations are also bound by oath of loyalty to the Führer.[24]

Oath-taking was just one of the many rituals that littered Nazi public life—indeed, it was possible for the same person to swear lifelong loyalty to his Führer on no less than six separate occasions.[25] The peculiar legal status of the civil service meant that it was particularly susceptible to co-optation within this recuperated notion of feudalism, but in Nazi Germany the ideology of leadership and vassalage was not confined to the civil service alone. No doubt the most notorious example was the SS, but the most familiar to contemporaries would probably have been the reconstruction of work-place relations effected by the Law for the Ordering of National Labour (*Arbeitsordnungsgesetz*,

[21] e.g. H. Seel, 'Das Beamtenrecht des Dritten Reiches', in H. Frank (ed.), *Deutsches Verwaltungsrecht* (Munich, 1937); A. Köttgen, 'Die Stellung des Beamtentums im völkischen Führerstaat', *JöR*, 25 (1938), 1–65.

[22] *Gesetz über die Vereidigung der Beamten und der Soldaten der Wehrmacht*, 20 Aug. 1934 (*RGBl*, 1934, i. 785); see also H. Gerber, *Politische Erziehung des Beamtentums im nationalsozialistischen Staat* (Tübingen, 1933), 29–31.

[23] E. R. Huber, *Die verfassungsrechtliche Stellung des Beamtentums* (Leipzig, 1941), 32.

[24] Neef, *Politische Forderung*, p. 10. See also F. Pansegrau, 'Die Neuformung des Beamtenrechts im nationalsozialistischen Staate', *ZADR*, 11 (1935), 820; Seel, 'Beamtenrecht' p. 161; E. R. Huber, *Verfassungsrecht des Grossdeutschen Reiches* (Hamburg, 1939), 404–7.

[25] On becoming an *Arbeitsmann*, soldier, SA trooper, NSDAP member, NSDAP official, and civil servant; see report by Amt für Kommunalpolitik, Saxony, Apr. 1938 (BA NS 25/430).

or AOG), adopted in January 1934. Together with the *Kraft durch Freude* and *Schönheit der Arbeit*, this represented the utopian promise of National Socialism to repair the complex dislocations of social harmony produced by industrial capitalism and to abolish class struggle.[26] This package, poised between ideological excess and managerial pragmatism, was as ambiguous as it was utopian, and the labour relationship aspect of civil-service policy belongs in the same context. The archaic metaphors of both civil-service and Nazi labour law disguised a pragmatic solution to the problem of work-place discipline, and did so in a form which, while verbally anti-capitalist, was not necessarily incompatible with either the industrial production process or a bureaucratized administration. The sources of National Socialism's ideological revision of bureaucracy may have been banal, and the re-baptism of the civil servant as a 'beamtete Volksgenosse'[27] or a 'Lehnsmann des Führers'[28] faintly absurd, but the generalization of this concept of social identity among civil servants was not in itself trivial, nor was the form it took accidental. Still, this propaganda was largely designed for internal consumption by civil servants, not for a wider audience. That it did not in the end save them from the opprobrium of bureaucratism will become clear.

II

There were some important respects, however, in which these new socio-political ideologies and identities were problematic. Considerable academic debate was roused after 1933 by the question of what the

---

[26] See T. W. Mason, 'Zur Enstehung des Gesetzes zur Neuordnung der nationalen Arbeit vom 20. Januar 1934: Ein Versuch über das Verhältnis "archaischer" und "moderner" Momente in der neuesten deutschen Geschichte', in H. Mommsen *et al.* (eds.), *Industrielles System und politische Entwicklung in der Weimarer Republik* (Düsseldorf, 1973), 322-51; B. Rüthers, *Die unbegrenzte Auslegung: Zum Wandel der Privatrechtsordnung im Nationalsozialismus* (Frankfurt, 1973), 382 ff.; A. Rabinbach, 'The Aesthetics of Production in the Third Reich', *JCH*, 11 (1976), 44-74; on 'modernism' and National Socialism, see H. A. Turner, 'Fascism and Modernization', *World Politics*, 24 (1972), 547-64, and J. Herf, *Reactionary Modernism: Technology, Culture and Politics in Weimar and the Third Reich* (Cambridge, 1984); on feudalism and National Socialism, see R. Koehl, 'Feudal Aspects of National Socialism', *American Political Science Review*, 65 (1960), 921-33.

[27] Köttgen, 'Stellung', p. 24.

[28] *Richtlinien*, 1937/8. In the course of the 1942 judicial reforms, judges were officially described as 'the Führer's vassal[s]'; see justice-ministry circular, 12 Oct. 1942 (BA R 22/4495).

Volksgemeinschaft meant in theory and practice, and especially how far the new Nazi order had superseded the conventional dualism of state and society, as well as the separation of powers and the positivist tradition in private and public law. Such discussions were hardly new in 1933, but they naturally took on a new significance after the political and constitutional upheaval of the Nazi seizure of power. The terms of debate were fraught with consequences for the status of the Third Reich in legal and political theory, not least for its claim—crucial in the eyes of its many conservative apologists—to be a *Rechtsstaat*.[29] The practical consequences of these debates were limited, of course, by the ability of the Nazi regime to free itself from normative regulation in selected policy domains, notably the expanded areas of police and racial/eugenic matters, and by the persistent unclarity of the new norms even where they (more or less) did exist. Academic jurisprudence and political theory circulated in a somewhat elliptical orbit between irrelevance to what was actually happening in crucial areas of the law, and, within certain limits, open debate about the nature of the Nazi state. In the space offered by specialist and limited-circulation academic journals, books, and pamphlets, and occasionally in the wider world of textbooks on constitutional and administrative law, theorists like Höhn, Huber, Koellreutter, and Gerber could calculate just how far self-interest and conscience might take them as they darted, moth-like, round the burning centre of the Nazi *Weltanschauung*.

The substance of these debates turned on some of the classic themes in German constitutional and legal theory, including the nature of the *Rechtsstaat*, the role of law in political organization, and the relationship between justice (*Recht*) and laws (*gesetztes Recht*). To these were added new issues peculiar to the circumstances of the Nazi polity: the legal and constitutional meaning of the *Volksgemeinschaft*, the status of the Führer, and the vexed political question of the relationship between the NSDAP and the state. The conundrum of how to domesticate these

---

[29] See in particular the work of O. Koellreutter, e.g. *Vom Sinn und Wesen der nationalen Revolution* (Berlin, 1933), 9-13; 'Der nationalsozialistische Rechtsstaat', in H. H. Lammers and H. Pfundtner (eds.), *Grundlagen, Aufbau und Wirtschaftsordnung des nationalsozialistischen Staates*, i. (Berlin, 1936), 16; *Volk und Staat in der Weltanschauung des Nationalsozialismus* (Berlin, 1935). For the following discussion, see M. Stolleis, 'Gemeinschaft und Volksgemeinschaft: Zur juristischen Terminologie im Nationalsozialismus', *VjhZ*, 20/1 (1972), 16-38, and his *Gemeinwohlformeln im nationalsozialistischen Recht* (Berlin, 1974), 236 ff.; D. Kirschenmann, *'Gesetz' im Staatsrecht und in der Staatsrechtslehre des Nationalsozialismus* (Berlin, 1970); R. Echterhölter, *Das öffentliche Recht im nationalsozialistischen Staat* (Stuttgart, 1970); Rüthers, *Unbegrenzte Auslegung*; E. Fraenkel, *The Dual State: A Contribution to the Theory of Dictatorship* (New York, 1941).

new issues into the conventions of theoretical discourse was virtually insoluble, just as the practical problems of party-state relations—indeed, of agreement on the basic nature of either of the two institutions— defeated bureaucrats and political leaders: the Nazi political system baffled its theorists and functionaries alike. One example can be taken as representative here: the specific problems that arose from the Nazi claim to have effectively revised the social order in the *Volksgemeinschaft*, and with it the meaning of individual rights and the status of contract. For, jejune though the rhetoric of feudalization may sound, it was rooted in fundamental principles of Nazi ideology, and the irresolution of legal theory and practice in this area carried concrete implications for all civil servants (indeed, for all citizens). The example also illustrates the parameters of permissible ideological debate in the 1930s.

The basic issue was the claim that the institution of the *Volksgemeinschaft* had superseded the conventional liberal dichotomy of state and society by swallowing them, along with all other social schisms, into a single totalizing whole. This claim rested ultimately on the assumption of a natural biological unity of the *Volk*, a word that connoted both race and nation and that acted as the Nazis' rhetorical antonym to class.[30] The indivisibility of the *Volk* was the foundation of the indivisibility of its *Gemeinschaft*. Although theorists differed, often sharply, in their constructions of the consequent status and interrelationship of terms such as state, politics, or the party, there was a substratum of agreement that the term *Volk* signalled the source and the specificity of the Nazi political order, and that the unity it constituted had supplanted the discord and confusion associated with the division of power in the 'liberal' state. For a theorist like Reinhard Höhn, who was committed to the elaboration of an effectively Nazified legal philosophy, the primacy of the *Volk* in political discourse was self-evident, and marked a wholesale disavowal of the principles and vocabulary of liberalism.[31] But even less iconoclastic writers who were still addicted to the state as an autonomous concept adulterated their defence of it with a large measure of *völkisch* concession:

In the *völkisch* sense the *Volk* is seen primarily as a living biological unity, as a natural community, for which blood and soil are the constitutive elements . . .

---

[30] C. Berning, *Vom 'Abstammungsnachweis' zum 'Zuchtwart': Vokabular des Nationalsozialismus* (Berlin, 1964), 191 ff.; G. Mosse, *The Crisis of German Ideology: Intellectual Origins of the Third Reich* (London, 1966).

[31] See e.g. R. Höhn, *Die Wandlung im staatsrechtlichen Denken* (Hamburg, 1934).

From this *völkisch* German reasoning there necessarily also flows the eternal value of the *Rechtsstaat*. For if every true legal order is only an expression of the shape of *völkisch* life, then the *Rechtsstaat* must possess eternal value, because it persists as long as the *Volk* continues to exist as a living unity.[32] The authority of the constitutional order, its claim to compliance and preservation, is based on the fact that it springs from the natural disposition and the historical task of the *Volk*, and from these endows the political reality of the *Volk* with an enduring form.[33]

But if the Nazi polity was thus 'founded on the fundamental order of *völkisch* unity and totality',[34] where did this leave the distinction between private and public law that corresponded to the distinction between society and the state, and that supported, among other things, the legal status of civil servants? Though linguistic constructions could soften the dissonance, this was a major issue for legal theory and practice, fraught with consequences for constitutional and administrative law and for the civil law of contract, not to mention the field of civil rights. Doubts were now raised about the competence of the administrative courts to review official acts and decisions, including civil servants' legal liability. Of equal significance, as far as civil servants were concerned, was the impact of the new ideology in the arena of subjective public law (*subjektives öffentliches Recht*), to which their own rights belonged. Was it now possible for civil servants to assert any rights *vis-à-vis* the state (indeed, for any citizen to claim such rights), when each individual was merely a component atom in the molecular community? Under National Socialism, as one authority put it:

The *Volksgenosse* does not confront the people as a whole [*Volksganze*] independently and with specified rights; rather, he is a member within the people's community, and thus cannot have a subjective right *as against* the community, but only a legal status *within it* . . . There exists no legal relationship between him and the totality attended with specific rights and duties, but a relationship between the whole and its parts.[35]

[32] Koellreutter, *Volk und Staat*, pp. 11 and 23; see also his *Der deutsche Führerstaat* (Tübingen, 1934).

[33] E. R. Huber, *Wesen und Inhalt der politischen Verfassung* (Hamburg, 1935), 37. The exception, of course, was Carl Schmitt, whose Origenist *Staat, Bewegung, Volk* (Hamburg, 1933) initiated his heretical deviation; see J. W. Bendersky, *Carl Schmitt: Theorist for the Reich* (Princeton, 1983), pt. 4.

[34] Huber, *Wesen und Inhalt*, p. 39.

[35] U. Scheuner, 'Die Rechtsstellung der Persönlichkeit in der Gemeinschaft', in Frank (ed.), *Verwaltungsrecht*, pp. 83-4. See also Oberverwaltungsgerichtsrat Krüger, 'Volksgemeinschaft statt subjektiver Rechte', *DV*, 1935, 37-41; and J. Danckwerts, 'Der Rechtsschutz in der Verwaltung', in Lammers and Pfundtner (eds.), *Grundlagen*, ii.

The concept of leadership—the *Führerprinzip*—only strengthened the point, for the authority of the Führer could not be bound by legal norms of any kind. As another legal theorist correctly pointed out in 1935: 'It is unanimously accepted that administrative review may not attempt to overturn Führer decisions'.[36] Or, in Hans Frank's more epigrammatic formula: 'The Führer's command is the destiny of the administration'.[37] Moreover, National Socialism rejected the liberal distinction between political and non-political spheres of state activity, as well as that between a sphere of individual life open to (legally sanctioned) state intervention and a private or 'state-free' sphere of the individual.[38] In the words of Koellreutter: 'The distinction drawn hitherto between government and administration derives from liberalism's denial of community, and has lost its meaning in the *völkisch* state. We must start from the presumption that political leadership and public administration share a common basis in the people as a political factor.'[39]

In the first few years after 1933, there was a—for the period and the topic—relatively lively debate about these matters, as commentators struggled to interpret legal developments under National Socialism in terms of familiar analytic categories. Contributors included not only academics and interested Nazi spokesmen like Hans Frank, but senior officials like Stuckart, who had to deal with the practical consequences of the new situation and who, in the German tradition, published widely on problems of the law and its administration. But there were no easy solutions, despite the spate of publication.[40] One reason was that where the problem had any immediate political bearing it was, not surprisingly, circumvented or solved in an *ad hoc* fashion, irrespective of theoretical sanction. Thus, in the crucial area of personal security and police procedure, administrative review of Gestapo acts was generally disallowed, before being formally abolished by the 1936 Gestapo law; the criminal law in general also retreated massively from the principles of *Rechtsstaatlichkeit*.[41] But in other, less critical areas,

---

[36] T. Maunz, 'Die Zukunft der Verwaltungsgerichtsbarkeit', *DR*, 19/20 (1935), 479.

[37] H. Frank, *Recht und Verwaltung* (Munich, 1939), 11.

[38] See e.g. W. Stuckart, 'Nationalsozialistischer Staat und Verwaltungsgerichtsbarkeit', *DV*, 1935, 161-4; also his longer notes, 'Gedanken zur Verwaltungsgerichtsbarkeit im 3. Reich' (BA R 18/5521); and E. R. Huber, *Neue Grundbegriffe des hoheitlichen Rechts* (Berlin, 1935).

[39] O. Koellreutter, *Deutsches Verwaltungsrecht* (Berlin, 1936), 5.

[40] See H. Muth, 'Zum Streit um die Verwaltungsgerichtsbarkeit', *DR*, 1938, 25.

[41] H. Buchheim *et al.*, *Anatomy of the SS State* (New York, 1968), 154-5; see also M. Broszat, *The Hitler State: The Foundation and Development of the Internal Structure of the Third Reich* (London and New York, 1981), ch. 10.

policy-makers ignored, or did not make a priority of solving, the problem of a comprehensive reform of administrative law and process. The courts were left to muddle on as best they could, while the stream of inconclusive academic debate substituted for the accomplishment of actual reform.

The problems they faced were familiar from other areas of administrative activity. The Third Reich inherited widely varying systems of administrative review from *Land* to *Land*, and proved unable to establish a new and uniform system.[42] Law and procedure remained virtually untouched until 1941, when a degree of reorganization and simplification was introduced by Führer decree,[43] but as late as 1944, academic writers still had to concede that the whole area remained in a provisional state.[44] As far as any shared conclusions were reached at a theoretical level, the tendency was to argue that although the separation of powers, administrative law, and individual rights in the liberal sense had clearly been superseded by the conditions of the National Socialist state, this did not necessarily mean either that laws as such were no longer needed, or that all forms of administrative law were nugatory. Typically, this argument involved reformulating the principle of the separation of powers and the consequent relationship between individual and state in terms more appropriate to Nazi ideology. Thus, Maunz distinguished between 'political leadership' (*politische Führung*) free of any controls, and 'political execution' (*politische Durchführung*) which must be held to the performance of instructions received from this unbound sovereign leadership.[45] The most common solution was to argue that administrative law did not protect the rights of individuals, but the needs of the community; the administrative court system could be seen as the 'guardian of the objective order', therefore, and continue to function.[46] This contrivance represented an acceptable theoretical justification for the persistence of administrative review, while explain-

[42] On the administrative court system, see A. Wagner, 'Die Umgestaltung der Gerichtsverfassung und des Verfahrens- und Richterrechts im nationalsozialistischen Staat', in *Die deutsche Justiz und der Nationalsozialismus*, i (Stuttgart, 1968), 329-38.

[43] *Führererlass über die Errichtung des Reichsverwaltungsgerichts*, 3 Apr. 1941 (*RGBl*, 1941, i. 201); documentation on its establishment in BA R 18/5773, R 43II/1161c, and R 2/11978. Its first president was Walter Sommer, previously head of department III in the StdF *Stab*; for his views on administrative jurisdiction, see his 'Die Verwaltungs-gerichtsbarkeit', *DVBl*, 1937, 425-30.

[44] A. Köttgen, *Deutsche Verwaltung* (Berlin, 1944), 242-4.

[45] T. Maunz, *Neue Grundlagen des Verwaltungsrechts* (Hamburg, 1934), 17.

[46] Stuckart, 'Gedanken', p. 9; W. Frick, 'Probleme des neuen Verwaltungsrechts', *Der Gemeindetag*, 21, 1 Nov. 1936; see also T. Maunz, 'Das Ende des subjektiven öffentlichen Rechts', *ZgStW*, 96 (1936), 71-111.

ing why its sphere of application was more narrowly constructed under National Socialism than before.

The debate and its attempted resolutions had a direct bearing on the position of civil servants. As Huber put it, writing in 1939:

> The public-service relationship is not a bundle of mutual 'subjective public rights', but an undivided life relationship that comprehends the entire person—that places him as a totality in a special bond with Führer, *Volk* and *Reich* . . . No individual 'subjective claims' are to be conceded, but rather the concrete legal status of each official marshalled in his cohort rests in its essence on the mutual bond that creates the relationship between leader and led.[47]

Theoretically, civil servants lost the constitutional protection of their vested rights, now deemed to be incompatible with the conditions of the *Volksgemeinschaft*, and with this their right to pursue them through the courts. In practice, though, as the previous discussion suggests, the situation was not quite so clear. The Weimar Constitution was violated and abridged in numerous ways after 1933, of course, sometimes 'lawfully', often without benefit of legal instrument. Thus, laws such as the BBG and DBG contravened the principles of Article 128 by abrogating equal eligibility for civil-service appointment; similarly, there was no doubt that the freedoms of political opinion and association guaranteed in Article 130 had been withdrawn. Yet although the 1934 *Neuaufbaugesetz* conferred on the Reich government the power to create new constitutional law, and hence *de facto* superseded the 1919 constitution, the latter was never formally repealed, and parts of it continued in force, through usage and absence of amendment. For example, when Frick decided in 1934 summarily to withdraw the right of civil servants to consult their personal files, demurrals from the justice ministry forced him to incorporate in his final instructions a statement to the effect that this was without prejudice to the other provisions of Article 129.[48] Civil-service representative committees (*Beamtenvertretungen*), instituted under Article 130, were abolished in 1933;[49] on the other hand, the 1937 Reich disciplinary code confirmed that civil servants still enjoyed a right of appeal. Many other statutory or administrative measures represented an express limitation of constitutional or vested rights, or withdrew administrative decisions affecting them from the competence of the courts—this was true of both the BBG and BRÄndG,

[47] Huber, *Verfassungsrecht*, pp. 415-16.
[48] See documentation in BA R 43II/424a.
[49] See Reich interior-ministry order, 15 June 1933 (BA R43I/1514); and *MBliV*, 1933, 601.

for example.[50] Where the courts' powers were not limited, however, they could continue to protect civil servants' formal material claims (*vermögensrechtliche Ansprüche*), even as their civil and political rights were being abridged. Thus, while the Reichsgericht would not prevent a Jewish civil servant from losing his job after the Nuremberg laws, it could, and did, protect his claim to a pension.[51] Moreover, the DBG expressly reserved civil servants' material claims to the competence of the administrative courts (in order to withdraw them from the less easily controllable civil courts).[52] Equally, in the absence of new legislation, Article 131 of the constitution continued to govern claims made by a third party in respect of a civil servant's dereliction of duty.[53] In other words, one reason why commentators found it so difficult to capture the new dispensation in administrative law was that its practice was such a salmagundi of precedent and pragmatism.

III

If civil servants lived in a state of some confusion with regard to the extent of their rights, the situation was little better in relation to their duties. Here the problem was not so much uncertainty, but rather the multiplication of the duties imposed on civil servants in the name of their status. The Prussian civil-service tradition of inner dedication offered a ready-made vessel into which the consequences of the new ideological standards could flow. 'In the Prussian tradition a civil-service career always demanded no less than the soul', explained Köttgen in 1938, a commonplace view echoed by many.[54] 'The civil service rests above all on conviction and inner bearing';[55] 'decisive for the value and effectiveness of the civil service is its *spirit*';[56] and, translated directly into the terms of the Third Reich: 'Our task is to give ever greater weight and meaning to the soldierly spirit of the German civil servant, as the loyal and ever-ready vassal of the Führer and

[50] Echterhölter, *Öffentliches Recht*, pp. 35-6.
[51] Ibid. 206-7.
[52] DBG, §142; see Huber, *Verfassungsrecht*, pp. 416-17. The clause abrogated a provision of WRV, Art. 129; see H. Weinkauff, 'Die deutsche Justiz und der National-sozialismus: Ein Überblick', in *Die deutsche Justiz*, i. 202.
[53] Ibid. 420.
[54] Köttgen, 'Stellung', p. 34.
[55] H. Neef, *Der Beamte im nationalsozialistischen Führerstaat* (Berlin, 1934), 10.
[56] F.-D. von der Schulenburg, 'Preussiches Beamtentum' (typescript *c.* 1931, Nachlass von der Schulenburg; private collection), 4.

the people's servant on the field of Germany's state administration.'[57] *Treue*, loyalty or fealty, was the key concept here; it was drawn from a still-current language of civil-service status and partially revised into meanings more specifically appropriate to the *Führerstaat*. Although the Weimar Republic had moved in a liberalizing direction as far as controls over civil servants' personal behaviour and political convictions were concerned, restrictions on political behaviour had been tightened in the early 1920s. Moreover, the disciplinary courts had been, and remained, notoriously conservative, and the thread of continuity with older standards was unbroken in Nazi Germany. The insistence on 'inner loyalty' and 'total devotion'—terms constantly in use in the rhetoric with which civil servants were addressed after 1933—explicitly denied the idea that limits could be set to what the civil servant owed the state-as-nation. Between them, the old concept of *Treue* and the more recent rhetoric of the national community raised the claims on civil servants to a new pitch.

To begin with, Nazi law created new standards of access to civil-service appointment itself, formally defining political, sex, and racial eligibility in unprecedented terms. By 1943, a list of exclusions governed admission to civil-service status:[58] no one could become a civil servant if he was not of German or 'related' blood, with the same conditions applying to his spouse; if he was not a German citizen, politically reliable, and a member or ex-member of the Nazi party or one of its formations; if he was legally incapacitated, including by reason of criminal conviction; and, in certain grades, if he had been a Freemason after January 1933. Furthermore, a civil servant was to be dismissed or retired if he concealed the fact that he or his spouse were of non-German blood, or if he married a non-German without permission; if he was sentenced to certain criminal penalties; refused to take the oath of loyalty; or if his political reliability came into doubt. Though exceptions were permitted in a number of these cases, between them they amounted to a far-reaching set of proscriptions. In addition, the provisions of the BRÄndG and the continuing discrimination against women meant that by the later 1930s the senior ranks of the civil service were even more exclusively male than hitherto.[59] Nevertheless,

[57] Neef, *Soldatentum*, p. 23.

[58] See memo prepared by Rüdiger for Pfundtner, 27 Jan. 1943 (BA R 18/5452).

[59] In 1937, Hitler decided that in principle women should no longer be appointed as either judges or prosecutors, or to the senior grade in general; see justice-ministry circular, 16 Jan. 1937, and interior-ministry circular, 24 Aug. 1938 (BA R 43II/427). In 1940, Frick directed that posts in the senior grade should not be established for women *Assessoren* (GBV circular, 20 May 1940; ibid.). See also U. von Gersdorff, *Frauen im Kriegsdienst 1914-1945* (Stuttgart, 1969), 39-41, 279-85.

although the propaganda image of the rank-and-file civil service was obsessively masculine, with its invocations of vassals and soldiers, in practice the proportion of women employed in the public sector increased between 1933 and 1939, notably in clerical and secretarial posts.[60]

The racial definitions of the 1935 citizenship laws (which offered the first legal definitions and gradations of 'Jewish' as opposed to 'non-Aryan', and mixed racial with religious criteria in doing so) were on the whole less exacting than those already imposed on civil servants by the BBG, but party circles maintained pressure for further turns of the screw as anti-Semitic policies intensified.[61] This was especially strong in the case of the so-called 'Mischlinge', or mixed-race persons, who from the party's point of view had got off too lightly in 1935. Racial standards varied from ministry to ministry, in fact, depending on the degree of resistance they could put up and the expected level of disruption to administrative activities; the law offered a number of opportunities for procrastination in any case. The finance ministry feared that the Nuremberg laws would adversely affect its staffing; the interior ministry found itself overwhelmed with business relating to stipulations on race and Freemasonry; the justice ministry noted staffing problems following the exclusion of *Mischlinge* in 1937.[62] During the war, Bormann demanded the dismissal of any remaining civil servants married to Jews or *Mischlinge*.[63] Standards of exemption were tightened, but there was a good deal of foot-dragging in the ministries to evade Bormann's final pressure for the dismissal of the last remaining handful in connection with the 1944 July plot.[64]

By comparison with racial and political standards, the consequences of religious belief were less drastic for civil servants, at least in the case of orthodox Protestant and Catholic Christianity; but policy here

---

[60] J. Stephenson, *Women in Nazi Society* (London, 1975), 177.

[61] The effects of anti-Semitic policies in the civil service are discussed in U. D. Adam, *Judenpolitik im Dritten Reich* (Düsseldorf, 1979), 51-64, 132-41, 147-9, 166-8.

[62] See Pfundtner to Frick, 30 Oct. 1935 (BA R 18/5438); note from dept. II to Frick, 28 July 1938 (BA R 18/5531); justice ministry to finance ministry, 2 Nov. 1937 (BA R 2/24040). Note that the exclusion of *Mischlinge* was achieved largely by use of §§5 and 6 of the BBG: see interior-ministry circulars, 8 Apr. 1937 (BA R 43II/422a) and 16 Aug. 1937 (GStA P 134/3139); pension rights were severely curtailed; Adam, *Judenpolitik*, pp. 167, 214.

[63] See Bormann to Frick, 30 Jan. 1942 (BA R 18/5318), and interior-ministry circular, 11 Aug 1942 (BA R 43II/458).

[64] See documentation in R 43II/599.

reflected the broader contradictions in the Nazi handling of religion and the Churches. In September 1933, Frick issued a directive observing that the alleged mass defection of civil servants from church membership had been a regrettable feature of the Weimar years, and expressing a pious wish that many strayed sheep would now return to the fold.[65] But those who drew strong moral conclusions from the teachings of Christianity were liable to find themselves in difficulties. Many of the cases arising from §71 of the DBG involved officials whose religious convictions had brought them into conflict with the political demands of National Socialism. Thus, a Catholic senior teacher in Bamberg was forcibly retired in 1942 on the grounds that, although he was entitled to hold his convictions, he was not allowed to use his job to 'indoctrinate' children with them.[66] Characteristically, Hitler was concerned about the disturbing effects of excessive zeal—such as Bormann's—in pressing these religious cases, and Lammers was able to use the Führer's caution to protect a number of suspect individuals or mitigate their punishment. In a long-drawn-out case in 1938-40, for example, chancellery officials successfully defended a *Regierungsrat* associated with the Confessing Church, ensuring that he suffered only a transfer rather than the forcible retirement demand by Bormann.[67]

Although a private and quietist religious affiliation might be tolerated under civil-service law, more public declarations and forms of association were clearly unacceptable. Civil servants were forbidden to join professional confessional associations,[68] and were unwise to give their children a religious education.[69] Adventists, who, like Mormons, maintained an uneasy equilibrium with the Nazi state, were not apparently persecuted for their beliefs in the civil service, but they were given no encouragement.[70] Though not a religious association as such,

---

[65] Interior-ministry circular, 26 Sept. 1933 (GStA Rep. 318/804); a circular of 3 Jan. 1938 stated that no civil servant should suffer adverse consequences from religious belief (BA R 43II/422a).

[66] Documentation in BA R 43II/448 (Oberstudienrat Dr W. S.). For §71, see also Ch. 5, pp. 179-80, above.

[67] Documentation in BA R 43II/448 (M. von S.).

[68] Interior-ministry circular, 4 Oct. 1938 (*RMBliV*, 1938, 1645); see also Echterhölter, *Öffentliches Recht*, pp. 37, 204-5.

[69] H. Matzerath, *Nationalsozialismus und kommunale Selbstverwaltung* (Berlin, 1970), 256.

[70] Interior-ministry circular, 8 Mar. 1937 (*RMBliV*, 1937, 379), withdrawing special leave facilities from Adventists; on the smaller denominations in general, see C. King, *The Nazi State and the New Religions: Five Case Studies in Non-Conformity* (New York, 1982). Jehovah's Witnesses were the object of special persecution; see ibid. 147-79, and M. Kater, 'Die ernsten Bibelforscher im Dritten Reich', *VjhZ*, 17/2 (1969), 181-218; for

Freemasons were another group that suffered disadvantages in the civil service. They were already ineligible for NSDAP membership, and Hess in particular was anxious that they should also be considered unreliable *per se*, and excluded from leading posts. Hitler, on the other hand, regarded the question as relatively trivial, and it would appear that the interior ministry left the first initiatives on this front to the party. In 1935, presumably in response to persistent party pressure, the ministry began to arrange the collection of information on civil servants who belonged to lodges; a year later, restrictions were placed on their employment and promotion, including a ban on their handling personnel matters.[71]

A host of other regulations and expectations requisitioned the behaviour and personality of civil servants for the Nazi cause. The DBG listed their official duties virtually at the beginning of the law (§§3–20), starting with the general premise that civil-service status demanded from each incumbent 'a sincere love of country, a spirit of self-sacrifice, full commitment of labour power, obedience to superiors and comradeship to colleagues. He should be a model of conscientious duty to all *Volksgenossen*. To the Führer, who guarantees him his special protection, he owes loyalty unto death.' His duties of loyalty to the state and NSDAP were prominently enumerated, of course. In general, civil servants were obligated to a standard of behaviour on their own and their family's part which was consistent with the status and respect due to their office, and which included the obligation to live in orderly moral and economic circumstances.[72] These were staples of German civil-service law, and so too were other duties, such as the maintenance of official secrecy, obedience to superiors, or the declaration of a personal interest. But the DBG also introduced new principles, such as the stipulation that salary increments could be withheld if an official's standard of work fell below the expected norm (§21).[73] That these various demands were not always mutually compatible must be clear by now: most obviously, the frequent incompatibility of party loyalty with official secrecy and obedience to superiors had caused the disciplinary cases against civil servants on the grounds of membership of the Witnesses, see OVG IV. D 1.38 (BA R 148/27), and III. D 64.39 (BA R 148/24).

[71] Details of membership collected under instructions issued on 10 July 1935 (*RMBliV*, 1935, 888a); restrictions on employment and promotion enumerated in instructions issued on 2 Sept. 1936 (*RMBliV*, 1936, 1186) 22 Apr., and 12 May 1937 (*RMBliV*, 1937, 646 and 752).

[72] See R. Schneider, *Kommentar zum Deutschen Beamtengesetz* (Berlin, 1937), 56–80.

[73] On 3 Mar. 1944, Himmler issued instructions that poor performance would be regarded as a disciplinary offence (BA R 43II/435b).

problems which led to, but were not fully solved by, the provisions of §42 of the DBG.[74] But the DBG catalogue did not exhaust the official and informal demands placed on civil servants. Offered the opportunity of a group of *Volksgenossen* who could be held officially to specific standards and styles of life, interested parties flocked to impose their own patterns. Thus, the Prussian wing of the BNSDJ proposed that reading *Mein Kampf* ought to be made an official duty; the Reich interior ministry issued instructions that civil servants should not only subscribe to the *Völkischer Beobachter*, but read it 'as a matter of course'.[75] Civil servants were also urged to keep themselves in physical shape by taking part in sports and gymnastics.[76] The interior ministry asked that appointments, promotions, and other such official acts should be timed to coincide with the new national festivals, including 30 January and the Führer's birthday (20 April).[77] Non-Jewish civil servants experienced the tenets of racial purity in passive form, as Jewish Germans were driven out of economic and social life. Among other restrictions, they were warned not to patronize Jewish banks, or apprentice their children to enterprises owned by Jews; and certificates of ill health issued by Jewish doctors were declared invalid in 1936.[78]

Comradeship—eventually made an official duty by the DBG—was in great demand from civil servants, as evidence that class barriers and the mores of the authoritarian state were being dismantled. Thus, civil servants on official visits to factories were instructed to greet representatives of the work-force as well as the management; others were reminded that polite behaviour to the public was a duty, and that use of the traditional and distancing third person in official communications was not consistent with the new German spirit. Similarly, civil servants were sent out on street collections for the *Winterhilfswerk* in carefully mixed-rank groups, the clerk rattling his box shoulder by shoulder with

[74] See Ch. 5, pp. 176-8, above.

[75] See Bochum BNSDJ to Prussian Staatsministerium, 6 July 1933 (GStA Rep. 90/2326), and interior-ministry circular, 3 Dec. 1935 (*MBliV*, 1935, 1443).

[76] Interior-ministry circular, 27 May 1935 (*MBliV*, 1935, 717).

[77] Interior-ministry instructions, 6 Nov. 1934 (*MBliV*, 1935, 227).

[78] On banks, justice-ministry instruction, 8 June 1936 (BA R 22/1628); on apprenticeships, see documentation from Nov. 1937 in BA R 22/4471; on doctors, interior-ministry instruction, 9 Oct. 1936 (*RMBliV*, 1936, 1330). Social relations with Jews might become the subject of disciplinary proceedings: see OVG. IV. D 77.37 and IV. D 33.38 (R 148)—the latter a case in which an officer in the welfare police allowed Jewish children into his home and 'to show themselves at the window, so that neighbours took exception to the fact that a civil servant of the Third Reich still maintained these relations in spite of national policy'; also Echterhölter, *Öffentliches Recht*, pp. 203-4.

the *Ministerialrat*.[79] They were also expected to be generous givers themselves, on the basis that they were financially better placed than many of their fellow citizens. Gauleiter Bürckel even issued instructions in 1937 that senior and middle-ranking civil servants who joined the party would be expected to pay the membership dues of two or three workers for the next two years as a sign of their goodwill.[80] Care was taken to ensure that the correct form of the *Hitlergruss* was used, verbally, physically, and in official communications, including the issue of special instructions for those whose loss of their right arm placed them at a disadvantage in this test of politeness and political duty.[81] The fatal combination of bureaucratic with political pedantry no doubt led to many such quixotic effects.

In dealing with civil servants' offences against these rules, the disciplinary courts did attempt to distinguish sheer political tactlessness from acts of motivated hostility to National Socialism. A teacher who sang his class an insulting song about the BDM was judged guilty of a 'pedagogical lapse', but was not taken to be politically suspect.[82] On the other hand, a school janitor who mocked the *Hitlergruss* by raising his fist and proclaiming 'Heil Moskau' and 'Rotfront' lost his pension, despite the fact that he was drunk at the time.[83] More complicated was the case of a teacher who refused to accept an award of a silver medal from Hitler, not for political reasons but because of long-standing quarrels with the school authorities; he was sentenced to lose his job, on the grounds that the refusal constituted 'a moral insult to the Führer [by which] the civil servant violated in the most serious manner the duty of loyalty imposed upon him'.[84] Wartime disciplinary judgements reflected the increasing severity of the penal code. An Austrian civil servant sentenced in the criminal court for listening to an enemy radio station also lost his pension; a policeman sentenced for black-market offences was dismissed. Another policeman lost his job for, among

[79] Interior-ministry instructions, 22 Nov. 1935 (*MBliV*, 1935, 1404); on official style, see Prussian Staatsministerium circular, 6 Mar. 1934 (*MBliV*, 1934, 604), and interior-ministry circulars 17 Aug. 1934 (*MBliV*, 1934, 1095) and 29 July 1936 (*RMBliV* 1936, 1053). Because comradeship was an official duty, failure to show it might result in disciplinary proceedings: e.g. a teacher who, among other offences, refused to go on a door-to-door collection for the WHW was fined in 1938; OVG. IV. D 4.38 (BA R 148); and see also Schneider, *Deutsches Beamtengesetz*, p. 76.
[80] Reprinted in *Frankfurter Zeitung*, 12 Nov. 1937.
[81] Prussian interior-ministry instructions, 20 July 1933 (*MBliV*, 1933, 859) and 27 Nov. 1933 (copy in GStA Rep. 318/805).
[82] OVG IV. D 58.37 (BA R 148/27).
[83] OVG IV. D 12.37 (ibid.).
[84] RVG I. D 21.42 (R 148).

other things, lying about his war service in Poland by claiming that he had shot over a hundred Poles and was therefore a murderer.[85]

In accordance with the premisses of disciplinary law, civil servants could expect severer standards to be demanded of them than of the general public. Their private and family lives had always been hedged around with prescriptions and prohibitions, for the convention was that a civil servant was never simply a private person. Sexual delicts had usually been heavily penalized, though the courts had varied in the severity with which they viewed adultery: the stricter penalties of dismissal or a heavy fine had usually been reserved for cases which became publicly known or in which a marriage was destroyed.[86] Standards of judgement probably became more severe under National Socialism, given the procreative significance of marriage.[87] They certainly became no lighter. One of the reasons a building engineer lost his job was the fact that cohabitation with his fiancée was judged 'reprehensible' and liable to dishonour him in the eyes of the public.[88] A forester who helped procure an abortion was dismissed after serving his prison sentence.[89] Homosexual offences were especially severely punished by the Nazis.[90] Men convicted of offences against §175 of the criminal code normally lost their job automatically, and might be dismissed even in the absence of any criminal prosecution;[91] the same was true of sexual offences against minors, male or female.[92] Though §53 of

[85] Respectively, RVG I. D 53.42, I. D 47.42, and I. D 35.42 (R 148).

[86] Schneider, *Deutsches Beamtengesetz*, pp. 77-8.

[87] A 1938 judgement against a woman accused of adultery declared that: 'Marriage is strictly protected in law precisely because it represents the germ cell of the national community'; OVG IV. D 67.38 (R 148/28). See also e.g. OVG IV. D 35.38 (R 148/28). However, an attempt by the interior ministry to set uniform guidelines for judgements on adultery was overturned by Hitler in 1937, on the grounds that it was inappropriate to treat private behaviour in this way; see interior-ministry draft circulated to ministries, 14 Dec. 1936, and subsequent documentation in BA R 43II/443.

[88] OVG IV. D 22.37 (R 148/27); contrast with RVG I. D 9.42 (R 148), where a number of mitigating circumstances reduced the penalty on appeal.

[89] OVG IV. D 66.37 (ibid.).

[90] On the amendment of §175 of the criminal code in 1935, see H.-G. Stümke and R. Finkler, *Rosa Winkel, Rosa Listen: Homosexuelle und 'Gesundes Volksempfinden' von Auschwitz bis heute* (Frankfurt, 1981), 212-17.

[91] For criminal cases, see e.g. OVG IV. D 81.37 and IV. D 72.37 (R 148/27); for cases not apparently the subject of a criminal prosecution, see OVG IV. D 65.37 (R 148/26) and IV. D 80.37 (R 148/27). See also RVG I. D 37.42, where the fact that a man stayed overnight in the same bed with a male friend was enough to secure a conviction under §175 and dismissal from his job as a tax inspector (R 148); and IV. D 86.37, where mere suspicion of homosexuality was enough to justify a heavy financial penalty against an *Oberregierungsrat* (R 148/128).

[92] OVG IV. D 25.28 (R 148/28).

the DBG mandated dismissal in certain criminal cases, civil servants might also find themselves facing disciplinary charges in the absence of any criminal offence. Thus, a Catholic municipal official under suspicion of conspiracy to treason was dismissed despite the fact that the criminal charges against him had been dropped for lack of evidence.[93] Non-sexual cases of personal failure also remained liable to disciplinary proceedings. For example, a tax official who suffered from a general aura of personal inadequacy lost his job because he was chronically indebted and his wife was incompetent; a teacher dismissed for embezzlement was criticized for not standing up to his wife, whose poor management had led the household into financial difficulties.[94] The effect of party membership on standards of judgement and sentencing underwent an important shift after about 1939. Whereas earlier practice had been to regard party membership as grounds for more exacting standards of judgement and more severe sentences, within a few years it was being regularly cited as a 'mitigating circumstance'.[95]

Much of this regulation of behaviour was hardly peculiar to the Nazi period. As with many other routine cases not discussed here, involving such matters as embezzlement, drunkenness at work, absenteeism, and other uncontroversial forms of misbehaviour, the disciplinary courts were largely continuing to apply the accepted standards for civil servants' behaviour through the usual apparatus of control. However, the standards of judgement as well as the offences themselves reflected the priorities of the new regime in political and moral cases, and it was not unusual for a political element to enter into cases ostensibly about some other matter. In spite of this, the disciplinary courts did not enjoy much of a reputation in party circles, where they were seen as populated largely by superannuated bureaucrats who protected their fellow officials by the most pettifogging and pedantic application of the rules. It was a supreme irony that Walter Sommer, one of those in the StdF *Stab* who had called attention to the use of the administrative courts as a final resting-place for ageing bureaucrats, was eventually to find himself kicked upstairs to head the new Reichsverwaltungsgericht when it was finally established in 1941.

Sommer was also prominent, as we shall see, in another aspect of civil

[93] OVG III. D 15.40 (R 148/24).
[94] RVG I. D 15.42 (R 148); OVG IV. D 44.38 (R 148/28).
[95] Compare e.g. OVG IV. D 23.37 (R 148/27), IV. D 8.37 (R 148/26), and IV. D 31.38 (R 148/28), with OVG III. D 46.39 (R 148/24), RVG I. D 33.42, and I. D 29.42 (R 148). See also StdF instructions 20/37, 29 Jan. 1937, that the expulsion of a civil servant from the party should not be automatic grounds for loss of his job (BA NS 6/vorl. 225).

servants' personal behaviour which, while it did not fall into the purview of the courts, was an issue of some concern to policy-makers: the question of marriage and procreation. Nazi population policies were concerned not only with selection between races, but also with eugenic standards within the permitted racial categories.[96] Anxiety about the alleged racial degeneration of the Germans was manifested not only in the 'anti-dysgenic' policies of forced abortion and sterilization, or in the infamous euthanasia action after 1939, but also in 'positive' eugenic programmes which attempted to encourage procreation on the part of people deemed worthy to pass their genetic material on to their heirs. On the whole, the fate of these pro-natalist policies amply bears out Martin Broszat's observation that the Nazi regime was, disastrously, more successful at achieving its negative than its positive aims.[97] Perhaps this was inevitable, given the familiar insusceptibility of reproductive behaviour to simple manipulation. Despite the apparent success of the marriage loan scheme, for example, it now appears clear that early increases in nuptiality and child-bearing after 1933 were compensations for a previous period of deficit rather than heralds of a new era of reproductive enthusiasm among Germans.[98] By the late 1930s, it was evident that Nazi policies had done nothing to reverse the trend, fixed since the 1880s, for 'persons in higher social classes [to have] lower fertility than those in classes below them'.[99] Civil servants and salaried employees had led the decline in fertility at the end of the nineteenth century, establishing a pattern that persisted through the 1930s.[100] Studies among state and NSDAP officials carried out in Thuringia in 1936 confirm this picture.[101] By comparison with the white-collar workers and peasants surveyed, the civil servants studied

[96] On Nazi eugenics, see G. Bock, 'Racism and Sexism in Nazi Germany: Motherhood, Compulsory Sterilization and the State', in R. Bridenthal *et al.*, (eds.), *When Biology Became Destiny: Women in Weimar and Nazi Germany* (New York, 1984), 271-96; also J. Noakes, 'Nazism and Eugenics: The Background to the Nazi Sterilization Law of 14 July 1933', in R. J. Bullen *et al.* (eds.), *Ideas Into Politics: Aspects of European History 1880-1950* (London, 1984), 75-94.

[97] Broszat, *The Hitler State*, pp. 354-5.

[98] T. Mason, 'Women in Nazi Germany, Part I', *History Workshop Journal*, 1 (1976), 95-105.

[99] J. E. Knodel, *The Decline of Fertility in Germany, 1871-1939* (Princeton, 1974), 147.

[100] Ibid. 127.

[101] K. Astel and E. Weber, 'Die unterschiedliche Fortpflanzung: Untersuchung über die Fortpflanzung von 12 000 Beamten und Angestellten der Thüringschen Staatsverwaltung', *Politische Biologie*, 9 (1939), and *Die Kinderzahl der 29 000 politischen Leiter des Gaues Thüringen der NSDAP und die Ursachen der ermittelten Fortpflanzungshäufigkeit* (Berlin, 1943).

(including teachers) married late, waiting until they had achieved established appointment before assuming family responsibilities. The average age at marriage of those surveyed was 28½ in 1930, compared to 27 before 1914 (the white-collar workers surveyed had married at about 26½, the peasants at 26); by 1936 this had risen to 30, as a result of the lengthier training and terms of labour and military service that delayed established appointment. The age at marriage of civil servants' wives also rose in this period, remaining at a constant average of some five years below their husbands'.[102] Virtually all births occurred within the first ten years of marriage; indeed, the wife's average age at her last confinement was only thirty-one, meaning that her theoretical pro-creative span of thirty years was narrowed in practice to no more than seven.[103] The completed family size of civil servants married in 1890-1900 averaged between two and three children, compared with the artisans' five; for marriages up to 1929, i.e. seven years before the survey, it had fallen to 1.5. Senior civil servants averaged fewer than two children per marriage, and those in the lower grade just over two, a pattern of social differentials in fertility that corresponded to national and long-term trends.[104] Since 1933, it was true, there had been a 50 per cent increase in civil servants' marital fertility, and this was almost twice the national increase of 28 per cent; but the base level was so low that even this increase came nowhere near the desired norm of four children per civil-service family. This goal was determined less by a calculation of what was feasible than by the authors' belief that civil servants constituted an 'elite professional stratum' (*ausgelesene Berufs-schicht*) that ought to produce disproportionately large families in order to contribute to the genetic improvement of the nation as a whole. On present trends, they argued: 'The diminution of the genetic capital (*Erbanlage*) of civil servants is proceeding with unprecedented speed, and with it the loss of their nationally valuable, indeed indispensable characteristics.'[105] Based on an analysis of the likely causes of the problem, suggested remedies included in particular the encouragement of earlier marriage by shortening the educational and training process; and a far-reaching adjustment of salaries to family size.[106]

[102] Astel and Weber, 'Unterschiedliche Fortpflanzung', pp. 29-34.
[103] Ibid. 115.
[104] Ibid. 116, 73-5.
[105] Ibid. 116, 118.
[106] Child allowances for the third and subsequent children in all families were intro-duced in 1940 (law of 9 Dec. 1940; *RGBl*, 1940, i. 1571). Allowances for civil servants were changed in 1941 (law of 15 Jan. 1941; *RGBl*, 1941, i. 33; and see documentation in BA R 43II/433a).

Similar arguments were advanced by Sommer in a long memorandum about reproductive trends among higher civil servants which he sent to Lammers in 1937, with the hope that he might be able 'to interest the Führer in the matter'.[107] He pointed out that although 'we must not overestimate the man with a university education [*Akademiker*], he is certainly a member of an ēlite—an intellectual if not a physical one'. The *Akademikerstand* in general was important to the nation, but it was not producing enough children to renew itself from within: it was, in Sommer's mechanistic language, a 'Zuschussgebiet', a deficiency area that had to be subsidized by inputs from other sections of the nation: 'Because of the childlessness of the *Akademiker* valuable hereditary stock is being wasted . . . and the *Akademikerstand* is becoming the cemetery of the German nation's genes . . . There is a justifiable anxiety that this mismanagement of the German nation's gene pool will result in the exhaustion of their source.' Like the Thuringian researchers, Sommer argued that late marriages were the key to the problem, and that one remedy lay in the reform of training schedules. Candidates for the higher grade did not qualify until the age of about twenty-eight; the RGS then prescribed four years of probationary service before established appointment was permitted. His practical suggestions turned on giving education and training a stronger vocational and selective cast, and preparing recruits for established appointment by the age of twenty-five. Sommer lent his views weight by indicating that they drew on opinions expressed by Hess and Bormann, though they also clearly reflected his own concern for the fate of his peers. The immediate consequence of his proposals—an index of the issue's importance—was an amendment to the RGS to cut the period of probationary service by half for both the higher and intermediate grades.[108]

More unconventional attempts to alleviate the problem were also made from time to time. In 1937, Gauleiter Schwede-Coburg of Pomerania issued instructions that all unmarried civil servants over the age of twenty-five must be reported to his office, with a view to having their promotion blocked. His move was immediately countermanded by the interior ministry, concerned as much to preserve its own authority as to protect civil servants from this crude and punitive intervention. Frick issued his own directive that unmarried civil servants were to be

[107] Memo dated 1 July 1937 (BA R 43II/450a). A version was also published as 'Akademiker und Bevölkerungspolitik', *Der Altherrenbund*, 1/2 (1938).

[108] See report of discussion on 10 Mar. 1937, and subsequent documentation in BA R 43II/450a; amendment issued 7 June 1938 (*RGBl*, 1938, i. 969).

asked on appointment why they were single and when they intended to remedy the situation; those married but still childless after two years were to be tactfully asked to explain in writing why their union remained unfruitful.[109] This was a purely tactical contrivance, however, and the information was not collected for any practical purpose; moreover, when the matter later came to Hitler's attention, he insisted that the inquiries be dropped.[110] Despite Hitler's squeamishness about probing into civil servants' personal lives, the issue came up again intermittently, suggesting that civil servants faced persistent background nagging over their procreative behaviour.[111] In the longer term, the problems of late marriage and low birth rates among civil servants figured prominently in debates about the financial and social status of civil servants, and about the problems of recruitment, and in the attempts by the interior ministry to initiate reforms in the salary and training systems. In these contexts, it was deployed as signal evidence of the structural crisis within the civil service which the interior ministry invoked in its campaign to reconstruct the prestige and power of the German administration.

IV

The sense that the civil service had suffered a catastrophic fall in prestige under National Socialism was inescapable by the later 1930s. The most solid evidence of this was the growing difficulty in recruiting and retaining administrative personnel. From about 1937, a swelling chorus of complaints was rising from central and field offices, alleging that staffing patterns showed cause for serious concern; this was especially true in the technical branches and in the senior grade, where competition with other employers was at its most acute. The advent of this problem was partly a function of the economic recovery, which pushed up the demand for trained personnel. When the Nazis came to power in 1933, the issue had not been a shortage of administrative personnel, but a surplus. Where possible, public agencies had cut back

109 Schwede-Coburg's instructions, 10 Apr. 1937, and subsequent documentation in BA R 22/4471; interior-ministry circular, 14 Dec. 1937 (GStA Rep. 90/2340).
110 Interior-ministry circular, 9 May 1938 (BA R 18/5564).
111 See e.g. circulars from the aviation ministry, 22 Oct. 1940 (BA R 55/22) and justice ministry, 22 Apr. 1939 (BA R 22/1628). The Reichsbund der Kinderreichen also kept up pressure on the ministries; see its notes to the justice ministry, 10 Feb. 1937 (BA R 22/4471) and 14 Sept. 1937 (BA R 22/1636).

on their staff during the depression, and, as we have seen, the BBG was used to eliminate surplus and incompetent officials in some branches. At the same time, the senior grade of the civil service could rely on a large pool of potential applicants among the swollen university-student population, which peaked in mid-1931.[112] Enrolments in the law faculties, in which prospective civil servants studied, had remained buoyant after 1918, reaching a high point of 22,743 in 1923, and returning to an almost as numerous 22,200 in 1928.[113] Many of these students were attracted by the prospect of state employment in the absence of other professional opportunities, especially after 1929. In the first years of the Nazi regime, the outlook for young graduates seemed poor: a BNSDJ investigation in 1935 showed that 12,000 graduates were currently working as *Referendare*, while as many as 5,000 *Assessoren* were said to be underemployed or unemployed.[114] It was expected that the supply of trained candidates for public appointments would continue to rise in the immediate future. Although the finance ministry, as early as 1934, offered a cautious prediction that 'in some sections of the administration we may see a certain shortfall in suitable recruits in the foreseeable future', shortages did not begin to appear until about 1938.[115] These were in fact in some specific, mainly technical sectors, especially those connected with construction and civil engineering, and in local government; all these branches were now alleged to be suffering from the departure of staff to other employment, as well as from a fall-off in new recruitment.[116] The technical sectors of the administration found themselves in competition for qualified

[112] M. H. Kater, *Studentenschaft und Rechtsradikalismus in Deutschland, 1928-1933: Eine sozialgeschichtliche Studie zur Bildungskrise in der Weimarer Republik* (Hamburg, 1975), 209, table 3; J. R. Pauwels, *Women, Nazis, and Universities: Female University Students in the Third Reich, 1933-1945* (Westport, 1984), 36.

[113] Report of conference held by justice-ministry recruitment review office (Amt für Nachwuchsfragen), 8-10 June 1944 (BA R 22/4449).

[114] BNSDJ to Reich finance ministry, 30 Apr. 1935 (BA R 2/24068); see also P. Hüttenberger, 'Interessenvertretung und Lobbyismus im Dritten Reich', in G. Hirschfeld and L. Kettenacker (eds.), *The 'Führer State': Myth and Reality. Studies on the Structure and Politics of the Third Reich* (Stuttgart, 1981), 431. On the problems of professional employment in general, see K. H. Jarausch, 'The Crisis of the German Professions 1918-1933', *JCH*, 20/3 (1985), 379-98, and 'The Perils of Professionalism: Lawyers, Teachers, and Engineers in Nazi Germany', *German Studies Review*, 9/1 (1986), 107-37.

[115] Reich finance-ministry memo, 'Die Herabsetzung der Altersgrenze im Verbindung mit der Frage der Förderung des Beamtennachwuchses', drafted 7 Apr. 1934 (BA R 2/22015).

[116] Finance-ministry circular, 23 Mar. 1938 (BA R 43II/418); interior-ministry departmental note to dept. I, 4 Apr. 1939 (BA R 18/2009).

personnel with the armed services and the quasi-military undertakings associated with rearmament; local government was especially badly hit because salaries for its technical staff tended to be low.[117] Between 1937 and 1939, the Deutscher Gemeindetag and the NSDAP's Hauptamt für Kommunalpolitik received numerous reports from municipalities throughout Germany, complaining that their staffing shortages were becoming intolerable. A leading city official in Munich drew a characteristic picture of how local government was losing the race for personnel:

Even those school students who show any interest at all in the public service today have the opportunity once again to enter professions which have better prospects and which correspond more closely to their abilities and preferences. The first place here is taken by the armed forces, which offer rich opportunities to the young person choosing his career. The 'secure' position of the civil servant . . . is now no longer an attraction. The kind of education the young person gets in school, Hitler Youth, labour service and army is not apt to fill him with enthusiasm for the professional civil service.[118]

However, the crisis of recruitment to the civil service which framed official discourse after 1937 is not immediately visible from the crude statistics of public employment in Nazi Germany. Although statistical data are hard to locate and verify, aggregate state employment in the categories of federal, state, and local administration appears to have grown by about 20 per cent between 1933 and 1939.[119] The sense that Germany was experiencing what the Reich statistical office described in 1936 as a process of 'bureaucratization' (*Verbehördlichung*) was inescapable,[120] and denunciations of this were widespread throughout the Nazi period, including by those who shared the responsibility for these developments. The deficiencies identified by the later 1930s, therefore, were due not to an absolute decline in the numbers of administrative personnel, but rather to increased demand, accompanied by cumulative

[117] See Matzerath, *Nationalsozialismus*, pp. 330-4; also labour ministry to army high command, 13 Dec. 1939 (BA R 41/53).
[118] Tempel (deputy mayor of Munich) to HfK, 26 Aug. 1938 (BA NS 25/682). The same file contains evidence submitted by other major cities and *Gaue*, as well as representations from the HfK to the StdF *Stab*; see also HfK to StdF *Stab*, 8 Aug. 1938 (BA NS 25/431). See also evidence submitted to the Deutscher Gemeindetag, collected in e.g. BA R 36/51.
[119] J. P. Cullity, 'The Growth of Governmental Employment in Germany', Ph.D. thesis (Columbia, 1964), 98, and table 3, p. 77.
[120] See note from Graevell (Reich statistical office) to Wienstein (chancellery), 5 Oct. 1936 (BA R 43II/418).

fears about its quality and distribution. Moreover, the issue as a whole cannot be separated from the nexus of problems associated with the duplication and overlapping of offices and functions—in other words, the mismanagement and wastage of labour in a heavily bureaucratized society.

The interior ministry argued that the aggregate staffing of local government had barely increased in real terms since the depression. The apparent growth from 334,002 *Beamte* and *Angestellte* in 1933 to 356,759 in 1936 masked the previous decline during the depression: by comparison with the 1930 figure, the increase up to 1936 was a relatively insignificant 5,000.[121] (Nevertheless, at the beginning of 1939, the interior ministry did initiate an inquiry into the causes of what seems to have been a cumulative increase in local-government staffing by then, and into the more efficient use of personnel.[122]) By then, shortfalls were being noted in the technical departments of local government, and in financial departments like savings banks and insurance, all of which suffered growing competition from the armed services, from new or expanding branches of the administration, or from the private sector.[123] It was because of such developments that, at the end of 1938, Frick tried unsuccessfully to promote action on local-government salaries, and the special problems of local government figured prominently in his overall salary relief campaign.[124]

The public service also suffered from the competition of employment in the NSDAP and its associated formations, a sector which expanded galactically after 1933. The Reichsleitung offices in Munich alone employed 2,546 paid officials at the end of 1936, and over 3,000 a year later.[125] Hundreds more were employed by the *Gauleitungen*, thousands more by the network of party formations like the SA, and affiliated associations like the RDB. The bureaucratization of the SS also proceeded apace after 1933, and attracted considerable numbers of jurists into its ranks.[126] Civil servants provided disproportionate

[121] Changes in staffing are discussed in detail in an interior-ministry internal note from dept. V to dept. I R, 4 Apr. 1939 (BA R 18/2099).

[122] Interior-ministry circular, 4 Jan. 1939 (ibid.). On the work of local government, see Matzerath, *Nationalsozialismus*, ch. 6.

[123] Interior-ministry note, 4 Apr. 1939 (see n. 121 above); also, HfK to StdF *Stab*, 22 Sept. 1936, about loss of savings bank personnel (BA NS 25/409).

[124] Interior ministry to finance ministry, 15 Dec. 1938 (BA R 43II/573b); see also Ch. 7, below.

[125] D. Orlow, *The History of the Nazi Party: 1933-1945* (Pittsburgh, 1973), 202; see also 170 ff., 222 ff., 253 ff., 323-4, etc. Salaries were the largest item in *Gau* budgets.

[126] G. C. Boehnert, 'The Jurists in the SS-Führerkorps, 1925-1939', in Hirschfeld and Kettenacker (eds.) *The 'Führer State'*, pp. 361-74; R. Koehl, *The Black Corps: The Structure and Power Struggles of the Nazi SS* (Madison, 1983), ch. 6.

numbers of party officials, paid and honorary, and the numbers involved were hardly insignificant. In 1934, the NSDAP and its affiliates had altogether over a million functionaries, paid and unpaid (not all of them party members, of course). [127] Of the corps of *politische Leiter*, over 17 per cent were civil servants in 1935. [128] Some 28 per cent of those civil servants (including teachers) who belonged to the party were *politische Leiter*, a percentage only equalled by peasants (the comparable figure for workers, for example, was just under 15 per cent). [129] A 1939 Thuringian study reported that over 23 per cent of *politische Leiter* were civil servants (including teachers), virtually all from the middle and lower grades. [130] The RDB alone mustered some 50,000 officials for its 900,000 or so members, the majority of them unpaid. [131] In other words, civil servants (including teachers) were not only over-represented as party members, but, as members or not, they were even more disproportionately likely to hold some kind of office, paid or unpaid, in the party or its affiliates. Frick pointed out that these civil servants—most of whom had not joined the party until after 1933—were expected to put in many extra hours of unpaid work for the party. A finance-administration investigation in 1939 found that over 75 per cent of civil servants were 'active' in some arm of the party, compared with 69.5 per cent of *Angestellte* and only 30 per cent of *Arbeiter*. [132] By contrast, the authors of the 1935 *Partei-Statistik* complained that old party members who had acquired civil-service jobs after 1933 were inclined to see this as a sufficient discharge of their obligations to National Socialism, and were no longer willing to work actively for the party—though they still expected to be recognized by high party ranking. This may have thrown further burdens on to non-party *Beamte*, whose organizational skills and official connections were what made them valuable to the party. In any case, it vividly illustrated the inescapable interdependence of party and state as linked bureaucracies,

---

[127] Orlow, *History of the Nazi Party: 1933-1945*, p. 92; see also Matzerath, *National-sozialismus*, p. 374.

[128] *NSDAP Partei-Statistik* (Berlin, 1935) ii. *Politische Leiter*, 158.

[129] Ibid. 160.

[130] Astel and Weber, 'Unterschiedliche Fortpflanzung', p. 14.

[131] *NSDAP Partei-Statistik*, iii. *Gliederungen, Ämter, Verbände*, 14.

[132] Finance-ministry memo, 25 Aug. 1939 (BA R 2/22583). Tax officials were in particular demand by the party; in 1935, and again in 1937, the StdF *Stab* was induced to issue instructions limiting the party's use of them, especially during working hours; instructions 77/35, 26 Apr. 1935 (BA NS 6/vorl. 218) and 124/37, 1 Oct. 1937 (NS 6/vorl. 227).

and it is not surprising that the party itself shared some of the same staffing problems as the civil service, along with its other bureaucratic characteristics. By 1940-1, when the NSDAP finally managed to issue its own long-planned consolidated salary code—which was closely modelled on the state system in form and content—party spokesmen too were complaining of the difficulty of attracting adequate personnel. Indeed, this was one of the principal justifications for issuing the code, which included substantial rate increases, in the middle of the war.[133]

The overall pattern of administrative employment had long begun to bear out the finance ministry's 1934 projection of personnel shortages linked to economic recovery. The problems were partly due to the expansion of the machinery of administration and the armed forces, but competition from the private sector increased after 1938, as a result of the economic expansion. In March 1938, Krosigk authorized the selective postponement of retirement in individual cases, to relieve 'the temporary shortage' of technical civil servants.[134] Later that year, Ohnesorge, the postal minister, claimed that his department was facing virtually insuperable staffing problems, and reported that one office was about to lose sixty female personnel who had given notice for the beginning of October.[135] Teachers were in increasingly short supply by the same date, a fact that led to a major policy turn-around in the employment of women.[136] As we shall see, the arguments deployed by Frick in his salary campaign after 1937 drew heavily on the problem of attracting and keeping civil servants.[137] As far as the senior grade of the civil service was concerned, trends in university enrolments were also giving grounds for concern. The student population declined by 50 per cent between 1931 and 1938, mainly due to the smaller birth cohort that came of age in the 1930s, but in the law faculties the decline was sharper and more severe. Numbers fell by half between 1933 and 1935; thereafter, enrolments fluctuated for some years (partly in response to the introduction of military conscription), but by 1939 there were no more than 5,800 students registered, compared with a peak of 22,200 in 1928, and over 14,000 in 1933.[138]

---

[133] See documentation in BA NS 1/417 and 2277; also BA S Sch. 363; Orlow, *History of the Nazi Party: 1933-1945*, pp. 218 ff.

[134] Finance-ministry circular, 23 Mar. 1938 (BA R 43II/418).

[135] Post ministry to finance ministry, 29 Aug. 1938 (BA R 43II/437a).

[136] On women's careers, see Stephenson, *Women in Nazi Society*, pp. 176-80. On the problem of teachers, see documentation collected by the StdF *Stab* after 1939 in BA NS 6/322.

[137] See Ch. 7, pp. 249-52, below.

Germany's expansionist foreign policy after 1938 brought further pressures, which were vastly aggravated by the outbreak of the war. Frick claimed that before the *Anschluss* only 3,413 of the interior administration's 3,820 senior posts were filled, and that although 637 officials had then been seconded from the Austrian and Sudeten administrations, by 1939, 1,449 senior posts in the Austrian, Sudeten, and Czech administrations remained unoccupied.[139] At the same time, the problem of the *Nachwuchsmangel* persisted during the war as a relatively independent issue that was not entirely subsumed by the larger procurement and deployment problem, even if that lent an air of greater urgency. The DGT and HfK, for example, continued to collect evidence of the difficulties experienced by local government in meeting its needs, especially in sectors where more interesting alternatives beckoned. Communities large and small were equally hit: Frankfurt am Main reported that it could not find any recruits to the intermediate grade of the technical service; the town of Zscherndorf (pop. 3,400), that it was struggling along with semi-qualified staff.[140] A circular from the Brandenburg Amt für Kommunalpolitik in November 1940 described the recruitment problem as 'everywhere the greatest anxiety of all official authorities and other responsible agencies. Without exception it is recognized that there is little interest in civil-service careers. Young male school-leavers presently try as far as possible for jobs in the private sector, where they will get ahead faster and not be at the mercy of public criticism.'[141] The circular referred to the low pay and sunken prestige of the civil service as the main cause of its inability to attract recruits, and suggested that after the war, when the expected economic boom made conditions even more adverse, civil servants should be forbidden to leave their jobs without permission. The DGT's civil-service committee, meeting in September 1941, likewise stressed the collapse of civil-service prestige, though it recommended financial incentives during training as the practical means of improving recruitment.[142] A DGT investigation in 1941 into local-government recruit-

138 Pauwels, *Women, Nazis, and Universities*, pp. 36 ff; also justice-ministry recruitment review office conference, 8-10 June 1944 (BA R 22/4449).

139 'Kriegsaufgaben der Staatsverwaltung', *NSBZ-Der deutsche Verwaltungsbeamte*, 11 May 1941, 161-4; also report of Neef speech in Berlin, *Steuer-Warte*, 4 Oct. 1942. The additional strains imposed by the war, and the attempts at administrative rationalization, will be discussed in Ch. 8 below.

140 *Oberbürgermeister* of Frankfurt to DGT, 12 Aug. 1941; *Bürgermeister* of Zscherndorf to DGT, 13 Aug. 1941 (BA R 36/370).

141 Sent to DGT by the DGT Dienststelle Osten, 13 Dec. 1940 (BA R 36/86).

142 Report of meeting 16 Sept. 1941 (BA R 36/5).

ment to the intermediate grade suggested that while most, though not all, communities were able to cover their needs, many complained that the selection of recruits was narrow and their quality poor, and some that recruits left after training in order to take advantage of the better opportunities in the private sector.[143] Reports of the worsening problems of local government continued throughout the war, suggesting the build-up of a post-war crisis about which little was being done.[144]

The object of local government's particular concern was the intermediate grade of the civil service from which the bulk of its officials were drawn, but the situation in the senior grade was little better. Enrolment in university law faculties continued to decline after 1939: on the eve of the war, law students comprised 10 per cent of the student population, compared with 23 per cent in 1932; by 1942, this had fallen to 4 per cent—far below any adequate replacement ratio.[145] As we shall see, training reform schemes developed by the interior and justice ministries after 1940 were direct responses to the deterioration in recruitment and the expectation of worse to come. In the summer of 1941, a major interministerial conference was held in the interior ministry to explore the recruitment crisis; its deliberations are worth considering at some length, both because they illustrate the thinking of the central bureaucracy on the problem, and because, despite the note of extreme urgency they struck, they produced so little in the way of practical results.[146]

The interior minister's expert, Rüdiger, opened the proceedings by summarizing the issues on the table. Although he conceded that salaries were a factor in falling recruitment, he argued that the real problem lay in the massive loss of prestige suffered by the civil service as a profession, compared with its status in the Kaiserreich. Rüdiger explained that the root causes of this were to be sought in the Weimar period, when 'a few system bosses, who had managed by means of their connections to get into the civil service and reach leading positions, gave Germans and the world an unbelievably grossly distorted image of the German civil servant'. Under National Socialism, the civil service had then been 'purified from [this] dross', but it had not been able to

[143] DGT circular, 17 Oct. 1941 (BA R 36/129).

[144] See e.g. DGT replies to queries from DGT Landesstelle Baden (27 June 1942) and the *Oberbürgermeister* of Hindenburg (14 Sept. 1942) (BA R 36/129).

[145] Justice-ministry recruitment review office conference, 8-10 June 1944 (BA R 22/4449).

[146] Minutes of conference (13 pp.), 20 June 1941 (BA R 18/5817).

recover the reputation it deserved. Choosing his language carefully to avoid imputing agency, Rüdiger attributed this to the fact that the civil service was the butt of public criticism in speeches and the press, which generalized the failings of individuals and 'maliciously' presented civil servants as 'ossified bureaucrats'. 'The result of this destruction of the civil service's prestige was that not only the sons of civil servants, but also the children of other professionals . . . had increasingly been opting for other careers which enjoyed a better reputation.' Ultimately, the victim of this state of affairs was not the civil servant, but 'in increasing measure the National Socialist state and thus the entire German people . . . *The most weighty national interests were thus at stake.*'

Rüdiger's views were evidently shared by his colleagues. The general consensus of the meeting was that:

Young people were already rejecting the civil service as a career, because it was seen as a second-class career. Thus the basis for a new kind of 'modern class struggle' was being laid, and the state could stand by no longer . . . The greatest stress was laid on the fact that the authority of the state would already be in question if the reputation of the German civil servant and respect for the German civil service continued to be undermined without restraint.

When it came to proposals for action, unanimous support was given to the suggestion by a representative of the labour ministry that Hitler himself should be asked to offer a public tribute to the 'selfless, tireless and loyal work of the civil service . . . and thus to honour the [concept] of the civil servant as the bearer of the state's administration and thus of its authority . . . Only then would it be possible to win young people for a civil-service career.' The conference regarded this as 'the *most essential* prerequisite' for a solution to the crisis; it also proposed that practical steps should be taken to deter public attacks on the civil service, to educate the public about the importance of the civil service, and to consider the introduction of a civil-service uniform, as well as to increase the number of medals and honorary titles conferred on civil servants.[147]

The complaints registered by the conference participants agreed with a growing sense that, under National Socialism, the civil service enjoyed only fitful public acclaim, if at all. Although figures like Frick, Pfundtner, and Neef repeatedly applauded and encouraged civil servants in their own professional circles, they also offered some bracing

---

[147] In Sept., the interior ministry asked to be kept informed of all instances of serious public attacks on the civil service; circular, 10 Sept. 1941 (BA R 36/86).

doses of criticism; meanwhile, the strong streak of disdain for the bureaucrat which had characterized Nazi attitudes before 1933 continued to influence public discourse in the Third Reich. Had Nazi propaganda activity in general not been so sedulous, the absence of a publicly fostered image for the civil service would doubtless not have been so obvious. But, given the ceaseless political noise and ceremonial pomposities of the Third Reich, the neglect of the civil service in favour of an alternative pantheon of national heroes was the more blatant, at any rate to its victims. A leading figure like Hans Frank might tell an audience of administrative civil servants in 1934 that they were 'the brain and heart of the National Socialist state',[148] but this was no substitute for the attention of the only leader whose interest ultimately mattered, and that was never forthcoming. Hitler was reluctant to offer public praise to the civil service, and his general scorn for the profession was presumably common knowledge among ministers and senior officials. Pfundtner repeatedly raised the question of Hitler's discrimination against the civil service in the matter of public honours. In 1934, he suggested that signed photographs of the Führer should be given to officials who had worked hard for the new Germany, and in 1938, for the elections; in November 1938, he complained that Hitler had honoured the army's role in the annexation of the Sudetenland by gazetting a large number of promotions, but had done nothing to mark the equally deserving contribution of the administration; and he protested that a reception held by Hitler for the armed-services chiefs at the beginning of 1939 should be paralleled by one for the heads of the civil administration.[149] Similarly, Hans Fabricius, a long-time Nazi now in the interior ministry, approached the chancellery in 1935 with a request that Hitler address a mass meeting of Nazi civil-servant activists, in order to counter the impression that the party was hostile to the civil service.[150] He pointed out that the NSDAP and the Wehrmacht were always being hailed as pillars of the Nazi state, whereas the civil service attracted only criticism from party leaders.

Though direct evidence is patchy, a mounting *malaise* can be detected in the civil service in the 1930s, provoked partly by their lack of public esteem, and also by the salary situation and the new political pressures

[148] Report of speech to Reichsfachgruppe Verwaltungsjuristen, 4 May 1934 (BA R 53/194).

[149] Pfundtner to Lammers, 14 Dec. 1934 (BA R 18/5524); Pfundtner to Frick, 11 Apr. 1938; Pfundtner to Lammers, 29 Nov. 1938; Pfundtner to Frick, 26 Jan. 1939 (all BA R 18/5565).

[150] Fabricius to Meerwald, 14 Nov. 1935 (BA R 43I/261).

on them. Not only were they subject to persistent pressure to conform
to the new standards imposed by law and convention, but they also felt
the demoralizing effects of seeing party members treated preferentially,
as Popitz pointed out in a long critique of Prussian appointments policy
in September 1936.[151] Senior civil servants experienced the frustrations
of working in a system in which party officials constantly intervened in
administrative decision-making and made no secret of their hostility
towards the permanent civil service; the rank and file felt exposed to
public grumbling and party suspicion. In 1937, Hess had to issue
instructions to the NSDAP that wholesale attacks on the civil service
were inconsistent with party discipline.[152] Plans were made by
Lammers in 1939 to establish a small committee to initiate discussions
intended to lead to a submission to Hitler on the problem of civil-
service prestige, but these appear to have come to nothing.[153] However,
the line between the ingratiation of the civil service with its new masters
and excessive and demoralizing self-criticism was itself hard to gauge.
Thus, Fabricius found himself the object of complaint in 1941 when,
in an article entitled 'Soldatisches Berufsbeamtentum', he inveighed
publicly against 'timid and anaemic pen-pushers who amuse themselves
with their mildewed duties on ground fertilized with the blood of
German warriors'.[154]

Fabricius's language, and the reaction it provoked, were symptomatic
of the additional pressures placed on civil servants during the war, with
the disparaging contrast between the bureaucrat safe at home and the
soldier at the front. Criticism of the civil service multiplied; the press,
avid to report the deeds of Germany's military heroes, neglected to
cover the more mundane contributions to the war effort by civil
servants; Hitler's silence became even more painful. The *SD-Meldungen*
repeatedly reported the poor state of morale among civil servants, their
overwork, and their increasing desire to volunteer for the army.[155] The
HfK opened a file labelled hopefully 'Rehabilitation of the Civil

---

[151] Popitz to Frick and Göring, 2 Sept. 1936 (GStA Rep. 90/2339).

[152] StdF instruction 44/37, 3 Apr. 1937 (BA NS 6/vorl. 225); see also BA SS 55,
13 Apr. 1937. The kind of thing at issue was e.g. a case in which a *Kreisleiter* described
the civil service as 'aktenstauberbleichten Arschbackenakrobaten'; see Stapo Magdeburg
report to Stapo Berlin, 13 Feb. 1934 (NG 3331). The SS newspaper, *Schwarze Korps*,
was especially guilty of unbridled attacks, notably on the judicial civil service; see
examples collected by the justice ministry 1937-42 (IfZ MA 118).

[153] Documentation, Jan./Feb. 1939, in GStA P 134/3019.

[154] DGT Dienststelle Ost to DGT, 16 Dec. 1941 (BA R 36/86).

[155] e.g. *SD-Meldungen aus dem Reich*, 86, 9 May 1940, 16-17 (BA R 58/184); 254, 26
Jan. 1942 (R 58/168) and 295, 29 June 1942 (R 58/172).

Service', and collected evidence of criticism from every quarter.[156] Two areas in which the civil service felt itself to be the object of damaging discrimination were the awarding of medals and other tokens of official recognition, and the evaluation of their military service. The first had already arisen as an issue before the war, with Pfundtner's efforts to secure an adequate share of symbolic rewards for the civil service's contribution to the tasks of national renewal. After the outbreak of war, similar complaints were registered at the relatively small number of *Kriegsverdienstkreuzen* made available to the administrative authorities by comparison with the party and the police. Thus, a *Regierungspräsident* complained in 1942 that local distribution gave each *Kreisleiter* fifty or sixty medals to hand out, while *Landräte* disposed of only two or three.[157]

The evaluation of war service for political purposes was a far more serious bone of contention, since it was part of the complex issue of the politicization of personnel policies. In 1941, Borman rejected proposals by the justice minister, Gürtner, that a civil servant's service at the front should be taken into consideration in evaluating political reliability: it was, Bormann argued, specious to suggest that a duty expected of all citizens should be regarded as a substitute for the special political test required of civil servants.[158] On the level of the individual case, the argument may have been correct, though it accords rather poorly with the Nazi addiction to war as the supreme national proving-ground. But it was also symptomatic of the fact that by this time, as Mommsen points out, there was no realistic test of political acceptability from Bormann's point of view.[159]

When the interior ministry brought this matter to Lammers's attention in November, it also enclosed an appeal to Hitler, drafted by Pfundtner in Frick's name, which was intended to serve as the basis for a meeting with the Führer.[160] Though this appeal appears not to have been submitted to Hitler, it offers an insight into the anxieties and

---

[156] Material collected 1941-4, in BA NS 25/919.

[157] *Regierungspräsident* in Merseburg to interior ministry, 8 Aug. 1942 (GStA P 134/3019); see also *Lagebericht* of *Generalstaatsanwalt* in Celle, 29 Jan. 1944 (IfZ Fa 58/1a).

[158] Bormann to interior ministry, 2 Feb. 1941 (BA R 43II/424); reprinted in H. Mommsen, *Beamtentum im Dritten Reich* (Stuttgart, 1966), 198-200, and see also 87 ff.

[159] Ibid. 86-7. See also Ch. 8, p. 282, below.

[160] Copy in BA R 43II/424, enclosed with letter dated 14 Nov. 1941; reprinted in Mommsen, *Beamtentum*, pp. 200-2.

frustrations of the civil-service ēlite. Pfundtner opened on a note of militarized urgency:

My Führer! World empires have always been created by military might. But their survival and development were ever dependent upon their political leadership and internal administration. It was for this reason that you yourself, my Führer, declared the civil service, the bearer of the administration, to be a pillar of the state. This pillar is threatened by severe blows. The German civil service has fallen into calamity.

He went on to construct a picture of an institution whose members had traditionally never sought material riches, but had felt recompensed by the esteem in which they were held. The state, in its turn, was well served by men drawn to their profession by such honourable motives— but if the prestige and reputation enjoyed by civil servants were withdrawn, the state would attract only time-servers and mediocrities. This was what now threatened the German civil service:

The unanimous observations of my own and all other departments show increasingly that civil servants are imbued with an embittering sense that their work and service is not valued and that they are unjustly slighted. A discouraging feeling of utter abandonment is beginning to cripple the best creative spirits . . . It is absolutely impossible to say any more that the professional civil service enjoys the special trust of our national leadership.

All the elements discussed above figured in the catalogue of woes: the lack of decorations, the public attacks 'reminiscent of the worst period of class struggle', the discrimination against career civil servants in favour of party appointees, the heavy burden of voluntary party work carried by civil servants. And a final flourish:

I implore you, my Führer, to take heed of the spiritual distress of the Greater German civil servant. Give him a word of thanks and recognition for all that he has accomplished since 1933, particularly during the war; let him enjoy the public honour and esteem he deserves; prove your confidence in him by entrusting him with great new tasks. Two million of Germany's best sons will thank you, my Führer . . .

The appeal was emblematic of the bureaucratic ēlite's reading of the crisis of the German civil service by the second year of the war. It was equally symptomatic that, not only was Frick driven to the stratagem of a written approach to Hitler because he could not secure a personal audience, but that even in this written form the appeal was ultimately never delivered. In any case, at much the same time that it was being drafted, Hitler was delivering one of his private diatribes against Germany's 'best sons', and declaring his own principles for its reorganization:

The Civil Service has reached the point of being a blind machine. . . . The chief condition for decentralisation is that the system of appointment by seniority shall be abandoned in favour of appointment to posts . . . The allowance allocated in addition to the basic salary should be in inverse ratio to the number of colleagues employed by a head of department . . . When I think of the organisation of the Party, which has always been exemplary from every point of view . . . I can see all the more clearly the weaknesses of our Ministries . . .[161] The Civil Service is the refuge of mediocre talents, for the State does not apply the criterion of superiority in the recruitment and use of its personnel.[162]

A few months later, Hitler repeated these sentiments in public, in the address to the Reichstag on 26 April 1942 in which he called for absolute powers of command over every German soldier and official:

In times like these no one can be allowed to presume on his vested rights, but everyone must realize that today there are only duties . . . It is of no interest to me in our present emergency whether in every individual case, say of a civil servant or a clerk, leave-time can be given or not, and I also will not stand for leave being credited against the future if it can't be given now. If anyone has any right at all to demand leave, then it is in the first place our soldier at the front, only him, and in second place the worker or woman worker for the front.[163]

Clearer confirmation of the problem identified in Pfundtner's appeal could hardly be found. The civil service, far from having been integrated into the National Socialist community, appeared to its political masters an alien, and to its own leaders an alienated, institution. But although by 1942 the scope for policy was becoming increasingly limited, the interior ministry had not confined its efforts to the level of sentiment alone. As the following chapters will show, the implementation of practical policies had been attempted in a number of important fields since the later 1930s, in a bid to identify and resolve the crisis of the civil service under National Socialism.

---

[161] *Hitler's Table Talk 1941–1944* introd. H. Trevor-Roper (London, 1973), 1/2 Nov. 1941, 103–5.

[162] Ibid., 10/11 Nov. 1941, p. 119.

[163] *Sten. Berichte*, 8. Sitzung, 26 Apr. 1942, 117; also *Beschluss des Grossdeutschen Reichstags*, 26 Apr. 1942 (*RGBl*, 1942, i. 247). New regulations on civil-service leave allowances had been introduced on 11 Apr. (*RGBl*, 1942, i. 168). See also *Table Talk*, p. 240, for Hitler's declaration that he could 'never make up my mind to praise publicly the body of officials generally'.

7

The Politics of Remuneration
1937-1939: A Case-Study

The debates and conflicts over the role of the civil service in the National Socialist polity, and over the public status of civil servants as members of the Nazi *Volksgemeinschaft*, were the flagrant and often public evidence of the indeterminacy of political structure and policy-making in the Nazi state. Less obvious, but no less revealing of the fundamental tensions in the hobbled process of state formation in the Third Reich, was the course of policy in fields internal to the functioning of the civil service. The hierarchical structure and integrity of the bureaucracy were heavily dependent on the linked systems of recruitment, training, and salaries, all of which were thrown into flux under the pressure of the competing projects of political reconstruction after 1933. As policy fields, they generated the critical technical standards of civil-service organization. In particular, they defined the role of merit as a criterion for institutional structure and individual advancement, and they helped to determine the capacity of some civil servants to function as an ēlite, in relation both to other personnel in the public administration and to the competing ēlites of the Nazi political and social order. Training and salary policies were thus imbued with meaning for those problems of status and morale which, as developments before 1933 had already shown, were of paramount significance for the self-image and the political and social role of the civil service.

On top of this, as archetypes of the arcana of administrative technique, these policy fields lent themselves to manipulation, under the guise of expert privilege, in the interests of broader policy objectives. Both the finance and justice ministries were occupied with their own sectional agendas in salary and training policy respectively, but it was the interior ministry that was most dedicated to this strategy and most persistent in utilizing it. Frick and his senior officials were engaged in the 1930s in a complex campaign of administrative reorganization, premised on an expansion of ministry powers which would consolidate it as the *Beamtenministerium* and the pivot of a reconstituted bureaucratic regime. The technical points of salary policy in particular were expedient instruments in this campaign. They were relatively removed from such overtly politicized issues as the role of party membership in civil-service affairs or the powers of party officials in appointments and promotions, and were familiar and congenial areas of business to the permanent ministerial staff. Moreover, the policy agenda in this field had not been exclusively set by the Nazi assumption of power, but, like the bigger questions of *Reichsreform*, had been carried over from the republic. In other words, administrative policy in the technical sense was an area in which the traditional ministries and their expert personnel had the upper hand over the newcomers in the Nazi Reich—a position which they could exploit for political ends. Both salary and training policy were highly contentious during the Nazi regime, there-fore, with their intrinsic narrowness being overtaken by the political conflicts that became attached to them. They thus lend themselves as case-studies in the conditions of administrative policy-making in Nazi Germany, as this and the following chapter will demonstrate.

I

The parameters for salary policy after 1933 were set initially by the two major considerations of overall economic and fiscal policy, and of the structural changes associated with *Reichsreform*. The first determined that civil-service salaries would have no priority in relation to the broader problems of economic recovery and rearmament, despite the depth of the Brüning cuts and the political capital the party had made of them in the early 1930s. It was agreed that salaries would not be further reduced,[1] but the validity of the Brüning cuts was twice extended, the second time indefinitely.[2] Moreover, the June 1933 BRÄndG re-enacted in effect the provisions of the 1920 salary limitation law (*Besoldungssperrgesetz*) by mandating the reduction of *Länder* and *Gemeinde* salaries to comparable Reich levels.[3] This measure, which, as

[1] In a cabinet meeting, 14 July 1933 (copy of minutes in BA R 43II/431). The Papen government had also rejected further pay cuts at the end of 1932; see minutes of cabinet, 18 Nov. 1932 (copy in BA R 43I/1458-9, ff. 341 ff.).

[2] The *Verordnung des Reichpräsident über Massnahmen auf dem Gebiete der Finanzen, der Wirtschaft und der Rechtspflege*, 16 Mar. 1933 (*RGBl*, 1933, i. 109), extended the decrees to 31 Mar. 1934. The *Gesetz zur Änderung und Ergänzung von Vorschriften auf dem Gebiete des Finanzwesens*, 23 Mar. 1934 (*RGBl*, 1934, i. 232), extended them 'until further notice' (Article 7, §1).

[3] BRÄndG, 30 June 1933, ch. VIII; for the scope of the law as a whole, see Ch. 5, pp. 149-52, above. The second of the Brüning decrees had not granted sufficient powers to enforce mandatory parity on *Gemeindebeamte* (decree of 5 June 1931, §7(2)), a position the BRÄndG and subsequent orders aimed to remedy; see L. Ambrosius, *Das Besoldungsrecht der Beamten: Kommentar* (Düsseldorf, 1954), 131-2.

we have seen, drew heavily on pre-1933 plans, was consistent with the Nazi programme of enforced defederalization and the establishment of uniform standards and practices throughout the Reich. In further moves in 1935/7, Reich salary law was declared applicable to *Länder* civil servants.[4] However, as always it proved easier to enact than to enforce such sweeping measures, and it is clear that the finance ministry was unable to impose standardization on the *Länder*, despite their nominal subordination to the Reich after the *Reichsreform* measures of 1933-5.[5] The problem was exacerbated by the accumulation of piecemeal supplements to the salary schedule (*Besoldungsordnung*) as new agencies were established or new departments and posts added to existing ones.[6] The constitutional and administrative changes initiated by the Nazi regime introduced more confusion than clarity into the state apparatus and its attendant machinery, especially given the abrupt foreclosure of co-ordination policy on Hitler's orders in 1935.

The attempt to impose uniform salary scales throughout the Reich had the inevitable effect of depressing some rates—this was, after all, its intent—and in certain cases the regime was cast in a role similar to that of Brüning which the party had so bitterly castigated in 1930-2. This unhappy irony was not lost on officials of the Berlin Amt für Beamte, who in 1935 had to explain to several thousand of their lowest-paid colleagues why they faced salary cuts as a result of the implementation of national legislation.[7] A summary of morale reports submitted to the Reich chancellery via the Berlin Gauleitung included numerous complaints: the move was the exact reverse of what had been expected from the Nazi government; local party officials were at a loss to defend the measure; lower-paid civil servants were precisely those who had risked most for the party before 1933. In this case, Hitler intervened

4 By the 24th and 29th amendments to the salary law respectively, 13 Dec. 1935 (*RGBl*, 1935, i. 1489) and 19 Mar. 1937 (*RGBl*, 1937, i. 342); see Oberregierungsrat Wichert, 'Das Gesetz über die 24. Änderung des Reichsbesoldungsgesetzes vom 13. Dezember 1935', *Beamtenjahrbuch*, Feb. 1936, 71-6.

5 As always, it was the pay of *Gemeindebeamte* that was most recalcitrant to regulation: see interior-ministry memo of 6 Jan. 1936, in connection with an attempt by Goerdeler, *Oberbürgermeister* in Leipzig, to raise his officials' pay (copy in R 43II/572b). Some of the problems at *Land* level are mentioned in a finance-ministry circular to the *Länder* governments (except Prussia, which had already issued parity regulations), 24 Jan. 1936 (BA R 2/22822).

6 For example, the 13th amendment added new posts to the schedule in respect of the aviation ministry and the general inspectorate of roads (5 July 1934; *RGBl*, i. 601); the 17th added the labour trustees (29 Mar. 1935; *RGBl*, 1935, i. 461); the 23rd, posts in the labour service (13 Dec. 1935; *RGBl*, 1935, i. 1485); and so on.

7 The documentation for this account is in BA R 43II/571.

personally to soften the blow, with characteristic insouciance of the procedural havoc he was causing. But the episode coincided with some of the first serious discussions within the government about the difficulty of maintaining steady wage and cost-of-living rates, and with the growing evidence that industrial wage rates throughout Germany were diverging, as arms-related industries began to outpace other sectors.[8] It was in this context that Hess, in one of his many moves to stall progress on the civil-service code, had made it pointedly clear that he would reject any draft containing financial improvements.[9] Similarly, it was Hess who blocked attempts by the interior ministry to regrade certain senior posts, or otherwise raise the status and salaries of its own officials.[10] In so far as Germany was experiencing an incipient armaments-led boom, civil servants were among those who risked being left behind.

The interior ministry was thus unable to seize the initiative in salary policy until 1937, when it drove a wedge into the narrow opening offered by the accumulating evidence of economic recovery. This year was something of watershed for the internal development of the Nazi state, marking a moment of regroupment in alliances and strategies. In civil-service politics, the new code had finally been adopted, yet it was also becoming evident that this was the end rather than the beginning of the reform programme espoused by the interior ministry. Of itself, the Nazi regime would not present clear opportunities for any fundamental remodelling of the civil service, far less for the elevation of its political status desired by the bureaucratic reformers. Those who had hoped for advances along these paths were forced on to the defensive or else into

[8] See the basic ministerial discussion of wage policy, 2 May 1935, at which ministers opposed any shift from a strict wage policy (copy of minutes in BA R 43II/541). For the economic context in general, see T. W. Mason, *Sozialpolitik im Dritten Reich: Arbeiterklasse und Volksgemeinschaft* (Opladen, 1977), esp. 147 ff.

[9] Hess to interior ministry, 26 Apr. 1935 (GStA Rep. 90/2329); see also memo by Killy on this point, 1 Feb. 1936 (BA R 43II/419a). Interestingly, this point was subsequently made public: see O. Fischbach, 'Das DBG vom 26. 1. 1937: Entstehungsgeschichte und Überblick', *Beamtenjahrbuch*, Feb. 1937, 45. For the DBG, see Ch. 5, pp. 174-83, above. For rank-and-file Nazi views on the excessive salaries paid to senior *Beamte*, see report of Göttingen Kreisleitung, 23 Feb. 1934 (BA NS 22/vorl. 618). I am grateful to Jeremy Noakes for this reference.

[10] This was pointed out in a letter from Oberpräsident Stürtz in Brandenburg/Posen-Westpreussen to the interior ministry, 22 May 1937: 'I know that the ministers concerned basically share the view expressed here [that the post of *Regierungsvizepräsident* should be upgraded], and are prepared to draw the consequences from it [but] that only the Führer's deputy, minister Hess, has vetoed it as a matter of principle for the time being, and that therefore the proposed readjustment has not taken place' (BA R 43II/433) (see also n. 14 below).

the exploitation of technical procedures in default of a frontal engagement with the political structure of the Nazi state. The pressures for a salary increase after 1937 were taken as a *point d'appui* for the wider issue of reforms in the salary system, and beyond that in the administration itself. A certain unanimity of motive can thus be seen among proponents of reform, notably Frick's senior staff, their backers in the chancellery and the heads of those ministries with large numbers of employees, together with some of the rank-and-file, nominally party spokesmen for civil-service interests: anxiety about the quality of recruitment at all levels, concern for the service's strength and efficiency, disquiet at the regime's neglect of civil servants' morale and their generally depressed status. The structural reform schemes drafted in the interior ministry also make it clear that senior officials were not only pursuing the ministry's plans for self-aggrandizement, but were aiming in addition to recover and enhance the status of the élite bureaucracy in general by widening the grade differentials built into the salary system. This was an attempt to continue the trend we have already observed away from the egalitarian principles of the 1920 salary law, a trend initiated after stabilization, formalized in the provisions of the 1927 salary law, and powered by the specific interests of the senior officials charged with the conduct of salary policy.[11] Despite the ostensible populism of the Nazi programme, this was another case in which the residual power of an entrenched élite enabled it to look after its own, even though it was unable to achieve the structural changes which would have furnished the financial ballast for its grander dreams.

Opposition to these campaigns came from a variety of quarters, not all of them equally animated by a rejection of the vision of bureaucracy redivivus. For the finance minister, Krosigk, for example, the debate was partly just the latest in the long round of territorial conflicts between the two ministries over responsibility for civil-service policy, conflicts which long antedated the Nazi regime. To some extent, it was because the ultimate tendency of the interior ministry's imperialism was so clear to a career professional like Krosigk that he resisted most of Frick's plans. On the other hand, Krosigk's very background also indicated a certain measure of sympathy for the restorationism of his colleague, and although he himself retained strong fiscal reservations about the wisdom of salary increases, as well as professional scepticism about the viability of Frick's grand designs, he was not entirely immune to arguments drawn from the armoury of status recovery. Economic

[11] See Ch. 3, pp. 76-90, above.

arguments remained uppermost for other opponents, like the labour minister, Seldte, or the price commissioner, Wagner, both of whom were necessarily drawn into the debates. The most powerful oppositional voices were undoubtedly those of Hess and Bormann, with their radical lack of sympathy for the bureaucracy and their profound hostility to Frick's ambitions. A somewhat more idiosyncratic critic was the Prussian finance minister, Popitz, a man of strong opinions and considerable administrative experience, who was committed to his own radical vision of bureaucratic rule. This led him at first to argue that salary issues were merely a diversion from the real problems facing the state in the 1930s, but he was later to alter his views, as the growing urgency of the matter convinced him that a solution would become necessary long before the maturation of his own increasingly precarious reform schemes. Popitz was also, of course, the most notable among those members of the bureaucratic élite whose disdain for the Nazi leadership and fears for Germany's future were eventually to lead them, like some army officers, into various degrees of open opposition.

Thus, the debate about salary policy after 1937 ranged over a far wider field than simply the achievement of pay increases through the abrogation of the Brüning cuts. This was only the starting-point for a programme of revision that was linked to the grander schemes of administrative reorganization. Reform of the salary system on the interior-ministry model aimed initially to restore balance and intelligibility to the increasingly tattered 1927 schedules (which between 1933 and 1937 had undergone some twenty-eight statutory amendments as well as numerous supplementary regulations), but it would also serve the interests of status restoration and administrative reform. In the first period of negotiations until 1939, pay increases were the central issue, but a general investigation of the potential for structural reform was subsequently agreed upon. The war, with its dislocating effects on the administrative machine, immediately gave additional impetus to plans for full-scale reform, plans which had been in abeyance since 1935. Not surprisingly, they faded into the background as Germany's military prospects also paled. These themes, then, represent the successive stages in the interior ministry's struggle to realize its policies. The abrogation of the pay cuts was an initial demand which was more or less achieved, with perhaps surprising speed under the circumstances: but the no less urgently pressed campaign for structural reform made no headway against the interest-motivated inertia of the regime. This failure marked the final defeat of the ministry as an initiator of policy in the Third Reich, and the loss of its residual authority to more power-ful competitors from the Nazi party's own bureaucratic systems. The present chapter will analyse the salary increase campaign up to 1939, leaving the issue of reform, and the defeat of the interior ministry, to Chapter 8.

II

The first steps towards the abrogation of the Brüning cuts were the indirect result of fears that the salary system was nearing final disintegration under the impact of piecemeal amendments. In 1937, the interior ministry was trying to press home a previously unsuccessful bid to regrade or financially improve some senior field posts, and was linking this to a further attempt to promote a number of ministerial posts to higher salary groups. The argument was the same in both cases: that the interior administration was losing some of its most experienced senior officials, notably *Landräte* and *Ministerialräte*, as they reached the salary ceiling for these posts and took off in search of more lucrative openings in other areas of the administration.[12] At the same time, the foreign ministry was petitioning for across-the-board special allowances for its senior civil servants to offset expenses allegedly incurred in the course of their official duties. At this point, the propaganda minister entered the fray, insisting that his officials were also entitled to the same consideration. Both sets of demands illustrate the pitfalls of salary policy in the Third Reich, as ministries scrambled for status and qualified staff in circumstances of extreme competitiveness. Upwards reclassification and the payment of supplementary allowances were selective technical alternatives to general pay increases, but they also threatened such fundamental principles of salary policy as the uniformity of scales in each rank irrespective of ministry. Indeed, this was already being eroded by this time, as ministries sought to retain their departmental experts by offering them barely legitimate forms of

[12] The post of *Ministerialrat* was at the top of schedule A (incremental salaries), and was the highest rank a ministerial official could reach before promotion to a scarce departmental headship. A senior *Ministerialrat* was a key official for his ministry, probably having long years of experience in his area of expertise, and was someone a minister could ill afford to lose. *Landräte* were fixed at a lower point in schedule A, with no prospects of further increments after reaching the top of the salary group. Thus, the only way a senior man in these and some other posts could increase his income was by taking a different appointment, in or out of the civil service.

additional income. Killy, the chancellery's expert on civil-service matters, was disturbed by this trend: 'If one or more departments', he commented, 'are singled out above the others in the manner requested, the natural result will be that the latter will not be reconciled to this inequity, but will endeavour to restore comparability. The kind of unrest and unhappiness that this process will evoke is surely undesirable.'[13] On the other hand, a competitive payment structure of this kind, in which uniformity was sacrificed to special needs or interests, reflected the growing interest in a merit system of salaries, which, as we shall see, was to become increasingly prominent in government circles.

The interior ministry had already decided to make a strong case for its demands, and brought up a particularly flagrant example of financial distress to press its arguments home. The chancellery was asked to bring Hitler's attention to this: it concerned an application for financial aid by an *Oberpräsident*'s deputy—a post of some standing and responsibility. Pfundtner described it as a 'cry of distress', and insisted that it 'cast such an indicative and glaring light on the distress of civil servants with large families, even those in the highest posts, that in the interests of the state the matter can no longer be avoided'.[14] Whether or not in collusion with chancellery officials, the interior ministry was beginning to make some progress in pursuing the question of pay increases. In September, Pfundtner returned from Nuremberg and instructed his officials to prepare for preliminary talks with him on a 'step-by-step rollback of the pay reduction orders'.[15] In December, some of the reclassification demands were incorporated in a fresh amendment to the salary schedule. When this matter was considered by the cabinet, discussion soon turned from the details of the amendment

[13] Internal memo by Killy, 25 Nov. 1937 (BA R 43II/431b). Note, however, that the chancellery had achieved special supplements for its own senior officials by the 19th amendment (29 Mar. 1935; *RGBl*, 1935, i. 464), and that Killy and his colleagues were currently trying to maintain this preferential status by creating the new rank of *Reichskabinettsrat*; this was achieved in the 31st amendment (9 Dec. 1937; *RGBl*, 1937, i. 1355). There was some force to the chancellery argument that its *Ministerialräte* had unusual responsibilities which justified this special treatment, but of course this also opened the way for the similar special pleading deplored by Killy himself.

[14] Pfundtner to Lammers, 25 May 1937, with enclosure from the *Oberpräsident* in Brandenburg/Posen-Westpreussen (see n. 10 above). This was a personal note, and Pfundtner suggested that Lammers might show the material to Hitler in order to 'give the Führer and Reich chancellor a picture of the precarious financial circumstances of even civil servants in leading and responsible positions'.

[15] Internal note from Pfundtner to dept. II of the interior ministry, 17 Sept. 1937 (BA R 18/5564). It is not clear what prompted this note, though presumably Pfundtner had held conversations at the party rally.

to the general question of salary rates.[16] Krosigk opposed any general improvement on economic grounds, though he conceded that there was a risk that an 'educated proletariat' was being created. But Hitler referred to the 'grotesque imbalance' between pay in the civil service and private sectors, warning that action was urgently needed. His favoured prescription was the introduction of competitive merit payments, on the grounds that this would be 'fairer than a purely schematic salary system'. Though no one demurred in the cabinet, this suggestion was anathema to the conventions that Killy and others were trying to defend. Nevertheless, Frick took up Hitler's suggestion a few weeks later, and put forward an enthusiastic proposal for the establishment of a special fund out of which payments could be made to deserving civil servants, a proposal which remained an undercurrent in the more substantial negotiations of the ensuing months.[17]

Hitler closed his remarks by observing that 'an inadequately paid public servant could hardly represent the state in a proper manner', and by noting 'unanimous agreement that something must happen soon in the direction discussed'. The Reich chancellery had in fact drawn up an extensive internal memorandum examining the financial position of civil servants, and although it is scarcely likely that Hitler drew on this for his own arguments, the evidence that was to figure in the coming debate was now being marshalled.[18]

The author of this document was Leo Killy, a man of experience and authority, whose strong professional commitment to the civil service made him a more consistent defender of its interests than his politically ambitious superior, Lammers. Killy drew much of his statistical evidence from a confidential report prepared in the finance ministry for the use of Hess's subordinate, Sommer. This showed that the rise in the official cost-of-living index from 115.9 in April 1933 to 126 in August 1937 had effectively lowered the real value of civil servants' incomes by 8 per cent; another 5 per cent of their pay was swallowed up in fees and contributions to professional, political, and social organizations (NSDAP, SA, RDB, WHW, etc.), while tax increases were claiming a further 1 to 2.75 per cent. Thus, civil-service incomes could be said to

---

[16] Minutes of cabinet, 9 Dec. 1937 (copy in BA R 43II/431b). The discussion was of the 31st amendment; see n. 13 above.

[17] Frick to Krosigk, 4 Jan. 1938 (BA R 18/5287). The chancellery, which received a copy of the letter, was not sympathetic to the idea: see its 19-pp. memorandum, 'Die besoldungspolitische Lage der deutschen Beamten' (marked 'Streng vertraulich!'), 13 July 1938, 18 (BA R 43II/432).

[18] See n. 13 above.

have suffered a *de facto* reduction of 14 to 15.75 per cent, on top of the 19 to 23 per cent cuts imposed by Brüning. Against this, the economic position of other members of the working population appeared to be improving. According to a public statement by Fritz Reinhardt, the party's expert in the finance ministry, the gross national income had risen by some 50 per cent since 1932; and according to a highly confidential statement from the labour ministry, the gross wages of workers had grown from 12 milliard RM in 1933 to 18.6 milliard RM in 1936. Although the bulk of this growth was accounted for by the absorption of the unemployed in the economy and by an increase in hours worked, it was still claimed that hourly pay rates had risen by 8 per cent since 1933, and weekly wages by 19 per cent.

Assessment of this data is complicated by the unreliability of much of the statistical evidence available for the Nazi period, as well as by the divergence between data produced by different sources and for different purposes. Following Mason's evaluation of economic indices, however, the basic outlines sketched by Killy were not incorrect in terms of the information available to him. Reinhardt's public claim for gross national income in 1937 was somewhat inflated, but the increase shown for gross industrial wages accords with the figure for all wages and salaries noted by Mason, as do the figures for hourly and (less closely) weekly wage rates also.[19] At 8 per cent, Killy's figure for the increase in the cost of living from 1933 to 1937 stands somewhat nearer to the official 6 per cent than to Mason's revised estimate of 12 to 13 per cent for workers alone.[20] The surprisingly large 5 per cent of income said to be taken by subscriptions and dues may be slightly exaggerated in the light of a group of civil-service budgets, collected in 1938, which show between 2.4 and 4.5 per cent of monthly salaries devoted to these purposes.[21] However, this did represent a new level of outlay by civil servants, and seems to have been much resented. In the 1920s, such expenditure had claimed only about 1 per cent of their income—less than half what workers were used to paying for union and association dues.[22] In sum, then, although there is no doubt that real wages in

---

[19] See the table in Mason, *Sozialpolitik*, p. 149, compiled from a range of primary and secondary sources.

[20] Ibid. and p. 153.

[21] Materials submitted to the interior ministry by the *Regierungspräsidenten* of Merseburg and Magdeburg, 31 Mar. 1938 and 10 June 1938 (copies in BA R 43II/432). See also n. 30 below.

[22] See *Die Lebenshaltung von 2000 Arbeiter-, Angestellten- und Beamtenhaushaltungen* (*Einzelschriften zur Statistik des Deutschen Reichs*, 22; Berlin 1932), 51.

Germany had *not* returned to pre-depression levels by 1937, or even 1938, there had been a recovery since the bottom of the slump in 1932 from which civil servants were excluded.[23]

Nevertheless, the labour ministry's review of wage statistics for the second quarter of 1938 was to show that the relative adversity of civil servants could easily be exaggerated.[24] Despite the Brüning cuts, civil-service incomes had not fallen in full proportion to the drop in national income between 1929 and 1933, and thus only since the beginning of 1938 could it be said that civil servants were really being left behind. It is in any case difficult to make meaningful comparisons between civil-service and other incomes after 1933, or to interpret how civil servants understood their own situation. Civil servants were distributed throughout the income scale in Germany, except at the absolute extremities; the top end, which included ministers as well as state secretaries and other senior posts, fell into the upper 10 per cent of incomes, the bottom into the lowest 88 per cent, and the Brüning cuts had not disturbed this significantly.[25] Direct comparison with other earners is difficult, especially for the senior grade of the service, whose work was comparable with professional and private-sector jobs for which little research data exists for this period.[26] Even reaching an acceptable average figure for the different grades was a tricky and debated business, as we have seen.[27] Except for the salaries paid in the most senior posts, rates were incremental and subject to complicated seniority calculations. The basic rates were also supplemented with

[23] See principally Mason, *Sozialpolitik*, ch. 4, and G. Bry, *Wages in Germany 1871-1945* (Princeton, 1960), 75-7, 233-54.

[24] Labour-ministry report, 'Die Entwicklung der tatsächlichen Arbeitsverdienste im 2. Vierteljahr 1938', sent to the chancellery on 3 Jan. 1939, and chancellery memo on this, 26 Jan. (both in BA R 43II/541).

[25] Computed from the schedules of the 1927 salary law, and from tables in H. Schiedt, *Die Gehälter der Beamten und die Dienstbezüge der Angestellten* (Berlin, 1939), and D. Petzina, W. Abelshauser, and A. Faust (eds.), *Sozialgeschichtliches Arbeitsbuch*, iii. *Materialien zur Statistik des Deutschen Reiches 1914-1945* (Munich, 1978), 105.

[26] For the status of professionals, see K. H. Jarausch, 'The Perils of Professionalism: Lawyers, Teachers and Engineers in Nazi Germany', *German Studies Review*, 9/1 (1986), 107-37; also D. Schoenbaum, *Hitler's Social Revolution: Class and Status in Nazi Germany 1933-1939* (New York, 1966), ch. 4; P. Hüttenberger, 'Interessenvertretung und Lobbyismus im Dritten Reich', in G. Hirschfeld and L. Kettenacker (eds.), *The 'Führer State': Myth and Reality. Studies on the Structure and Politics of the Third Reich* (Stuttgart, 1981), 431-44. For engineers, see the pioneering study by K.-H. Ludwig, *Technik und Ingenieure im Dritten Reich* (Düsseldorf, 1979); for doctors, see M. H. Kater, 'The Burden of the Past: Problems of a Modern Historiography of Physicians and Medicine in Nazi Germany', *German Studies Review*, 10/1 (1987), 31-56.

[27] See Ch. 3 n. 42, above.

variable local weightings and child allowances, which might add up to half as much again. Non-contributory pensions and dependants' allowances were obviously a considerable hidden benefit of civil-service employment; in the 1920s, the proportion of civil-service household income spent on insurance, including these items, had been between 50 and 75 per cent less than in comparable blue- and white-collar workers' households. On top of these calculable features of civil-service pay, one must also consider less measurable advantages, especially the enjoyment of steady employment during the depression years, or (to the extent that this is an advantage) the fact that civil servants' wives did not 'have' to go out to work.[28]

All this only underlines the familiar point that wage and salary rates are entangled in specific histories, a point which the 1920s salary debates had already amply confirmed. Objectively, civil servants' nominal salaries remained as low in 1937 as they had been in the middle of the depression; their real incomes, preserved to some extent by the price falls of the depression, were also being reduced by then as the economy picked up again. The Brüning cuts, as we have seen, had wiped out the effect of the 1927 salary law; allowing for price movements, it is safe to say that, historically speaking, civil servants were somewhere back in the early 1920s as far as their salaries were concerned, though with the proviso that the differential structure was less egalitarian than had been the case then.

The aggregate data can be illuminated by the extensive documentation of civil-service distress which made its way into the interior ministry in 1938 and 1939. This material was evidently submitted in response to Frick's first salvo in his campaign for across-the-board salary increases, a passionately worded letter to the finance ministry, which, in defiance of convention, he also circulated among the other ministries.[29] Frick began by stating that the Brüning cuts had reduced already modest civil-service salaries to an insupportably low level; new expenditures by civil servants, including the cost of subscriptions, party donations, and uniforms, and the rise in the cost of living since 1932, had added such heavy burdens that civil servants could make ends meet only 'by means of the most meticulous economizing, by the adoption of

[28] *Die Lebenshaltung*, p. 41. 12 per cent of civil-servant households surveyed had some income from a working wife, compared with almost 50 per cent of working-class and 15 per cent of white-collar households.

[29] Frick to finance minister, with copies to the chancellery, Reich ministers, Führer's deputy, Prussian minister-president, and Prussian finance minister, 4 Jan. 1938 (copy in BA R 43II/432).

a more than modest style of life, and by giving up many perfectly reasonable expenditures'. He suggested that civil servants were being forced to withdraw from the nation's cultural life, and that the old tradition of generations of service to the nation was dying because civil servants could no longer afford to educate their children:

Whereas previously it was the civil servant who went without other necessities in order to provide considerable sums for the education of his children, and thus presented the state with valuable recruits for the civil service and officer corps, as well as advancing beneficially up the social scale . . . now he can barely scrape together the means to give his children the same education he himself received. . . . Far from there being upward social mobility now, there is no more than a standstill or indeed a decline; we have a downwards, not an upwards movement. It is hardly necessary to argue that this is harmful not only to the individual civil servant and his family, but to the entire German people.

Frick called for the utmost speed in meeting 'the exceptional economic plight of the civil service', and as an initial step he proposed the repeal of the first of Brüning's emergency orders, which would amount to a 6 per cent increase on current rates. He may have weakened his case somewhat by suggesting, as a possible compromise, an adjustment of housing allowances alone, which would take account of rising rents, but all in all this was a strong initial sally.

As a result of Frick's unorthodox procedure, his future arguments were able to draw on considerable information about civil servants' hardships, including individual cases and budgets, which now flowed in from sources in the field, among them a number of *Regierungspräsidenten* as well as offices in the judicial administration and the Reichsbahn.[30] This material took up the cues supplied by Frick;

[30] The following materials are considered here: (1) Report and enclosures from *Regierungspräsident* in Merseburg to interior ministry, 31 Mar. 1938; circulated with 10-pp. letter by Frick, 20 Apr. 1938 (BA R 43II/432) (2) Report and enclosures from *Regierungspräsident* in Magdeburg to interior ministry, 10 June 1938; sent to Lammers with 10-pp. letter by Frick, 25 June 1938 (ibid.) (3) Letter from transport ministry to interior ministry, 18 June 1938, enclosing 31 statements from Reichsbahn officials collected by the HfB; sent by Frick to Lammers (ibid.) (4) Report and enclosures from *Regierungspräsident* in Düsseldorf to interior ministry, 21 July 1938; sent to Lammers by Frick, 29 July 1938 (BA R 43II/431b) (5) Letter (29-pp.) from justice ministry to Frick, including information from the *Generalstaatsanwalt* in Düsseldorf, the *Oberlandesgerichtspräsident* in Naumburg, and the *Landesgerichtspräsident* in Halle, 2 Feb. 1939; sent to Krosigk with 4-pp. letter by Frick, and copy to chancellery, 2 Mar. 1939 (BA R 43II/432b). These were the only materials circulated by Frick, though it is possible that additional information was acquired by the ministry. (In the following discussion, further references to the sources are given only where the provenance is not clear from the text.)

it vividly illustrates the chronic financial difficulties suffered by civil servants at all levels, as well as the anxious conclusions drawn by their superiors. A good deal of it came from industrial areas where private-sector wages were relatively high, and housing was expensive and hard to find. From Merseburg, for example, came a report that local industrial employers were paying far more than the tariff wages, so that workers in a local machine-building factory were making as much as 70 RM per week, while others were being rewarded with Christmas bonuses or a thirteenth month's pay; the *Regierungspräsident* here complained that he was unable to find an official driver. From Magdeburg came similar news that a shorthand typist could double her pay by leaving the state for the private sector, along with a table of statistics on local wage movements between 1933 and 1938 drawn up in consultation with the DAF and the local works trustees. The Naumburg *Oberlandesgerichtspräsident* reported that weekly wages of up to 200 RM were not uncommon in the industrial zones of his region. All this was presented as evidence that the official figures for industrial wages underestimated actual facts, and that the already noticeable gap between industrial and civil-service incomes was widening. As the Merseburg report put it:

the material distress of civil servants is further aggravated, from the psychological point of view, by the fact that in my region, as a result of the industrial growth prompted by activity under the Four Year Plan, the standard of living of the workers has been considerably enhanced by the heavy wage increases noted above, while for civil servants . . . it has noticeably worsened.

The housing shortage in Magdeburg was allegedly the cause of peculiar problems for civil servants:

it is very hard to maintain the [official] rental rates, because no-one who is looking for housing complains about the rent but is happy to find available housing, even at a sacrifice. A state employee in search of housing is, on the one hand, helpless in the face of competitors from the private sector. On the other hand, his department insists that he move quickly. A civil servant who offers a rent higher than the officially permitted rate, in order to get any kind of housing at all, damages himself in two ways: he has to pay a rent beyond his means . . . and then he also risks being penalized by the Price Control Board, as has already happened here.

For civil servants themselves the effects were both psychologically depressing and economically devastating, especially when low pay was supplemented by borrowing. The *Regierungspräsident* in Magdeburg recorded that the sums paid out as advances on salary had doubled between 1933 and 1937, and his counterpart in Merseburg confirmed that a quarter of the employees in his department had received advances in 1937. Both the Naumburg *Oberlandesgerichtspräsident* and the *Generalstaatsanwalt* in Düsseldorf voiced great anxiety at the indebtedness of civil servants—both what they knew about and what they suspected was being kept quiet out of embarrassment; the former asserted that existing arrangements supposed to help indebted civil servants were inadequate, mainly because the debts were so high and the methods of repayment were too expensive. Conscious of the traditional expectation that a civil servant should live within his income, the Merseburg *Regierungspräsident* insisted that 'the civil service cannot be reproached on account of this indebtedness. Incomes are genuinely insufficient to cover even the barest necessities.'

What this meant for individuals was demonstrated in the case histories collected by these rapporteurs. The Naumburg report mentioned an official who, under a party-organized scheme, would have to pay 10,792 RM over eight years to clear a debt of 6,830 RM. A *Regierungsinspektor* in Merseburg had no more than 10 per cent of his monthly income (35 RM) left for non-recurrent essentials like clothing;[31] in his application for an emergency grant he was driven to mention the no doubt embarrassing fact that his wife suffered from menopausal ailments, despite which they could not afford any domestic help. An official in the senior grade similarly insisted that he could only keep his debts within limits by virtually renouncing all but essential expenditures. Three of the Naumburg report's thirteen pages were devoted to an examination of the expenditures made by civil servants for purposes connected with the Nazi party and its associated activities; many of these were funded by public subscriptions which were virtually obligatory for civil servants. These burdens might include membership dues, newspaper subscriptions, payments for national, regional, and local rallies, donations to the SA or to the SS for needy members, special collections for the *Winterhilfswerk*, for the 'Mother and Child' scheme, for uniforms for the NSKK in the Sudetenland, and more. The burden was heaviest on those civil servants who were also members of the NSDAP, SA, and so on. To make matters even more galling, the reports made it clear that the public had highly exaggerated ideas of what civil servants earned: 'A *Regierungsrat* is simply assumed to be

---

[31] This appears to be about half the comparable sum for 1927; see *Die Lebenshaltung*, p. 43.

worth 800 to 1,000 RM a month [a more likely figure would be 400 to 700 RM], and anyone who tries to contradict this assumption is thought unreasonable. A worker on the kind of wages mentioned previously can only with difficulty be convinced that he earns as much as or more than a *Regierungsrat*.'[32] This left the civil servant in an unfortunate dilemma. He was expected to contribute to funds and collections according to his assumed means: if he did, he incurred an expense he could ill afford, but if he did not, 'he runs the risk of being thought a bad comrade, if the consequences are not even more unpleasant'.

The point about this kind of information is not that it was evidence of total destitution among civil servants—the *Regierungsinspektor* mentioned above acknowledged that many *Volksgenossen* were worse off than himself—but that it demonstrated that, even with careful budgeting, civil servants of all ranks were unable to afford a *standesgemäss* style of life. It was this, as much as any more absolute problems, that attracted the anxious attention of the rapporteurs. As one report put it, civil servants had reached the point where they were no longer contributing to or handing down 'the cultural heritage of the nation'.[33] They could not afford cultural and educational activities in their own lives; worse, they were unable to provide their children with an appropriate education, except at great financial sacrifice. The reports from the judicial administration stressed the importance of the quasi-official socializing which allowed judges to compare sentencing practice, for example, or officials of different ranks to mingle together in an office *Kameradschaftsabend*; but this cost money, and so too did other quasi-professional requirements, such as a judge's need for an up-to-date personal reference library.[34] This sense of offended *ständisch* propriety comes out strongly in the meticulous grading of complaints; that the least well-paid civil servants' clothes are patched and darned, that men in the middle grade cannot afford big enough apartments, that higher civil servants cannot tip the tradesmen at New Year or 'mix socially with attorneys, doctors, the bigger merchants or the better sort of manufacturers and tradespeople'.[35] This was a litany of protest by a privileged class which sensed its loss of automatic access to status and esteem; the fixation here on the material sources of erosion stood in for a more complex set of fears of social disqualification.

[32] Merseburg *Regierungspräsident* report, p. 4.
[33] Ibid. 5.
[34] Justice-ministry materials, pp. 24-5.
[35] Ibid. 22-4.

Similar anxieties were mirrored in complaints which also had a wider social and political resonance. There was some emphasis on the damaging demographic consequences of low salaries, especially late marriage and the disincentive to large families.[36] More serious were the fears that the deteriorating financial situation of the service was making it an increasingly unattractive career. Low rewards obviously did not encourage job satisfaction; it was also claimed that people were leaving the service for private-sector jobs, and, worst of all, that future recruitment was jeopardized.[37] The allegations of a personnel shortage will be analysed further in the following chapter, but a couple of points might be noted at this stage. First, there appears to have been more discussion of the temptations to move elsewhere, and of the disadvantages of staying in the service, than hard information about actual loss of personnel to the private sector. Indeed, it also looks as if some of the official disquiet was occasioned simply by the fact that civil servants were changing jobs *within* the civil service, including the shift from *Beamte* to *Angestellte* status if this was financially advantageous.[38] These men were not lost to the administration, but what *was* threatened was the belief that the civil service ought to be a steady lifetime career of service to the state, and should not be treated as a casual source of livelihood. Given that some officials may have been using the opportunities of the state labour market in this way, they could seem to be imitating the worst features of the private sector, from which the state was thought to be immune. Secondly, much of this anxiety about staffing was not fixed in current problems, but was displaced to the future—to the fear that new recruitment would suffer. As one report put it, piling on the conditionals:

If these aims [economic security and public recognition] were not to be achieved, by far the greater part of the current civil service would, it is true, not fail; but we would not be able to expect a new generation of similar quality, and in particular not from the civil service itself—something I regard as important in terms of tradition and for other reasons. To this it is essential, however, that the life of the civil servant is not only a model to his children, but also a goal worth striving for.[39]

[36] This was the substance, for example, of a letter from the *Landrat* in Dinslaken (von Werder) to the *Regierungspräsident* in Düsseldorf, included among the latter's enclosures.
[37] These issues were raised in all the reports (except the HfB report), but see especially the one from the *Regierungspräsident* in Magdeburg and the justice-ministry materials.
[38] See the case described by the *Landrat* in Dinslaken (n. 36 above). For another light on the problem, see Krosigk's letter to the HfB, 21 Dec. 1934 (BA R 43II/431).
[39] Justice-ministry letter, p. 7.

A forcible elision of future and present was clearly expressed in this comment. The outlook for the civil service was grim, it claimed, and this then became tantamount to saying that a crisis *already* existed. In the eyes of its partisans, the civil service was an historic institution that could not be neglected without compromising its essential character. A regime that courted this risk already made itself responsible for catastrophe.

The association of low pay and status decline in predictions of a troubled future for the civil service clearly echoed some of the concerns and uncertainties of the 1920s, when the civil service had experienced other pressures towards redefinition which it cannot be said to have mastered. In the 1930s, salary and recruitment problems became the focus of intensified fears and disappointments which had few other practical outlets. These culminated in a discourse of 'crisis' in the civil service, generated internally and brought out on to the political stage as evidence of a danger threatening the very survival of the Nazi state, indeed of Germany itself. This movement from internal problem to national peril was to be fast, accelerated not only by the salary issue but also by the war. Indeed, the war was not only a real crisis which brought new problems for the administration, but it also offered a context and a vocabulary of menace in which these issues were given fresh meaning and urgency.

The function of the salary campaign as a focus of displaced anxieties is clearly illustrated in the progress of Frick's campaign. Starting in January 1938, eighteen months were to elapse before the achievement of any across-the-board salary increases. In the annals of government procedure, this might almost count as speedy, even if the periodicity of Nazi activity was unusually unpredictable, alternating between literally interminable delay and sudden bursts of movement. At any event, Frick fought a battle which approached the verbally excessive, given that there was virtually no disagreement among his immediate cabinet colleagues that the situation was intolerable both for the administration and for civil servants themselves. The great majority of them strongly endorsed his demands, volunteering their own information on the position in their departments.[40] Even most of Frick's opponents—Wagner, Seldte, Popitz, and Krosigk himself—conceded the seriousness of the

---

[40] See the series of letters in Jan. and Feb. 1938 from the economics, forestry, foreign, church, food and agriculture, education, postal, and justice ministries (copies in BA R 43II/432).

problem as such, disagreeing only about the best or available means for its solution. Of course, acquiescence is cheap in the absence of action, but there is no mistaking Krosigk's tone: 'Your basic position in the question of civil-service pay, and the apprehension you express at the continuation of the present situation, I accept now as before without reservation in every respect';[41] but he could see no way to accept the remedy proposed by Frick, given the existence of higher budgetary priorities and the risk of an inflationary spiral. Popitz, too, recognized the accuracy of the dismal picture painted by Frick ('The consequences in the entire public administration—departure of experienced civil servants to the private sector, lack of recruits, lowering of standards— have long been the object of serious concern'), but recommended that one should look first at whether the German economy could afford a bureaucracy of the size it now shouldered, including the party apparatuses.[42] Both Popitz and Wagner drew attention to the non-economic problems of the civil service, Wagner querying somewhat ambiguously 'whether at present economic considerations are uppermost in [the problem of] strengthening the place of civil servants in the German community', and remarking that it was not the first time that civil servants would have to offer sacrifices in the public interest.[43]

Behind these concerns lay ministers' full awareness of the narrowing economic and fiscal options open to the government, as armaments claimed a growing share of public expenditure after 1936, and as the sectorally booming economy generated dangerous inflationary pressures. Frick's policy *démarche* coincided with the debates that culminated in the decree on wage formation issued on 25 June 1938, an attempt to impose the wage controls that had been in the offing since 1935.[44] The plain fact was that by 1938 *some* workers in the private sector had been able to increase their wages by methods that were usually unavailable to civil servants. The latter were dependent on a state which, by contrast with its role in the private sector, had a relatively secure control over their salaries; they were thus suffering the inevitable disadvantage of those on fixed incomes in a time of rising wages and prices. Thus Krosigk refused point-blank to finance salary

---

[41] Krosigk to Frick, 14 June 1938 (copy in BA R 43II/432a).

[42] Popitz to Krosigk, 21 June 1938 (copy in BA R 43II/432).

[43] Price commissioner Wagner to interior minister, 11 June 1938 (copy in BA R 43II/432).

[44] *Verordnung über die Lohngestaltung*, 25 June 1938 (*RGBl*, 1938, i. 691). For the full context of Nazi wages policy, see Mason, *Sozialpolitik*. chs. 4 and 6.

increases by means of public borrowing.[45] A planned wages and incomes policy might have attempted to equalize the advances made by workers in the private and public sectors, but this was quite out of the question in Nazi Germany, of course, where a theoretical commitment to planning masked a reality of indecision, ignorance, and anarchy. However, as the experience of the 1920s had shown, an orderly civil-service salary policy did not seem a government forte in any case, not only because of the tumultuous state of public finance but also because the principles of salary structure were so undecided.

Frick's position in the late 1930s in many ways resembled that of Köhler ten years previously, with the obvious difference that the former was not minister of finance, and thus could not call the fiscal tune. Even though there was not the same public debate on the question as there had been in the 1920s, the role of the bureaucracy in government ensured that in the 1930s too its views would be well represented, with Frick as well tuned to civil servants' interests as Köhler had been. Indeed, given the absence of competing spokesmen for the civil service, apart from the ineffective Hauptamt für Beamte, Frick and others were able to reconstruct the image of cohesion that had been fractured by the actual divisions in the civil service in the 1920s, a reconstruction which inevitably reflected the vantage-point of the men responsible for it. However, ordinary civil servants were not ignorant of the negotiations being conducted in 1938. In an ironic parallel to Köhler's 1927 Magdeburg speech, Frick prematurely leaked his ministry's plans in a public speech in Königsberg in June 1938, arousing considerable unrest among civil servants.[46] The final point of similarity was, of course, that both ministers eventually won their case; and even if Köhler's victory had been the faster and more complete, both were perhaps equally pyrrhic as far as civil servants were concerned.

What the interior ministry wanted, in fact, shifted somewhat as nego-tiations unfolded. Frick continued to make use both of the aggregate statistics where these suited his purpose, and of the case histories that came into his hands, but he faced an apparently obdurate opponent in Krosigk. His initial proposal had already contained the seeds of a compromise, however. When it was rebuffed,[47] he returned with

[45] Krosigk to Frick, 14 June 1938 (copy in BA R 43II/432a).
[46] Frick's speech reported in *VB*, 19 June 1938. For Köhler's speech, see Ch. 3, p. 87, above.
[47] From information in the chancellery memo of 13 July 1938 (see n. 17 above), it is clear that Krosigk called an immediate meeting on receipt of Frick's letter: ministers met on 11 Jan. i.e. within a week, and before most official responses had been received in the

another pair of proposals, this time for an immediate backdated 6 per cent increase, or alternatively a redistribution of funds to favour civil servants with large families.[48] Again, these demands were justified in the strongest language, in which the odds at stake were already being raised:

> I can no longer permit the further postponement of the measures necessary for alleviating this emergency; their urgency is not in the slightest doubt considering the actual situation; and indeed cannot be doubted. These measures should have been initiated long ago, for day by day the plight of civil servants becomes more oppressive and intolerable, their indebtedness increases, their efficiency and job satisfaction threaten to decline under the pressure of financial worries, to the great detriment of the public, and the morale and strength of character of civil servants may suffer irreparable damage. Not least among what is involved here is the question of securing competent recruits. If the civil service comes to be recruited from among people who have been unable to find alternative jobs because of their below-average abilities, it will be unable to master its tasks as the agent of the public will [*Willensträger des Staates*]. Even if this has not yet become the case, it cannot be doubted that we are today already on the path that must lead to this immeasurably harmful result. Almost daily I realize from reports and information of the most varied kind that the circumstances sketched in [the Merseburg report] are by no means exceptional, but are the general rule.
>
> I am therefore unable to share your opinion that at the present time civil-service pay cannot be increased, for reasons of fiscal politics and because of more urgent demands on public monies. Rather, I regard the question of reforming civil-service salaries as one of the most urgent of tasks. If it proves impossible to maintain—indeed to raise—the efficiency of the civil service, then all the other tasks of the Reich, the *Länder*, and the *Gemeinde* will only be imperfectly carried out. It is the people as a whole who will be the ultimate sufferers unless the already visible damage is undone by means of far greater expenditure than has yet been assigned to this problem. I must therefore insist that the available funds be distributed in such a way that civil-service salaries may be raised.

interior ministry. The meeting (the attendance is not clear from this source) decided that a salary increase was impossible, and that the matter should henceforth be considered secret. Minutes of this important meeting could not be located; however, a further reference to it (in a communication from the justice to the finance minister, 17 Feb. 1938, in BA R 43II/432) implies that Krosigk had not been unwilling to consider action of some kind. If so, this would lend support to the inference that although Krosigk was fiscally opposed to a salary increase, he was personally sympathetic to the situation described by Frick.

48 Frick to Krosigk, 20 Apr. 1938 (copy in BA R 43II/432).

Who was Frick trying to impress with his extravagant language and predictions of national catastrophe? He still had little opposition in the cabinet, after all: his colleagues rallied in support, as before, emphasizing this time the direness of the recruitment problem.[49] Frick's rhetoric seems to have had two purposes. From Krosigk and Wagner, the prophets of economic doom, he needed to extract a recognition that civil-service pay was a matter of such extraordinary national priority that other considerations retreated before it. With Krosigk, Frick may also have been playing an elaborate game in which both exaggerated their respective positions in order to impress a third party, for Krosigk had, as we have seen, fully conceded the principle of Frick's argument. The third party was that portion of the Nazi leadership that stood outside the narrow circle of mainly bourgeois nationalist and ex-*Beamte* cabinet ministers. The crucial figures here were Hitler himself and Hess, certainly heavily encouraged in the background by Bormann. Hitler's fitful interventions in policy could not be relied on to enforce a consistent line. He had a dilettantish interest in the idea of competitive merit pay, and was currently being asked to deal with questions of military pay, but it is unlikely that he was directly involved in this stage of the salary negotiations.[50] But, in the summer of 1938, as headway was being made towards a compromise between Frick and Krosigk, Frick addressed another of his long and impassioned letters to Lammers, as the basis for securing a direct decision by Hitler.[51] This

[49] See the series of ministerial responses in Apr. and May (copies in BA R 43II/432).

[50] Cf. Hitler's comments in the cabinet of 9 Dec. 1937 (see p. 237, above). The question of military salaries was a sensitive one. Military (and police) personnel had been spared some of the effects of the Brüning cuts in 1930-2; the interior ministry was anxious that the consequent loss of parity between a number of military and civil grades should not become fixed, which would be likely if the military authorities adopted a device for incorporating the lower rates into the military salary schedule. This 'net rate' scheme, which would have re-fixed the scheduled rates at the amount actually being paid (instead of leaving them at the nominal or pre-reduction rate), was under discussion for both military and civil salaries. Frick himself favoured a net-rate scheme for the civil schedules, but only if it were accompanied by the increases he was presently seeking (see his letter to Krosigk, 9 Mar. 1938; copy in BA R 43II/432); he opposed a one-sided move to military net rates, for fear that it would embalm the more advantageous military rates and prevent any future restoration of civil parity. For the ministry's view, see the important letter from Pfundtner to Lammers, 9 July 1938, 7-12, in which he reviewed this and the other basic arguments about the salary issue (BA R 43II/432).

[51] Frick to Lammers, 25 June 1938 (BA R 43II/452). Frick listed his 6 lengthy letters to the finance ministry since the beginning of the year (3 of them in June alone), reviewed the evidence, and demanded that the matter be brought before Hitler. Lammers had received copies of all Frick's letters to Krosigk, plus all the supporting evidence; Pfundtner's letter a fortnight later (see previous footnote) was obviously a further attempt to maintain the pressure and provide Lammers with the evidence he needed to pursue the case.

ceremonial statement called on both rhetoric and evidence to paint
Frick's case in the most lurid colours:

As the Reich minister responsible to the Führer and Reich chancellor for civil-
service policy, I believe that the situation in respect of civil-service salaries has
today reached a point which, *in the interests of the people as a whole*, is no longer
tolerable. I am not exaggerating when I state that to begin with the indebtedness
of civil servants has already reached *an unprecedented* scale . . . and that,
secondly, as a result of the lack of recruits at even a minimum level of quality
and quantity (quite apart from the large numbers of those who are leaving the
public service in order to take better-paying jobs in the private sector), the time
is drawing ever closer at which the machinery of state *in all its branches* will no
longer be in a position to master its tasks, however hard it tries.

A month or so later, Hess, who was routinely included in the cabinet
circulation of Frick's salvoes, made a somewhat belated intervention
with a laconic and uncompromising refusal to sanction any salary
increase. His arguments were quite predictable: civil servants had not
suffered as much as most Germans in the depression; only some
workers had improved their wages since 1933, and many of the rest
were still struggling near the poverty line. He closed with the comment
that 'workers still suffering under this principle [the wage, salary, and
price freeze] would not understand it if I renounced my rigid stance in
the case of civil-service salaries, but still kept to it in theirs'.[52]

It appears, however, that Hess was too late to modify an interim
agreement that had at last been reached by Frick and Krosigk, though,
as we shall see, he did his best to sabotage the next set of negotiations at
the last minute.[53] The financial concessions in the compromise that was
finally adopted at this stage were issued as an amendment to the salary
schedule.[54] The most important provisions included increases of

[52] Hess to Frick, 13 July 1938 (copy in BA R 43II/431b). This was forwarded to
Lammers by Frick, along with another batch of supporting data (the report from the
Düsseldorf *Regierungspräsident*; see n. 30 above). Hess remained unreconciled; see the
report of his views in a ministerial conference on personnel policy called by Hess's
office, 31 Aug. 1938 (GStA Rep. 90/2340).

[53] See pp. 254-7, below.

[54] 32nd amendment, 27 Sept. 1938 (*RGBl*, 1938, i. 1205). This began as the 33rd
amendment, circulated by the finance minister on 9 July; for its terms, and the terms of
the agreement between the finance and interior ministers, see chancellery internal
memorandum, 15 July 1938 (BA R 43II/431b); also finance-ministry internal
memorandum (signed by Wever), 4 Aug. 1938 (BA R 2/4450). The cause of the delay
between July and Sept. was a fresh dispute about the status of supplements payable to
chancellery officials; the chancellery's attempt to insert a revision of this in the new
amendment was resisted by the finance ministry, and threatened the whole package; see
Frick to Lammers, 18 Aug. 1938 (BA R 43II/431b). See also W. Frick, 'Stellung und
Aufgaben des Beamten', *NSBZ-Deutsche Zollbeamtenzeitung*, 13 Nov. 1938, 385-6.

between 4 and 8 per cent in the rates paid to the lowest seven salary groups; and a modest backdated increase in the allowances for the fourth and subsequent children, together with the raising of the maximum age to which they were payable. They thus took account of some of the specific problems and complaints highlighted in the interior ministry's campaign and the submissions it had reviewed. But they were far from being a direct step towards the abrogation of the Brüning cuts—those remained in force, even if their effect was mitigated. The basic question remained unresolved, therefore, but Krosigk had agreed that it would be reconsidered in the light of economic developments by the beginning of the next fiscal year in April 1939.

III

Despite this agreement, however, Frick had to fight the battle for salaries once again in 1939, though this time with an unexpected ally in the person, or rather the nominal support, of Hitler. For this second round, the interior ministry and the chancellery worked in close collaboration. Lammers secured Hitler's approval for the progressive abrogation of the Brüning cuts sometime in May, and he and his staff worked together with the interior ministry on the timing and wording of Frick's communications with Krosigk. The latter had responded very negatively to Frick's first broaching of the matter towards the end of 1938, citing the fiscal effects of mounting military expenditures and of the new administrative burdens imposed by Germany's expansionist foreign policy. The capital market was overextended, and Krosigk flatly refused to fund any new outlays by the risky method of printing currency: in his view, therefore, there was no chance that salaries could be increased in 1939.[55] This was in January 1939; it was followed by a campaign very like the one fought by Frick in the previous year, though this time he relied on Lammers for his support rather than on the entire

---

[55] Frick's opening letter of 28 Nov. 1938 does not appear to have survived; Krosigk's response on 5 Jan. 1939 exists in a copy in the chancellery files (BA R 43II/433). Evidently, Frick also raised the possibility of an exhaustive review of the salary system; see reference to this in a note from Pfundtner to Lammers, 13 Feb. 1939 (BA R 43II/422a).

cabinet.[56] If the tactics were different, the arguments were much the same. Once again, Frick emphasized the desperate straits of civil servants and the risk to the safety of the Reich, falling now into the military trope suggested by the times:

It is not enough that in times of danger the army defends the borders of the Reich: rather, the state apparatus must also be in a position to master whatever difficulties arise . . . To improve the situation of German civil servants as the bearers of the machinery of state . . . is thus, like the provision of the necessary weapons for the German military, a question of arming the German nation.[57]

When Krosigk responded with a cautious admission that some upward rounding-off might accompany a determined effort to tidy up the salary system, Frick, at the chancellery's instigation, more than doubled his previous demand: he now bid for a 15 rather than a 6 per cent increase, which would represent the abrogation of the first and third Brüning cuts.[58] Frick's staff was now working in close collusion with Lammers'. His note, drafted at the end of April, was not dispatched until late May, in order to give Lammers time to secure the approval by Hitler to which the final version of Frick's note referred. This was presumably secured by the end of May, or at the latest by 10 June, when Lammers invited the handful of cabinet members involved (including Hess) to a minis-terial conference on 15 June, invoking the fact that 'the Führer wants immediate attention to the salary question'.[59] Although Lammers had

<hr />

[56] Frick's major approaches to Krosigk were dated 2 Mar. and 28 Apr. 1939; with the former he included the extensive report from the justice ministry on the state of his field personnel (see n. 30 above; and for the April letter see also n. 58 below) (copies in BA R 43II/432b).

[57] Frick to Krosigk, 2 Mar. 1939 (ibid.).

[58] Krosigk's response dated 29 Mar. 1939 (copy in ibid.). Frick justified his stepped-up demand in ample terms: '[Since 1938] the economic position of the civil service . . . has already become so wretched and their aggregate indebtedness so enormous that the removal of only 6 per cent of the cuts will now no longer provide a really perceptible improvement, and thus would have no psychological effect . . . in these circumstances the only question that now remains, and that demands an immediate answer, is how a genuinely perceptible improvement for the civil service can be achieved . . . I am therefore of the opinion that a reduction of the Brüning cuts by 6 per cent is no longer sufficient to produce the necessary settlement; a perceptible improvement will only be achieved by abolishing the cuts imposed by both the first and the third pay reduction orders, i.e. 6 plus 9 per cent, totalling 15 per cent altogether.' (Frick to Krosigk, 28 Apr. 1939; ibid.) The chancellery's suggestion of a higher percentage increase was made in a note from Lammers to Pfundtner, 3 Apr. 1939 (BA R 43II/422a).

[59] Lammers returned the draft to the interior ministry on 21 May, with some suggestions for strengthening it, and stated that he would be bringing the matter to Hitler's attention 'on the next suitable occasion' (BA R 43II/432b). His invitation of 10

stressed the importance of personal attendance at this meeting, Hess, still the principal opponent of the scheme, did not appear. Instead, he sent Sommer as his representative, a man more clearly an ally of the chancellery and interior ministry in this case. Sommer subsequently informed the chancellery that Hess had had a change of heart, and was writing to Hitler to give up his opposition.[60] Within a few more days, the ministries directly concerned met to draft the decrees decided upon at the conference: their effect would be to increase salaries by 9 to 11 per cent.[61]

At this very moment, however, Hess, far from renouncing his opposition, was doing the exact opposite—writing a long memo to Hitler in which he restated his objections and confirmed that his views remained unchanged.[62] His central argument was the vital necessity of maintaining an effective wage and price freeze (a point with which Wagner concurred).[63] The fact that this had not been entirely successful was no excuse for the government to abandon the principle officially. Instead of the dangerously inflationary proposals made by Frick, Hess offered four alternative schemes: a 10 per cent increase, plus massive personnel reductions; postponement until official wage increases could be sanctioned; suspension by means of issuing salary bonds redeemable in the future; or restriction to the most needy grades. The sabotage was

June was sent to the finance and interior ministers, the Führer's deputy, and the price commissioner (ibid.). The latter, Wagner, had still not renounced his opposition to a salary increase (see p. 247 and n. 43 above), though he was now suggesting that an administrative reform which reduced the number of senior posts and restored a realistic differential system would free enough funds to allow the government to secure the services of top-flight men—and he did concede the urgency of this; see his letter to Göring, 29 Apr. 1939 (copy in ibid.). A long (8-pp.) memo prepared for Frick on 18 June in the interior ministry (by Ministerialrat Bommel) briefed him for the conference by reviewing the grounds of Wagner's and Hess's opposition, and providing Frick with arguments against them. Bommel also reported that Hitler was said to have agreed to a progressive abrogation of all the cuts over a period of one to two years, and that the proposed method was to be not a published statute but a secret directive empowering the interior and finance ministries to issue the necessary regulations (his source for this information was probably his chancellery counterpart, Killy) (BA R 18/5561).

[60] Sommer to Lammers, 16 June 1939 (BA R 43II/432b). Popitz had also abandoned his objections, agreeing finally that the issue was too urgent to await a comprehensive administrative reform; see his letter to Göring (as Prussian minister-president), 15 June 1939 (copy in BA R 43II/432b).

[61] Chancellery memo, 19 June 1939 (BA R 43II/432b). Rumours of action on salaries were circulating by this time: see report of speech by Neef in May, *NSBZ-Deutsche Zollbeamtenzeitung*, 11 June 1939, 353-4.

[62] Hess to Lammers, 21 June 1939, enclosing the memorandum he had already shown Hitler (BA R 43II/432b).

[63] See n. 59 above.

effective: Hitler was now reported to have agreed to the last-named scheme.[64]

It was Lammers who orchestrated the final counter-attack to this unorthodox and unwelcome intervention, pulling together information from the finance and labour ministries and persuading Krosigk to ally himself with Frick in a long statement of what was now their joint case.[65] Hess's arguments were refuted point by point, including his fears of inflation: the NSDAP, after all, paid a thirteenth month's salary annually, and the Christmas bonuses paid out by industry in December 1938 had released on to the market in one month more than twice what the proposed salary increases would amount to over a whole year. Krosigk also summarized his own reasons for finally abandoning his opposition to the scheme, the key point being the fact that unauthorized and ultimately intolerable methods were being used by state agencies to improve the financial position of their staffs. In order to attract and retain personnel, public authorities had been driven to such stratagems as paying unofficial grants and tax-free expense allowances; creating promotion posts or reclassifying posts in the salary schedule so that higher salaries could be paid; even helping civil servants to moonlight, to the detriment of their official duties. The worst areas were, not surprisingly, such technical services as civil engineering, naval architecture, mining, or medicine, where competition from the private sector was greatest, and also the expanded police and security forces. The extra cost over and above the official salary bill was estimated to amount to several hundred million RM per annum; in one individual case cited, payments by the SD to its flight staffs had more than doubled their scheduled rates. It was clear to everyone involved that these methods were creating total anarchy in the salary system, but all claimed that there was no other way to compete effectively with the private sector. It was this 'avalanche-like anarchy and contempt for the law' that had driven Krosigk to set aside his grave economic reservations and accept official salary increases as the less objectionable of two poor alternatives.

[64] See n. 62 above.

[65] The memo, drawn up by Bommel, Killy, and Wever (the interior-ministry, chancellery, and finance-ministry experts respectively), was approved by Frick and Krosigk on 30 June, after a week of urgent debate about tactics. One aborted choice was a long and emotional petition to Hitler signed by Frick on 24 June, but never delivered; its arguments ('The figure of the incorruptible civil servant, which has served the whole world as a model, is now slowly, but at an ever-increasing pace, vanishing') were presumably judged less effective than the factual document eventually used (all documentation in BA R 43II/432b).

With these arguments, Hitler was induced to go back to his original decision and sign the decree drafted in June.[66] At the same time, he insisted that the process of issuing and executing the orders implementing the pay increases must take place in the utmost secrecy, without any publicity. The number of persons informed of the measure was to be kept to an absolute minimum, and instructions were to be given verbally as far as possible, not in writing. If civil servants queried the raise, they were to be told, in Hitler's own laconic phrase: 'Die Abzüge haben sich vermindert'—a reflexive, agent-less, 'The reductions have diminished'. Hitler also directed that a committee composed of Lammers, Krosigk, and Frick was to supervise the process and also begin discussions on a general reform of the salary system. But this was not all. To Frick's fury and Lammers' embarrassment, Hitler made a belated crucial modification of his decision within hours of reaching it. Fritz Reinhardt, ex-*Gauleiter* and NSDAP financial expert, and since 1933 state secretary in Krosigk's ministry, persuaded Hitler to reconsider a version of Hess's bond scheme; and Lammers, sensing defeat, had to concede a compromise whereby the first increase would be reduced to 6 per cent, instead of the 9 to 11 per cent already approved by Hitler.[67] Reinhardt had obviously been put up to this intervention by Hess or Bormann, a display of irresponsibility with regard to his own minister's policy that was equalled only by Hitler's own. Reinhardt was engaged in a deliberate act of sabotage, but Hitler was scarcely capable of functioning as the supreme decision-maker he represented in theory, least of all in issues which did not capture his undisguised interest. On his own insistence, he was not kept informed about the details of policy development, and thus frequently lacked the basis for a secure decision when an issue ultimately reached him. The salary decision of 1939 bears all the hallmarks of Hitler's *modus operandi*: the lack of a real sense of priorities; the grudging approval secured only by playing on his fears of unpreparedness and weakness on the German home front; his obsession with the secrecy and non-accountability of its implementation; and his unpredictable openness to the reversal of a previous decision.

[66] Lammers to Krosigk, 6 July 1939, enclosing a copy of the decree signed by Hitler (ibid.).

[67] For this acount of events, which took place that evening at a state banquet for the Bulgarian prime minister, see the internal memorandum for Frick, based on information from Pfundtner and Seel, 7 July 1939 (BA R 18/5561). For the subsequent exchange between Reinhardt and Frick, see their letters of 13 and 15 July respectively (copies in BA R 43II/433).

The problems lay deeper than this, however. The episode is also instructive as an example of the political process in the Third Reich. None of its individual elements—the indiscipline of a senior official, the tangled chains of communication, the shifting and sometimes devious alliances, the vacillations by the head of government—was unique to Nazi Germany. Bureaucratic sabotage is a structural feature of modern government, as any student of recent British or French policy-making knows; so is political indecision. But what was strikingly specific to the Third Reich was the fact that this devious and unsettled system of policy-making was not exceptional but the norm. Governmental process rested on a structure of superimposed, concurrent, and disconnected authorities, powered by different or non-existent concepts of administrative practice as well as by widely varying policy goals, and dealing in a coin of imprecise legal instruments. The principle of majority decision by cabinet agreement had long been abandoned—indeed, the cabinet was no longer meeting by now—but no alternative decision-making system had been devised, and nothing was proof against Hitler's interventions or vetoes. The normal flow of government business, complex enough in any case, had little chance in this heady atmosphere of indiscipline and infighting. It was perhaps a tribute to the tenacity of Frick and his allies in the chancellery that the salary decision went through at all; a tribute, too, to the mounting anxiety that Frick, for all his rhetoric, might not be far wrong in the picture he painted of the state of German administration.

The secret circular that was finally issued by the finance ministry on 12 July authorized the abrogation of 6 per cent of the Brüning cuts from 1 July, and stated that the rest would be dealt with as the economic situation permitted.[68] In the event, only one further stage was reached, in December 1940, and the 1927 salary rates were not formally restored in Germany until the 1950s. But by the end of 1940, civil servants were in receipt of 94 per cent of their officially scheduled rates.[69]

How much of an achievement was this? Ordinary civil servants were apparently not overjoyed at what Frick had done for them.[70] Although

[68] Finance-ministry circular (marked 'Secret! For internal use only'), 12 July 1939 (copy in BA R 43II/432b). Jews were not eligible for the new rates: see interior-ministry circular, 19 Aug. 1939 (copy in GStA P 134/3194).
[69] Finance-ministry circular, 23 Dec. 1940 (copy in BA R 18/5561). See also Ch. 8, p. 294, below. For the final restoration of 1927 salary levels, in 1949-51, see Ambrosius, *Besoldungsrecht*, pp. 148-9.
[70] *SD-Meldungen aus dem Reich*, 147, 5 Dec. 1940, 15-19 (BA R 58/156); 155, 20 Jan. 1941, 15-16 (R 58/157); 167, 3 Mar. 1941, 16-17 (R 58/158); 168, 10 Mar. 1941, 15-16 (R 58/158).

they must have welcomed any increase in their income, they were per-plexed and resentful at the way in which this had been accomplished. The secrecy of the decrees was both pointless—they all knew beforehand what was in the offing—and infuriating, for it suggested that they were not entitled to the money. In civil servants' eyes, their raise did not breach the wage freeze, but righted a wrong done them by the republic, and it ought to have been publicized as such. Moreover, there were some legal problems as a result of the secrecy, which surely added to this sense of irritation. It was obviously a complex matter to recalculate individual salaries, and there were bound to be disputes about the outcome. The question then arose as to whether the courts were competent to review such disputes, as they were in civil servants' material interests in general. The finance ministry wanted to withdraw the matter from the courts' jurisdiction, and to treat the whole affair as falling under civil servants' duty of official secrecy. The ministry got its way, but not without the justice ministry pointing out that, legally, the only way to keep the courts out would be to declare that the pay raise did not restore a right (which would have been legally enforceable under Article 129 of the constitution) but was simply an 'ex gratia payment' (*freiwillige Zuwendung*).[71]

These problems apart, it was still something of a success for Frick that he had almost fully realized his abrogation policy in a period of three years in which strenuous attempts were being made to maintain a wage freeze. The fact that these efforts were unsuccessful only strained the salary question further: the failure was bound to strengthen the determination of Wagner, Hess, and initially Krosigk to enforce the freeze, while it further aggravated the adverse comparison between salaries and wages. Tariff wages continued to be exceeded throughout the later 1930s, sometimes by spectacular proportions, though far from evenly across industry. As a terse marginal comment by Killy on a letter from a colleague in the labour ministry noted, against a passage on the wages of military masons, 'more than a Reg. Vizepräs. or MinRat'.[72] This confusion of hierarchy was particularly offensive, no doubt. However, it is clear that the public sector had its own equivalent of this unofficial and uneven upwards drift, in the form of those adventitious supplements and other unauthorized payments deplored by Krosigk in June 1939. The true extent of these cannot be gauged, unfortunately,

---

[71] See justice-ministry internal memorandum, 8 Apr. 1941, and additional documentation on the issue, in BA R 22/4489.

[72] Knolle to Killy, 5 July 1939, 2 (BA R 43II/432b).

but they ought not be ignored when evaluating the comparative economic standing of civil servants in the later 1930s. Some officials, mainly in the senior ranks, were obviously drawing more than their scheduled income, just as some workers had opportunities to earn more than the tariff rates, and for the same basic reason: their skills were in short supply. Yet, as we have already noted, this invasion of the civil service by the standards of the market-place was not unproblematic. The loss of uniformity and clarity in the salary system disturbed the deep-seated principles on which the system had theoretically been based for the past half century or more. This was troubling to traditionalists like Krosigk, as well as to anyone who actually had the job of administering the disintegrating system. On the other hand, Germany in the 1930s rang even more loudly than in the 1920s with calls for rewards to be based on merit and achievement (*Leistung*) rather than on fixed rules of advancement. These had some resonance among civil servants, including policy-makers, as we shall see shortly. There was thus a certain tension, paralleling some of the debates of the 1920s, between defence of the more traditional principles and openness to new standards of evaluation.

This was to become more evident in the course of wartime discussions of the linked issues of salaries, recruitment, and training. Before turning to this, however, one further point should be made. If, as has been suggested, the salary question was the focus of a broader anxiety about the direction of civil-service politics in the 1930s, then the abrogation of the Brüning cuts could not of itself alleviate this anxiety. It is true that the primary aim stressed by Frick in his long and impassioned correspondence had been the achievement of the salary increase, and that he had refused to be fobbed off with promises of more fundamental action in the future. But a no less stridently conveyed message was that the German civil service was in deep trouble, in terms of both of morale and effectiveness. Frick's overwrought rhetoric had a tactical purpose in terms of decision-making, but it also expressed a fantasy of professional degeneration that far exceeded any individual symptom. It is not possible to believe that the profound crisis Frick purported to describe could be alleviated by anything as straightforward as a pay raise. And if we examine the state of affairs after the measures of 1939 and 1940, it is clear that it was not. By then, however, the war was also radically altering the conditions of administrative policy, rendering the constraints more severe and the chances of alleviation in either the long or short term increasingly dim.

8

The Crisis of Policy
1939-1945

I

From 1939, German administrative policy was increasingly dictated by the exigencies and timetable of the war. In no modern state has the transition from peace to large-scale war been a simple process, nor have the political and administrative apparatuses developed in the course of a prolonged and intensive conflict been fully foreseeable at the start.[1] The difficulties and deficiencies of German administrative politics during the Second World War were scarcely unique, therefore, any more than the fact that the war was seen by some as a fresh opportunity to canvass solutions for older problems, or to shift the distribution of power in preparation for the post-war period. But Nazi Germany was singular in several aspects of its wartime experience which directly affected its process of government. In the first place, the war was not simply an instrument of policy from which specific gains were expected: as Martin Broszat has put it, echoing a widespread judgment: 'Through the war National Socialism came into its own . . . and returned to its true element.'[2] This meant not only that mobilization for war in some sense corresponded to the deepest aspirations of National Socialism as a movement and an ideology, but also that the functional rationality of specific war aims was constantly undercut by the metaphysics of struggle as such—what Hitler in 1942 called 'the cement which will bind into one indissoluble whole all the races of the German Reich'.[3] A territorial and spiritual refoundation of Germany was the ultimate goal of this war, linking the home and the military fronts in a vast project of totalizing regeneration. Yet although the process of war was supposed to have this purgatory effect, the outline of the New

[1] See e.g. K. Burk (ed.), *War and the State: The Transformation of British Government, 1914-1919* (London, 1982); P. Fraser, 'The Impact of the War of 1914-1918 on the British Political System', in M. R. D. Foot (ed.), *War and Society* (London, 1973), 123-39.
[2] M. Broszat, *The Hitler State: The Foundation and Development of the Internal Structure of the Third Reich* (London, 1981), 307.
[3] *Hitler's Table Talk 1941-44*, introd. H. Trevor-Roper (London, 1973), 20 May 1942, 492.

Order that would arise at the end of the combat remained cloudy and indistinct. Temporization and deferral marked the wartime planning that did occur—as if institutions, like cities, must first be reduced to rubble by the accidents of war before they could be cleared and rebuilt. The solvent effects of these dreams of racial renewal were felt especially in central and eastern Europe, whose fragile boundaries and ethnic intricacies were brutally dismantled by Nazi conquest. The forced population transfers and expulsions, the genocide of Jews, gypsies, Poles, and other 'misfits' were contributions to the amorphous vision of a new Nazi polity; so too were the other grand strategies of the SS in the east, including the promise of a symbolic and safely contained eternal war zone with which to ensure the survival of the soldierly myth and the race itself. One is bound to question the practical feasibility of such schemes, but in any case they were certainly incompatible with the less hysterical plans for military administration and economic exploitation which motivated other partners in the Nazi war of conquest. The goals of geopolitics and of the *Grossraumwirtschaft* could not be realized together, though both were pursued simultaneously.[4] But because clear priorities and lines of policy were never negotiated, and because, by contrast with western Europe, the indigenous regimes in the east were so thoroughly displaced, Nazi administration there intensified the fragmented and competitive bureaucratism that already reigned in the Altreich. Old rivalries were exported to the occupied and annexed territories to thrive anew, and the wild irregularities of rule in the eastern territories also had a corrosive effect on the conditions of government inside Germany itself.[5] The political melting-pot of eastern Europe was thus the source of some of the most salient shifts in the internal balance of power in the Third Reich. In particular, the old tensions between centralism and particularism which had already strained the Nazi regime were wound to an even higher pitch.

If the war stimulated or reinforced ambitions to participate in a refoundation of Nazi Germany, not only the conditions of conquest but also the attitude of Hitler himself virtually ruled out any systematic progress towards this end. Already a distant figure in relation to the ordinary business of government, Hitler more or less vanished as the head of civil government after 1939, swallowed up entirely by his role as commander-in-chief. Physically, he was more often at his military headquarters than in Berlin; politically, his involvement in the process

---

[4] A. Milward, *The German Economy at War* (London, 1965), 153-65.
[5] M. Broszat, *Nationalsozialistische Polenpolitik 1939-1945* (Frankfurt, 1965), ch. 3.

of government was increasingly fitful and arbitrary. But no alternative machinery was installed as a substitute for the role Hitler no longer filled; indeed, it was as if he believed that government and administration could somehow be held in abeyance for the duration. Thus, he insisted that no fundamental decisions affecting the structure of government or the distribution of political authority were to be made during the war.[6] This duplicated and strengthened Hitler's 1935 moratorium on further constitutional reform; it had been then, too, after the political stabilization of the regime, that he had begun his own retreat from active participation in government. But this new veto on policies and decisions likely to affect 'the ultimate shape of the Reich', as the phrase went, could not hold back the tide. As in the pre-war period, indecision produced not stasis or a vacuum, but unplanned and unregulated shifts in the power structure instead of planned and formal ones.

'A war of each against all', was how General Thomas described the procurement situation two months into the war, and his comment was equally appropriate to the struggle for the resources of political mobilization in Germany.[7] The weaker protagonists in this were Frick and Göring, whose proposals for the redistribution of governnmental power or for administrative rationalization were serially deflected by Lammers. The latter was able initially to preserve his own authority as the interpreter of the *Führerwille*. But meanwhile Himmler, Bormann, and Goebbels contrived to press ahead with their own machinations, deriving a less easily side-tracked authority from their powerful party roles, and foreshadowing the new dispositions of power that occurred shortly before the final demise of the regime. Moreover, these were all men who enjoyed easy access to Hitler at a time when his figurative and geographical remoteness from Berlin hindered communication with him. Whether he exercised his power directly or not, Hitler retained a crucial authority to define the scope of legitimate authority and policy. Ministers like Frick were dependent on the uncertain patronage of intermediaries to secure an audience with the Führer or to have a matter brought to his attention, a brokerage operated largely by Lammers and Bormann in their respective roles as chiefs of the Reich and party

---

[6] An unpublished *Führererlass über eine vorübergehende Einschränkung der Rechtssetzung*, 5 June 1940, suspended work on all matters not related to defence for 6 months; it was extended for a further 6 months in Dec. 1940, and then indefinitely on 16 May 1941 (BA R 43II/604).

[7] B. Carroll, *Design for Total War: Arms and Economics in the Third Reich* (The Hague, 1968), 210.

chancelleries. Inevitably, this too became a matter of contestation between them, with Bormann managing to achieve a virtual monopoly by mid-1943.[8] The competition fostered by the endemic de-centring of power in Germany after 1939 ensured that the vision of a reconstructed polity was no more likely to be realized during the war than in peacetime. But the business of administration had to continue, of course, and complex responses had to be made to the circumstances of war, even if these were simultaneously caught up in continuing power struggles. In fact, the vicissitudes of the war made for a sequence of quite rapid modifications in administrative policy, just as it did in economic mobilization; indeed, the two were closely linked. Between 1939 and 1941, the administrative apparatus was partially adjusted to the conditions of limited war: some decision-making processes were streamlined, restrictions were placed on the conduct of non-essential business, and the first steps were taken to mobilize additional personnel to replace officials conscripted into the armed forces. By 1942, however, the duration of the war and the growing problems of labour procurement were creating new strains that demanded a more resolute rationalization of government business. Complaints about over-centralization accumulated from the beginning of 1941; early in 1942, both Frick and Göring made equally unsuccessful bids to secure new personal powers to supervise redoubled programmes of administrative rationalization. Following Speer's appointment as minister for munitions in February, and the adoption of new initiatives on the armaments and procurement front, labour mobilization took on a new urgency. The administration was combed for conscripts, and pressure on the remaining personnel intensified. The final phase of policy can be dated from mid-1943, when Frick lost his post as interior minister to Himmler, and when the conversion to the policy of total war was initiated. With Goebbels' appointment as plenipotentiary for total war in August 1944, a final

[8] Broszat, *The Hitler State*, pp. 312-18. Bormann had replaced Hess after his flight to England on 12 May 1941; at the same time, the StdF *Stab* was reorganized and renamed as the party chancellery, emphasizing its parallelism with Lammers' Reich chancellery. Bormann's ministerial rank was confirmed by a Hitler decree of 29 May 1941 (*RGBl*, 1941, i. 295; and see executive order, 16 Jan. 1942; *RGBl*, 1942, i. 35). In Apr. 1943, Hitler conferred the title 'Führer's secretary' on him; see Bormann memo, 8 May 1943, and Reich chancellery circular, 8 May 1943 (BA NS 6/159). For Bormann's consolidation of his power, see P. Diehl-Thiele, *Partei und Staat im Dritten Reich: Untersuchungen zum Verhältnis von NSDAP und allgemeiner und innerer Staatsverwaltung* (Munich, 1969), 241-57, and D. Orlow, *The History of the Nazi Party 1933-1945* (Pittsburgh, 1973), 422 ff.

process of rationalization was attempted. Politically, however, the direction had changed radically. The emergence of a new tripartite power relationship between Goebbels, Himmler, and Bormann meant that the struggle over the administration was conducted by men with autonomous power bases and political agendas; the internal administrative issues so important to Frick were increasingly only the backdrop to struggles within the Nazi leadership for the dwindling inheritance of their regime.

II

The interior ministry played a prominent and embattled role in these processes of adaptation, constantly seeking to ensure that wartime rationalization furthered its concentration strategy, while blocking independent moves by other governmental agencies. The situation at the beginning of the war in some ways paralleled that during the seizure of power in 1933-4, especially in the sense of reproducing the struggles between central and regional sources of power and between party and state legitimations. As in 1933, so the onset of the war brought a sudden access of power and responsibility to Nazi party officials, and similar challenges to the established state authorities; military and procurement needs also mandated the creation of new authorities, as well as attempts at high-level co-ordination. Thus, the contradictory impulses towards the dispersal and concentration of power were both reinforced. This process had to some extent pre-dated the war itself, as the German polity struggled to accommodate the earlier fruits of Hitler's diplomatic adventures. The *Reichsgau* system of administration, established in Austria and the Sudentenland in 1938-9, in some measure implemented Frick's project of defederalization and the establishment of a concentrated *Mittelstufe*, or intermediate level, contained within his ministry's field hierarchy. By contrast with the *Länder* of the Altreich, where the process of amalgamating Reich and *Land* authorities remained incomplete and the *Reichsstatthalter* and *Oberpräsidenten* stood outside the direct chain of command, the *Reichsgaue* were subordinate regions in a unitary state structure, and the *Reichsstatthalter* were integrated into the field administration. In theory, this created a single chain of command, running from the Reich interior ministry through the *Reichsstatthalter* to the subordinate offices of the interior administration.[9] However, Frick's authority over the *Reichsstatthalter* turned out to be more nominal than authentic; the process of defederalization and concentration enhanced not his own power, but the autonomy of the *Gauleiter-Reichsstatthalter* under Hitler. When Poland was overrun in 1939, a similar structure was installed in the newly annexed *Reichsgaue* of Danzig-Westpreussen and the Wartheland. These regions became the site of particularly painful disputes between Frick and the two wilful and ambitious *Gauleiter*, Forster and Greiser, who insisted on an unfettered freedom to make their own administrative appointments and generally to run their *Gaue* as they saw fit.[10] In the short term the ministry recovered a modicum of control, but in the longer term it was unable to prevent the expansion of particularist power in these regions.

This was not the only example of the tendency towards particularist fragmentation. At the beginning of September 1939, power had been further redistributed to the party and the periphery by the appointment of all *Gauleiter-Reichsstatthalter/Oberpräsidenten* to the new post of defence commissioner (*Reichsverteidigungskommissar*); like the *Reichsstatthalter/Oberpräsidenten* themselves, these new commissioners were assigned powers of 'direction' (*Steuerung*) *vis-à-vis* most of the state field agencies.[11] The offices were thus administratively redundant, in that they duplicated powers already held by their occupants. Their rationale was more political than administrative, for they served to exclude the army from the civil role it had played in 1914-18, and asserted the leadership claims of the NSDAP. They also created new and needless problems of co-ordination between the commissioners and the central ministries; while many *Gauleiter* had not been appointed as commissioners, and resented their exclusion. When, in 1942, all *Gauleiter* were eventually appointed as defence commissioners, and the *Gaue* and

[9] For contemporary accounts of administration at the *Mittelinstanz*, see C. Johanny and O. Redelberger, *Volk, Partei, Reich* (Berlin, Leipzig, and Vienna, 1941), 145-56, and A. Köttgen, *Deutsche Verwaltung* (Berlin, 1944), 64-71; also A. V. Boerner, 'Toward Reichsreform: The Reichsgaue', *American Political Science Review*, 33 (1939), 1059-81.

[10] On these developments, see Broszat, *The Hitler State*, pp. 121-9; H. Mommsen, *Beamtentum im Dritten Reich* (Stuttgart, 1966), 110-13; Diehl-Thiele, *Partei und Staat*, pp. 123-44. On the modalities of *Gauleiter* authority in the war, see P. Hüttenberger, *Die Gauleiter: Studie zum Wandel des Machtgefüges in der NSDAP* (Stuttgart, 1969), ch. 4. An attempt by the interior ministry to insert itself into the administration of the western European occupied territories quickly came to grief; see Stuckart to Lammers, 3 June 1940, and subsequent documentation in BA R 43II/641.

[11] *VO über die Bestellung von Reichsverteidigungskommissaren*, 1 Sept. 1939 (*RGBl*, 1939, i. 1565); Hüttenberger, *Gauleiter*, pp. 152 ff.

defence zones were made coterminous, this further shifted power towards the regions and the NSDAP. Moreover, the enormous resources of power being amassed by Himmler's SS and police apparatus in the occupied territories not only paralleled the original process by which Himmler had concentrated police authority in his hands after 1933, but represented an additional and independent amalgamation of state and party authority. In important respects, the SS also constituted a new centralizing focus in the governmental structure. By comparison with the NSDAP's organizational structure, it was far less subject to the fragmentation and parcellization of power (at least at this stage of its existence). In this context it was perfectly logical, therefore, that in 1943 Himmler should have become the heir to Frick's entire administrative apparatus.

Problems of co-ordination existed at the top as well as in the field. Just as any semblance of collegial decision-making had quickly disappeared after the seizure of power, so in 1939 a paper project for a species of war cabinet was stillborn. At the end of August 1939, a six-man ministerial council for national defence (Ministerialrat für die Reichsverteidigung) was established, with Göring as chairman and Lammers as secretary.[12] It had the power to issue decrees, and in theory might have functioned as an adequate substitute for Hitler in non-military affairs. But the apparent logic of its creation was deceptive. Orderly political collaboration had little chance in Nazi Germany, and the council soon became more significant as a source of additional legitimation for its members than as a collective body. Moreover, it was typical that the council should be added on to the existing set of policy-making institutions, rather than replacing any of them. By this date, there were at least four independent legislators in Nazi Germany: the Führer (and through him the government (Reichsregierung) and Reichstag), the ministerial council, the council's inner 'committee of three' (Dreierkollegium), and the head of the Four-Year-Plan. Although some limitations and demarcations did exist, there was no systematic

12 *Erlass des Führers über die Bildung eines Ministerrats für die Reichsverteidigung,* 30 Aug. 1939 (*RGBl,* 1939, i. 1539); for its procedures and powers, see Reich chancellery to StdF, GBV, GBW, and OKW, 3 Sept. 1939, and Reich chancellery to ministerial council, 20 Feb. 1940 (BA R 43II/604); also G. Meinck, 'Der Reichsverteidigungsrat', *Wehrwissenschaftliche Rundschau,* 6/8 (1956), 411-22; Broszat, *The Hitler State,* pp. 308-12; on the cabinet in general, see L. Gruchmann, 'Die "Reichsregierung" im Führerstaat: Stellung und Funktion des Kabinetts im nationalsozialistischen Herrschaftssystem', in G. Doeker and W. Steffani (eds.), *Klassenjustiz und Pluralismus: Festschrift für Ernst Fraenkel* (Hanover, 1973), 187-223.

distribution of legislative authority, nor any superior mechanism for determining conflicts of authority, apart from Hitler himself.[13] Furthermore, special authorizations were issued by Hitler for particular fields of policy which often impinged on others, and these were not always publicly promulgated or, indeed, recorded in written form. The elusive authority to undertake the 'final solution' is only the most notorious of these.[14] In another and related case, Himmler was invested with extensive independent powers in October 1939 as 'Reichskommissar für die Festigung deutschen Volkstums', by means of an unpublished Führer decree countersigned by three members of the ministerial defence council, Göring, Keitel, and Lammers.[15] The range of capacities and co-signatories available to the legislators often seems baffling; and as far as derived powers are concerned, the structures of authority over the economy and the allocation of special powers for procurement and labour mobilization during the war created a system of particularly mind-boggling complexity.[16]

In this maze of new authorities, legitimations, and shifts in the scope of governmental power, the challenge to Frick's ministry to assert its own authority as the central source of administrative policy-making was more difficult than it had been in 1933. Yet he may have thought himself in a stronger position than for some years. He was a member of the ministerial council, and, with the new title of 'Plenipotentiary for the Administration' (*Generalbevollmächtigter für die Reichsverwaltung*), he joined Funk and Keitel in the committee of three. Under Hitler's August 28 decree, he was empowered to issue or countersign measures to implement administrative rationalization, after consultation with the other appropriate central authorities. In October, Frick established a committee, headed by Stuckart and including representatives from the other main central authorities, to investigate the potential for rationalization.[17] The priorities were to maintain a 'smooth and speedy process of public administration with a minimum of personnel and resources', and to ensure that 'every citizen has direct and immediate

[13] D. Kirschenmann, '*Gesetz*' *im Staatsrecht und in der Staatsrechtslehre des Nationalsozialismus* (Berlin, 1970), 112-18.

[14] See M. Broszat, 'The Genesis of the "Final Solution"', in H. W. Koch (ed.), *Aspects of the Third Reich* (London, 1985), 390-429.

[15] R. L. Koehl, *RKFDV: German Resettlement and Population Policy 1939-1945* (Cambridge, Mass., 1957), 49-70, 247-9.

[16] Carroll, *Design for Total War*, pp. 232-3; L. Herbst, *Der Totale Krieg und die Ordnung der Wirtschaft: Die Kriegswirtschaft im Spannungsfeld von Politik, Ideologie und Propaganda 1933-1945* (Stuttgart, 1982), 111-17; Broszat, *The Hitler State*, p. 304.

[17] Interior-ministry circular, 15 Oct. 1939 (BA R 18/5450).

access to the offices of the administration without having to go through innumerable agencies'.[18] The ministry's programme of objectives included some obvious expedients to suspend non-essential offices, to delegate some decisions, and to ensure that responsibilities were clearly assigned and demarcated, so that splits and duplications were avoided. However, they were also witness to the ministry's ulterior aim of using wartime planning to pursue its old strategy of centralization and concentration. Thus, the interior administration was to be the beneficiary of these various measures, just as the ministry itself would be in charge of them. Any essential business left homeless by an agency's suspension would be assigned to the interior administration, which would also be expected to take over tasks now deemed inappropriate for the ministries currently in charge of them (for example, the finance ministry could hand over the administration of marriage loans and child allowances), and tasks of general scope, such as school inspection or social insurance. Responsibilities shared among different agencies of the interior administration were to be concentrated in the hands of the *Regierungspräsidenten*. Likewise, tasks currently distributed among several different administrative branches were also to be concentrated in interior-administration hands—for instance the administration of protective legislation, currently divided between six separate branches (police, labour offices, labour trustees, the industrial inspectorate, accident insurance, and DAF). By the spring of 1942, 264 separate measures had been adopted; these included the delegation to subordinate authorities of numerous routine decisions, such as the withdrawal of licenses for dental practice; various simplifications to legal procedures; and general attempts to rationalize offices and procedures.[19] Steps were also taken to simplify and adjust some civil-service procedures and to start exploring the personnel situation: new powers were quickly adopted for the compulsory transfer of civil servants, while the stipulation that *Beamtinnen* must retire on marriage was rescinded, and retired officials were required to register themselves.[20]

Thus, the war offered new opportunities for the interior ministry's pursuit of its four principal objectives: centralizing administrative and civil-service policy by bringing the residual *Länder* institutions under the effective control of the Reich interior ministry; narrowing the

[18] 'Grundsätze für die Verwaltungsvereinfachung', 18 Oct. [1939] (BA R 18/5450, ff. 129-41).

[19] See list sent by Lammers to Göring, 24 May 1942 (BA R 43II/708).

[20] *VO über Massnahmen auf dem Gebiet des Beamtenrechts*, 1 Sept. 1939 (*RGBl*, 1939, i. 1603).

competence of the specialist administrations and transferring the bulk of their responsibilities to the field offices of the interior administration, notably the *Regierungspräsident* and *Landrat*; clearly demarcating the tasks of party and state agencies at this intermediate field level; and procuring wider powers for the interior ministry to implement these policies. Equally unchanged was the opposition these strategies provoked among Frick's colleagues. For example, an ambitious attempt at the end of 1939 to destroy the remnants of administrative autonomy in the *Länder* came to nothing, though it illustrates the continued centrality of the civil service to Frick's vision. A July 1939 measure, the Law for the Unification of Administrative Structure, had nominally assimilated *Länder* agencies and staffs to the authority of the Reich, but had not really disturbed the status quo, whereby the *Reichsstatthalter* and *Land* ministries retained practical authority over appointments and personnel budgeting.[21] This meant that *Länder* authorities could easily obstruct the Reich's personnel policies, at the cost, Frick claimed, of a debilitating wastage of time and staff, and to the detriment of his campaign to create 'a *uniform* type of National Socialist civil servant'.[22] He now proposed a new distribution of competences between Reich and *Länder*. The lion's share would fall to the Reich, so that the majority of civil servants would come under central control and be incorporated in the Reich's budget. Otherwise, he argued, the fragmentation of the administration would proceed unchecked: bits and pieces of *Land* authority would continue to be hived off into independent agencies, which had already happened with the police, the waterways, and some other units; the prospect of a 'uniform, organic and planned process of administrative unification [*Gesamtverreichlichung*]' would recede even further. This strenuous attempt at centralization, which Stuckart had wanted to push even farther than Frick, came to nothing, though there were echoes of it in a subsequent bid by the interior ministry in 1941 to incorporate into the Reich

---

[21] *Gesetz über die Vereinheitlichung im Behördenaufbau*, 5 July 1939 (*RGBl*, 1939, i. 1197). The interior ministry had been trying to achieve an effectively unitary national civil service since 1936, coupling in its aims the end of '*Länder* civil-service particularism' with the creation of 'a single Reich civil service to restore to the erstwhile *Länder* civil servants that professional idealism which is indispensable for the welfare of the people': see interior ministry's draft law and official memorandum, 29 Dec. 1936, and other documentation in BA R 43II/422a.

[22] See Frick to Reich chancellery *et al.*, 23 Feb. 1940, and other documentation in BA R 18/5450.

budget senior civil servants in the *Länder* interior administrations.[23] A strong opponent of this scheme was Krosigk, by now busy resisting a whole series of claims by Frick to sole jurisdiction in many areas of civil-service policy, even when a financial interest was clearly indicated. Frick's position was that, 'As the Reich's civil-service minister I have the leadership in the field of civil-service politics, and the responsibility for the fate of the German civil service.'[24] By the autumn of 1942, a senior interior-ministry official was describing the finance ministry's attitude as 'grotesque', and claiming that, 'in my view things are coming to such a pass that any kind of systematic and enterprising leadership in civil-service policy is being sabotaged'.[25] But Krosigk's position, stated in distinctly unministerial language, was that he saw 'no reason to alter . . . the demarcation of authority in the field of civil-service law which has been assigned to me historically, appears to me appropriate, corresponds to statutory provisions, and has until now been recognized by you'.[26] And in June, Killy was led to remark that: 'Recently it has frequently become obvious that the Reich interior minister is endeavouring to make his status as civil-service minister into an exclusive one, and to force back the influence of the finance minister by defining as many issues as possible as aspects of "general civil-service policy"'.[27]

The deteriorating relations between Frick and Krosigk testified to the trials Frick was preparing for himself as he continued his efforts to implement his concepts of civil-service and administrative policy. His ministry lacked the necessary authority to impose its leadership, and this had an awkward feedback effect on its own position. Administration continued to be plagued by overwork and incoherence, and this did not go unnoticed by Frick's enemies. In an attempt to remedy this, Stuckart approached Göring in May 1940 with an urgent request for a categorical ban on all non-essential business, pointing out that Frick's attempts to abolish these offices had repeatedly been obstructed and that stronger measures were clearly overdue.[28] He specifically argued that it was

[23] See documentation July-Nov. 1941 in BA R 43II/1135a. The initiative was abandoned because of the enormous scope of the accompanying administrative reforms that it would have required.

[24] Frick to Krosigk, 27 Oct. 1941 (BA R 43II/429b). This was in response to a complaint by Krosigk that Frick had called an interministerial conference on reclassification without consulting him.

[25] Rüdiger memo, Aug./Sept. 1942 (BA R 18/5562).

[26] Finance minister to interior minister, 21 July 1942 (BA R 43II/143a, which also documents a series of such disputes).

[27] Memo, 19 June 1942 (ibid.).

[28] Stuckart to Göring, 11 May 1940 (BA R 43II/641).

crucial that the party should not be allowed to take on any of the tasks temporarily suspended by state agencies. But although Stuckart enclosed the draft of a suitably draconian decree in which, playing the civilian counterpart to General Thomas, he invoked the imperatives of 'total war', the initiative was side-stepped by Göring and Lammers. A somewhat weakly worded general reminder of administrative priorities was eventually issued in October,[29] but well before this Lammers had contrived the issue of an unpublished Führer decree, which declared that 'until further notice any laws and decrees that have no direct connection with national defence are to be deferred'.[30] Although superficially similar to the kind of measure urged by Stuckart, in practice this decree was unsatisfactory from the interior ministry's point of view. Not only was it a general injunction rather than a catalogue of specific instructions, but the concept of 'the national defence' was restrictive rather than empowering as far as the interior ministry was concerned. Moreover, it emanated from the Führer, not from the ministerial council of which Frick was a member, and gave no specific powers to his ministry.

This deflection of interior-ministry plans was engineered by Lammers, who was to repeat the process less than a year later in response to further initiatives by both Frick and Göring. In the meantime, Lammers contributed to the pressure on Frick by orchestrating a damaging chorus of protests from the *Reichsstatthalter* about over-centralization. The *Reichsstatthalter* had long fretted under their unresolved status between party, state, and Führer. Most of them were simultaneously NSDAP *Gauleiter* and delegates of the Reich government, and in the latter capacity, but not the former, were subject to interior-ministry supervision. Complaints about their status had been endemic since 1935, and they now used the emergency of the war for another rebellion against central-government tutelage. In the spring of 1941, a huge dossier of accusations began to flow into the chancellery, solicited by Lammers at Bormann's request. Hitler's own mandate hovered over this investigation, for, following complaints from three of the Austrian *Reichsstatthalter* about recent governmental decisions, Hitler had expressed himself forcefully and typically on the subject of central control. According to Bormann, Hitler had dismissed as absurd the idea that delegating financial responsibilities to the *Reichsstatthalter*

[29] GBV circular, 10 Oct. 1940 (ibid.).
[30] *Erlass des Führers über eine vorübergehende Einschränkung der Rechtssetzung*, 5 June 1940 (BA R 43II/604); and see n. 6 above.

would encourage separatist ambitions; equally, he had ridiculed the fact that the permission of 'some little *Regierungsrat*' in Berlin was required every time a *Reichsstatthalter* wanted to promote a janitor to head janitor.[31] Lammers accordingly circularized the *Reichsstatthalter*, asking them for their views on centralization, and in particular for examples of budgetary and personnel matters in which they felt they were subject to unnecessary interference by the central Reich authorities.

The *Reichsstatthalter* responded with enthusiasm to this invitation to state their case against the central-government bureaucracy. Without exception, they bitterly criticized their dependence on the central authorities for the most minute of decisions and approvals, though there was some division of opinion as to whether this sin was to be laid at the door mainly of the interior ministry or of central government as a whole. Karl Röver of Oldenburg protested that Berlin bureaucrats were incapable of distinguishing between 'government' and 'administration', and that, as a result, minor officials in the Berlin ministries made themselves responsible for local decisions for which they had no sensitivity.[32] From Saxony, Martin Mutschmann submitted a 39-page memorandum—not the longest by any means—detailing examples of 'the exaggerated centralism and bureaucratization of the administration since the takeover of power' that was hampering his work;[33] and, to show that the situation was little better in the new model *Reichsgaue*, Jury of the Lower Danube filed an equally copious documentation.[34] In an ironic echo of his old career, Sprenger complained that he acted as little more than 'the government's postman', while Jordan of Magdeburg-Anhalt called for the 'restoration of the old rights of the *Reichsstatthalter*' under the original 1933 law.[35] The burden of virtually all the responses was that a fundamental reform of relations between the *Reichsstatthalter*, the Reich, and the *Länder* governments was essential as soon as the war was over, and that this should involve the withdrawal of the *Reichsstatthalter* from interior-ministry supervision, and their

---

[31] Bormann to Lammers, 1 Mar. 1941 (BA R 43II/1394); the full set of 20 *Reichsstatthalter* reports is in R 43II/1394a and b; see also E. Peterson, *The Limits of Hitler's Power* (Princeton, 1969), 116-19.
[32] Röver to chancellery, 3 June 1941 (R 43II/1394a).
[33] Mutschmann to chancellery, 28 Apr. 1941 (ibid.).
[34] Jury to chancellery, 5 Apr. 1941 (R 43II/1394b).
[35] Sprenger to chancellery, 26 Apr. 1941, and Jordan to chancellery, 8 Apr. 1941 (R 43II/1394a).

installation as an effective *Mittelinstanz* under the direct command of the Führer.

The *Reichsstatthalter* reports stimulated a fresh round of conferences about the problem of administrative simplification, and of proposals by interested parties for the creation of new powers to tackle it. In January 1942, Göring sent Lammers, as secretary of the ministerial council, an ambitious proposal to establish a new administrative rationalization commission. It was to be composed of the state secretaries from the finance and interior ministries, Reinhardt and Stuckart, and would be given powers 'to issue or cause to be issued all measures appropriate to the achievement of the aims enumerated', namely, administrative rationalization, the saving of manpower, and the release of personnel for arms production.[36] Lammers was quick to deflect this attempt by the Reichsmarschall to recoup the authority he had squandered by neglecting his role as head of the ministerial council.[37] He brought the matter to Hitler's attention within three days of Göring's letter, and recorded that:

The Führer does *not* agree with the proposal . . . The Führer stated in general that he did not wish the Reichsmarschall to take the rationalization of the administration into his hands. Moreover, the two ministers who would *pro forma* compose the commission, equally their two state secretaries, were absolutely the least qualified to enforce rationalization on other authorities, for these two ministries were precisely those where rationalization was most urgently needed, yet where it had not yet occurred.[38]

Happily, Lammers was also able to report Hitler's view that: 'If any office was in a position to force rationalization in the administration and to supervise the process . . . this was the chief of the Reich chancellery, who would also be in a permanent position to obtain his—the Führer's—decision.' Accordingly, Göring's plan was rejected outright; four days later a totally different Führer decree was issued.[39] Worded as a personal instruction from Hitler, this unpublished decree did not create any new powers or agencies, but leant on the August 1939 rationaliza-

---

[36] See Göring to Lammers, 19 Jan. 1942, and further documentation in BA R 43II/706a.

[37] Goebbels later took a dim view of Göring's failure to use his powers; see L. P. Lochner (ed.), *The Goebbels Diaries* (London, 1948), 201-3 (entry for 2 Mar. 1943).

[38] Lammers memo, 21 Jan. 1942 (BA R 43II/706a). See also Hitler's repetition of these comments a few days later, recorded in *Table Talk*, 24 Jan. 1942, no. 121, pp. 237 ff.

[39] *Erlass des Führers über die weitere Vereinfachung der Verwaltung*, 25 Jan. 1942 (BA R 43II/706a).

tion decree and declared the need for redoubled efforts. Its central content was a list of fifteen commandments of administrative good behaviour, followed by instructions to the Reich authorities to keep Lammers informed of their progress in adopting these various stratagems. These included instructions that government agencies were to yield all personnel conscripted by the armed forces, substituting women and older men; hours of work were to be maximized and leaves cut to the minimum; clear priorities were to be established so that non-urgent business gave way to war-related work; rationalization measures were to be designed in such a way that they did not themselves lead to more work; and, importantly, all post-war planning was to be suspended and not resumed 'until permitted by the military situation and required by the prospect of the war's end'.

Lammers' strategy and criteria here are instructive. He clearly believed that a commission composed, in effect, of Reinhardt and Stuckart would lack the authority to force rationalization on the central authorities themselves. It would be forced to confine its measures to the subordinate echelons, while the more urgent business of disciplining their masters would be dissipated in endless discussions, sub-commissions, and official investigations, leading ultimately to 'a paper war about whether rationalization was necessary or not'.[40] On the other hand, Lammers was equally reluctant to see Göring given the additional powers he would need, as head of the ministerial council, to authorize the measures outlined in his original proposal. Göring's clout was still such that Lammers may have felt that he had to move with alacrity to deflect both these possibilities: the entire process from proposal to Führer decree lasted less than a week. It is clear, then, that Lammers had no interest in reviving any kind of cabinet, least of all one headed by the vainglorious and lazy Göring (an opinion which Hitler evidently shared). Indeed, he evinced the greatest doubt that the members of the government could be persuaded to work together in any organized fashion whatsoever; rather, he pinned his hopes on leaving each minister to work independently in his own sphere, reporting directly to Hitler via himself. Finally, of course, he saw an opportunity to enhance his own power, though without actually altering the formal disposition of authority.

Similar considerations were at work in Lammers' handling of a concurrent attempt by the interior ministry to enlarge its own powers following the *Reichsstatthalter* inquiry. Towards the end of 1941,

[40] Lammers memo, 23 Jan. 1942 (ibid.).

Stuckart had approached Lammers with a fresh proposal for a Führer decree which would enforce some decentralization, but at the same time enhance his ministry's overall authority.[41] The commodious draft he submitted to the chancellery basically proposed that considerable powers should be delegated to the lower and intermediate agencies of the administration, notably to the *Reichsstatthalter* in the *Reichsgaue*, and that the interior administration should act as the focus for all administrative business in the field. The GBV or the interior ministry was to be endowed with sweeping powers of supervision and adjudication, some of them riding roughshod over the existing disposition of authority among the ministries; for example, the interior ministry was to acquire unprecedented authority to make regulations for the entire civil service, with the other ministries guaranteed no more than a right of consultation.

Lammers' generally low opinion of Frick and his staff made it inevitable that he would resist such an extension of their authority. Their ambitious document, envisaged as an extension of Hitler's August 1939 decree, cut no ice in the chancellery, whose copy is peppered with Killy's sceptical marginalia, notably in respect of the danger of dispersing too much authority to the *Mittelstufe* and the extent of the powers claimed by the GBV.[42] Lammers expressed himself in favour of some reform in principle, but was doubtful that Frick's 'very general and excessively textbook-like formulations' would find much favour among other ministers. He therefore procrastinated, refusing to show Hitler the proposal until other ministries and the party chancellery had had time to comment on it.[43] Between December 1941 and February 1942, the interior ministry held high-level consultations with other ministers, members of the ministerial council, and a number of *Reichsstatthalter/Oberpräsidenten*. At one of these, in mid-January, Stuckart's insistence that decentralization was essential, and that new powers were needed to override the tenacious resistance of the central authorities, was countered by representatives of the Reich and party chancelleries and the finance ministry, who argued that the point was to make better use of existing powers. They were also reluctant to give the impression that Hitler's decree of August 1939 had failed.[44] The results

[41] The first draft was handed to the chancellery in confidence in Sept. 1941 (BA R 43II/707a).
[42] Draft of 3 Dec. 1941; see also the subsequent draft, and official memorandum, dated 26 Jan. 1942 (ibid.).
[43] See Lammers to Bormann, and Lammers to Stuckart, 14 Dec. 1941 (ibid.).
[44] Minutes of conference, 13 Jan. 1942 (BA R 18/5451).

of these discussions were ambiguous. By the end of January, it had apparently been agreed that the measure should take the form of a ministerial council decree, not a Führer decree, and an amended draft was put into circulation. At a meeting of *Reichsstatthalter/Oberpräsidenten* in early February, Frick and Stuckart seem to have been partially successful in winning over these enemies of central government by courting them as allies against the Berlin specialist ministries. However, Lammers now fought back against the enactment of a measure to which he remained hostile. At a meeting in the chancellery the following day, which was intended to be a forum for the free discussion of basic issues, Lammers, Stuckart, and Neumann, the state secretary from the Four-Year Plan office, argued out the different positions.[45] Stuckart insisted that existing powers were inadequate to deal with the mounting manpower crisis. In his view, the root causes of this were the continuing and intractable problems of over-centralization, fragmentation, and parallel organization, and it is clear that he numbered the swollen ranks of the party's numerous bureaucracies among the worst offenders. Though Lammers agreed with this diagnosis, he also demurred at the proposed expansion of GBV powers, as well as at the idea of issuing a single massive instrument. He repeatedly emphasized his reluctance to bring such a compendious measure before the Führer, who would not welcome being asked to approve so much new law at once. Against Stuckart's objections, Lammers insisted that the measure should be broken into a series of separate instruments, possibly a series of orders deriving from an overarching Führer decree.

Lammers' proposal was clearly designed to eviscerate Frick's measure and ensure that the chancellery retained control over whatever instruments were eventually adopted. Frick, of course, was bitterly affronted by this move. In an angry letter to Lammers, he reiterated the fact that (against Lammers' original expectations) ministers, *Reichsstatthalter*, and even Bormann had all supported his measure, and he reminded Lammers that he himself had approved its content in principle. Declaring his convictions at the level of language as well as policy, Frick insisted on the importance of a single, indivisible measure: 'By dividing the decree into a series of instructions and orders, its integral material and psychological effect is lost. Only as a co-ordinated whole will the decree's stipulations lead to real decentralization and real manpower

---

[45] Minutes of conference, 5 Feb. 1942; also present were Kritzinger from the Reich chancellery, and Ehrensberger of the GBV (ibid.).

savings. It is precisely the form of the decree that gives the most emphatic signal of the urgency of the measures to those concerned.'[46] However, Lammers set about soliciting criticisms of Frick's plan from other ministries, secured Hitler's approval of his own scheme, and arranged the drafting in the chancellery of the new series of Führer decrees and orders.[47] The three new decrees, which delegated or simplified procedures in civil-service appointments, civil-service law, and the preparation of the budget, were signed by Hitler on 9 March; they were followed by three further orders, issued under the signatures of Göring, Frick, Funk, and Lammers (i.e. the civilian members of the ministerial council), which delegated some licensing and supervisory powers, and set out in declaratory form the principles of wartime administrative practice.[48] Though the wording of these measures largely followed the original interior-ministry drafts, there was no trace of the cumulative assignment of new powers to the interior ministry/GBV: Frick was left with the bark, but not the bite.

The issue of these orders was accompanied by another of the procedural rows that were so characteristic of government in the Third Reich. Frick had asked Lammers to delay promulgating the decrees in the *Reichsgesetzblatt* until the executive orders were also settled and signed. When Frick still did not have the final wording ready by March 13, Lammers sent the decrees for publication anyway, and was furious to discover, six days later, that Frick had countermanded this. Threatening literally to report Frick to the Führer, Lammers finally secured their prompt publication.[49]

This rather petty row is instructive of something more, however. As in his letter to Lammers on 12 February, Frick's insistence on the form and appearance of the legislation mirrored his obsessive preoccupation with administrative coherence and uniformity; and it was this strategy

[46] Frick to Lammers, 12 Feb. 1942 (BA R 43II/707a). See also Bürckel to Lammers, 2 Mar. 1942 (BA R 43II/706).

[47] Marginal note on letter of 12 Feb., referring to 2 meetings between Lammers and Hitler on 9 and 15 Feb. and concluding: 'Der Führer billigt meine Auffassungen'; see also other documentation in BA R 43II/707a; and Lammers to Frick, 19 Feb. 1942 (BA R 18/5451).

[48] *Erlass des Führers zur Dezentralisierung der Personalverwaltung; Erlass des Führers zur personalrechtlichen Vereinfachung;* and *Erlass des Führers über Vereinfachungen in der Ausführung des Haushaltsplans,* all 9 Mar. 1942 (*RGBl,* 1942, i. 119, 120, and 120); *VO zur Dezentralisierung des Erlaubniswesens* and *VO zur Dezentralisierung der Aufsicht über Körperschaften, Stiftungen und Anstalten des öffentlichen Rechts,* both 19 Mar. 1942 (*RGBl,* 1942, i. 129 and 130); *Anordnung zur Entlastung der Verwaltungsbehörden bei der Verwaltungsdurchführung und Verwaltungsaufsicht,* 19 Mar. 1942 (*MBliV,* 1942, 582).

[49] Documentation in BA R 43II/707a.

that was so suspect to Lammers. As the final shape of the decrees of both January and March 1942 suggests, Lammers was anxious to establish his chancellery as the locus of a co-ordinated supervision of wartime rationalization policies. However, although personal ambition obviously played a strong part in this, it also appears that Lammers and his senior officials were troubled by the practical implications of Frick's combined strategy of concentration and decentralization. Frick was evidently willing to concede authority to the *Reichsstatthalter/Oberpräsidenten* in the field, including powers wrested from the specialist ministries in the name of administrative concentration. What Lammers and his colleagues doubted was whether Frick and his apparatus were strong enough to control the centrifugal forces that this process of delegation would release. As Killy put it in one of his comments on the September 1941 draft decree: 'Not decentralization but centralization at the intermediate level [*Mittelstufe*], together with the disempowerment of the central offices, is the effect that has in practice been achieved. Or *has* the R. d. In. [interior ministry] still any decisive influence over the *Reichsstatthalter*?'[50] Lammers also doubted that the interior minister was in any position to implement the kind of authority over the specialist ministers that he was claiming through this decree. In other words, Lammers foresaw a situation in which key powers were vested in an agency which was too weak to utilize them effectively, leaving the administrative field more exposed to the forces of disintegration and particularism. Lammers' moves can thus be seen as an attempt to step into this potentially dangerous vacuum at the centre, filling it with an authority legitimated by the Führer himself, the ultimate arbiter of the party as well as of the state apparatus. Serious attention could then be paid to the increasingly urgent question of administrative rationalization. But although Lammers did have, as he claimed, regular access to Hitler at this time, and thus an ultimate sanction from above for his authority, he had no independent means for its implementation on the ground: he had the commander, so to speak, but not the troops. This was in strong contrast to the interior ministry itself, which, as Frick repeatedly stressed, already possessed a considerable field apparatus of its own, and therefore claimed both the right and the obligation to take the lead in administrative policy. Moreover, in Hitler, Lammers had, as he well knew, a superior who was quite uninterested in the concrete business of administrative practice, and thus Lammers' legitimation

---

[50] Marginal note to draft of 27 Sept. 1941 (ibid.).

was itself insecurely anchored in the soft ground of the Führer's attention. Yet the fiction of Hitler's supreme and effective authority had to be maintained: in all the toing and froing of complaints and criticisms in 1941 and later, the one thought that remained unspeakable was the possibility that Hitler himself was at fault. So, although Lammers' authority was probably at its height at this point, it was not an authority that could easily be translated into real power.

Thus, the first phase of wartime administrative activity ended in measures which must be seen more as responses to the power flux than as effective attempts to cope with administrative shortcomings. The spring of 1942 was in any case a period of rapid change in the direction of the war, following America's entry into the conflict and the start of the Russian counter-attack in December 1941. War production became an inescapable priority in the economic sphere, and the reorganization of the civilian economy, including labour allocation, was not far behind.[51] Albert Speer, appointed to the munitions ministry after Todt's sudden death in February 1942, moved fast to consolidate and extend his powers, a strategy that within a month brought the establishment of a central planning board to control raw materials allocation and the appointment of a plenipotentiary for labour supply. These appointments themselves are illustrations of the indiscriminacy of administrative development in Nazi Germany: Speer was the archetypal technocrat who dedicated himself to building effective independent authority over civilian as well as military production in order to co-ordinate the two, while labour plenipotentiary Sauckel was the 'typical, ambitious party functionary',[52] whose programme leant heavily on the Gauleiter and furthered the assimilation of administrative to party authority that had begun with their appointment as defence commissioners in 1939. In their different ways, however, both threatened the existing distribution of power in the administrative system, and were scarcely welcome to an interior ministry struggling to retain its own authority. From now on the ministry was acutely concerned to protect both its powers and its personnel from the direct and indirect depredations of the new regime of war production.

Shortly before this, however, when the prospects for post-war planning still looked bright, plans had begun circulating in the interior

[51] For these developments, see Carroll, *Design for Total War*, pp. 230-41; Herbst, *Der Totale Krieg*, pt. 3; E. L. Homze, *Foreign Labor in Nazi Germany* (Princeton, 1967), chs. 5 and 6.
[52] Ibid. 111.

ministry for renewed reform in the civil-service training and salary systems. These were intended to revive the status and morale of the bureaucratic ēlite of the interior administration in particular, and to ensure it a role in the post-war world. That they were largely to come to nothing was due not only to the increasingly unfavourable military situation, but also to the weakness of the interior ministry, and its growing marginalization as a source of policy and authority.

III

Two years previously, after a lapse of some years, the interior ministry had resumed its interest in the training of senior administrators, largely in the hope that sweeping reforms would help attract high-quality recruits into the civil service. In 1937, as we have seen, the interior ministry had accepted an interim and unsatisfactory compromise regulation, which had divided administrative and legal training and had also left open the important question of how to prepare candidates for the specialist branches. That episode had also ended in a brush between Frick and Hitler, which had presumably not helped the authority of the final ruling. Moreover, the StdF *Stab* was beginning to take an increasing interest in training procedures in the later 1930s, as it struggled to develop appropriate standards and procedures for the Nazification of the civil service.[53] The ministry returned to the question in mid-1940, when Pfundtner, who was to retain close personal control over the discussions that ensued, instructed his fellow state secretary, Stuckart, and three senior officials to prepare proposals for a thoroughgoing revision of the training programme for the senior grade of the administrative civil service. This initiative may have been Pfundtner's own, without Frick's mandate, but it was clearly a response to the progress of the war—as Pfundtner said, it anticipated the 'exceptional . . . demands that are bound to be placed on civil servants of the senior administration at the end of a victorious war'.[54] The plans that were developed in the ministry in the next two years indicated that strenuous efforts were being made to adapt official thinking to both the opportunities offered by German imperialism and the challenges presented by the party.

[53] See ch. 5, above.
[54] Pfundtner to Stuckart, Schütze, and Suren, 27 June 1940 (BA R 18/5667).

The remit drafted by Pfundtner for the guidance of his colleagues already indicated some important new departures. By contrast with Frick's earlier position, he argued that 'the training of senior administrative officials must be *totally* separate from that of pure jurists', including at university level, where he proposed the introduction of a new course of study in administration. At all stages, practice was to be emphasized as much as theory and law; special provisions should also take account of the need to attract ex-army officers, who 'in point of character and decisiveness will undoubtedly be a highly desirable addition to the administration'. Pfundtner was anxious to embark on a programme of reform, since other departments were also beginning to lay their own plans for the future; he placed great emphasis on the need to develop a single, uniform, training and examination system for all branches of the administration, suggesting that the ministry would need to call on the backing of Göring and the party in order to overwhelm the cries of protest that would surely arise from the specialist branches.

The demand for a separate and distinctive administrative training was the most telling of these criteria, and suggests that senior administrators had now decided that they had a good deal more to lose than to gain from a close association with jurists. Hitler's deep contempt for jurists was notorious, and had been made explicit during the 1937 fracas. It might well be worth sacrificing the neatness of a combined training if the interior administration could thereby be liberated from the opprobrium attached to the law and its practitioners in the Nazi state. The alternative that was now developed in intra-ministerial discussions, therefore, not only threw over the joint training, but also sought to minimize the role of law as such in the administrative training; instead of legal 'theory' and 'abstraction', the new emphasis was on administration as a practical science. The schemes that emerged drew self-consciously on the tradition of cameralistics that had been ruptured by the nineteenth-century turn to the primacy of law in the German public sphere. They also put a strong emphasis on the vocational aspects of university education for future administrators, linking this to a critique of legal education as being both too abstract and too subordinated to the demands of legal careers alone.

Preparation of the reform measures was limited to the handful of civil servants immediately involved; the specialist ministries were deliberately kept at a distance, and only the chancellery and the party chancellery were directly consulted. Yet it appears that within this restricted circle a major effort at reconceptualizing the role of the civil-service élite was underway, not least in response to pressures exerted by the party in its effort to pursue the Nazification of the civil service. These objectives were not stable, however. Apparently at Hess's insistence, new regulations on admission to the civil service, issued in 1939, had stipulated membership of the NSDAP or one of its associated formations as a condition of entry.[55] But, as we have seen, Hess's staff had already begun to revise earlier views that party membership was the best gauge of a civil servant's political virtue. Remarks by Walter Sommer in 1938 had suggested that the party was shifting its ground, discounting the importance of membership for rank-and-file officials, and looking to a more exacting set of criteria for the most important posts.[56] In 1941, Bormann was formally to adopt this as his position. He informed the interior ministry that the NSDAP was not interested in enrolling civil servants who were only seeking to advance their careers, but that all leading civil servants would be expected not simply to be party members, but to have 'given fully reliable service to the party or one of its formations'.[57]

The NSDAP's shifting position had considerable significance for training policy, for it implied that the party was developing its own views about the composition of a new administrative élite. Its spokesman here tended to be Walter Sommer, whose interests spanned the relationship between training, salary structure, social mobility, and procreation. His arguments were aimed at making the civil service more accessible and attractive in an era when more enticing careers beckoned venturesome and independent young men. As he put it, without a substantial rethinking of its principles, the civil service risked being left with 'those people who do not feel strong enough to live their life without seniority systems, fixed increments and the like, *i.e.* bureaucrats, a class less welcome in today's state than ever before'.[58]

On the interior ministry's side, the most authoritative contributor to these debates was undoubtedly the state secretary, Stuckart, who had devoted some attention to the question since the beginning of the

[55] *VO über die Vorbildung und Laufbahnen der deutschen Beamten*, 28 Feb. 1939 (*RGBl*, 1939, i. 371), Art 1, §2; and see R. Schneider *et al.*, *Kommentar zur Verordnung über die Vorbildung und die Laufbahnen der deutschen Beamten* (Berlin, 1939). Membership of the HJ, now virtually compulsory, qualified.

[56] See Ch. 5, pp. 186-8, above.

[57] Bormann to Frick, 21 Aug. 1941, and related documentation in BA R 43II/421a.

[58] Sommers to Lammers, 1 July 1937 (BA R 43II/450a) (and see also Ch. 6, pp. 214-15, above); also W. Sommer, 'Die Ausbildung des Nachwuchses der höheren Verwaltungsbeamten', *DVBl*, 1937, 360-3.

regime, and now found himself in charge of it. While still in the education ministry in 1934, he had worked on a reform of the university law curriculum.[59] Subsequently, he developed at greater length his ideas on the 'crisis in law' that had been gathering strength in Germany since the turn of the century: the growing tension between 'lawyers' law' on the one hand, and the people's 'innate sense of justice' (*gesundes Volksempfinden*), which was beginning to make inroads into statute and practice.[60] Lawyers' law, according to Stuckart, was Roman, materialist, abstract, over-conceptual, a matter of pure theory and formal logic—alien and remote from the everyday life of the ordinary citizen. But this *Juristenrecht* was opposed by a *Volksrecht* that derived from the moral values of the national community, from the 'heroic-idealistic life-view' of the German people. The challenge for the National Socialist regime was to find the means of expressing an ideology which embodied these healthy and sound values, as a *Rechtsordnung*, a legal order: 'The legal maxim and the law of life must be restored to full harmony.' In future, therefore, the representatives of the legal order—lawyers, judges, civil servants—must be both mentally and politically equipped to accomplish their role in this, by means of a legal training that took full account of the new principles of the law. Stuckart conceded that the civil service had, rightly, forfeited to the NSDAP its claim to act as a 'staatstragende Volksschicht', but he strongly implied that a legal revival would redeem its practitioners and enable them to recover something of their status; indeed, he was insistent that the law remained the best education for administrators, as long as it was interspersed with bouts of practical apprenticeship.

As the interior-ministry discussions began in 1940, Stuckart prepared a long unpublished essay in which he sought to clarify his views further.[61] He now reversed his opinions about the status and value of the law for the administration, arguing that it was pointless to try to maintain a combined training for jurists and administrators: their tasks were quite different, and required distinctive skills. Under National Socialism, the law was no longer the supreme standard it had been in the nineteenth century; for administrators, creative initiative within a broadly defined sphere of action was the new order of the day, not the

[59] W. Stuckart, 'Ziel und Weg einer nationalsozialistischen Studienreform', *ZADR*, 2 (1934), 53–5.
[60] W. Stuckart, *Nationalsozialistische Rechtserziehung* (Frankfurt, 1935); also his 'Rechtswahrer und Staat', *DV*, 1935, 353–61.
[61] 'Grundgedanken zur Neuordnung des Ausbildungsganges der höheren Verwaltungsbeamten', 5 Aug. 1940; Nachlass von der Schulenburg (private collection).

application of technical rules. The administrator 'must nowadays take part in the preservation and shaping of the state and the community in his department. What we need are men who are pioneers of culture, colonizers and economic innovators in the best sense of these words.'

Stuckart's shift of opinion was exemplary for the direction of his ministry's reform discussions, though whether it was a principled revision of his ideas or a more pragmatic response to the drastic collapse in the prestige of the law and lawyers is less easy to determine. As Stuckart quite explicitly argued: 'It is now high time for the senior administrative civil servant to be liberated from the odium of the jurist, someone he neither is nor should be if he is to understand his profession correctly and perform his duties correctly.' The heavy emphasis placed by Stuckart and others on the practical and creative side of administrative work was both a response to the opportunities offered by the war, and an attempt to grasp these in terms not wholly foreign to the corporate ideology of their profession. Stuckart's vocabulary of pioneers and colonizers makes sense only in the context of the drama of conquest unfolding in Europe at this time; it declares a desire that the establishment of German dominion be seen as part of the proper tasks of the civil service, and at the same time conveys a willingness to adapt to these new challenges, ensuring that the civil service will possess a right of co-determination in Germany's future, alongside the National Socialist political leadership. The character who most effectively symbolized these aspirations, and assimilated them to a powerful bureaucratic heritage, was the Prussian *Landrat*, an official long prominent in administrative discourse as the archetype of the versatile and practical administrator. It was on this idealized figure drawn from a composite tradition that the hopes of the reformers were focused as they attempted to develop a newly strengthened corps of modern officials.

Apart from Stuckart, however, few other professionals or academics had devoted much attention to the specific question of civil-service training since 1933. An official charged with summarizing the available opinion on the matter found very little material from outside the administration itself.[62] Business men were said to believe that senior officials should be better informed about economic principles and policies now that the state was more directly involved in planning; they were seconded by academic economists and authorities such as the price commissioner, who urged that skills in economics and planning were in

[62] See memo (40-pp. plus appendices) by Oberregierungsrat Ernst, May 1941 (BA R 18/5567).

many cases more important than a knowledge of the law, and should be learned before officials were set loose in the real world. Among the administration's own experts, there were virtually no defenders of the existing training system, though a few were prepared to argue for a legal training on the grounds that it was the archetype of all disciplined analysis. In terms of concrete proposals for reform, the main division concerned the relative importance attached to theoretical and to practical work. Bormann, not surprisingly, was known to favour a predominantly practical process of education and in-service training, consistent with his strong preference for a generally more flexible personnel policy, in which the application of any rules on training would be tempered by discretion in the appointment of men without formal qualifications. His subordinate, Sommer, was another severe critic of the role of law and of theory in training, and was said to have argued (like Stuckart) that 'above all the administrative civil servant must be *politically* freed from the curse of being a jurist'. By contrast, Köttgen, one of the few academics who had published on the subject, was strongly attached to the theoretical component of education and training, for it was this that guaranteed what he called 'the mental synthesis within the civil-service corps', which, as we have seen, guaranteed in his eyes the coherence of the administration.

Pfundtner wanted a regulation issued as soon as possible, presumably on the assumption that the inauguration of the post-war world was just around the corner. However, his first push for action in 1941 was unsuccessful. A year or so later the ministry produced a set of 'guidelines for a training regulation for the senior public service', representing the sum of two years of investigation and internal discussion, and embodying bureaucratic revivalism at its height, not least in its linguistic usage.[63] Senior officials were now being collectively characterized as the 'Verwaltungsführerkorps'—taking at face value the language long purveyed in the propaganda literature—while for trainees, the eccentric title of 'Regierungsjunker' was coined. The vocational emphasis in selection and training was pronounced, as was the unspoken intention to exclude women entirely. Candidates for admission to training would be mustered annually at a camp (the term employed was not 'Lager', but 'Kameradschaft'), to be reviewed by a selection board consisting of a *Landrat* and another senior official, a doctor, a psychologist, and representatives of the interior ministry and

[63] Guidelines dated 15 May 1942; see also minutes of intraministerial discussions, 15 May and 21 July (BA R 18/5567).

the party chancellery. Before entering university, candidates would fulfil a four- to six-week preparatory placement (*Vorpraxis*) with a *Landrat*. The university curriculum would then cover a catholic expanse of administrative science and practice, studied, at Stuckart's suggestion, in a new faculty to be called 'Wissenschaft von Volk und Staat'; and at his suggestion, too, the suffix 'Recht' was to be dropped as far as possible, so that students would no longer take their courses in 'Finanzrecht', but in 'Finanz', 'Verwaltung', and so on. University vacations would include periods of manual labour in mines, factories, or farms, a second placement with a *Landrat*, and another with a *Kreisleitung*. All students and trainees would receive modest financial support. The university education terminated in an examination supervised by a special board of ministerial and party representatives, further emphasizing the vocational nature of the process. Successful candidates, who would have taken their final vows while at university, so to speak, would then complete a two-year probationary training, when they could opt to join a specialist branch such as finance or transport, if staffing allowed. In-service training followed the existing pattern of short periods in the main agencies of the administration, including party offices. The final hurdle was not a second written examination, but attendance at a six- to eight-week camp, possibly to be associated with the NSDAP's Bad Tölz camp, which would test and encourage the recruit's fitness for leadership and command. The final decision on qualification was to be taken by the interior ministry or the specialist ministry as appropriate. There remained only some dispute over whether the newly qualified civil servant should be eligible for immediate established appointment, the counter-argument being that if this innovation were permitted civil servants would be looking for promotion too soon.

In the event, these schemes came to nothing, despite the advanced stage they had reached in the ministry by 1942. That year saw a spate of articles on civil-service training in the academic press, notably a long series in *Deutsche Verwaltung*, no doubt promoted by Pfundtner.[64] At the end of 1942, or possibly in early 1943, an exhaustive executive order was drafted in the interior ministry, intended to accompany a proposed Hitler decree implementing the reform, but neither was promulgated.[65] The only specific measure adopted was in 1942, when *Diplomvolkswirte*

---

[64] See e.g. *DV*, 1942, 61-7, 125-30, 164-8, 168-70, 335-8, 447-53; also an article by Pfundtner himself, in *ZADR*, 8, 1942.
[65] Undated draft, annotated by Pfundtner (BA R 18/5567).

were admitted to the administration on the same terms as law graduates, a move that went some way towards meeting the concerns of business and of the government's own economic departments.[66]

The reason for this failure is unclear. Possibly the scheme had remained Pfundtner's own, and did not enjoy the full backing of Frick, who appears never to have been directly involved and may not have been reconciled to the change of strategy.[67] It is also conceivable that Bormann helped to engineer its demise; certainly, his man in the interior ministry, von Helms, had not been very co-operative, and appears to have been responsible for some of the delays that hampered the scheme in 1941. Moreover, the non-civil servants on Bormann's staff were not necessarily impressed by plans which clung to the principles of academic training, even if other party interests were taken into account.[68] There remain two other considerations. One is the question of timing. Discussions had been initiated in 1940 at the height of optimism about Germany's future; they were abandoned as the outcome of the war was looking more and more dubious, and at a time when, as we have seen, other major policy initiatives in the ministry were also collapsing. But the military situation alone may not account directly for the demise of the project. A second problem was that the interior ministry had become increasingly isolated and impotent as it pursued schemes that rode roughshod over the sectional interests of other departments. Frick's desire to control a uniform and concentrated administration, and to be the decisive authority in civil-service affairs, took little account of the real conditions of government and administration in Nazi Germany—or perhaps the problem was that they took too much account of this. The paradox was that the splintering of power that Frick and his officials so accurately identified as the organizing principle of the Third Reich was also their own nemesis. The more the fragmentation advanced, the more it might have vindicated the ministry's own concept of administration; and yet, the more it also suggested that the ministry itself was part of, rather than a solution to, the problem.

66 Interior ministry to finance ministry, 27 Mar. 1942, enclosing draft of this (ibid.). The measure was issued on 24 Apr. 1942 (*RGBl*, 1942, i. 241).

67 All the evidence discussed here is to be found in Pfundtner's *Handakten*, or personal files, which break off abruptly at this point. Departmental files, if any, do not seem to have survived, and records from other ministries are also extremely fragmentary.

68 For an indication of later party thinking on civil-service training, see Orlow, *History of the Nazi Party: 1933-1945*, p. 433.

By the early 1940s, friction between Frick and Krosigk on this score had become endemic, as we have seen, and relations with the justice ministry, the third major protagonist in civil-service policy, also deteriorated sharply as the interior ministry's proposed training reform became known. The justice ministry cannot have been ignorant of interior-ministry thinking on the subject, and certainly knew about the new plans by the autumn of 1942, if not earlier.[69] The ministry remained deeply opposed to the separation of administrative and judicial training. As Freisler pointed out in 1943: 'The judicial administration . . . has always emphasized that, with all due respect to the naturally different duties that fall to justice and administration, the *joint course of study* at university must continue. Knowledge of the principles of law and its components, not a specialist vocational training, must stand in the foreground at the university.'[70] In its resistance to the idea of an independent curriculum in administrative science, the justice ministry was backed by the education ministry, which saw its own precarious authority over the educational process being threatened by interior-ministry plans for the staffing of administration faculties with non-academics, and the establishment of an outside examination board.

The dispute here was not simply about departmental authority, or even about the extent to which education should be dictated by vocational criteria. Rather, the authority of the law in general was the larger issue that lent an edge to jurists' arguments. In Nazi Germany, as we have seen, they found themselves in an almost surreal world in which the authority of the law was still asserted in principle, while the security of *Rechtsstaatlichkeit* had vanished in practice. The radicalization of legal practice and ideology intensified considerably from the beginning of the war, notably after the death in January 1941 of Gürtner, a nationalist who had remained largely unsympathetic to the ideas of such Nazi jurists as Frank, Freisler, and Thierack. In April 1942, in a move designed expressly to show Hitler's displeasure with judges and the law, the Reichstag underwrote Hitler's unbounded right to dismiss from his post any German, 'whether simple soldier or officer,

---

[69] See memo by Segelken of the justice ministry, 9 Oct. 1942, noting a meeting between Rothenberger, Rust, and Frick; the divergent views on training were made clear, and it was agreed that they would form the subject of further discussion in the near future (BA R 22/1730; further documentation has not survived).

[70] R. Freisler, 'Die neue Studienordnung', 18 Nov. 1943 (BA R 22/1730a).

inferior or senior civil servant or judge, leading or subordinate party functionary, worker or clerk'.[71] Four months later, Hitler brought to an end the interregnum that had followed Gürtner's death, and replaced the acting minister, Schlegelberger (a trained jurist and career civil servant of the same stripe as Gürtner), by the Nazi jurist, Otto Thierack. Simultaneously, in sharp contrast to the moratorium on administrative reform, a Führer decree empowered Thierack, in consultation with Lammers and Bormann, to begin 'the construction of a National Socialist legal system'.[72] The man charged with the initial work on this was Curt Rothenberger, a jurist who had been active in the Nazi movement since 1931, and who had come to Hitler's attention in March 1942, when he had sent the Führer a copy of his long analysis of the *Justizkrise*.[73] Rothenberger pointed out that the judicial system and its personnel had become isolated, defenceless, and unrespected, that they lacked the Führer's confidence, and were incapable of fulfilling their political duty of service to the German community and the ideology of National Socialism. Many of his prescriptions aimed at restoring the reputation of the judiciary, and he urged the replacement of the 'beamtete Berufsrichter' of the nineteenth century with a new 'Urtyp des deutschen Richter'. The authority of this select élite would derive not from their traditional official status, but from their organic identification with the values of the Nazi community: leadership, honour, national comradeship, loyalty, the values of the yeoman and the soil.

Though Rothenberger was to resign after less than eighteen months, having failed to secure the confidence of either his minister or the party authorities, his memorandum exemplified the sense of crisis that was felt throughout the judicial system, and his remedies paralleled those circulating in interior-ministry circles to alleviate the related distress of the civil service. Both aimed at establishing new professional élites who would not only conform to the ostensible demands of National Socialism, as far as these could be ascertained, but who would also

[71] *Beschluss des Grossdeutschen Reichstags*, 26 Apr. 1942 (*RGBl*, 1942, i. 247). On the radicalization process after 1942, see H. Weinkauff, 'Die deutsche Justiz und der Nationalsozialismus', in *Die deutsche Justiz und der Nationalsozialismus* (Stuttgart, 1968), i. 150-69.

[72] *Erlass des Führers über besondere Vollmachten des Reichsministers der Justiz*, 20 Aug. 1942 (*RGBl*, 1942, i. 535).

[73] 'Gedanken über eine nationalsozialistische Justizreform', 31 Mar. 1942 (BA R 43II/1560b). See also views expressed at a conference between the party chancellery and 'party members in the public service', 23-5 Sept. 1944, noted in a NSDAP treasury memo (BA NS 1/557).

recover the authority and status of the governmental agencies they represented. Both were attempts, in other words, to find a middle way between the beleaguered expectations of a tradition élite and the disdainful negligence of its parvenu political masters. The interior ministry wanted to establish the administrative élite as a corps of creative participants in the work of German government, and asserted its own expertise as the best guide on how to achieve this. The justice ministry, if anything even more alarmed at the vanishing prestige of the law and lawyers, was being urged by Thierack and Rothenberger to abandon the vestiges of positivism and to develop an equally imaginative role in the administration of justice. Neither wanted to see the work of their profession reduced to the mechanical execution of policies developed by a capricious and unsympathetic political leadership. It is striking, of course, that so little intra-administration solidarity was manifested in these efforts at self-defence. The disagreements stemmed partly from the old contest in German public life between the claims of *Recht* and *Verwaltung*, for the interior ministry's plans represented a notable departure from the principles of the *Juristenmonopol*. But they assumed a sharper edge from the judicial authorities' fear that independent initiatives by the administration would leave them naked and alone, marked as sole representatives of a now openly despised legal tradition. As a justice-ministry official commented when the interior-ministry schemes for separate university courses first came to his attention in October 1942: 'Such a development would be extremely ill-advised . . . It would represent a highly undesirable [and] retrograde development counter to the healthy objective of offering the jurist a comprehensive education and restoring him once again to the *universitas literarum*.'[74]

However, jurists themselves were undecided about the rival claims of *Bildung* and vocational training as a suitable preparation for young lawyers and an appropriate response to their tribulations under National Socialism. The wartime years saw the culmination of moves by the justice and education ministries to revise the university law curriculum in line with some of the changes that had overtaken the law and its interpreters in Nazi Germany.[75] A series of modifications in the subjects of study were under discussion, including lengthier instruction

[74] Memo by Segelken, 9 Oct. 1942 (BA R 22/1730).

[75] The curriculum had been revised once in 1935; for the resumption of work in 1938, initiated by the Akademie für Deutsches Recht, see documentation in BA R 22/1729 and R 61/99.

in public law; it was also proposed, somewhat controversially, that students might gain experience beyond the class-room in vocational 'practical workshops', to be conducted by professional lawyers as well as by academics.[76] These ideas developed partly in response to party pressure for a more practice-oriented legal education, and to the need for training courses suitable for older wartime entrants as well as young men continuing their university studies on temporary military leave. But they were also a reaction to the interior ministry's own schemes, and they were clearly intended to undermine the latter's plans for a separate administrative curriculum and faculty. For in addition, the justice and education ministries were responding to another glaring facet of the crisis in law: the drain of recruitment into both the university law faculties and the judicial civil service. As one jurist pointed out in 1943: 'No young person has any desire to enter a commonly abused profession.'[77] The fear of a recruitment crisis was not, as we have seen, confined to this branch of the public service, but had long figured in the interior ministry's campaign on behalf of the administration. If law remained the privileged route of entry, the future prospects of the senior civil service were not encouraging. On the eve of the war, law students comprised 10 per cent of the student population, compared with a high of 23 per cent in 1923; by 1942, this had fallen to 4 per cent—far below any adequate replacement ratio.[78] In absolute numbers, 1941 was the worst year, with only 2,306 students enrolled; even the slightly higher figures for 1942 and 1943 gave little cause for confidence, especially since the proportion of female law students was increasing (from 2.4 per cent in 1939, to over 16 per cent in 1944). The number of men entering the judicial training as *Referendare* had not declined quite so precipitously at the beginning of the war, as a result of eased entry regulations for ex-officers, but by far the majority of them left after qualifying as *Assessoren*; thus, in 1941 there were 7,577 *Referendare* but only 2,120 *Assessoren*. The ratio as such was not atypical, since all prospective lawyers and some other professionals

[76] On these 'Praktikerarbeitsgemeinschaften' see principally documentation in BA R 22/4508-4510. The universities and the education ministry were unhappy at the proposal because it denigrated academics and over-emphasized the vocational aspects of education.

[77] Neumann (Dresden), at conference of the justice-ministry recruitment review office (Amt für Nachwuchsfragen), 12 Nov. 1943 (BA R 22/4447).

[78] This and following data are drawn from recruitment review office conferences and reports in June, July, and Oct. 1944 (BA R 22/4449 and 4451); see also J. Pauwels, *Women, Nazis, and Universities: Female University Students in the Third Reich, 1933-1945* (Westport, 1984), 101.

qualified first as *Referendare* before choosing private employment; but because the absolute numbers were by now so low, recruitment to the civil service was no longer adequately covered. The problem was not only how to increase enrolments in the law faculties, but also how to ensure that a larger proportion of graduates wound up in the civil service. This was the more important given the vast additional territories that Germany now had to police.

As far as many established professionals were concerned, this was a virtually hopeless task, given the lamentable state of the judiciary and the legal profession in National Socialist Germany. The recruitment review office (Amt für Nachwuchsfragen) established in the justice ministry in 1943 gave its interpretation of the origins of the crisis in June 1944, at one of a series of conferences on the problem.[79] Discussion turned quickly from the problem of recruitment as such, to the crisis in legal practice in general. For the past ten years, delegates complained, the law and jurisprudence had undergone almost continuous change. There was a mania for issuing new and supposedly definitive laws, but hardly had these been passed when ideas and circumstances altered, and new enactments became necessary: indeed, the more definitive a law set out to be, the more likely it was to need early amendment. It was scarcely possible to be sure from one day to the next which laws were in force and which were not—even supposing that the various regulations could be found, which was frequently impossible, given the lack of up-to-date textbooks. Ministers constantly issued new directives without troubling to consult the justice ministry, creating a chaos of contradictory provisions and of superseded, but not formally annulled, legislation; the sources of law were innumerable, their places of publication (if any, one might add) equally legion, yet there was no single comprehensive reference work in which they were all collated and available for easy consultation.[80] In short, the justice ministry had been deprived of its natural, deserved, and traditional status as the centre for the collation of legislation, its role having been usurped by the party chancellery, where the interests and needs of the law were 'naturally not much considered'. So it went on; individual cases were cited, particular offenders identified, and frustrations vented. The most

[79] 8-10 June 1944 (BA R 22/4449). For the foundation of the office, see documentation in BA R 22/4447.

[80] This 'book famine' was a serious matter: see remarks by Landesgerichtsrat Zeller at the recruitment review office's conference of 8-10 June 1944, and also a major attempt to assemble a textbook bibliography, also in 1944 (documentation in BA R 22/4454).

favoured remedy appeared to be a total ban on all new legislation until the present mess had been sorted out and the indispensable reference work compiled. With this massive sense of inferiority and impending calamity in the judicial system, it was hardly surprising that the justice ministry was alarmed by the interior ministry's plans to develop an entirely separate training system. Evidently, however, after almost two years of tensions, some kind of compromise was reached with the interior ministry. The exact procedure whereby this agreement was finally achieved cannot be reconstructed with confidence, though it is likely that pressure for an immediate revision of the curriculum for students on release from the services played an important part.[81] The interior ministry had evidently dropped its own plans for separate administrative faculties sometime in 1943. One index of progress towards this was a speech delivered by Stuckart to students returning to the army at the end of the 1942-3 winter semester, in which he declared that: 'I myself, after exhaustive consideration, see the possibility of a combined university curriculum continuing in the future . . . with the proviso that justice, adminis-tration and the economy receive equal treatment'.[82] Stuckart went on to recant his earlier views, observing that:

Justice, administration and the economy face the same task . . . of freeing themselves from the present type of the jurist and the superseded concepts and teaching methods of existing training . . . Thus in the future too an academic education, but no longer training in the capacity for formal-legal thought and tuition in the elements of positivist law. Rather, the main aim [is] the education of the complete National Socialist personality . . .

By the spring of 1944, Stuckart's ministry was confining itself to arguments about details—whether, for example, the new course should be entitled 'Rechts- und Staatswissenschaften' or 'Staats- und Rechts-wissenschaften'.[83] The new curriculum for university law studies was eventually issued by the education ministry in July 1944, to come into force the following semester.[84] The preamble spoke of preparing students to become 'creative, effective and responsible bearers of the

[81] Interior-ministry views on this summarized by Rüdiger in a memo for Pfundtner, 17 May 1943 (BA R 18/5567).
[82] Extracts/résumé in BA R 22/4452. Stuckart also mentions that 'in the summer of the previous year' (i.e. 1941/2) the talk had all been of separation.
[83] Education ministry to justice ministry, 29 Mar. 1944 (BA R 22/4511).
[84] See documentation in BA R 22/4511. The curriculum was published in *Deutsche Wissenschaft, Erziehung und Volksbildung*, 1944, 17.

creative forces of the German people'. It included enhanced attention to administrative and economic topics (dropping the suffix '-recht' from most of these), the introduction of two practical workshops, and provisions for the first examination to be conducted not by the universities but by the justice ministry (through the *Oberlandesgerichtspräsidenten*), a procedure which surely cannot have pleased either the education or the interior ministry. Although it was certainly a considerable achievement, given the deep divisions among the interested parties, the new curriculum was far less than the major training reform originally conceived by the interior ministry. Whatever hopes for the status of the civil service the ministry had placed in its plans were thus frustrated.

IV

A similar fate awaited the interior ministry's attempts in the course of the war to revise the civil-service salary system. During the campaign over the Brüning cuts, the slogan of abrogation had disguised a more fundamental demand for major structural changes in the salary system, in the interests both of rationalization and a revised distribution of salary resources. As the issue of salary policy became complicated by the pressures of the war, the relationship between structural reform and immediate partial alleviation became more entangled. Frick had pressed strongly for the abrogation measure of July 1939 as a first priority, and had refused to be fobbed off with vague promises of future comprehensive measures. When he returned to the question of the remaining cuts in December 1940, his arguments for further action continued to be couched in the fervent tones of his earlier campaign. He still catalogued much lurid evidence of need, including claims that some civil servants' salaries were too low to pay for all the rations to which they were entitled, and that the high suicide rate testified to the depressed state of civil servants' morale.[85] Interior-ministry strategy was torn between

---

[85] Interior ministry to finance ministry, 13 Dec. 1940 (BA R 18/5561). This second measure was supposed to be as secret as the first, but for evidence of the failure of this, see StdF *Stab* to *Reichsorganisationsleiter*, 28 Jan. 1941 (BA NS 22/714). This report also revealed that Ley had not been consulted about the measure; for the DAF's critique, see the report (rather muddled in its arguments) made by the DAF's Arbeitswissenschaftliches Institut, 'Die Wiederaufbesserung der Beamtenbezüge in ihrem Verhältnis zu der Lohnentwicklung in der Wirtschaft', sent by Pohl to General Thomas, 15 Feb. 1941 (BA(F) Wi/IF5/575); and see also Frick's 25-pp. letter to Ley, 10 June 1941, explaining it and justifying his salary policy in general (BA R 18/5566).

Frick's desire for immediate action to defend the status of his administration and its civil servants, and his acceptance of the fact that, in the long run, staff shortages and the defects of the heavily amended salary system could not be overcome either by merely restoring the 1927 salary schedules, or by *ad hoc* adjustments. It was this repeated process of papering over the cracks that had brought the salary system to the verge of disintegration as a coherent structure by the outbreak of the war, and that lent urgency to plans for a new salary law. Thus, the interior ministry's salary policy after 1940 reflected its interest in both immediate action and long-range planning; at the same time, it was understandably anxious that the existence of long-term plans should not be used to defer short-term measures. On the one hand, therefore, Frick kept hammering away at his provisional measure—abrogation of the remaining Brüning cuts and amendments to the salary schedules. On the other hand, the salary reform committee foreseen in the first abrogation order of July 1939 finally began to meet in 1941, and to discuss the principles of a more systematic reform of salary law.[86] Though the surviving documentation is somewhat fragmentary, the deliberations of this committee, and the policy moves initiated by Frick, offer further evidence of the ministry's attempts to link and solve the mounting pressures on the civil service and on its own authority.

The committee saw its brief as the replacement of the 1927 salary code by something more appropriate to the times. The first objective of a rewritten code was thus declared to be, 'not the claim of the individual civil servant to a higher salary, but the state's need to maintain and establish a civil service competent to carry out the tasks of national policy'.[87] More precisely, the 1927 system was regarded as most deficient in its treatment of the higher and superior grades of the service (*höherer* and *gehobener Dienst*):

The present level of salaries in these grades has led to the social decline of civil servants and thus at the same time to an exodus of the most capable . . . One of the essential tasks of salary reform is thus to get rid of the levelling of grades inherited from the Marxist period and to give greater recognition to the merit principle [*Leistungsgedanke*].[88]

What this might mean in practice was shown by notional pay rates worked out subsequently in the interior ministry: the senior grade would average an increase of 37 per cent on existing salary rates, the

---

[86] Lammers to Krosigk, 6 July 1939 (BA R 43II/432b).
[87] Minutes of meeting, 26 June 1941 (BA R 43II/429b).
[88] Ibid.

superior about 24 per cent, the intermediate (*einfacher mittlerer*) 12 per cent, and the lower (*unterer*) a somewhat more generous 19 per cent.[89] This demonstrated a clear commitment to the expansion of differentials in order to restore the status of the higher ranks that had been eroded by inflation and policy in the early 1920s, and only partially restored in the 1927 schedule.

It is significant that Bormann's representative on the committee, the career civil servant, Gerhard Klopfer, recorded his personal approval of this move, but indicated that Bormann and the Hauptamt für Beamte might not share his opinion.[90] Although it is likely that the committee's position was motivated primarily by the self-interest of a hard-pressed élite, and it certainly followed the trend initiated by the relatively non-egalitarian 1927 schedule, it did try to write up its proposals in terms acceptable to the premisses of Nazi social theory. The watchword here was 'merit' (*Leistung*), which stood for an open system of incentives and rewards for ability rather than a fixed structure of seniority and regulated increments. The latter had in any case been deeply shaken by ten years of Nazi practice. In the words of one of the committee's minutes:

Administrative procedure in practice has . . . undermined the seniority system in recent years. Whether a single outsider enters the administration or an entire administrative branch is newly incorporated (e.g. of the latter: Labour Service, NSKK etc.), in every case the civil servants involved, as well as their superiors, claim and receive a new calculation of their seniority status. This ignores regulations and is set according to age and previous experience in the private sector and in the public service.

The other public authorities, especially local government, have recklessly evaded all rules on seniority.[91]

The committee was unable to devise anything that would close all the loopholes—after all, the problem lay not only in the existing arrangements but in the certainty that any system would be equally abused. However, it did work out ways of incorporating the merit principle into the promotion system more effectively. Of some importance, too, were its discussions of how to weight the incremental structure, the aim here being to fix starting salaries at a level that would enable younger officials to support children early in life, as well as to compete with the

[89] Rüdiger memo, 28 July 1942 (BA R 18/5562).
[90] Minutes of meeting attended by representatives of the Reich chancellery, interior and finance ministries, and party chancellery, 20 Aug. 1941 (BA R 43II/429b).
[91] Minutes of meeting, 26 June 1941 (ibid.).

more attractive military and police officer scales, which were by definition designed for young men.

The committee touched here on the two critical points in a civil-service career: the time of entry, when immediate conditions as well as future prospects would either attract or deter the potential recruit, and the moment or moments later on, when an excessively rigid incremental or promotion system and an ungenerous rate of remuneration would put the civil servant at a disadvantage compared with his peers in other fields of employment.[92] In tackling them, the committee was beginning to develop a substantially new set of criteria for the salary system, in which internal incentives and the comparison with outside incomes were both far more prominent than before. These ideas had obviously made a good deal of headway before 1933, when the computation of civil-service salaries had emerged from the obscurity that had shrouded it in imperial Germany, and had become the object, if not of direct negotiation, then at least of open and sharp debate. Their more explicit adoption, now albeit in ministerial discussions rather than public debate, testified to the prominence in contemporary social thought of concepts of competition, merit, and achievement, as well as the determination (in theory) to dislodge the old élites from their protected and privileged status and to provide 'an open path for the best' (*freie Bahn den Tüchtigen*), as the slogan put it. The DAF was the tolerated organ for the residues of the Nazi populist promise, while the archetype of the newly emancipated achiever in the Third Reich was doubtless the engineer, a new and relatively classless occupation, whose skills conveniently spanned military and civilian uses, precision and monumental tasks, 'head' and 'hand', in a neat synthesis of Nazi ideals. Though the RDB faced a hopeless task in promoting its own members' nobility of labour by comparison, it nevertheless made prodigious efforts in this unrewarding direction, as we have seen. It fell to the interior ministry, however, to use the slogans of Nazi egalitarianism to serve the interests of an élite.[93]

Both the RDB and the ministry's policy-makers were animated as much by fears of the status loss suffered by the civil service as by their financial slippage—not that these were unrelated, of course. Although, given the earlier shift in the 1920s away from *Unterhalt* and towards the *Leistungstheorie*, it was no longer unheard-of to compare the civil service

92 Killy memo, 11 Nov. 1941 (ibid.).
93 For an attempt to introduce the merit principle into the Berlin municipal salary system in 1943, see documentation in BA R 36/197.

with the private labour market, this was a departure from the convention that civil-service salaries formed a closed system that operated in disjunction from the professions or private employees, and that was determined by its own, partly non-monetary, factors. The comparison with outside salaries, not with past civil-service levels, had been the linchpin of Frick's pre-war relief campaign, and it was now presented as the explicit criterion for a new salary system. Both potential recruits and established civil servants were allegedly making this comparison themselves, and drawing their own conclusions, to the growing detriment of the administration. Thus, the ostensible irrelation between civil-service and private-sector emoluments was exposed as illusory in practice—just as it was no longer plausible to assume that civil servants enjoyed automatic public status, far less that this compensated for any deficiency in pay. In this context of adverse comparisons at every level, both the banal propaganda purveyed by Neef and his cohorts and the principles formulated in the interior ministry were attempts to seize the initiative and reverse the terms, by insisting on the capacity and right of the civil service to be enrolled under the new banner of meritocracy.

The suggested arrangements for promotion also illustrated the way in which predictable rules could be combined with a degree of flexibility, and offered one solution to the problem of how to incorporate dynamic incentives into a basically fixed hierarchical system.[94] In each service grade, promotion would be standardized according to a three- or four-stage sequence, consisting of the starting position, one guaranteed promotion post, and then a limited number of higher promotion posts attainable by competition. Taken in conjunction with adjustments to the incremental and seniority systems (which would enable the civil servant to achieve a fairly high salary at the time when his family commitments were likely to be greatest), this model would permit a balance between hierarchy and competitive merit. It was hoped that it would offer attractive opportunities to the ambitious and gifted recruit, especially in the senior grade, while also satisfying the more average.

The system was also intended as a contribution to administrative rationalization, since it would abolish the confusing coexistence of up to five equally classed posts of the same rank, and would thus help to reduce the number of separate salary classes. The benefits of this would be felt not only in the operation of the salary system, but, more importantly, in the rationalization of the structure and functioning of

[94] See decisions of conference, 20 Aug. 1941 (BA R 43II/429b), and Rüdiger memo, 28 July 1942 (BA R 18/5562).

the administration as a whole. Administrative simplication was also behind the proposal that civil-service salaries should be restored to tax-free status (having been proportionately reduced). This net-rate scheme would have the advantage of relieving the tax authorities of a substantial amount of work, but against this stood the fact that the initial implementation of the scheme would be time-consuming, and that it might provoke popular resentment as taxed workers compared themselves with untaxed civil servants. Although the interior ministry was on the whole in favour of the scheme, it was opposed by the finance ministry on largely financial grounds, and by the party chancellery on political ones; it was dropped for the time being in 1942.[95]

As these ideas were being developed, Frick was also making efforts to achieve immediate revisions in the salary system. His practical programme in 1941 consisted of three linked objectives: first, the creation of more promotion posts in the interior ministry, justified by the stagnation of opportunity for upward movement; second, the upward reclassification of a large number of posts, designed to bring remuneration more into line with their allegedly expanded responsibilities; finally, the payment of supplementary allowances to some key officials, which, as we have seen in the context of pre-war policies, was a form of back-door pay increase. In detail, these schemes consisted of a long series of individual and highly technical alterations to the existing salary schedules; they did not form the basis of the systematic reform under discussion in the committee, therefore, but nevertheless served a broadly similar purpose. As Frick put it in a major *démarche* to the finance ministry in June 1941:

The problem of guaranteeing a quantitatively and qualitatively sufficient level of recruitment into the civil service at all grades, which I have been pursuing for several years with particular anxiety, will never find a satisfactory solution unless through an adequate provision of promotion posts and an appropriate valuation of the same in salary terms, which will assure candidates that the merit principle [*Leistungsgrundsatz*], to which the National Socialist state pays special regard, is also duly recognized in the civil-service profession too . . . The necessary measures . . . must be adopted straight away, and indeed with all possible expedition. To postpone them until the end of the war is unacceptable, because the process of attracting recruits . . . must begin forthwith.[96]

[95] Arguments for and against listed by Krosigk in a note to Lammers, 18 Apr. 1942 (BA R 43II/657a).

[96] See 23-pp. letter from Frick to Krosigk, 27 June 1941; full list entitled 'Anträge des RdI. betr. Besoldungsaufbesserung', probably July 1941 (both BA R 43II/429b). Frick had broached some of these issues a year earlier: see the exchange of correspondence in May and June 1940, passed to the chancellery by Krosigk, 19 June 1941 (ibid.).

Frick went on to argue that the war, annexations, and occupations had expanded the work-loads and responsibilities of certain posts, especially in the interior ministry, and that this demanded recognition. It was no accident, of course, that his specific proposals emphasized some of the key posts in the interior administration, including those of *Landrat*, *Regierungsvizepräsident*, and departmental heads in the *Oberpräsidien* and *Regierungspräsidien*, together with corresponding posts in the subordinate staffs of these offices. The point about this list of senior posts was that it was made up of the most elevated positions to which career civil servants could now aspire in the course of a normal career, since the highest ranks (the *Oberpräsident* and *Regierungspräsident*) had largely become the province of political appointments from outside the professional bureaucracy. Frick's claims on their behalf were thus designed to bolster the standing of the professional civil service (the impossible alternative would have been to abolish political nomination to posts at the apex of the administrative apparatus). Similarly troubling problems of status were revealed in the comparisons he drew between old and newly created posts: as an example, he pointed out that the recently increased salaries of the *Höhere SS- und Polizeiführer* were higher than those of the *Oberpräsidenten* to whom they were nominally subordinate.[97]

Frick's proposals were greeted with scepticism in the finance ministry, where Krosigk regarded them as an attempt to anticipate the systematic reform for which planning had only just got under way. Accordingly, Krosigk decided to 'let the matter rest' until Frick raised it again;[98] without responding directly to Frick, he allowed one of his officials to indicate that the finance ministry was not impressed by his proposals, since they favoured the interior administration and, if adopted, were likely to provoke similar demands from other ministries.[99] The Reich chancellery, to which Frick had looked for support, was equally unimpressed by his arguments. Its expert, Killy, commented that 'the Reich interior minister is pursuing almost exclusively his own interests', and he recommended Lammers to 'exercise restraint in meeting [Frick's] request for support'.[100] Like Krosigk, Killy also argued that stopgap measures would frustrate the long-range process of reform, which he envisaged as something that ought to be prepared

---

[97] On this, see documentation in BA R 43II/433b.
[98] Wever to Killy, 19 Sept. 1941 (BA R 43II/429b).
[99] Minute of conference, 25 July 1941 (ibid.).
[100] Memo on Frick's letter, 2 July 1941 (ibid.).

comprehensively and down to the last detail, ready for promulgation the moment the war ended.

Although the reform committee's discussions continued over the summer, it took another salvo from Frick, in October, to revive the question of immediate action on his requests. In a stiffly worded note to Krosigk, Frick summoned a ministerial conference, asserting that:

the severe crisis that the professional civil service is now undergoing demands immediate and drastic measures. You have surely been informed of the many endeavours I have been making, especially recently, to consolidate and raise the status of the civil service by all possible means. As much as I am aware that the main task lies in the ethical-political sphere, the material side of the problem cannot be ignored . . . An unacceptable disadvantage of our present salary system is the lack of sufficient promotion posts; this is a point which highlights the fact that our present salary law dates from the parliamentary and liberal epoch . . . Only the smallest number of civil servants have a chance to rise into a post commensurate with their performance. The greatest part have, by contrast, no prospect of securing an appropriate remuneration. An unacceptable and—for the *National Socialist* state—unworthy situation![101]

He also developed at length his justification for emphasizing the role of the interior administration. Not only had it been particularly hard hit by the promotion crisis, but 'the civil servant of the interior is far more the focus of the public interest than the civil servant of other branches . . . it is precisely the interior administration that bears the heaviest burden in the debates about the existence of the professional civil service, and whose strengthening is a matter of political importance of the first order'.

Krosigk regarded Frick's initiative as an unwarranted intrusion on his own authority as finance minister; he also argued that Frick's proposals would set off similar demands from other ministries, especially in relation to the armed forces.[102] Frick in turn was outraged, declaring that as minister for the civil service he had the right 'to issue invitations to a conference on questions that are so important and decisive for the fate of the civil service . . . even when these have consequences for financial policy. Otherwise the competence of every minister would have no more than paper value!'[103] The ultimate outcome of all this bad

---

[101] Frick to Krosigk, 20 Oct. 1941 (ibid.). Frick was now including the abrogation of the final 6 per cent of cuts in his list of demands; for finance-ministry views on this, see statement by Krosigk, 6 Dec. 1941 (BA R 2/22009c).

[102] Finance ministry to Reich chancellery, 22 Oct. 1941 (BA R 43II/429b).

[103] Interior ministry to finance ministry, 27 Oct. 1941 (ibid.).

feeling—a compromise conference in November, attended by Lammers, Krosigk, Frick, and Popitz, which established general guidelines for future procedure on salary issues—can hardly have satisfied Frick.[104] Although much of his argumentation about promotions and salary levels was accepted in principle—as, indeed, had long been the case in certain circles—the conference decided that this should only be adopted in the new salary system, to come into force as soon as the war ended. Frick did get some support from Popitz for his insistence on building up a strong *Mittelinstanz*, and it was agreed that preparations for the new law should forge ahead 'with all possible speed', but this must have been a disappointing outcome to the consistent pressure he had been applying.

In any event, as we have seen, work on the salary reform began to run out of steam a year later, as post-war prospects dimmed. The interior ministry resumed its demands for immediate measures, arguing that the unforeseen continuation of the war and the postponement of salary reform rendered the principles established in November 1941 no longer applicable.[105] Regular battles were now taking place over the annual budget draft, as Frick (and other ministers) tried to achieve their ends by padding their estimates rather than by amendments to the salary law. Moreover, in order to justify a measure it was increasingly important to argue that it was 'strategically necessary' (*kriegswichtig*) according to the narrowing criteria now being adopted. For by 1942, the manpower problems that had loomed on the horizon since the beginning of the war were becoming inescapable, leading to growing pressures on the staffing and operation of the civil administration.

V

When Lammers had drawn up his lengthy critical comments on Göring's plan for a rationalization commission in 1942, the issue of manpower deployment was uppermost in his mind: 'As a top priority it is essential that the Führer give the Wehrmacht the command to be ruthless in its conscription of all [public employees] in question. Objections to this must be impermissible in principle . . . Only in this way, by means of

---

[104] Minutes of conference, 25 Nov. 1941 (ibid.).

[105] See documentation in GStA P 134/338, especially interior ministry to Prussian finance ministry, 5 Jan. 1943. An interim measure, the 36th amendment to the salary law, which raised salaries in the top, non-incremental ranks, was eventually adopted on 30 Mar. 1943 (*RGBl*, 1943, i. 189).

an absolute compulsion to renounce part of their staffs, will the authorities be brought to the point of introducing the concrete rationalization that is required.'[106] The urgency of the situation in the third year of war was hardly surprising. Civilian-labour procurement and deployment, including meeting the demands of the administrative apparatus, had already been identified before 1939 as a key area of weakness for a prospective war economy, and in theory steps had been taken to identify the worst dangers in peacetime and plan for their alleviation.[107] Yet the outbreak of war did not lead to the implementation of any systematic plans for labour procurement. Although the labour shortage was becoming increasingly critical by 1942, it is well known that severe limitations were placed on the recruitment of labour to the military and civilian war effort by the unwillingness or inability of the German government to exploit its native resources to the utmost. Civilian conscription was less comprehensive and effective than in wartime Britain, for example, notably in respect of the reserve army of female labour. The reasons for this have become the subject of considerable debate among historians, and are not in themselves the central issue here.[108] What is important is the fact that the labour shortages had growing repercussions on administrative policy and planning.

Although there may have been greater offenders than Frick as far as effective labour distribution and utilization were concerned, he took the blame for his apparent inability to control the manpower needs of the largest consumer of administrative labour power in the German political system. Thus, as the shortages intensified after 1941, the interior administration came under increasing suspicion of protecting its own and failing to deliver its quota of personnel to the armed forces and to essential war work. Criticism focused particularly on the growth of the ministry's own central staff—between 1937 and 1941, for example, it

[106] Lammers memo, 23 Jan. 1942 (BA R 43II/706a).
[107] See meetings of Reichsverteidigungsrat in 1938-9, especially in 2nd session, 23 June 1939 (BA(F) Wi/F5/560 (1), 4-14).
[108] For Britain, see M. Gowing, 'The Organisation of Manpower in Britain during the Second World War', *JCH*, 7 (1972), 147-62; P. Summerfield, *Women Workers in the Second World War* (London, 1984). For Germany, see U. von Gersdorff, *Frauen im Kriegsdienst 1914-1945* (Stuttgart, 1969); T. Mason, 'Women in Nazi Germany, Part I', *History Workshop Journal*, 1 (1976), 74-113, and 'Women in Germany, 1925-1940: Family, Welfare and Work', *History Workshop Journal*, 2 (1976), 5-32; D. Winkler, *Frauenarbeit im 'Dritten Reich'* (Hamburg, 1977); L. J. Rupp, *Mobilizing Women for War: German and American Propaganda* (Princeton, 1978).

had grown from 371 officials to 463, by 1942, to 687[109]—and on the persistent problem of the *Mittelinstanz*, where the coexistence of *Reichsstatthalter* and *Regierungspräsidenten* continued to present a glaring instance of the very duplication that ministry officials deplored so frequently.[110] With the growing pressure on manpower, it was inevitable that authorities would fight to retain their own staffs, and point the finger at other culprits instead; moreover, it was easy enough to find examples of others' egregious failings with which to counter or forestall criticisms of one's own. But from the point of view of the administrative policy-makers themselves, the pressures on the civilian bureaucracy to yield more of its members to military service intensified fears that the civil service was being wilfully shorn of the staff necessary for the adequate performance of its duties, so that these could be reassigned to the party's own agencies. As before, the interior ministry identified itself closely with the interests of the bureaucracy as such, sometimes ingenuously, but often with the ulterior motive of maintaining its own competitive status in the struggle for personnel. These anxieties only thinly masked the underlying fear that the civil service was losing its battle for authority and status to intrusive competitors from the party, the SS, and the secondary bureaucratic apparatuses of the occupied territories—not to mention the armed forces themselves—all of which were now swallowing up vast numbers of personnel. And once again, the question of the relative quality and status of the officials staffing these competitive bureaucratic systems was just as important as the issue of sheer numbers.

The sense of imminent crisis became more acute during the war, when the further radical shift of political priorities intensified fears that civil servants had been abandoned by Germany's political leadership. Frick's early wartime efforts on this score were intended as much to assert the administrative interests he claimed to represent as to alleviate manpower problems as such. He repeatedly linked the evidence of crisis to his own programme of solutions, arguing that only his model of administrative reform would finally put an end to the chronic problems of understaffing and overwork. After Frick's departure in 1943, however, it seems that the interior ministry no longer pressed its case quite so strongly; indeed, some of its senior officials appeared to doubt that the personnel shortage was really as critical as it had been painted, with

[109] See list, 'Planstellen im RMdI', May 1941 (BA R 2/11664), and GBV to Reich and party chancelleries, 23 Feb. 1942 (BA R 43II/708a).

[110] For this problem, which was most acute in Prussia, see Diehl-Thiele, *Partei und Staat*, ch. 3.

the implication that the profession was even willing to sabotage the war effort in order to defend its sectional interests. In other words, the evidence on this issue must be read not simply as an account of a 'real' crisis in staffing levels. More tellingly, it may be seen as symptomatic of the profession's fears of status decline, and of the obsessive protectionism of its defenders.

The manpower question thus consisted of two distinct but related components: the crisis of recruitment (*Nachwuchsmangel*) in the civil service, which dated from well before the war, and the wartime manpower deployment problem. These issues were separate to the extent that the latter was largely a problem of the efficient utilization of personnel, while the former was a problem of the attraction of personnel, all other things being equal. They were related through the argument that if the administration as a whole were more efficiently organized, the alleged recruitment and staffing crisis would shrink to more manageable proportions. But if both problems remained recalcitrant to solution, they would continue in a spiral of mutual exacerbation. This would then redound to the discredit of the interior ministry, as both the ministry responsible for civil-service affairs, as well as a massive employer of administrative personnel: it would be exposed as capable of mastering neither its business nor its own staff. Although all branches of the administration, indeed, all employers of labour, were under increasing pressure from the growing manpower crisis in Germany after 1941, it was the interior ministry that took upon itself the special burden of managing the crisis of the professional civil service.

The rationalization measures already discussed were largely designed to reduce the staffing needs of the administrative apparatus within Germany in order to release personnel to the armed forces and for the occupation staffs. As the pace of the war accelerated after 1941, Germany began to suffer from an acute labour shortage that could be relieved in one sector only by competition with another. New tasks were now falling to the share of the administration in Germany and the occupied territories: mobilization, requisitioning, and evacuation, the supervision of the multiplying apparatuses of economic control and of German and foreign labour, the growing burdens of social welfare. Later, air raids and evacuations further aggravated the conditions of everyday work: communications were disrupted, offices of paperwork were scattered or destroyed. All this had to be survived with severely reduced staffs. By January 1943, the interior administration had lost about half of its nominal establishment, and was relying heavily on older men (including many plucked out of retirement) and on women; staff losses in the judicial administration at the same date ranged from 55 per cent of senior civil servants, to 83 per cent of those in the lowest grade.[111] The annexed and occupied territories also took thousands of personnel away from the Reich, especially eastwards: already by November 1939, some 70-80,000 German officials had been seconded to the *Ostgebiete*.[112] Of 8,108 officials (*Beamte* and *Angestellte*) enumerated in a partial survey of the establishments of the central Reich authorities in 1942, over a thousand had been seconded to duties in the annexed eastern provinces, on top of the 1,856 conscripted into the armed forces.[113] The judicial administration alone was providing over 6,000 officials in the occupied and annexed territories in mid-1942.[114] By 1943, the occupied territories were consuming the efforts of 263,593 seconded personnel, mainly from the transportation and financial/customs branches.[115] Morale among those sent to these unfamiliar and hostile areas was usually said to be poor,[116] and government policy, which wavered between identifying service in the east as an honour and as a punitive transfer, was confusing.[117] These cumulative staff losses sapped the capacities of the administrations from which they were taken, yet they were still not sufficient to meet the demand. Foreign labour, which was used extensively if inefficiently in industry and agriculture, was not supposed to make quite the same contribution to administration, but nevertheless had to be employed, if reluctantly.[118]

By 1942, Krosigk was describing the staffing position of the finance

[111] For the interior administration, see preliminary discussion notes prepared in the interior ministry, 4 Jan. 1943 (BA R 18/5476); also interior ministry to OKW, 26 Feb. 1943 (BA R 18/5568). For the judicial administration, see appendix to Reich chancellery memo, 3 Mar. 1943 (BA R 43II/661).

[112] *SD-Meldungen aus dem Reich*, 22 Jan. 1940, 43, 8-9 (BA R 58/147).

[113] GBV to Reich and party chancelleries, 23 Feb. 1942 (BA R 43II/708a).

[114] Führer-Information, 13, 1942, 21 May 1942 (copy in BA R 43II/1559a).

[115] 'Übersicht über die in die Gebiete ausserhalb der Reichsgrenze abgeordneten Bediensteten der Zivilverwaltung', dated 'Frühjahr 1943' (BA R 43F/3511); and see also Krosigk circular to Göring, Frick, the Reich chancellery, and other ministries, 4 Sept. 1942, deploring the personnel and financial chaos and wastage of administration in the east (BA NS 6/166).

[116] *SD-Meldungen aus dem Reich*, e.g. 24 June 1940, 99, 18-19 (BA R 58/151), 28 Nov. 1940, 145, 27-8 (R 58/156).

[117] See e.g. GBV circular to Reich ministries, 18 Apr. 1940, deploring a case in which a civil servant was offered transfer to the east as an alternative to imprisonment, and much similar documentation, in BA R 43II/425.

[118] See e.g. interior ministry to *Regierungspräsident* in Kattowitz, 14 Apr. 1942, re local employment of Poles (BA R 18/1916).

administration as 'catastrophic', and threatening that he could not take responsibility for the consequences if he lost yet more personnel.[119] In the interior ministry, Stuckart, a keen critic of administrative disorganization, identified the overall problem as one of rational deployment:

It is not conceivable that if the current prodigal use of manpower continues we will be capable of an effective reconstruction of Europe or leadership of the continent. As a result of the existing double and treble organization of business in Germany, not only are people being detained in the Altreich when they are urgently needed for the development of the new territories, but we face the danger that the error of overlapping organization will be exported to the new territories and will lead to the same failings there.[120]

On the ground, too, the problems looked no less daunting: 'I see the time not far off', wrote a Pomeranian *Landrat* in 1942, 'when the authorities will no longer be able to meet their obligations; their failure will certainly have intolerable consequences. What this would mean for the conduct of the war and the war economy hardly needs to be specified.'[121]

The Hitler decrees of January and March 1942 had stimulated a further burst of departmental reviews which Frick struggled to maintain some semblance of supervising. Executive instructions issued by Lammers in February made it clear that the January decree had not created any new powers, but had merely reiterated the original rationalization decree of 28 August 1939. All measures of 'general' scope were still to be cleared with Frick, as plenipotentiary, and he was also to ensure that personnel released from inessential work in one department were transferred expeditiously to other more urgent tasks. Given all prior experience of bureaucratic imperialism in Nazi Germany, it was hardly surprising that Lammers specifically urged that ancient rivalries should now be set aside, and that departments should not try to take over jurisdictions vacated by their colleagues.[122] (During the dis-

119 Krosigk to Lammers, 17 Mar. 1942, objecting to his ministry's inclusion in schemes by which personnel were shifted from one branch to another in response to work-loads (BA R 43II/657).

120 Stuckart, in meeting with Lammers, 5 Mar. 1942 (BA R 18/5451). See also his 'Zentralgewalt, Dezentralisation und Verwaltungseinheit', in *Festgabe für Heinrich Himmler* (Berlin, 1941), 1-32; *Führung und Verwaltung im Kriege* (Berlin, 1941); and 'Die Vereinfachung der Verwaltung im Kriege', *DV*, 1942, 121-4.

121 Report from the *Landrat* in Stolp, sent by Schwede-Coburg to the interior ministry, 29 Oct. 1942 (BA R 18/5476).

122 Reich chancellery instructions, 4 Feb. 1942 (BA R 43II/706a). A reminder was issued on 6 Mar. 1943 (BA R 43II/657a).

cussions of the March decrees he had expressed a particular fear that party organizations would try to leap into breaches opened by state agencies.) Decentralization and labour-saving measures now adopted by the interior ministry included the elimination of one level of the administrative court system, the transfer of certain decisions to subordinate authorities, and the suspension of such inessential business as the changing of street names. Similarly, the finance ministry rationalized or abolished some low-yielding taxes, and took steps to simplify the income tax system. The interior ministry aimed to reduce its central staffing to 50 per cent of its 1939 male complement, the economics ministry to 40 per cent; the education ministry reported that its central senior staff now numbered no more than 94 civil servants, who oversaw the 300,000 personnel of the educational system.[123] When Göring complained to Lammers in April that 'virtually nothing has been accomplished in the question of administrative simplification', Lammers was able to send him a bundle of forty reports on the rationalization measures adopted in the different branches of the administration since January. These included a nineteen-page summary of the 264 measures adopted in the interior administration alone since the January decrees, along with a further 130 pages of detailed reports—a massive documentation that was clearly intended to overwhelm Göring's criticisms.[124]

Yet the process of rationalization was far from straightforward, as the following example shows. By the end of the year, a small internal commission appointed by Frick in June 1942 was reporting on its investigation into the local effects of the new round of rationalization in the interior administration, and offering proposals for further measures.[125] The commission consisted of four interior-ministry officials (the most senior being Ministerialdirigent Danckwerts), one representative from the Prussian finance ministry, and one each from the offices of a *Reichsstatthalter/Oberpräsident* and a *Regierungspräsident*. Its findings, which were based on a study of three *Oberpräsidien* and ten *Regierungen*, illustrate the professional bureaucracy's opinion of the state of the field administration after ten years of Nazi rule, at a point when, in the commission's own words, 'the interior

[123] For these and similar measures, see Reich chancellery memos, 3 and 26 Mar. 1942 (BA R 43II/708, ff. 53-9).

[124] Lammers to Göring, 24 May 1942, with enclosures (ibid., ff. 80-91).

[125] 'Bericht der vom GBV eingesetzten Kommission 2' (45-pp. plus appendix), 25 Nov. 1942 (BA R 18/2898a).

administration clearly stands before a fateful turning-point'. The war had obviously imposed severe strains of its own, notably in the loss of some 40 to 50 per cent of personnel in the two senior grades of the field administration, but the commission also identified as the principal problem a state of affairs that had long pre-dated the war, and that was indeed a *de facto* principle of Nazi government. This was the creation of numerous special offices and agencies that lacked 'exact delimitations of responsibility':

It is one of the most characteristic organizational principles of the National Socialist state that tasks of great political priority, which can be solved in a timely fashion only by deploying maximum resources of power, are assigned not to agencies with clearly defined competences, but to *a trusted individual* [*Vertrauensperson*] *furnished with sweeping powers*. In organizational terms this is unobjectionable if the existing administrative agencies are put at the disposal of this kind of commissar and if—functioning simply as a central authority—he makes use of them and does not create a new apparatus of his own. But it leads ineluctably to the gravest difficulties if commissars of this kind turn up at *Gau* or *Kreis* level, and if sooner or later they acquire the form of a new authority equipped with its own comprehensive powers.

In other words, special commissions were being vastly over-used in the Third Reich, and in particular had been allowed to develop into entire ramified systems with their own chains of command and field offices—precisely what the interior ministry wanted to combat in the name of a uniform and concentrated field administration. The examples singled out included the complex of administrative authorities in the conquered territories of eastern Europe, notably Himmler's Commissariat for the Strengthening of Germandom, and the Haupttreuhandstelle Ost, an arm of Göring's Four-Year Plan. The commission was doubtless correct in drawing particular attention to the peculiar and threatening context of eastern European administration, but the problem also existed within the Altreich, where the Four-Year Plan maintained another complex of agencies and offices, and where numerous special commissions for everything from road-building to school-books worked away unfettered by subordination to any central authority.[126] Moreover, as the report continued, these new authorities were now unable to secure enough experienced staff to run efficiently the business assigned to them. The commission saw little hope of

---

[126] See list dated 31 Jan. 1942 (BA R 43II/706). For Bormann's not dissimilar views on the proliferation of independent commissions, see his internal memo for Friedrichs, 22 Mar. 1942 (BA R 2/31904).

improvement during the war and while 'the final picture of the nature and organization of the state' remained unclear. It argued, however, that administrative concentration was indispensable, and that only the classic specialist ministries (justice, finance, posts, and railways) should maintain their own field systems. The rest—i.e. virtually the entire administrative amoeba spawned since 1933, if not earlier—ought, it implied, to be assigned to the interior administration, which otherwise risked 'being shunted aside into the role of a specialist administration' if what it called the 'pluralistic imperialism' that now characterized German administration continued to gain ground. If the interior administration failed to fight back immediately, it would have lost its role by the time the war ended: it had already, for example, forfeited to special commissions or new ministries most of its powers in public works, energy, transport, and more:

It appears certain that under its own leadership the interior administration has not had the strength to withstand effectively the increasing tendencies towards fragmentation, for in the great game of power it is after all a basically unpolitical body. In the revolutionary dynamics of our times the administration does not carry enough weight to impress its own stamp upon the continuing process of development.

The interesting conclusion to which the authors came was that since the interior administration lacked independent power, it ought to attach itself to one of the more effective power centres in Nazi Germany, either the NSDAP or the SS. To this end, the commission envisaged an extension and formalization of dual office-holding between party and state in such a way as to eliminate some of the worst points of friction: for example, not only could the *Gauleiter-Oberpräsident* system be made more uniform, but the old and vexed question of the relationship between *Oberpräsidenten* and *Regierungspräsidenten*, who shared authority at the intermediate level, could be solved if the two were merged. The means were radical, but the commission's aim was still the restoration of concentrated and effective authority on the interior administration—assuming that it could survive this political transfusion unchanged. In practical terms, the commission claimed that its survey of the field apparatus indicated that the specialist administrations had been far more successful than the interior administration in retaining their staffs, and that this posed a serious threat to the latter's status: 'This danger should not be made light of, for it is likely to shake the interior administration to its core.' It recommended that the ministry show no generosity in releasing its younger age-groups to the armed services, on the telling basis that this would have no appreciable effect on the prestige of the administration and carried considerable disadvantages. The answer to the problem of manpower procurement within the administrative apparatus was, it suggested, the establishment of a neutral commission which would be free of suspicions of bias in its decisions.

The immediate fate of these proposals is unclear, but they appear to have influenced interior-ministry thinking during the next round of administrative rationalization. This had been inaugurated a few days previously, when a review commission of sorts had in fact been established, apparently in an attempt to rationalize and unify the process of labour procurement in order to provide the general staff with the million new soldiers it was requesting. The origin of this commission, as well as its authorization, is obscure. The instrument of appointment was an 'instruction' (*Anordnung*) of the Führer, which was also signed by the three members of the so-called 'Drei-Männer-Ausschuss' (Three-Man committee), Keitel, Bormann, and Lammers (not to be confused with the Dreierkollegium of the ministerial council). It appointed the infantry general, von Unruh, as a special commissioner (*Sonderbeauftragter*), with the task of 'examining whether in view of the demands of the war all forces are being appropriately deployed and fully utilized'.[127] Von Unruh was authorized to establish his own staff, and given powers, overriding existing statutory provisions if necessary, to demand that underused personnel be 'made available' and that offices he deemed to be non-strategic should be abolished or reorganized. These were nominally substantial powers to be invested in a single person. However, their impact was muted by the stipulation that any measures 'of substantial political or other extensive significance' could be submitted by those Reich authorities affected to Hitler's decision, via Lammers. Moreover, Keitel was delegated with this power for measures affecting the armed forces, Bormann for those affecting the party, and Göring for the economy.

The instruction marked the beginning of a new stage in the linked processes of labour procurement and administrative rationalization. Its simultaneous concentration and dispersal of authority were also typical

---

[127] Instruction, 22 Nov. 1942 (copy in BA R 43II/604a, ff. 139-40). For the Drei-Männer-Ausschuss, see Carroll, *Design for Total War*, p. 242, and Homze, *Foreign Labor*, p. 210, though in these sources its origin is dated to Jan. and Feb. 1943 respectively; *Goebbels Diaries*, p. 198.

of those delicate gyrations among the powerful of which this period affords so many examples. The winter of 1942-3, with defeat looming at Stalingrad, was a period of intense political struggle over the future direction of German mobilization, with Bormann, Sauckel, and Göring resisting the pressures exerted by Speer and Goebbels for a total mobilization.[128] Hitler's decisions throughout 1943 wavered under the impact of these different pressures, responding now to the one, now to the other. The direction of policy was not clear-cut; rather, the build-up to the ceremonial declaration of the total war strategy in July 1944 emerged piecemeal. Von Unruh's appointment was followed by the issue, early in January 1943, of a Führer decree 'For the Comprehensive Mobilization of Men and Women for the Tasks of National Defence', in which the term 'total war' made its first statutory appearance.[129] The stated purpose of this decree was to release all suitable manpower for conscription and for arms production by applying stringent criteria for all exemptions, and by ensuring that only strategically essential employment would be permitted. Once more, the civilian authorities were enjoined to suspend non-essential work, and they were empowered to deviate from existing law. Hitler's previous rationalization decree of 25 January 1942 (itself basically a repetition of the August 1939 decree) was 'to be applied in more strenuous measure', and a total ban on post-war planning was imposed. The decree also instructed Sauckel to begin the registration of all non-mobilized adults (those employed by public authorities were among the exempted categories), which was duly embarked upon.[130] Once again, the authorizations conferred by this decree were politically dispersed, partly in view of the already chequered map of authority in existence, partly in response to the disposition of other vested interests. It was counter-signed, following Hitler's signature, by the members of the Three-Man Committee. Göring's authority to issue instructions as air force minister and chief of the Four-Year Plan was confirmed, however, to be supplemented by measures issued by the Reich authorities and the *Reichsverteidigungs-*

---

[128] Homze, *Foreign Labor*, pp. 209 ff. On labour mobilization in this period, see also D. Eichholtz, *Geschichte der deutschen Kriegswirtschaft 1939-1945* (E. Berlin, 1985), ii. *1945-1943*, ch. 4; Herbst, *Der Totale Krieg*, pp. 198-218; Winkler, *Frauenarbeit*, ch. 7.

[129] *Erlass des Führers über den umfassenden Einsatz von Männern und Frauen für Aufgaben der Reichsverteidigung*, 13 Jan. 1943 (unpublished) (BA R 43II/604a); reprinted in Gersdorff, *Frauen im Kriegsdienst*, pp. 375-7. Like the Nov. decree, this was signed by Hitler, and counter-signed by the 'Three Wise Men' (Goebbels' term for the Drei-Männer-Ausschuss).

[130] *VO über die Meldung von Männern und Frauen für Aufgaben der Rechtsverteidigung*, 27 Jan. 1943 (*RGBl*, 1943, i. 67); Winkler, *Frauenarbeit*, pp. 134-42.

kommissare. In addition, the committee was instructed to keep Hitler informed about those measures implemented and further ones required, and empowered to issue further orders, but at the same time it was to keep in close contact with Goebbels; and von Unruh was instructed to 'support them in their actions and conduct his commission in agreement with [the committee]'.

These measures provided the framework for the further progress of administrative rationalization until the total mobilization decree of July 1944.[131] Labour procurement for military and civilian purposes was now in theory under the supervision of the Three-Man Committee and von Unruh, but Sauckel and Speer retained considerable independent authority. As far as procurement from the government sector was concerned, von Unruh's initial appointment had been followed by some discussion of administrative strategies, in which Stuckart set out the interior ministry's accomplishments and future plans.[132] The interior administration had given up 35 per cent of its senior civil servants to the army, and a further 15 per cent was on secondment; overall, it was now largely staffed by 50- to 60-year-olds. The interior administration proper was now said to muster some 5,000 senior civil servants, with about 24,000 in all other grades; local government, including municipal enterprises, still employed about half a million *Beamte,* along with 350,000 *Angestellte* and 650,000 *Arbeiter*—enough, no doubt, to whet Sauckel's appetite—but women represented about 50-60 per cent of this. Moreover, throughout 1942 and 1943 the interior administration continued to resist the army's and Sauckel's unremitting demands for manpower, arguing that it had reached the limit of its capacity to release personnel, and threatening dire consequences for the administration if more were forcibly taken. Thus, a chancellery memo in August 1943 asserted that the latest figures demanded by Sauckel (15,000 from the GBV, 10,000 from the finance administration) were 'bureaucratic inventions', and that 'the administrations have already been bled bonedry, and can hardly perform even the most urgent, life-and-death tasks'.[133] On a local level, the *Landrat* of Düren reported in January 1942 that staffing in the county administration had '*reached a point*

131 See also the executive order for the administration issued by Lammers, 17 Jan. 1943 (BA R 43II/604a).

132 Internal memo by Stuckart, 30 Dec. 1942, and notes for discussion, undated; also minutes of meeting with von Unruh, 4 Jan. 1943; and draft of interior ministry to Lammers, Jan. 1943 (all BA R 18/5476).

133 Reich chancellery memo, 23 Aug. 1943 (BA R 43II/656a); see also interior ministry to OKW, 26 Feb. 1942 (BA R 18/5568).

beyond which an orderly performance of work in this sector of the administration is no longer possible', and warned of an impending '*catastrophe*', while the *Regierungspräsident* in Potsdam spoke of '*signs of a danger of collapse*' in the interior administration.[134] Even so, civil-service numbers continued to shrink: between mid-1942 and mid-1943, the personnel of state administration and self-government fell by some twenty thousand, from 568,074 to 547,993.[135] In March 1943, the *Regierungspräsident* in Kattowitz reported that: 'There are large administrative offices which no longer have a single *Beamte*, and where an acting official, who is often also only an acting official for a neighbouring district, has to conduct the administration with a few entirely unreliable ethnic German or Polish assistants.'[136]

In Stuckart's view, further labour-saving depended upon the solution of some of those problems of administrative disorganization which he had pilloried for so long, and which had figured in the Danckwerts commission's deliberations. But many of these suggestions had been expressly forbidden by Hitler, including the amalgamation of neigh-bouring *Landratsämter*, the incorporation of offices at *Regierung* level with those of the *Reichsstatthalter/Oberpräsidenten*, and, indeed, any measures which involved territorial changes or affected the 'basic structure' of the administration.[137] After an apparently constructive meeting between ministry staff and von Unruh at the beginning of January, Frick prepared for another round of efforts on behalf of his rationalization strategy, sending Lammers and Bormann an identical account of the problems and soliciting their good offices in securing Hitler's support for his solutions.[138] He rehearsed once more the now familiar trinity of administrative chaos: fragmentation, duplication, and centralism. As to the first of these, he pointed out that 'hardly any office can enforce measures independently without the involvement of another authority. I recently learned from a *Landrat*'s report that he has

[134] Enclosures in Frick to Lammers, 12 Feb. 1942 (BA R 43II/707a).

[135] Calculated from figures given in a memo by Kritzinger, 17 July 1944 (BA R 43II/664a).

[136] *Regierungspräsident* in Kattowitz to interior ministry, 15 Mar. 1943 (BA R 18/3710) (the problem here was that Greiser, against ministry advice, had volunteered the age cohorts of 1901 and below for conscription, thereby depriving himself of what had been, on the whole, a fairly young staff).

[137] This veto obstructed, for example, territorial changes proposed by Schwede-Coburg and Mutschmann in 1942, though both were finally implemented (see documentation in BA R 18/5313 and R 43II/658b respectively).

[138] Frick to Lammers and Bormann, 1 Apr. 1943 (copy in BA R 18/5476). An undated 14-pp. set of recommendations for action under the Jan. decree, possibly by Stuckart, may have served as notes for this letter (BA R 18/5452).

to work with 67 separate offices at *Kreis* level!' The second count brought evidence of tasks shared among different state, party, and private authorities—for example, youth welfare was split between the *Jugendämter, Regierungspräsidenten, Landesjugendämter*, courts of guardians (*Vormundschaftsrichter*), HJ, NSV, labour office, DAF, 'and so on'. Frick also drew particular attention to the continuing parallelism of *Landrat* and *Kreisleiter*, and hinted that this was causing increasing friction as the *Kreisleiter*, taking advantage of the reduced staffs of the *Landräte*, refused to confine themselves to their task of 'Menschen-führung' and intervened in administrative tasks.[139] On the third count, centralism was encouraged by this state of affairs in general; where competences were divided at the subordinate level, appeals constantly had to be made to the central authorities to adjudicate disputes. Frick ended by reiterating his commitment to decentralization, but only where there was also a strong central authority, discipline, and compliance.

The ministry's practical proposals for implementing the January decree now included continuing plans to amalgamate some party and state offices and other attempts to end parallel organization, as well as further simplifications in civil-service law. These were discussed at a ministerial conference in February which was attended, among others, by Frick, Krosigk, Lammers, Bormann, and Goebbels, and at which the interior and finance ministers bargained over which rights in civil-service law each was prepared to renounce.[140] It proved easier to reach agreement on the simplification of details in civil-service law than on the vexed question of party-state relations; but the situation was acknowledged to be sufficiently chaotic for all to agree to research concrete examples of the latter problem in order to get some response from Hitler.

This February conference, which set the terms of the interior ministry's policies until the middle of 1944, was one of numerous similar discussions with Reich ministries conducted by Goebbels and the Three-Man Committee. In the course of the next eighteen months, hundreds of separate measures were adopted to speed the release of men to the army and to register and redeploy manpower in the economy. By July 1944, over 800,000 men had been conscripted, over 1.6 million

[139] The problem of *Kreisleiter-Landrat* relations is discussed in Diehl-Thiele, *Partei und Staat*, pp. 193-7; also Mommsen, *Beamtentum*, pp. 111-23, 223-41.
[140] Minutes of conference, 10 Feb. 1943, and see also internal preliminary notes, undated (BA R 18/5452).

men and women had been registered for labour, and almost half a million others had been redeployed.[141] All ministries claimed to have made numerous new moves to simplify procedures and to close down dispensable offices—the finance ministry, for example, had closed or amalgamated many of its local finance offices, the justice ministry had done the same with some lower courts. Similar steps had been taken by the party, including closing the HfB. Frick and Krosigk had managed to agree on a measure, known as the 'Stoperlass', which simplified major elements of civil-service law; it included a ban on amendments to the salary system and on exemptions from certain training and appointment regulations.[142] But Hitler persisted in his veto on those more far-reaching measures of regional reorganization which would have affected the existing disposition of political authority; thus, many of the most serious problems of administrative disorganization were never tackled.[143]

This was the context in which the final push for the adoption of a total war strategy was developed. By the end of 1943, Speer was arguing strenuously that the measures adopted under the January 1943 Hitler decree had been insufficient to meet the demand for manpower, and that plenipotentiary powers for a total mobilization should be concentrated on a single person.[144] On 22 July—two days after the attempt on Hitler's life—the chief participants in the mobilization debate (including Bormann, Keitel, Goebbels, Speer, Sauckel, and Funk, along with Lammers, Stuckart, and other ministerial representatives, but not including Frick, Göring, or any representative of the foreign ministry) met in the chancellery to discuss a draft decree for total

[141] Figures from memo by Boley (Reich chancellery), 'Zusammenfassung der Massnahmen unter Führererlass 13. 1. 43', 22 July 1944 (BA R 43II/664).

[142] Reich chancellery instructions, 17 Feb. 1943 (copy in BA R 2/22207). Its severity was subsequently mitigated in several respects (see further documentation here and in BA R 43II/654a). For examples of the problem of granting exemptions, see Lammers' memo on propaganda-ministry promotions practices, 24 Oct. 1942 (BA R 43II/458a); documentation on the regrading of senior SS and police officers, 1941-2 (BA R 18/5568); also the 36th amendment to the salary law, 30 Mar. 1943 (*RGBl*, 1943, i. 189), which raised salaries in some of the top, non-incremental posts.

[143] For examples of such issues, see documentation in BA R 43II/656 (attempted amalgamation of *Regierungspräsidien* with *Oberpräsidien*, 1943-4), and 658 (incorporations of *Länder* ministries, 1943); also, the dissolution of Popitz's Prussian finance ministry, proposed by Krosigk in Feb. 1943, but accomplished only after the 1944 July plot on political grounds (BA R 43II/1363c).

[144] For Speer's position and arguments in 1943, see Milward, *German Economy*, pp. 151-5; Herbst, *Der Totale Krieg*, pp. 255-76; and Broszat, *The Hitler State*, pp. 312-3.

mobilization, devoting a good deal of their time to the tactical question of how to present it to Hitler.[145] Lammers summarized the effects of the Three-Man Committee's efforts, explaining that it had used its powers as best it could, but that the present situation was so critical that a committee was no longer appropriate: one man had to take charge, and the most suitable man was Goebbels. Goebbels then spoke at length, emphasizing the propaganda challenge of convincing a reluctant nation that this really was total war. All resistance to the delivery of manpower for the war effort now had to be broken; von Unruh had proved unable to stand up to the civil authorities, and had not accomplished enough; the essential aim of providing manpower for munitions was now the priority.[146] After some further discussion of Goebbels's powers and the measures that might be taken, and some argument about whether administration was swallowing up more labour than it merited, Lammers was delegated as the group's spokesman. Three days later, he submitted the revised draft of the decree to Hitler, who approved it and instructed Lammers to summon a meeting of ministers and state secretaries at which Goebbels would announce his appointment; 'No debate was to take place in this session'.

The published decree, signed by Hitler, Lammers, and Bormann, obfuscated its own origins by stating that Göring, as head of the (long defunct) ministerial council, was to nominate for Hitler's approval a plenipotentiary for total war, whose responsibility it would be 'to ensure that all public institutions are fitted for the objective of total war and do not deprive army and munitions of manpower'.[147] There ensued inevitable arguments about the effect of the decree in centralizing decision-making, with Bormann protesting that it fettered freedom of action at *Gau* level, where the *Gauleiter* and *Reichsverteidigungskommissare* represented a form of party field administration under his authority.[148]

As far as administrative policy was concerned, total mobilization was merely a tightening of the screw. In August, the justice ministry was expected to provide 28,000 men for the armed services, while the education and postal administrations were to hand over 35,000 between

---

[145] This account is reconstructed from documentation in BA R 43II/664a.

[146] As we have seen, his authority had been drafted in such a way as to make resistance not only possible, but inevitable.

[147] *Erlass des Führers über den totalen Kriegseinsatz*, 25 July 1944 (*RGBl*, 1944, i. 161). See also Herbst, *Der Totale Krieg*, pp. 343-4; Homze, *Foreign Labor*, pp. 223-9.

[148] See documentation in BA R 43II/666a, leading to Reich chancellery circular, 25 Sept. 1944; Hüttenberger, *Gauleiter*, pp. 188 ff., 200-3.

them;[149] the intermediate levels of the interior administration were ordered to yield 30 per cent of their usable staffs.[150] Discussions of further simplifications in civil-service law continued, with wrangling over proposals for both a promotion bar and a ban on all salary adjustments continuing to the bitter end; the salary issue roused all the old arguments about the value placed on civil servants' work.[151] Another old and insoluble issue was the amalgamation and suspension of subordinate offices, including some *Regierungen* and *Landratsämter*, which continued to fall victim to the known opposition of Hitler.[152]

The last of these issues was of more than merely technical importance, for it was part of the latest and final round of power struggles in which the interior ministry was now involved. Long before the final turn towards total mobilization, a change of regime had taken place in the ministry: on 24 August 1943, Himmler had replaced Frick as minister.[153] Frick's loss of office followed a campaign of criticism against him during the early summer, documented in Goebbels' diaries, which was well-tuned to Hitler's now increasing distrust of his administrative apparatus.[154] That the interior ministry was nevertheless still a prize worth possessing is indicated by the fact that both Goebbels and Bormann had hoped to win it, and that Daluege congratulated the victor on having achieved what had been 'so long striven for'.[155] In practice, Himmler left a good deal of the day-to-day business to Stuckart, the senior state secretary since Pfundtner had departed with his master, but there is no doubt that he saw his new position as an additional base on which to build an authority counter to Bormann's. Among the most important aspects of this was his commitment to the construction of a new relationship between Berlin and the field apparatus. As he explained in a speech in November 1943:

I see my principal task very clearly before me: to establish the authority of the Reich in the administration and in the interior, and where necessary to restore it

[149] Führer-information, A 1/462, 9 Aug. 1944 (copy in BA R 43II/666b).

[150] Mentioned in Stuckart to Lammers, 13 Sept. 1944 (BA R 43II/656).

[151] For the promotion bar, see material in BA R 43II/455, up to Mar. 1945; for the salary moratorium, see the documentation in BA R 2/22042, up to Feb. 1945.

[152] Stuckart to Lammers, 13 Sept. 1944 (BA R 43II/656).

[153] See Diehl-Thiele, *Partei und Staat*, pp. 196-200.

[154] *Goebbels Diaries*, pp. 283, 286 ff., 291-6, 381. Frick became head of the protectorate of Bohemia-Moravia, where he was overshadowed by his state secretary, K. H. Frank; see G. Rhode, 'The Protectorate of Bohemia and Moravia', in V. Mamatey and R. Luza (eds.), *A History of Czechoslovakia* (Princeton, 1973), 316.

[155] Daluege to Himmler, 28 Aug. 1943 (BDC Himmler).

... If we were to try and decide every single detail in the ministry in Berlin ... things that can be done better out there in the field, then we ought not to be surprised if a spirit of resistance develops in the *Reichsgaue*, if a *Reichsstatthalter* finds his position undignified and if people out there say: we'll make ourselves independent of the centre. I see the task of the centre as giving as much in the way of stimulus as possible, devolving outwards as much regional decision-making as possible, making it possible for creative people, who possess the capacity for leadership, to work.[156]

Or, as he put it a few months earlier, he wanted through decentralization to create 'happy *Gaue* and happy *Länder*'.[157] Programmatically, Himmler indicated his acceptance of the fact that major issues, including the fate of the *Regierungspräsidenten*, could not be decided during the war; that he felt less strongly than Frick on the issue of administrative concentration; and that his inclination to devolution would make him tolerant of local deviations in minor issues, but not in major ones.[158] In terms of civil-service policy, Himmler acknowledged an attachment to the ethical image of the civil service: 'In the future it will once more be the case that the civil service, and especially the administrative civil servant, will be imbued with a distinctive and prideful *esprit de corps*, and this will also once again prove attractive to young men inspired by it and by a yearning for action, and thus provide a new generation of recruits.'[159] Still, he was also determined to introduce legislation to overturn tenure, so that any 'incapable' civil servant could be turned out of office as required.[160] In other respects, however, Himmler's administrative programme was not so very different from Frick's—with the one major exception that Himmler was in a far better position to accomplish his. Both sought to decentralize or devolve, both wanted the services of a respected élite, and both realized that success would depend on the ministry's capacity to enforce compliance with its orders and respect for its objectives as well as its personnel. This was what Frick had never been able to achieve; Himmler's chances, given his enormous power in the SS-police apparatus, were infinitely superior. Nevertheless, the battle between Himmler and Bormann for mastery in the field was undecided by the war's end; the

---

[156] Speech in Krakau, 18 Nov. 1943 (BA R 18/1250).
[157] Speech to representatives of German justice, 25 May 1944 (BA NS 19HR/19).
[158] Report of *Regierungspräsidenten* conference in Breslau, 13 Jan. 1944 (BA R 43II/425a). See also report of speech on 28 Oct. 1944, in Diehl-Thiele, *Partei und Staat*, p. 199.
[159] Krakau speech; see n. 156 above.
[160] Breslau speech; see n. 158 above.

authority of the *Gauleiter* continued to expand as the last days of the Third Reich unfolded, and they took over civil and military tasks alike.[161]

This, then, was the final stage of Germany's political, administrative, and territorial dissolution, as the government fragmented in the face of the Allied armies. In the last few months of the war, the interior ministry was dispersed; 'work became less and less as the rapid occupation of German territory proceeded and communications became worse and worse', until, in March 1945, there was simply nothing left to do.[162]

---

[161] Hüttenberger, *Gauleiter*, pp. 192-5.

[162] Memoir by Ministerialrat Heinrichs, 1962 (BA K1 Erw, 215/2). In Jan., Himmler had imposed the death penalty for any leader of a civilian office who abandoned his post without orders; see GBV circular, 1 Feb. 1945 (BA R 22/4435).

9

State Formation and Political Representation in Nazi Germany

I

In April 1933, Fritz-Dietlof Graf von der Schulenburg, a *Regierungsrat* in the Königsberg Oberpräsidium and active member of the NSDAP since 1931 set out an optimistic programme for the role of the German civil service in National Socialist Germany, and sent it to his ministry.[1] With a sense of urgency, he described the challenges facing the new regime:

> The National Socialist leaders face the task of constructing a National Socialist state. The leaders are political fighters and are not well versed in the techniques of administration. The co-operation of the bureaucracy, which has the expert knowledge and experience of administrative techniques, is indispensable . . . the rebuilding of the state depends upon the penetration of each and every office by the political spirit of National Socialism.

For Schulenburg, the scion of an old Prussian aristocratic family, National Socialism promised the enactment of Prussian political ideals in a new form; chief among these was the regeneration of the civil-service élite, both as a moral force and as a partner in the political revolution which was to transform his homeland.

Barely four years later, Schulenburg, by now a *Landrat* in East Prussia, addressed another memorandum to his friends in the Berlin ministries. In this one, entitled 'Civil Service: Crisis and Remedy', he described the disaster that he saw threatening the civil service, and with it the future of Germany reborn.[2] Three problems troubled him. First, 'the *technically clear task* of the civil service and the individual civil servant *is increasingly vanishing*, for the once concentrated authority of

---

[1] Memorandum, 'Neuaufbau des höheren Beamtentums', reprinted in H. Mommsen, *Beamtentum im Dritten Reich* (Stuttgart, 1966), 137-42; see also H. Mommsen, 'Fritz-Dietlof Graf von der Schulenburg und die preussiche Tradition', *VjhZ*, 32/2 (1984), 213-39, and A. Krebs, *Fritz-Dietlof Graf von der Schulenburg: Zwischen Staatsraison und Hochverrat* (Hamburg, 1964), 101-3.

[2] Memorandum of Sept. 1937, reprinted in Mommsen, *Beamtentum*. pp. 146-9.

the state is fragmented into innumerable specialist agencies, the party and corporative organizations are working in the same areas without any clear demarcation of responsibilities . . .'. Secondly, although the personnel of the civil service had been politically purified and rebuilt since 1933:

it is publicly *ridiculed* as a 'bureaucracy', disparaged as a mechanistic apparatus without any leadership or community role or power, decried as remote from the public and even perfidious . . . The civil servant . . . is exposed to attacks that are really aimed at the state as such; when disputes arise, he is regularly left without political protection, even when he is simply doing his duty . . . But the historical accomplishments of the civil service . . . are unthinkable without honour and recognition. If the *honour of the civil service is no longer protected, one cannot expect its service in the long run.*

And, finally: 'the civil service is economically largely proletarianized', the result of war and inflation, followed by the Brüning salary cuts. Schulenburg's remedies matched his diagnosis. He wanted immediate action to restore coherence and unity to the state apparatus and to clarify the distribution of governmental tasks; to rid the civil service of political suspicion and return personnel policies to the administrators themselves; and to alleviate its financial distress, by raising salaries, improving promotion prospects, or increasing emergency allowances. For, as he concluded: 'The situation is clear: the civil service finds itself as a result of all these constraints *in a crisis that is consuming its very substance*—something that even the System [Weimar] was unable to destroy.'

The disintegration of Schulenburg's hopes represents a typical experience of civil servants under National Socialism, whether or not they had shared his initial enthusiasm for the regime. No one who has studied the intricacies and contradictions of policy in the Third Reich can doubt that this was a period of profound assault on the personnel and principles of the German administration. At one level, the fragmentation of the apparatus of government, the chronic conflicts in policy-making and execution, and the persistent violation of procedural norms resulted from the destructive impact of National Socialist rule on the standards of administrative practice previously developed in Germany. This was not because the Nazi leadership had adopted a deliberate strategy of displacing the existing structures of administration and substituting a set of newly legitimated institutions. The subversion of the civil service was piecemeal and *ad hoc*, the effect of incompetence, impatience, and neglect rather than the pursuit of a clear alternative vision. In what Hans Mommsen has described as a 'parasitic' process, the Nazi regime dissolved the institutional apparatuses it had inherited, and consumed the sources of its own survival as a functioning political system.[3] If this was an example of Nazi social Darwinism in practice, its effect was one of negative selection, the survival of the unfittest.

The image of a functionally rational state under assault by a dynamic and undisciplined party has become widely accepted in the historical literature, and it appears to be solidly confirmed by the archival evidence. Much of the material in this book documents the repeated clashes between the defenders of bureaucratic practice and the agents of party assertion, and we have reviewed ample evidence of the anxiety and anger expressed by men like Frick, Pfundtner, Lammers, Killy, Krosigk, and Popitz, who deplored the corrosion of familiar administrative standards and practices by the terms of Nazi rule. Yet it is questionable whether the character of Nazi administration can be best explained as the effect of a collision between the principles of bureaucratic rationalism on the one hand, and the elemental dynamism of the Nazi movement on the other. In acknowledging the existence of a party-state dichotomy in Nazi Germany, we need also to avoid confusing the functional rationality of the bureaucratic process with the substantive quality of bureaucratic rule as a political system.[4] The latter was at least as great an object of contention as the former; the defence of the civil service as a privileged institution in the structure of government was a political rather than an administrative issue. Moreover, the evidence from which historians have assembled the dualist construct, documents conflict not only between 'party' and 'state' as such, but also between rival representations of what was rational in administrative terms and what was chaotic. It was as part of this strategy of representation that particular interests depicted themselves and their actions as rational, and those of others as the opposite, irrespective of their real character and effects. It can be argued, in other words, that the dualism of state and party was over-determined by this partisan battle of representation, in which the two institutions figured respectively and polemically as embodiments of stability and dynamism, even when they were not. For it is perfectly clear to any outside observer that the Nazi party was quite as bureaucratic as the civil administration, and that,

3 Ibid. 13.
4 This is discussed in my essay, 'Bureaucracy, Politics and the National Socialist State', in P. Stachura (ed.), *The Shaping of the Nazi State* (London, 1978), 234-56.

similarly, the civil administration was itself responsible for a good deal of the confusions and complexities of the Nazi state.[5] The assignation of the bureaucracy to the category of administration and order, and of the Nazi party to that of politics and disorder, needs, therefore, to be stripped of its rhetorical associations in the documentary representations from which the historical narrative is drawn. Of course there were real clashes between bureaucracy and party, administration and politics; but there were also powerful motives among the protagonists for perpetrating and exaggerating this very set of contrasts, and for suppressing or ignoring contrary evidence. Partisans of bureaucratic rule could legitimate their own status and press their arguments home by magnifying the degree of external pressure on the bureaucratic process; conversely, a party mired in its own bureaucratic apparatuses and procedures had good reason to divert criticism elsewhere.

II

This was the context in which the administrative and civil-service policies that have formed the substance of this book were developed, and in which the frustrations of their sponsors accumulated. The conventions of bureaucratic loyalty and the apolitical nationalism of the ministerial élite meant, however, that few of the men whose labours we have examined fell by the wayside until their patience with the regime was finally exhausted by the additional provocations of the war and the threat of defeat. Schulenburg himself was among the best known of these; his defection was shared by Popitz, Goerdeler, and some other representatives of the German administration who eventually put themselves in open opposition to the regime they had served. Among the men whose careers tell a large part of the story of bureaucratic policy-making in this period, Killy was forced to resign in 1944, while Stuckart evidently made a series of unsuccessful attempts to volunteer for the army after 1940. Less conspicuously, and hardly on their own initiative, Frick and Pfundtner both left the interior ministry in 1943.[6]

[5] This point was made long ago by F. Neumann, in *Behemoth: The Structure and Practice of National Socialism* (London, 1942), 72-3.

[6] H. von Borch, *Obrigkeit und Widerstand: Zur politischen Soziologie des Beamtentums* (Tübingen, 1954), remains the classic study of the problem of bureaucratic resistance. See also P. Hoffmann, *Widerstand, Staatsstreich, Attentat: Der Kampf der Opposition gegen Hitler* (Frankfurt, 1970), ch. 6, and H. Mommsen, 'Social Views and Constitutional Plans of the Resistance', in H. Graml *et al.*, *The German Resistance to Hitler* (London, 1970), 55-147.

To remain in office was not necessarily a signal of active consent—yet what exactly was the disaffection with the quality of administrative policy which was so frequently and clamorously voiced by the men responsible for it? How correct were they in their diagnosis of the crisis which, they claimed, National Socialist leadership had brought upon the state and its works—a diagnosis which subsequent historians have tended to confirm?

Two rhetorics dominated the official discourse about governmental structure and civil-service policy in Nazi Germany: the rhetoric of unity, concentration, and rationalization, and the rhetoric of crisis. These represented the polarities of administrative experience: on the one hand, an aspiration for clarity of structure, decision-making, and policy execution; on the other, a recognition that this had entirely eluded policy-makers, and that the ostensible bearers of the structure were themselves in equal disarray. Men like Frick, Schulenburg, Pfundtner, Lammers, and Killy, along with many of their lesser colleagues like Seel or Fabricius, looked to the Prussian tradition for their models of the administration and its personnel. At the same time, they saw National Socialism as the bearer of a revived national unity that would also necessarily require and rebuild the authority of the civil service. Other senior officials, among them ministers like Popitz, Krosigk, and Gürtner, were perhaps always more sceptical of the promises of National Socialism, but they could nevertheless accept this vision of national recovery, even if they preferred to keep their distance from the party in whose name it was to be achieved. Yet between them, these representatives of Germany's politico-administrative élite presided over the disintegration of their own ideals, in so far as these were embodied in the institutions and practices of the civil administration. Schulenburg had been right to argue that the National Socialist state could not dispense with the help of the bureaucracy in 1933. But what he saw as a principled and collaborative effort of renewal, in which a political division of labour assigned one set of tasks to the party and another to the civil administration, fast collapsed into a morass of mutual rivalries and suspicions. The conflicts this engendered were evidence not only of the *differences* between the two institutions, but also of their *shared* characteristics as bureaucratic apparatuses. They also demonstrated the practical impossibility of differentiating between 'leadership' and 'administration' in a political system which vigorously rejected the separation of powers.

A critical example of this was the destructive competition for the appropriation of the resources of administrative reproduction in the Nazi polity. After its already damaging experience in the Weimar Republic, the civil service faced new competitors for these in the multitude of quasi-bureaucratic institutions spawned in the Third Reich: the DAF, the PO (the NSDAP's political organization), the SS, and other party formations, together with such new state foundations as the propaganda and aviation ministries. The salary campaign of the later 1930s demonstrated the extent of disagreement about access to the financial resources for the reproduction of the civil service, both as an institution and as a social group or *Stand*. Certain non-financial resources were equally finite and were similarly the focus of intense competition. The most important of these was the pool of trained personnel out of which the professional civil service recruited and reproduced itself. The attempts at training reform, especially during the war, disclosed a series of arguments about the terms of access to personnel. First, the reformers claimed that the next generation of professionals was not being produced in sufficient numbers to cover actual or expected demand. Secondly, those that were being trained by the institutions of professional education (the universities, schools, army, etc.) were being appropriated by other competitors for bureaucratic labour power, notably the party, the armed services, and the SS. Thirdly, the process by which, so to speak, the 'raw material' of candidates for the civil service was converted into the finished product of the *Berufsbeamtentum* as a corporate institution, was not adequately controlled by the administrative élite itself. Finally, the structure of government mandated a wasteful use of resources, in which the staff that was available was inefficiently deployed; this, too, represented a weakening of the concept of bureaucratic administration as a system ostensibly characterized by efficiency. This was closely connected to another aspect of resource competition: the struggle for the appropriation of 'honour', or political and social esteem in the Weberian sense. If this was not in itself a finite commodity, it was at any rate true that the concept of prestige and access to it were defined by a powerful new competition of values under National Socialism, in which soldiers, party fighters, and probably even mothers took precedence over administrators. Weber's classic claim that 'the honor of the civil servant [comprises his] wages'[7] was repeatedly echoed in the complaints by

---

[7] M. Weber, 'Politics as Vocation' (1918), in H. H. Gerth and C. Wright Mills (eds.), *From Max Weber: Essays in Sociology* (London, 1948), 80.

Frick and others that civil servants were being deprived of their due in this sphere, and in their threats that loss of honour undermined the capacity of the civil service to perform its allotted tasks. In all these ways, the professional civil service was being deprived of access to the means of its own reproduction as a political and social élite. Yet this was the result of competition on its own ground, and not simply the effect of an alien assault.

As the early chapters of this book have suggested, this fear that the civil service might simply vanish was not confined to the National Socialist period, but had its roots in the possibility, identified in the 1920s at the latest, that the *Berufsbeamtentum* was in danger of being effaced by bureaucracy. Earlier debates had turned on the question of how an élite professional civil service might be salvaged from the probably inevitable growth of bureaucracy, as the state's tasks continued to expand and differentiate in the twentieth century. After 1933, the issue reappeared, transmogrified, in the endless debates about the division of labour between party 'leadership' and bureaucratic 'administration'. The National Socialist period did not invent the issue, in other words, but it did vastly exacerbate the problem of bureaucratization, and turned it in new directions, not least in its own ranks. The extreme discourse of crisis in the civil service after the mid-1930s is testimony to the double disappointment of those who had thought that National Socialism might offer a solution to the problems threatening the civil service in the Weimar period, of which politicization was only one example; the problems of honour or prestige and of economic status figured equally. This may help to explain why the rhetoric of crisis arose so fast: by 1937-8, the protagonists were already speaking in terms of some kind of final crisis of the *Berufsbeamtentum*, of damage which was already virtually irreparable.[8] This was partly due to the simultaneous speed and inconclusiveness with which Nazi politicization had proceeded, to be sure; yet that was only one aspect of the Nazi failure to address a problem of élite reproduction that was already on the agenda in Weimar and before.

---

[8] e.g. Frick to Krosigk, 20 Apr. 1938: 'the morale and strength of character of civil servants may suffer irreparable damage' (BA R 43II/432); or the draft of Frick to Hitler, 24 June 1939: 'The figure of the incorruptible civil servant, which has served the whole world as a model, is now slowly, but at an ever-increasing pace, vanishing' (BA R 43II/432b); see also Ch. 7 above.

III

The ideological stake in this struggle was the question of who was to fulfil the National Socialist regime's claim to represent the unity of the nation. One of the most striking paradoxes of the National Socialist political system is the contradiction between, on the one hand, the immense concentration of power it embodied and the ideological unity it espoused, and, on the other, the extreme fragmentation of its structure and processes in practice. This dualism between concentration and fragmentation as historical characteristics of National Socialist rule is mirrored in the current historiography, which is itself deeply fractured between 'intentionalist' and 'structuralist' interpretations of the Third Reich. On the one hand, historians such as Hans Mommsen and Martin Broszat have depicted the Nazi state as a grossly decentred polyocracy circulating around a 'weak dictator'. Against this, Klaus Hildebrand, among others, has argued that Nazi Germany constituted a more or less effective *Führerdiktatur* in which ultimately, even if not universally, Hitler's intentions and authority determined the distribution and the uses of power.[9] The debate between these two interpretations has had extremely important implications, not only for the analysis of the Nazi state in general, but also for the explanation of its most catastrophic policies, notably the transition from anti-Semitism to genocide. For intentionalists, policy originated, in the last analysis, in the ideology and will of Hitler and perhaps of other leading Nazis, with the bureaucratic agencies being primarily the executants of political decisions external to their own operations.[10] The structuralist interpretation, by contrast, has argued for an active relationship between the structure and function of the state, or in other words, for the way in which the mechanisms and processes of administration contributed to the content of policy as well as to its technical

[9] See M. Broszat, *The Hitler State* (London, 1981); G. Hirschfeld and L. Kettenacker (eds.), *The 'Führer State': Myth and Reality. Studies on the Structure and Politics of the Third Reich* (Stuttgart, 1981), pt. 1. The contemporary literature is discussed in two recent surveys: J. Hiden and J. Farquharson, *Explaining Hitler's Germany: Historians and the Third Reich* (London, 1983), ch. 3, and I. Kershaw, *The Nazi Dictatorship. Problems and Perspectives of Interpretation* (London, 1985), ch. 4. The term 'Polykratie' appears to have been introduced into the literature by Gerhard Schulz in 1960; see K. D. Bracher, W. Sauer, and G. Schulz, *Die nationalsozialistische Machtergreifung: Studien zur Errichtung des totalitären Herrschaftssytems in Deutschland 1933/34* (Cologne and Opladen, 1962), 599.

[10] e.g. G. Fleming, *Hitler and the Final Solution* (Oxford, 1986).

implementation.[11] On this basis, the close analysis of bureaucratic processes offers one of the best means of describing and explaining the course of any field of policy in Nazi Germany, including that of the bureaucracy itself.

The structuralist interpretation of National Socialism has been deeply grounded in such detailed empirical studies, but to some extent its interpretations were predicated on a prior revival of Marxist political theory. This did much to reinvigorate the analysis of European fascism in the 1960s, by turning towards political questions the attention that had previously been concentrated on the issue of the social sources of fascism. Both the concept of the 'primacy of politics' (Mason) and that of the 'relative autonomy' of politics and the state (Poulantzas) bear more than a coincidental resemblance to the main tenets of the subsequent structuralist position.[12] Marxists and structuralists equally dismiss the idea that policy is the effect of a relatively straightforward process of transitive causation, whether this flows from an intentionalist concept of ideology, or from a reductionist view of class. This is true even of the more functionalist Marxist 'state derivation' literature, which developed in Germany in the 1960s and 1970s. Although deeply critical of the Poulantzian separation of the political and economic instances, state derivationism in its less reductionist versions problematized the internal form of the state as well as its functional relation to capital.[13] Nevertheless, despite its origins in debates about the crisis of capitalism, and its concern with the key question of why social relations in bourgeois society appear separately as economic and political relations, this school has had little direct influence on the analysis of the fascist state as such. Rather, it is the structuralist and autonomist models that have offered the most useful tools for analysis, for they focus directly and specifically on the internal constitution of, and relations between, the apparatuses of the state.

On the whole, however, the influence of political theory has been

11 See H. Mommsen, 'The Realization of the Unthinkable: The "Final Solution of the Jewish Question" in the Third Reich', in G. Hirschfeld (ed.), *The Policies of Genocide: Jews and Soviet Prisoners of War in Germany* (London, 1986), 93-144.

12 T. W. Mason, 'The Primacy of Politics: Politics and Economics in National Socialist Germany', in S. J. Woolf (ed.), *The Nature of Fascism* (London, 1968), 165-95; N. Poulantzas, *Fascism and Dictatorship: The Third International and the Problem of Fascism* (London, 1974); also J. Caplan, 'Theories of Fascism: Nicos Poulantzas as Historian', *History Workshop Journal*, 3 (1977), 83-100.

13 See J. Holloway and S. Picciotto (eds.), *State and Capital: A Marxist Debate* (London, 1978); B. Jessop, *The Capitalist State: Marxist Theories and Methods* (New York and London, 1982), ch. 3.

more implicit than explicit in current academic debates among western historians about the nature of National Socialist rule.[14] Historians have not on the whole taken up the challenge of changes in theories of the state, whether Marxist or non-Marxist; an unemphatic Weberianism still sponsors most discussions. Rather than flowing together with recent theoretical debates about the capitalist state, the intentionalist-structuralist debate has tended to lean on the past twenty-five years of intense empirical research into the political history of National Socialism, its governing institutions and administrative processes. With all the recent proliferation of empirical and theoretical literature on the workings of the National Socialist state, the issues under debate have in fact been remarkably stable over the fifty years since the Nazi seizure of power. They continue to reappear, in appropriately different guises, in both the empirical and the theoretical literature. In essence, the interpretive debates have circulated around two central problematics: on the one hand, the class location and significance of the National Socialist regime in and for capitalism; and on the other, the relationship between Hitler's power and the political mechanisms of policy-making and execution. In different ways, this was true of the earliest contributions to the scholarly analysis of National Socialism, such as Ernst Fraenkel's *The Dual State* (1941), Franz Neumann's *Behemoth* (1942), and the essays of some of the other contemporary German theorists like Pollock or Kirchheimer, all of whom emphasized the technical rationality of at least some aspects of bureaucratic rule under National Socialism.[15] The subsequent enquiries in the 1950s into the concept of totalitarianism in the works of Arendt, Friedrich, and others took up many of the same basic questions, though in a much broader historical context;[16] and they remain, as we have seen, central to the most recent discussions of polyocracy and relative autonomy, as also to the expanding field of publications on the social history of the Third Reich. Neumann in particular has had an enduring effect on later work,

[14] The outstanding attempt to apply Poulantzian categories to modern German history is D. Abraham's *The Collapse of the Weimar Republic: Political Economy and Crisis* (New York, 1986), which by its nature stops short of an analysis of the Nazi regime.

[15] E. Fraenkel, *The Dual State: A Contribution to the Theory of Dictatorship* (New York, 1941); Neumann, *Behemoth*; O. Kirchheimer, 'The Legal Order of National Socialism', *Studies in Philosophy and Social Science*, 9 (1941), 456-75; F. Pollock, 'Is National Socialism a New Order?', ibid. 440-55; Mason's use of the term 'primacy of politics' is anticipated by Pollock's discussion of the concept (p. 453).

[16] H. Arendt, *The Origins of Totalitarianism* (New York, 1951); C. J. Friedrich and Z. K. Brzezinski, *Totalitarian Dictatorship and Autocracy* (Cambridge, Mass., 1956).

and the influence of his core propositions about the quadripartite distribution of power among competing élites in Nazi Germany can easily be detected in both structuralist and autonomist theories. Thus, Michael Geyer has recently fused the concept of relative autonomy with Weberian and Frankfurt School approaches, to theorize the Nazi state as a system not of politics but of domination.[17] According to this argument, politics under National Socialism was not about co-operation or even competition in the distribution of resources, but was a process of negotiation aimed at maintaining a structure of distances between the several producers of domination, whose power rested on their relative independence from one another. The deformation of the political process followed from the collapse of politics into crude domination, and from the simultaneous dissolution under National Socialism of the liberal boundaries between state, economy, and society: a double destruction of the mediations otherwise essential to the polities associated with modern capitalism.

Nevertheless, if the issues have tended to remain stable, what has changed more radically is the nature of the evidence available for resolving these questions, the sources of enquiry, and the scope of explanation. Essentially, since the 1940s and 1950s the leadership in scholarly debates about National Socialism has shifted from political sociology to history, in conformity with one of the conventions of the academic division of labour. With this has come a certain narrowing of the perspective of enquiry and explanation. As the study of National Socialism has fallen further into the purview of historians' archival investigations, and has flowered in empirical detail, so we have perhaps come to learn more but understand less about its meaning and place in history. Some may regard this as an inevitable and desirable state of affairs, in that the habits of history as a practice enforce a healthy scepticism in respect of immodest theoretical projects.[18] Historians are deterred by the conventions of the discipline from asking, for example, Franz Neumann's ticklish question: 'Is Germany a State?'.[19] Yet Tim Mason's call, twenty years ago, for a co-operative effort among scholars

[17] M. Geyer, 'The State in National Socialist Germany', in C. Bright and S. Harding (eds.), *Statemaking and Social Movements: Essays in History and Theory* (Ann Arbor, 1984), 193-232.
[18] This seems to be the view of Hiden and Farquharson, *Explaining Hitler's Germany*, p. 82.
[19] The title of one of his final chapters, *Behemoth*, p. 382. It is echoed in Pollock's expression of 'grave doubts as to whether it makes sense to call the National Socialist system a state'; 'Is National Socialism a New Order', p. 450.

to integrate 'the immense quantities of newly available documentary evidence into an interpretative framework'[20] has rarely been heeded, and Neumann's question remains a provocative place to begin. How can historians use the insights that derive from a close analysis of the workings of the Nazi state to develop our understanding of its place in the history of the formation and reproduction of the German state?

IV

The initial proposition for such a project is that the problems of state structure and administrative function in Nazi Germany will not be adequately explained if they are seen only as the contingent products of the political circumstances of that period. Rather, they need to be set in the context of the more profound structural problem of German state formation. That term usually denotes the long-term process of the differentiation of the modern state as such from earlier or alternative forms of political organization, such as clan or tribe, theocracy or universal state; studies in state formation tend to cover the *longue durée* of European history since the sixteenth century or earlier. To restrict this concept to a local and partial case may appear to mistake the process of political change within a state for the formation of the state as such. However, there are good reasons for suggesting that the process of state formation in Germany has, as John Gillis has put it, not been 'one sequence, but a repeated series of sequences', in which the basic problem of forging the link between state and nation was an issue that arose repeatedly and was subjected to only temporary resolutions.[21] Thus the relatively sophisticated development of state apparatuses in the German states in the eighteenth century was followed by a tenacious resistance to the subsequent process of nation-state formation in the nineteenth, which Bismarck side-stepped rather than solved. The civil service was crucial in this as the point at which, rhetorically and in practice, the problems of both particularism and class plurality were supposedly resolved: its corporate identity and mentality offered a technical closure to the question of creating substantive nationhood. That the German political system was under strain by the end of the nineteenth

[20] Mason, 'The Primacy of Politics', p. 168.
[21] J. Gillis, 'Germany', in R. Grew (ed.), *Crises of Political Development in Europe and the United States* (Princeton, 1979), 325. See also G. Eley, 'State Formation, Nationalism and Political Culture: Some Thoughts on the Unification of Germany', in id., *From Unification to Nazism: Reinterpreting the German Past* (London, 1986), 61-84.

century is well known, whatever the different judgements as to its capacity for refoundation.[22] But there was also an administrative counterpart in this, in the growth of a bureaucratic sector which could no longer fulfil the role of linkage and mediation assigned to it. It was neither neutral nor homogeneous, nor could it subsist within the supposed terms of the state-society dichotomy. The German civil service belonged both to the state and to society, as the tensions discussed in Chapters 2 and 3 suggest, and it became increasingly specious to argue that it was uniquely able to transcend this dichotomy.

In terms of this model, 1918-19 marked a deliberate attempt to establish an effective nation-state in Germany. It was presided over by an unstable centre-populist hegemonic bloc, resting on a new set of alliances among the political representatives of classes and class fractions previously kept at a distance from the German political process. When the post-war political settlement began to collapse in the systemic crisis after 1930, another departure was attempted, this time on the basis of a right-populist alliance whose fissiparity became increasingly obvious from 1933, but which was held in place by the dictatorial nature of the Nazi regime.[23] Both in 1918-19 and after 1930, political tendencies towards the centralization and concentration of power were bounded by powerful forces of regional and institutional particularism. The convening and mediating roles assigned to the civil service were contested by alternative ideologies and institutions, among them, in 1919, the sovereign people, the constitution and parliament, and, in 1933, the *Volk*, the NSDAP, and the Führer, nested in each other like a set of Russian dolls. In the crisis of the early 1930s, National Socialism presented a tripartite solution to the problems of real and representational unity that had bedevilled the process of German state formation since the nineteenth century, offering to efface the distinction between state and society, to unify the people, and to establish the authority of a totalizing ideology. Administratively, the significant characteristic of the National Socialist phase of German state formation was the attempt to realize those tendencies towards strict centralization which had been inherent in the process since the mid-nineteenth century, but had never been

---

[22] This debate is, of course, directly linked to the question of the origins of National Socialism; see D. Blackbourn and G. Eley, *The Peculiarities of German History* (Oxford, 1984); H. Grebing, *Der 'deutsche Sonderweg' in Europa 1806-1945* (Stuttgart, Bern, Cologne, and Mainz, 1986); R. Evans, 'The Myth of Germany's Missing Revolution', *New Left Review*, 149 (Jan./Feb. 1985), 67-94.

[23] The problems of class representation and bloc formation in the republic are discussed in Abraham, *Collapse of the Weimar Republic.*

fully accomplished. The participation of the civil service was essential to the establishment of a unitary state, and the interior ministry assumed the thankless task of trying to embody an ideological commitment to unity in an appropriately concrete structure and process of administration. But because the National Socialist regime was also supposed to have overcome the state-society dichotomy, it effectively excluded a refoundation of the state in its nineteenth-century form.

Before 1933, the party had claimed to represent the totality and universality of the (racial) nation in a period of extreme decomposition; after the seizure of power, it was faced with the challenge of translating this proposition from the realm of ideology into that of politics. This, however, proved virtually impossible, for it was based on the false premiss of a straightforward correspondence between representational and real unity, which would also efface conflict. It was one thing to propose Hitler as the representation of unity—a symbolic function which is attached to every head of state—but National Socialism went well beyond this.[24] In a banal form, this confusion was captured in Hans Frank's proposition that Hitler would perform every task if he could, but that since one man could not actually do this, a corps of subsidiaries was necessary.[25] More sophisticated, but no less erroneous versions of the premiss that this symbol of unity could in fact be made concrete pervaded the political and legal ideology of the Nazi regime, and helped to obstruct the development of any effective theory of the state. As Dietrich Kirschenmann has observed: 'The National Socialist concept of law inserts the word Führer wherever the reality of rule threatens to come into contradiction with the basic unit of ideology [Ideologeme] . . . In short: it bonds deed and theory in the last instance to a Führer removed from reality and at the same de-realized: it makes use of a Führer-formula.'[26]

Nazi ideology was indeed hostile to the concept of the state as well as its practices, a fact that left political theory under National Socialism largely in the hands of conservatives. But only a few of these, including

[24] Cf. Geyer's concept of 'ideological politics'; 'The State in National Socialist Germany', p. 208.

[25] H. Frank, *Recht und Verwaltung* (Munich, 1939), 14. This was Frank's justification for the existence of a hierarchical bureaucracy, to which he was strongly committed.

[26] D. Kirschenmann, *'Gesetz' im Staatsrecht und in der Staatsrechtslehre des Nationalsozialismus* (Berlin, 1970), 17. I have translated the term 'Ideologeme' by analogy with Foucault's 'episteme'. See also T. Mason, 'Intention and Explanation: A Current Controversy about the Interpretation of National Socialism', in Hirschfeld and Kettenacker (eds.), *The 'Führer State'*, p. 35; and I. Kershaw, *The Hitler Myth* (Oxford, 1987).

Schmitt, and perhaps Höhn and Forsthoff, had any claim to be original political or legal theorists.[27] Most of the rest of the academics and practitioners who continued to write on political or constitutional theory after 1933 took on the secondary task of accommodating what they believed to be National Socialist ideology into their university lectures and textbooks. Here they attempted to legitimate not only the Nazi regime, but also their own professional right as theorists to speak authoritatively about the new dispensation. The greatest problems they faced were, first, to distance themselves from the traditions of both positivism and of the state as an end in itself; secondly, to conceptualize the relationship between *Volk*, Führer, NSDAP, and state; and thirdly, to make sense of the fact that the rule of law itself was so shaky in the new Germany. The result was a series of largely formulaic representations, in which the concepts of the *Volk* and Führer took rhetorical and explanatory primacy. Thus, Walter Sommer characterized the new state as neither a 'state without a people', nor a 'civil service state', nor a 'state as end in itself', but 'the state of the German people, of the German people embodied in the NSDAP'.[28] Otto Koellreutter argued in a lecture to the Kant Society in Halle that: 'For a *völkisch* system of thought, the state as an independent value falls into the background', and cited the Nazi ideologue, Alfred Rosenberg, as his authority for this: 'We do not want the total state, but the totality of the National Socialist movement in the state; we do not want a corporative state, but a political power structure of corporative construction.'[29] For Ernst Huber, the state was to be seen neither as an end in itself nor a mere instrument: 'precisely by being permeated by the essence and spirit of the people [*Volk*] the state has obtained a new dignity and authority . . . this state is the people itself in its political form'.[30] What these and many similar formulas share is the effort to capture the total character of the Nazi polity, without falling into the trap of identifying this with the state as such. Most of them date from the period before 1935, when this polity appeared to be in the process of formation; the

27 On Schmitt and his fate under National Socialism, see J. W. Bendersky, *Carl Schmitt: Theorist for the Reich* (Princeton, 1983), chs. 9-12.

28 W. Sommer, 'Die NSDAP als Verwaltungsträger', in H. Frank (ed.), *Deutsches Verwaltungsrecht* (Munich, 1937), 169.

29 O. Koellreutter, *Volk und Staat in der Weltanschauung des Nationalsozialismus* (Berlin, 1935), quoting Rosenberg from *Völkischer Beobachter*, 9 Jan. 1934. Koellreutter's lecture was a critique of Carl Schmitt.

30 E. R. Huber, *Neue Grundbegriffe des hoheitlichen Rechts* (Berlin, 1935).

rate of publication fell markedly after Hitler's ban on further public discussion of the issue.

Thus, the representation of the as yet unknown unity of the National Socialist system replicated the problem of its practical realization. Irresolution and mediocrity marked both, and the issue of what 'really' constituted the Nazi state was displaced to an unspecified future.[31] What had been achieved so far was regarded as provisional and subject to later substantiation or revision, yet it was frequently treated as if it constituted the logical first steps in a deliberate process of refoundation. But as Walter Sommer put it in 1937, it was 'futile to write learned treatises about the nature of the new state, here our pens will scratch in vain', because only Hitler knew what the state would look like ten years from now, and he would not be influenced by what academics had to say.[32] However, what was never realized was the simplistic division of labour between the party cadres as 'leadership' and the state apparatus as 'administration' (Führung and Verwaltung). Instead of this dualism, there was a contest over the ground itself. Hess and Bormann maintained their pressure to Nazify civil-service personnel; Frick's policies tended towards the creation of a strong state on the authoritarian model, in which the civil service would enjoy a clearly legitimated primacy. To use Geyer's terms, these strategies threatened the structure of distances between the 'producers of domination' by asserting the overriding claims of one of these over the others. Moreover, on a more abstract level, Frick's administrative strategy also threatened to expose the fallacy at the heart of the Nazi claim to represent a real unity or conflict-free totality. Not only did the civil service constitute an historically legitimated rival in this field, but Frick's insistence on the achievement of administrative unity, centralization, and concentration was intolerable to Nazi ideologues and to political leaders like Hitler or Goebbels, precisely because it exposed the fact that unity was open only to partial and symbolic representation, not to total and concrete realization. Even if deliberate sabotage of the Nazi project was not Frick's intention, his rhetorical obsession with unity was highly counter-productive. In the Nazi polity, totality had to be either everywhere or only in Hitler, but it could not be fixed in the intermediate structures required by a hierarchical administration. This was the circle Hans Frank kept trying to square in his writings on administration; and institutionally it was

---

[31] The best discussion of this at the level of political and legal theory is M. Stolleis, *Gemeinwohlformeln im nationalsozialistischen Recht* (Berlin, 1974).

[32] Quoted in Kirschenmann, *'Gesetz' im Staatsrecht*, p. 198.

reflected in the persistent strife which, as we have seen, arose from the structure and staffing of the *Mittelinstanz*. Similarly, individuals rather than offices were repeatedly charged with the performance of new tasks, culminating in the appointment of Goebbels as plenipotentiary for total war: a pleonastic function if ever there was one. Yet ultimately, Frick's claims on behalf of the civil service also rested on the assertion that it, too, embodied a representational totality. To be sure, the civil service's claim was more firmly rooted in German political history; and partly for this reason, it also relied on an elaborate code of substantive and procedural rules as well as a real division of labour. But the ultimate clash was not between the administrative rationality of the state and the dynamic parasitism of the party, but between two political concepts that were equally dynamic and irrational in terms of the realities of political representation and mediation in the modern state. If National Socialism sought to achieve a system of government without administration, the civil-service ideal was an administration that effaced government as a political process.

Some twenty years ago, Karl Dietrich Bracher exposed the presiding illusion of Nazi society in forceful terms: 'The better organized and more effective "order" of totalitarian one-man rule is . . . the lie that animates all authoritarian movements . . . its matrix is an ideology of order which vilifies the pluralistic character of modern society, subjugating it to a misanthropic as well as unreal ideal of efficiency modelled on technical perfection and military order.'[33] There was enough in this to attract a certain kind of bureaucratic mind, of course, and to create a link of some kind with the traditions of bureaucratic rule, even if in Germany the civil service had seen itself as something other, or more, than a mere bureaucracy. Both National Socialists and civil servants sought to legitimate their right to rule by claiming to represent the totality of the people. Though all political representation tends to displace power to some extent, the claim advanced by these two institutions and their presiding ideologies was that conflict within the nation could be effaced entirely: the bureaucracy by subjecting it to procedural solution, National Socialism by building a society in which domestic conflict no longer existed, as a springboard for the real issue of international struggle. This was what made bureaucracy and National Socialism a potentially deadly combination. For the Nazis, conflict

[33] K. D. Bracher, *The German Dictatorship: The Origins, Structure and Effects of National Socialism* (Harmondsworth, 1973; orig. edn., 1969), 297.

within the nation was unrecognizable, just as conflict between nations was inevitable; all they could do with their enemies was, ultimately, to kill them. And only when efficiency came to be equated with fanaticism did this conflict with the expectations of the German civil service.[34] But by then it was too late.

[34] H. Mommsen, 'Hitlers Stellung im nationalsozialistischen Herrschaftssystem', in Hirschfeld and Kettenacker (eds.), *The 'Führer State'*, p. 67. R. J. Lifton's reflections on the mentality of the physicians involved in the bureaucratic process of genocide are also pertinent here; see *The Nazi Doctors: Medical Killing and the Psychology of Genocide* (New York, 1986), 14-18, 495-500.

BIBLIOGRAPHY

I. UNPUBLISHED SOURCES

1. Bundesarchiv, Koblenz (BA)

Note: The process of archival reorganization has affected some of the classes and file numbers cited in the text since I consulted these holdings. I have endeavoured to bring citations up to date as far as possible; additional corrections from readers would be welcome.

R 2: Reichsfinanzministerium.
R 18: Reichsministerium des Innern.
R 21: Reichsministerium für Erziehung, Wissenschaft und Volksbildung.
R 22: Reichsjustizministerium.
R 36: Deutscher Gemeindetag.
R 41: Reichsarbeitsministerium.
R 43I: Alte Reichskanzlei (to 1933).
R 43II: Neue Reichskanzlei.
R 43F: Reichskanzlei microfilm.
R 48: Reichspostministerium.
R 53: Reichsvizekanzlei.
R 55: Reichspropagandaministerium.
R 58: Reichssicherheitshauptamt.
R 61: Akademie für Deutsches Recht.
R 115: Reichsprüfungsamt für den höheren und gehobenen Verwaltungsdienst.
R 148: Reichsdienststrafhof.
P 135: Preussisches Justizministerium.
NS 1: Reichsschatzmeister der NSDAP.
NS 6: Stellvertreter des Führers/Partei-Kanzlei.
NS 16: Nationalsozialistischer Rechtswahrerbund.
NS 20: NSDAP Kleine Erwerbungen.
NS 22: Reichsorganisationsleitung.
NS 25: Hauptamt für Kommunalpolitik.
NS 26: NSDAP Hauptarchiv.
NS 40: Hauptamt für Beamte/Reichswaltung des Reichsbunds der Deutschen Beamten.

Sammlung Schumacher.
Sammlung Sänger.
Nachlass Lüders.
Kleine Erwerbungen.

2. *Bundesarchiv, Militärarchiv Freiburg*

RW 6: Allgemeines Wehrmachtsamt.
Wi/IF5: Wehrwirtschaftsstab im Reichskriegsministerium/OKW.

3. *Geheimes Staatsarchiv, Berlin-Dahlem (GStA)*

Rep. 90: Preussisches Staatsministerium.
Rep. 77: Preussisches Ministerium des Innern.
Rep. 318: Reichsarbeitsministerium.
Rep. 184: Oberverwaltungsgericht.
P 134: Preussisches Finanzministerium.

4. *Berlin Document Centre (BDC)*

Personnel files of major civil servants and political figures.

5. *Institut für Zeitgeschichte, Munich (IfZ)*

ZS: Zeugenschrifttum.
MA; FA: Microfilm collections.

6. *Microfilms*

National Archives:
    T 175: Reichsführer-SS und Chef der deutschen Polizei.
    T 81: NSDAP miscellaneous.
Hoover Institution:
    NSDAP Hauptarchiv (HA).

II. PRINTED PRIMARY SOURCES

1. *Official Publications*

Deutscher Reichsanzeiger und Preussischer Staatsanzeiger, 1934-5.
Entscheidungen des Reichsgerichts in Zivilsachen, 1929.
Einzelschriften zur Statistik des Deutschen Reichs:
    No. 18: *Der Personalstand der öffentlichen Verwaltung im Deutschen Reich am*

31. März 1928 und am 31. März 1927 (Berlin, 1931).

No. 22: *Die Lebenshaltung von 2000 Arbeiter-, Angestellten- und Beamtenhaushaltungen*, 2 vols. (Berlin, 1932).

Ministerialblatt des Reichs- und preussischen Ministeriums des Innern, 1936-41.

Ministerialblatt für die preussische innere Verwaltung, 1933-5.

Preussische Gesetzsammlung, 1906-38.

Reichsgesetzblatt, i. 1873-1945.

Reichsministerialblatt, 1933-4.

Statistisches Jahrbuch für das Deutsche Reich, 1927-34.

Verhandlungen der verfassungsgebenden Deutschen Nationalversammlung, 1919-20.

Verhandlungen des Reichstags, 1919-33.

Wirtschaft und Statistik, 1925, 1930.

2. *Other Printed Primary Documents, Text Collections, Reference Works, etc.*

ABC des Deutschen Beamtengesetzes: Alphabetischer Führer durch das DBG (Berlin, 1938).

Akten der Reichskanzlei, ed. Karl Dietrich Erdmann (Boppard, 1968-).

Das Kabinett Scheidemann, ed. Hagen Schulze (1971).

Das Kabinett Bauer, ed. Anton Golecki (1980).

Das Kabinett Müller I, ed. Martin Vogt (1971).

Das Kabinett Fehrenbach, ed. Peter Wulf (1962).

Die Kabinette Wirth I und II, ed. Ingrid Schulze-Bidlingmaier (1973).

Das Kabinett Cuno, ed. Karl-Heinz Harbeck (1968).

Das Kabinett Stresemann, ed. Karl-Dietrich Erdmann and Martin Vogt (1978).

Die Kabinette Marx I und II, ed. Günter Abramowksi (1973).

Die Kabinette Luther I und II, ed. Karl-Heinz Minuth (1977).

Die Kabinette Brüning I und II, ed. Tilman Koops (1982).

Das Kabinett Hitler, i. ed. Karl-Heinz Minuth (1983).

Das Archiv.

BAYNES, NORMAN H. (ed.), *The Speeches of Adolf Hitler 1922-39* (Oxford, 1942).

BOBERACH, HEINZ (ed.), *Meldungen aus dem Reich: Auswahl aus den geheimen Lageberichten des Sicherheitsdienstes der SS 1939-44* (Munich, 1968).

BRAND, ARTHUR, *Das Deutsche Beamtengesetz* (Berlin, 1942).

DOMARUS, MAX (ed.), *Hitler: Reden und Proklamationen 1923-1945* (Würzburg, 1962-3).

FABRICIUS, HANS and STAMM, K., *Bewegung, Staat und Volk in ihrer Organisationen* (Berlin, 1935).

FISCHBACH, OSKAR, *Deutsches Beamtengesetz* (Berlin, 1940).

FRICK, WILHELM, *Die Nationalsozialisten im Reichstag 1924-28* (Munich, 1929).

—— *Die Nationalsozialisten im Reichstag 1924-31* (Munich, 1932).

—— *Die Tätigkeit der Nationalsozialisten im Reichstag 1928-1930* (n.p., n.d.).

Hitler's Table Talk 1941-44, introd. Hugh Trevor-Roper (London, 1973).

KLOSS, ERHARD (ed.), *Reden des Führers: Politik und Propaganda Adolf Hitlers 1922-1945* (Munich, 1967).

LOCHNER, LOUIS P. (ed.), *The Goebbels Diaries* (London, 1948).

Das Mitgliedschaftswesen im Reichsbund der Deutschen Beamten (Berlin, n.d.).

Mitteilungsblatt der Nationalsozialisten in den Parlamenten und gemeindlichen Vertretungskörpern.

MÜLLER, H. *et al.*, *Neues Beamtenrecht für Grossdeutschland* (Leipzig, 1944).

MÜNZ, LUDWIG, *Führer durch die Behörden und Organisationen* (Berlin, 1937).

―― and LEHMANN, CARL, *Führer durch die Behörden und Organisationen* (Berlin, 1934).

NSDAP Partei-Statistik, 3 vols. (Munich, 1935).

Organisationsbuch der NSDAP (Munich, 1937).

PETZINA, DIETMAR *et al.* (eds.), *Sozialgeschichtliches Arbeitsbuch*, iii. *Materialien zur Statistik des Deutschen Reiches 1914-1945* (Munich, 1978).

Reden gehalten auf der 1. Kundgebung der Berufsgruppe Verwaltungsbeamte im BNSDJ am 14. September 1933 (Berlin, 1933).

SAUER, FRANZ (ed.), *Beamtenrecht des Reichs: Sammlung der für die Beamten geltenden reichsrechtlichen Bestimmungen* (Berlin, 1933).

SCHÄFERS, KARL *et al.* (eds.), *Deutsches Beamtengesetz vom 26. Januar 1937* (Berlin, 1937).

SCHNEIDER, H. (ed.), *Richtlinien Propaganda und Schulung* (Reichsbund der Deutschen Beamten; Berlin, 1936-9).

SCHNEIDER, RICHARD, *Kommentar zum Deutschen Beamtengesetz* (Berlin, 1937).

―― *et al.*, *Kommentar zur Verordnung über die Vorbildung und die Laufbahnen der deutschen Beamten* (Berlin, 1939).

SEEL, HANNS and SCHNEIDER, RICHARD, *Laufbahnen der deutschen Beamten*, ii/4, *Allgemeine und innere Verwaltung: Höherer Dienst* (Berlin, 1940).

STUCKART, WILHELM and HOFFMAN, HORST (eds.), *Handbuch des Beamtenrechts* (Berlin and Leipzig, 1938).

Taschenbuch für Verwaltungsbeamte (Berlin, 1940-3).

Trials of the War Criminals before the Nuremberg Military Tribunals under Control Council Law No. 10 (Green Series), vols. 12-14 (Case 11: The Ministries Case) (Washington, 1950).

TREUE, WOLFGANG, *Deutsche Parteiprogramme 1861-1945* (Göttingen and Frankfurt, 1954).

[NSDAP], *Verfügungen, Anordnungen, Bekanntgaben*, vols. ii, iv, vi (Munich, 1942-4).

WEGNER, KONSTANZE and ALBERTIN, LOTHAR (eds.), *Linksliberalismus in der Weimarer Republik: Die Führungsgremien der Deutschen Demokratischen Partei und der Deutschen Staatspartei 1918-1933* (Düsseldorf, 1980).

III. CONTEMPORARY NEWSPAPERS AND PERIODICALS

Beamtenjahrbuch.
Die Deutsche Forstzeitung.
Deutsches Recht.
Der Deutsche Verwaltungsbeamte.
Deutsche Verwaltungsrecht.
Deutsche Zollbeamtenzeitung.
Nationalsozialistische Beamten-Zeitung.
Der Schulungsbrief.
Steuer-Warte.
Völkischer Beobachter.
Zeitschrift der Akademie für Deutsches Recht.

IV. SELECTED SECONDARY WORKS

ABRAHAM, DAVID, 'Labor's Way: On the Successes and Limits of Socialist Politics in Interwar and Post-World War II Germany', *International Labor and Working Class History*, 28 (1985), 1-24.
—— *The Collapse of the Weimar Republic: Political Economy and Crisis* (New York, 1986).
ABRAHAM, HANS F., *Intergovernmental Relations in Germany* (Cambridge, Mass., 1943).
ADAM, UWE, *Judenpolitik im Dritten Reich* (Düsseldorf, 1979).
ALLEN, WILLIAM S., *The Infancy of Nazism: The Memoirs of ex-Gauleiter Krebs 1923-1933* (New York, 1976).
Allgemeiner Deutscher Beamtenbund, *Der Nationalsozialismus: Eine Gefahr für das Berufsbeamtentum* (Berlin, 1932).
Almanach der Deutschen Beamten (Berlin, 1934).
AMBROSIUS, LORENZ, *Das Besoldungsrecht der Beamten: Kommentar* (Düsseldorf, 1954).
ANDERSON, MARGARET and BARKIN, KENNETH, 'The Myth of the Puttkamer Purge and the Reality of the Kulturkampf: Some Reflections on the Historiography of Imperial Germany', *JMH*, 54 (1982), 647-86.
ANDERSON, WILLIAM (ed.), *Local Government in Europe* (New York, 1939).
ANSCHÜTZ, GERHARD, *Die Verfassung des Deutschen Reiches* (Bad Homburg, 1960; orig. edn., 1921).
—— and THOMA, RICHARD (eds.), *Handbuch des deutschen Staatsrechts*, 2 vols. (Tübingen, 1932).
APELT, WILLIBALT, 'Die Entwicklung des öffentlichen Rechts im Freistaat Sachsen 1923-1930', *JöR*, 19 (1931), 34-57.
—— *Geschichte der Weimarer Verfassung* (Munich and Berlin, 1964; orig. edn., 1946).

ARENDT, HANNAH, *The Origins of Totalitarianism* (New York, 1951).

ARTZT, HEINZ, *Der Reichsstatthalter im Gemeinschaftsstaat* (Dresden, 1937).

ASTEL, KARL and WEBER, ERNA, 'Die unterschiedliche Fortpflanzung: Untersuchung über die Fortpflanzung der 12 000 Beamten und Angestellten der Thüringschen Staatsverwaltung', *Politische Biologie*, 9 (1939).

——*Die Kinderzahl der 29 000 politischen Leiter des Gaues Thüringen der NSDAP und die Ursachen der ermittelten Fortpflanzungshäufigkeit* (Berlin, 1943).

Die Ausbildung der deutschen Juristen: Veröffentlichungen des Arbeitskreises für Fragen der Juristenbildung, ii (Tübingen, 1960).

AY, KARL-LUDWIG, *Die Entstehung einer Revolution: Die Volksstimmung in Bayern während des Ersten Weltkrieges* (Berlin, 1968).

BADER, K. S., *Die deutsche Juristen* (Tübingen, 1947).

BARTELD, A., 'Die deutsche Beamtenbewegung', in Anton Erkelenz (ed.), *Zehn Jahre Deutscher Republik* (Berlin, 1929), 344-51.

BATOCKI, ADOLF et al. (eds.), *Staatsreferendar und Staatsassessor: Reformvorschläge für das Ausbildungs- und Berechtigungswesen der Juristen und Volkswirte* (Jena, 1927).

BAUER, KARL, *Querverbindung von Partei- und Staatsbehörden* (Tübingen, 1936).

BAUM, WALTER, ' "Reichsreform" im Dritten Reich', *VjhZ*, 3/1 (1955), 36-56.

Beamte, nicht leichtgläubig sein, das Zentrum hat euch was zu sagen (Berlin, 1928).

BECKER, JOSEF (ed.), *Heinrich Köhler: Lebenserinnerungen des Politikers und Staatsmannes 1878-1949* (Stuttgart, 1964).

BEETHAM, DAVID, *Max Weber and the Theory of Modern Politics* (London, 1974).

BEHREND, HANS-KARL, 'Zur Personalpolitik des preussischen Ministeriums des Innern: Die Besetzung der Landratsstellen in den östlichen Provinzen 1919- 1933', *Jahrbuch für die Geschichte Mittel- und Ostdeutschlands*, 6 (1957), 173-214.

BENDERSKY, JOSEPH, 'The Expendable Kronjurist: Carl Schmitt and National Socialism 1933-36', *JCH*, 14/2 (1979), 309-28.

—— *Carl Schmitt: Theorist for the Reich* (Princeton, 1983).

BENDIX, REINHARD, 'Social Stratification and Political Power', *APSR*, 46 (1952), 357-75.

BENTIN, LUTZ-ARWED, *Johannes Popitz und Carl Schmitt: Zur wirtschaftlichen Theorie des totalen Staates in Deutschland* (Munich, 1972).

BERNING, CORNELIA, *Vom 'Abstammungsnachweis' zum 'Zuchtwart': Vokabular des Nationalsozialismus* (Berlin, 1964).

BESSEL, RICHARD and FEUCHTWANGER, E. J. (eds.), *Social Change and Political Development in Weimar Germany* (London, 1981).

BESSON, WALDEMAR, *Württemberg und die deutsche Staatskrise* (Stuttgart, 1959).

BEST, WERNER, *Die deutsche Polizei* (Darmstadt, 1941).

BIEGERT, HANS H., 'Gewerkschaftspolitik in der Phase des Kapp-Lüttwitz-Putsches', in Hans Mommsen et al. (eds.), *Industrielles System und politische Entwicklung in der Weimarer Republik* (Düsseldorf, 1974), 190-205.

BLACHLY, FREDERICK F. and OATMAN, MIRIAM E., *The Government and Administration of Germany* (Baltimore, 1928).

BLACKBOURN, DAVID and ELEY, GEOFF, *The Peculiarities of German History* (Oxford, 1984).

BLEEK, WILHELM, *Von der Kameralausbildung zum Juristenprivileg: Studium, Prüfung und Ausbildung der höheren Beamten des allgemeinen Verwaltungsdienstes in Deutschland im 18. und 19. Jahrhundert* (Berlin, 1972).

BOAK, HELEN L., 'Women in Weimar Germany: The "Frauenfrage" and the Female Vote', in Richard Bessel and E. J. Feuchtwanger (eds.), *Social Change and Political Development in Weimar Germany* (London, 1981), 155-73.

BOCK, GISELA, 'Racism and Sexism in Nazi Germany: Motherhood, Compulsory Sterilization and the State', in Renate Bridenthal *et al.* (eds.), *When Biology Became Destiny: Women in Weimar and Nazi Germany* (New York, 1984), 271-96.

BÖCKENFÖRDE, ERNST WOLFGANG, *Gesetz und gesetzgebende Gewalt* (Berlin, 1958).

BOEHNERT, GUNNAR C., 'The Jurists in the SS-Führerkorps, 1925-1939', in Gerhard Hirschfeld and Lothar Kettenacker (eds.), *The 'Führer State': Myth and Reality. Studies on the Structure and Politics of the Third Reich* (Stuttgart, 1981), 361-74.

BOERNER, ALFRED V., 'Toward Reichsreform: The Reichsgaue', *APSR*, 33 (1939), 1059-81.

BOHLEN, A., *Besoldungsreform und höhere Beamte* (Berlin [1925]).

—— *Die höheren Beamten nach drei Gehaltskürzungen* (Berlin, 1931).

BORCH, HERBERT von, *Obrigkeit und Widerstand: Zur politischen Soziologie des Beamtentums* (Tübingen, 1954).

—— 'Obrigkeit und Widerstand', *VjhZ*, 3/3 (1955), 297-310.

BORN, LESTER K., 'The Ministerial Collecting Center near Kassel, Germany', *The American Archivist*, 13 (1950), 237-58.

BORNHAK, KONRAD, *Preussisches Verwaltungsrecht* (Freiburg, 1889).

BOWEN, RALPH H., *German Theories of the Corporative State* (New York and London, 1947).

BRAATZ, WERNER E., 'Franz von Papen and the Preussenschlag, 20 July 1932: A Move by the "New State" towards Reichsreform', *European Studies Review*, 3 (1973), 157-80.

BRACHER, KARL DIETRICH, *Die Auflösung der Weimarer Republik: Eine Studie zum Problem des Machtverfalls in der Demokratie* (Düsseldorf, 1978; orig. edn., 1955).

—— 'Brünings unpolitische Politik und die Auflösung der Weimarer Republik', *VjhZ*, 19/2 (1971), 113-23.

—— SAUER, WOLFGANG, and SCHULZ, GERHARD, *Die nationalsozialistische Machtergreifung: Studien zur Errichtung des totalitären Herrschaftssystems in Deutschland 1933/34* (Cologne and Opladen, 1962).

BRAND, ARTHUR, *Das Beamtenrecht: Die Rechtsverhältnisse der preussischen Staats- und Kommunalbeamten* (Berlin, 1928).

BRANDT, EDMUND, *Die politische Treuepflicht: Rechtsquellen zur Geschichte des deutschen Berufsbeamtentums* (Karlsruhe and Heidelberg, 1976).

BRAUN, OTTO, *Von Weimar zu Hitler* (New York, 1940).

BRAUSSE, HANS BERNHARD, *Die Führungsordnung des deutschen Volkes: Grundlegung einer Führungslehre* (Hamburg, 1941).

BRECHT, ARNOLD, *Reichsreform: Warum und Wie?* (Berlin, 1931).

—— 'Civil Service', *Social Research*, 3 (1936), 202-21.

—— 'Bureaucratic Sabotage', *Annals of the American Academy of Political Science*, 189 (1937), 48-57.

—— 'The Relevance of Foreign Experience', in Fritz Morstein Marx (ed.), *Public Management and the New Democracy* (New York, 1940), 107-29.

—— *Federalism and Regionalism in Germany: The Division of Prussia* (New York, 1945).

—— 'Personnel Management', in Edward H. Litchfield (ed.), *Governing Post-War Germany* (Ithaca, 1953), 263-93.

—— *Aus nächster Nähe: Lebenserinnerungen eines beteiligten Beobachters 1886-1927* (Stuttgart, 1966).

—— *Mit der Kraft des Geistes: Lebenserinnerungen zweite Hälfte 1927-1967* (Stuttgart, 1967).

—— *The Political Education of Arnold Brecht: An Autobiography 1884-1970* (Princeton, 1970).

——and GLASER, COMSTOCK, *The Art and Technique of Administration in German Ministries* (Cambridge, Mass., 1940).

BRIDENTHAL, RENATE and KOONZ, CLAUDIA, 'Beyond *Kinder, Küche, Kirche*: Weimar Women in Politics and Work', in Renate Bridenthal *et al.* (eds.), *When Biology Became Destiny: Women in Weimar and Nazi Germany* (New York, 1984), 33-65.

BRILL, HERMANN, *Der Kampf um die Erhaltung des Berufsbeamtentums* (Berlin, 1926).

BROMBACH, H., 'Leistungsgrundsatz und Personalverwaltung', *Deutsche Verwaltungsblätter*, 1937, 86-9.

BROSZAT, MARTIN, *Nationalsozialistische Polenpolitik 1939-1945* (Frankfurt, 1965).

—— 'Soziale Motivation und Führer-Bindung des Nationalsozialismus', *VjhZ*, 18/4 (1970), 392-409.

—— (ed.), *Bayern in der NS-Zeit*, i. *Soziale Lage und politisches Verhalten der Bevölkerung im Spiegel vertraulicher Berichte* (Munich and Vienna, 1977).

—— *The Hitler State: The Foundation and Development of the Internal Structure of the Third Reich* (London, 1981).

BRUCK, W. F., *Das Ausbildungsproblem des Beamten in Verwaltung und Wirtschaft: Geschichtliches und Reformvorschläge* (Leipzig, 1926).

BRUNET, RENÉ, *The New German Constitution* (New York, 1922).

BRÜNING, HEINRICH, *Memoiren 1918-1934*. 2 vols. (Munich, 1972).

BRUNS, H., *Das Prinzip verfassungsrechtlicher Sicherung der Beamtenrechte* (Bad Godesberg, 1955).

BRY, GERHARD, *Wages in Germany 1871-1945* (Princeton, 1960).

BUCHHEIM, HANS *et al.*, *Anatomy of the SS State* (New York, 1968).

BURIN, FREDERIC S., 'Bureaucracy and National Socialism', in Robert K. Merton *et al.* (eds.), *Reader in Bureaucracy* (Glencoe, 1952), 33-47.

BURK, KATHLEEN (ed.), *War and the State: The Transformation of British Government, 1914-1919* (London, 1982).

CAMPBELL, G. A., *The Civil Service in Britain* (London, 1965).

CAPLAN, JANE, 'The Politics of Administration: The Reich Interior Ministry and the Germany Civil Service 1933-1943', *Historical Journal*, 20/3 (1977), 707-36.

—— 'Theories of Fascism: Nicos Poulantzas as Historian', *History Workshop Journal*, 3 (1977), 83-100.

—— 'Bureaucracy, Politics and the National Socialist State', in Peter D. Stachura (ed.), *The Shaping of the Nazi State* (London, 1978), 234-56.

—— '"The Imaginary Universality of Particular Interests": The "Tradition" of the Civil Service in German History', *Social History*, 4/2 (1979), 299-317.

—— 'Recreating the Civil Service: Issues and Ideas in the Nazi Regime', in Jeremy Noakes (ed.), *Government, Party and People in Nazi Germany* (Exeter, 1980), 34-56.

—— 'Strategien und Politik in der Ausbildung der Beamten im Dritten Reich', in Manfred Heinemann (ed.), *Erziehung und Schulung im Dritten Reich*, ii. *Hochschule, Erwachsenenbildung* (Stuttgart, 1980), 246-60.

—— 'Civil Service Support for National Socialism', in Gerhard Hirschfeld and Lothar Kettenacker (eds.), *The 'Führer State': Myth and Reality. Studies on the Structure and Politics of the Third Reich* (Stuttgart, 1981), 167-93.

—— 'Speaking the Right Language: The Nazi Party and the Civil Service Vote in the Weimar Republic', in Thomas Childers (ed.), *The Formation of the Nazi Constituency 1918-1933* (London, 1986), 182-201.

CARROLL, BERNICE, *Design for Total War: Arms and Economics in the Third Reich* (The Hague, 1968).

CHAPMAN, BRIAN, *The Profession of Government* (London, 1959).

—— *Police State* (London, 1970).

CHILDERS, THOMAS, 'National Socialism and the New Middle Class', in Reinhard Mann (ed.), *Die Nationalsozialisten: Analysen faschistischer Bewegungen* (Stuttgart, 1980), 19-33.

—— 'Inflation, Stabilization and Political Realignment in Germany 1924-1928', in Gerald D. Feldman *et al.* (eds.), *Die deutsche Inflation: Eine Zwischenbilanz* (Berlin and New York, 1982), 409-31.

—— *The Nazi Voter: The Social Foundations of Fascism in Germany, 1919-1933* (Chapel Hill, 1983).

—— (ed.), *The Formation of the Nazi Constituency 1918-1933* (London, 1986).

COHN, E. J., *Manual of German Law*, i (London, 1968).

COLE, TAYLOR, 'Italy's Fascist Bureaucracy', *APSR*, 32 (1938), 1143-57.

—— 'Corporative Organisation of the Third Reich', *Review of Politics*, 2/4 (1940), 438-62.

COYNER, SANDRA, 'Class Consciousness and Consumption: The New Middle Class during the Weimar Republic', *Journal of Social History*, 10 (1977), 310-31.

CROZIER, MICHEL, *The Bureaucratic Phenomenon* (London, 1964).

CULLITY, JOHN P., 'The Growth of Governmental Employment in Germany', Ph.D. thesis (Columbia, 1964).

—— 'The Growth of Governmental Employment in Germany, 1882-1950', *ZgStW*, 123 (1967), 201-17.

DAHM, GEORG, *Deutsches Recht* (Stuttgart, 1963).

DANCKWERTS, JULIUS, 'Der Rechtsschutz in der Verwaltung', in Hans Heinrich Lammers and Hans Pfundtner (eds.), *Grundlagen, Aufbau und Wirtschaftsordung des nationalsozialistischen Staates*, ii/1 (26) (Berlin, 1936-9).

DANIELS, HANS, *Das Deutsche Beamtengesetz vom 26. Januar 1937* (Berlin, 1937).

DANIELS, HEINRICH, 'Pflichten und Rechten der Beamten', in Gerhard Anschütz and Richard Thoma (eds.), *Handbuch des deutschen Staatsrechts*, ii (Tübingen, 1932), 41-9.

DELBRÜCK, CLEMENS von, *Die Ausbildung für den höheren Verwaltungsdienst in Preussen* (Jena, 1917).

Deutscher Beamtenbund: Ursprung, Weg, Ziele (Bad Godesberg, 1968).

DICKMANN, FRITZ, 'Die Regierungsbildung in Thüringen als Modell der Machtergreifung: Ein Brief Hitlers aus dem Jahre 1930', *VjhZ*, 14 (1966), 454-64.

DIEHL-THIELE, PETER, *Partei und Staat im Dritten Reich: Untersuchungen zum Verhältnis von NSDAP und allgemeiner und innerer Staatsverwaltung* (Munich, 1969).

DIMPKER, HEINRICH, *Die 'Wiederherstellung des Berufsbeamtentums': Nationalsozialistische Personalpolitik in Lübeck*, (Kiel, 1981).

DÖHRING, ERICH, *Geschichte der deutschen Rechtspflege seit 1500* (Berlin, 1953).

DOMRÖSE, ORTWIN, *Der NS-Staat in Bayern von der Machtergreifung bis zum Röhm-Putsch* (Munich, 1974).

DORN, WALTER A., 'The Prussian Bureaucracy in the Eighteenth Century', *Political Science Quarterly*, 46 (1931), 403-23; 47 (1932), 75-94, 259-73.

DREWS, BILL, *Grundzüge einer Verwaltungsreform* (Berlin, 1917).

DUGGAN, PAUL R., 'Currents of Administrative Reform in Germany 1907-1918', Ph.D. thesis (Harvard, 1968).

EBELING, CARL-OTTO, *Grundlagen und wesentliche Merkmale des Beamtenverhältnisses im nationalsozialistischen Staat* (Hamburg, 1936).

ECHTERHÖLTER, RUDOLF, *Das öffentliche Recht im nationalsozialistischen Staat* (Stuttgart, 1970).

EHNI, HANS-PETER, 'Zum Parteienverhältnis in Preussen 1918-1932', *Archiv für Sozialgeschichte*, 11 (1971), 241-88.

— *Bollwerk Preussen? Preussenregierung, Reich-Länder Problem und Sozialdemokratie 1928-1932* (Bonn and Bad Godesberg, 1975).

EICHHOLTZ, DIETER, *Geschichte der deutschen Kriegswirtschaft 1939-1945*, ii (E. Berlin, 1985).

EIMERS, ENNO, *Das Verhältnis von Preussen und Reich in den ersten Jahren der Weimarer Republik (1918-1923)* (Berlin, 1969).

ELBEN, WOLFGANG, *Das Problem der Kontinuität in der deutschen Revolution 1918-1919* (Düsseldorf, 1965).

ELEY, GEOFF, *From Unification to Nazism: Reinterpreting the German Past* (London, 1986).

EMERSON, RUPERT, *State and Sovereignty in Modern Germany* (Yale, 1928).

Entwicklung und Reform des Beamtenrechts: Veröffentlichung der Vereinigung der deutschen Staatsrechtslehrer (Berlin and Leipzig, 1932).

ERGER, JOHANNES, *Der Kapp-Lüttwitz-Putsch: Ein Beitrag zur deutschen Innenpolitik 1919/20* (Düsseldorf, 1970).

ESCHENBURG, THEODOR, 'Politik und Verwaltung', *Universitas*, 1948, 917-30.

— *Der Beamte in Partei und Parlament* (Frankfurt, 1952).

— *Ämterpatronage* (Stuttgart, 1961).

— 'Eine Beamtenvernehmung im 3. Reich', *VjhZ*, 11/2 (1963), 210-12.

— *Die improvisierte Demokratie: Gesammelte Aufsätze zur Weimarer Republik* (Munich, 1963).

EVANS, RICHARD, 'The Myth of Germany's Missing Revolution', *New Left Review*, 149 (Jan./Feb. 1985), 67-94.

EYCK, ERICH, *A History of the Weimar Republic*, 2 vols. (New York, 1967).

FABRICIUS, HANS, *Der Beamte einst und im neuen Reich* (Berlin, 1933).

— *Dr. Frick: Der revolutionäre Staatsmann* (Berlin [1933]).

— 'Gedanken über nationalsozialistische Verwaltungspolitik', *ZADR*, 1935, 46-8.

— 'Das Deutsche Beamtengesetz', *ZADR* 1937.

— *Dr. Frick: Ein Lebensbild des Reichsministers des Innern* (Berlin, 1938).

— 'Soldatisches Beamtentum', *Der Prignitzer*, 18 Nov. 1941.

FALKENBERG, ALBERT, *Die deutsche Beamtenbewegung nach der Revolution* (Berlin, 1920).

FAUSER, MANFRED, 'Das Gesetz im Führerstaat', *AöR*, 26 (1935), 129-54.

— 'Verwaltungsverfahren und verwaltungsgerichtliches Verfahren nach dem Führererlass vom 28. August 1939', *AöR*, 31 (1940), 186-93.

FELDMAN, GERALD D. *et al.* (eds.), *Die deutsche Inflation: Eine Zwischenbilanz / The German Inflation Reconsidered: A Preliminary Balance* (Berlin, 1982).

FENSKE, HANS, 'Monarchisches Beamtentum und demokratischer Rechtsstaat: Zum Problem der Bürokratie in der Weimarer Republik', in *Demokratie und Verwaltung: 25 Jahre Hochschule für Verwaltung Speyer* (Berlin, 1972), 117-36.

—— 'Preussische Beamtenpolitik vor 1918', *Der Staat*, 12 (1973), 339-56.

Festgabe für Heinrich Himmler (Berlin, 1941).

FINER, HERMANN, *The British Civil Service* (London, 1927).

—— 'The Principles and Practice of Remuneration in the British Civil Service', in Wilhelm Gerloff (ed.), *Die Beamtenbesoldung im modernen Staat* (Munich and Leipzig, 1932).

—— *The Theory and Practice of Modern Government*, i (London, 1932).

FINER, SAMUEL E., *Comparative Government* (Harmondsworth, 1974).

FISCHBACH, OSKAR, 'Voraussetzungen für die Schaffung von Beamtenstellen', *Beamtenjahrbuch*, 1935, 659-67.

—— 'Das DBG vom 26. 1. 1937: Entstehungsgeschichte und Überblick', *Beamtenjahrbuch*, 1937, 44-53.

—— *Deutsches Beamtengesetz* (Berlin, 1940).

FLEINER, FRITZ, *Beamtenstaat und Volksstaat* (Tübingen, 1916).

—— *Institutionen des deutschen Verwaltungsrechts* (Aalen, 1963; orig. edn., 1928).

FLEMING, GERALD, *Hitler and the Final Solution* (Oxford, 1986).

FLETCHER, WILLARD A., 'The German Administration in Luxemburg 1940-1942', *Historical Journal*, 13 (1970), 533-44.

FORSTHOFF, ERNST, *Der totale Staat* (Hamburg, 1933).

—— *Die Verwaltung als Leistungsträger* (Stuttgart, 1938).

—— *Lehrbuch des Verwaltungsrechts*, i (Berlin, 1966).

FRAENKEL, ERNST, *The Dual State: A Contribution to the Theory of Dictatorship* (New York, 1941).

FRANK, ELKE, 'The Role of the Bureaucracy in Transition', *Journal of Politics*, 27 (1966), 724-53.

FRANK, HANS, (ed.), *Deutsches Verwaltungsrecht* (Munich, 1937).

—— 'Staat und Recht', *Nationalsozialistisches Jahrbuch*, 1937, 244-9.

—— *Rechtsgrundlegung des nationalsozialistischen Führerstaates* (Munich, 1938).

—— *Recht und Verwaltung* (Munich, 1939).

—— *Die Technik des Staates* (Berlin, Leipzig, and Vienna, 1942).

—— *Im Angesicht des Galgens* (Munich, 1953).

FRASER, PETER, 'The Impact of the War of 1914-1918 on the British Political System', in M. R. D. Foot (ed.), *War and Society* (London, 1973), 123-39.

FREYMUTH, A., FALCK, ERNST, and WÄGER, HERMANN, *Sozialdemokratie und Berufsbeamtentum* (Berlin, 1927).

FREYTAGH-LORINGHOVEN, AXEL FREIHERR von, *Die Weimarer Verfassung in Lehre und Wirklichkeit* (Munich, 1924).

FRICK, WILHELM, *Wir bauen das Dritte Reich* (Berlin, 1934).

—— 'Probleme des neuen Verwaltungsrechts', *Der Gemeindetag*, 21, 1 Nov. 1936.

—— 'Vier Jahre Aufbau des 3. Reiches', *ZADR* 1937.

—— 'Erst Deutsche, dann Beamte!', *Deutsches Nachrichtenbüro* 148, 19 Oct. 1937.

FRICKE, DIETER, 'Reichsbund der höheren Beamten (RhB) 1918-1934', in Dieter Fricke (ed.), *Handbuch der bürgerlichen Parteien und anderer bürgerlicher Interessenorganisationen*, ii (Leipzig, 1968), 493-500.

FRIEDRICH, CARL J., 'The Continental Tradition of Training Administrators in Law and Jurisprudence', *JMH*, 11 (1939), 129-48.

—— and COLE, TAYLOR, *Responsible Bureaucracy: A Study of the Swiss Civil Service* (New York, 1932).

—— and BRZEZINSKI, ZBIGNIEW K., *Totalitarian Dictatorship and Autocracy* (Cambridge, Mass., 1956).

FRIESENHAHN, ERNST, 'Zur Legitimation und zum Scheitern der Weimarer Verfassung', in Karl Dietrich Erdmann and Hagen Schulze (eds.), *Weimar: Selbstpreisgabe einer Demokratie* (Düsseldorf, 1980), 81-108.

GAST, HUBERT, *Die Beamtenbesoldung im Reich und in den Ländern* (Berlin, 1922).

GEIB, E., 'Die Ausbildung des Nachwuchses für den höheren Verwaltungsdienst', *AöR*, 80 (1955/6), 307-45.

GEIGER, THEODOR, 'Panik im Mittelstand', *Die Arbeit*, 10 (1930), 637-54.

GERBER, CARL FRIEDRICH von, *Grundzüge des deutschen Staatsrechts* (Leipzig, 1880).

GERBER, HANS, 'Vom Begriff und Wesen des Beamtentums', *AöR*, 18 (1930), 1-85.

—— *Politische Erziehung des Beamtentums in nationalsozialistischen Staat* (Tübingen, 1933).

—— *Auf dem Wege zum neuen Reiche: Eine Sammlung politischer Vorträge und Aufsätze aus deutscher Notzeit 1919-1931* (Stuttgart and Berlin, 1934).

—— and MERKL, ADOLF, *Entwicklung und Reform des Beamtenrechts* (Berlin and Leipzig, 1932).

GERLACH, HELLMUTH von, *Meine Erlebnisse in der preussischen Verwaltung* (Berlin, 1919).

GERLOFF, WILHELM (ed.), *Die Beamtenbesoldung im modernen Staat* (Munich and Leipzig, 1932).

GERSDORFF, URSULA von, *Frauen im Kriegsdienst 1914-1945* (Stuttgart, 1969).

GERTH, H. H. and WRIGHT MILLS, C. (eds.), *From Max Weber: Essays in Sociology* (London, 1948).

GEYER, MICHAEL, 'The State in National Socialist Germany', in Charles Bright and Susan Harding (eds.), *Statemaking and Social Movements: Essays in History and Theory* (Ann Arbor, 1984), 193-232.

GILBERT, FELIX (ed.), *The Historical Essays of Otto Hintze* (New York, 1975).

GILLIS, JOHN P., 'Aristocracy and Bureaucracy in Nineteenth-Century Prussia', *Past and Present*, 41 (1968), 105-29.

—— *The Prussian Bureaucracy in Crisis, 1840-1860: Origins of an Administrative Ethos* (Stanford, 1971).

—— 'Germany', in Raymond Grew (ed.), *Crises of Political Development in Europe and the United States* (Princeton, 1979), 313-45.

GLEES, ANTHONY, 'Albert C. Grzesinski and the Politics of Prussia, 1926-1930', *English Historical Review*, 89 (1974), 814-34.

GMELIN, H., 'Bericht über die Gesetzgebung in Hessen in den Jahren 1921 und 1922', *JöR*, 12 (1923/4), 113-25.

—— 'Die Entwicklung des öffentlichen Rechts in Hessen von 1923 bis Ende 1928', *JöR*, 17 (1929), 172-200.

GOEBBELS, JOSEF, *Preussen muss wieder preussisch werden!* (Munich, 1932).

GOWING, MARGARET, 'The Organisation of Manpower in Britain during the Second World War', *JCH*, 7/1-2 (1972), 147-62.

GRABOWSKY, ADOLF (ed.), *Die Reform des deutschen Beamtentums* (Gotha, 1917).

GRAIS, HUE de and PETERS, HANS, *Handbuch der Verfassung und Verwaltung in Preussen und dem Deutschen Reich* (Berlin, 1926).

GREBING, HELGA, *Der 'deutsche Sonderweg' in Europa 1806-1945* (Stuttgart, Bern, Cologne, and Mainz, 1986).

GRILL, JOHNPETER HORST, *The Nazi Movement in Baden, 1920-1945* (Chapel Hill, 1983).

GROTH, KARL, *Die Reichsfinanzverwaltung* (Berlin, 1937).

GRUCHMANN, LOTHAR, 'Die "Reichsregierung" im Führerstaat', in Günther Doeker and Winfried Steffani (eds.), *Klassenjustiz und Pluralismus* (Hanover, 1973), 187-223.

GRZESINSKI, ALBERT C., 'Verwaltungsreform und demokratische Republik', *Deutsche Republik*, 3 (1929), 1164-7.

—— *La Tragie-Comédie de la République allemande* (Paris, 1934).

GÜNTHER, A., 'Die Folgen des Krieges für Einkommen und Lebenshaltung der mittleren Volksschichten Deutschlands', in R. Meerwarth *et al.*, *Die Einwirkung des Krieges auf Bevölkerungsbewegung, Einkommen und Lebenshaltung in Deutschland* (Stuttgart, Berlin, Leipzig, and New Haven, 1932), 99-279.

HAHN, CLAUDIA, 'Der öffentliche Dienst und die Frauen: Beamtinnen in der Weimarer Republik', in Frauengruppe Faschismusforschung, *Mutterkreuz und Arbeitsbuch: Zur Geschichte der Frauen in der Weimarer Republik* (Frankfurt, 1981), 49-78.

HALLOWELL, JOHN H., *The Decline of Liberalism as an Ideology: With Particular Reference to German Politico-Legal Thought* (Berkeley, 1943).

HAM, CHRISTOPHER and HILL, MICHAEL, *The Policy Process in the Modern Capitalist State* (New York, 1984).

HAMILTON, RICHARD, *Who Voted for Hitler?* (Princeton, 1982).

HANKO, HELMUT, 'Kommunalpolitik in der "Hauptstadt der Bewegung" 1933-1935: Zwischen "revolutionärer" Umgestaltung und Verwaltungskontinuität', in Martin Broszat *et al.* (eds.), *Bayern in der NS-Zeit*, iii. *Herrschaft und Gesellschaft im Konflikt* (Munich and Vienna, 1981), 329-441.

HANSMEYER, KARL-HEINRICH (ed.), *Kommunale Finanzpolitik in der Weimarer Republik* (Stuttgart, Cologne, Berlin, and Mainz, 1973).

HARTMANN, F., 'Führer und Beamter', *DR*, 8 (1935), 212-4.

HARTUNG, FRITZ, *Studien zur Geschichte der preussischen Verwaltung*, i. *Vom 16. Jahrhundert bis zum Zusammenbruch des alten Staates im Jahre 1806* (Berlin, 1942).

—— *Zur Geschichte des Beamtentums in 19. und 20. Jahrhundert* (Berlin, 1948).

—— *Staatsbildende Kräfte der Neuzeit* (Berlin, 1961).

—— *Deutsche Verfassungsgeschichte vom 15. Jahrhundert bis zur Gegenwart* (Stuttgart, 1969; orig. edn., 1950).

HATTENHAUER, HANS, *Geschichte des Beamtentums* (Cologne, 1980).

HAUFF, LILY, *Die Entwickelung der Frauenberufe in den letzten drei Jahrzehnten* (Berlin, 1911).

HAUNGS, PETER, *Reichspräsident und parlamentarische Kabinettsregierung: Eine Studie zum Regierungssystem der Weimarer Republik in den Jahren 1924 bis 1929* (Cologne and Opladen, 1968).

HEGEL, GEORG WILHELM FRIEDRICH, *Philosophy of Right*, trans. T. M. Knox (Oxford, 1967).

HELD, DAVID, *Introduction to Critical Theory: Horkheimer to Habermas* (London, 1980).

HELFRITZ, H., 'Die Entwicklung des öffentlichen Rechts in Preussen', *JöR*, 14 (1926), 246-69.

HELLER, HERMANN, 'Das Berufsbeamtentum in der deutschen Demokratie', *Die neue Rundschau*, 41 (1930), 721-32.

—— 'Politische Demokratie und soziale Homogenität', in *Gesammelte Schriften*, ii (Leiden and Tübingen, 1971), 421-33.

HENNING, HANS-JOACHIM, *Das westdeutsche Bürgertum in der Epoche der Hochindustrialisierung 1860-1914: Soziales Verhalten und soziale Strukturen*, i. *Das Bildungsbürgertum in den preussischen Westprovinzen* (Wiesbaden, 1972).

—— *Die deutsche Beamtenschaft im 19. Jahrhundert* (Stuttgart, 1984).

HERBST, LUDOLF, 'Die Krise des nationalsozialistischen Regimes am Vorabend des Zweiten Weltkrieges und die forcierte Aufrüstung', *VjhZ*, 26/3 (1978), 347-92.

—— *Der Totale Krieg und die Ordnung der Wirtschaft: Die Kriegswirtschaft im Spannungsfeld von Politik, Ideologie and Propaganda 1933-1945* (Stuttgart, 1982).

HERF, JEFFREY, *Reactionary Modernism: Technology, Culture and Politics in Weimar and the Third Reich* (Cambridge, 1984).

HERZ, JOHN H., 'German Adminstration under the Nazi Regime', *APSR*, 40 (1946), 682-702.

—— 'Political Views of the West German Civil Service', in Hans Speier and W. P. Davison (eds.), *West German Leadership and Foreign Policy* (Evanston and New York, 1957), 96-135.

HERZFELD, HANS, 'Johannes Popitz: Ein Beitrag zur Geschichte des deutschen Beamtentums', in *Forschungen zu Staat und Verfassung: Festgabe für Fritz Hartung* (Berlin, 1958), 343-65.

HIDEN, JOHN and FARQUHARSON, JOHN, *Explaining Hitler's Germany: Historians and the Third Reich* (London, 1983).

HINTZE, OTTO, 'Behördenorganisation und allgemeine Verwaltung in Preussen beim Regierungsantritt Friedrichs II', *Acta Borussica*, 6/1 (Berlin, 1901).

—— *Der Beamtenstand* (Leipzig, 1911).

—— 'Bismarcks Stellung zur Monarchie und zum Beamtentum', in Fritz Hartung (ed.), *Gesammelte Abhandlungen*, iii (Leipzig, 1943), 653-93.

—— 'Geist und Epoche der preussischen Geschichte', in Fritz Hartung (ed.), *Gesammelte Abhandlungen*, iii (Leipzig, 1943), 9-37.

—— 'Der Commissarius und seine Bedeutung in der allgemeinen Verwaltungsgeschichte', in Otto Hintze, *Staat und Verfassung* (Göttingen, 1962), 242-74.

—— 'Der österreichische und der preussische Beamtenstaat im 17. und 18. Jahrhundert', in Otto Hintze, *Staat und Verfassung* (Göttingen, 1962), 321-58.

—— 'Der preussische Militär- und Beamtenstaat im 18. Jahrhundert', in Otto Hintze, *Regierung und Verwaltung* (Göttingen, 1967), 419-28.

HIRSCHFELD, GERHARD and KETTENACKER, LOTHAR (eds.), *The 'Führer State': Myth and Reality. Studies on the Politics and Structure of the Third Reich* (Stuttgart, 1981).

HITLER, ADOLF, *Mein Kampf* (London, 1939).

HOFFMANN, FRIEDRICH, 'Die Ausbildung für Verwaltung und Praxis im deutschen Kameralismus', *ZgStW*, 103 (1943), 177-208.

HOFFMANN, GABRIELE, *Sozialdemokratie und Berufsbeamtentum: Zur Frage nach Wandel und Kontinuität im Verhältnis der Sozialdemokratie zum Berufsbeamtentum in der Weimarer Zeit* (Hamburg, 1972).

HOFFMANN, PETER, *Widerstand, Staatsstreich, Attentat: Der Kampf der Opposition gegen Hitler* (Frankfurt, 1970).

HÖHN, REINHARD, *Die Wandlung im staatsrechtlichen Denken* (Hamburg, 1934).

—— *Rechtsgemeinschaft und Volksgemeinschaft* (Hamburg, 1935).

—— 'Der Beamte', *DR*, 1937, 98-102.

—— 'Staat und Rechtsgemeinschaft', *ZgStW*, 103 (1943), 656-90.

—— MAUNZ, THEODOR, and SWOBODA, ERNST, *Grundfragen der Rechtsauffassung* (Munich, 1938).

HÖHNDORF, E., 'Beamter und öffentlicher Amtsträger', *ZgStW*, 97 (1937), 147-87.

HOLLOWAY, JOHN and PICCIOTTO, SOL (eds.), *State and Capital: A Marxist Debate* (London, 1978).

HOMZE, EDWARD L., *Foreign Labor in Nazi Germany* (Princeton, 1967).

HUBER, ERNST RUDOLF, 'Die Totalität des völkischen Staates', *Die Tat*, 1934.

—— 'Die deutsche Staatswissenschaft', *ZgStW*, 95 (1935), 1-65.

—— *Neue Grundbegriffe des hoheitlichen Rechts* (Berlin, 1935).

—— *Wesen und Inhalt der politischen Verfassung* (Hamburg, 1935).

—— 'Die Selbstverwaltung der Berufsstände', in Hans Frank (ed.), *Deutsches Verwaltungsrecht* (Munich, 1937), 239-61.

—— 'Einheit und Gliederung des völkischen Rechts', *ZgStW*, 98 (1938), 310-58.

—— *Verfassungsrecht des Grossdeutschen Reiches* (Hamburg, 1939).

—— *Bau und Gefüge des Reichs* (Hamburg, 1941).

—— *Die verfassungsrechtliche Stellung des Beamtentums* (Leipzig, 1941).

—— *Dokumente zur deutschen Verfassungsgeschichte*, 3 vols. (Stuttgart, 1961-6).

HUNT, RICHARD N., *German Social Democracy 1918-1933* (Chicago, 1970).

HÜTTENBERGER, PETER, *Die Gauleiter: Studie zum Wandel des Machtgefüges in der NSDAP* (Stuttgart, 1969).

—— 'Nationalsozialistische Polykratie', *Geschichte und Gesellschaft*, 2 (1976), 417-42.

—— 'Interessenvertretung und Lobbyismus im Dritten Reich', in Gerhard Hirschfeld and Lothar Kettenacker (eds.), *The 'Führer State': Myth and Reality. Studies on the Structure and Politics of the Third Reich* (Stuttgart, 1981), 429-57.

JACOB, HERBERT, *German Administration since Bismarck: Central Authority versus Local Autonomy* (New Haven and London, 1963).

JACOBY, HENRY, *The Bureaucratization of the World* (Berkeley and Los Angeles, 1973).

JAMES, HAROLD, *The German Slump: Politics and Economics 1924-1936* (Oxford, 1986).

JAMES, HERMANN GERLACH, *Principles of Prussian Administration* (New York, 1913).

JARAUSCH, KONRAD H., 'The Crisis of the German Professions 1918-33', *JCH*, 20/3 (1985), 379-98.

—— 'The Perils of Professionalism: Lawyers, Teachers and Engineers in Nazi Germany', *German Studies Review*, 9/1 (1986), 107-37.

JASPER, GOTTHARD, *Der Schutz der Republik: Studien zur staatlichen Sicherung der Demokratie in der Weimarer Republik* (Tübingen, 1963).

JAY, MARTIN, *The Dialectical Imagination: A History of the Frankfurt School and the Institute of Social Research 1923-1950* (Boston, 1973).

JELLINEK, WALTER, 'Revolution und Reichsverfassung', *JöR*, 9 (1920), 1-128.

—— 'Die Rechtsformen des Staatsdienstes: Begriff und rechtliche Natur des Beamtenverhältnisses', in Gerhard Anschütz and Richard Thoma (eds.), *Handbuch des deutschen Staatsrechts*, ii (Tübingen, 1932), 20-33.

—— *Verwaltungsrecht* (Berlin, 1966).

JESSEN, JENS, *Deutsche Finanzwirtschaft* (Hamburg, 1937).

JESSOP, BOB, *The Capitalist State: Marxist Theories and Methods* (London and New York, 1982).

JOHANNY, CARL and REDELBERGER, OSKAR, *Volk, Partei, Reich* (Berlin, Leipzig, and Vienna, 1941).

JOHE, WERNER, *Die gleichgeschaltete Justiz* (Frankfurt, 1967).

JOHNSON, HUBERT C., *Frederick the Great and his Officials* (New Haven and London, 1975).

JONES, LARRY E., 'The Dying Middle: Weimar Germany and the Fragmentation of Bourgeois Politics', *Central European History*, 5 (1972), 23-54.

KAHN-FREUND, OTTO, *Labour Law and Politics in the Weimar Republic* (Oxford, 1981).

KALMER, GEORG, 'Beamtenschaft und Revolution: Eine sozialgeschichtliche Studie über die Voraussetzungen und Wirklichkeit des Problems', in Karl Bosl (ed.), *Bayern im Umbruch* (Munich, 1969), 201-61.

KATER, MICHAEL., 'Die ernsten Bibelforscher im Dritten Reich', *VjhZ*, 17/2 (1969), 181-218.

—— *Studentenschaft und Rechtsradikalismus in Deutschland, 1928-1933: Eine sozialgeschichtliche Studie zur Bildungskrise in der Weimarer Republik* (Hamburg, 1975).

—— *The Nazi Party: A Social Profile of Members and Leaders, 1919-1945* (Cambridge, Mass., 1983).

—— 'Sozialer Wandel in der NSDAP im Züge der nationalsozialistischer Machtergreifung', in Wolfgang Schieder (ed.), *Faschismus als soziale Bewegung: Deutschland und Italien im Vergleich* (Göttingen, 1983), 25-67.

—— 'The Burden of the Past: Problems of a Modern Historiography of Physicians and Medicine in Nazi Germany', *German Studies Review*, 10/1 (1987), 31-56.

KEHR, ECKART, *Der Primat der Innenpolitik: Gesammelte Aufsätze zur preussisch-deutschen Sozialgeschichte im 19. und 20. Jahrhundert* (Berlin, 1965).

KENNEDY, ELLEN, 'The Politics of Toleration in Late Weimar: Hermann Heller's Analysis of Fascism and Political Culture', *History of Political Thought*, 5/1 (1984), 109-27.

—— 'Carl Schmitt und die "Frankfurter Schule": Deutsche Liberalismuskritik im 20. Jahrhundert', *Geschichte und Gesellschaft*, 12/3 (1986), 380-419.

KERN, ERNST, 'Berufsbeamtentum und Politik', *AöR*, 77 (1951/2), 107-10.

KERSHAW, IAN, *Popular Opinion and Political Dissent in the Third Reich* (Oxford, 1983).

—— *The Nazi Dictatorship: Problems and Perspectives of Interpretation* (London, 1985).

—— *The 'Hitler Myth': Image and Reality in the Third Reich* (Oxford, 1987).

KING, CHRISTINE, *The Nazi State and the New Religions: Five Case Studies in Non-Conformity* (New York, 1982).

KIRCHHEIMER, OTTO, 'The Legal Order of National Socialism', *Studies in Philosophy and Social Science*, 9 (1941), 456-75.

—— *Politik und Verfassung* (Frankfurt, 1964).

—— *Funktionen des Staats und der Verfassung: Zehn Analysen* (Frankfurt, 1972).

KIRSCHENMANN, DIETRICH, *'Gesetz' im Staatsrecht und in der Staatsrechtslehre des Nationalsozialismus* (Berlin, 1970).

KITSON-CLARK, G. R., '"Statesmen in Disguise": Reflections on the History of the Neutrality of the Civil Service', *Historical Journal*, 2/1 (1959), 19-39.

KLENNER, JOCHEN, *Verhältnis von Partei und Staat 1933-1945: Dargestellt am Beispiel Bayerns* (Munich, 1974).

KLOTZ, HELMUT, *Nationalsozialismus und Beamtentum* (Berlin, 1931).

KLUGE, RUDOLF and KRÜGER, HEINRICH, *Verfassung und Verwaltung im Grossdeutschen Reich* (Berlin, 1941).

KNAUTH, R., 'Die Entwicklung des öffentlichen Rechts in Thüringen in den Jahren 1923-1927', *JöR*, 16 (1928), 1-50.

— 'Die Entwicklung des öffentlichen Rechts in Thüringen von 1928 bis Mitte 1931', *JöR*, 19 (1931), 58-112.

KNODEL, JOHN E., *The Decline of Fertility in Germany, 1871-1933* (Princeton, 1974).

KNOPP, G., *Die preussische Verwaltung des Regierungsbezirks Düsseldorf in den Jahren 1899-1919* (Cologne, 1974).

KOCH, H. W., *A Constitutional History of Germany in the Nineteenth and Twentieth Centuries* (London, 1984).

KOCKA, JÜRGEN, 'The First World War and the "Mittelstand": German Artisans and White-Collar Workers', *JCH*, 8/1 (1973), 101-23.

— *Klassengesellschaft im Krieg: Deutsche Sozialgeschichte 1914-1918* (Göttingen, 1973).

— *Die Angestellten in der deutschen Geschichte 1850-1980* (Göttingen, 1981).

— 'Otto Hintze, Max Weber und das Problem der Bürokratie', *Historische Zeitschrift*, 223 (1981), 65-105.

KOEHL, ROBERT, *RKFDV: German Resettlement and Population Policy 1939-1945. A History of the Reich Commission for the Strengthening of Germandom* (Cambridge, Mass., 1957).

— 'Feudal Aspects of National Socialism', *APSR*, 65 (1960), 921-33.

— *The Black Corps: The Structure and Power Struggles of the Nazi SS* (Madison, 1983).

KOELLREUTTER, OTTO, *Grundriss der allgemeinen Staatslehre* (Tübingen, 1933).

— *Vom Sinn und Wesen der nationalen Revolution* (Berlin, 1933).

— *Der deutsche Führerstaat* (Tübingen, 1934).

— *Volk und Staat in der Weltanschauung des Nationalsozialismus* (Berlin, 1935).

— *Deutsches Verwaltungsrecht* (Berlin, 1936).

— *Grundfragen unserer Volks- und Staatsgestaltung* (Berlin, 1936).

— 'Der nationalsozialistische Rechtsstaat', in Hans Heinrich Lammers and Hans Pfundtner (eds.), *Grundlagen, Aufbau und Wirtschaftsordnung des nationalsozialistischen Staates*, i (Berlin, 1936).

— 'Wesen und Gestaltung der ersten juristischen Staatsprüfung', *ZADR*, 1938, 255-8.

KOENIG, K., 'Der Rechtsweg wegen vermögensrechtliche Ansprüche nach dem DBG', *Deutsche Verwaltungsblätter*, 1937, 83-6.

KÖHLER, LUDWIG von, *Grundlehren des deutschen Verwaltungsrechts* (Stuttgart and Berlin, 1936).

KOLB, EBERHARD, *Die Arbeiterräte in der deutschen Innenpolitik 1918-1919* (Düsseldorf, 1962).

KORDT, ERICH, 'The Public Servant in Germany', *Public Administration*, 16/2 (1938), 173-84.

KOSELLECK, REINHARD, *Preussen zwischen Reform und Revolution: Allgemeines Landrecht, Verwaltung und soziale Bewegung von 1791 bis 1848* (Stuttgart, 1967).

KOSHAR, RUDY, *Social Life, Local Politics, and Nazism: Marburg 1880-1935* (Chapel Hill, 1986).

KÖTTGEN, ARNOLD, *Das deutsche Berufsbeamtentum und die parlamentarische Demokratie* (Berlin and Leipzig, 1928).

—— *Beamtenrecht* (Breslau, 1929).

—— 'Zur Frage des Erwerbs der Beamteneigenschaft', *AöR*, NF 18 (1930), 225-34.

—— 'Die Entwicklung des deutschen Beamtenrechts und die Bedeutung des Beamtentums im Staat der Gegenwart', in Gerhard Anschütz and Richard Thoma (eds.), *Handbuch des deutschen Staatsrechts*, ii (Tübingen, 1932), 1-19.

—— 'Aufgaben und verfassungsrechtliche Stellung des Berufsbeamtentums im modernen Staat', in Fritz Berber (ed.), *Zum Neuaufbau der Verfassung* (*Jahrbuch für politische Forschung*, 1; Berlin, 1933), 101-28.

—— 'Die Ausbildung der höheren Verwaltungsbeamten', *RVBl*, 1935, 465-9.

—— 'Die Entwicklung des öffentlichen Rechts in Preussen', *JöR*, 22 (1935), 273-338.

—— 'Die Stellung des Beamtentums im völkischen Führerstaat', *JöR*, 25 (1938), 1-65.

—— *Deutsche Verwaltung* (Berlin, 1944).

—— 'Das Beamtenurteil des Bundesverfassungsgerichts', *AöR*, 19 (1953/4), 350-68.

KREBS, ALBERT, *Fritz-Dietlof Graf von der Schulenburg: Zwischen Staatsraison und Hochverrat* (Hamburg, 1964).

KROSIGK, LUTZ GRAF SCHWERIN von, *Es geschah in Deutschland* (Tübingen and Stuttgart, 1951).

—— *Staatsbankrott: Die Geschichte der Finanzpolitik des Deutschen Reiches von 1920 bis 1945* (Göttingen, 1974).

KRÜGER [OBERVERWALTUNGSGERICHTSRAT], 'Volksgemeinschaft statt subjektiver Rechte', *DV*, 1935, 37-41.

KRÜGER, HERBERT, *Das Leistungsprinzip als Verfassungsgrundsatz* (Cologne, 1957).

KÜLZ, W., 'Beamtenschaft und politischer Radikalismus', *Der Beamtenfreund* (1932), 7.

KUNZ, ANDREAS, 'Stand versus Klasse: Beamtenschaft und Gewerkschaften im Konflikt um den Personalabbau 1923/24', *Geschichte und Gesellschaft*, 8 (1982), 55-86.

— 'Verteilungskampf oder Interessenkonsensus? Einkommensentwicklung und Sozialverhalten von Arbeitnehmergruppen in der Inflationszeit 1914 bis 1924', in Gerald D. Feldman *et al.* (eds.), *Die deutsche Inflation: Eine Zwischenbilanz* (Berlin, 1982), 347-84.

— *Civil Servants and the Politics of Inflation in Germany 1914-1924* (Berlin and New York, 1986).

KÜSTER, OTTO, 'Zur Frage des Berufsbeamtentums', *AöR*, 77 (1951/2), 364-6.

LAMMERS, HANS HEINRICH, 'Zum 30. Januar 1934', *RVBl*, 1943, 41-4.

— and PFUNDTNER, HANS (eds.), *Grundlagen, Aufbau und Wirtschaftsordnung des nationalsozialistischen Staates* (Berlin, 1936-9).

LASKI, HAROLD, 'Bureaucracy', *Encyclopaedia of the Social Sciences*, iii (London, 1930), 70-3.

LASSAR, G., 'Reichseigene Verwaltung unter der Weimarer Verfassung', *JöR*, 14 (1926), 1-231.

LAUBINGER, HANS-WERNER, 'Die Treuepflicht des Beamten im Wandel der Zeiten', in Karl König *et al.* (eds.), *Öffentlicher Dienst: Festschrift für Carl Hermann Ule* (Cologne, 1977), 89-110.

LEDERER, EMIL and MARSCHAK, JAKOB, 'Der neue Mittelstand', *Grundriss der Sozialökonomik*, 9 (Tübingen, 1926), 121-41.

LEPAWSKY, ALBERT, 'The Nazis Reform the Reich', *APSR*, 30 (1936), 324-50.

LEPPERT-FÖGEN, ANNETTE, *Die deklassierte Klasse: Studien zur Geschichte und Ideologie des Kleinbürgertums* (Frankfurt, 1974).

LIEBEL, HELEN, P., 'Enlightened Bureaucracy versus Enlightened Despotism in Baden, 1750-1792', *Transactions of the American Philosophical Society*, NS 55/5 (1965).

LIERMANN, H., 'Die Entwicklung des öffentlichen Rechts in Baden bis Ende 1928', *JöR*, 17 (1929), 142-71.

LIFTON, ROBERT JAY, *The Nazi Doctors: Medical Killing and the Psychology of Genocide* (New York, 1986).

LINDENLAUB, DIETER, *Richtungskämpfe im Verein für Sozialpolitik* (Wiesbaden, 1967).

LINGG, ANTON, *Die Verwaltung der Nationalsozialistischen Deutschen Arbeiterpartei* (Munich, 1939).

LITCHFIELD, EDWARD H. (ed.), *Governing Postwar Germany* (Ithaca, 1953).

LOTZ, ALBERT, *Geschichte des deutschen Beamtentums* (Berlin, 1914).

LÖWITZ, KARL, 'Max Weber und Karl Marx', *Archiv für Sozialwissenschaft und Sozialpolitik*, 67 (1932), 53-99.

LUDWIG, KARL-HEINZ, *Technik und Ingenieure im Dritten Reich* (Düsseldorf, 1979).

MCLENNAN, GREGOR *et al.* (eds.), *The Idea of the Modern State* (Milton Keynes and Philadelphia, 1984).

MÄDING, ERHARD, *Die staatsrechtliche Stellung der NSDAP* (Leipzig, 1936).

MANNHEIM, KARL, *Ideology and Utopia* (New York, 1936).

MARKÜLL, F., 'Führung und Verwaltung', *RVBl*, 1936, 777-81.

MARX, FRITZ MORSTEIN, 'Berufsbeamtentum in England', *ZgStW*, 90 (1930), 449-95.

—— 'German Bureaucracy in Transition', *APSR*, 28 (1934), 467-80.

—— 'Civil Service in Germany', in Leonard D. White *et al.*, *Civil Service Abroad* (New York, 1935), 161-275.

—— 'Germany's New Civil Service Act', *APSR*, 31 (1937), 878-83.

—— *Government in the Third Reich* (New York, 1937).

—— 'Bureaucracy and Dictatorship', *Review of Politics*, 3 (1941), 100-17.

—— *The Administrative State: An Introduction to Bureaucracy* (Chicago, 1957).

MARX, KARL, 'Critique of Hegel's Doctrine of the State', in *Karl Marx: Early Writings* (Harmondsworth, 1975), 57-198.

MASCHKE, W., *Der höheren Beamten niedrige Besoldung* (Berlin, 1927).

MASON, TIMOTHY W., 'The Primacy of Politics: Politics and Economics in National Socialist Germany', in Stuart J. Woolf (ed.), *The Nature of Fascism* (London, 1968), 165-95.

—— 'Zur Entstehung des Gesetzes zur Neuordnung der nationalen Arbeit vom 20. Januar 1934: Ein Versuch über das Verhältnis "archaischer" und "moderner" Momente in der neuesten deutschen Geschichte', in Hans Mommsen et al. (eds.), *Industrielles System und politische Entwicklung in der Weimarer Republik* (Düsseldorf, 1973), 322-51.

—— *Arbeiterklasse und Volksgemeinschaft: Dokumente und Materialen zur deutschen Arbeiterpolitik 1936-1939* (Opladen, 1975).

—— 'Women in Germany, 1925-40: Family Welfare and Work', *History Workshop Journal*, 2 (1976), 5-32.

—— 'Women in Nazi Germany, Part I', *History Workshop Journal*, 1 (1976), 74-113.

—— *Sozialpolitik im Dritten Reich: Arbeiterklasse und Volksgemeinschaft* (Opladen, 1977).

—— 'Intention and Explanation: A Current Controversy about the Interpretation of National Socialism', in Gerhard Hirschfeld and Lothar Kettenacker (eds.), *The 'Führer State': Myth and Reality. Studies on the Structure and Politics of the Third Reich* (Stuttgart, 1981), 23-42.

MATTHIAS, ERICH, *Zwischen Räten und Geheimräten: Die deutsche Revolutionsregierung 1918/19* (Düsseldorf, 1970).

—— and MORSEY, RUDOLF (eds.), *Das Ende der Parteien* (Düsseldorf, 1979).

MATZERATH, HORST, *Nationalsozialismus und kommunale Selbstverwaltung* (Berlin, 1970).

MAUNZ, THEODOR, *Neue Grundlagen des Verwaltungsrechts* (Hamburg, 1934).

—— 'Die Entwicklung des deutschen Verwaltungsrechts seit dem Jahre 1933', *ZgStW*, 95 (1935), 311-40.

—— 'Die Führergedanke in der Verwaltung', *DR*, 1935, 219-21.

—— 'Die Zukunft der Verwaltungsgerichtsbarkeit', *DR*, 1935, 478-81.

—— 'Das Ende des subjektiven öffentlichen Rechts', *ZgStW*, 96 (1936), 71-111.

—— *Deutsches Staatsrecht* (Munich and Berlin, 1957).

MEDICUS, FRANZ ALBRECHT, 'Reichsverwaltung und Landesverwaltung', in Hans Heinrich Lammers and Hans Pfundtner (eds.), *Grundlagen, Aufbau und Wirtschaftsordnung des nationalsozialistischen Staates*, 24 (Berlin, 1936-9).

—— *Das Reichsministerium des Innern: Geschichte und Aufbau* (Berlin, 1940).

MEINCK, GERHARD, 'Der Reichsverteidigungsrat', *Wehrwissenschaftliche Rundschau*, 6 (1956), 411-22.

MEINCK, JÜRGEN, *Weimarer Staatslehre und Nationalsozialismus: Ein Studie zum Problem der Kontinuität im staatsrechtlichen Denken in Deutschland 1928 bis 1936* (Frankfurt and New York, 1978).

MEISSNER, OTTO, *Das neue Staatsrecht des Reiches und seiner Länder* (Berlin, 1921).

—— *Staatssekretär unter Ebert—Hindenburg—Hitler* (Hamburg, 1950).

—— and KAISENBERG, G., *Staats- und Verwaltungsrecht im Dritten Reich* (Berlin, 1935).

MENGES, FRANZ, *Reichsreform und Finanzpolitik: Die Aushöhlung der Eigenstaatlichkeit Bayerns auf finanzpolitischem Wege in der Zeit der Weimarer Republik* (Berlin, 1971).

MERTON, ROBERT K. *et al.* (eds.), *Reader in Bureaucracy* (Glencoe, 1952).

MEYER, SIBYLLE, 'Die mühsame Arbeit des demonstrativen Müssiggangs: Über die häuslichen Pflichten der Beamtenfrauen im Kaiserreich', in Karin Hausen (ed.), *Frauen suchen ihre Geschichte* (Munich, 1983), 172-94.

MICHEL, ERNST, 'Das Beamtenproblem', *Deutsche Republik*, 3 (1929), 1469-72, 1501-7.

MIETH, WALTER, 'Vorbildung und Bevölkerungspolitik', *DR*, 1938.

MILLER, SUSANNE, *Die Bürde der Macht: Die deutsche Sozialdemokratie 1918-1920* (Düsseldorf, 1978).

MILWARD, ALAN, *The German Economy at War* (London, 1965).

MISES, LUDWIG von, *Bureaucracy* (New Haven, 1944).

MÖLLER, HORST, 'Die preussischen Oberpräsidenten der Weimarer Republik als Verwaltungselite', *VjhZ*, 30/1 (1982), 1-26.

MOMMSEN, HANS, 'Aufgabenkreis und Verantwortlichkeit des Staatssekretärs der Reichskanzlei Dr. Wilhelm Kritzinger', in *Gutachten des Instituts für Zeitgeschichte*, ii (Stuttgart, 1966), 369-98.

—— *Beamtentum im Dritten Reich* (Stuttgart, 1966).

—— 'Ein Erlass Himmlers zur Bekämpfung der Korruption in der inneren Verwaltung vom Dezember 1944', *VjhZ*, 16/3 (1968), 295-309.

—— 'Social Views and Constitutional Plans of the Resistance', in Hermann Graml *et al.*, *The German Resistance to Hitler* (London, 1970), 55-147.

—— 'Die Stellung der Beamtenschaft in Reich, Ländern und Gemeinden in der Ära Brüning', *VjhZ*, 21/2 (1973), 151-65.

—— 'Staat und Bürokratie in der Ära Brüning', in Gotthard Jasper (ed.),

Tradition und Reform in der deutschen Politik: Gedenkschrift für Waldemar Besson (Frankfurt, 1976), 81-137.

—— 'Hitlers Stellung im nationalsozialistischen Herrschaftssystem', in Gerhard Hirschfeld and Lothar Kettenacker (eds.), *The 'Führer State': Myth and Reality. Studies on the Structure and Politics of the Third Reich* (Stuttgart, 1981), 43-72.

—— 'Fritz-Dietlof Graf von der Schulenburg und die preussische Tradition', *VjhZ*, 32/2 (1984), 213-39.

—— 'The Realization of the Unthinkable: The "Final Solution of the Jewish Question" in the Third Reich', in Gerhard Hirschfeld (ed.), *The Policies of Genocide: Jews and Soviet Prisoners of War in Germany* (London, 1986), 93-144.

—— *et al.* (eds.), *Industrielles System and politische Entwicklung in der Weimarer Republik* (Düsseldorf, 1973).

Mommsen, Wolfgang J., 'The German Revolution 1918-1920: Political Revolution and Social Protest Movement', in Richard Bessel and E. J. Feuchtwanger (eds.), *Social Change and Political Development in the Weimar Republic* (London, 1981), 21-54.

—— *Max Weber and German Politics 1890-1920* (Chicago and London, 1984).

Morsey, Rudolf, *Die oberste Reichsverwaltung unter Bismarck 1867-1890* (Münster, 1957).

—— 'Zur Beamtenpolitik des Reiches von Bismarck bis Brüning', in *Demokratie und Verwaltung: 25 Jahre Hochschule für Verwaltung Speyer* (Berlin, 1972).

—— 'Staatsfeinde im öffentlichen Dienst (1929-1932): Die Beamtenpolitik gegenüber NSDAP-Mitgliedern', in Klaus König *et al.* (eds.), *Öffentlicher Dienst: Festschrift für Carl Herman Ule* (Cologne, 1977), 111-35.

—— 'Beamtenschaft und Verwaltung zwischen Republik und "Neuem Staat"', in Karl Dietrich Erdmann and Hagen Schulze (eds.), *Weimar: Selbstpreisgabe einer Demokratie* (Düsseldorf, 1980), 151-68.

Mosse, George, *The Crisis of German Ideology: Intellectual Origins of the Third Reich* (London, 1966).

Most, Otto, 'Zur Wirtschafts- und Sozialstatistik der höheren Beamten in Preussen', *Schmollers Jahrbuch*, 34 (1915), 181-218.

Müller, Christoph and Staff, Ilse (eds.), *Der soziale Rechtsstaat: Gedächtnisschrift für Hermann Heller 1891-1933* (Baden-Baden, 1984).

Müller, Hans-Eberhard, *Bureaucracy, Education, and Monopoly. Civil Service Reforms in Prussia and England* (Berkeley, 1984).

Müller [Heinrich], *Beamtentum und Nationalsozialismus* (Munich, 1931).

Müller, Heinz *et al.*, *Neues Beamtenrecht für Grossdeutschland* (Berlin, 1944).

Muncy, Lysbeth, 'The Junkers and the Prussian Administration from 1918 to 1939', *Review of Politics*, 9 (1947), 482-501.

—— *The Junker in the Prussian Administration under William II 1888-1914* (New York, 1970).

—— 'The Prussian Landräte in the Last Years of the Monarchy: A Case Study of Pomerania and the Rhineland in 1890-1918', *CEH*, 6/4 (1973), 299-338.

MURSINSKY, ERICH and BRILL, JUSTIN, *Die Organisation der nationalsozialistischen Beamten* (Berlin, 1940).

MUTH, HEINRICH, 'Zum Streit um die Verwaltungsgerichtsbarkeit', *DR*, 1938, 25-6.

NAUMANN, FRIEDRICH, *Die Stellung der Beamten im Haushalte des Staates* (Berlin, 1910).

NAWIASKY, HANS, *Die Stellung des Berufsbeamtentums im parlamentarischen Staat* (Munich, 1926).

NEEF, HERMANN, *Die Aufgaben des Beamten im Dritten Reich* (Berlin, 1934).

—— *Der Beamte im nationalsozialistischen Führerstaat* (Berlin, 1934).

—— 'Aufgabe und Arbeit des Ausschüsses für Beamtenrecht bei der Akademie für Deutsches Recht', *ZADR*, 1935, 340-2.

—— *Das Beamtenorganisationswesen im nationalsozialistischen Staat* (Berlin, 1935).

—— *Die politisch-weltanschauliche Reorganisation der deutschen Beamten im Sinn und Geist des Nationalsozialismus* (Berlin, 1935).

—— *Der Beamte im Geschehen der Zeit* (Berlin, 1936).

—— 'Nationalsozialistisches Beamtenrecht', *ZADR*, 1936.

—— *Die neue geistige Grundhaltung des Beamten* (Berlin, 1936).

—— *Das Soldatentum des deutschen Beamten* (Berlin, 1936).

—— *Die politische Forderung an den Beamten in Recht und Gesetzgebung* (Berlin, 1937).

—— *Fünf Jahre nationalsozialistischer Beamteneinheitsorganisation* (Berlin, 1938).

NEESSE, GOTTFRIED, 'Das Verhältnis von Partei und Staat in der Gemeinde', *DV*, 1935, 175-8.

—— *Partei und Staat* (Hamburg, 1936).

—— *Staatsdienst und Staatsschicksal* (Hamburg, 1955).

NETZBAND, K. B. and WIDMAIER, H. P., *Währungs- und Finanzpolitik der Ära Luther 1923-1925* (Tübingen, 1964).

NEUBERT, REINHARD, 'Beamtentum und Nationalsozialismus', *DR*, 1931.

Neues Beamtentum: Beiträge zur Neuordnung des öffentlichen Dienstes, ed. Institut zur Förderung öffentlicher Angelegenheiten (Frankfurt, 1951).

NEUMANN, FRANZ, *Behemoth: The Structure and Practice of National Socialism* (London, 1942).

—— 'The Social Significance of the Basic Laws in the Weimar Constitution', *Economy and Society*, 10 (1981), 329-47.

NICHOLLS, ANTHONY J., 'Die höhere Beamtenschaft in der Weimarer Zeit: Betrachtungen zu Problemen ihrer Haltung und ihrer Fortbildung', in Lothar Albertin and Werner Link (eds.), *Politische Parteien auf dem Weg zur parlamentarischen Demokratie in Deutschland: Entwicklungslinien bis zur Gegenwart* (Düsseldorf, 1981), 195-207.

NICOLAI, HELMUT, *Grundlagen der kommenden Verfassung über den staatsrechtlichen Aufbau des Dritten Reiches* (Berlin, 1933).

—— *Der Staat im nationalsozialistischen Weltbild* (Leipzig, 1933).

—— *Der Neuaufbau des Reiches nach dem Reichsreformgesetz vom 30. Januar 1934* (Berlin, 1934).

NOAKES, JEREMY, *The Nazi Party in Lower Saxony 1921-1933* (Oxford, 1971).

—— (ed.), *Government, Party and People in Nazi Germany* (Exeter, 1980).

—— 'Nazism and Eugenics: The Background to the Nazi Sterilization Law of 14 July 1933', in R. J. Bullen *et al.* (eds.), *Ideas into Politics: Aspects of European History 1880-1950* (London, 1984), 75-94.

—— and PRIDHAM, GEOFFREY (eds.), *Nazism 1919-1945*, i. *The Rise to Power 1919-1934* (Exeter, 1983); ii. *State, Economy and Society 1933-1939* (Exeter, 1984).

NORBECK, A., *Die Formen der Zusammenarbeit von Partei und Staat auf dem Gebiet der Verwaltung*, Ph.D. thesis (Munich and Zeulenroda, 1938).

NORDEN, WALTER, 'Zur Ausbildungsfrage der höheren Verwaltungsbeamten', *ZgStW*, 86 (1929), 107-17.

NSDAP Reichsorganisationsleitung, *Quo Vadis Deutsches Berufsbeamtentum?* (Frankfurt, 1932).

NYOMARKAY, JOSEPH, *Charisma and Factionalism in the Nazi Party* (Minneapolis, 1967).

OERTZEN, PETER von, *Die soziale Funktion des staatsrechtlichen Positivismus: Eine wissenssoziologische Studie über die Entstehung des formalistischen Positivismus in der deutschen Staatsrechtswissenschaft* (Frankfurt, 1974).

OPPLER, KURT and ROSENTHAL-PELLDRAM, ERICH, *Die Neugestaltung des öffentlichen Dienstes* (Frankfurt, 1950).

ORLOW, DIETRICH, *The History of the Nazi Party: 1919-1933* (Pittsburgh, 1969).

—— *The History of the Nazi Party: 1933-1945* (Pittsburgh, 1973).

PAUWELS, JACQUES R., *Women, Nazis, and Universities: Female University Students in the Third Reich* (Westport, 1984).

PEREZ-DIAZ, VICTOR M., *State, Bureaucracy and Civil Society: A Critical Discussion of the Political Theory of Karl Marx* (London, 1978).

PETERSON, EDWARD N., 'The Bureaucracy and the Nazi Party', *Review of Politics*, 28 (1966), 172-92.

—— *The Limits of Hitler's Power* (Princeton, 1969).

PEUKERT, DETLEV, *Inside Nazi Germany: Conformity, Opposition and Racism in Everyday Life* (New Haven and London, 1987).

PFUNDTNER, HANS, *Dr. Wilhelm Frick und sein Ministerium* (Munich, 1937).

—— 'Der Einheitsgedanke in der deutschen Verwaltung', *ZADR*, 1937.

—— 'Deutsche Verwaltung im Kriege', *RVBl*, 1942, 441-6.

PIKART, EBERHARD, 'Preussische Beamtenpolitik 1918-33', *VjhZ*, 6/2 (1958), 119-37.

—— 'Berufsbeamtentum und Parteienstaat: Eine Fallstudie', *Zeitschrift für Politik*, NF 1960, 225-40.

POETZSCH-HEFFTER, FRITZ, 'Vom Staatsleben unter der Weimarer Republik', *JöR*, 17 (1929), 1-141.

—— 'Vom deutschen Staatsleben', *JöR*, 22 (1935), 1-272.

POGGI, GIANFRANCO, *The Development of the Modern State: A Sociological Intro-duction* (London, 1978).

POLAK, KARL, *Zur Dialektik in der Staatslehre* (E. Berlin, 1963).

POLLOCK, FREDERICK, 'Is National Socialism a New Order?', *Studies in Philosophy and Social Science*, 9 (1941), 440-55.

POLLOCK, JAMES K., *The Government of Greater Germany* (New York, 1938).

POTTHOFF, HEINRICH, 'Verfassungsväter ohne Verfassungsvolk? Zum Problem von Integration und Desintegration nach der Novemberrevolution', in Gerhard A. Ritter (ed.), *Gesellschaft, Parlament und Regierung: Zur Geschichte des Parlamentarismus in Deutschland* (Düsseldorf, 1974), 339-54.

—— *Gewerkschaften und Politik zwischen Revolution und Inflation* (Düsseldorf, 1979).

POTTHOFF, HEINZ, *Probleme des Arbeitsrechts* (Jena, 1912).

—— *Grundfragen des künftigen Beamtenrechts* (Berlin, 1923).

POULANTZAS, NICOS, *Political Power and Social Classes* (London, 1973).

—— *Fascism and Dictatorship: The Third International and the Problem of Fascism* (London, 1974).

—— *Classes in Contemporary Capitalism* (London, 1975).

PRELLER, LUDWIG, *Sozialpolitik in der Weimarer Republik* (Düsseldorf, 1978; orig. edn., 1949).

PRERADOVICH, NIKOLAUS von, *Die Führungsschichten in Österreich und Preussen 1806-1918* (Wiesbaden, 1955).

PREUSS, HUGO, *Staat, Recht und Freiheit: Aus 40 Jahren deutscher Politik und Geschichte* (Hildesheim, 1964).

QUANTE, PETER, 'Die Kinderzulagen in der deutschen Beamtenbesoldung', *Zeitschrift des preussischen Statistischen Landesamts*, 62 (1922), 225-69.

RABINBACH, ANSON, 'The Aesthetics of Production in the Third Reich', *JCH*, 11 (1976), 44-74.

RAMM, THILO, 'Labor Relations in the Public Sector of the Federal Republic of Germany: The Civil Servant's Role', in Charles M. Rehmus (ed.), *Public Employment Labor Relations: An Overview of Eleven Nations* (Ann Arbor, 1975), 101-24.

RATHKE, A., *Wie werde ich Beamter?* (Berlin, 1940).

REBENTISCH, DIETER, 'Die "politische Beurteilung" als Herrschaftsinstrument der NSDAP', in Detlev Peukert and Jürgen Reulecke (eds.), *Die Reihen fast geschlossen: Beiträge zur Geschichte des Alltags unterm Nationalsozialismus* (Wuppertal, 1981), 107-25.

REHBERGER, HORST, *Die Gleichschaltung des Landes Baden 1932/33* (Heidelberg, 1966).

REJEWSKI, HARRO-JÜRGEN, *Die Pflicht zur politischen Treue im preussischen Beamtenrecht 1850-1918* (Berlin, 1973).

RIDLEY, FREDERICK F. (ed.), *Specialists and Generalists* (London, 1968).

RINGER, FRITZ K., 'Higher Education in Germany in the Nineteenth Century', *JCH*, 12/3 (1973), 123-38.

ROHDE, GOTTHOLD, 'The Protectorate of Bohemia and Moravia', in Victor Mamatey and Radomir Luza (eds.), *A History of Czechoslovakia* (Princeton, 1973), 296-321.

RÖHL, JOHN C. G., 'Higher Civil Servants in Germany, 1890-1900', *JCH*, 2/3 (1967), 101-21.

ROLOFF, ERNST-AUGUST, *Bürgertum und Nationalsozialismus: Braunschweigs Weg im Dritten Reich* (Hanover, 1961).

ROSENBERG, HANS, *Bureaucracy, Aristocracy and Autocracy: The Prussian Experience 1660-1815* (Boston, 1966).

ROSENTHAL, E., 'Der staatliche Aufbau des Landes Thüringen', *JöR*, 12 (1923/4), 75-112.

RUESCHEMEYER, DIETRICH, *Power and the Division of Labour* (Stanford, 1986).

RUNGE, WOLFGANG, *Politik und Beamtentum im Parteienstaat: Die Demokratisierung der politischen Beamten in Preussen zwischen 1918 und 1933* (Stuttgart, 1965).

RUPP, LEILA, *Mobilizing Women for War: German and American Propaganda* (Princeton, 1978).

RÜRUP, REINHARD (ed.), *Arbeiter- und Soldatenräte im rheinisch-westfälischen Industriegebiet: Studien zur Geschichte der Revolution 1918/19* (Wuppertal, 1975).

RÜTHERS, BERND, *Die unbegrenzte Auslegung: Zum Wandel der Privatrechtsordnung im Nationalsozialismus* (Frankfurt, 1973).

SAAGE, RICHARD (ed.), *Solidargemeinschaft und Klassenkampf: Politische Konzeptionen der Sozialdemokratie zwischen den Weltkriegen* (Frankfurt, 1986).

SAEMISCH, [MORITZ], *Der Reichssparkommissar und seine Aufgaben* (Berlin, 1930).

SARTORIUS, C., 'Die Entwicklung des öffentlichen Rechts in Württemberg in den Jahren 1925-1932', *JöR*, 20 (1932), 168-94.

SAUER, P., *Das Reichsjustizministerium* (Berlin, 1939).

SAUER, PAUL, *Württemberg in der Zeit des Nationalsozialismus* (Ulm, 1975).

SCHAAP, KLAUS, *Die Endphase der Weimarer Republik im Freistaat Oldenburg 1928-1933* (Düsseldorf, 1978).

SCHÄRL, WALTER, *Die Zusammensetzung der bayrischen Beamtenschaft 1806-1918* (Kallmünz, 1955).

SCHEUNER, ULLRICH, 'Die Rechtsstellung der Persönlichkeit in der Gemeinschaft', in Hans Frank (ed.), *Deutsches Verwaltungsrecht* (Munich, 1937), 82-97.

SCHEURL, EBERHARD FREIHERR von, 'Probleme der Juristenbildung', *AöR*, NF 5 (1923), 137-81.

—— 'Die Persönlichkeit in der deutschen Verwaltung: Eine verwaltungspolitische Untersuchung', *AöR*, NF 25 (1934), 1-29.

SCHIEDT, HANS, *Die Gehälter der Beamten und die Dienstbezüge der Angestellten* (Berlin, 1939).

SCHLESINGER, RUDOLF, *Federalism in Central and Eastern Europe* (New York, 1945).

SCHLEUNES, KARL A., *The Twisted Road to Auschwitz: Nazi Policy towards German Jews 1933-1939* (Urbana, Chicago, and London, 1979).

SCHMAHL, HERMANNJOSEF, *Disziplinarrecht und politische Betätigung der Beamten in der Weimarer Republik* (Berlin, 1977).

SCHMIDT, GEORG, 'Reform der Ausbildung für den höheren Dienst', *DV*, 1942, 61-7.

SCHMIER, L. E., 'Martin Bormann and the Nazi Party 1941-1945', Ph.D. thesis (Chapel Hill, 1968).

SCHMITT, CARL, *Staat, Bewegung, Volk* (Hamburg, 1933).

—— *Staatsgefüge und Zusammenbruch des Zweiten Reiches* (Hamburg, 1934).

—— 'Was bedeutet der Streit um den Rechtsstaat?', *ZgStW*, 95 (1935), 189-201.

—— *Positionen und Begriffe im Kampf mit Weimar-Genf-Versailles 1923-1939* (Hamburg, 1940).

—— 'Wohlerworbene Beamtenrechte und Gehaltskürzungen' (1931), in Carl Schmitt, *Verfassungsrechtliche Aufsätze* (Berlin, 1958), 174-80.

—— *Der Hüter der Verfassung* (Berlin, 1962; orig. edn., 1931).

SCHMOLLER, GUSTAV, 'Über Behördenorganisation, Amtswesen und Beamtentum', *Acta Borussica*, 1 (Berlin, 1894), 13-143.

—— *Preussische Verfassungs-, Verwaltungs- und Finanzgeschichte* (Berlin, 1921).

SCHNEIDER, WERNER, *Die Deutsche Demokratische Partei in der Weimarer Republik 1924-1930* (Munich, 1978).

SCHOENBAUM, DAVID, *Hitler's Social Revolution: Class and Status in Nazi Germany 1933-1939* (New York, 1966).

SCHÖNFELDT, JOBST von, *Die allgemeine und innere Verwaltung* (Berlin, 1943).

SCHRON, E., 'Deutscher Beamtenbund (DBB) 1918-1933', in Dieter Fricke (ed.), *Handbuch der bürgerlichen Parteien und anderer bürgerlicher Interessenorganisationen*, i (Leipzig, 1968), 422-8.

SCHÜCKING, LOTHAR ENGELBERT (pseud.), *Die Reaktion in der inneren Verwaltung Preussens* (Berlin, 1908).

SCHULZ, GERHARD, *Zwischen Demokratie und Diktatur: Verfassungspolitik und Reichsreform in der Weimarer Republik, i. Die Periode der Konsolidierung und der Revision des Bismarckschen Reichsaufbaus 1919-1930* (Berlin, 1963).

SCHÜSTEREIT, HARTMUT, *Linksliberalismus und Sozialdemokratie in der Weimarer Republik* (Düsseldorf, 1975).

SCHÜTZE, ERWIN, 'Beamtenpolitik im Dritten Reich', in Hans Pfundtner (ed.), *Dr. Wilhelm Frick und sein Ministerium* (Berlin, 1937), 47-65.

SCHWARZ, FRANZ-XAVIER, 'Das Finanz- und Verwaltungswesen der NSDAP', *ZADR*, 1936, 150-4.

SCHWARZ, OTTO, *Die Entwicklung der Ausgaben und Einnahmen Deutschlands*,

Englands, Frankreichs und Italiens vor und nach dem Weltkriege (Magdeburg, 1921).

SEEL, HANNS, *Der Beamte im neuen Staat* (Berlin, 1933).

—— *Erneuerung des Berufsbeamtentums* (Berlin, 1933).

—— *Gesetz zur Wiederherstellung des Berufsbeamtentums* (Berlin, 1933).

—— *Die Neuordnung des Beamtenrechts* (Berlin, 1933).

—— 'Ausklang des Berufsbeamtengesetzes: Neues Beamtenrecht', *ZADR*, 1934, 148-9.

—— 'Deutsches Beamtenrecht', in Hans Heinrich Lammers and Hans Pfundtner (eds.), *Die Verwaltungs-Akademie: Ein Handbuch für den Beamten im nationalsozialistischen Staat* (Berlin n.d. [?1935]).

—— 'Das Beamtenrecht des Dritten Reiches', in Hans Frank (ed.), *Deutsches Verwaltungsrecht* (Munich, 1937), 151-65.

—— *Das neue Beamtengesetz vom 26. Januar 1937* (Berlin, 1937).

SELF, PETER, *Administrative Theories and Politics: An Inquiry into the Structure and Processes of Modern Government* (London, 1972).

SEVERING, CARL, *Mein Lebensweg*, 2 vols. (Cologne, 1950).

SHARP, WALTER R., *The French Civil Service: Bureaucracy in Transition* (New York, 1931).

SMEND, RUDOLF, 'Der Einfluss der deutschen Staats- und Verwaltungsrechtslehre des 19. Jahrhunderts auf das Leben in Verfassung und Verwaltung', in Rudolf Smend, *Staatsrechtliche Abhandlungen und andere Aufsätze* (Berlin, 1968), 326-45.

SOLCH, OTTO, 'Insbesondere Besoldungen und Hinterbliebenenversorgung', in Gerhard Anschütz and Richard Thoma (eds.), *Handbuch des deutschen Staatsrechts*, i (Tübingen, 1932), 68-76.

SOMMER, WALTER, 'Die Ausbildung des Nachwuchses der höheren Verwaltungsbeamten', *DVBl*, 1937, 360-3.

—— 'Die NSDAP und das Deutsche Beamtengesetz', *DVBl*, 1937, 81-3.

—— 'Die NSDAP als Verwaltungsträger', in Hans Frank (ed.), *Deutsches Verwaltungsrecht* (Munich, 1937), 166-75.

—— 'Die Verwaltungsgerichtsbarkeit', *DVBl*, 1937, 425-30.

SONTHEIMER, KURT, *Antidemokratisches Denken in der Weimarer Republik* (Munich, 1978).

—— and BLEEK, WILHELM, *Abschied vom Berufsbeamtentum? Perspektiven einer Reform des öffentlichen Dienstes in der Bundesrepublik Deutschland* (Hamburg, 1973).

SPEIER, HANS, *Die Angestellten vor dem Nationalsozialismus: Ein Beitrag zum Verständnis der deutschen Sozialstruktur 1918-1933* (Göttingen, 1977).

STACHURA, PETER D., *Gregor Strasser and the Rise of Nazism* (London, 1983).

STEPHENSON, JILL, *Women in Nazi Society* (London, 1975).

STOLLEIS, MICHAEL, 'Gemeinschaft und Volksgemeinschaft: Zur juristischen Terminologie im Nationalsozialismus', *VjhZ*, 20/1(1972), 16-38.

—— *Gemeinwohlformeln im nationalsozialistischen Recht* (Berlin, 1974).

STRAKOSCH, HENRY E., *State Absolutism and the Rule of Law: The Struggle for the Codification of Civil Law in Austria 1753-1811* (Sydney, 1967).

STRUVE, WALTER, *Elites against Democracy: Leadership Ideals in Bourgeois Political Thought in Germany, 1890-1933* (Princeton, 1973).

STUCKART, WILHELM, 'Ziel und Weg einer nationalsozialistischen Studienreform', *ZADR*, 1934, 53-5.

— *Nationalsozialistische Rechtserziehung* (Frankfurt, 1935).

— 'Nationalsozialistischer Staat und Verwaltungsgerichtsbarkeit', *DV*, 1935, 161-4.

— 'Partei und Reich', *DV*, 1935, 196-9.

— 'Rechtswahrer und Staat', *DV*, 1935, 353-61.

— 'Nationalsozialismus und Staatsrecht', in Hans Heinrich Lammers and Hans Pfundtner, (eds), *Grundlagen, Aufbau und Wirtschaftsordnung des nationalsozialistischen Staates*, 1 (Berlin, 1936).

— *Führung und Verwaltung im Kriege* (Berlin, 1941).

— 'Zentralgewalt, Dezentralisation und Verwaltungseinheit', in *Festgabe für Heinrich Himmler* (Berlin, 1941), 1-32.

— 'Die Vereinfachung der Verwaltung im Kriege', *DV*, 1942, 121-4.

— 'Die Probleme der inneren Gestaltung des Grösseren Reiches', in *Das Grössere Reich* (Berlin, 1943), 139-68.

— and NEESSE, GOTTFRIED, *Partei und Staat* (Vienna, 1938).

— and SCHEERBARTH, WALTER, *Verwaltungsrecht* (Leipzig, 1941).

— and SCHIEDERMAYER, ROLF, *Neues Staatsrecht* (Leipzig, 1944).

STÜMKE, HANS-GEORG and FINKLER, RUDI, *Rosa Winkel, Rosa Liste: Homosexuelle und 'Gesundes Volksempfinden' von Auschwitz bis heute* (Frankfurt, 1981).

STÜRMER, MICHAEL, 'Parliamentary Government in Weimar Germany 1924-1928', in Anthony J. Nicholls and Erich Matthias (eds.), *German Democracy and the Triumph of Hitler* (London, 1971), 59-77.

SUMMERFIELD, PENNY, *Women Workers in the Second World War* (London, 1984).

SWEET, WILLIAM, 'The Volksgerichtshof: 1934-45', *JMH*, 46/2 (1974), 314-29.

TATARIN-TARNHEYDEN, E., 'Grundlagen des Verwaltungsrechts im neuen Staat', *AöR*, NF 24 (1934), 345-58.

TEPPE, KARL, *Provinz, Partei, Staat: Zur provinziellen Selbstverwaltung im Dritten Reich untersucht am Beispiel Westfalens* (Münster, 1977).

THIERACK, OTTO, 'Die Justizausbildungsordnung', *ZADR*, 1943, 90-2.

TIEBEL, FRITZ, *Die Beamtenschaft Adolf Hitlers* (Berlin, 1940).

TISCH, HEINRICH, *Das Problem des sozialen Auf- und Abstieges im deutschen Volk, dargestellt an Hand einer Erhebung über die soziale Herkunft der Beamten in der Saarpfalz* (Heidelberg, 1937).

TRACEY, DONALD R., 'Reform in the Early Weimar Years: The Thuringian Example', *JMH*, 44 (1976), 195-212.

TURNER, HENRY A., 'Fascism and Modernization', *World Politics*, 24 (1972), 547-64.

UNGER, ARYEH L., *The Totalitarian Party: Party and People in Nazi Germany and Soviet Russia* (Cambridge, 1974).

VIALON, FRIEDRICH K., 'Die Stellung des Finanzministers', *VjhZ*, 2/2 (1954), 136-48.

VIERHAUS, RUDOLF, 'Ständewesen und Staatsverwaltung in Deutschland im späteren 18. Jahrhundert', in Rudolf Vierhaus and Manfred Botzenhart (eds.), *Dauer und Wandel der Geschichte: Festgabe für Kurt von Raumer* (Münster, 1966), 337-60.

VOCKE, ANNEMARIE, *Grundrechte und Nationalsozialismus* (Leipzig, 1938).

VOGEL, JULIUS (ed.), *Deutsches Berufsbeamtentum: Kernsätze aus Reden, Schriften und Aufsätzen des Reichsbeamtenführers Hermann Neef* (Berlin, 1942).

VOIGT, ERICH, *Die Reichsregierung und die Reichszentralbehörden* (Jena, 1941).

VÖLTER, HANS, 'Die deutsche Beamtenbesoldung', in Wilhelm Gerloff (ed.), *Die Beamtenbesoldung im modernen Staat* (Munich and Leipzig, 1932), 1-96.

WACKE, GERHARD, 'Zwischen Arbeitsrecht und Beamtenrecht', *ZADR*, 1937, 496-9.

—— 'Zur Neugestaltung des Beamtenrechts', *AöR*, 76 (1950/1), 385-434.

WAGNER, ALBRECHT, 'Die Umgestaltung der Gerichtsverfassung und des Verfahrens- und Richterrechts im nationalsozialistischen Staat', in *Die deutsche Justiz und der Nationalsozialismus*, i (Stuttgart, 1968), 191-366.

WALDECKER, LUDWIG, 'Entwicklungstendenzen im deutschen Beamtenrecht', *AöR*, NF 7 (1924), 129-71.

WALKER, HARVEY, *Training Public Employees in Great Britain* (New York, 1935).

WEBER, MAX, *Gesammelte politische Schriften* (Tübingen, 1958).

WEBER, WERNER 'Führererlass und Führerverordnung', *ZgStW*, 102 (1942), 102-37.

—— *Das Berufsbeamtentum im demokratischen Rechtsstaat* (Cologne, 1952).

—— NEESSE, GOTTFRIED, and BARING, M., *Der deutsche Beamte heute* (Baden-Baden, 1959).

WEINKAUFF, HERMANN, 'Die deutsche Justiz und der Nationalsozialismus: Ein Überblick', in *Die deutsche Justiz und der Nationalsozialismus*, i (Stuttgart, 1968), 19-188.

WELLS, ROGER, 'Reichsreform and Prussian Verwaltungsreform in 1932', *APSR*, 27 (1933), 237-43.

—— 'The Liquidation of the German Länder', *APSR*, 30 (1936), 350-61.

WERMUTH, ADOLF, *Ein Beamtenleben: Erinnerungen* (Berlin, 1922).

WICHERT, Dr., 'Das Gesetz über die 24. Änderung des Reichsbesoldungsgesetzes vom 13. Dezember 1935', *Beamtenjahrbuch*, 1936, 71-6.

WIESE, HANSALBRECHT, *Wehrmacht und Beamtentum* (Berlin, 1937).

WIESE, WALTER, *Der Staatsdienst in der Bundesrepublik Deutschland: Grundlagen, Probleme, Neuordnung* (Neuwied and Berlin, 1972).

WILHELM, THEODOR, *Die Idee des Berufsbeamtentums* (Tübingen, 1933).

WINKLER, DÖRTE, *Frauenarbeit im 'Dritten Reich'* (Hamburg, 1977).

WINTER, FRITZ, *Der Deutsche Beamtenbund: Seine Enstehung und Entwicklung* (Berlin, 1931).

WITT, PETER-CHRISTIAN, 'Der preussische Landrat als Steuerbeamte 1891-1918: Bemerkungen zur politischen und sozialen Funktion des deutschen Beamtentums', in Immanuel Geiss and Bernd-Jochen Wendt (eds.), *Deutschland in der Weltpolitik des 19. und 20. Jahrhunderts* (Düsseldorf, 1973), 205-19.

—— 'Reichsfinanzminister und Reichsfinanzverwaltung: Zum Problem des Verhältnisses von politischer Führung und bürokratischer Herrschaft in den Anfangsjahren der Weimarer Republik', *VjhZ*, 23/1 (1975), 1-61.

WITTLAND, Dr., 'Die Reichsgrundsätze über Einstellung, Anstellung und Beförderung der Reichs- und Landesbeamten', *Beamtenjahrbuch*, 1936, 599-614.

WUNDER, BERND, *Geschichte der Bürokratie in Deutschland* (Frankfurt, 1986).

GLOSSARY OF GERMAN TERMS AND CIVIL-SERVICE GRADES

Angestellter: In public service: employee without *Beamte* status and privileges.

Beamte: Career civil servant.

Berufsbeamtentum: Professional civil service.

Grundgehalt: Basic pay.

Hinterbliebenenversorgung: Surviving dependants' allowances.

Landrat: County director.

Leistungsgrundsatz: Achievement or merit principle.

Ministerialdirektor: Division director.

Ministerialdirigent: Subdivision head.

Ministerialrat: Principal, 1st class.

Mittelinstanz: Intermediate echelon of Reich or *Land* administration in the field.

Oberpräsident: Provincial governor.

Oberregierungsrat: Principal, 2nd class (ministerial); senior promotion grade in field offices.

Polizeipräsident: Police commissioner.

Regierungspräsident: District officer.

Regierungsrat: Assistant principal (ministerial); principal grade in field offices.

Reichsstatthalter: Reich governor.

Ruhestand: Retirement.

Staatssekretär: Permanent under-secretary.

Stand: Estate, in corporative sense.

Standesgemäss: Socially appropriate.

Unterhaltssystem: 'Alimentation': salary system based on socially assessed need, not remuneration of labour.

Wartestandsbeamte: Civil servant in provisional retirement.

Wohlerworbene Rechte: Vested rights: the privileges of tenure, etc. attached to civil-service status.

Civil-Service Grade Structure

I. *Unterer* or *einfacher Dienst* (elementary or lower service): clerical, mechanical, and unskilled posts, generally requiring minimum school qualification (*Volksschule*), e.g. caretaker, messenger, telephone operator, clerical assistant, prison warder (salary scales A12–A9).

II. *Mittlerer* or *einfacher mittlerer Dienst* (intermediate service): skilled trades and more senior clerical posts (*Assistenten*), requiring superior school achievement or apprenticeship, e.g. tax clerk, chancellery clerk, police lieutenant, lithographer, army bootmaker (salary scales A8-A4d).

III. *Gehobener* or *gehobener mittlerer Dienst* (superior service): executive grade (*Inspektor* and *Amtmann*), requiring 12-year schooling (*Mittelschule*) or technical training, e.g. marine engineer, postmaster, tax inspector, principal's clerk (salary scales A4c2-A3).

IV. *Höherer Dienst* (senior or higher service): administrative grade, requiring full university education and higher technical qualification where appropriate (except exempted posts), e.g. ministerial principal, architect, judge, professor, field office director, etc. (salary scales A2c2 up, and all Schedule B (non-incremental) posts).

INDEX

administrative courts 201-3, 209-11
administrative policy:
    before 1933: 26-8, 55-6, 58, 88, 90-1
    National Socialist 133-7, 152-9,
        260-80 *passim*, 322-4, 325-7, 333-4,
        336-8
    wartime rationalization 260-80 *passim*,
        300, 302-18
    see also Frick, Wilhelm; NSDAP:
        relations with state; Reich-*Land*
        relations; Reich ministries and
        administrations
Adventists 206
Alimentation:
    see civil·service salaries: *standesgemässer
        Unterhalt*
Allgemeiner Deutscher Beamtenbund
    18, 59, 69, 73-4, 80, 85, 89, 95 n.,
    97, 101, 111-12
Allgemeiner Deutscher Gewerkschafts-
    bund 37
Allgemeiner Freier Angestelltenbund 37
Angestellte (white-collar workers) 7, 12,
    47, 53-6, 61, 68, 69, 72, 99, 107,
    143, 170, 172, 191, 219, 245
Apelt, Willibalt 27
Arbeitsordnungsgesetz (AOG):
    see Law for the Ordering of National
        Labour
Arendt, Hannah 330
Austria 209, 221, 264, 271

Baden 30, 31, 49, 124, 126
Bavaria 7, 27, 39, 124, 139-40, 157
Beamte:
    see civil servants; civil service; higher
        civil servants
Beamtenrechtsänderungsgesetz (BRÄndG):
    see Law for the Amendment of
        Regulations in Civil-Service, Salary
        and Pensions Law
Berlin 20, 34-5, 231
Berufsbeamtengesetz (BBG):

see Law for the Restoration of the
    Civil Service
Berufsbeamtentum:
    see civil service: tradition
Betriebsverwaltung, Betriebsbeamte:
    see civil service: industrial
Bismarck, Otto von 332
Bormann, Martin
    and civil servants 205, 206, 226, 285,
        287
    and civil servants as NSDAP members
        169, 172, 282
    and civil service salaries 234, 250,
        256, 296
    and DBG 177, 178, 180
    as head of party chancellery 163-4,
        172, 262-3, 264, 271-2, 276, 311,
        312-19 *passim*
    see also party chancellery
Bracher, Karl Dietrich 337
Bracht, Franz 125-6
Braun, Otto 123
Braunschweig 115
Brecht, Arnold 27, 35
Broszat, Martin 212, 260, 328
Brüning, Heinrich 28, 35, 87, 90-6,
    100-1, 126-9
Bund Nationalsozialistischer Deutscher
    Juristen 116, 208
Bürckel, Josef 209
bureaucracy 11, 13, 15, 24, 52, 60-6,
    90-1, 103, 137, 171, 217, 218, 229,
    261, 282, 307, 322, 323-4, 325, 327,
    330, 333, 337

cameralistics 6, 281
Catholics 46, 49, 122, 206, 211
    see also Centre Party
Centre Party 46, 48, 74, 86-8, 93, 100,
    122, 128, 146
civil servants:
    conscription in war 263, 274, 302-4,
        306-8, 311, 313-18 *passim*

civil servants (*cont.*):
criticism 66 n., 102-4, 221, 223-8,
291, 322
duties 2, 32-3, 39-40, 175, 203-4,
206-11
see also civil service: disciplinary law
legal status (*Beamtenverhältnis; Dienst-
und Treueverhältnis*) 4-9 *passim*,
11-12, 23, 25, 33-4, 64-70, 73-6,
96, 101, 150-1, 194-6
lower (*unterer*) 7, 34-5, 36-7, 74-5, 77,
78, 81, 91, 95, 107, 252, 296
loyalty (*Treue*) 31-4, 39-41, 74, 124,
126, 194, 204, 207
see also civil service: oath
marital and sexual behaviour 210,
212-15, 245
material claims
see civil servants: rights, vested rights
middle (*mittlerer*) 7, 34-5, 36-7, 74,
77, 78, 222, 295-6
morale 224-8, 231, 233, 244-6, 247,
249, 253, 258, 259, 289-90, 291,
294
NSDAP membership 116-30, 132-4,
146, 159, 161, 165-71, 176-9, 182,
187, 211, 219, 282
'political' (*politische, disponible*) 6, 23,
29, 39, 42-9, 73-4, 139, 166, 177, 179
political behaviour and rights 9,
12-13, 15-21, 25-6, 28-30, 33,
34-41, 42-4, 47-9, 94, 112, 114,
116-30 *passim*, 140, 142, 165
see also civil servants: NSDAP
membership
political control after 1933: 119, 142-9,
150, 159-60, 164-74 *passim*, 177,
179-80, 182-3, 191, 204, 282
qualifications 2, 6-7, 44-5, 142-3, 150,
165, 171-4, 186-7
see also civil servants: training; civil
service: 'outsiders'
racial restrictions 106, 108, 114,
142-5 *passim*, 150, 170, 177, 180,
203, 204, 205, 208
religious restrictions 205-7
retirement 42-4, 52-6, 142, 179-80,
278
see also civil servants: 'political';
Wartestandsbeamte; civil service:
appointments policy
rights 24-5, 28, 55, 56, 74-5, 112-13,
143, 175, 180, 199-203, 258

see also civil servants: tenure, vested
rights
senior:
see higher civil servants
social origins 3, 7, 46, 49
tenure 5-6, 24, 52-7, 75, 142, 147,
148, 180
training 2-3, 6-7, 44-5, 49-50, 171-4,
183-8, 214, 221, 222, 229, 280-94,
326
see also civil servants: qualifications
Versorgungsanwärter 7, 106, 109, 170
vested rights (*wohlerworbene Rechte*)
22, 24, 59, 73, 95-6, 112-13, 133,
148, 149-50, 202, 228
see also civil servants: rights, tenure
Wartestandsbeamte 108, 148
women 8, 17, 46-7, 52, 53, 56,
97-100, 150-1, 180, 204-5, 220,
268, 274, 306
see also civil service; higher civil
servants; civil service salaries
civil service:
appointments policy before 1933: 20,
29-31, 42-9, 107
appointments policy, National Socialist
106, 108, 114-15, 138-40, 150,
159, 161, 164-74 *passim*, 179,
181-3, 204
see also civil servants: political
control; civil service: promotion
policy
associations 9, 17-18, 21, 55-6, 57, 76,
78, 80, 87, 89, 93, 94-5, 97, 101,
117, 120, 191 n., 193
see also individual associations
councils (*Beamtenräte*) 19
'crisis' after 1933: 215, 223, 227-8,
246, 259, 301, 304-5, 321-3,
325-7
see also civil servants: morale; civil
service: falling prestige
disciplinary law and courts 5, 9,
39-42, 123, 125, 152, 169, 181,
189, 204, 209-11
as élite 2, 17, 65, 75, 80, 85, 92, 110,
135, 182, 183, 213, 214, 229, 233,
280, 282, 285, 289-90, 296, 297,
319, 321, 323-7 *passim*
falling prestige 215, 222-8, 246, 247,
297-8, 300, 301, 305, 326-7
see also civil servants: morale; civil
service: 'crisis' after 1933

industrial (*Betriebsbeamte*) 9, 17, 60, 73, 74, 127-8
law reform 50, 56, 73-5, 142, 146-7, 149-52, 159, 174-83, 316
  see also individual laws
neutrality 30, 34, 38
  see also civil service: tradition
oath 3, 23, 25 n., 31-3, 36, 63, 194-5, 204
'outsiders' (*Aussenseiter*) 43, 44, 45, 48, 171
  see also civil servants: qualifications
personnel shortage 180 n., 216-23, 233, 245, 247, 249, 251, 294, 302, 305-7, 309-14
promotion policy 45, 58, 114-15, 166, 170-4, 181-3, 255, 298-301
  see also civil service: appointments policy
purged by Nazis 113-15, 138-40, 141-9, 222
recruitment 183, 184, 215-23, 233, 245, 247, 249, 251, 255, 282, 292-3, 298, 299, 305
  see also civil service: personnel shortage
size and composition 8, 9, 13, 47, 51, 53-6, 60-1, 217-18, 220-2, 304, 305-7, 308-9, 314
  see also civil service: personnel shortage
in South Germany 6, 49
as *Stand* 11-12, 15, 21, 26, 105, 110, 191, 326
tradition 1, 10-12, 21, 28, 33-4, 57, 59, 60, 62-4, 66, 79, 81, 91, 93-4, 101, 102, 109, 113, 187-8, 203, 227, 243, 245, 289, 319, 322, 325, 337
  see also civil service: as élite, *Stand*
works councils (*Beamtenvertretungen*) 24, 202
  see also civil servants; civil service salaries; higher civil servants
Civil Service Disciplinary Code (RDStrO, 1937) 181
civil service salaries 47, 59, 76-100, 217, 229-59, 294-302, 316
  abrogation of Brüning cuts (1937-40) 229-59, 294
  Brüning cuts (1930-2) 76, 88, 89, 90-101, 110-15 *passim*, 128, 322
  ceiling 85, 86 n., 151, 230-1

child allowances 77, 79, 80, 92 n., 109, 213 n., 240, 252
dependants' allowances (*Hinterbliebenenversorgung*) 4, 22, 176
differentials 77, 78-9, 80, 82-4, 89, 239, 296
housing and local allowances 77, 79, 89, 240, 241
law of 1909: 77, 78
law of 1920: 78-9, 81-2, 85, 89, 233
law of 1927: 59, 76, 86-91, 93, 233, 234, 257, 295
merit principle (*Leistungsprinzip*) 79-84, 96, 259, 295-6, 297-9
National Socialist policy 180, 207, 218, 220, 229-59, 294-302, 326
pensions 22, 53, 88, 92, 98, 108, 176, 178
standesgemässer Unterhalt 4, 79, 80, 96, 244, 297-8
supplementary payments 89, 108, 235-6, 255, 258-9, 299
Committee of Three (*Dreierkollegium*) 266
Communist Party (KPD) 74-5, 88, 123-5
communists 142, 145
Confessing Church 206
constitutional reform before 1933: 29, 90-1, 100

Daluege, Kurt 145, 318
Danzig-Westpreussen 265
Dawes Plan 87, 106
Deutsche Demokratische Partei (DDP) 16, 18, 30, 44, 48, 74, 98, 122
Deutscher Arbeitsfront 191
Deutscher Beamtenbund 18, 23, 24, 35, 36-7, 38, 57, 59, 69, 73, 78, 80, 82-5, 87, 89, 91, 94-7, 101, 111, 119
Deutscher Beamtengesetz (DBG)
  see German Civil Service Law (1937)
Deutscher Gemeindetag 217, 221-2
Deutsche Volkspartei (DVP) 30, 34, 41, 48, 74, 122
Deutschnationale Volkspartei (DNVP) 16, 23, 30, 33, 34, 39, 74, 86, 107, 115, 122, 132, 165
Dietrich, Hermann 126, 128
'double earners' 98, 99, 149, 151

Ebert, Friedrich 19
Enabling Act (1933) 140, 149

Epp, Franz Xaver Ritter von 139-40
eugenics:
  see civil servants: marital and sexual behaviour; population policy

Fabricius, Hans 128, 224, 225
Finer, Hermann 1
Forsthoff, Ernst 335
Four-Year Plan 242, 266, 276, 309, 312
Fraenkel, Ernst 330
Frank, Hans 200, 224, 288, 334, 336
Freemasons 207
Freisler, Roland 288
Frick, Wilhelm:
  administrative strategy 134, 136-7, 153-7, 159 n., 184, 229-30, 263-5, 267-71 passim, 275-8, 287, 304, 314-16, 336-7
  and BBG 141
  before 1933: 108-9, 115, 124, 131, 134
  and civil service 'crisis' 246, 248, 250-1, 253, 259, 294-5, 301
  civil service policy 137, 166, 182, 202, 206, 214-15, 219, 221, 229, 268, 287, 299-302
  and civil service salaries 218, 229-30, 233, 237, 240-59 passim, 294-302 passim
  and civil service training 184-7, 281, 287
  and DBG 174-7
  and Hess 160, 162
  and Krosigk 246-56 passim, 270, 288, 300-2
  leaves Reich interior ministry 304, 318, 324
  and RGS 171-4
  see also Hitler: and Frick; plenipotentiary for the administration; Reich ministries and administrations: interior
Friedrich, Carl J. 330
Friedrichs, Helmuth 163, 168-9
Funk, Walter 277

Gauleiter 141, 155, 160, 165, 167, 264-6, 271, 279, 310, 317, 320
Geiger, Theodor 71
Generalbevollmächtigter für die totale Krieg
  see plenipotentiary for total war
Generalbevollmächtigter für die Verwaltung
  see plenipotentiary for the administration

Gerber, Hans 62-3
German Civil Service Law (DBG, 1937) 152, 174-83, 187, 202, 203, 206, 207-8, 232
Gesamtverband Deutscher Beamtengewerkschaften 18 n.
Geyer, Michael 331, 336
Gilbert, Parker 87-8
Gillis, John 10, 332
Goebbels, Josef 114, 172, 262, 263-4, 312, 313, 315-17 passim, 337
Goerdeler, Carl-Friedrich 324
Göring, Hermann 139, 159, 177, 262, 263, 266, 270-1, 273, 274, 277, 302, 308, 312
Grauert, Ludwig 131 n.
Greiser, Arthur 113, 265
Groener, Wilhelm 126-7
Grzesinski, Albert 41, 44, 48, 113
Gürtner, Franz 179, 226, 289

Haas, Ludwig 30
Hamburg 124, 126
Haushofer, Karl 157
Hegel, Georg Wilhelm Friedrich 10
Heine, Wolfgang 43
Helms, Hans von 166-7, 287
Hess, Rudolf 157, 158, 174
  and civil servants 186-7, 207
  and civil servants as NSDAP members 176-7, 187, 207, 282
  and civil service salaries 232, 234, 250, 251, 253-6
  and DBG 175-8
  as Führer's deputy 160-4, 172, 181-2
  see also staff of the Führer's deputy
Hessen 124, 126, 156
Heydebrand und der Lasa, Ernst von 133
higher civil servants 7, 16, 20, 34-6, 42-50, 74-5, 77, 78, 81, 87, 108-9
  and National Socialism 119, 122, 135, 143, 145, 166, 171-4, 182, 183-8, 204, 220-1, 225, 232, 282, 284, 295-6, 313
  see also civil servants: 'political'
Hildebrand, Klaus 328
Himmler, Heinrich 164, 262, 263-4, 266, 267, 309, 318-19
Hindenburg, Paul von 111
Hinterbliebenenversorgung
  see civil service salaries: dependants' allowances

Hintze, Otto 1, 10, 11-12, 62
Hirsch, Paul 43
Hitler, Adolf 114, 117, 260
  and BBG 143, 144, 148
  and civil servants as NSDAP members
    167, 168, 182
  and civil service salaries 236, 237,
    250-6 passim
  and DBG 176-80
  and Frick 115, 131, 134, 137, 155,
    158, 187, 252, 314, 315
  and Nazi takeover 138, 140, 141
  as NSDAP leader 126, 132, 155-6
  and Reich-Land relations 155-8, 262,
    316, 318
  and Reichsstatthalter 155-6
  role in political system after 1933:
    153, 155-6, 159, 160, 165, 174,
    180, 194-5, 200, 266-7, 271, 273,
    274, 276, 277-9, 311, 312, 317,
    328, 333-6 passim
  see also Hitler: style of government
  style of government 158, 176, 177-8,
    250, 256-7, 261-2, 267, 276,
    278-9
  views on civil service 102-3, 104, 105,
    138-9, 187, 206, 207, 215, 224,
    226, 227-8, 281, 288-9
Hitler Youth (HJ) 116
Höhn, Reinhard 198, 335
Huber, Ernst Rudolf 202, 355

Imbusch, Heinrich 87, 88
Independent Social Democratic Party
  (USPD) 20, 24
inflation 51, 58, 77, 78

Jews
  see civil servants: racial restrictions
Joel, Curt 128
Juristenmonopol 6, 49, 187, 290
Justizausbildungsordnung (JAO; 1934) 185

Kapp putsch 33, 34-8, 42, 43
Keitel, Wilhelm 267, 311, 316
Kerrl, Hans 125
Killy, Leo 177, 236, 237-8, 258, 270,
  275, 278, 300, 324
Kirchheimer, Otto 330
Kirschenmann, Dietrich 334
Klopfer, Gerhard 161 n., 164, 296
Koellreutter, Otto 200, 335
Köhler, Heinrich 86-9, 248

Köttgen, Arnold 14, 32, 63, 64-5, 203,
  285
Kraft durch Freude (KdF) 196
Krebs, Albert 134
Krosigk, Lutz Graf Schwerin von 136,
  162, 171, 220, 233, 237, 246,
  247-8, 250-8 passim, 270, 288,
  300-2, 306, 315
  see also Reich ministries and adminis-
    trations: finance

labour law 4, 62, 73-5, 96, 195
Lammers, Hans Heinrich
  as channel to Hitler 178, 214, 226,
    253-4, 262-3, 311, 314
  and NSDAP before 1933: 133
  role in government after 1933: 179,
    206, 225, 252, 255, 256, 266, 271-9,
    300, 302-3, 307-8, 316-18 passim
  see also Reich chancellery
Länder 27-8, 50, 59, 85, 88, 96, 134,
  136, 139-41, 145, 151, 152-9, 231
  see also individual Länder; Reich-Land
    relations
Landrat 42-3, 45-6, 155, 165, 226,
  235, 284, 285, 286, 300, 315
law:
  National Socialist concepts 281, 283-4,
    285, 288-93, 334
  students 216, 220, 222, 290-2, 293
  see also Juristenmonopol; civil
    servants: training
Law, Reich Civil Service
  see German Civil Service Law; Reich
    Civil Service Law
Laws:
  Concerning the Duties of Civil
    Servants for the Security of the
    Republic (1922) 38
  see also Laws for the Protection of
    the Republic
  for the Amendment of Regulations in
    Civil-Service, Salary and Pensions
    Law (BRÄndG, 1933) 69-70,
    149-52, 166, 203, 204, 230
  for the Co-ordination of the Länder
    with the Reich, 1st (1933) 140
  for the Co-ordination of the Länder
    with the Reich, 2nd (1933) 140-1
  for the Ordering of National Labour
    (AOG, 1934) 195-6
  for the Reconstruction of the Reich
    (Neuaufbaugesetz, 1934) 152-5, 202

Laws (cont.):
  for the Restoration of the Civil Service
    (BBG, 1933) 141-9, 152, 159,
    166, 174, 202, 205
  for the Unification of Administrative
    Structure (1939) 269
Laws for the Protection of the Republic
    (Republikschutzgesetze, 1922) 31,
    38-41, 44, 110, 123
Laws, Nuremberg:
  see Nuremberg Laws
Lederer, Emil 71, 72
Leistungsprinzip:
  see civil service salaries: merit principle
local government 8, 9, 59, 85, 93, 139,
    146, 151, 216-18 passim, 221-2, 313
Loeper, Wilhelm Friedrich 133
Lüdemann, Hermann 30
Lüders, Marie-Elisabeth 98-9

Marschak, Jakob 71, 72
Marx, Karl 11
Marx, Wilhelm 85, 88
Mason, Tim 238, 239, 331-2
Medicus, Franz Albrecht 157-8
Ministerial Defence Council 266, 267
Mittelinstanz 136, 154, 169, 264-5, 273,
    275, 278, 302, 304
Mittelstand 12, 23, 71-2, 129
Mommsen, Hans 323
Mormons 206
Munich 146, 147, 217
Mutschmann, Martin 272

National Club 132, 133
Nationalsozialistische Beamten-Zeitung
    (NSBZ) 119, 121, 193
Nationalsozialistische Betriebszellen-
    organisation (NSBO) 117, 119, 127
Nationalsozialistische Deutsche Arbeiter-
    partei (NSDAP) 26, 29, 40, 48, 88,
    97, 101
  civil servants' support before 1933:
    116-17, 119-30 passim, 132-4,
    169-70, 173
  civil service organization before 1933:
    116-23, 127-8, 129-30
  civil service policy before 1933:
    114-16, 124, 131-4
  civil service programme (1924) 106,
    113
  civil service propaganda 41, 92,

102-14, 118-21, 129-30, 190-6, 224,
    298
  criticism of civil service 102-4, 190,
    221, 223-8, 291, 322
  emergency programme (1931) 110
  1932 election campaign 110-15
  organizational structure 116-21, 132,
    161-4, 168-9, 218-20, 325-6
  party courts 176, 179
  party programme (1920) 113-14
  Reichstag fraction 108, 110, 118
  relations with state 137-8, 155-69
    passim, 175, 197-8, 207-8, 225,
    264-6, 269, 271, 273, 279, 304,
    323, 333-7 passim
Neef, Hermann 119, 121, 128, 192-5
Neuaufbaugesetz:
  see Law for the Reconstruction of the
    Reich
Neumann, Franz 330, 331, 332
Nicolai, Helmut 133-4, 137, 157-8
Noske, Gustav 35, 37
NSDAP-Hauptamt für Beamte 190-2,
    296, 316
NSDAP-Hauptamt für Kommunalpolitik
    165, 217, 221, 225
NSDAP-party chancellery:
  see party chancellery
Nuremberg Laws (1935) 205

Oberpräsident 42-3, 46, 153-6, 264-5,
    275, 278, 300, 310, 314
Oldenburg 114-16
Order to Reduce Reich Personnel
    Expenditure (PAV, 1923) 31, 46,
    51-7, 58, 65, 97, 107, 108, 141, 148
Orlow, Dietrich 131

Papen, Franz von 125
party chancellery 162 n., 281, 299
  see also Bormann, Martin; staff of the
    Führer's deputy
Personalabbauverordnung (PAV):
  see Order to Reduce Reich Personnel
    Expenditure
Personalunion 165, 168-9, 310
Pfundtner, Hans:
  and BBG 143, 148
  and civil service morale 224, 226-8
  and civil service salaries 236
  and civil service training 184, 187,
    280-1, 285, 287
  and DBG 174-5

leaves Reich interior ministry 324
and NSDAP before 1933: 132-3
Planck, Erwin 139
plenipotentiary for the administration
267, 275-7, 307
see also Frick, Wilhelm
plenipotentiary for total war 267, 317,
337
see also Goebbels, Josef
Pollock, Frederick 330
Popitz, Johannes 135, 147, 149, 175,
185, 225, 234, 246, 247, 302, 324
population policy 212-15
see also civil servants: marital and
sexual behaviour
Poulantzas, Nicos 329
Preuss, Hugo 18, 23, 24, 26
Prussia 1-3, 5, 6-7, 8, 9, 29, 30, 31,
41-50, 111-12, 113-14, 123-7, 135,
139, 145, 153, 184
finance administration 147, 149
interior administration 139, 145, 154,
165, 166
judicial administration 145

rationalization 51, 61, 81, 84
Rechtsstaat 1, 197, 199-200, 288
Regierungspräsident 42-3, 46, 154-5,
241 n., 242, 243, 268, 300, 304,
310, 319
Reich chancellery 236, 237, 262-3, 281
see also Pfundtner, Hans
Reich Civil Service Law (1873, 1907)
38, 52-3, 150, 174
Reich defence commissioners 265-6,
311-12, 317
Reich-Land relations 26-8, 29, 39,
49-50, 52, 85, 90, 97, 134-8
under National Socialism 140-1,
152-9, 231, 268-70, 271-4
Reich ministries and administrations:
aviation 154, 172
finance 68, 69, 89, 144-5, 146, 148,
149, 172-4, 186, 205, 216, 268,
299, 306-7, 313
see also Krosigk, Lutz Schwerin von
foreign 235
interior 60, 66-7, 134-7, 141, 146,
149, 152-8, 172-5, 183, 218,
222-3, 229, 232, 233, 234-5,
241-3, 264-5, 266, 267-71, 277-90
passim, 293-4, 300-1, 303-5,
308-11, 313, 318-19, 320, 334

see also Frick, Wilhelm
justice 153, 241-4, 288-90, 292-3,
306, 317
labour 154
postal 8, 17, 60, 99-100, 117, 126-8,
147, 154, 180 n., 220, 317
propaganda 154, 172, 235, 316 n.
Reichsbahn 106, 128, 154, 241
Reichsbund der Deutschen Beamten
191-3, 219, 294
Reichsbund der höheren Beamten 18,
69, 80, 85, 95-6
Reichsdienststraforordnung (RDStrO):
see Civil Service Disciplinary Code
Reichsgaue 264-5, 275
Reichsgrundsätze (RGS, 1921) 171-2
Reichsgrundsätze (RGS, 1936) 173-4,
182, 214
Reichsreform:
see Reich-Land relations
Reichsstatthalter 140-1, 153, 154-7, 160,
165, 167, 169, 264-5, 269, 271-6
passim, 278, 304, 314
Reichsstatthalter Law, 2nd (1935) 152,
156-7
Reichsverteidigungskommissare:
see Reich defence commissioners
Reichsverteidigungsrat:
see Ministerial Defence Council
Reinhardt, Fritz 238, 256, 273
Republikschutzgesetze:
see Laws for the Protection of the
Republic
revolution of 1918: 14-15, 18-20
Ring Deutscher Beamtenverbände 18 n.
Rosenberg, Alfred 335
Rothenberger, Curt 289-90
Röver, Karl 114, 115, 272
Rüdiger, Hans 222-3

SA (Sturm-Abteilung) 116, 127, 170,
173, 176
Saemisch, Moritz 58, 65-6
Sauckel, Fritz 156 n., 279, 312, 313,
316
Saxony 49, 156
Schätzel, Georg 126-7
Schlegelberger, Franz 289
Schleicher, Kurt 127
Schmitt, Carl 96, 335
Schoenbaum, David 189
Schulenburg, Fritz-Dietlof von der
185, 321-2, 324, 325

Schwede-Coburg, Franz 214
SD (*Sicherheitsdienst*) 255
Seeckt, Hans von 35
Seel, Hanns 148
Seldte, Franz 234, 246
Severing, Carl 41, 43, 48, 125 n.
Silverberg, Paul 93 n.
social democracy 9, 12, 70-3
Social Democratic Party (SPD) 20,
    23-4, 30, 33, 36, 38, 43, 44, 48,
    74, 88, 111, 122
social democrats 41, 48, 49, 85, 113,
    146
Sommer, Walter 161, 163, 178, 182-3,
    186, 211, 214, 254, 282, 285, 335,
    336
Speer, Albert 263, 279, 312, 313, 316
Sprenger, Jakob 112-13, 118-20, 121,
    128, 191-2, 272
SS (*Schutzstaffel*) 116, 127, 170, 176,
    261, 266, 300, 316 n., 319
staff of the Führer's deputy (StdF Stab)
    161-4, 165, 167, 171, 182, 280
    see also Hess, Rudolf; party chancellery
Stegerwald, Adam 87, 93
'Stoperlass' (1943) 316
Strasser, Gregor 117, 118, 132
Stresemann, Gustav 55, 57
Stuckart, Wilhelm 318, 324
    and administrative reform 267, 269,
        270-6 *passim*, 307, 313, 316
    and NSDAP before 1933: 132
    and training policy 280, 282-4, 293
    views on law 200, 283-4
Sudetenland 221, 264

Thierack, Otto 288, 289
Thomas, Georg 262
Three-Man Committee (*Dreierausschuss*)
    311, 312, 313, 315, 317
Thuringia 115, 124
trade unions 9, 18, 59, 85, 91

Unruh, General von 311, 312, 313, 314,
    317

Verfassungsreform:
    see constitutional reform before 1933
Verwaltungsreform:
    see administrative policy
Volksgemeinschaft 83-4, 110, 112, 189,
    197-9, 229

wages 232, 238-40, 242, 247-8, 251,
    254, 258
Wagner, Adolf 140, 157
Wagner, Josef 234, 246, 250, 254, 258
Wartheland 265
Weber, Max 11, 326, 330
Weimar coalition 38, 41
Weimar Constitution 18-19, 21-9, 32,
    40, 46, 135, 152, 202
    Article 39: 25 n.
    Article 48: 95
    Article 109: 46
    Article 118: 25
    Article 128: 25, 46, 151, 202
    Article 129: 22-5, 95, 96, 129, 258
    Article 130: 25-6, 33, 202
    Article 131: 25 n., 203
    Article 176: 25 n.
    see also constitutional reform before
        1933
white-collar workers:
    see Angestellte
Wirth, Joseph 38, 127
Witt, Peter-Christian 15
wohlerworbene Rechte:
    see civil servants: vested rights
Württemberg 30, 39, 49, 124

Young Plan referendum 123, 126

Zweigert, Erich 139